THE MASSES OF
HOLY WEEK
&
TENEBRAE

PALM SUNDAY
TENEBRAE
SACRED TRIDUUM

Palm Sunday

The Blessing of the Palms

A -spér- ges me, * Dó- mi- ne, hyssó-po, et mundá- bor :

la-vá- bis me, et su-per ni-vem de- albá- bor. Ps. 50. Mi- se-ré-

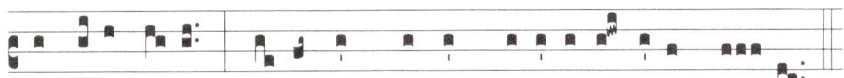

re me- i, De- us, * se-cúndum magnam mi-se-ri-cór-di- am tu- am.

ANTIPHON: Thou shalt sprinkle me, O Lord, with hyssop, and I shall be cleansed; Thou shalt wash me, and I shall become whiter than snow. Psalm 50. Have mercy on me, O God, according to Thy great mercy.

V. Osténde nobis, Dómine, misericórdiam tuam.

R. Et salutáre tuum da nobis.

V. Dómine, exáudi oratiónem meam.

R. Et clamor meus ad te véniat.

V. Dóminus vobíscum.

R. Et cum spíritu tuo.

V. Show us, O Lord, Thy mercy.

R. And grant us Thy salvation.

V. O Lord, hear my prayer.

R. And let my cry come before Thee.

V. The Lord be with you.

R. And with thy spirit.

ORÉMUS.   LET US PRAY.

EXÁUDI nos, Dómine sancte, Pater omnípotens, ætérne Deus, et míttere dignéris sanctum Angelum tuum de cælis, qui custódiat, fóveat, prótegat, vísitet atque deféndat omnes habitántes in hoc habitáculo. Per Christum Dóminum nostrum.

℟. Amen.

HEAR us, O holy Lord, almighty Father, everlasting God, and vouchsafe to send Thy holy Angel from heaven, to guard, cherish, protect, visit and defend all that are assembled in this place: through Christ our Lord.

℟. Amen.

After the holy water has been sprinkled, the celebrant in violet cope, with his ministers also vested in violet, proceeds to the blessing of the palms, or of branches of olive or other trees which are placed on the epistle side of the altar. The choir sings first the following anthem:

ANTIPHON   MATTHEW 21: 9

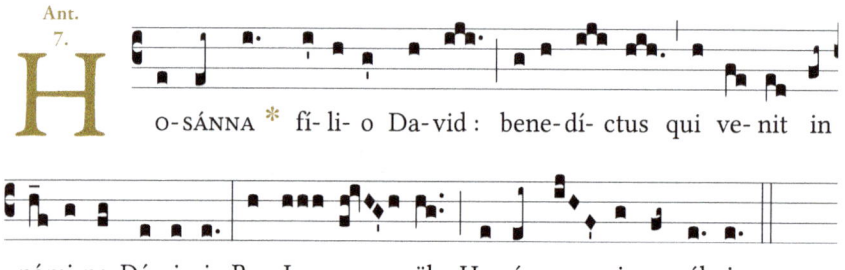

Ho-sánna * fí-li-o Da-vid : bene-dí-ctus qui ve-nit in nómi-ne Dómi-ni. Rex Is- ra- ël : Ho-sánna in excél-sis.

ANTIPHON: Hosanna * to the Son of David! Blessed is He that cometh in the Name of the Lord. O King of Israel: Hosanna in the highest!

℣. Dóminus vobíscum.   ℣. The Lord be with you.
℟. Et cum spíritu tuo.   ℟. And with thy spirit.

ORÉMUS.   LET US PRAY.

DEUS, quem dilígere et amáre justítia est, ineffábilis grátiæ tuæ in nobis dona multíplica: et qui fecísti nos in morte Fílii tui speráre quæ crédimus; fac nos eódem resurgénte perveníre quo téndimus: Qui tecum vivit et regnat in unitáte Spíritus

O GOD, whom to love above all is righteousness, multiply in us the gifts of Thine ineffable grace: and since Thou hast given us in the death of Thy Son to hope for those things which we believe, grant us by the Resurrection of the same to attain the

Sancti Deus per ómnia sǽcula sæculórum.

R. Amen.

end to which we aspire. Who livest and reignest with God the Father, in the unity of the Holy Ghost, God, world without end.

R. Amen.

LESSON FROM THE BOOK OF EXODUS
Exodus 15: 27; 16: 1-7

IN diébus illis: Venérunt fílii Israël in Elim, ubi erant duódecim fontes aquárum et septuagínta palmæ: et castrametáti sunt juxta aquas. Profectíque sunt de Elim, et venit omnis multitúdo filiórum Israël in desértum Sin, quod est inter Elim et Sínai: quintodécimo die mensis secúndi, postquam egréssi sunt de terra Ægýpti. Et murmurávit omnis congregátio filiórum Israël contra Móysen et Aaron in solitúdine. Dixerúntque fílii Israël ad eos: Utinam mórtui essémus per manum Dómini in terra Ægýpti, quando sedebámus super ollas cárnium, et comedebámus panem in saturitáte: cur eduxístis nos in desértum istud, ut occiderétis omnem multitúdinem fame? Dixit autem Dóminus ad Móysen: Ecce, ego pluam vobis panes de cælo: egrediátur pópulus, et cólligat quæ suffíciunt per síngulos dies: ut tentem eum, utrum ámbulet in lege mea an non. Die autem sexto parent quod ínferant: et sit duplum, quam collígere sciébant per síngulos dies. Dixerúntque Móyses et Aaron ad omnes fílios Israël: Véspere sciétis, quod Dóminus edúxerit vos de terra Ægýpti: et mane vidébitis glóriam Dómini.

IN those days the children of Israel came into Elim, where there were twelve fountains of water, and seventy palm trees; and they encamped by the waters. And they set forward from Elim, and all the multitude of the children of Israel came into the desert of Sin, which is between Elim and Sinai: the fifteenth day of the second month after they came out of the land of Egypt. And all the congregation of the children of Israel murmured against Moses and Aaron in the wilderness. And the children of Israel said to them: Would to God we had died by the hand of the Lord in the land of Egypt, when we sat over the fleshpots and ate bread to the full. Why have you brought us into this desert, that you might destroy all the multitude with famine? And the Lord said to Moses: Behold I will rain bread from heaven for you; let the people go forth and gather what is sufficient for every day; that I may prove them whether they will walk in My law or not. But the sixth day let them provide for to bring in; and let it be double to that they were wont to gather every day. And Moses and Aaron said to the children of Israel: In the evening you shall know that the Lord hath brought

you forth out of the land of Egypt; and in the morning you shall see the glory of the Lord.

℟. Deo grátias.

℟. Thanks be to God.

RESPONSORY   JOHN 11: 47-49, 50, 53

Resp. 2.

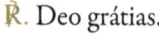

COL- LE- GÉ- RUNT * pon-tí- fi-ces et pha-ri-sǽ- i con- cí- li- um, et di- cé-bant : Quid fá- ci- mus, qui- a hic ho- mo multa signa fa- cit? Si dimít-timus e- um sic, o- mnes cre- dent in e- um : * Ne forte vé- ni- ant Romá- ni, et tol- lant nostrum lo- cum, et gen- tem. ℣. Unus au- tem ex il- lis, Cá- i-phas nómi- ne, cum esset pónti- fex anni il-lí- us, prophetá- vit di- cens : Expe-dit vo- bis,

ut unus mo-ri- á-tur homo pro pó- pu- lo, et non to-ta gens pér-

e- at. Ab il-lo ergo di- e co-gi-ta-

vé- runt interfí-ce-re e- um, di-cén-tes. Ne forte.

R. The chief priests and the Pharisees gathered a council and said: What do we, for this man doth many miracles? If we let Him alone so, all will believe in Him; And the Romans will come, and take away our place and nation. V. But one of them, called Caiphas, being the high priest that year, prophesied, saying: It is expedient for you that one man should die for the people, and that the whole nation perish not. From that day, therefore, they devised to put Him to death, saying: And the Romans will come, and take away our place and nation.

ANOTHER RESPONSORY   MATTHEW 26: 39, 41

N mon- te O-li-vé- ti o-rá- vit ad Pa-

trem: Pa- ter, si fí- e-ri pot- est, tránse- at a me ca-lix i-

ste. Spí- ri-tus qui- dem promptus est, ca- ro autem in-

fír- ma: fí- at vo-lún-tas tu- a. V. Vi-gi-lá-te,

et o-rá- te, ut non intré-tis in ten- ta-ti-ó- nem. *

Spí- ri-tus.

℟. On mount Olivet He prayer to His Father: Father, if it may be, let this chalice pass from Me. * The spirit is indeed willing, but the flesh weak; Thy will be done. ℣. Watch and pray, that ye enter not into temptation. * The spirit is indeed willing, but the flesh weak; Thy will be done.

CONTINUATION ✠ OF THE HOLY GOSPEL
ACCORDING TO ST. MATTHEW
Matthew 21: 1-9

IN illo témpore: Cum appropinquásset Jesus Jerosólymis, et venísset Béthphage ad montem Olivéti: tunc misit duos discípulos suos, dicens eis: Ite in castéllum, quod contra vos est, et statim inveniétis ásinam alligátam et pullum cum ea: sólvite et addúcite mihi: et si quis vobis áliquid díxerit, dícite, quia Dóminus his opus habet, et conféstim dimíttet eos. Hoc autem totum factum est, ut adimplerétur, quod dictum est per Prophétam, dicéntem: Dícite fíliæ Sion: Ecce, Rex tuus venit tibi mansuétus, sedens super ásinam et pullum, fílium subjugális. Eúntes autem discípuli, fecérunt, sicut præcépit illis Jesus. Et adduxérunt ásinam et pullum: et imposuérunt super eos vestiménta sua, et eum désuper sedére tecérunt. Plúrima autem turba stravérunt vestiménta sua in via: álii autem cædébant ramos de arbóribus, et sternébant in

AT that time, when Jesus drew nigh to Jerusalem, and was come to Bethphage, unto Mount Olivet, then He sent two disciples, saying to them: Go ye into the village that is over against you, and immediately you shall find an ass tied, and a colt with her; loose them and bring them to Me; and if any man shall say anything to you, say ye that the Lord hath need of them; and forthwith he will let them go. Now all this was done that it might be fulfilled which was spoken by the prophet, saying: Tell ye the daughter of Sion: Behold thy King cometh to thee meek, and sitting upon an ass, and a colt the foal of her that is used to the yoke. And the disciples going did as Jesus commanded them. And they brought the ass and the colt, and laid their garments upon them, and made Him sit thereon. And a very great multitude spread their

via: turbæ autem, quæ præcedébant et quæ sequebántur, clamábant, dicéntes: Hosánna fílio David: benedíctus, qui venit in nómine Dómini.

garments in the way, and others cut boughs from the trees, and strewed them in the way, and the multitudes that went before and that followed cried, saying: Hosanna to the Son of David; Blessed is He that cometh in the Name of the Lord.

The celebrant then blesses the branches.

V. Dóminus vobíscum.
R. Et cum spíritu tuo.

V. The Lord be with you.
R. And with thy spirit.

ORÉMUS.

LET US PRAY.

AUGE fidem in te sperántium, Deus, et súpplicum preces cleménter exáudi: véniat super nos múltiplex misericórdia tua: bene ✠ dicántur et hi pálmites palmárum, seu olivárum: et sicut in figúra Ecclésiæ multiplicásti Noë egrediéntem de arca, et Móysen exeúntem de Ægýpto cum fíliis Israël: ita nos, portántes palmas et ramos olivárum, bonis áctibus occurrámus óbviam Christo: et per ipsum in gáudium introëámus ætérnum: Qui tecum vivit et regnat in unitáte Spíritus Sancti Deus.

INCREASE, O God, the faith of them that hope in Thee, and in Thy mercy hear the prayers of Thy suppliant people; let Thy multiplied mercy descend upon us, and may these branches of palm-olive-trees be blessed; ✠ and as in a figure of Thy Church Thou didst multiply Noah going forth from the ark, and Moses going out of Egypt with the children of Israel, so may we go forth to meet Christ with good works, bearing palms and olive branches; and enter through Him into everlasting joy; Who livest and reignest with God the Father, in the unity of the Holy Ghost, God:

PER ómnia sǽcula sæculórum.
R. Amen.
V. Dóminus vobíscum.
R. Et cum spíritu tuo.
V. Sursum corda.
R. Habémus ad Dóminum.

V. Grátias agámus Dómino Deo nostro.
R. Dignum et justum est.

WORLD without end.
R. Amen.
V. The Lord be with you.
R. And with thy spirit.
V. Lift up your hearts.
R. We have them lifted up to the Lord.
V. Let us give thanks to the Lord our God.
R. It is meet and just.

VERE dignum et justum est, æquum et salutáre, nos tibi semper et ubíque grátias ágere: Dómine sancte, Pater omnípotens, æterne Deus: Qui gloriáris in consílio Sanctórum tuórum. Tibi enim sérviunt creatúræ tuæ: quia te solum auctórem et Deum cognóscunt, et omnis factúra tua te colláudat, et benedícunt te Sancti tui. Quia illud magnum Unigéniti tui nomen coram régibus et potestátibus hujus sǽculi líbera voce confiténtur. Cui assístunt Angeli et Archángeli, Throni et Dominatiónes: cumque omni milítia cæléstis exércitus hymnum glóriæ tuæ cóncinunt, sine fine dicéntes.

IT is truly meet and just, right and availing unto salvation, that we should always and in all places give thanks unto Thee, O Lord, Father almighty, everlasting God. Who dost glory in the assembly of Thy Saints. For Thy creatures serve Thee, because they acknowledge Thee as their only Creator and God; and Thy whole creation praiseth Thee, and Thy Saints bless Thee. For with free voice they confess that great Name of Thine only-begotten Son before the kings and powers of this world. Around whom the Angels and Archangels, the Thrones and Dominions stand; and with all the host of the heavenly army, sing the hymn of Thy glory, saying without ceasing:

SANCTUS   XVIII

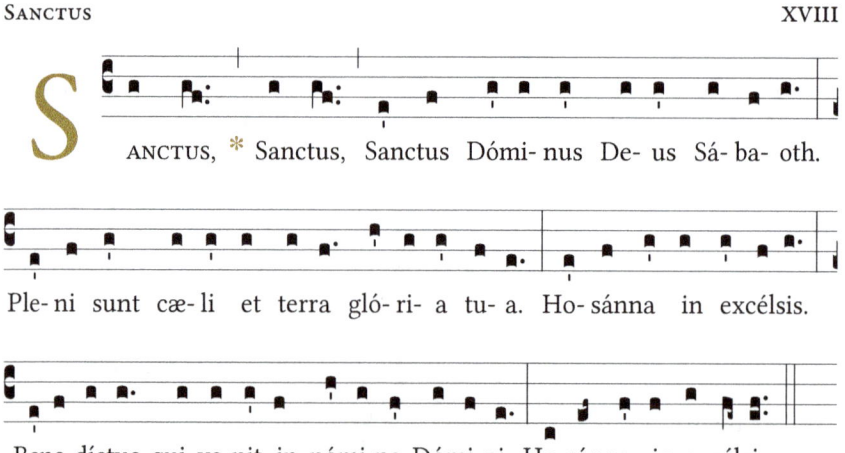

SANCTUS, * Sanctus, Sanctus Dómi-nus De-us Sá-ba-oth.

Ple-ni sunt cæ-li et terra gló-ri-a tu-a. Ho-sánna in excélsis.

Bene-díctus qui ve-nit in nómi-ne Dómi-ni. Ho-sánna in excélsis.

SANCTUS: Holy, * Holy, Holy, Lord God of hosts. Heaven and earth are full of Thy glory. Hosanna in the highest. Blessed is He that cometh in the Name of the Lord. Hosanna in the highest.

℣. Dóminus vobíscum.
℟. Et cum spíritu tuo.

℣. The Lord be with you.
℟. And with thy spirit.

Orémus.

Pétimus, Dómine sancte, Pater omnípotens, ætérne Deus: ut hanc creatúram olívæ, quam ex ligni matéria prodíre jussísti, quamque colúmba rédiens ad arcam próprio pértulit ore, bene✠dícere et sanct✠ficáre dignéris: ut, quicúmque ex ea recéperint, accípiant sibi protectiónem ánimæ et córporis: fiátque, Dómine, nostræ salútis remédium tuæ grátiæ sacraméntum. Per Dóminum nostrum Jesum Christum, Fílium tuum: qui tecum vivit et regnat in unitáte Spíritus Sancti Deus, per ómnia sæcula sæculórum.

℟. Amen.

Orémus.

Deus, qui dispérsa cóngregas, et congregáta consérvas: qui pópulis, óbviam Jesu ramos portántibus, benedixísti: béne✠dic étiam hos ramos palmæ et olívæ, quos tui fámuli ad honórem nóminis tui fidéliter suscípiunt; ut, in quemcúmque locum introdúcti fúerint, tuam benedictiónem habitatóres loci illíus consequántur: et, omni adversitáte effugáta, déxtera tua prótegat, quos rédemit Jesus Christus, Fílius tuus, Dóminus noster: Qui tecum vivit et regnat in unitáte Spíritus Sancti Deus per ómnia sæcula sæculórum.

℟. Amen.

Let us pray.

We beseech Thee, O holy Lord, almighty Father, everlasting God, that Thou wouldst vouchsafe to bless ✠ and hallow ✠ this creature of the olive tree, which Thou didst cause to shoot out of the substance of the wood, and which the dove when returning to the ark brought in its mouth: that whosoever shall receive it may find protection of soul and body; and that it may be to us, O Lord, a saving remedy and the sacred sign of Thy grace. Through Jesus Christ, Thy Son our Lord, Who liveth and reigneth with Thee, in the unity of the Holy Ghost, God, world without end.

℟. Amen.

Let us pray.

O God, who dost gather what is dispersed abroad, and preserve what is gathered together; who didst bless the people who went forth to meet Jesus, bearing branches of palms; bless ✠ likewise these branches of palm and olive, which Thy servants receive faithfully in honor of Thy Name; that into whatsoever place they shall be brought, those who dwell in that place may obtain Thy blessing, and all adversities being removed, Thy right hand may protect those who have been redeemed by our Lord Jesus Christ, Thy Son. Who livest and reignest with God the Father, in the unity of the Holy Ghost, God, world without end.

℟. Amen.

ORÉMUS.

Deus, qui miro dispositiónis órdine, ex rebus étiam insensibílibus, dispensatiónem nostræ salútis osténdere voluísti: da, quǽsumus; ut devóta tuórum corda fidélium salúbriter intéllegant, quid mýstice desígnet in facto, quod hódie, cælésti lúmine affláta, Redemptóri óbviam procédens, palmárum atque olivárum ramos vestígiis ejus turba substrávit. Palmárum igitur rami de mortis príncipe triúmphos exspéctant; súrculi vero olivárum spirituálem unctiónem advenísse Quodámmodo clamant. Intelléxit enim jam tunc illa hóminum beáta multitúdo præfigurári: quia Redémptor noster, humánis cóndolens misériis, pro totíus mundi vita cum mortis príncipe esset pugnatúrus ac moriéndo triumphatúrus. Et ídeo tália óbsequens administrávit, quæ in illo ei triúmphos victóriæ et misericórdiæ pinguédinem declarárent. Quod nos quoque plena fide, et factum et significátum retinéntes, te, Dómine sancte, Pater omnípotens, ætérne Deus, per eúndem Dóminum nostrum Jesum Christum supplíciter exorámus: ut in ipso atque per ipsum, cujus nos membra fíeri voluísti, de mortis império victóriam reportántes, ipsíus gloriósæ resurrectiónis partícipes esse mereámur:

LET US PRAY.

O God, who, by the wonderful order of Thy disposition, hast been pleased to manifest the dispensation of our salvation even from things insensible: grant, we beseech Thee, that the devout hearts of Thy faithful may understand to their benefit what is mystically signified by the fact that on this day the multitude, taught by a heavenly illumination, went forth to meet their Redeemer, and strewed branches of palms and olive at His feet. The branches of palms, therefore, represent His triumphs over the prince of death; and the branches of olive proclaim, in a manner, the coming of a spiritual unction. For that pious multitude understood that these things were then prefigured; that our Redeemer, compassionating human miseries, was about to fight with the prince of death for the life of the whole world, and, by dying, to triumph. For which cause they dutifully ministered such things as signified in Him the triumphs of victory and the richness of mercy. And we also, with full faith, retaining this as done and signified, humbly beseech Thee, O holy Lord, Father almighty, everlasting God, through the same Jesus Christ our Lord, that in Him and through Him, whose members Thou hast been pleased to make us, we may become victorious over the empire of death, and may deserve to be partakers of His glorious Resurrection.

Qui tecum vivit et regnat in unitáte Spíritus Sancti Deus per ómnia sǽcula sæculórum.

℟. Amen.

ORÉMUS.

DEUS, qui, per olívæ ramum, pacem terris colúmbam nuntiáre jussísti: præsta, quǽsumus; ut hos olívæ ceterarúmque árborum ramos cælésti bene✠dictióne sanctífices: ut cuncto pópulo tuo profíciant ad salútem. Per Christum, Dóminum nostrum.

℟. Amen.

ORÉMUS.

BÉNE✠DIC, quǽsumus, Dómine, hos palmárum seu olivárum ramos: et præsta; ut, quod pópulus tuus in tui veneratiónem hodiérna die corporáliter agit, hoc spirituáliter summa devotióne perfíciat, de hoste victóriam reportándo et opus misericórdiæ summópere diligéndo. Per Dóminum nostrum Jesum Christum, Fílium tuum: qui tecum vivit et regnat in unitáte Spíritus Sancti Deus, per ómnia sǽcula sæculórum.

℟. Amen.

Who livest and reignest with God the Father, in the unity of the Holy Ghost, God, world without end.

℟. Amen.

LET US PRAY.

O GOD, who by an olive branch didst command the dove to proclaim peace to the earth: hallow, we beseech Thee, by Thy heavenly blessing ✠ these branches of the olive and other trees; that they may profit all Thy people unto salvation. Through Christ our Lord.

℟. Amen.

LET US PRAY.

BLESS, ✠ we beseech Thee, O Lord, these branches of palm or olive: and grant that what Thy people today bodily perform for Thy honor, they may perfect spiritually with the utmost devotion, by gaining the victory over the enemy, and ardently loving every work of mercy. Through Jesus Christ, Thy Son our Lord, Who liveth and reigneth with Thee, in the unity of the Holy Ghost, God, world without end.

℟. Amen.

The celebrant puts incense in the thurible , sprinkles the palms three times with holy water, and then incenses them three times. He then says:

℣. Dóminus vobíscum.

℟. Et cum spíritu tuo.

℣. The Lord be with you.

℟. And with thy spirit.

ORÉMUS.

LET US PRAY.

Dᴇᴜs, qui Fílium tuum Jesum Christum, Dóminum nostrum, pro salúte nostra in hunc mundum misísti, ut se humiliáret ad nos et nos revocáret ad te: cui étiam, dum Jerúsalem veníret, ut adimpléret Scriptúras, credéntium populórum turba, fidelíssima devotióne, vestiménta sua cum ramis palmárum in via sternébant: præsta, quæsumus; ut illi fídei viam præparémus, de qua, remóto lápide offensiónis et petra scándali, fróndeant apud te ópera nostra justítiæ ramis: ut eius vestígia sequi mereámur: Qui tecum vivit et regnat in unitáte Spíritus Sancti Deus per ómnia sǽcula sæculórum.

O Gᴏᴅ, who for our salvation didst send into this world Thy Son Jesus Christ our Lord, that He might humble Himself unto our state, and call us back to Thee; for whom also, as He entered into Jerusalem to fulfill the Scriptures, a multitude of faithful people, with zealous devotion, strewed their garments, with palm branches, in the way: grant, we beseech Thee, that we may prepare for Him the way of faith, from which the stone of offense and rock of scandal being removed, our works may flourish before Thee with branches of justice, that so we may be found worthy to follow His footsteps: Who livest and reignest with God the Father, in the unity of the Holy Ghost, God, world without end.

℟. Amen.

℟. Amen.

The palms are then distributed to the clergy and to the laity, during which the following antiphons are sung:

ANTIPHON   JOHN 12: 13

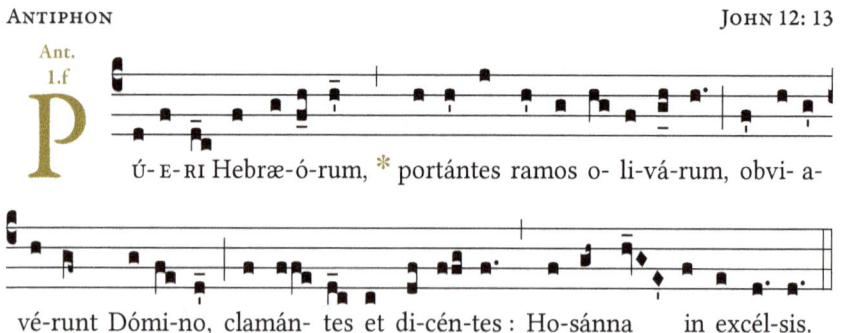

Pú- ᴇ-ʀɪ Hebræ-ó-rum, * portántes ramos o- li-vá-rum, obvi-a-vé-runt Dómi-no, clamán- tes et di-cén-tes : Ho-sánna in excél-sis.

ANTIPHON: The Hebrew children * bearing olive branches, went forth to meet the Lord, crying out, and saying, Hosanna in the highest.

It was customary before 1955 to sing verses of the Psalms;
after 1955 this was formalized with the verses given below.

Psalm 23: 1-2, 7-10

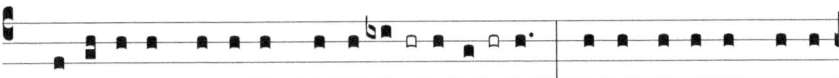

1. Dómi-ni est terra, et ple-ni-**tú**- do **e**- jus: * orbis terrá-rum, et u-

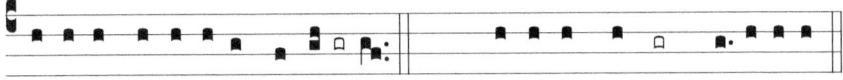

ni-vérsi qui há-bi-*tant in* **e**- o.   *Flex:* prínci-pes, vestras, †

1. The earth is the Lord's and the fulness thereof: * the world, and all they that dwell therein.

2. Quia ipse super mária fundávit eum, * et super flúmina præpa*rávit* eum.

repeat Púeri *as above.*

2. For He hath founded it upon the seas; * and hath prepared it upon the rivers.

7. Attóllite portas, príncipes, vestras: † et elevámini, portæ æternáles: * et introí*bit Rex* **glóriæ.**

8. Quis est iste Rex glóriæ? † Dómi-nus **for**tis et **po**tens: * Dóminus po-*tens* in **prǽ**lio.

repeat Púeri *as above.*

7. Lift up your gates, O ye princes, † and be ye lifted up, O eternal gates: * and the King of Glory shall enter in.

8. Who is this King of Glory? † the Lord who is strong and mighty: * the Lord mighty in battle.

9. Attóllite portas, príncipes, vestras: † et elevámini, portæ æternáles: * et introí*bit Rex* **glóriæ.**

10. Quis est iste Rex **glóriæ**? * Dóminus virtútum ipse *est Rex* **glóriæ.**

repeat Púeri *as above.*

9. Lift up your gates, O ye princes, † and be ye lifted up, O eternal gates: * and the King of Glory shall enter in.

10. Who is this King of Glory? * the Lord of hosts, He is the King of Glory.

11. Glória **Patri**, et **Fí**lio, * et Spirí-*tui* **San**cto.

12. Sicut erat in princípio, et **nunc**, et **sem**per, * et in sǽcula sæcu*lórum.* **A**men.

repeat Púeri *as above.*

11. Glory be to the Father, and to the Son, * and to the Holy Ghost.

12. As it was in the beginning, is now, * and ever shall be, world with-out end. Amen.

ANTIPHON   MATTHEW 21: 8,9

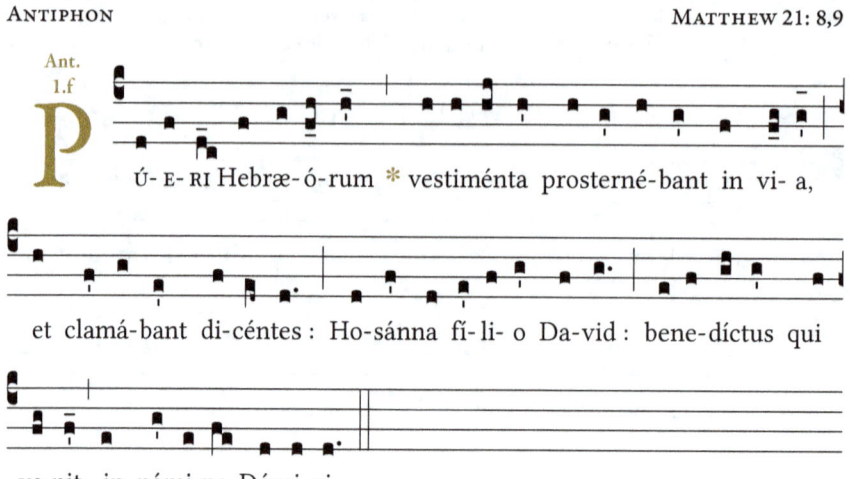

Pú-e-ri Hebræ-ó-rum * vestiménta prosterné-bant in vi- a, et clamá-bant di-céntes : Ho-sánna fí-li- o Da-vid : bene-díctus qui ve-nit in nómi-ne Dómi-ni.

ANTIPHON: The Hebrew children * spread their garments in the way, and cried out, saying: Hosanna to the Son of God: blessed is He that cometh in the Name of the Lord.

It was customary before 1955 to sing verses of the Psalms;
after 1955 this was formalized with the verses given below.

PSALM 46

1. Omnes Gentes, **pláu**di-te **má**-ni-bus : * ju-bi-lá-te De- o in vo-ce exsul*ta-ti-* **ó-** nis.

1. O clap your hands, all ye nations: * shout unto God with the voice of joy.

2. Quóniam Dóminus ex**cél**sus,   2. For the Lord is high, terrible: *
terríbilis, * Rex magnus super *omnem*   a great king over all the earth.
ter*ram.

repeat Púeri *as above.*

3. Subjécit pópulos nobis : * et gentes sub pédibus nostris.

3. He hath subdued the people under us; * and the nations under our feet.

4. Elégit nobis hereditátem suam : * spéciem Jacob, *quam di*léxit.

4. He hath chosen for us His inheritance, * the beauty of Jacob which he hath loved.

repeat Púeri *as above.*

5. Ascéndit **De**us in júbilo : * et Dóminus in *voce* **tub**æ.

5. God is ascended with jubilee, * and the Lord with the sound of trumpet.

6. Psállite Deo **no**stro, **psáll**ite : * psállite Regi *nostro*, **psáll**ite.

6. Sing praises to our God, sing ye: * sing praises to our king, sing ye.

repeat Púeri *as above.*

7. Quóniam Rex omnis **terr**æ **De**us : * psállite *sapi***én**ter.

7. For God is the king of all the earth: * sing ye wisely.

8. Regnábit Deus **su**per **gen**tes : * Deus sedet super sedem *sanctam* **su**am.

8. God shall reign over the nations: * God sitteth on His holy throne.

repeat Púeri *as above.*

9. Príncipes populórum congregáti sunt cum **Deo Á**braham : * quóniam dii fortes terræ veheménter *ele*váti sunt.

9. The princes of the people are gathered together, with the God of Abraham: * for the strong gods of the earth are exceedingly exalted.

repeat Púeri *as above.*

10. Glória **Pa**tri, et **Fí**lio, * et Spirí-*tui* **San**cto.

10. Glory be to the Father, and to the Son, * and to the Holy Ghost.

11. Sicut erat in princípio, et **nunc**, et **sem**per, * et in sǽcula sæcu*lórum*. **A**men.

11. As it was in the beginning, is now, * and ever shall be, world without end. Amen.

repeat Púeri *as above.*

The antiphons are repeated as necessary until the distribution of branches is completed, after which the celebrant says:

℣. Dóminus vobíscum.

℣. The Lord be with you.

℟. Et cum spíritu tuo.

℟. And with thy spirit.

ORÉMUS.

OMNÍPOTENS sempitérne Deus, qui Dóminum nostrum Jesum Christum super pullum ásinæ sedére fecísti, et turbas populórum vestiménta vel ramos árborum in via stérnere et Hosánna decantáre in laudem ipsíus docuísti : da, quǽsumus; ut illórum innocéntiam imitári possímus, et eórum méritum cónsequi mereámur. Per eúndem Dóminum nostrum Jesum Christum Fílium tuum, qui tecum vivit et regnat in unitáte Spíritus Sancti, Deus, per ómnia sǽcula sæculórum.

℞. Amen.

LET US PRAY.

ALMIGHTY and everlasting God, who didst ordain that our Lord Jesus Christ should sit upon the foal of an ass, and didst teach the multitude to spread their garments or branches of trees in the way and to sing Hosanna to His praise: grant, we beseech Thee, that we may be able to imitate their innocence and deserve to partake of their merit. Through the same Jesus Christ, Thy Son, Our Lord, Who liveth and reigneth with Thee in the unity of the Holy Ghost, God, world without end.

℞. Amen.

THE PROCESSION

When the celebrant places incense in the thurible, the deacon, turning towards the people, sings:

℣. Procedámus in pace.

℟. In nómine Christi. Amen.

℣. Let us go forth in peace.

℟. In the name of Christ. Amen.

The thurifer precedes with the smoking censer, followed by the subdeacon, bearing the processional cross between two acolytes carrying lighted candles. Then follow the clergy in order of rank, and finally the celebrant with the deacon on his left. All carry palms, and all or some of them sing the following anthems, during the whole time the procession lasts.

ANTIPHON   MATTHEW 21: 1-3, 7-9

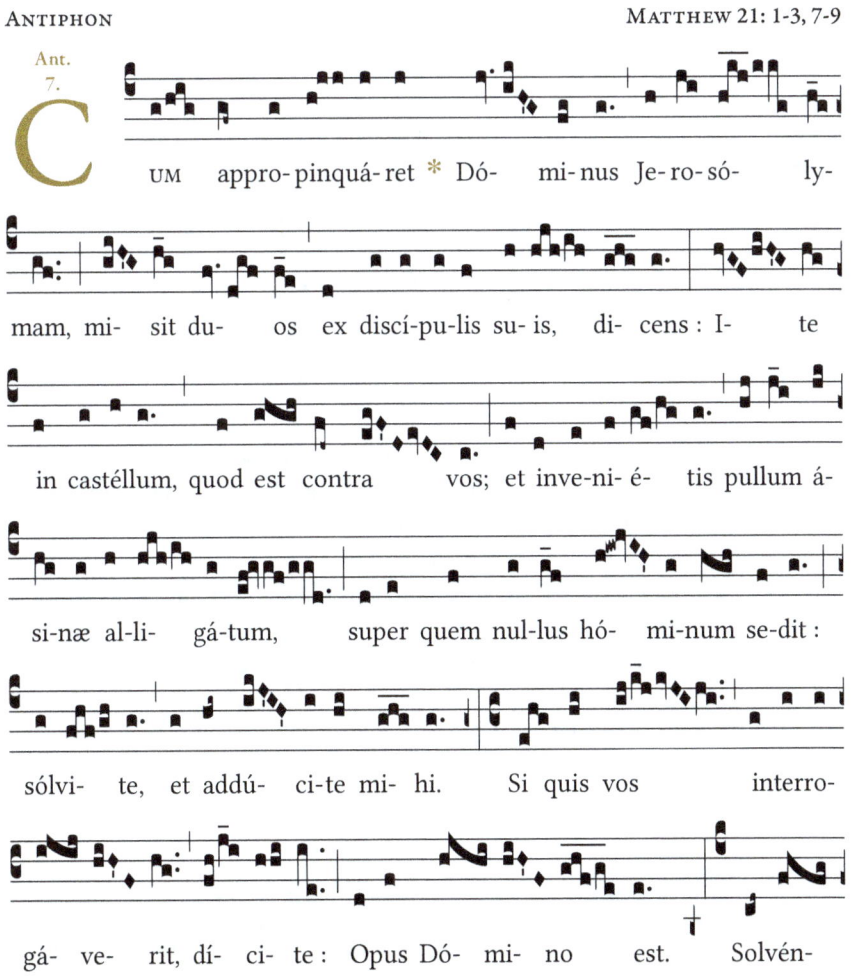

Cum appro-pinquá-ret * Dó- mi-nus Je-ro-só- ly-mam, mi- sit du- os ex discí-pu-lis su- is, di- cens : I- te in castéllum, quod est contra vos; et inve-ni-é- tis pullum á-si-næ al-li- gá-tum, super quem nul-lus hó- mi-num se-dit : sólvi- te, et addú- ci-te mi- hi. Si quis vos interro-gá- ve- rit, dí- ci- te : Opus Dó- mi- no est. Solvén-

tes   ad-du-xé-runt ad Je-sum: et impo-su- é-runt il- li vesti-mén-

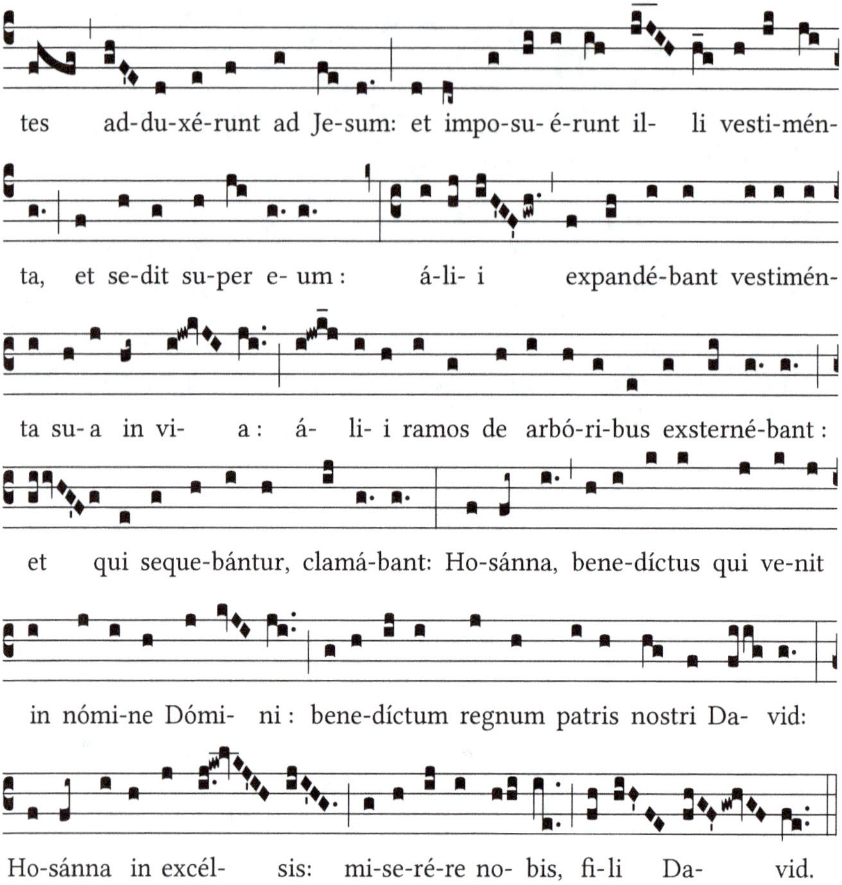

ta,   et se-dit su-per e- um :   á-li- i   expandé-bant vestimén-

ta su- a in vi-   a :   á- li- i ramos de arbó-ri-bus exsterné-bant :

et   qui seque-bántur, clamá-bant: Ho-sánna, bene-díctus qui ve-nit

in nómi-ne Dómi- ni : bene-díctum regnum patris nostri Da- vid:

Ho-sánna in excél- sis: mi-se-ré-re no- bis, fi-li Da- vid.

ANTIPHON: When our Lord drew nigh to Jerusalem, He sent two of His disciples, saying: Go ye into the village over against you; and you shall find an ass's colt tied, on which no man hath sat: loose it, and bring it to Me. If any man shall question you, say: The Lord hath need of it. They loosed it and brought it to Jesus, and laid their garments upon it, and He seated Himself on it; some spread their garments in the way; others strewed branches from the trees; and those who followed cried out: Hosanna! Blessed is He that cometh in the Name of the Lord; blessed be the reign of our father David! Hosanna in the highest! O Son of David, have mercy on us!

ANTIPHON   JOHN 12: 12-13

Ant. 7.

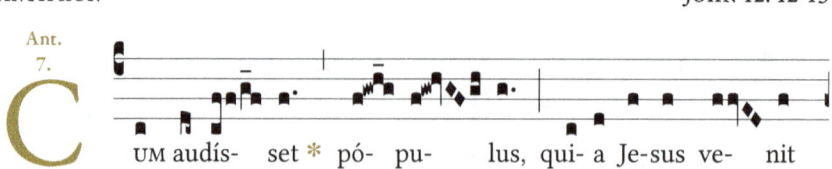

C UM audís- set * pó- pu- lus, qui- a Je-sus ve- nit

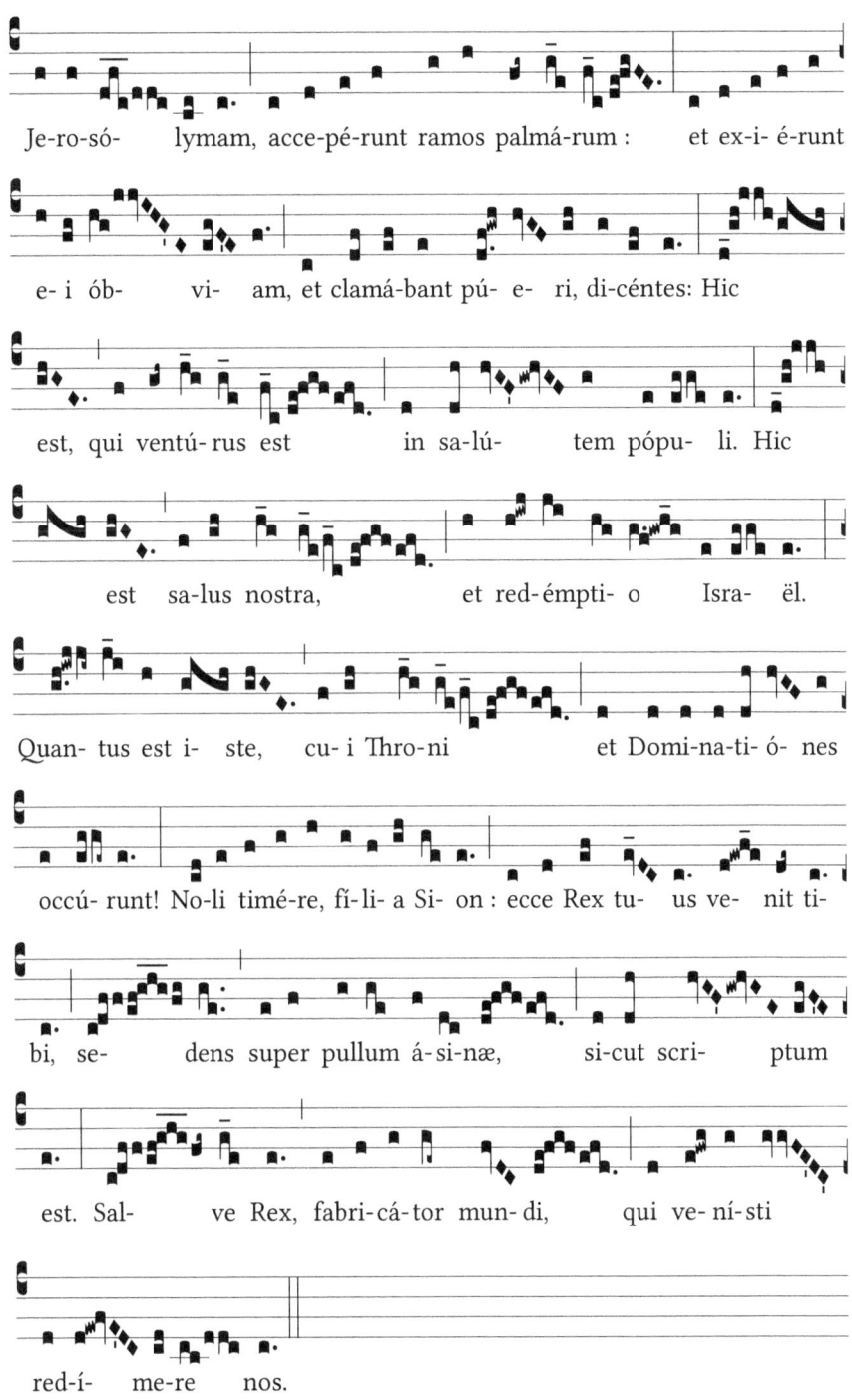

Je-ro-só- lymam, acce-pé-runt ramos palmá-rum : et ex-i- é-runt

e- i ób- vi- am, et clamá-bant pú- e- ri, di-céntes: Hic

est, qui ventú- rus est in sa-lú- tem pópu- li. Hic

est sa-lus nostra, et red-émpti- o Isra- ël.

Quan- tus est i- ste, cu- i Thro-ni et Domi-na-ti- ó- nes

occú- runt! No-li timé-re, fí-li- a Si- on : ecce Rex tu- us ve- nit ti-

bi, se- dens super pullum á-si-næ, si-cut scri- ptum

est. Sal- ve Rex, fabri-cá-tor mun- di, qui ve- ní-sti

red-í- me-re nos.

ANTIPHON: When the people heard that Jesus was coming to Jerusalem, they took palm branches, and went forth to meet Him; and the children cried out, saying: This is He that is come for the salvation of the people. He is our salvation, and the redemption of Israel. How great is He whom the Thrones and Dominions go forth to meet! Fear not, O daughter of Sion; behold thy King cometh to thee sitting on an ass's colt, as it is written. Hail, O King, Creator of the world, who art come to redeem us!

ANTIPHON

Ant. 8.

A NTE sex di- es   * so- lémnis   Paschæ, quando ve- nit Dómi- nus in ci- vi- tá- tem Je- rú- sa- lem,   occurré- runt e- i pú- e-ri : et in má-ni-bus portá-bant ramos palmá- rum, et clamá-bant vo-ce magna di-céntes : Ho-sánna in excélsis : bene-díctus qui ve-ní-sti in mul-ti-tú- di-ne mi-se-ri-cór- di- æ : Ho-sánna   in excélsis.

ANTIPHON: Six days before the solemn feast of the Passover, when our Lord came into the city of Jerusalem, the children met Him: and in their hands they carried palm branches, and they cried out with a loud voice, saying: Hosanna in the highest! Blessed art Thou who art come in the multitude of Thy mercy. Hosanna in the highest!

ANTIPHON

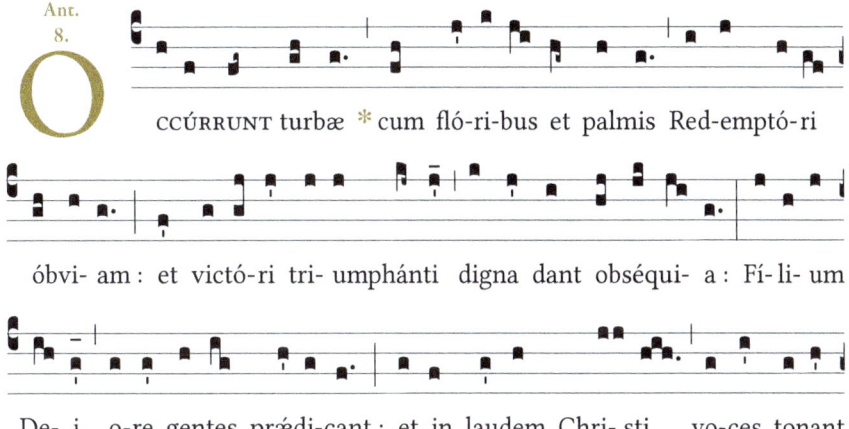

Ant. 8.

Occúrrunt turbæ *cum fló-ri-bus et palmis Red-emptó-ri óbvi- am : et victó-ri tri- umphánti digna dant obséqui- a : Fí- li- um De- i o-re gentes prǽdi-cant : et in laudem Chri- sti vo-ces tonant per nú-bi-la : Ho-sánna.

ANTIPHON: The multitude goeth forth to meet our Redeemer with flowers and palms, and payeth the homage due to a triumphant Conqueror: the Gentiles proclaim the Son of God; and their voices thunder through the skies in praise of Christ: Hosanna in the highest!

ANTIPHON

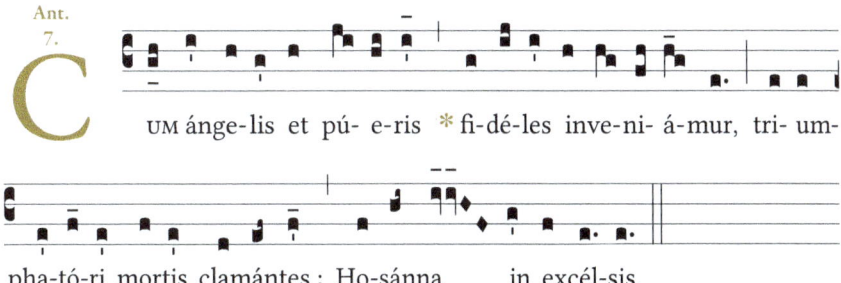

Ant. 7.

Cum ánge-lis et pú- e-ris *fi-dé-les inve-ni- á-mur, tri- umpha-tó-ri mortis clamántes : Ho-sánna in excél-sis.

ANTIPHON: Let the faithful join with the Angels and children, singing to the Conqueror of death: Hosanna in the highest!

ANTIPHON

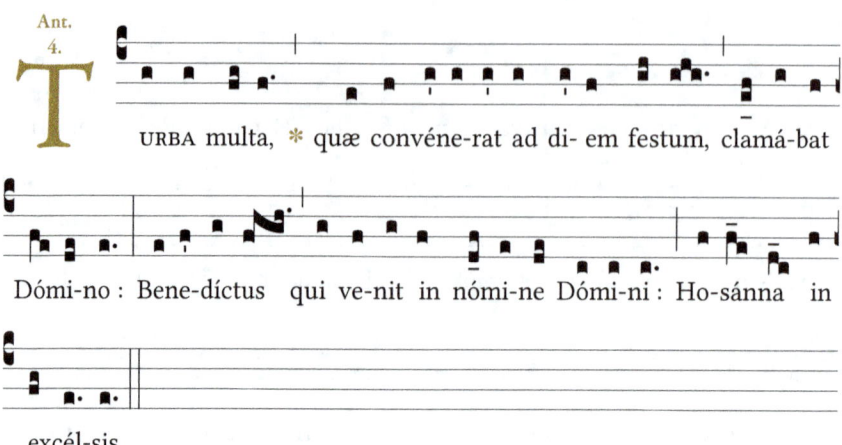

TURBA multa, * quæ convéne-rat ad di-em festum, clamá-bat

Dómi-no: Bene-díctus qui ve-nit in nómi-ne Dómi-ni: Ho-sánna in

excél-sis.

ANTIPHON: A great multitude that was met together at the festival cried out to the Lord: Blessed is He that cometh in the Name of the Lord: Hosanna in the Highest!

At the return of the procession two or four cantors go into the church and, shutting the door, stand facing towards the procession, singing the hymn Glória, laus. *The celebrant then repeats this with those who are outside the church.*

The other verses, all or in part as may be found desirable, are then sung by those within, those remaining outside answering Glória, laus *after every verse.*

HYMN   THEODULF, BISHOP OF ORLEANS † 821

LÓ-RI-A, laus et honor ti-bi sit, Rex Christe Red-émptor :

Cu-i pu-e-rí-le de-cus prompsit Ho-sánna pi-um.

HYMN: Glory, praise and honor to Thee, O King Christ, the Redeemer: to whom children poured their glad and sweet Hosanna's song.

1. Isra- ël es tu Rex, Da-ví-dis et íncli-ta pro-les : Nómi-ne qui in Dó-

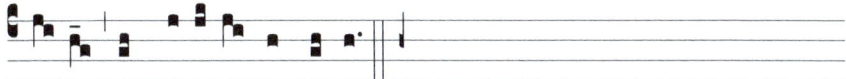

mi- ni, Rex bene-dí-cte, ve-nis.   ℟. Glória, laus.

1. Hail, King of Israel! David's Son of royal fame! Who comest in the Name of the Lord, O Blessed King.

2. Cœ-tus in ex-cél-sis te laudat cǽ-li-cus omnis, Et mortá-lis ho-mo,

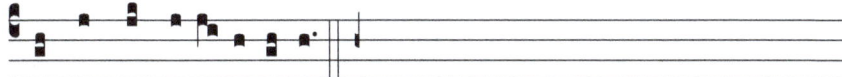

et cuncta cre- á- ta simul.   ℟. Glória, laus.

2. The Angel host laud Thee on high, on earth mankind, with all created things.

3. Plebs Hebrǽa ti- bi cum palmis óbvi- a ve-nit : Cum pre-ce, vo-to,

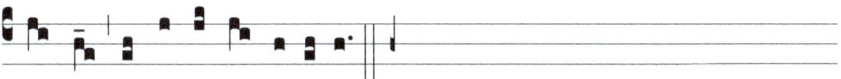

hymnis, ádsumus ec-ce ti-bi.   ℟. Glória, laus.

3. With palms the Jews went forth to meet Thee. We greet Thee now with prayers and hymns.

4. Hi ti-bi pas-sú- ro solvé-bant mú-ni- a laudis : Nos ti-bi re-gnán-ti

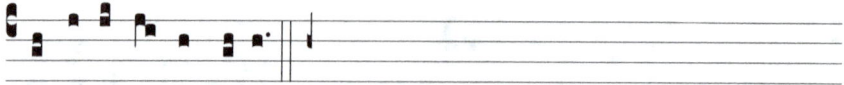

pángimus ec-ce me-los.   ℟. Glória, laus.

4. On Thy way to die, they crowned Thee with praise; We raise our song to Thee, now King on high.

5. Hi pla-cu- é-re   ti- bi, plá-ce- at de-vó-ti- o nostra : Rex bone, Rex

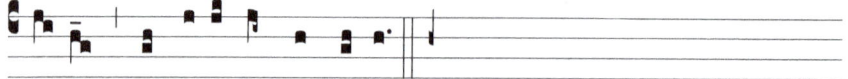

clemens, cui bona cuncta pla-cent.   ℟. Glória, laus.

5. Their poor homage pleased Thee, O gracious King! O clement King, accept too ours, the best that we can bring.

After this, the subdeacon knocks on the door with the shaft of the processional cross: when the door is opened, the procession enters the church, singing:

RESPONSORY   INGREDIÉNTE DÓMINO

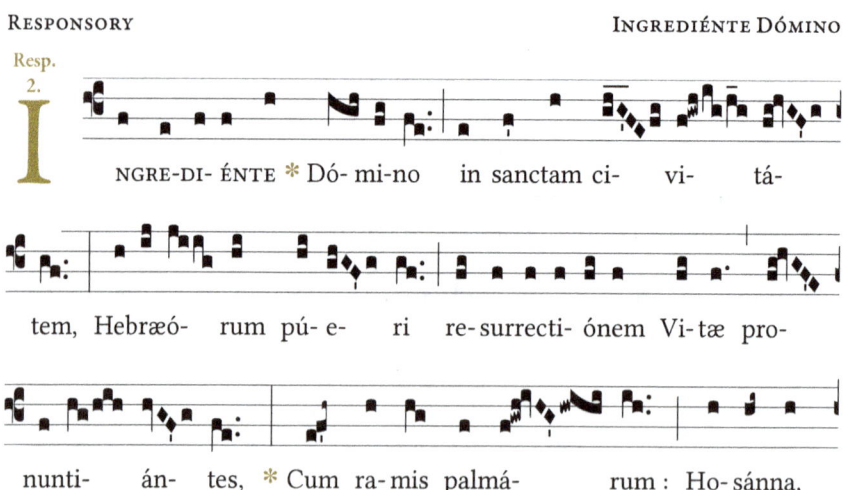

NGRE-DI- ÉNTE * Dó- mi-no in sanctam ci- vi- tá-

tem, Hebræó- rum pú- e- ri re-surrecti- ónem Vi-tæ pro-

nunti- án- tes, * Cum ra-mis palmá-   rum : Ho-sánna,

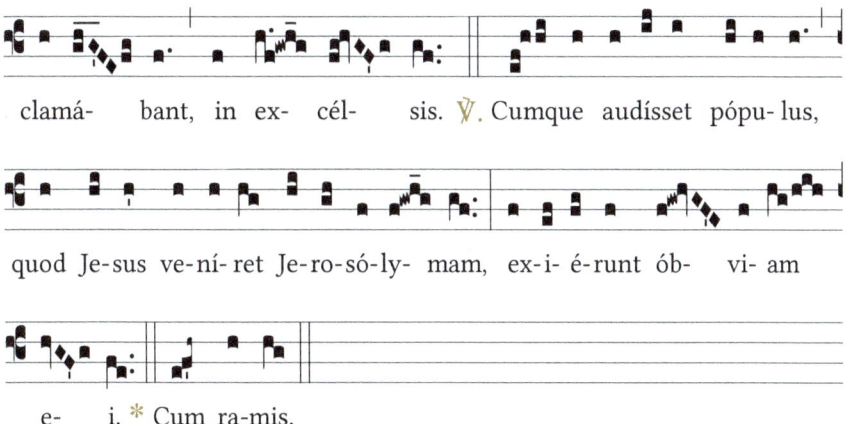

clamá- bant, in ex- cél- sis. ℣. Cumque audísset pópu- lus,

quod Je-sus ve-ní- ret Je-ro-só-ly- mam, ex-i- é-runt ób- vi- am

e- i. * Cum ra-mis.

℟. As our Lord entered the holy city, the Hebrew children, declaring the resurrection of life, * With palm branches, cried out: Hosanna in the highest. ℣. When the people heard that Jesus was coming to Jerusalem, they went forth to meet Him: * With palm branches, cried out: Hosanna in the highest.

The Mass is then celebrated, and at Mass all hold the palms in their hands while the Passion and Gospel are sung.

THE MASS

PRAYERS AT THE FOOT OF THE ALTAR

The celebrant bows before the altar and makes the sign of the cross saying:

IN nómine Patris, ✠ et Fílii, et Spíritus Sancti.
Amen.

IN the Name of the Father, ✠ and of the Son, and of the Holy Ghost.
Amen.

℣. Introíbo ad altáre Dei.

℟. Ad Deum, qui lætíficat juventútem meam.

℣. Adjutórium nostrum ✠ in nómine Dómini.

℟. Qui fecit cælum et terram.

℣. I will go in to the altar of God.

℟. To God who giveth joy to my youth.

℣. Our help ✠ is in the Name of the Lord.

℟. Who made heaven and earth.

CONFÍTEOR

The celebrant bows low and says:

CONFÍTEOR Deo omnipoténti, beátæ Maríæ semper Vírgini, beáto Michaéli Archángelo, beáto Joánni Baptístæ, sanctis Apóstolis Petro et Paulo, ómnibus Sanctis, et vobis, fratres: quia peccávi nimis cogitatióne, verbo et ópere: **(Pércutit sibi pectus ter, dicens)** mea culpa, mea culpa, mea máxima culpa. Ideo precor beátam Maríam semper Vírginem, beátum Michaélem Archángelum, beátum Joánnem Baptístam, sanctos Apóstolos Petrum et Paulum, omnes Sanctos, et vos, fratres, oráre pro me ad Dóminum, Deum nostrum.

℟. Misereátur tui omnípotens Deus, et, dimíssis peccátis tuis, perdúcat te ad vitam ætérnam.

℣. Amen.

I CONFESS to almighty God, to the blessed Mary ever Virgin, blessed Michael the Archangel, blessed John the Baptist, the holy Apostles Peter and Paul, to all the Saints, and to you, brothers, that I have sinned exceedingly in thought, word, and deed, **(The priest strikes his breast three times, saying:)** through my fault, through my fault, through my most grievous fault. Therefore I beseech the blessed Mary, ever Virgin, blessed Michael the Archangel, blessed John the Baptist, the holy Apostles Peter and Paul, all the Saints, and you, brothers, to pray to the Lord our God for me.

℟. May almighty God be merciful to thee, and forgiving thy sins, bring thee to everlasting life.

℣. Amen.

The server bows and says:

Cᴏɴꜰíᴛᴇᴏʀ Deo omnipoténti, beátæ Maríæ semper Vírgini, beáto Michaéli Archángelo, beáto Joánni Baptístæ, sanctis Apóstolis Petro et Paulo, ómnibus Sanctis, et tibi, pater: quia peccávi nimis cogitatióne, verbo et ópere: (**Pércutit sibi pectus ter, dicens**) mea culpa, mea culpa, mea máxima culpa. Ideo precor beátam Maríam semper Vírginem, beátum Michaélem Archángelum, beátum Joánnem Baptístam, sanctos Apóstolos Petrum et Paulum, omnes Sanctos, et te, pater, oráre pro me ad Dóminum, Deum nostrum.

℣. Misereátur vestri omnípotens Deus, et, dimíssis peccátis vestris, perdúcat vos ad vitam ætérnam.

℟. Amen.

℣. Indulgéntiam, ✠ absolutiónem et remissiónem peccatórum nostrórum tríbuat nobis omnípotens et miséricors Dóminus.

℟. Amen.

The celebrant bows and continues:

℣. Deus, tu convérsus vivificábis nos.

℟. Et plebs tua lætábitur in te.

℣. Osténde nobis, Dómine, misericórdiam tuam.

℟. Et salutáre tuum da nobis.

℣. Dómine, exáudi oratiónem meam.

℟. Et clamor meus ad te véniat.

℣. Dóminus vobíscum.

℟. Et cum spíritu tuo.

Oʀéᴍᴜs.

I ᴄᴏɴꜰᴇss to almighty God, to the blessed Mary ever Virgin, blessed Michael the Archangel, blessed John the Baptist, the holy Apostles Peter and Paul, to all the Saints, and to you, Father, that I have sinned exceedingly in thought, word, and deed, (**Now strike your breast three times, saying:**) through my fault, through my fault, through my most grievous fault. Therefore I beseech the blessed Mary, ever Virgin, blessed Michael the Archangel, blessed John the Baptist, the holy Apostles Peter and Paul, all the Saints, and you, Father, to pray to the Lord our God for me.

℣. May almighty God be merciful to thee, and forgiving thy sins, bring thee to everlasting life.

℟. Amen.

℣. May the ✠ almighty and merciful Lord grant us pardon, absolution, and remission of our sins.

℟. Amen.

℣. O God, Thou wilt turn again and quicken us.

℟. And thy people shall rejoice in Thee.

℣. Show us, O Lord, Thy mercy.

℟. And grant us Thy salvation.

℣. O Lord, hear my prayer.

℟. And let my cry come before Thee.

℣. The Lord be with you.

℟. And with thy spirit.

Lᴇᴛ ᴜs ᴘʀᴀʏ.

The celebrant ascends to the altar and says silently:

AUFER a nobis, quǽsumus, Dómine, iniquitátes nostras: ut ad Sancta sanctórum puris mereámur méntibus introíre. Per Christum, Dóminum nostrum. Amen.

Orámus te, Dómine, per mérita Sanctórum tuórum, quorum relíquiæ hic sunt, et ómnium Sanctórum: ut indulgére dignéris ómnia peccáta mea. Amen.

TAKE away from us our iniquities, we beseech Thee, O Lord, that we may be worthy to enter with pure minds into the Holy of Holies, through Christ our Lord. Amen.

We beseech Thee, O Lord, by the merits of Thy Saints, whose relics are here, and of all the Saints, that Thou wouldst vouchsafe to forgive me all my sins. Amen.

INTROIT

The celebrant reads the Introit *from the Epistle side of the altar:*

INTROIT   PSALM 21: 20, 22

Dó- MINE, * ne longe fá- ci- as auxí- li- um tu- um a me, ad defensi- ónem me- am áspi- ce: lí- be- ra me de o- re le- ó- nis, et a córni- bus u- ni-cornu- ó- rum humi-li-tá- tem me- am. *Ps.* De- us, De- us me- us, réspi-ce in me, * qua-re me de-re-liquí-sti? longe a sa-lú-te me- a verba de-lictó- rum me- ó-rum.

Introit: O Lord, be not far from me; O my help, hasten to aid me. Save me from the lion's mouth; from the horns of the wild bulls, my wretched life. **Ps. 21:2** My God, my God, look upon me, why have You forsaken me? Far from my salvation are the words of my sins.

The celebrant moves to the middle of the altar and alternately recites the Kyrie *with the server.*

Kyrie

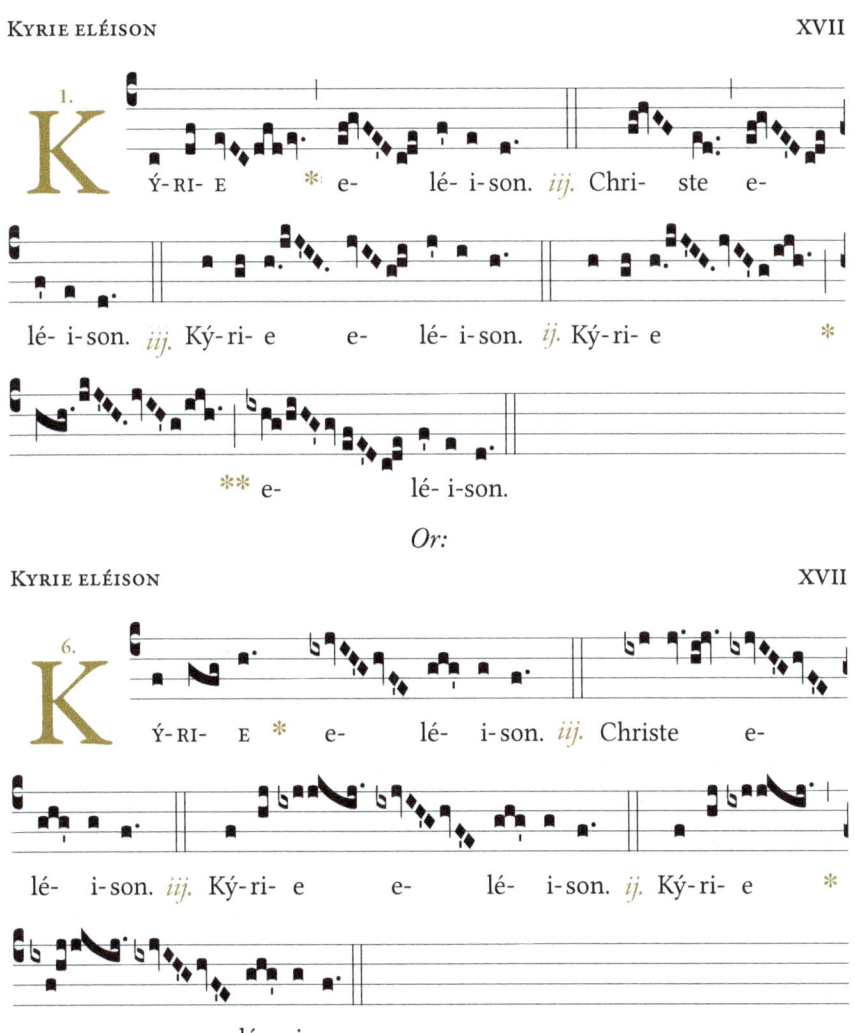

Kyrie: Lord, have mercy. (**3x**) Christ, have mercy. (**3x**) Lord, have mercy. (**3x**)

COLLECT

The celebrant turns to the people and says:

℣. Dóminus vobíscum.

℟. Et cum spíritu tuo.

℣. The Lord be with you.

℟. And with thy spirit.

ORÉMUS.

LET US PRAY.

Omnípotens sempitérne Deus, qui humáno géneri, ad imitándum humilitátis exémplum, Salvatórem nostrum carnem súmere et crucem subíre fecísti: concéde propítius; ut et patiéntiæ ipsíus habére documénta et resurrectiónis consórtia mereámur. Per eúndem Dóminum nostrum Jesum Christum Fílium tuum, qui tecum vivit et regnat in unitáte Spíritus Sancti, Deus, per ómnia sǽcula sæculórum.

℟. Amen.

Almighty, eternal God, Who, to provide mankind an example of humility for it to imitate, willed that the Saviour should assume our flesh and suffer death upon the Cross, mercifully grant that we may be found worthy of the lesson of His endurance and the fellowship of His resurrection. Through the same Jesus Christ, Thy Son, Our Lord, Who liveth and reigneth with Thee in the unity of the Holy Ghost, God, world without end.

℟. Amen.

The celebrant reads the Lesson from the Epistle side of the altar, or at a Solemn High Mass the subdeacon sings it:

LESSON FROM THE LETTER OF ST. PAUL TO THE PHILIPPIANS
Philippians 2: 5-11

Fratres: Hoc enim sentíte in vobis, quod et in Christo Jesu: qui, cum in forma Dei esset, non rapínam arbitrátus est esse se æquálem Deo: sed semetípsum exinanívit, formam servi accípiens, in similitúdinem hóminum factus, et hábitu invéntus ut homo. Humiliávit semetípsum, factus obédiens usque ad mortem, mortem autem crucis. Propter quod et Deus exaltávit illum: et donávit illi nomen, quod est super omne nomen: *(hic genuflectitur)* ut in nómine Jesu omne genu flectátur cæléstium,

Brethren: Have this in mind in you which was also in Christ Jesus, Who, though He was by nature God, did not consider being equal to God a thing to be clung to, but emptied Himself, taking the nature of a slave and being made like unto men. And appearing in the form of man, He humbled Himself, becoming obedient to death, even to death on a cross. Therefore God also has exalted Him and has bestowed upon Him the Name that is above every name, *(Kneel)* so that at the Name of Jesus

terréstrium et infernórum: et omnis lingua confiteátur, quia Dóminus Jesus Christus in glória est Dei Patris.

every knee should bend of those in heaven, on earth and under the earth and every tongue should confess that the Lord Jesus Christ is in the glory of God the Father.

℟. Deo grátias.

℟. Thanks be to God.

GRADUAL   PSALM 72: 24, 1-3

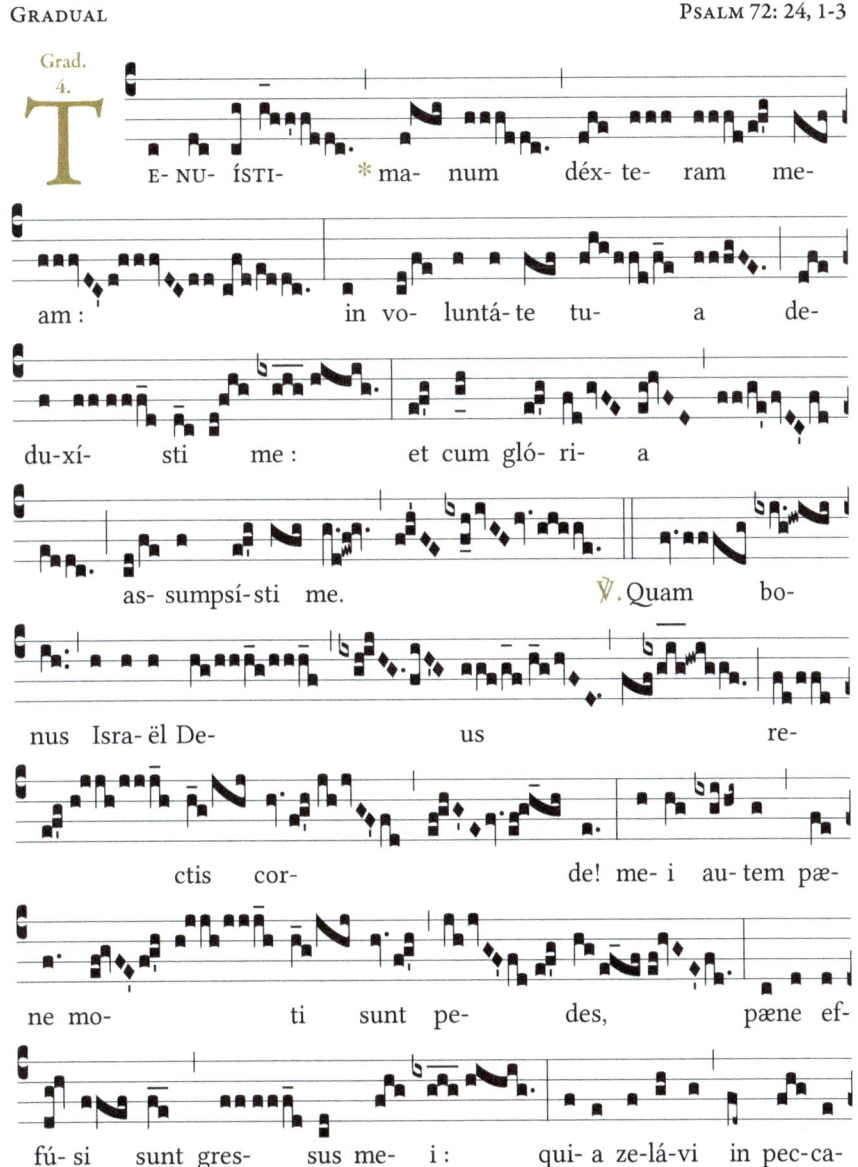

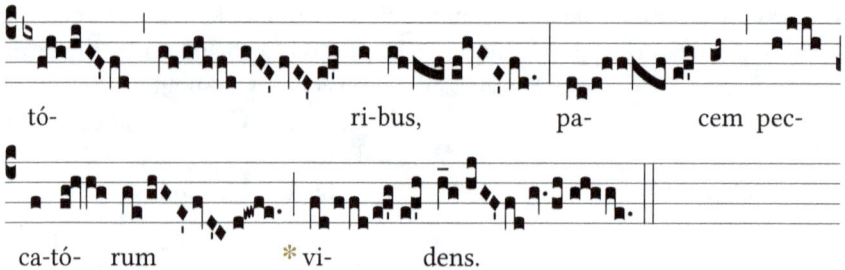

tó- ri-bus, pa- cem pec-

ca-tó- rum   * vi- dens.

GRADUAL: You have hold of my right hand; with Your counsel You guide me; and in the end You will receive me in glory. ℣. How good God is to Israel, to those who are clean of heart! But, as for me, I almost lost my balance; my feet all but slipped, because I was envious of sinners when I saw them prosper though they were wicked.

TRACT   PSALM 21: 2-9, 18-19, 22, 24, 32

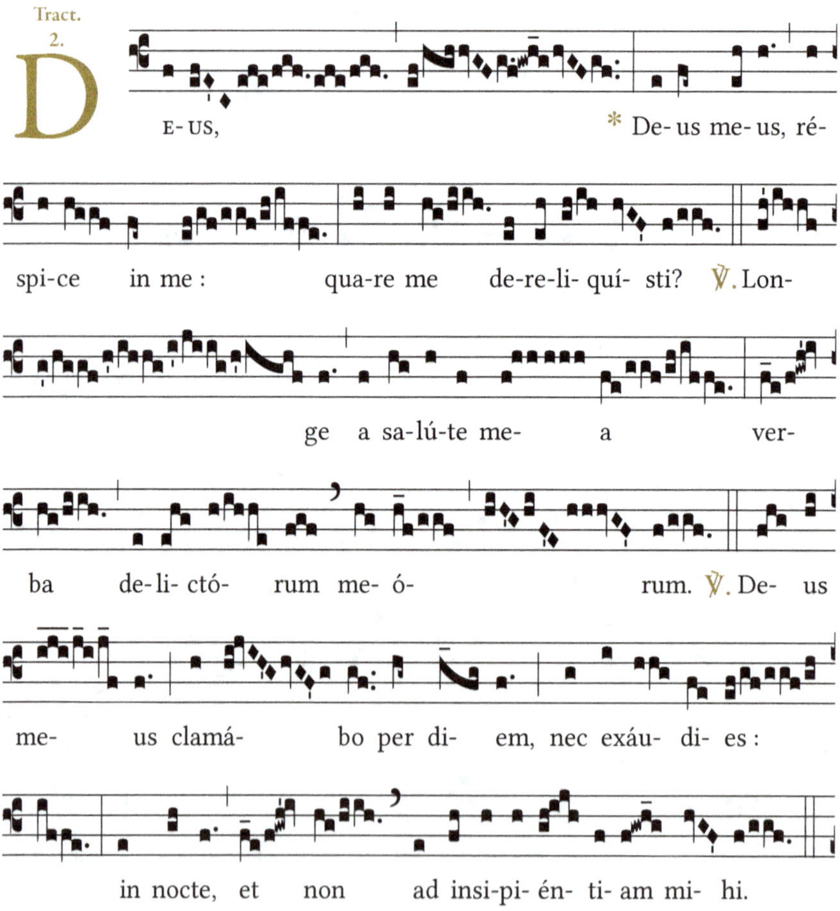

Tract.
2.

D

E- US,   * De- us me- us, ré-

spi-ce   in me :   qua-re me   de-re-li- quí- sti?   ℣. Lon-

ge   a sa-lú-te me-   a   ver-

ba   de-li-ctó- rum me- ó-   rum. ℣. De- us

me-   us clamá-   bo per di-   em, nec exáu- di- es :

in nocte, et   non   ad insi-pi- én- ti- am mi- hi.

℣. Tu au- tem in sancto há- bi- tas,

laus Is- ra- ël. ℣. In te spe-ra-vé- runt

patres no- stri : spe-ra-vé- runt, et li- be- rásti

e- os. ℣. Ad te cla-ma-vé- runt, et sal-vi fa- cti sunt :

in te spe-ra-vé- runt, et non sunt confú- si.

℣. Ego au- tem sum vermis, et non ho-

mo : oppróbri- um hó- mi-num, et abjécti-

o ple- bis. ℣. Omnes qui vi- dé- bant me, a-

sperna-bán- tur me : lo-cú-ti sunt lá- bi- is

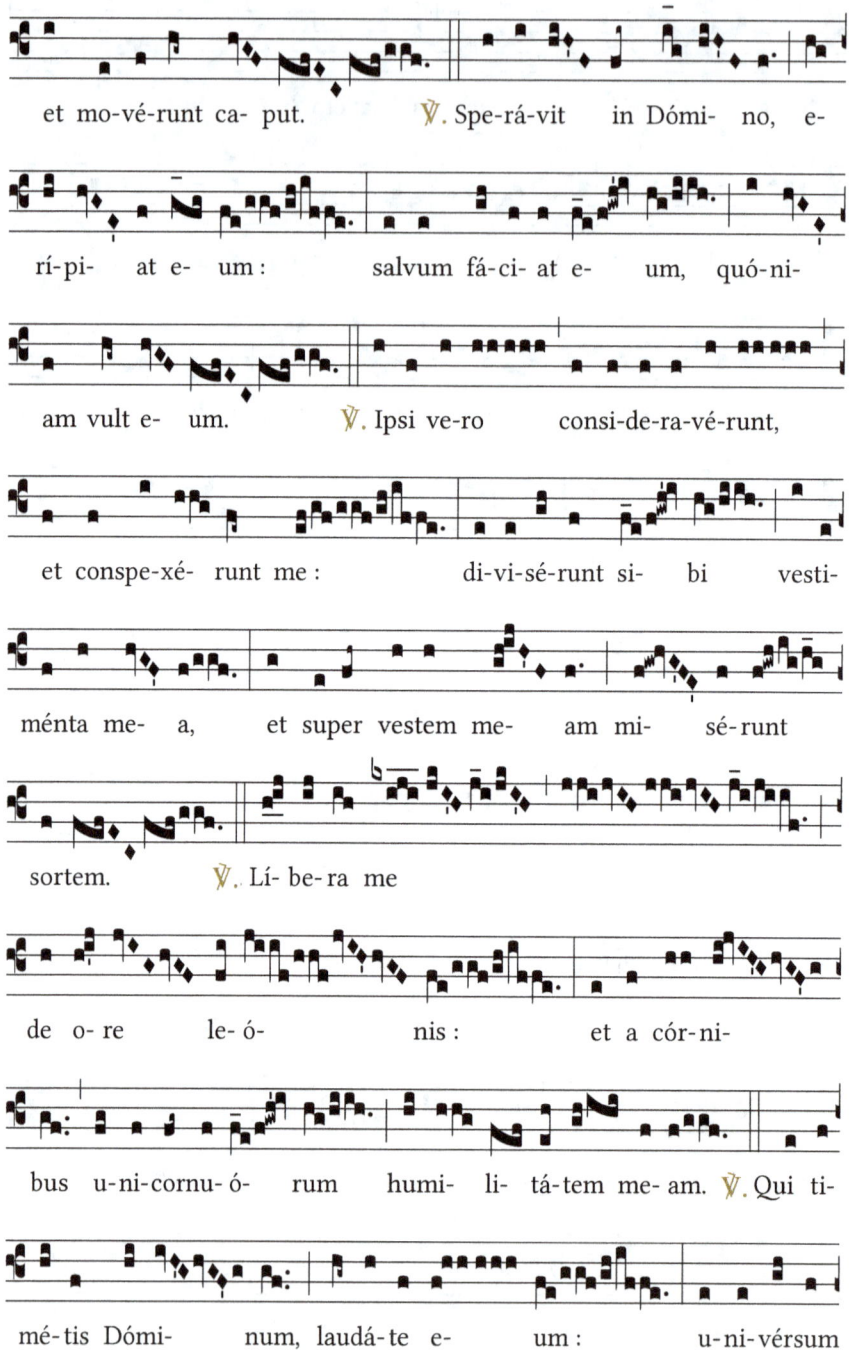

et mo-vé-runt ca- put. ℣. Spe-rá-vit in Dómi- no, e-

rí-pi- at e- um : salvum fá-ci- at e- um, quó-ni-

am vult e- um. ℣. Ipsi ve-ro consi-de-ra-vé-runt,

et conspe-xé- runt me : di-vi-sé-runt si- bi vesti-

ménta me- a, et super vestem me- am mi- sé-runt

sortem. ℣. Lí- be-ra me

de o- re le- ó- nis : et a cór-ni-

bus u-ni-cornu- ó- rum humi- li- tá-tem me-am. ℣. Qui ti-

mé-tis Dómi- num, laudá-te e- um : u-ni-vérsum

semen Ja- cob, magni- fi- cá-te e- um. ℣. Annunti- á-bi-

tur Dómi- no ge-ne-rá-ti- o ventú- ra : et

annunti- ábunt cæ- li justí- ti- am e-

jus. ℣. Pó-pu-lo qui nascé- tur, quem fe- cit

* Dó- mi-nus.

TRACT: My God, my God, look upon me: why have You forsaken me? ℣. Far from my salvation, are the words of my sins. ℣. O my God, I cry out by day and You answer not; by night, and there is no relief. ℣. But You are enthroned in the holy place, O glory of Israel! ℣. In You our fathers trusted; they trusted and You delivered them. ℣. To You they cried, and they escaped; in You they trusted, and they were not put to shame. ℣. But I am a worm, not a man; the scorn of men, despised by the people. ℣. All who see me, scoff at me; they mock me with parted lips, they wag their heads. ℣. He relied on the Lord; let Him deliver him, let Him rescue him, if He loves him. ℣. But they look on and gloat over me; they divide my garments among them, and for my vesture they cast lots. ℣. Save me from the lion's mouth; from the horns of the wild bulls, my wretched life. ℣. You who fear the Lord, praise Him: all you descendants of Jacob, give glory to Him. ℣. There shall be declared to the Lord a generation to come: and the heavens shall show forth His justice. ℣. To a people that shall be born, which the Lord has made.

THE PASSION ✠ OF OUR LORD JESUS CHRIST
ACCORDING TO MATTHEW
Matthew 26: 1-75; 27: 1-66

J: Our Lord Jesus Christ | C: Narrator | *S: Other speaker(s)*

IN illo témpore: Dixit Jesus discípulis suis:

J. Scitis, quid post bíduum Pascha fiet, et Fílius hóminis tradétur, ut crucifigátur.

C. Tunc congregáti sunt príncipes sacerdótum et senióres pópuli in átrium príncipis sacerdótum, qui dicebátur Cáiphas: et consílium fecérunt, ut Jesum dolo tenérent et occíderent. Dicébant autem :

S. *Non in die festo, ne forte tumúltus fíeret in pópulo.*

C. Cum autem Jesus esset in Bethánia in domo Simónis leprósi, accéssit ad eum múlier habens alabástrum unguénti pretiósi, et effúdit super caput ipsíus recumbéntis. Vidéntes autem discípuli, indignáti sunt, dicéntes:

S. *Ut quid perdítio hæc? pótuit enim istud venúmdari multo, et dari paupéribus.*

C. Sciens autem Jesus, ait illis:

J. Quid molésti estis huic mulíeri? opus enim bonum operáta est in me. Nam semper páuperes habétis vobíscum: me autem non semper habétis. Mittens enim hæc unguéntum hoc in corpus meum, ad sepeliéndum me fecit. Amen, dico

AT that time Jesus said to His disciples:

J. You know that after two days shall be the Pasch, and the Son of Man shall be delivered up to be crucified.

C. Then were gathered together the chief priests and ancients of the people, into the court of the high priest, who was called Caiphas; and they consulted together, that by subtlety they might apprehend Jesus, and put Him to death. But they said:

S. *Not on the festival day, lest perhaps there should be a tumult among the people.*

C. And when Jesus was in Bethania, in the house of Simon the leper, there came to Him a woman having an alabaster box of precious ointment and poured it on His head as He was at table. And the disciples seeing it had indignation, saying:

S. *To what purpose is this waste? For this might have been sold for much and given to the poor.*

C. And Jesus knowing it, said to them:

J. Why do you trouble this woman? For she hath wrought a good work upon Me. For the poor you have always with you; but Me you have not always. For she, in pouring this ointment upon My Body, hath done it for My burial. Amen I say to

vobis, ubicúmque prædicátum fúerit hoc Evangélium in toto mundo, dicétur et, quod hæc fecit, in memóriam ejus.

C. Tunc ábiit unus de duódecim, qui dicebátur Judas Iscariótes, ad príncipes sacerdótum, et ait illis:

S. *Quid vultis mihi dare, et ego vobis eum tradam?*

C. At illi constituérunt ei trigínta argénteos. Et exínde quærébat opportunitátem, ut eum tráderet.

Prima autem die azymórum accessérunt discípuli ad Jesum, dicéntes:

S. *Ubi vis parémus tibi comédere pascha?*

C. At Jesus dixit:

J. Ite in civitátem ad quendam, et dícite ei: Magíster dicit: Tempus meum prope est, apud te fácio pascha cum discípulis meis.

C. Et fecérunt discípuli, sicut constítuit illis Jesus, et paravérunt pascha. Véspere autem facto, discumbébat cum duódecim discípulis suis. Et edéntibus illis, dixit:

J. Amen, dico vobis, quia unus vestrum me traditúrus est.

C. Et contristáti valde, cæpérunt sínguli dícere:

S. *Numquid ego sum, Dómine?*

C. At ipse respóndens, ait:

J. Qui intíngit mecum manum in parópside, hic me tradet. Fílius quidem hóminis vadit, sicut scriptum est de illo: væ autem hómini illi, per quem Fílius hóminis tradétur: bonum erat ei, si natus non fuísset homo ille.

you, wheresoever this gospel shall be preached in the whole world, that also which she hath done shall be told for a memory of her.

C. Then went one of the twelve, who was called Judas Iscariot, to the chief priests, and he said to them:

S. *What will you give me; and I will deliver Him unto you?*

C. But they appointed him thirty pieces of silver. And from thenceforth he sought opportunity to betray Him.

And on the first day of the Azymes the disciples came to Jesus, saying:

S. *Where wilt Thou that we prepare for Thee to eat the pasch?*

C. But Jesus said:

J. Go ye into the city to a certain man, and say to him: The master saith, My time is near at hand, with thee I make the pasch with My disciples.

C. And the disciples did as Jesus appointed to them; and they prepared the pasch. But when it was evening, He sat down with His twelve disciples; and whilst they were eating, He said:

J. Amen I say to you that one of you is about to betray Me.

C. And they, being very much troubled, began every one to say:

S. *Is it I, Lord?*

C. But He answering, said:

J. He that dippeth his hand with Me in the dish, he shall betray Me. The Son of Man indeed goeth, as it is written of Him; but woe to that man by whom the Son of Man shall be betrayed; it were better for him, if that man had not been born.

C. Respóndens autem Judas, qui trádidit eum, dixit:

S. *Numquid ego sum, Rabbi?*

C. Ait illi:

J. Tu dixísti.

C. Cenántibus autem eis, accépit Jesus panem, et benedíxit, ac fregit, dedítque discípulis suis, et ait:

J. Accípite et comédite: hoc est corpus meum.

C. Et accípiens cálicem, grátias egit: et dedit illis, dicens:

J. Bíbite ex hoc omnes. Hic est enim sanguis meus novi Testaménti, qui pro multis effundétur in remissiónem peccatórum. Dico autem vobis: non bibam ámodo de hoc genímine vitis usque in diem illum, cum illud bibam vobíscum novum in regno Patris mei.

C. Et hymno dicto, exiérunt in montem Olivéti. Tunc dicit illis Jesus:

J. Omnes vos scándalum patiémini in me in ista nocte. Scriptum est enim: Percútiam pastórem, et dispergéntur oves gregis. Postquam autem resurréxero, præcédam vos in Galilǽam.

C. Respóndens autem Petrus, ait illi:

S. *Et si omnes scandalizáti fúerint in te, ego numquam scandalizábor.*

C. Ait illi Jesus:

J. Amen, dico tibi, quia in hac nocte, ántequam gallus cantet, ter me negábis.

C. Ait illi Petrus:

S. *Etiam si oportúerit me mori tecum, non te negábo.*

C. And Judas that betrayed Him, answering said:

S. *Is it I, Rabbi?*

C. He saith to him:

J. Thou hast said it.

C. And whilst they were at supper, Jesus took bread, and blessed and broke and gave to His disciples, and said:

J. Take ye and eat; this is My Body.

C. And taking the chalice, He gave thanks and gave to them, saying:

J. Drink ye all of this. For this is My blood of the new testament, which shall be shed for many unto the remission of sins. And I say to you, I will not drink from henceforth of this fruit of the vine until that day when I shall drink it with you new in the kingdom of My Father.

C. And a hymn being said, they went out unto Mount Olivet. Then Jesus saith to them:

J. All you shall be scandalized in Me this night; for it is written: I will strike the shepherd, and the sheep of the flock shall be dispersed; but after I shall be risen again, I will go before you into Galilee.

C. And Peter, answering, said to Him:

S. *Although all shall be scandalized in Thee, I will never be scandalized.*

C. Jesus said to him:

J. Amen I say to thee, that in this night, before the cock crow, thou wilt deny Me thrice.

C. Peter saith to Him:

S. *Yea, though I should die with Thee, I will not deny Thee.*

C. Simíliter et omnes discípuli dixérunt.

Tunc venit Jesus cum illis in villam, quæ dícitur Gethsémani, et dixit discípulis suis:

J. Sedéte hic, donec vadam illuc et orem.

C. Et assúmpto Petro et duóbus fíliis Zebedǽi, cæpit contristári et mæstus esse. Tunc ait illis:

J. Tristis est ánima mea usque ad mortem: sustinéte hic, et vigiláte mecum.

C. Et progréssus pusíllum, prócidit in fáciem suam, orans et dicens:

J. Pater mi, si possíbile est, tránseat a me calix iste: Verúmtamen non sicut ego volo, sed sicut tu.

C. Et venit ad discípulos suos, et invénit eos dormiéntes: et dicit Petro:

J. Sic non potuístis una hora vigiláre mecum? Vigiláte et oráte, ut non intrétis in tentatiónem. Spíritus quidem promptus est, caro autem infírma.

C. Iterum secúndo ábiit et orávit, dicens:

J. Pater mi, si non potest hic calix transíre, nisi bibam illum, fiat volúntas tua.

C. Et venit íterum, et invénit eos dormiéntes: erant enim óculi eórum graváti. Et relíctis illis, íterum ábiit et orávit tértio, eúndem sermónem dicens. Tunc venit ad discípulos suos, et dicit illis:

J. Dormíte jam et requiéscite: ecce, appropinquávit hora, et Fílius

C. And in like manner said all the disciples.

Then Jesus came with them into a country place which is called Gethsemani; and He said to His disciples:

J. Sit you here, till I go yonder and pray.

C. And taking with Him Peter and the two sons of Zebedee, He began to grow sorrowful and to be sad. Then He saith to them:

J. My soul is sorrowful even unto death; stay you here and watch with Me.

C. And going a little further, He fell upon His face, praying and saying:

J. My Father, if it be possible, let this chalice pass from Me; nevertheless, not as I will, but as Thou wilt.

C. And He cometh to His disciples, and findeth them asleep. And He saith to Peter:

J. What! Could you not watch one hour with Me? Watch ye, and pray that ye enter not into temptation. The spirit indeed is willing, but the flesh is weak.

C. Again the second time, He went and prayed, saying:

J. My Father, if this chalice may not pass away, but I must drink it, Thy will be done.

C. And He cometh again, and findeth them sleeping, for their eyes were heavy. And leaving them, He went again and He prayed the third time, saying the self-same word. Then He cometh to His disciples, and saith to them:

J. Sleep ye now and take your rest; behold, the hour is at hand, and the

hóminis tradétur in manus peccatórum. Súrgite, eámus: ecce, appropinquávit, qui me tradet.

C. Adhuc eo loquénte, ecce, Judas, unus de duódecim, venit, et cum eo turba multa cum gládiis et fústibus, missi a princípibus sacerdótum et senióribus pópuli. Qui autem trádidit eum, dedit illis signum, dicens:

S. *Quemcúmque osculátus fúero, ipse est, tenéte eum.*

C. Et conféstim accédens ad Jesum, dixit:

S. *Ave, Rabbi.*

C. Et osculátus est eum. Dixítque illi Jesus:

J. Amíce, ad quid venísti?

C. Tunc accessérunt, et manus injecérunt in Jesum et tenuérunt eum.

Et ecce, unus ex his, qui erant cum Jesu, exténdens manum, exémit gládium suum, et percútiens servum príncipis sacerdótum, amputávit aurículam ejus. Tunc ait illi Jesus:

J. Convérte gládium tuum in locum suum. Omnes enim, qui accéperint gládium, gládio períbunt. An putas, quia non possum rogáre Patrem meum, et exhibébit mihi modo plus quam duódecim legiónes Angelórum? Quómodo ergo implebúntur Scriptúræ, quia sic opórtet fíeri?

C. In illa hora dixit Jesus turbis:

J. Tamquam ad latrónem exístis cum gládiis et fústibus comprehéndere me: quotídie apud vos sedébam docens in templo, et non me tenuístis.

Son of Man shall be betrayed into the hands of sinners. Rise, let us go; behold, he is at hand that will betray Me.

C. As He yet spoke, behold Judas, one of the twelve, came, and with him a great multitude with swords and clubs, sent from the chief priests and the ancients of the people. And he that betrayed Him gave them a sign, saying:

S. *Whomsoever I shall kiss, that is He; hold Him fast.*

C. And forthwith coming to Jesus, he said:

S. *Hail, Rabbi.*

C. And he kissed Him. And Jesus said to him:

J. Friend, whereto art thou come?

C. Then they came up and laid hands on Jesus, and held Him.

And behold one of them that were with Jesus, stretching forth his hand, drew out his sword, and striking the servant of the high priest, cut off his ear. Then Jesus saith to him:

J. Put up again thy sword into its place; for all that take the sword shall perish with the sword. Thinkest thou that I cannot ask My Father, and He will give Me presently more than twelve legions of Angels? How then shall the Scriptures be fulfilled, that so it must be done?

C. In that same hour Jesus said to the multitudes:

J. You are come out, as it were to a robber, with swords and clubs to apprehend Me. I sat daily with you, teaching in the temple, and you laid not hands on Me.

C. Hoc autem totum factum est, ut adimpleréntur Scriptúræ Prophetárum. Tunc discípuli omnes, relícto eo, fugérunt.

At illi tenéntes Jesum, duxérunt ad Cáipham, príncipem sacerdótum, ubi scribæ et senióres convénerant. Petrus autem sequebátur eum a longe, usque in átrium príncipis sacerdótum. Et ingréssus intro, sedébat cum minístris, ut vidéret finem. Príncipes autem sacerdótum et omne concílium quærébant falsum testimónium contra Jesum, ut eum morti tráderent: et non invenérunt, cum multi falsi testes accessíssent. Novíssime autem venérunt duo falsi testes et dixérunt:

S. Hic dixit: Possum destrúere templum Dei, et post tríduum reædificáre illud.

C. Et surgens princeps sacerdótum, ait illi:

S. Nihil respóndes ad ea, quæ isti advérsum te testificántur?

C. Jesus autem tacébat. Et princeps sacerdótum ait illi:

S. Adjúro te per Deum vivum, ut dicas nobis, si tu es Christus, Fílius Dei.

C. Dicit illi Jesus:

J. Tu dixísti. Verúmtamen dico vobis, ámodo vidébitis Fílium hóminis sedéntem a dextris virtútis Dei, et veniéntem in núbibus cæli.

C. Tunc princeps sacerdótum scidit vestiménta sua, dicens:

S. Blasphemávit: quid adhuc egémus téstibus? Ecce, nunc audístis

C. Now all this was done that the Scriptures of the prophets might be fulfilled. Then the disciples, all leaving Him, fled.

But they holding Jesus led Him to Caiphas the high priest, where the scribes and the ancients were assembled. And Peter followed Him afar off, even to the court of the high priest. And going in, he sat with the servants, that he might see the end. And the chief priests and the whole council sought false witness against Jesus, that they might put Him to death. And they found none, whereas many false witnesses had come in. And last of all there came two false witnesses; and they said:

S. This man said, I am able to destroy the temple of God, and after three days to rebuild it.

C. And the high priest, rising up, said to Him:

S. Answerest Thou nothing to the things which these witness against Thee?

C. But Jesus held His peace. And the high priest said to Him:

S. I adjure Thee by the living God, that Thou tell us if Thou be the Christ the Son of God.

C. Jesus saith to him:

J. Thou hast said it. Nevertheless I say to you, hereafter you shall see the Son of Man sitting on the right hand of the power of God, and coming in the clouds of heaven.

C. Then the high priest rent his garments, saying:

S. He hath blasphemed; what further need have we of witnesses?

blasphémiam: quid vobis vidétur?

C. At illi respondéntes dixérunt:

S. *Reus est mortis.*

C. Tunc exspuérunt in fáciem ejus, et cólaphis eum cecidérunt, álii autem palmas in fáciem ejus dedérunt, dicéntes:

S. *Prophetíza nobis, Christe, quis est, qui te percússit?*

C. Petrus vero sedébat foris in átrio: et accéssit ad eum una ancílla, dicens:

S. *Et tu cum Jesu Galiléo eras.*

C. At ille negávit coram ómnibus, dicens:

S. *Néscio, quid dicis.*

C. Exeúnte autem illo jánuam, vidit eum ália ancílla, et ait his, qui erant ibi:

S. *Et hic erat cum Jesu Nazaréno.*

C. Et íterum negávit cum juraménto:

S. *Quia non novi hóminem.*

C. Et post pusíllum accessérunt, qui stabant, et dixérunt Petro:

S. *Vere et tu ex illis es: nam et loquéla tua maniféstum te facit.*

C. Tunc cæpit detestári et juráre, quia non novísset hóminem. Et contínuo gallus cantávit. Et recordátus est Petrus verbi Jesu, quod díxerat: Priúsquam gallus cantet, ter me negábis. Et egréssus foras, flevit amáre.

Mane autem facto, consílium iniérunt omnes príncipes sacerdótum et senióres pópuli advérsus Jesum, ut eum morti tráderent. Et vinctum

Behold, now you have heard the blasphemy. What think you?

C. But they answering, said:

S. *He is guilty of death.*

C. Then they did spit in His face and buffeted Him; and others struck His face with the palms of their hands, saying:

S. *Prophesy unto us, O Christ, who is he that struck Thee?*

C. But Peter sat without in the court, and there came to him a servant maid, saying:

S. *Thou also wast with Jesus the Galilean.*

C. But he denied it before them all, saying:

S. *I know not what thou sayest.*

C. And as he went out of the gate, another maid saw him, and she saith to them that were there:

S. *This man also was with Jesus of Nazareth.*

C. And again he denied it with an oath:

S. *I know not the man.*

C. And after a little while, they came that stood by and said to Peter:

S. *Surely thou also art one of them; for even thy speech doth discover thee.*

C. Then he began to curse and to swear that he knew not the man; and immediately the cock crew. And Peter remembered the words of Jesus which He had said: before the cock crow, thou wilt deny Me thrice. And going forth, he wept bitterly.

And when morning was come, all the chief priests and ancients of the people took counsel against Jesus, that they might put Him to death. And they

adduxérunt eum, et tradidérunt Póntio Piláto præsidi.

Tunc videns Judas, qui eum trádidit, quod damnátus esset, pæniténtia ductus, réttulit trigínta argénteos princípibus sacerdótum et senióribus, dicens:

S. *Peccávi, tradens sánguinem justum.*

C. At illi dixérunt:

S. *Quid ad nos? Tu vidéris.*

C. Et projéctis argénteis in templo, recéssit: et ábiens, láqueo se suspéndit.

Príncipes autem sacerdótum, accéptis argénteis, dixérunt:

S. *Non licet eos míttere in córbonam: quia prétium sánguinis est.*

C. Consílio autem ínito, emérunt ex illis agrum fíguli, in sepultúram peregrinórum. Propter hoc vocátus est ager ille, Hacéldama, hoc est, ager sánguinis, usque in hodiérnum diem. Tunc implétum est, quod dictum est per Jeremíam Prophétam, dicéntem: Et accepérunt trigínta argénteos prétium appretiáti, quem appretiavérunt a fíliis Israël: et dedérunt eos in agrum fíguli, sicut constítuit mihi Dóminus.

Jesus autem stetit ante præsidem, et interrogávit eum præses, dicens:

S. *Tu es Rex Judæórum?*

C. Dicit illi Jesus:

J. Tu dicis.

C. Et cum accusarétur a princípibus sacerdótum et senióribus, nihil respóndit. Tunc dicit illi Pilátus:

brought Him bound, and delivered Him to Pontius Pilate the governor.

Then Judas, who betrayed Him, seeing that He was condemned, repenting himself, brought back the thirty pieces of silver to the chief priests and ancients, saying:

S. *I have sinned in betraying innocent blood.*

C. But they said:

S. *What is that to us? Look thou to it.*

C. And casting down the pieces of silver in the temple, he departed, and went and hanged himself with a halter.

But the chief priests having taken the pieces of silver, said:

S. *It is not lawful to put them into the corbona, because it is the price of blood.*

C. And after they had consulted together, they bought with them the potter's field, to be a burying-place for strangers. For this cause that field was called Haceldama, that is, the field of blood, even to this day. Then was fulfilled that which was spoken by Jeremias the prophet, saying: And they took the thirty pieces of silver, the price of Him that was prized, whom they prized of the children of Israel: and they gave them unto the potter's field, as the Lord appointed to me.

And Jesus stood before the governor, and the governor asked Him, saying:

S. *Art Thou the King of the Jews?*

C. Jesus saith to him:

J. Thou sayest it.

C. And when He was accused by the chief priests and ancients, He answered nothing. Then Pilate saith to Him:

S. Non audis, quanta advérsum te dicunt testimónia?

C. Et non respóndit ei ad ullum verbum, ita ut mirarétur præses veheménter. Per diem autem sollémnem consuéverat præses pópulo dimíttere unum vinctum, quem voluíssent. Habébat autem tunc vinctum insígnem, qui dicebátur Barábbas. Congregátis ergo illis, dixit Pilátus:

S. Quem vultis dimíttam vobis: Barábbam, an Jesum, qui dícitur Christus?

C. Sciébat enim, quod per invídiam tradidíssent eum. Sedénte autem illo pro tribunáli, misit ad eum uxor ejus, dicens:

S. Nihil tibi et justo illi: multa enim passa sum hódie per visum propter eum.

C. Príncipes autem sacerdótum et senióres persuasérunt populis, ut péterent Barábbam, Jesum vero pérderent. Respóndens autem præses, ait illis:

S. Quem vultis vobis de duóbus dimítti?

C. At illi dixérunt:

S. Barábbam.

C. Dicit illis Pilátus:

S. Quid ígitur fáciam de Jesu, qui dícitur Christus?

C. Dicunt omnes:

S. Crucifigátur.

C. Ait illis præses:

S. Quid enim mali fecit?

C. At illi magis clamábant, dicéntes:

S. Crucifigátur.

S. Dost not Thou hear how great testimonies they allege against Thee?

C. And He answered to him never a word, so that the governor wondered exceedingly. Now upon the solemn day the governor was accustomed to release to the people one prisoner, whom they would. And he had then a notorious prisoner that was called Barabbas. They therefore being gathered together, Pilate said:

S. Whom will you that I release to you: Barabbas, or Jesus that is called Christ?

C. For he knew that for envy they had delivered Him. And as he was sitting in the place of judgment his wife sent to him, saying:

S. Have thou nothing to do with that just man, for I have suffered many things this day in a dream because of Him.

C. But the chief priests and ancients persuaded the people that they should ask Barabbas, and take Jesus away. And the governor answering, said to them:

S. Whither will you of the two to be released unto you?

C. But they said:

S. Barabbas.

C. Pilate saith to them:

S. What shall I do then with Jesus that is called Christ?

C. They all call:

S. Let Him be crucified.

C. The governor said to them:

S. Why, what evil hath He done?

C. But they cried out the more, saying:

S. Let Him be crucified.

C. Videns autem Pilátus, quia nihil profíceret, sed magis tumúltus fíeret: accépta aqua, lavit manus coram pópulo, dicens:

S. *Innocens ego sum a sánguine justi hujus: vos vidéritis.*

C. Et respóndens univérsus pópulus, dixit:

S. *Sanguis ejus super nos et super fílios nostros.*

C. Tunc dimísit illis Barábbam: Jesum autem flagellátum trádidit eis, ut crucigerétur.

Tunc mílites præsidis suscipiéntes Jesum in prætórium, congregavérunt ad eum univérsam cohórtem: et exuéntes eum, chlámydem coccíneam circumdedérunt ei: et plecténtes corónam de spinis, posuérunt super caput ejus, et arúndinem in déxtera ejus. Et genu flexo ante eum, illudébant ei, dicéntes:

S. *Ave, Rex Judæórum.*

C. Et exspuéntes in eum, accepérunt arúndinem, et percutiébant caput ejus.

Et postquam illusérunt ei, exuérunt eum chlámyde et induérunt eum vestiméntis ejus, et duxérunt eum, ut crucifígerent. Exeúntes autem, invenérunt hóminem Cyrenæum, nómine Simónem: hunc angariavérunt, ut tólleret crucem ejus. Et venérunt in locum, qui dícitur Gólgotha, quod est Calváriæ locus.

Et dedérunt ei vinum bíbere cum felle mixtum. Et cum gustásset, nóluit bíbere. Postquam autem crucifixérunt eum, divisérunt vestiménta ejus, sortem mitténtes: ut implerétur, quod dictum est per Prophétam dicéntem: Divisérunt sibi vestiménta

C. And Pilate seeing that he prevailed nothing, but that rather a tumult was made, taking water washed his hands before the people, saying:

S. *I am innocent of the blood of this just man; look you to it.*

C. And the whole people answering, said:

S. *His blood be upon us and upon our children.*

C. Then he released to them Barabbas, and having scourged Jesus, delivered Him unto them to be crucified.

Then the soldiers of the governor, taking Jesus into the hall, gathered together unto Him the whole band; and stripping Him they put a scarlet cloak about Him. And platting a crown of thorns they put it upon His head and a reed in His right hand. And bowing the knee before Him, they mocked Him, saying:

S. *Hail, King of the Jews.*

C. And spitting upon Him, they took the reed and struck His head.

And after they had mocked Him, they took off the cloak from Him, and put on Him His own garments, and led Him away to crucify Him. And going out, they found a man of Cyrene, named Simon; him they forced to take up His cross. And they came to the place that is called Golgotha, which is, the place of Calvary.

And they gave Him wine to drink mingled with gall; and when He had tasted He would not drink. And after they had crucified Him, they divided His garments, casting lots; that it might be fulfilled which was spoken by the prophet, saying: They divided

mea, et super vestem meam misérunt sortem. Et sedéntes, servábant eum. Et imposuérunt super caput ejus causam ipsíus scriptam: Hic est Jesus, Rex Judæórum. Tunc crucifíxi sunt cum eo duo latrónes: unus a dextris et unus a sinístris.

Prætereúntes autem blasphemábant eum, movéntes cápita sua et dicéntes:

S. *Vah, qui déstruis templum Dei et in tríduo illud reædíficas: salva temetípsum. Si Fílius Dei es, descénde de cruce.*

C. Simíliter et príncipes sacerdótum illudéntes cum scribis et senióribus, dicébant:

S. *Alios salvos fecit, seípsum non potest salvum fácere: si Rex Israël est, descéndat nunc de cruce, et crédimus ei: confídit in Deo: líberet nunc, si vult eum: dixit enim: Quia Fílius Dei sum.*

C. Idípsum autem et latrónes, qui crucifíxi erant cum eo, improperábant ei.

A sexta autem hora ténebræ factæ sunt super univérsam terram usque ad horam nonam. Et circa horam nonam clamávit Jesus voce magna, dicens:

J. Eli, Eli, lamma sabactháni?

C. Hoc est:

J. Deus meus, Deus meus, ut quid dereliquísti me?

C. Quidam autem illic stantes et audiéntes dicébant:

S. *Elíam vocat iste.*

C. Et contínuo currens unus ex eis, accéptam spóngiam implévit acéto et

My garments among them, and upon my vesture they cast lots. And they sat and watched Him. And they put over His head His cause written: This is Jesus the King of the Jews. Then were crucified with Him two thieves; one on the right hand and one on the left.

And they that passed by blasphemed Him, wagging their heads, and saying:

S. *Vah, Thou that destroyest the temple of God and in three days dost rebuild it, save Thine own self. If Thou be the Son of God, come down from the cross.*

C. In like manner also the chief priests with the scribes and ancients, mocking, said:

S. *He saved others, Himself He cannot save; if He be the king of Israel, let Him now come down from the cross, and we will believe Him; He trusted in God, let Him now deliver Him if He will have Him; for He said: I am the Son of God.*

C. And the self-same thing the thieves also that were crucified with Him reproached Him with.

Now from the sixth hour there was a darkness over the whole earth, until the ninth hour. And about the ninth hour, Jesus cried out with a loud voice, saying:

J. Eli, Eli, lamma sabacthani?

C. That is:

J. My God, My God, why hast Thou forsaken Me?

C. And some that stood there and heard said:

S. *This man calleth Elias.*

C. And immediately one of them running took a sponge and filled it

impósuit arúndini, et dabat ei bíbere. Céteri vero dicébant:

S. *Sine, videámus, an véniat Elías líberans eum.*

C. Jesus autem íterum clamans voce magna, emísit spíritum.

with vinegar and and gave Him to drink. And the others said:

S. *Let be; let us see whether Elias will come to deliver Him.*

C. And Jesus again crying with a loud voice, yielded up the ghost.

Here all kneel and pause for a few moments.

E T ecce, velum templi scissum est in duas partes a summo usque deórsum: et terra mota est, et petræ scissæ sunt, et monuménta apérta sunt: et multa córpora sanctórum, qui dormíerant, surrexérunt. Et exeúntes de monuméntis post resurrectiónem ejus, venérunt in sanctam civitátem, et apparuérunt multis. Centúrio autem et qui cum eo erant, custodiéntes Jesum, viso terræmótu et his, quæ fiébant, timuérunt valde, dicéntes:

A ND behold the veil of the temple was rent in two from top even to the bottom; and the earth quaked and the rocks were rent; and the graves were opened, and many bodies of the saints that had slept arose, and coming out of the tombs after His resurrection, came into the holy city, and appeared to many. Now the centurion and they that were with him watching Jesus, having seen the earthquake and the things that were done, were sore afraid, saying:

S. *Vere Fílius Dei erat iste.*

C. Erant autem ibi mulíeres multæ a longe, quæ secútæ erant Jesum a Galilǽa, ministrántes ei: inter quas erat María Magdaléne, et María Jacóbi, et Joseph mater, et mater filiórum Zebedǽi. Cum autem sero factum esset, venit quidam homo dives ab Arimathǽa, nómine Joseph, qui et ipse discípulus erat Jesu. Hic accéssit ad Pilátum, et pétiit corpus Jesu. Tunc Pilátus jussit reddi corpus. Et accépto córpore, Joseph invólvit illud in síndone munda. Et pósuit illud in monuménto suo novo, quod excíderat in petra. Et advólvit saxum magnum ad óstium monuménti, et ábiit. Erat autem ibi María Magdaléne et áltera María, sedéntes contra sepúlcrum.

S. *Indeed this was the Son of God.*

C. And there were there many women afar off, who had followed Jesus from Galilee, ministering unto Him: among whom was Mary Magdalen, and Mary the mother of James and Joseph, and the mother of the sons of Zebedee. And when it was evening, there came a certain rich man of Arimathea, named Joseph, who also himself was a disciple of Jesus. He went to Pilate and asked the body of Jesus. Then Pilate commanded that the body should be delivered. And Joseph taking the body wrapt it up in a clean linen cloth, and laid it in his own new monument, which he had hewed out in a rock. And he rolled a great stone to the door of the monument

and went his way. And there was Mary Magdalen and the other Mary, sitting over against the sepulchre.

The deacon says the Munda cor *and asks for the celebrant's blessing, before singing the end of the Passion, the Gospel of the Mass.*

Munda cor meum ac lábia mea, omnípotens Deus, qui lábia Isaíæ Prophétæ cálculo mundásti igníto: ita me tua grata miseratióne dignáre mundáre, ut sanctum Evangélium tuum digne váleam nuntiáre. Per Christum, Dóminum nostrum. Amen.

D. Jube, domne, benedícere.

℣. Dóminus sit in corde tuo et in lábiis tuis : ut digne et competénter annúnties Evangélium suum : In nómine Patris, et Fílii, ✠ et Spíritus Sancti.

Amen.

Cleanse my heart and my lips, O almighty God, who didst cleanse the lips of the prophet Isaias with a burning coal, and vouchsafe, through Thy gracious mercy, so to purify me, that I may worthily announce Thy holy Gospel. Through Christ our Lord. Amen.

D. Sir, give me thy blessing.

℣. The Lord be in thy heart and on thy lips, that thou mayst worthily and in a becoming manner, proclaim His holy Gospel. In the name of the Father, and of the Son, ✠ and of the Holy Ghost. Amen.

The deacon concludes singing the Passion:

Altera autem die, quæ est post Parascéven, convenérunt príncipes sacerdótum et pharisǽi ad Pilátum, dicéntes: Dómine, recordáti sumus, quia sedúctor ille dixit adhuc vivens: Post tres dies resúrgam. Jube ergo custodíri sepúlcrum usque in diem tértium: ne forte véniant discípuli ejus, et furéntur eum, et dicant plebi: Surréxit a mórtuis; et erit novíssimus error pejor prióre. Ait illis Pilátus: Habétis custódiam, ite, custodíte, sicut scitis. Illi autem abeúntes, muniérunt sepúlcrum, signántes lápidem, cum custódibus.

And the next day, which followed the day of preparation, the chief priests and the Pharisees came together to Pilate, saying: Sir, we have remembered that that seducer said, while He was yet alive: After three days I will rise again. Command therefore the sepulchre to be guarded until the third day, lest perhaps His disciples come and steal Him away and say to the people: He is risen; and the last error shall be worse than the first. Pilate saith to them: You have a guard; go, guard it as you know. And they departing, make the sepulchre sure, sealing the stone and setting guards.

CREDO

The celebrant returns to the middle of the altar and says the Credo:

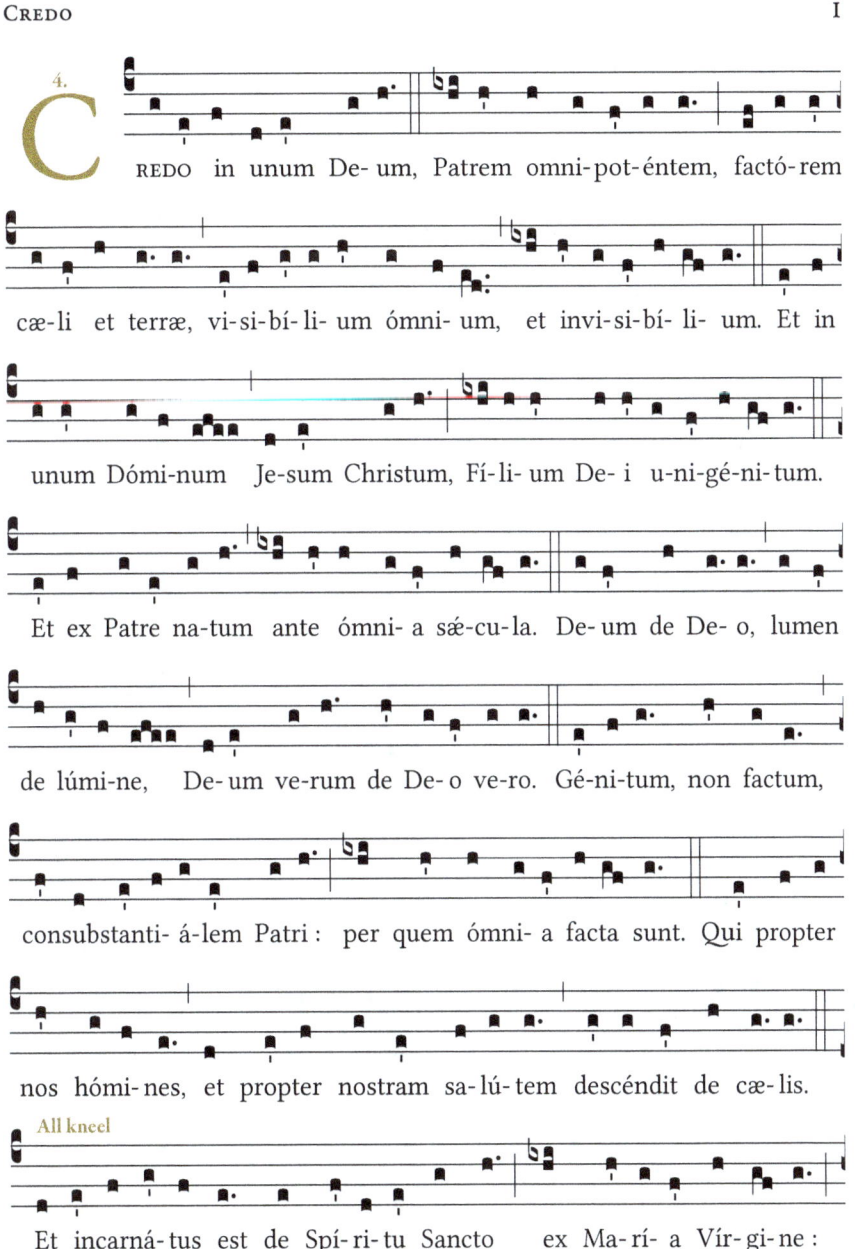

CREDO in unum De- um, Patrem omni- pot- éntem, factó- rem cæ- li et terræ, vi- si- bí- li- um ómni- um, et invi- si- bí- li- um. Et in unum Dómi- num Je- sum Christum, Fí- li- um De- i u- ni- gé- ni- tum. Et ex Patre na- tum ante ómni- a sǽ- cu- la. De- um de De- o, lumen de lúmi- ne, De- um ve- rum de De- o ve- ro. Gé- ni- tum, non factum, consubstanti- á- lem Patri : per quem ómni- a facta sunt. Qui propter nos hómi- nes, et propter nostram sa- lú- tem descéndit de cæ- lis.

All kneel

Et incarná- tus est de Spí- ri- tu Sancto ex Ma- rí- a Vír- gi- ne :

Alternate chants for the Credo *may be found in the Appendix.*

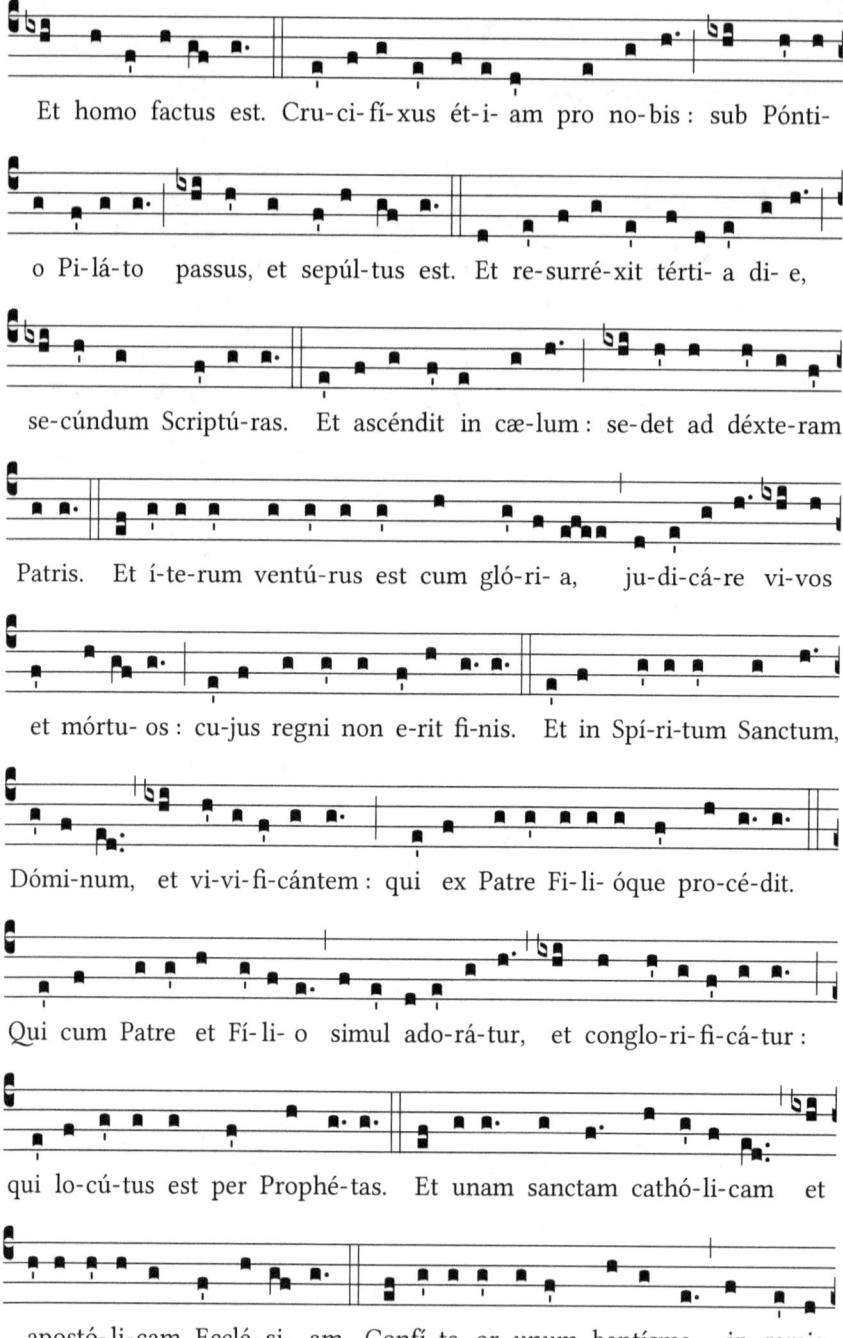

Et homo factus est. Cru-ci-fí-xus ét-i- am pro no-bis : sub Pónti-

o Pi-lá-to   passus, et sepúl-tus est. Et re-surré-xit térti- a di- e,

se-cúndum Scriptú-ras.   Et ascéndit in cæ-lum : se-det ad déxte-ram

Patris. Et í-te-rum ventú-rus est cum gló-ri- a,   ju-di-cá-re vi-vos

et mórtu- os : cu-jus regni non e-rit fi-nis.   Et in Spí-ri-tum Sanctum,

Dómi-num, et vi-vi-fi-cántem : qui ex Patre Fi-li- óque pro-cé-dit.

Qui cum Patre et Fí-li- o simul ado-rá-tur, et conglo-ri-fi-cá-tur :

qui lo-cú-tus est per Prophé-tas. Et unam sanctam cathó-li-cam   et

apostó-li-cam Ecclé- si- am. Confí-te- or unum baptísma   in remis-

si- ónem pecca-tó-rum. Et exspécto re-surrecti- ónem mortu- ó-rum.

Et vi-tam ventú-ri sǽ-cu-li. A- men.

CREED: I believe in one God, the Father almighty, Maker of heaven and earth, and of all things, visible and invisible.

And in one Lord Jesus Christ, the only begotten Son of God. And born of the Father, before all ages. God of God: Light of Light: true God of true God. Begotten, not made, consubstantial with the Father, by Whom all things were made. Who, for us men, and for our salvation, came down from heaven. (Kneel down.) And became incarnate by the Holy Ghost of the Virgin Mary: and was made man. He was crucified also for us, suffered under Pontius Pilate, and was buried. And the third day He rose again according to the Scriptures. And ascended into heaven, and sitteth at the right hand of the Father. And He shall come again with glory to judge both the living and the dead, of whose kingdom there shall be no end.

And in the Holy Ghost, the Lord and Giver of Life, proceeding from the Father and the Son. Who together, with the Father and the Son, is adored and glorified: Who spoke by the prophets. And in one, holy, Catholic and Apostolic Church. I confess one baptism for the remission of sins. And I look for the resurrection of the dead. And the life of the world to come. Amen.

OFFERTORY

The celebrant kisses the altar, turns to the people and says:

℣. Dóminus vobíscum.
℟. Et cum spíritu tuo.

ORÉMUS.

℣. The Lord be with you.
℟. And with thy spirit.

LET US PRAY.

OFFERTORY

PSALM 68: 21-22

M- PRO- PÉ- RI- UM * exspectá- vit cor me-

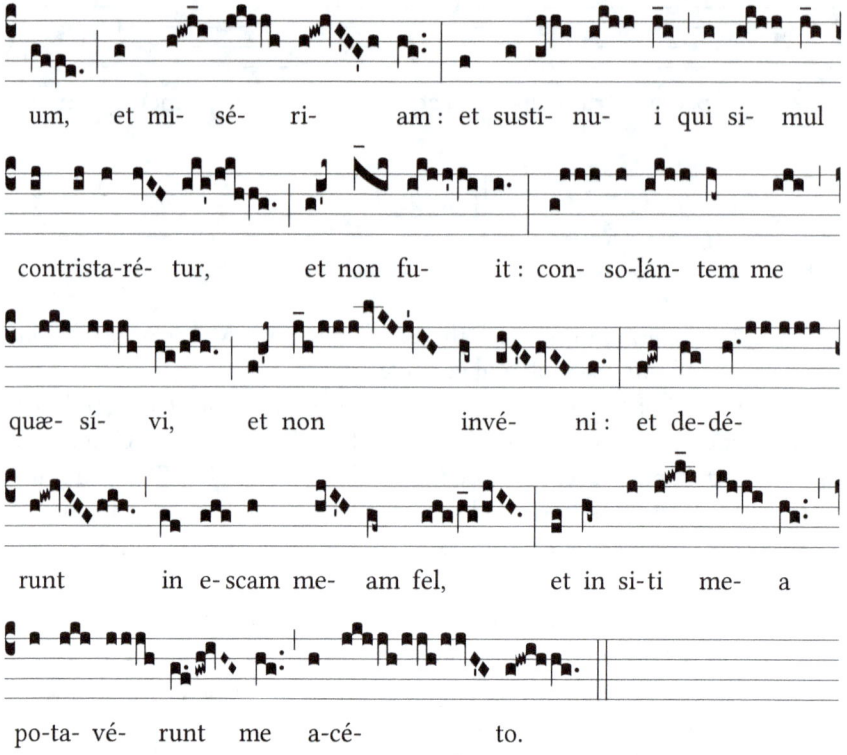

um, et mi- sé- ri- am: et sustí- nu- i qui si- mul

contrista-ré- tur, et non fu- it: con- so-lán- tem me

quæ- sí- vi, et non invé- ni: et de-dé-

runt in e-scam me- am fel, et in si-ti me- a

po-ta- vé- runt me a-cé- to.

OFFERTORY: Insult has broken my heart, and I am weak; I looked for sympathy, but there was none; for comforters, and I found none. Rather they put gall in My food and in My thirst they gave Me vinegar to drink.

At Solemn High Mass the subdeacon wearing the Humeral Veil brings the covered chalice to the altar and gives it to the deacon, who then gives the chalice and paten with host to the celebrant. The celebrant then uncovers the chalice and says:

SÚSCIPE, sancte Pater, omnípotens ætérne Deus, hanc immaculátam hóstiam, quam ego indígnus fámulus tuus óffero tibi Deo meo vivo et vero, pro innumerabílibus peccátis, et offensiónibus, et neglegéntiis meis, et pro ómnibus circumstántibus, sed et pro ómnibus fidélibus christiánis vivis atque defúnctis: ut mihi, et illis profíciat ad salútem in vitam ætérnam. Amen.

ACCEPT, O Holy Father, almighty and eternal God, this unspotted host, which I, Thy unworthy servant, offer unto Thee, my living and true God, for my innumerable sins, offenses, and negligences, and for all here present: as also for all faithful Christians, both living and dead, that it may avail both me and them for salvation unto life everlasting. Amen.

DEUS, ✠ qui humánæ substántiæ dignitátem mirabíliter condidísti, et mirabílius reformásti: da nobis per hujus aquæ et vini mystérium, ejus divinitátis esse consórtes, qui humanitátis nostræ fíeri dignátus est párticeps, Jesus Christus, Fílius tuus, Dóminus noster: Qui tecum vivit et regnat in unitáte Spíritus Sancti Deus: per ómnia sǽcula sæculórum. Amen.

O GOD, ✠ who, in creating human nature, didst wonderfully dignify it, and still more wonderfully restore it, grant that, by the Mystery of this water and wine, we may be made partakers of His divine nature, who vouchsafed to be made partaker of our human nature, even Jesus Christ our Lord, Thy Son, who with Thee, liveth and reigneth in the unity of the Holy Ghost, God: world without end. Amen.

OFFÉRIMUS tibi, Dómine, cálicem salutáris, tuam deprecántes cleméntiam: ut in conspéctu divínæ majestátis tuæ, pro nostra et totíus mundi salúte, cum odóre suavitátis ascéndat. Amen.

WE OFFER unto Thee, O Lord, the chalice of salvation, beseeching Thy clemency, that it may ascend before Thy divine Majesty, as a sweet savor, for our salvation, and for that of the whole world. Amen.

IN SPÍRITU humilitátis et in ánimo contríto suscipiámur a te, Dómine: et sic fiat sacrifícium nostrum in conspéctu tuo hódie, ut pláceat tibi, Dómine Deus.

ACCEPT US, O Lord, in the spirit of humility and contrition of heart, and grant that the sacrifice which we offer this day in Thy sight may be pleasing to Thee, O Lord God.

VENI, sanctificátor omnípotens ætérne Deus: et béne ✠ dic hoc sacrifícium, tuo sancto nómini præparátum.

COME, O almighty and eternal God, the Sanctifier, and bless ✠ this Sacrifice, prepared for the glory of Thy holy Name.

INCENSING

At Solemn High Mass the sacrificial gifts and the altar are incensed respectively, the celebrant first blessing the incense saying:

PER intercessiónem beáti Michaélis Archángeli, stantis a dextris altáris incénsi, et ómnium electórum suórum, incénsum istud dignétur Dóminus bene✠dícere, et in odórem suavitátis accípere. Per Christum, Dóminum nostrum. Amen.

MAY the Lord, by the intercession of blessed Michael the Archangel, who standeth at the right side of the altar of incense, and of all His Elect, vouchsafe to bless ✠ this incense and receive it as an odor of sweetness: through Jesus Christ our Lord. Amen.

The celebrant receives the thurible from the deacon and incenses the sacrificial gifts saying:

INCÉNSUM istud a te benedíctum ascéndat ad te, Dómine: et descéndat super nos misericórdia tua.

MAY THIS incense, which Thou hast blessed, O Lord, ascend to Thee, and may Thy mercy descend upon us.

The celebrant then incenses the altar, reciting from Psalm 140:

DIRIGÁTUR, Dómine, orátio mea, sicut incénsum, in conspéctu tuo: elevátio mánuum meárum sacrifícium vespertínum. Pone, Dómine, custódiam ori meo, et óstium circumstántiæ lábiis meis: ut non declínet cor meum in verba malítiæ, ad excusándas excusatiónes in peccátis.

LET MY prayer, O Lord, be directed as incense in Thy sight: the lifting up of my hands as an evening sacrifice. Set a watch, O Lord, before my mouth, and a door round about my lips. May my heart not incline to evil words, to make excuses for sins.

The celebrant returns the thurible to the deacon saying:

ACCÉNDAT in nobis Dóminus ignem sui amóris, et flammam ætérnæ caritátis. Amen.

MAY THE Lord enkindle within us the fire of His love, and the flame of everlasting charity. Amen.

LAVÁBO

The celebrant then moves to the Epistle side and washes his fingers, reciting from Psalm 25:

LAVÁBO inter innocéntes manus meas: et circúmdabo altáre tuum, Dómine: Ut áudiam vocem laudis, et enárrem univérsa mirabília tua. Dómine, diléxi decórem domus tuæ et locum habitatiónis glóriæ tuæ. Ne perdas cum ímpiis, Deus, ánimam meam, et cum viris sánguinum vitam meam: In quorum mánibus iniquitátes sunt: déxtera eórum repléta est munéribus. Ego autem in innocéntia mea ingréssus sum: rédime me et miserére mei. Pes meus stetit in dirécto: in ecclésiis benedícam te, Dómine.

I WILL wash my hands among the innocent: and I will compass Thine altar, O Lord That I may hear the voice of praise: and tell of all Thy wonderous works. I have loved, O Lord, the beauty of Thy house and the place where Thy glory dwelleth. Take not away my soul, O God, with the wicked: nor my life with blood-thirsty men. In whose hands are iniquities, their right hand is filled with gifts. But I have walked in my innocence: redeem me, and have mercy on me. My foot hath stood in the direct way, in the churches I will bless Thee, O Lord.

The celebrant returns to the middle of the altar, bows down and prays:

Súscipe, sancta Trínitas, hanc oblatiónem, quam tibi offérimus ob memóriam passiónis, resurrectiónis, et ascensiónis Jesu Christi, Dómini nostri: et in honórem beátæ Maríæ semper Vírginis, et beáti Joannis Baptistæ, et sanctórum Apostolórum Petri et Pauli, et istórum et ómnium Sanctórum: ut illis profíciat ad honórem, nobis autem ad salútem: et illi pro nobis intercédere dignéntur in cælis, quorum memóriam ágimus in terris. Per eúndem Christum, Dóminum nostrum. Amen.

Receive, O holy Trinity, this oblation which we make to Thee, in memory of the Passion, Resurrection and Ascension of our Lord Jesus Christ, and in honor of Blessed Mary, ever Virgin, blessed John the Baptist, the holy Apostles Peter and Paul, and of all the Saints, that it may avail unto their honor and our salvation, and may they vouchsafe to intercede for us in heaven, whose memory we celebrate on earth. Through the same Christ our Lord. Amen.

The celebrant kisses the altar and then turns to the people saying:

℣. ORÁTE, FRATRES: ut meum ac vestrum sacrifícium acceptábile fiat apud Deum Patrem omnipoténtem.

℟. Suscípiat Dóminus sacrifícium de mánibus tuis vel meis ad laudem et glóriam nominis sui, ad utilitátem quoque nostram, totiúsque Ecclésiæ suæ sanctæ.

℣. Amen.

℣. BRETHREN, PRAY that my Sacrifice and yours may be acceptable to God the Father almighty.

℟. May the Lord receive the Sacrifice from thy hands, to the praise and glory of His Name, to our benefit and that of all His holy Church.

℣. Amen.

SECRET

Concéde, quǽsumus, Dómine: ut óculis tuæ majestátis munus oblátum, et grátiam nobis devotiónis obtíneat, et efféctum beátæ perennitátis acquírat. Per Dóminum nostrum Jesum Christum, Fílium tuum: qui tecum vivit et regnat in unitáte Spíritus Sancti Deus, per ómnia sǽcula sæculórum.

℟. Amen.

Grant, we beseech You, almighty God, that the gift offered in the sight of Your majesty may obtain for us the grace of reverent devotion and assure us eternal happiness. Through Jesus Christ, Thy Son our Lord, Who liveth and reigneth with Thee, in the unity of the Holy Ghost, God, world without end.

℟. Amen.

PREFACE OF THE HOLY CROSS

ℙER ómnia sǽcula sæculórum.
℟. Amen.
℣. Dóminus vobíscum.
℟. Et cum spíritu tuo.
℣. Sursum corda.
℟. Habémus ad Dóminum.

℣. Grátias agámus Dómino Deo nostro.
℟. Dignum et justum est.

ₓVERE dignum et justum est, æquum et salutáre, nos tibi semper et ubíque grátias ágere: Dómine sancte, Pater omnípotens, ætérne Deus: Qui salútem humáni géneris in ligno Crucis constituísti: ut, unde mors oriebátur, inde vita resúrgeret: et, qui in ligno vincébat, in ligno quoque vincerétur: per Christum, Dóminum nostrum. Per quem majestátem tuam laudant Angeli, adórant Dominatiónes, tremunt Potestátes. Cæli cælorúmque Virtútes ac beáta Séraphim sócia exsultatióne concélebrant. Cum quibus et nostras voces ut admítti júbeas, deprecámur, súpplici confessióne dicéntes:

ℙWORLD without end.
℟. Amen.
℣. The Lord be with you.
℟. And with thy spirit.
℣. Lift up your hearts.
℟. We have them lifted up to the Lord.
℣. Let us give thanks to the Lord our God.
℟. It is meet and just.

IT is truly meet and just, right and for our salvation, that we should at all times, and in all places, give thanks unto Thee, O holy Lord, Father almighty, everlasting God; Who didst establish the salvation of mankind on the tree of the Cross; that whence death came, thence also life might arise again, and that he, who overcame by the tree, by the tree also might be overcome: Through Christ our Lord. Through whom the Angels praise Thy Majesty, the Dominations worship it, the Powers stand in awe. The Heavens and the heavenly hosts together with the blessed Seraphim in triumphant chorus unite to celebrate it. Together with these we entreat Thee that Thou mayest bid our voices also to be admitted while we say with lowly praise:

The bells are rung and the faithful kneel for the Sanctus.

SANCTUS   XVII

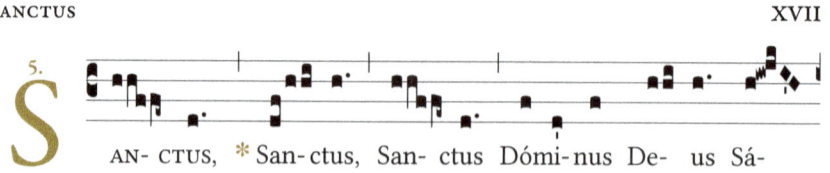

SAN- CTUS, * San- ctus, San- ctus Dómi- nus De- us Sá-

ba-oth. Ple-ni sunt cæ- li et ter- ra gló-ri- a tu- a. Ho- sán-

na in excél- sis. Be-ne-díctus qui ve-nit in nómi-ne Dómi-ni.

Ho- sánna in excél- sis.

Sanctus: Holy, Holy, Holy, Lord God of Sabaoth. Heaven and earth are full of Thy glory. Hosanna in the highest. Blessed is He that cometh in the Name of the Lord. Hosanna in the highest.

The Canon of the Mass

The celebrant joins his hands and bows over the altar, silently praying:

Te ígitur, clementíssime Pater, per Jesum Christum, Fílium tuum, Dóminum nostrum, súpplices rogámus, ac pétimus, uti accépta hábeas et benedícas, hæc ✠ dona, hæc ✠múnera, hæc ✠ sancta sacrifícia illibáta, in primis, quæ tibi offérimus pro Ecclésia tua sancta cathólica: quam pacificáre, custodíre, adunáre et régere dignéris toto orbe terrárum: una cum fámulo tuo Papa nostro **N.** et Antístite nostro **N.** et ómnibus orthodóxis, atque cathólicæ et apostólicæ fídei cultóribus.

Meménto, Dómine, famulórum famularúmque tuarum **N.** et **N.** et ómnium circumstántium, quorum tibi fides cógnita est et nota devótio, pro quibus tibi offérimus: vel qui tibi

We therefore humbly pray and beseech Thee, most merciful Father, through Jesus Christ; Thy Son, our Lord, that Thou wouldst vouchsafe to accept and bless these ✠ gifts, these ✠ presents, these ✠ holy unspotted Sacrifices, which in the first place we offer Thee for Thy holy Catholic Church to which vouchsafe to grant peace, as also to preserve, unite, and govern it throughout the world, together with Thy servant **N.,** our Pope, and **N.,** our Bishop, and all orthodox believers and professors of the Catholic and Apostolic Faith.

Be mindful, O Lord, of Thy servants and handmaidens, **N.** and **N.,** and of all here present, whose faith and devotion are known unto Thee, for whom we offer, or who offer up to

ófferunt hoc sacrifícium laudis, pro se suísque ómnibus: pro redemptióne animárum suárum, pro spe salútis et incolumitátis suæ: tibíque reddunt vota sua ætérno Deo, vivo et vero.

Communicántes, et memóriam venerántes, in primis gloriósæ semper Vírginis Maríæ, Genetrícis Dei et Dómini nostri Jesu Christi: sed et beatórum Apostolórum ac Mártyrum tuórum, Petri et Pauli, Andréæ, Jacóbi, Joánnis, Thomæ, Jacóbi, Philíppi, Bartholomǽi, Matthǽi, Simónis et Thaddǽi: Lini, Cleti, Cleméntis, Xysti, Cornélii, Cypriáni, Lauréntii, Chrysógoni, Joánnis et Pauli, Cosmæ et Damiáni: et ómnium Sanctórum tuórum; quorum méritis precibúsque concédas, ut in ómnibus protectiónis tuæ muniámur auxílio. Per eúndem Christum, Dóminum nostrum. Amen.

Thee, this sacrifice of praise for themselves, their families and friends, for the redemption of their souls, for the health and salvation they hope for; and who now pay their vows to Thee, the everlasting, living and true God.

We pray in union with and honor the memory, especially of the glorious ever Virgin Mary, mother of our God and Lord Jesus Christ: and of the blessed Apostles and Martyrs Peter and Paul, Andrew, James, John, Thomas, James, Philip, Bartholomew, Matthew, Simon, and Thaddeus; Linus, Cletus, Clement, Xystus, Cornelius, Cyprian, Lawrence, Chrysogonus, John and Paul, Cosmas and Damian, and of all Thy Saints, through whose merits and prayers, grant that we may in all things be defended by the help of Thy protection. Through the same Christ our Lord. Amen.

The bell is rung as the celebrant extends his hands over the oblation and says:

HANC ígitur oblatiónem servitútis nostræ, sed et cunctæ famíliæ tuæ, quǽsumus, Dómine, ut placátus accípias: diésque nostros in tua pace dispónas, atque ab ætérna damnatióne nos éripi, et in electórum tuórum júbeas grege numerári. Per Christum, Dóminum nostrum. Amen.

QUAM oblatiónem tu, Deus, in ómnibus, quǽsumus, bene✠díctam, adscríp✠tam, ra✠tam, rationábilem, acceptabilémque fácere dignéris: ut nobis Cor✠pus, et San✠guis fiat dilectíssimi Fílii tui, Dómini nostri Jesu Christi.

WE therefore beseech Thee, O Lord, graciously to accept this oblation of our service, as also of Thy whole family; and to dispose our days in Thy peace, preserve us from eternal damnation, and rank us in the number of Thine Elect. Through the same Christ our Lord. Amen.

WHICH oblation do Thou, O God, vouchsafe in all respects, to bless, ✠approve, ✠ ratify, ✠ make worthy and acceptable; that it may be made for us the Body ✠ and Blood ✠ of Thy most beloved Son Jesus Christ our Lord.

QUI PRÍDIE quam paterétur, accépit panem in sanctas ac venerábiles manus suas, elevátis óculis in cælum ad te Deum, Patrem suum omnipoténtem, tibi grátias agens, bene✠díxit, fregit, dedítque discípulis suis, dicens: Accípite, et manducáte ex hoc omnes.

WHO, THE DAY before He suffered, took bread into His holy and venerable hands, and with His eyes lifted up towards heaven unto Thee, God, His almighty Father, giving thanks to Thee, He blessed ✠ it, broke it and gave it to His disciples saying: Take and eat ye all of this.

Hoc est enim Corpus Meum.

For this is My Body.

The celebrant kneels before the Host and adores. He then elevates the Sacred Host as the bell is rung. The celebrant then uncovers the chalice and says:

SÍMILI modo postquam cenátum est, accípiens et hunc præclárum Cálicem in sanctas ac venerábiles manus suas: item tibi grátias agens, bene✠díxit, dedítque discípulis suis, dicens: Accípite, et bíbite ex eo omnes.

IN LIKE manner, after He had supped, taking also this excellent chalice into His holy and venerable hands He blessed ✠, and gave it to His disciples, saying: Take and drink ye all of this.

Hic est enim Calix Sánguinis mei, novi et ætérni testaménti; mystérium fidei: qui pro vobis et pro multis effundétur in remissiónem peccatórum.

For this is the Chalice of my Blood, of the new and eternal testament; the mystery of faith: which shall be shed for you and for many unto the remission of sins.

Hæc quotiescúmque fecéritis, in mei memóriam faciétis.

As often as ye shall do these things, ye shall do them in memory of me.

The celebrant kneels before the Precious Blood and adores. He then elevates the Precious Blood as the bell is rung. Following this the celebrant continues:

UNDE et mémores, Dómine, nos servi tui, sed et plebs tua sancta, ejúsdem Christi Fílii tui, Dómini nostri, tam beátæ passiónis, nec non et ab ínferis resurrectiónis, sed et in cælos gloriósæ ascensiónis: offérimus præcláræ majestáti tuæ de tuis donis ac

WHEREFORE, O Lord, we Thy servants, as also Thy holy people, calling to mind the blessed Passion of the same Christ, Thy Son, our Lord, and also His Resurrection from the dead and His glorious Ascension into heaven: do offer unto Thy most

datis, hóstiam ✠ puram, hóstiam ✠ sanctam, hóstiam ✠ immaculátam, Panem ✠ sanctum vitæ ætérnæ, et Cálicem ✠ salútis perpétuæ.

SUPRA quæ propítio ac seréno vultu respícere dignéris: et accépta habére, sicúti accépta habére dignátus es múnera púeri tui justi Abel, et sacrifícium Patriárchæ nostri Abrahæ: et quod tibi óbtulit summus sacérdos tuus Melchísedech, sanctum sacrifícium, immaculátam hóstiam.

SÚPPLICES te rogámus, omnípotens Deus: jube hæc perférri per manus sancti Angeli tui in sublíme altáre tuum, in conspéctu divínæ majestátis tuæ: ut, quotquot ex hac altáris participatióne sacrosánctum Fílii tui Cor ✠ pus, et Sán ✠ guinem sumpsérimus, omni benedictióne cælésti et grátia repleámur. Per eúndem Christum, Dóminum nostrum. Amen.

excellent Majesty of Thine own gifts, bestowed upon us, a pure ✠ Host, a holy ✠ Host, an unspotted ✠ Host, the holy ✠ Bread of eternal life, and the Chalice ✠of everlasting salvation.

UPON which vouchsafe to look with a propitious and serene countenance, and to accept them, as Thou wert graciously pleased to accept the gifts of Thy just servant Abel, and the sacrifice of our patriarch Abraham, and that which Thy high priest Melchisedech offered to Thee, a holy Sacrifice, and unspotted Victim.

WE MOST humbly beseech Thee, almighty God, command these offerings to be borne by the hands of Thy holy Angel to Thine altar on high, in the sight of Thy divine majesty, that as many as shall partake of the most holy Body ✠ and Blood ✠ of Thy Son at this altar, may be filled with every heavenly grace and blessing. Through the same Christ our Lord. Amen.

The celebrant now commemorates and intercedes for the dead saying:

MEMÉNTO étiam, Dómine, famulórum famularúmque tuárum N. et N., qui nos præcessérunt cum signo fídei, et dórmiunt in somno pacis. Ipsis, Dómine, et ómnibus in Christo quiescéntibus locum refrigérii, lucis, et pacis, ut indúlgeas, deprecámur. Per eúndem Christum, Dóminum nostrum. Amen.

NOBIS quoque peccatóribus fámulis tuis, de multitúdine miseratiónum tuárum sperántibus, partem áliquam et societátem donáre dignéris, cum tuis sanctis Apóstolis et Martýribus: cum

REMEMBER also, O Lord, Thy servants and handmaids N. and N., who are gone before us with the sign of faith, and rest in the sleep of peace. To these, O Lord, and to all that rest in Christ, grant, we beseech Thee, a place of refreshment, light, and peace; Through the same Christ our Lord. Amen.

TO US ALSO, Thy sinful servants, confiding in the multitude of Thy mercies, vouchsafe to grant some part and fellowship with Thy holy Apostles and Martyrs, with John, Stephen,

Joánne, Stéphano, Matthía, Bárnaba, Ignátio, Alexándro, Marcellíno, Petro, Felicitáte, Perpétua, Agatha, Lúcia, Agnéte, Cæcília, Anastásia, et ómnibus Sanctis tuis: intra quorum nos consórtium, non æstimátor mériti, sed véniæ, quǽsumus, largítor admítte. Per Christum, Dóminum nostrum.

Matthias, Barnabas, Ignatius, Alexander, Marcellinus, Peter, Felicitas, Perpetua, Agatha, Lucy, Agnes, Cecilia, Anastasia, and with all Thy Saints, into whose company we beseech Thee to admit us, not weighing our merits, but pardoning our offenses. Through Christ our Lord.

The celebrant reverences the Sacred Host and Chalice and then continues:

PER quem hæc ómnia, Dómine, semper bona creas, sanctí✠ficas, viví✠ficas, bene✠dícis et præstas nobis.

BY Whom, O Lord, Thou dost ever create, sanctify, ✠ quicken, ✠ bless, ✠ and give unto us all these good things.

Per ip✠sum, et cum ip✠so, et in ip✠so, est tibi Deo Patri ✠ omnipoténti, in unitáte Spíritus ✠ Sancti, omnis honor, et glória.

By Him, ✠ and with Him, ✠ and in Him ✠ is to Thee, God the Father ✠ almighty, in the unity of the Holy ✠ Ghost, all honor and glory.

LORD'S PRAYER

PER ómnia sǽcula sæculórum.
℟. Amen.

ORÉMUS: Præcéptis salutáribus móniti, et divína institutióne formáti audémus dícere:

WORLD without end.
℟. Amen.

LET US PRAY. Instructed by Thy saving precepts, and formed by Thy divine institution, we are bold to say:

PATER noster, qui es in cælis, sanctificétur nomen tuum: advéniat regnum tuum: fiat volúntas tua, sicut in cælo et in terra. Panem nostrum quotidiánum da nobis hódie: et dimítte nobis débita nostra, sicut et nos dimíttimus debitóribus nostris: et ne nos indúcas in tentatiónem:
℟. Sed líbera nos a malo
℣. Amen.

OUR Father, who art in heaven, hallowed be Thy Name; Thy kingdom come; Thy will be done on earth as it is in heaven. Give us this day our daily bread. And forgive us our trespasses, as we forgive those who trespass against us. And lead us not into temptation.
℟. But deliver us from evil.
℣. Amen.

LÍBERA nos, quǽsumus, Dómine, ab ómnibus malis, prætéritis, præséntibus et futúris: et intercedénte beáta et gloriósa semper Vírgine Dei Genetríce María, cum beátis Apóstolis tuis Petro et Paulo, atque Andréa, et ómnibus Sanctis, da propítius pacem in diébus nostris, ut, ope misericórdiæ tuæ adjúti, et a peccáto simus semper líberi et ab omni perturbatióne secúri. Per eúndem Dóminum nostrum Jesum Christum, Fílium tuum. Qui tecum vivit et regnat in unitáte Spíritus Sancti Deus.

PER ómnia sǽcula sæculórum.
℟. Amen.
℣. Pax Dómini sit semper vobíscum.

℟. Et cum spíritu tuo.

DELIVER us, we beseech Thee, O Lord, from all evils, past, present, and to come; and by the intercession of the Blessed and glorious ever Virgin Mary, Mother of God, and of the holy Apostles, Peter and Paul, and of Andrew, and of all the Saints, mercifully grant peace in our days, that through the assistance of Thy mercy we may be always free from sin, and secure from all disturbance. Through the same Jesus Christ, Thy Son, our Lord. Who with Thee in the unity of the Holy Ghost liveth and reigneth God,

WORLD without end.
℟. Amen.
℣. The peace of the Lord be always with you.

℟. And with thy spirit.

The celebrant drops a particle of the Sacred Host into the chalice saying:

HÆC commíxtio, et consecrátio Córporis et Sánguinis Dómini nostri Jesu Christi, fiat accipiéntibus nobis in vitam ætérnam. Amen.

MAY THIS mixture and consecration of the Body and Blood of our Lord Jesus Christ be to us who receive it effectual unto eternal life. Amen.

The celebrant strikes his breast thrice and says:

AGNUS DEI   XVII

A-GNUS De- i, * qui tol- lis peccá- ta mundi : mi-se-ré-re

no- bis. Agnus De- i, * qui tol- lis peccá- ta mundi : mi-se-ré-re no-

bis. Agnus De- i, * qui tol- lis peccá- ta mundi : dona no-bis pa- cem.

Agnus Dei: Lamb of God, who takest away the sins of the world, have mercy on us. Lamb of God, who takest away the sins of the world, have mercy on us. Lamb of God, who takest away the sins of the world, grant us peace.

The celebrant continues:

DÓMINE Jesu Christe, qui dixísti Apóstolis tuis: Pacem relínquo vobis, pacem meam do vobis: ne respícias peccáta mea, sed fidem Ecclésiæ tuæ; eámque secúndum voluntátem tuam pacificáre et coadunáre dignéris: Qui vivis et regnas Deus per ómnia sǽcula sæculórum. Amen.

O LORD Jesus Christ, who saidst to Thine Apostles: Peace I leave you, My peace I give you: regard not my sins, but the faith of Thy Church; and vouchsafe to grant her that peace and unity which is agreeable to Thy will: Who livest and reignest God, world without end. Amen.

At Solemn High Mass the Kiss of Peace is given to the deacon:

℣. Pax tecum.
℟. Et cum spíritu tuo.

℣. Peace be with thee.
℟. And with thy spirit.

DÓMINE Jesu Christe, Fili Dei vivi, qui ex voluntáte Patris, cooperánte Spíritu Sancto, per mortem tuam mundum vivificásti: líbera me per hoc sacrosánctum Corpus et Sánguinem tuum ab ómnibus iniquitátibus meis, et univérsis malis: et fac me tuis semper inhærére mandátis, et a te numquam separári permíttas: Qui cum eódem Deo Patre et Spíritu Sancto vivis et regnas Deus in sǽcula sæculórum. Amen.

O LORD Jesus Christ, Son of the living God, who, according to the will of Thy Father, with the cooperation of the Holy Ghost, hast by Thy death given life to the world; deliver me by this Thy most sacred Body and Blood, from all my iniquities and from all evils; and make me always cleave to Thy commandments, and suffer me never to be separated from Thee, Who livest and reignest, with the same God the Father and the Holy Ghost, God, world without end. Amen.

PERCÉPTIO Córporis tui, Dómine Jesu Christe, quod ego indígnus súmere præsúmo, non mihi provéniat in judícium et condemnatiónem:

LET NOT the partaking of Thy Body, O Lord, Jesus Christ, which I, though unworthy, presume to receive, turn to my judgment and condemna-

sed pro tua pietáte prosit mihi ad tutaméntum mentis et córporis, et ad medélam percipiéndam: Qui vivis et regnas cum Deo Patre in unitáte Spíritus Sancti Deus, per ómnia sǽcula sæculórum. Amen.

tion; but let it, through Thy mercy, become a safeguard and remedy, both for soul and body; Who with God the Father, in the unity of the Holy Ghost, livest and reignest God, world without end. Amen.

The celebrant genuflects, rises and then says:

PANEM cæléstem accípiam, et nomen Dómini invocábo.

I WILL TAKE the Bread of heaven, and will call upon the Name of the Lord.

The celebrant strikes his breast and says three times:

DÓMINE, non sum dignus, ut intres sub tectum meum: sed tantum dic verbo, et sanábitur ánima mea.

LORD, I am not worthy that Thou shouldst enter under my roof; say but the word, and my soul shall be healed.

The celebrant makes the Sign of the Cross with the Sacred Host and says:

CORPUS Dómini nostri Jesu Christi custódiat ánimam meam in vitam ætérnam. Amen.

THE BODY of our Lord Jesus Christ preserve my soul unto life everlasting. Amen.

The celebrant consumes the Sacred Host and then purifies the paten saying:

QUID retríbuam Dómino pro ómnibus, quæ retríbuit mihi? Cálicem salutáris accípiam, et nomen Dómini invocábo. Laudans invocábo Dóminum, et ab inimícis meis salvus ero.

WHAT return shall I make to the Lord for all He has given to me? I will take the chalice of salvation, and call upon the Name of the Lord. Praising I will call upon the Lord, and I shall be saved from my enemies.

The celebrant makes the Sign of the Cross with the Chalice saying:

SANGUIS Dómini nostri Jesu Christi custódiat ánimam meam in vitam ætérnam. Amen.

THE BLOOD of our Lord Jesus Christ preserve my soul unto life everlasting. Amen.

The celebrant consumes the Precious Blood as the servers repeat the Confíteor. *At Solemn High Mass this is often chanted:*

CONFÍTEOR Deo omnipoténti, beátæ Maríæ semper Vírgini, beáto Michaéli Archángelo, beáto Joánni Baptístæ, sanctis Apóstolis Petro et Paulo, ómnibus Sanctis, et tibi, pater: quia peccávi nimis cogitatióne, verbo et ópere: (Pércutit sibi pectus ter, dicens) mea culpa, mea culpa, mea máxima culpa. Ideo precor beátam Maríam semper Vírginem, beátum Michaélem Archángelum, beátum Joánnem Baptístam, sanctos Apóstolos Petrum et Paulum, omnes Sanctos, et te, pater, oráre pro me ad Dóminum, Deum nostrum.

℣. Misereátur vestri omnípotens Deus, et, dimíssis peccátis vestris, perdúcat vos ad vitam ætérnam.

℟. Amen.

℣. Indulgéntiam, ✠ absolutiónem et remissiónem peccatórum nostrórum tríbuat nobis omnípotens et miséricors Dóminus.

℟. Amen.

I CONFESS to almighty God, to the blessed Mary ever Virgin, blessed Michael the Archangel, blessed John the Baptist, the holy Apostles Peter and Paul, to all the Saints, and to you, Father, that I have sinned exceedingly in thought, word, and deed, (Now strike your breast three times, saying:) through my fault, through my fault, through my most grievous fault. Therefore I beseech the blessed Mary, ever Virgin, blessed Michael the Archangel, blessed John the Baptist, the holy Apostles Peter and Paul, all the Saints, and you, Father, to pray to the Lord our God for me.

℣. May almighty God be merciful to thee, and forgiving thy sins, bring thee to everlasting life.

℟. Amen.

℣. May the ✠ almighty and merciful Lord grant us pardon, absolution, and remission of our sins.

℟. Amen.

The celebrant faces the people holding up one of the Sacred Hosts and says:

ECCE Agnus Dei, ecce qui tollit peccáta mundi.

BEHOLD the Lamb of God, behold Him Who taketh away the sins of the world.

The following is said three times:

DÓMINE, non sum dignus, ut intres sub tectum meum: sed tantum dic verbo, et sanábitur ánima mea.

LORD, I am not worthy that Thou shouldst enter under my roof; say but the word, and my soul shall be healed.

Ablutions

After distributing Holy Communion the celebrant purifies the sacred vessels. At Solemn High Mass the subdeacon takes the Chalice from the celebrant for purifying as the celebrant says:

QUOD ore súmpsimus, Dómine, pura mente capiámus; et de múnere temporáli fiat nobis remédium sempitérnum.

GRANT, O Lord, that what we have taken with our mouth, we may receive with a pure mind; and from a temporal gift may it become to us an eternal remedy.

CORPUS tuum, Dómine, quod sumpsi, et Sanguis, quem potávi, adhǽreat viscéribus meis: et præsta; ut in me non remáneat scélerum mácula, quem pura et sancta refecérunt sacraménta: Qui vivis et regnas in sǽcula sæculórum. Amen.

MAY THY Body, O Lord, which I have received, and Thy Blood which I have drunk, cleave to my bowels; and grant that no stain of sin may remain in me, who have been fed with this pure and holy Sacrament; Who livest and reignest for ever and ever. Amen.

Communion

The celebrant reads the Communion on the Epistle side of the altar:

COMMUNION   MATTHEW 26: 42

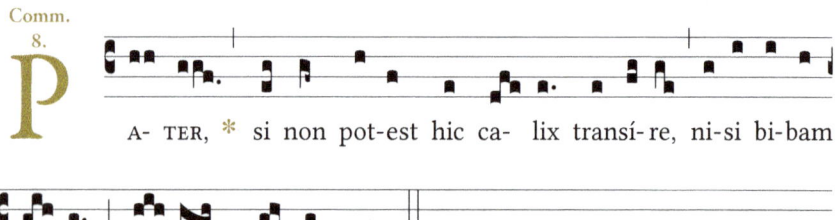

Comm. 8.

PA- TER, * si non pot-est hic ca- lix transí-re, ni-si bi-bam

il- lum : fi- at vo-lún-tas tu- a.

COMMUNION: Father, if this cup cannot pass away, unless I drink it, Your will be done.

Postcommunion

The celebrant turns to face the people saying:

℣. Dóminus vobíscum.
℟. Et cum spíritu tuo.

℣. The Lord be with you.
℟. And with thy spirit.

ORÉMUS.

PER hujus, Dómine, operatiónem mystérii: et vítia nostra purgéntur, et justa desidéria compleántur. Per Dóminum nostrum Jesum Christum, Fílium tuum: qui tecum vivit et regnat in unitáte Spíritus Sancti Deus, per ómnia sæcula sæculórum.

℟. Amen.

LET US PRAY.

BY the working of this sacred rite, O Lord, may our sins be erased and our just desires fulfilled. Through Jesus Christ, Thy Son our Lord, Who liveth and reigneth with Thee, in the unity of the Holy Ghost, God, world without end.

℟. Amen.

CONCLUSION

The celebrant turns to face the people saying:

℣. Dóminus vobíscum.
℟. Et cum spíritu tuo.

℣. The Lord be with you.
℟. And with thy spirit.

At Solemn High Mass the deacon chants the Benedicámus, Domino:

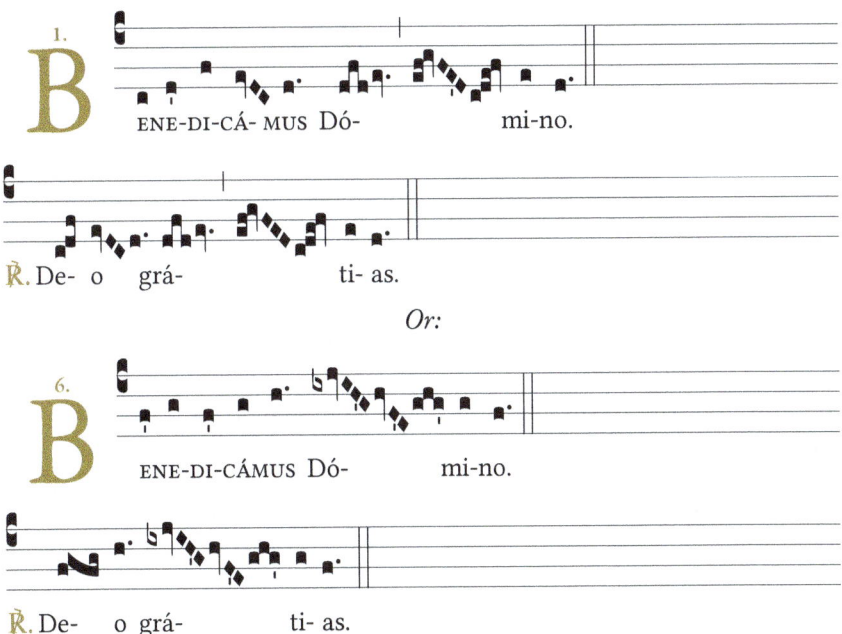

℣. Let us bless the Lord. ℟. Thanks be to God.

The celebrant bows over the altar and silently says:

Pláceat tibi, sancta Trínitas, obséquium servitútis meæ: et præsta; ut sacrifícium, quod óculis tuæ majestátis indígnus óbtuli, tibi sit acceptábile, mihíque et ómnibus, pro quibus illud óbtuli, sit, te miseránte, propitiábile. Per Christum, Dóminum nostrum. Amen.

May the performance of my homage be pleasing to Thee, O holy Trinity: and grant that the Sacrifice which I, though unworthy, have offered up in the sight of Thy Majesty, may be acceptable to Thee, and through Thy mercy, be a propitiation for me, and for all those for whom I have offered it. Through Christ our Lord. Amen.

The people kneel and the celebrant turns towards them for the blessing saying:

℣. Benedícat vos omnípotens Deus, Pater, et Fílius, ✠ et Spíritus Sanctus.
℟. Amen.

℣. May almighty God the Father, Son, ✠ and Holy Ghost, bless you.
℟. Amen.

The people stand as the celebrant moves to the Gospel side of the altar and reads the Last Gospel:

℣. Dóminus vobíscum.
℟. Et cum spíritu tuo.

℣. The Lord be with you.
℟. And with thy spirit.

THE BEGINNING ✠ OF THE HOLY GOSPEL
ACCORDING TO JOHN
John 1: 1-14

In princípio erat Verbum, et Verbum erat apud Deum, et Deus erat Verbum. Hoc erat in princípio apud Deum. Omnia per ipsum facta sunt: et sine ipso factum est nihil, quod factum est: in ipso vita erat, et vita erat lux hóminum: et lux in ténebris lucet, et ténebræ eam non comprehendérunt.

Fuit homo missus a Deo, cui nomen erat Joánnes. Hic venit in testimónium, ut testimónium perhibéret de

In the beginning was the Word, and the Word was with God, and the Word was God. The same was in the beginning with God. All things were made by Him, and without Him was made nothing that was made: in Him was life, and the life was the Light of men; and the Light shineth in darkness, and the darkness did not comprehend it.

There was a man sent from God, whose name was John. This man came for a witness, to testify concerning the

lúmine, ut omnes créderent per illum. Non erat ille lux, sed ut testimónium perhibéret de lúmine.

Erat lux vera, quæ illúminat omnem hóminem veniéntem in hunc mundum. In mundo erat, et mundus per ipsum factus est, et mundus eum non cognóvit. In própria venit, et sui eum non recepérunt. Quotquot autem recepérunt eum, dedit eis potestátem fílios Dei fíeri, his, qui credunt in nómine ejus : qui non ex sanguínibus, neque ex voluntáte carnis, neque ex voluntáte viri, sed ex Deo nati sunt.

(Genufléctit dicens:)

Et Verbum caro factum est, et habitávit in nobis: et vídimus glóriam ejus, glóriam quasi Unigéniti a Patre, plenum grátiæ et veritátis.

℟. Deo grátias.

Light, that all might believe through Him. He was not the Light, but he was to testify concerning the Light.

That was the true Light, which enlighteneth every man that cometh into this world. He was in the world, and the world was made by Him, and the world knew Him not. He came unto His own, and His own received Him not. But as many as received Him to them He gave power to become sons of God, to them that believe in His Name, who are born not of blood, nor of the will of the flesh, nor of the will of man, but of God.

(Here all kneel.)

And the Word was made flesh, and dwelt among us: and we saw His glory, the glory as of the Only begotten of the Father, full of grace and truth.

℟. Thanks be to God.

Suggested Rubrics for Tenebrae

Given that Tenebrae has little to no official rubrics, the following list of suggested rubrics is provided for what is customary in many places. These general rubrics are for Tenebrae as a whole; other rubrics specific to certain sections will be provided interlinearly. Not all notes here are achievable in all circumstances, so one should do the best one can.

Candle Ceremony

1. The altar should have a cross and six lighted candles with no additional ornamentation. These six candles are extinguished alternately during the *Benedíctus* at Lauds at every second verse so that the final candle is extinguished on the last verse.

2. A triangle-shaped candle holder which holds fifteen candles is set in front of the altar on the Epistle side. After each Psalm is sung one of the fifteen candles is alternately extinguished, starting from the bottom. There are thirteen Psalms and one Canticle, and thus the final lighted candle of these fifteen should be the uppermost.

3. This remaining candle should be removed and "hidden" (that is, taken out of sight) following the repetition of the antiphon of the *Benedíctus* at Lauds.

4. As the fifteenth candle is removed all additional and remaining lighting should be extinguished, including electric light. You may wish to coordinate supplemental and environmental lighting to complement the extinguishing of candles as far as is possible.

5. The "hidden" candle is brought back in following the *Strépitus*, after which all depart in silence.

Strépitus

The *Strépitus* is a loud, sustained noise created by banging which follows the removal of the final candle. This can be made in various ways, but is often produced by banging hard-bound books on kneelers, pewbacks, the floor, etc., although any reasonable means of producing the sound is acceptable. The *strépitus* should cease as the "hidden" candle is brought back into the sanctuary.

Psalms and Canticle

1. The antiphon for each Psalm is intoned by a cantor up to the * either from a lectern in between the choirs or in place, with the remaining choir joining for what follows after the *.

2. The choir typically stands while singing the initial antiphon. After the intonation of the first Psalm verse by a cantor the choirs are seated. For each subsequent antiphon only the cantor rises to intone the antiphon and is seated after intoning the first verse of the Psalm up to the *.

3. Each antiphon is sung in its entirety before and after each Psalm. For convenience the antiphon has been repeated below each Psalm to aid in this.

2. The Psalms are chanted antiphonally, alternating verses. The choir intoning the antiphon also chants the first Psalm verse following the antiphon.

3. A server or choir member may extinguish the candles following the Psalm during or immediately following the repeated antiphon.

Lessons, Responsories and Versicles

1. Each Lesson is typically chanted by one cantor while standing at a lectern between the choirs without the support of a choir.

2. Each Responsory is typically intoned by a cantor who also chants the ℣. with the choir joining in at the *. The intonation is done standing, after which the cantor sits.

3. At the versicles the ℣. is sung by a cantor and the ℟. by the choir. The versicles are typically said while the entire choir is standing.

Misc.

1. The *Aperi Dómine* may be said while kneeling before the Office begins.

2. The *Pater noster, Ave María* and *Credo* at the beginning of the Office are said silently. The *Pater noster* is also said silently following each Nocturn at Matins.

3. The prayer *Respíce quǽsumus* immediately precedes the *strépitus*.

4. The antiphon *Christus factus est* is sung while kneeling.

Holy Thursday

All kneel.

APERI Dómine, os meum ad benedicéndum nomen sanctum tuum: munda quoque cor meum ab ómnibus vanis, pervérsis et aliénis cogitatiónibus; intelléctum illúmina, afféctum inflámma, ut digne, atténte ac devóte hoc Offícium recitáre váleam, et exaudíri mérear ante conspéctum divínæ Majestátis túæ. Per Christum Dóminum nostrum.

℞. Amen.

DÓMINE, in unióne illíus divínæ intentiónis, qua ipse in terris laudes Deo persolvísti, has tibi Horas persólvo.

O Lord, open thou my mouth that I may bless Thy Holy Name. Cleanse my heart from all vain, evil, and wandering thoughts; enlighten my understanding, kindle my affections, that I may pray to, and praise Thee with attention and devotion; and may worthily be heard before the presence of Thy Divine Majesty. Through Christ our Lord.

℞. Amen.

LORD, in union with that Divine Intention wherewith Thou didst Thyself praise God, whilst Thou wast on earth, I offer these Hours unto Thee.

At Matins

The Pater noster, Ave María and Credo are said silently.

PATER NOSTER, qui es in cælis, sanctificétur nomen tuum: advéniat regnum tuum: fiat volúntas tua, sicut in cælo et in terra. Panem nostrum quotidiánum da nobis hódie: et dimítte nobis débita nostra, sicut et nos dimíttimus debitóribus nostris: et ne nos indúcas in tentatiónem: sed líbera nos a malo. Amen.

OUR FATHER, who art in heaven, hallowed be Thy name. Thy kingdom come. Thy will be done on earth as it is in heaven. Give us this day our daily bread. And forgive us our trespasses, as we forgive those who trespass against us. And lead us not into temptation: but deliver us from evil. Amen.

AVE MARÍA, grátia plena; Dóminus tecum: benedícta tu in muliéribus, et benedíctus fructus ventris tui Jesus. Sancta María, Mater Dei, ora pro nobis peccatóribus, nunc et in hora mortis nostræ. Amen.

CREDO in Deum, Patrem omnipoténtem, Creatórem cæli et terræ.

Et in Jesum Christum, Fílium ejus únicum, Dóminum nostrum: qui concéptus est de Spíritu Sancto, natus ex María Vírgine, passus sub Póntio Piláto, crucifíxus, mórtuus, et sepúltus: descéndit ad ínferos; tértia die resurréxit a mórtuis; ascéndit ad cælos; sedet ad déxteram Dei Patris omnipoténtis: inde ventúrus est judicáre vivos et mórtuos.

Credo in Spíritum Sanctum, sanctam Ecclésiam cathólicam, Sanctórum communiónem, remissiónem peccatórum, carnis resurrectiónem, vitam ætérnam. Amen.

HAIL MARY, full of grace; The Lord is with thee; blessed art thou amongst women, and blessed is the fruit of thy womb, Jesus. Holy Mary, Mother of God, pray for us sinners, now and at the hour of our death. Amen.

I BELIEVE in God, the Father almighty, Creator of heaven and earth.

And in Jesus Christ, His only Son, our Lord; who was conceived by the Holy Ghost, born of the Virgin Mary, suffered under Pontius Pilate, was crucified, died and was buried: He descended into hell; the third day He arose again from the dead; He ascended into heaven; sitteth at the right hand of God the Father almighty: from thence He shall come to judge the living and the dead.

I believe in the Holy Ghost, the holy Catholic Church, the communion of Saints, the forgiveness of sins. The resurrection of the body. And life everlasting. Amen.

1ST NOCTURN

1. Ant.
8.c

Z e-lus domus tu-æ * comé-dit me, et oppróbri- a expro-

bránti- um ti-bi ce-ci-dé-runt super me.

ANTIPHON: The zeal of Thine house * hath eaten me up, and the reproaches of them that reproached Thee are fallen upon me.

PSALM 68

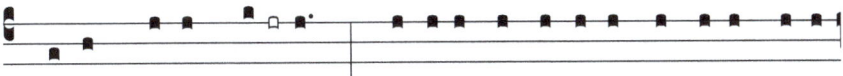

1. Salvum me fac, **De-** us: * quón-i- am intra-vé-runt aquæ usque ad

á-*nimam* **me-** am. *Flex:* tempéstas aquæ, †

1. Save me, O God: * for the waters are come in even unto my soul.

2. Infíxus sum in limo pro**fún**di : * et non *est sub***stán**tia.

2. I stick fast in the mire of the deep: * and there is no sure standing.

3. Veni in altitúdinem **maris** : * et tempé*stas de***mér**sit me.

3. I am come into the depth of the sea: * and a tempest hath overwhelmed me.

4. Laborávi clamans, raucæ factæ sunt fauces **meæ** : * defecérunt óculi mei, dum spero in *Deum* **me**um.

4. I have laboured with crying; my jaws are become hoarse: * my eyes have failed, whilst I hope in my God.

5. Multiplicáti sunt super capíllos cápitis **mei**, * qui odé*runt me* **gra**tis.

5. They are multiplied above the hairs of my head, * who hate me without cause.

6. Confortáti sunt qui persecúti sunt me inimíci mei in**jús**te : * quæ non rápui, tunc *exsol***vé**bam.

6. My enemies are grown strong who have wrongfully persecuted me: * then did I pay that which I took not away.

7. Deus, tu scis insipiéntiam **me**am : * et delícta mea a te non *sunt* *abs***cón**dita.

8. Non erubéscant in me qui ex- spéctant te, **Dó**mine, * Dómi*ne vir***tú**- tum

9. Non confundántur **su**per me * qui quærunt te, *Deus* **Is**raël.

10. Quóniam propter te sustínui op**pró**brium : * opéruit confúsio fá*ciem* **me**am.

11. Extráneus factus sum frátribus **me**is, * et peregrínus fíliis *matris* **me**æ.

12. Quóniam zelus domus tuæ comédit me : * et oppróbria expro- brántium tibi ceci*dérunt* **su**per me.

13. Et opérui in jejúnio ánimam **me**am : * et factum est in oppró*bri- um* **mi**hi.

14. Et pósui vestiméntum meum cilícium : * et factus sum illis *in* *pa***rá**bolam.

15. Advérsum me loquebántur, qui sedébant in **por**ta : * et in me psallébant qui bi*bébant* **vi**num.

16. Ego vero oratiónem meam ad te, **Dó**mine : * tempus beneplá*citi*, **De**us.

17. In multitúdine misericórdiæ tuæ ex**áu**di me, * in veritáte sa*lútis* **tu**æ :

18. Eripe me de luto, ut non in**fí**gar : * líbera me ab iis, qui odérunt me, et de profú*ndis* a**quá**rum.

19. Non me demérgat tempéstas aquæ, † neque absórbeat me pro**fún**- dum : * neque úrgeat super me púte*us* *os* **su**um.

7. O God, Thou knowest my foolishness; * and my offences are not hidden from Thee.

8. Let not them be ashamed for me, who look for Thee, O Lord, * the Lord of hosts.

9. Let them not be confounded on my account, * who seek Thee, O God of Israel.

10. Because for Thy sake I have borne reproach; * shame hath covered my face.

11. I am become a stranger to my brethren, * and an alien to the sons of my mother.

12. For the zeal of Thy house hath eaten me up: * and the reproaches of them that reproached Thee are fallen upon me.

13. And I covered my soul in fasting: * and it was made a reproach to me.

14. And I made haircloth my gar- ment: * and I became a byword to them.

15. They that sat in the gate spoke against me: * and they that drank wine made me their song.

16. But as for me, my prayer is to Thee, O Lord; * for the time of Thy good pleasure, O God.

17. In the multitude of Thy mercy hear me, * in the truth of Thy salva- tion.

18. Draw me out of the mire, that I may not stick fast: * deliver me from them that hate me, and out of the deep waters.

19. Let not the tempest of water drown me, † nor the deep swallow me up: * and let not the pit shut her mouth upon me.

20. Exáudi me, Dómine, quóniam benígna est misericórdia **tu**a : * secúndum multitúdinem miseratiónum tuárum ré*spice* **in** me.

21. Et ne avértas fáciem tuam a púero **tu**o : * quóniam tríbulor, velóci*ter* ex*áu*di me.

22. Inténde ánimæ meæ, et líbera eam : * propter inimícos meos é*ri*pe me.

23. Tu scis impropérium meum, et confusiónem **me**am, * et reveréntiam **me**am.

24. In conspéctu tuo sunt omnes qui tríbu**lant** me . * impropérium exspectávit cor meum, *et misé*riam.

25. Et sustínui qui simul contristaré-tur, et non **fu**it : * et qui consolarétur, et *non inv*éni.

26. Et dedérunt in escam **me**am fel : * et in siti mea potavérunt *me* ac*é*to.

27. Fiat mensa eórum coram ipsis in **lá**queum, * et in retributiónes, *et in* **scán**dalum.

28. Obscuréntur óculi eórum ne **ví**deant : * et dorsum eórum sem*per in***cúr**va.

29. Effúnde super eos iram **tu**am : * et furor iræ tuæ compre**hén**dat **e**os.

30. Fiat habitátio eórum des**ér**ta : * et in tabernáculis eórum non sit *qui in***há**bitet.

31. Quóniam quem tu percussísti, perse**cú**ti sunt : * et super dolórem vúlnerum meórum *addi***dé**runt.

20. Hear me, O Lord, for Thy mercy is kind; * look upon me according to the multitude of Thy tender mercies.

21. And turn not away Thy face from Thy servant: * for I am in trouble, hear me speedily.

22. Attend to my soul, and deliver it: * save me because of my enemies.

23. Thou knowest my reproach, and my confusion, * and my shame.

24. In Thy sight are all they that afflict me; * my heart hath expected reproach and misery.

25. And I looked for one that would grieve together with me, * but there was none: and for one that would comfort me, and I found none.

26. And they gave me gall for my food, * and in my thirst they gave me vinegar to drink.

27. Let their table become as a snare before them, * and a recompense, and a stumblingblock.

28. Let their eyes be darkened that they see not; * and their back bend Thou down always.

29. Pour out Thy indignation upon them: * and let Thy wrathful anger take hold of them.

30. Let their habitation be made desolate: * and let there be none to dwell in their tabernacles.

31. Because they have persecuted him whom Thou hast smitten; * and they have added to the grief of my wounds.

32. Appóne iniquitátem super iniquitátem eórum : * et non intrent in justítiam tuam.

32. Add Thou iniquity upon their iniquity: * and let them not come into Thy justice.

33. Deleántur de libro vivéntium : * et cum justis non scribántur.

33. Let them be blotted out of the book of the living; * and with the just let them not be written.

34. Ego sum pauper et dolens : * salus tua, Deus, suscépit me.

34. I am poor and sorrowful: * Thy salvation, O God, hath set me up.

35. Laudábo nomen Dei cum cántico : * et magnificábo eum in laude :

35. I will praise the name of God with a canticle: * and I will magnify Him with praise.

36. Et placébit Deo super vítulum novéllum : * córnua producéntem et úngulas.

36. And it shall please God better than a young calf, * that bringeth forth horns and hoofs.

37. Vídeant páuperes et læténtur : * quǽrite Deum, et vivet ánima vestra.

37. Let the poor see and rejoice: * seek ye God, and your soul shall live.

38. Quóniam exaudívit páuperes Dóminus : * et vinctos suos non despéxit.

38. For the Lord hath heard the poor: * and hath not despised his prisoners.

39. Laudent illum cæli et terra, * mare et ómnia reptília in eis.

39. Let the heavens and the earth praise Him; * the sea, and every thing that creepeth therein.

40. Quóniam Deus salvam fáciet Sion : * et ædificabúntur civitátes Juda.

40. For God will save Sion, * and the cities of Juda shall be built up.

41. Et inhabitábunt ibi, * et hereditáte acquírent eam.

41. And they shall dwell there, * and acquire it by inheritance.

42. Et semen servórum ejus possidébit eam : * et qui díligunt nomen ejus, habitábunt in ea.

42. And the seed of his servants shall possess it; * and they that love his name shall dwell therein.

1. Ant.
8.c

Z E-LUS domus tu-æ comé-dit me, et oppróbri- a expro-bránti- um ti-bi ce-ci-dé-runt super me.

The first candle is extinguished.

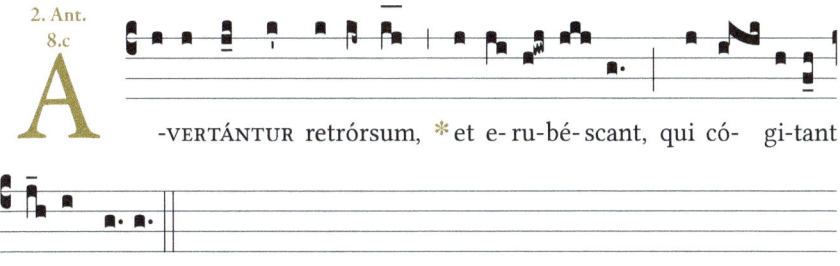

2. Ant.
8.c

A-VERTÁNTUR retrórsum, * et e- ru-bé- scant, qui có-   gi-tant

mi-hi ma-la.

ANTIPHON: Let them be turned backward * and put to confusion that desire my hurt.

PSALM 69

1. De- us, in adju-tó-ri- um me- um intén-de: * Dómi-ne ad adjuvándum

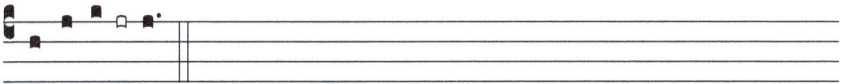

me festí- na.

1. O God, come to my assistance; * O Lord, make haste to help me.

2. Confundántur et revereántur, * qui quærunt ánimam meam.

3. Avertántur retrórsum, et erubéscant, * qui volunt mihi mala.

4. Avertántur statim erubescéntes, * qui dicunt mihi : Euge, euge.

5. Exsúltent et lætántur in te omnes qui quærunt te, * et dicant semper : Magnificétur Dóminus : qui díligunt salutáre tuum.

6. Ego vero egénus, et pauper sum : * Deus, ádjuva me.

7. Adjútor meus, et liberátor meus es tu : * Dómine, ne moréris.

2. Let them be confounded and ashamed * that seek my soul:

3. Let them be turned backward, and blush for shame * that desire evils to me:

4. Let them be presently turned away blushing for shame * that say to me: 'Tis well, 'tis well.

5. Let all that seek thee rejoice and be glad in thee; * and let such as love thy salvation say always: The Lord be magnified.

6. But I am needy and poor; * O God, help me.

7. Thou art my helper and my deliverer: * O Lord, make no delay.

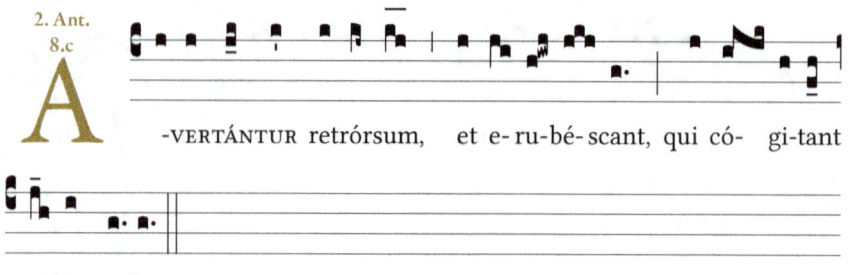

2. Ant.
8.c

A-VERTÁNTUR retrórsum, et e- ru-bé-scant, qui có- gi-tant

mi-hi ma-la.

The second candle is extinguished.

3. Ant.
8.c

D E- US me- us, *é- ri-pe me de manu pecca- tó- ris.

ANTIPHON: Deliver me, my God, * out of the hand of the wicked.

PSALM 70

1. In te, Dómi-ne, spe-rá-vi, non confúndar in æ-**tér**-num: * in justí-ti-

a tu-a lí-be-ra me, et *é-ripe* me. *Flex:* de-re-líquit e- um, †

℣. 2. **tu**- am, * *et* **sal**va me.

1. In thee, O Lord, I have hoped, let me never be put to confusion: * deliver me in thy justice, and rescue me.

2. Inclína ad me aurem **tu**am, * *et* **sal**va me.	2. Incline Thy ear unto me, * and save me.
3. Esto mihi in Deum protectórem, et in locum mu**ní**tum : * ut sal*vum me* **fá**cias.	3. Be Thou unto me a God, a protector, and a place of strength: * that Thou mayst make me safe.

4. Quóniam firmaméntum **meum**, * et refúgium *meum* **es** tu.

5. Deus meus, éripe me de manu peccatóris, * et de manu contra legem agéntis *et in*íqui :

6. Quóniam tu es patiéntia mea, **Dó**mine : * Dómine, spes mea a juven*túte* **me**a.

7. In te confirmátus sum ex **ú**tero : * de ventre matris meæ tu es pro*téctor* **me**us.

8. In te cantátio mea semper : tamquam prodígium factus sum **mul**tis : * et tu ad*jútor* **for**tis.

9. Repleátur os meum laude, ut cantem glóriam **tu**am : * tota die magni*túdinem* **tu**am.

10. Ne projícias me in témpore sene**ctú**tis : * cum defécerit virtus mea, ne *dere*lín**quas** me.

11. Quia dixérunt inimíci mei **mi**hi : * et qui custodiébant ánimam meam, consílium fecé*runt in* **u**num.

12. Dicéntes : Deus derelíquit eum, † persequímini, et comprehéndite eum : * quia non est *qui* erí**piat**.

13. Deus ne elongéris **a** me : * Deus meus, in auxílium *meum* ré**spice.**

14. Confundántur, et defíciant detrahéntes ánimæ **me**æ : * operiántur confusióne et pudóre, qui quærunt *mala* **mi**hi.

15. Ego autem semper sperábo : * et adjíciam super omnem *laudem* **tu**am.

16. Os meum annuntiábit justítiam **tu**am : * tota die salu*táre* **tu**um.

4. For Thou art my firmament * and my refuge.

5. Deliver me, O my God, out of the hand of the sinner, * and out of the hand of the transgressor of the law and of the unjust.

6. For Thou art my patience, O Lord: * my hope, O Lord, from my youth.

7. By Thee have I been confirmed from the womb: * from my mother's womb Thou art my protector.

8. Of Thee shall I continually sing: I am become unto many as a wonder, * but Thou art a strong helper.

9. Let my mouth be filled with praise, that I may sing Thy glory; * Thy greatness all the day long.

10. Cast me not off in the time of old age: * when my strength shall fail, do not Thou forsake me.

11. For my enemies have spoken against me; * and they that watched my soul have consulted together,

12. Saying: God hath forsaken him: † pursue and take him, * for there is none to deliver him.

13. O God, be not Thou far from me: * O my God, make haste to my help.

14. Let them be confounded and come to nothing that detract my soul; * let them be covered with confusion and shame that seek my hurt.

15. But I will always hope; * and will add to all Thy praise.

16. My mouth shall shew forth Thy justice; * Thy salvation all the day long.

17. Quóniam non cognóvi litteratúram, † introíbo in poténtias **Dó**mini : * Dómine, memorábor justítiæ tu*æ sol*íus.

18. Deus, docuísti me a juventúte **me**a : * et usque nunc pronuntiábo mirab*ília* **tu**a.

19. Et usque in senéctam et **sé**nium : * Deus, ne *derelín*quas me,

20. Donec annúntiem bráchium **tu**um * generatióni omni, *quæ vent*ú**ra** est :

21. Poténtiam tuam, et justítiam tuam, Deus, † usque in altíssima, quæ fecísti ma**gná**lia : * Deus, quis s*ímilis* **ti**bi ?

22. Quantas ostendísti mihi tribulatiónes multas et malas : † et convérsus vivifi**cá**sti me : * et de abýssis terræ íterum *redu***xí**sti me :

23. Multiplicásti magnificéntiam **tu**am : * et convérsus conso*látus* **es** me.

24. Nam et ego confitébor tibi in vasis psalmi veritátem **tu**am : * Deus, psallam tibi in cíthara, *Sanctus* **Is**raël.

25. Exsultábunt lábia mea cum cantávero **ti**bi : * et ánima mea, quam *red*e**mí**sti.

26. Sed et lingua mea tota die meditábitur justítiam **tu**am : * cum confúsi et revériti fúerint, qui quærunt *mala* **mi**hi.

17. Because I have not known learning, † I will enter into the powers of the Lord: * O Lord, I will be mindful of Thy justice alone.

18. Thou hast taught me, O God, from my youth: * and till now I will declare Thy wonderful works.

19. And unto old age and grey hairs: * O God, forsake me not,

20. Until I shew forth Thy arm * to all the generation that is to come:

21. Thy power, and Thy justice, O God, † even to the highest great things Thou hast done: * O God, who is like to Thee?

22. How great troubles hast Thou shewn me, many and grievous: † and turning Thou hast brought me to life, * and hast brought me back again from the depths of the earth:

23. Thou hast multiplied Thy magnificence; * and turning to me Thou hast comforted me.

24. For I will also confess to Thee Thy truth with the instruments of psaltery: * O God, I will sing to Thee with the harp,

25. My lips shall greatly rejoice, when I shall sing to Thee; * and my soul which Thou hast redeemed.

26. Yea and my tongue shall meditate on Thy justice all the day; * when they shall be confounded and put to shame that seek evils to me.

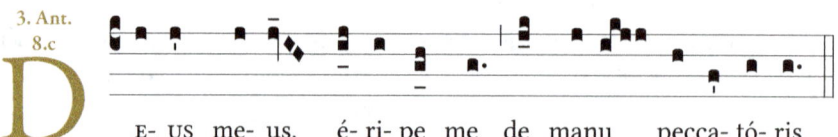

3. Ant.
8.c

D E- us me- us, é- ri- pe me de manu pecca- tó- ris.

The third candle is extinguished.

℣. Avertántur retrórsum, et e-ru-béscant. ℟. Qui có-gi-tant mí-hi má-la.

Or:

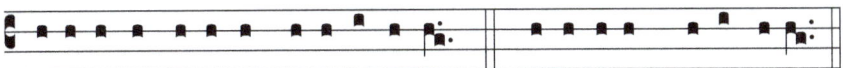

℣. Avertántur retrórsum, et e-ru-béscant. ℟. Qui có-gi-tant mí-hi má-la.

℣. Let them be turned backward and put to confusion.
℟. That desire my hurt.

The Pater noster *is said silently.*

LESSON 1   LAMENTATIONS 1 :1-5

IN-CI-PIT Lamentá-ti- o Je-remí- æ Prophé-tæ.   ALEPH.   Quómo-

do se-det so-la cí-vi-tas plena pópu-lo : facta est qua-si ví-du- a dó-

mi-na Génti- um : princeps pro-vinci- á-rum facta est sub tri-bú-to.

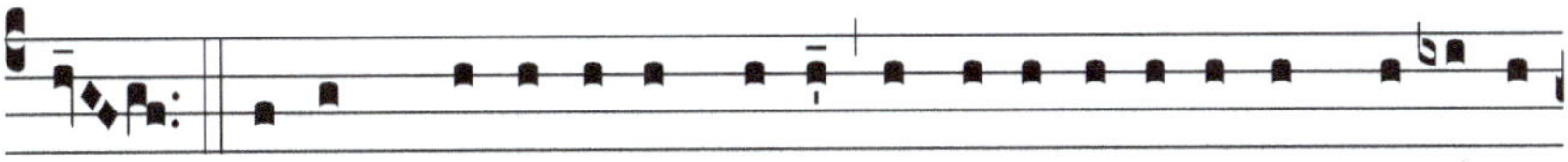

BETH.   Plo-rans plo-rá-vit in nocte, et lácrimæ e-jus in ma-xíl-lis

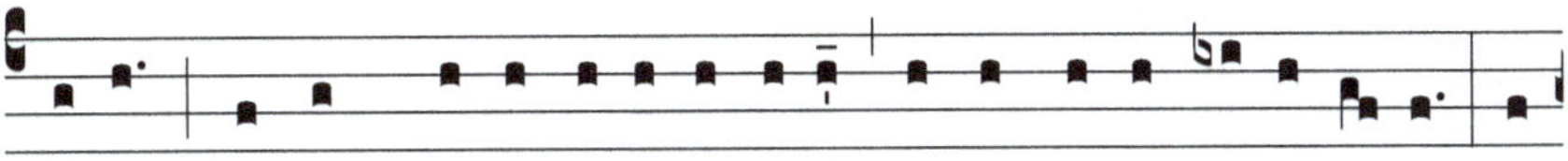

e-jus : non est qui conso-lé-tur e- am ex ómni-bus ca-ris e- jus : o-

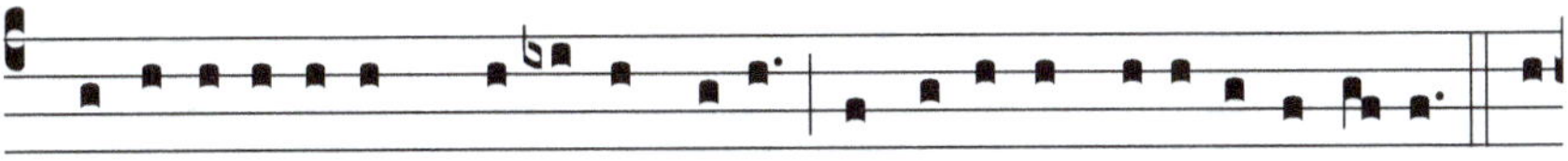

mnes amí-ci e-jus spre-vé-runt e- am, et facti sunt e- i in-i-mí-ci. GHI-

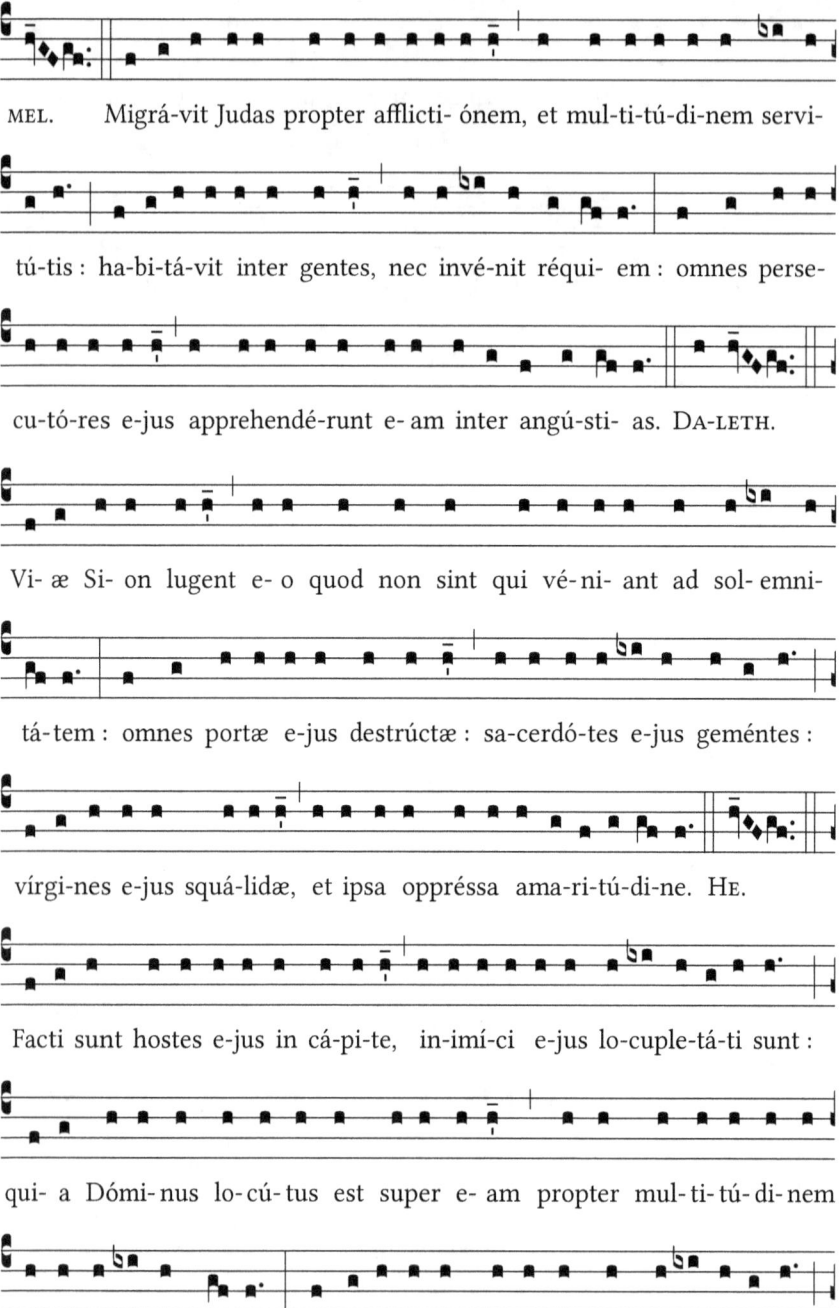

MEL. Migrá-vit Judas propter afflicti- ónem, et mul-ti-tú-di-nem servi-

tú-tis : ha-bi-tá-vit inter gentes, nec invé-nit réqui- em : omnes perse-

cu-tó-res e-jus apprehendé-runt e- am inter angú-sti- as. DA-LETH.

Vi- æ Si- on lugent e- o quod non sint qui vé-ni- ant ad sol- emni-

tá-tem : omnes portæ e-jus destrúctæ : sa-cerdó-tes e-jus geméntes :

vírgi-nes e-jus squá-lidæ, et ipsa oppréssa ama-ri-tú-di-ne. HE.

Facti sunt hostes e-jus in cá-pi-te, in-imí-ci e-jus lo-cuple-tá-ti sunt :

qui- a Dómi- nus lo-cú- tus est super e- am propter mul- ti-tú- di-nem

in-iqui- tá-tum e- jus : párvu-li e-jus ducti sunt in capti-vi-tá-tem,

ante fá-ci- em tri-bu-lántis. Je-rú-sa-lem, Je-rú-sa-lem, convérte-re ad

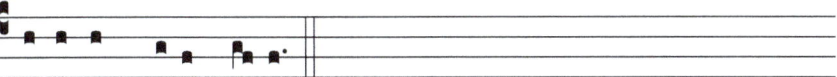

Dómi-num De- um tu- um.

LESSON 1: ALEPH. How doth the city sit solitary that was full of people! how is the mistress of the Gentiles become as a widow: the princes of provinces made tributary! **BETH.** Weeping she hath wept in the night, and her tears are on her cheeks: there is none to comfort her among all them that were dear to her: all her friends have despised her, and are become her enemies. **GHIMEL.** Juda hath removed her dwelling place because of her affliction, and the greatness of her bondage: she hath dwelt among the nations, and she hath found no rest: all her persecutors have taken her in the midst of straits. **DALETH.** The ways of Sion mourn, because there are none that come to the solemn feast: all her gates are broken down: her priests sigh: her virgins are in affliction, and she is oppressed with bitterness. **HE.** Her adversaries are become her lords, her enemies are enriched: because the Lord hath spoken against her for the multitude of her iniquities: her children are led into captivity: before the face of the oppressor. *Jerusalem, Jerusalem, return to the Lord thy God.*

RESPONSORY 1   IN MONTE OLIVÉTI

tré-tis in ten- ta- ti- ó-   nem. * Spí- ri-tus.

℟. At the Mount of Olives He prayed unto the Father: O My Father, if it be possible, let this cup pass from Me! * The spirit indeed is willing, but the flesh is weak. ℣. Watch and pray, that ye enter not into temptation. ℟. The spirit indeed is willing, but the flesh is weak.

LESSON 2   LAMENTATIONS 1: 6-9

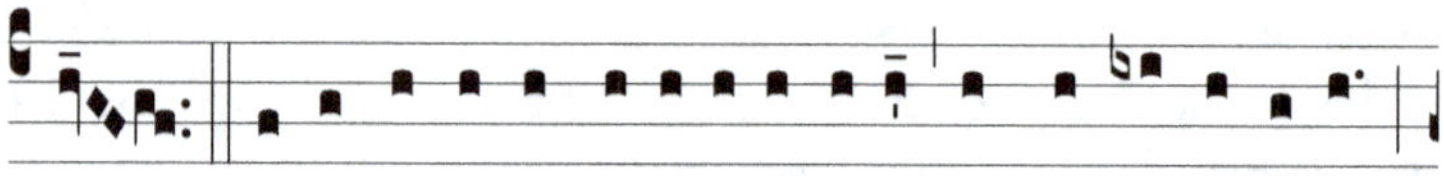

AU.   Et egréssus est a fí-li- a Si- on omnis de-cor e-jus :

facti sunt prínci-pes e-jus vel-ut a-rí- e-tes non inve-ni- éntes páscu-

a : et a-bi- é-runt absque forti-tú-di-ne ante fá-ci- em subsequéntis.

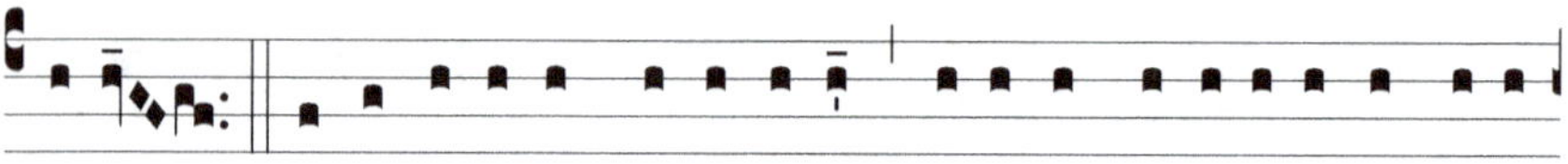

ZA- IN.   Re-cordá-ta est Je-rú-sa-lem di- é-rum afflicti- ó-nis su-æ

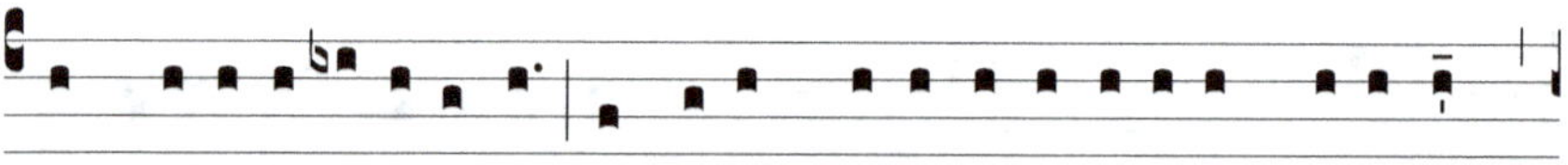

et præva-ri-ca-ti- ó-nis, ómni- um de-si-de-ra-bí- li- um su- ó-rum,

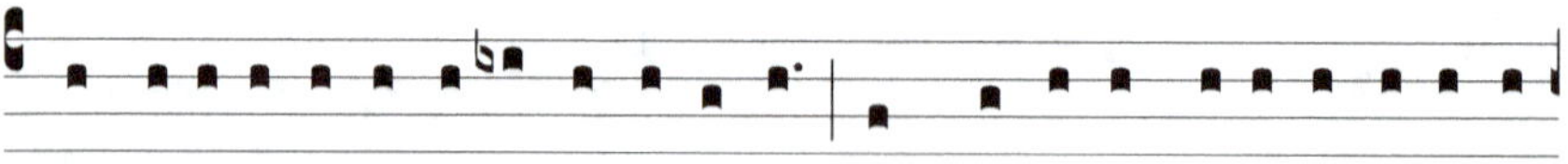

quæ habú- e-rat a di- é-bus antíquis, cum cá-de-ret pópu-lus e-jus in

manu hostí-li, et non esset au-xi-li- á- tor : vi-dé-runt e- am hostes,

et de-ri-sé-runt sábba-ta e- jus. HETH. Peccá-tum peccá-vit Je-rú-

sa-lem, propté-re- a instá-bi-lis facta est : omnes, qui glo-ri-fi-cá-bant

e- am, spre-vé-runt il-lam, qui- a vi-dé-runt igno-mí-ni- am e- jus :

ipsa autem gemens convérsa est re-trórsum. TETH. Sordes e-jus in

pé-di-bus e-jus, nec re-cordá-ta est fi-nis su- i : depó-si-ta est ve-

heménter, non ha-bens conso-la-tó-rem : vi-de, Dómi-ne, afflicti- ónem

me- am, quó-ni- am e-réctus est in-i-mí-cus. Je-rú-sa-lem, Je-rú-sa-lem,

convérte-re ad Dómi-num De- um tu- um.

LESSON 2: **VAU.** And from the daughter of Sion all her beauty is depart-ed: her princes are become like rams that find no pastures: and they are gone away without strength before the face of the pursuer. **ZAIN.** Jerusalem hath remembered the days of her affliction, and prevarication of all her desirable things which she had from the days of old, when her people fell in the enemy's hand, and there was no helper: the enemies have seen her, and have mocked at

her sabbaths. **HETH.** Jerusalem hath grievously sinned, therefore is she become unstable: all that honoured her have despised her, because they have seen her shame: but she sighed and turned backward. **TETH.** Her filthiness is on her feet, and she hath not remembered her end: she is wonderfully cast down, not having a comforter: behold, O Lord, my affliction, because the enemy is lifted up. *Jerusalem, Jerusalem, return to the Lord thy God.*

RESPONSORY 2   TRISTIS EST ÁNIMA MEA

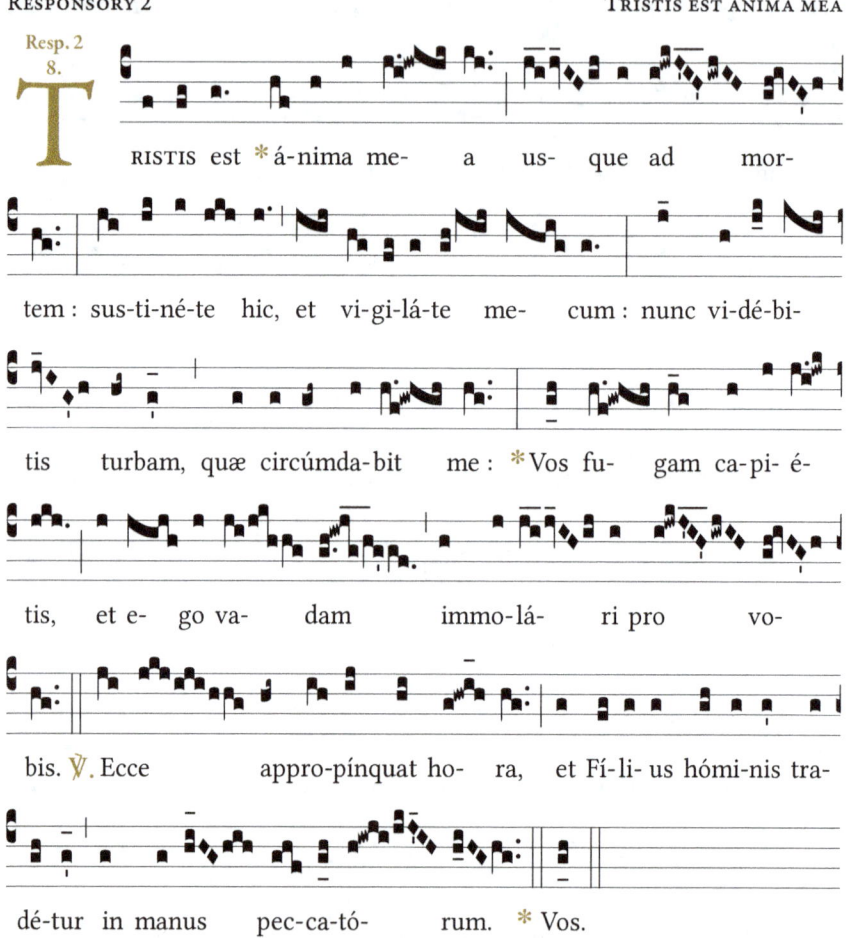

TRISTIS est *á-nima me- a us- que ad mor-tem : sus-ti-né-te hic, et vi-gi-lá-te me- cum : nunc vi-dé-bi-tis turbam, quæ circúmda-bit me : *Vos fu- gam ca-pi- é-tis, et e- go va- dam immo-lá- ri pro vo-bis. ℣. Ecce appro-pínquat ho- ra, et Fí-li- us hómi-nis tra-dé-tur in manus pec-ca-tó- rum. * Vos.

℟. My Soul is exceeding sorrowful, even unto death: tarry ye here and watch with Me * Yet a little while, and ye shall see the multitude close Me in. Ye shall flee; and I will go to be offered a sacrifice for you. ℣. Behold, the hour is at hand, and the Son of man is betrayed into the hands of sinners. ℟. Ye shall flee; and I will go to be offered a sacrifice for you.

J OD. Manum su- am mi-sit hostis ad ómni- a de-si-de-ra-bí-

li- a e-jus : qui- a vi-dit gentes ingréssas sanctu- á-ri- um su- um, de

qui-bus præcé-pe-ras ne intrá-rent in ecclé-si- am tu- am. CAPH.   O-

mnis pópu-lus e-jus gemens, et quæ-rens panem : de-dé-runt pre-ti- ó-

sa quæque pro ci-bo   ad re-fo-cil-lándam á-ni-mam. Vi-de, Dómi-ne,

et consí-de-ra, quó-ni- am facta sum vi- lis. LAMED.   O vos omnes,

qui transí- tis per vi- am, atténdi-te, et vi-dé-te si est do-lor sic-ut do-lor

me- us : quó-ni- am vindemi- á-vit me,   ut lo-cú-tus est Dómi-nus in

di- e i-ræ fu-ró-ris su- i. MEM.   De excélso mi-sit ignem in óssi-bus

me- is, et e-ru-dí-vit me : expándit re-te pé-di-bus me- is, convértit me

re-trórsum : pó-su- it me de-so-lá-tam, to-ta di- e moeró-re conféctam.

Nun.   Vi-gi-lá-vit jugum in-iqui- tá-tum me- á-rum : in manu e-jus

convo-lú-tæ sunt, et impó-si-tæ collo me- o : infirmá-ta est virtus

me- a : de-dit me Dómi-nus in manu, de qua non pót-e-ro súrge-re.

Je-rú-sa-lem, Je-rú-sa-lem, convérte-re ad Dómi-num De- um tu- um.

Lesson 3: Jod. The enemy hath put out his hand to all her desirable things: for she hath seen the Gentiles enter into her sanctuary, of whom thou gavest commandment that they should not enter into thy church. **Caph.** All her people sigh, they seek bread: they have given all their precious things for food to relieve the soul: see, O Lord, and consider, for I am become vile. **Lamed.** O all ye that pass by the way, attend, and see if there be any sorrow like to my sorrow: for he hath made a vintage of me, as the Lord spoke in the day of his fierce anger. **Mem.** From above he hath sent fire into my bones, and hath chastised me: he hath spread a net for my feet, he hath turned me back: he hath made me desolate, wasted with sorrow all the day long. **Nun.** The yoke of my iniquities hath watched: they are folded together in his hand, and put upon my neck: my strength is weakened: the Lord hath delivered me into a hand out of which I am not able to rise. *Jerusalem, Jerusalem, return to the Lord thy God.*

RESPONSORY 3   ECCE VÍDIMUS

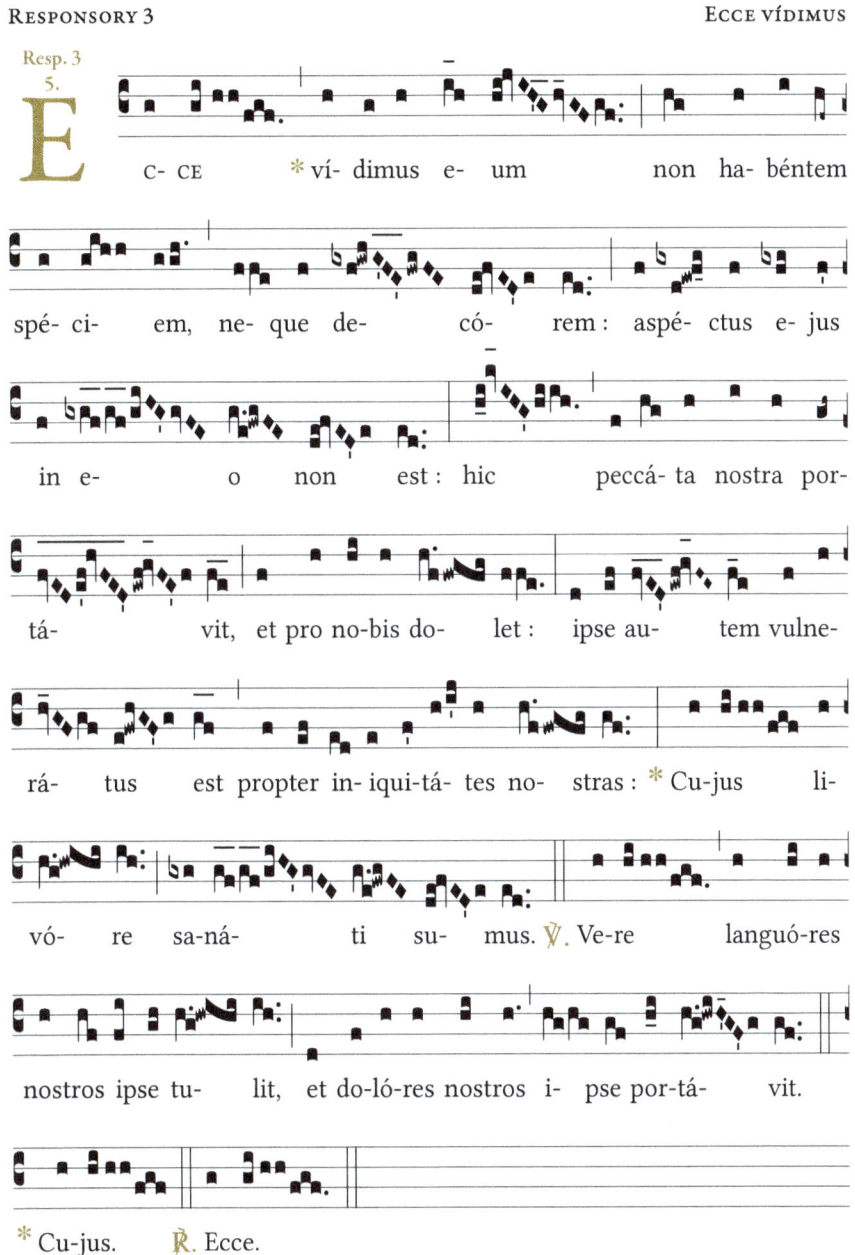

E-CE * ví- dimus e- um   non ha- béntem spé- ci- em, ne- que de- có- rem : aspé- ctus e- jus in e- o non est : hic peccá- ta nostra por- tá- vit, et pro no-bis do- let : ipse au- tem vulne- rá- tus est propter in- iqui-tá- tes no- stras : * Cu-jus li- vó- re sa-ná- ti su- mus. ℣. Ve-re languó-res nostros ipse tu- lit, et do-ló-res nostros i- pse por-tá- vit.

* Cu-jus.   ℟. Ecce.

℟. Behold, when we shall see Him, He hath no form nor comeliness: there is no beauty in Him: this is He Which hath borne our griefs and carried our sorrows; but He was wounded for our transgressions * And with His stripes we are healed. ℣. Surely He hath borne our griefs and carried our sorrows.

℟. And with His stripes we are healed. ℟. Behold, when we shall see Him, He hath no form nor comeliness: there is no beauty in Him; this is He Which hath borne our sins and carried our sorrows: but He was wounded for our transgressions, and with His stripes we are healed.

2ND NOCTURN

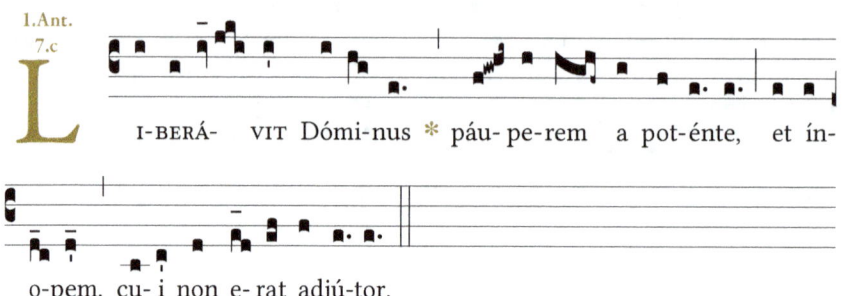

1.Ant.
7.c

L I-BERÁ- VIT Dómi-nus * páu- pe-rem a pot-énte, et ín-

o-pem, cu- i non e- rat adjú-tor.

ANTIPHON: The Lord shall deliver * the needy from the strong: the poor also, that hath no helper.

PSALM 71

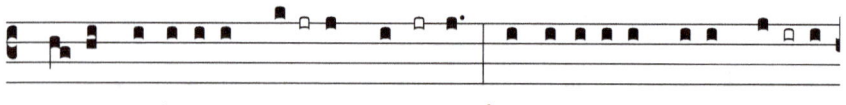

1. De- us, ju-dí-ci- um **tu-** um **re-**gi da : * et justí-ti- am tu-am **fí-**li- o

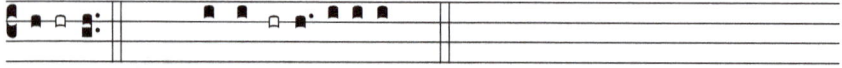

re- gis : *Flex :* A-rá-bi- æ, †

1. Give to the king Thy judgment, O God: * and to the king's son Thy justice:

2. Judicáre pópulum tuum **in** justítia, * et páuperes tuos **in** judício.

3. Suscípiant montes **pa**cem pópulo : * et **co**lles justítiam.

4. Judicábit páuperes pópuli, et salvos fáciet **fí**lios **páu**perum : * et humiliábit calum**niató**rem.

2. To judge thy people with justice, * and Thy poor with judgment.

3. Let the mountains receive peace for the people: * and the hills justice.

4. He shall judge the poor of the people, and He shall save the children of the poor: * and He shall humble the oppressor.

5. Et permanébit cum sole, et **an**te **lu**nam, * in generatióne et genera**tió**nem.

6. Descéndet sicut plúvia in **vel**lus : * et sicut stillicídia stillántia **super ter**ram.

7. Oriétur in diébus ejus justítia, et abun**dán**tia **pa**cis : * donec auferátur **lu**na.

8. Et dominábitur a mari **us**que ad **ma**re : * et a flúmine usque ad términos **or**bis ter**rá**rum.

9. Coram illo próci**dent** Æ**thí**opes : * et inimíci ejus **ter**ram **lin**gent.

10. Reges Tharsis, et ínsulæ **mú**nera **óf**ferent : * reges Arabum et Saba **do**na ad**dú**cent.

11. Et adorábunt eum omnes **reges ter**ræ : * omnes Gentes **sér**vient **ei** :

12. Quia liberábit páuperem **a** po**tén**te : * et páuperem, cui non **e**rat ad**jú**tor.

13. Parcet páupe**ri** et **í**nopi : * et ánimas páuperum **sal**vas **fá**ciet.

14. Ex usúris et iniquitáte rédimet áni**mas** e**ó**rum : * et honorábile nomen eórum **co**ram **il**lo.

15. Et vivet, et dábitur ei de auro Arábiæ, † et adorábunt de **i**pso **sem**per : * tota die bene**dí**cent ei.

16. Et erit firmaméntum in terra in summis móntium, † superextollétur super Líbanum **fru**ctus ejus : * et florébunt de civitáte sicut **fæ**num ter**ræ**.

5. And He shall continue with the sun, and before the moon, * throughout all generations.

6. He shall come down like rain upon the fleece; * and as showers falling gently upon the earth.

7. In His days shall justice spring up, and abundance of peace, * till the moon be taken away.

8. And He shall rule from sea to sea, * and from the river unto the ends of the earth.

9. Before Him the Ethiopians shall fall down: * and His enemies shall lick the ground.

10. The kings of Tharsis and the islands shall offer presents: * the kings of the Arabians and of Saba shall bring gifts:

11. And all kings of the earth shall adore Him: * all nations shall serve Him.

12. For He shall deliver the poor from the mighty: * and the needy that had no helper.

13. He shall spare the poor and needy: * and He shall save the souls of the poor.

14. He shall redeem their souls from usuries and iniquity: * and their names shall be honourable in His sight.

15. And He shall live, and to Him shall be given of the gold of Arabia, † for Him they shall always adore: * they shall bless Him all the day.

16. And there shall be a firmament on the earth on the tops of mountains, † above Libanus shall the fruit thereof be exalted: * and they of the city shall flourish like the grass of the earth.

17. Sit nomen ejus bene**dí**ctum in **sǽ**cula : * ante solem pérmanet **no**men **e**jus.

17. Let His name be blessed for evermore: * His name continueth before the sun.

18. Et benedicéntur in ipso omnes **tri**bus **terræ** : * omnes Gentes magni**fic**ábunt eum.

18. And in Him shall all the tribes of the earth be blessed: * all nations shall magnify Him.

19. Benedíctus Dóminus, **Deus Is**raël, * qui facit mira**bí**lia **so**lus.

19. Blessed be the Lord, the God of Israel, * who alone doth wonderful things.

20. Et benedíctum nomen majestátis ejus **in** ætérnum : * et replébitur majestáte ejus omnis terra : **fiat, fiat.**

20. And blessed be the name of His majesty for ever: * and the whole earth shall be filled with His majesty. So be it. So be it.

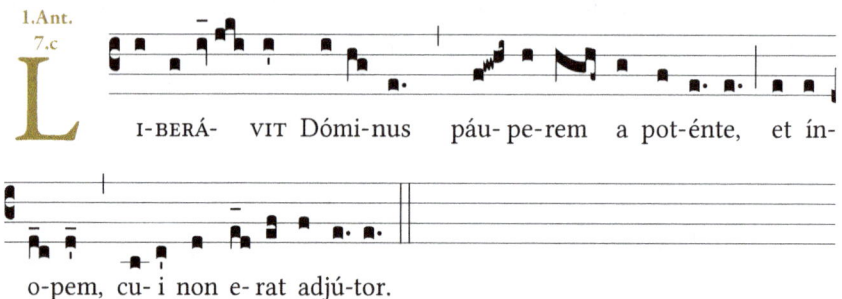

1.Ant.
7.c

L I-BERÁ- vit Dómi-nus páu- pe-rem a pot-énte, et ín-o-pem, cu- i non e- rat adjú-tor.

The fourth candle is extinguished.

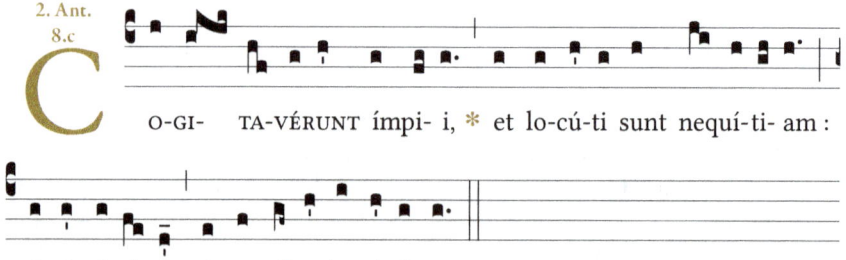

2. Ant.
8.c

C O-GI- TA-VÉRUNT ímpi- i, * et lo-cú-ti sunt nequí-ti- am : in-iqui- tá-tem in excélso lo-cú-ti sunt.

Antiphon: The ungodly think * and speak wickedness: they speak loftily concerning oppression.

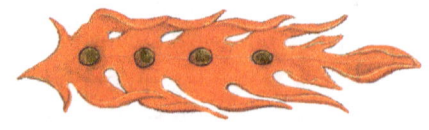

PSALM 72

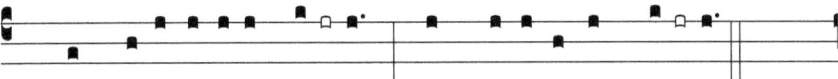

1. Quam bonus Isra- ël **De-** us, * his, qui re*cto sunt* **cor-** de!

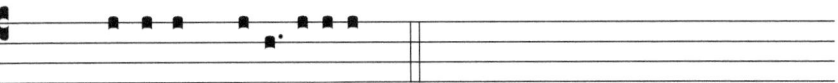

Flex : déxte-ram me- am : †

1. How good is God to Israel, * to them that are of a right heart!

2. Mei autem pene moti sunt **pe**des : * pene effúsi sunt *gressus* **me**i.

3. Quia zelávi super iníquos, * pacem pecca*tórum* **vi**dens.

4. Quia non est respéctus morti e**ó**rum : * et firmaméntum in pla*ga e***ó**rum.

5. In labóre hóminum **non** sunt : * et cum homínibus non flage*lla***bún**tur:

6. Ideo ténuit eos su**pér**bia, * opérti sunt iniquitáte et impie*táte* **su**a.

7. Pródiit quasi ex ádipe iníquitas e**ó**rum : * transiérunt in af*féctum* **cor**dis.

8. Cogitavérunt, et locúti sunt ne**quí**tiam : * iniquitátem in excél*so lo***cú**ti sunt.

9. Posuérunt in cælum os **su**um : * et lingua eórum trans*ívit in* **ter**ra.

10. Ideo convertétur pópulus **me**us hic : * et dies pleni inve*niéntur in* **ei**s.

11. Et dixérunt : Quómodo scit **De**us, * et si est sciéntia *in ex***cél**so?

2. But my feet were almost moved; * my steps had well nigh slipped.

3. Because I had a zeal on occasion of the wicked, * seeing the prosperity of sinners.

4. For there is no regard to their death, * nor is there strength in their stripes.

5. They are not in the labour of men: * neither shall they be scourged like other men.

6. Therefore pride hath held them fast: * they are covered with their iniquity and their wickedness.

7. Their iniquity hath come forth, as it were from fatness: * they have passed into the affection of the heart.

8. They have thought and spoken wickedness: * they have spoken iniquity on high.

9. They have set their mouth against heaven: * and their tongue hath passed through the earth.

10. Therefore will my people return here * and full days shall be found in them.

11. And they said: How doth God know? * and is there knowledge in the most High?

12. Ecce ipsi peccatóres, et abundántes in sǽculo, * obtinuérunt divítias.

13. Et dixi : Ergo sine causa justificávi cor meum, * et lavi inter innocéntes manus meas.

14. Et fui flagellátus tota die, * et castigátio mea in matutínis.

15. Si dicébam : Narrábo sic : * ecce natiónem filiórum tuórum reprobávi.

16. Existimábam ut cognóscerem hoc, * labor est ante me.

17. Donec intrem in Sanctuárium Dei : * et intélligam in novíssimis eórum.

18. Verúmtamen propter dolos posuísti eis : * dejecísti eos dum allevaréntur.

19. Quómodo facti sunt in desolatiónem, súbito defecérunt : * periérunt propter iniquitátem suam.

20. Velut sómnium surgéntium, Dómine, * in civitáte tua imáginem ipsórum ad níhilum rédiges.

21. Quia inflammátum est cor meum, et renes mei commutáti sunt : * et ego ad níhilum redáctus sum, et nescívi.

22. Ut juméntum factus sum apud te : * et ego semper tecum.

23. Tenuísti manum déxteram meam : † et in voluntáte tua deduxísti me, * et cum glória suscepísti me.

24. Quid enim mihi est in cælo? * et a te quid vólui super terram?

12. Behold these are sinners; and yet abounding in the world * they have obtained riches.

13. And I said: Then have I in vain justified my heart, * and washed my hands among the innocent.

14. And I have been scourged all the day; * and my chastisement hath been in the mornings.

15. If I said: I will speak thus; * behold I should condemn the generation of Thy children.

16. I studied that I might know this thing, * it is a labour in my sight:

17. Until I go into the sanctuary of God, * and understand concerning their last ends.

18. But indeed for deceits Thou hast put it to them: * when they were lifted up, Thou hast cast them down.

19. How are they brought to desolation? they have suddenly ceased to be: * they have perished by reason of their iniquity.

20. As the dream of them that awake, O Lord; * so in Thy city Thou shalt bring their image to nothing.

21. For my heart hath been inflamed, and my reins have been changed: * and I am brought to nothing, and I knew not.

22. I am become as a beast before Thee: * and I am always with thee.

23. Thou hast held me by my right hand; † and by Thy will Thou hast conducted me, * and with Thy glory Thou hast received me.

24. For what have I in heaven? * and besides thee what do I desire upon earth?

25. Defécit caro mea, et cor **me**um : * Deus cordis mei, et pars mea Deus *in æ*térnum.

25. For thee my flesh and my heart hath fainted away : * Thou art the God of my heart, and the God that is my portion for ever.

26. Quia ecce, qui elóngant se a te, períbunt : * perdidísti omnes, qui forni*cántur* **abs** te.

26. For behold they that go far from thee shall perish : * Thou hast destroyed all them that are disloyal to thee.

27. Mihi autem adhærére Deo **bo**num est : * pónere in Dómino Deo *spem* **me**am :

27. But it is good for me to adhere to my God, * to put my hope in the Lord God:

28. Ut annúntiem omnes prædicatiónes **tu**as, * in portis f*íliæ* **Si**on.

28. That I may declare all Thy praises, * in the gates of the daughter of Sion.

2. Ant.
8.c

C O-GI- TA-VÉRUNT ímpi- i, et lo-cú-ti sunt nequí-ti- am : in-iqui- tá-tem in excélso lo-cú-ti sunt.

The fifth candle is extinguished.

3.Ant.
1.g

EX-SÚRGE, Dómi-ne, * et jú-di-ca causam me- am.

ANTIPHON: Arise, O Lord, * and judge my cause.

PSALM 73

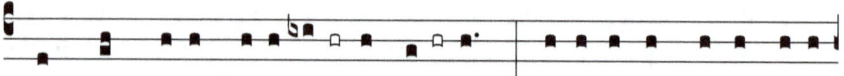

1. Ut quid, De- us, repu- lísti in **fi-** nem : * i-rá-tus est fu-ror tu- us

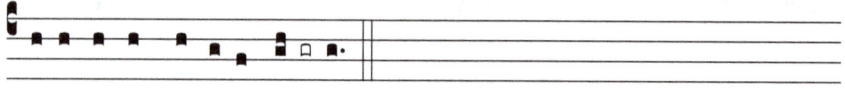

super o-ves pá*scu-æ* **tu-** æ?

1. O God, why hast Thou cast us off unto the end: * why is Thy wrath enkindled against the sheep of Thy pasture?

2. Memor esto congregatiónis **tuæ:** * quam possedísti *ab in*ítio.

2. Remember Thy congregation, * which Thou hast possessed from the beginning.

3. Redemísti virgam hereditátis **tuæ:** * mons Sion, in quo habitás*ti in* eo.

3. The sceptre of Thy inheritance which Thou hast redeemed: * mount Sion in which Thou hast dwelt.

4. Leva manus tuas in supérbias eórum in **fi**nem: * quanta malignátus est inim*ícus in* **san**cto!

4. Lift up Thy hands against their pride unto the end; * see what things the enemy hath done wickedly in the sanctuary.

5. Et gloriáti sunt **qui** o**dé**runt te: * in médio solemni*tátis* **tuæ.**

5. And they that hate Thee have made their boasts, * in the midst of Thy solemnity.

6. Posuérunt signa **su**a, **sig**na: * et non cognovérunt sicut in éxitu *super* **sum**mum.

6. They have set up their ensigns for signs, * and they knew not both in the going out and on the highest top.

7. Quasi in silva lignórum secúribus excidérunt jánuas ejus **in** idípsum: * in secúri et áscia deje*cérunt* **e**am.

7. As with axes in a wood of trees, they have cut down at once the gates thereof, * with axe and hatchet they have brought it down.

8. Incendérunt igni sanctuárium tuum: * in terra polluérunt tabernáculum nóminis tui.

9. Dixérunt in corde suo cognátio eórum simul: * Quiéscere faciámus omnes dies festos Dei a terra.

10. Signa nostra non vídimus, jam non est prophéta: * et nos non cognóscet ámplius.

11. Usquequo, Deus, improperábit inimícus: * irrítat adversárius nomen tuum in finem?

12. Ut quid avértis manum tuam, et déxteram tuam, * de médio sinu tuo in finem?

13. Deus autem Rex noster ante sǽcula: * operátus est salútem in médio terræ.

14. Tu confirmásti in virtúte tua mare: * contribulásti cápita dracónum in aquis.

15. Tu confregísti cápita dracónis: * dedísti eum escam pópulis Æthíopum.

16. Tu dirupísti fontes, et torréntes * tu siccásti flúvios Ethan.

17. Tuus est dies, et tua est nox: * tu fabricátus es auróram et solem.

18. Tu fecísti omnes términos terræ: * æstátem et ver tu plasmásti ea.

19. Memor esto hujus, inimícus improperávit Dómino: * et pópulus insípiens incitávit nomen tuum.

20. Ne tradas béstiis ánimas confiténtes tibi, * et ánimas páuperum tuórum ne obliviscáris in finem.

8. They have set fire to Thy sanctuary: * they have defiled the dwelling place of Thy name on the earth.

9. They said in their heart, the whole kindred of them together: * Let us abolish all the festival days of God from the land.

10. Our signs we have not seen, there is now no prophet: * and He will know us no more.

11. How long, O God, shall the enemy reproach: * is the adversary to provoke Thy name for ever?

12. Why dost Thou turn away Thy hand: and Thy right hand * out of the midst of Thy bosom for ever?

13. But God is our king before ages: * He hath wrought salvation in the midst of the earth.

14. Thou by Thy strength didst make the sea firm: * Thou didst crush the heads of the dragons in the waters.

15. Thou hast broken the heads of the dragon: * Thou hast given him to be meat for the people of the Ethiopians.

16. Thou hast broken up the fountains and the torrents: * Thou hast dried up the Ethan rivers.

17. Thine is the day, and thine is the night: * Thou hast made the morning light and the sun.

18. Thou hast made all the borders of the earth: * the summer and the spring were formed by Thee.

19. Remember this, the enemy hath reproached the Lord: * and a foolish people hath provoked Thy name.

20. Deliver not up to beasts the souls that confess to Thee: * and forget not to the end the souls of Thy poor.

21. Réspice in testaméntum tuum: * quia repléti sunt, qui obscuráti sunt terræ dómibus iniquitátum.

21. Have regard to Thy covenant: * for they that are the obscure of the earth have been filled with dwellings of iniquity.

22. Ne avertátur húmilis factus confúsus: * pauper et inops laudábunt nomen tuum.

22. Let not the humble be turned away with confusion: * the poor and needy shall praise Thy name.

23. Exsúrge, Deus, júdica causam tuam: * memor esto improperiórum tuórum, eórum quæ ab insipiénte sunt tota die.

23. Arise, O God, judge Thy own cause: * remember Thy reproaches with which the foolish man hath reproached Thee all the day.

24. Ne obliviscáris voces inimicórum tuórum: * supérbia eórum, qui te odérunt, ascéndit semper.

24. Forget not the voices of Thy enemies: * the pride of them that hate Thee ascendeth continually.

3. Ant.
1.g

E X-SÚRGE, Dómi-ne, et jú-di-ca causam me- am.

The sixth candle is extinguished.

℣. De-us me- us, é-ri-pe me de manu pecca-tó-ris.

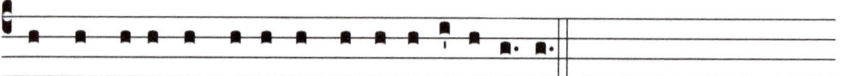

℟. Et de mánu contra lé-gem a-géntis et in-íqui.

Or:

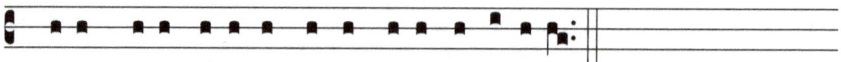

℣. De-us me- us, é-ri-pe me de manu pecca-tó-ris.

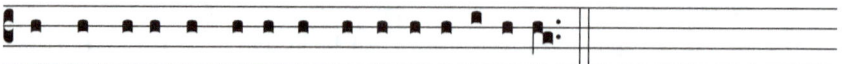

℟. Et de mánu contra lé-gem a-géntis et in-íqui.

℣. Let them be turned backward and put to confusion.

℟. That desire my hurt.

The Pater noster *is said silently.*

LESSON 4   ST. AUGUSTINE, BISHOP ON PSALM 54: 1

 x tractá-tu sancti Augustí-ni E-písco-pi super Psalmos.

Exáudi, De- us, o-ra-ti- ónem me- am, et ne despé-xe-ris depre-ca-ti-

ónem me- am : inténde mi-hi, et exáudi me. Sa-ta-géntis, sol-lí-ci-ti,

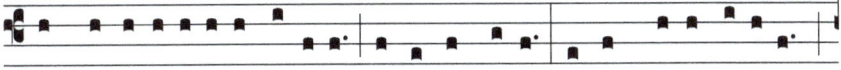

in tri-bu-la-ti- óne pó-si-ti, verba sunt ista.   O-rat multa pá-ti- ens,

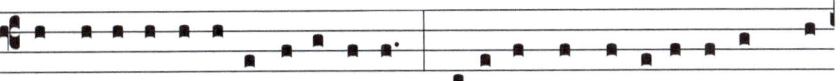

de ma-lo li-be-rá-ri de-sí-de-rans. Súpe-rest ut vi-de- ámus in quo

ma-lo sit : et cum dí-ce-re cóepe-rit, agnoscámus i-bi nos esse : ut com-

mu-ni-cá-ta tri-bu-la-ti- óne, conjungámus o-ra-ti- ónem. Contristá-tus

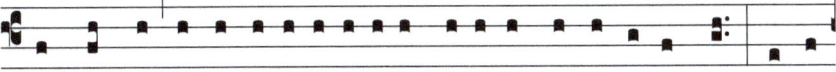

sum, inquit, in ex-erci-ta-ti- óne me- a, et conturbá-tus sum. U-bi

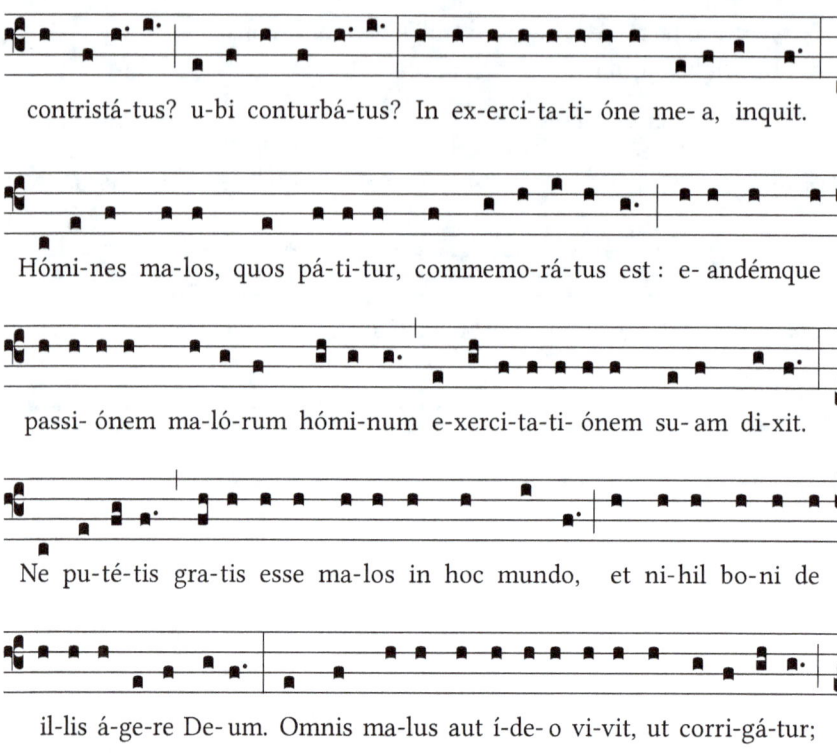

contristá-tus? u-bi conturbá-tus? In ex-erci-ta-ti- óne me- a, inquit.

Hómi-nes ma-los, quos pá-ti-tur, commemo-rá-tus est : e- andémque

passi- ónem ma-ló-rum hómi-num e-xerci-ta-ti- ónem su- am di-xit.

Ne pu-té-tis gra-tis esse ma-los in hoc mundo,   et ni-hil bo-ni de

il-lis á-ge-re De- um. Omnis ma-lus aut í-de-o vi-vit, ut corri-gá-tur;

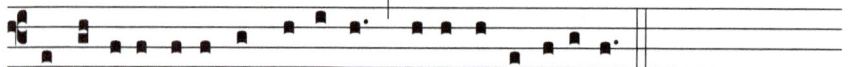

aut í-de- o vi-vit, ut per il-lum bonus ex-erce- á-tur.

From the Treatise of St. Augustine, Bishop, Upon the Psalms.

LESSON 4: Give ear to my prayer, O God, and despise not my supplication: attend unto me and hear me. These are the words of a man travailing, anxious, and troubled. He prayeth in the midst of much suffering, longing to be rid of his affliction. Our part is to see what that his affliction was, and when he hath told us, to acknowledge that we also suffer therefrom; that so, partaking in his trouble, we may take part also in his exercise, and am troubled. Wherein mourned he? Wherein was he troubled? He saith: In my exercise. In the next words he giveth us to know that his affliction was the oppression of the wicked, because of the voice of the enemy, and because of the oppression of the wicked, and this suffering which came upon him at the hands of wicked men, he hath called his exercise. Think not that wicked men are in this world for nothing, or that God doth no good with them. Every wicked man liveth, either to repent, or to exercise the righteous.

RESPONSORY 4 AMÍCUS MEUS ÓSCULI

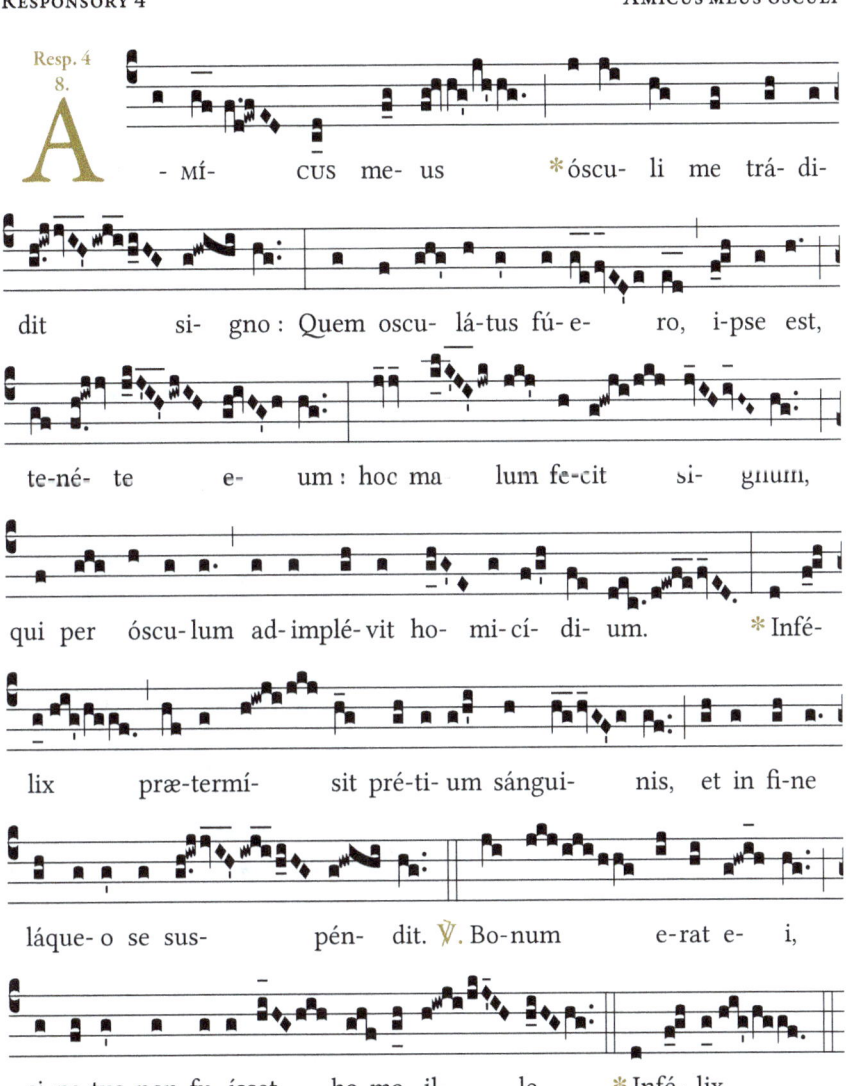

A-MÍ- cus me- us *óscu- li me trá- di-

dit si- gno : Quem oscu- lá-tus fú- e- ro, i-pse est,

te-né- te e- um : hoc ma lum fe-cit si- gnum,

qui per óscu-lum ad-implé- vit ho- mi-cí- di- um. *Infé-

lix præ-termí- sit pré-ti- um sángui- nis, et in fi-ne

láque- o se sus- pén- dit. ℣. Bo-num e-rat e- i,

si na-tus non fu- ísset ho-mo il- le. *Infé- lix.

℟. Mine own friend hath betrayed Me by the sign of a kiss: Whomsoever I shall kiss, That Same is He; hold Him fast. This was the traitorous sign which he gave, even he who murdered with a kiss. * Woe unto that man! He cast down the price of blood, and went, and hanged himself. ℣. It had been good for that man if he had not been born. ℟. Woe unto that man! He cast down the price of blood, and went, and hanged himself.

Lesson 5   St. Augustine, Bishop on Psalm 54: 1

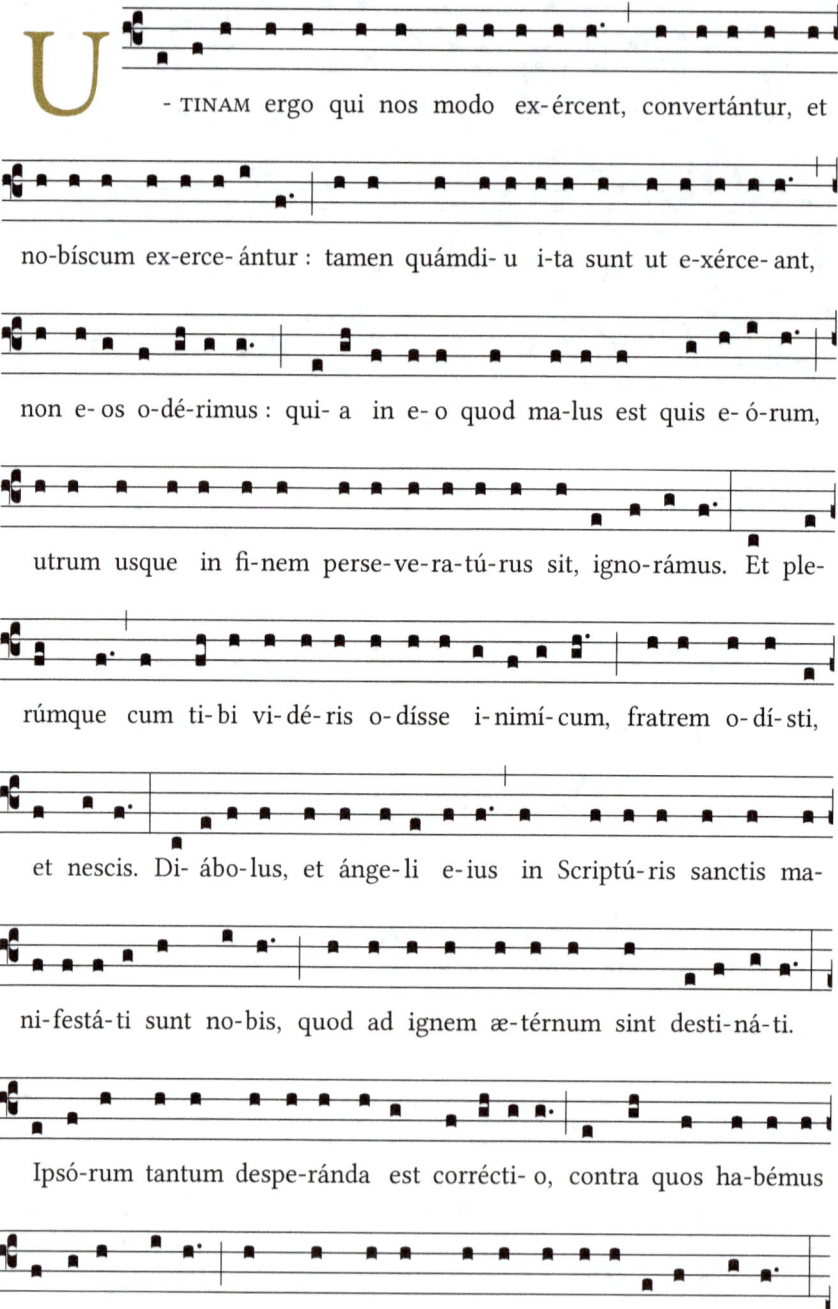

U- tinam ergo qui nos modo ex-ércent, convertántur, et

no-bíscum ex-erce-ántur : tamen quámdi- u i-ta sunt ut e-xérce- ant,

non e- os o-dé-rimus : qui- a in e- o quod ma-lus est quis e- ó-rum,

utrum usque in fi-nem perse-ve-ra-tú-rus sit, igno-rámus. Et ple-

rúmque cum ti- bi vi-dé- ris o-dísse i-nimí- cum, fratrem o- dí- sti,

et nescis. Di- ábo-lus, et ánge-li e-ius in Scriptú-ris sanctis ma-

ni-festá-ti sunt no-bis, quod ad ignem æ-térnum sint desti-ná-ti.

Ipsó-rum tantum despe-ránda est corrécti- o, contra quos ha-bémus

occúltam luctam : ad quam luctam nos armat Apósto-lus, di-cens :

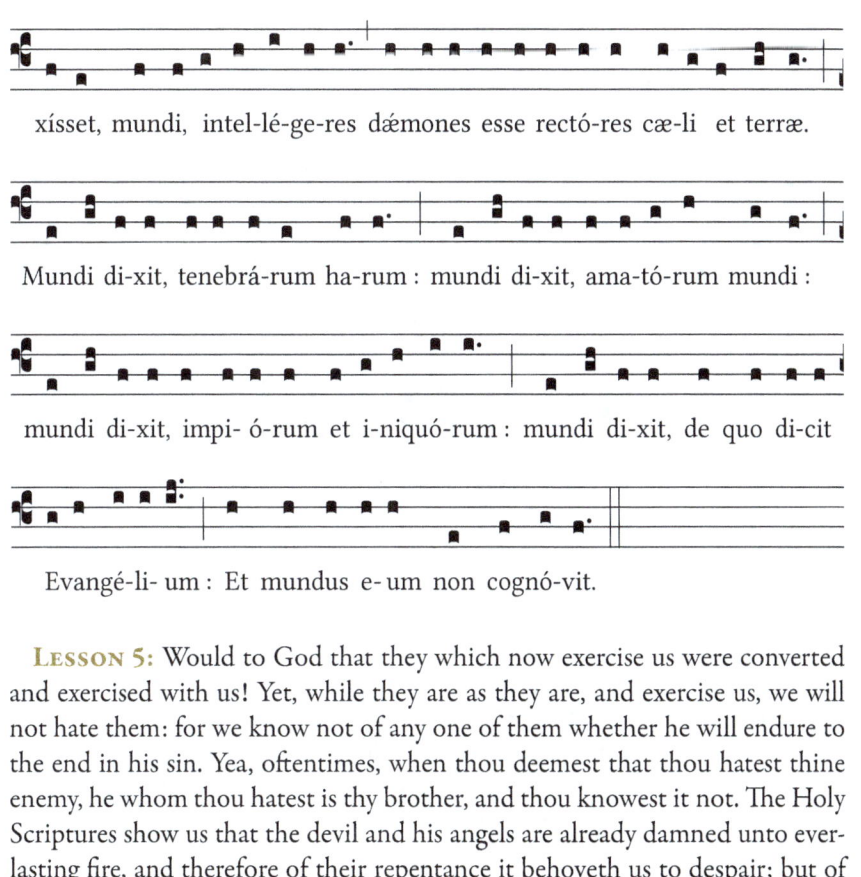

Non est no-bis colluctá-ti- o advérsus carnem et sángui-nem : id est,

non advérsus hómi-nes, quos vi-dé-tis, sed advérsus prínci-pes, et po-

testá-tes, et rectó-res mundi, tenebrá-rum ha-rum. Ne forte cum di-

xísset, mundi, intel-lé-ge-res dæmones esse rectó-res cæ-li et terræ.

Mundi di-xit, tenebrá-rum ha-rum : mundi di-xit, ama-tó-rum mundi :

mundi di-xit, impi- ó-rum et i-niquó-rum : mundi di-xit, de quo di-cit

Evangé-li- um : Et mundus e- um non cognó-vit.

Lesson 5: Would to God that they which now exercise us were converted and exercised with us! Yet, while they are as they are, and exercise us, we will not hate them: for we know not of any one of them whether he will endure to the end in his sin. Yea, oftentimes, when thou deemest that thou hatest thine enemy, he whom thou hatest is thy brother, and thou knowest it not. The Holy Scriptures show us that the devil and his angels are already damned unto everlasting fire, and therefore of their repentance it behoveth us to despair; but of theirs only.

These are they against whom we wrestle within; to the which wrestling the Apostle stirreth us up where he saith: We wrestle not against flesh and blood,

(that is, not against men whom we see,) but against principalities, against powers, against the rulers of the darkness of this world. He saith not the rulers of this world, lest perchance thou shouldest deem that devils are the lords of heaven and earth; what he doth say is, rulers of the darkness of this world, of that world which they love who love the world, of that world wherein the ungodly and unrighteous do prosper, of that world, in fine, of which the Gospel saith: And the world knew Him not.

Responsory 5   Judas mercátor péssimus

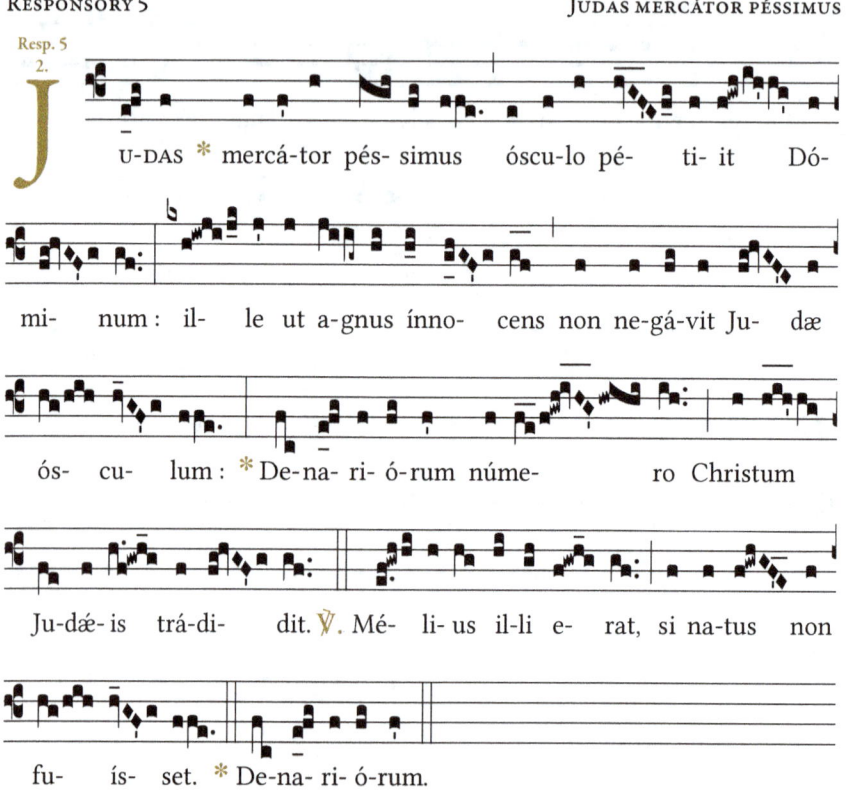

Ju-das * mercá-tor pés-simus óscu-lo pé-ti-it Dóminum : il-le ut a-gnus ínno-cens non ne-gá-vit Ju-dæ ós-cu-lum : * De-na-ri-ó-rum núme-ro Christum Ju-dǽ-is trá-di-dit. ℣. Mé-li-us il-li e-rat, si na-tus non fu-ís-set. * De-na-ri-ó-rum.

℟. The vile trader Judas came to the Lord to kiss Him, and He, as a guileless Lamb, refused not a kiss to Judas, * Who, for a certain number of pence, betrayed Christ to the Jews. ℣. It had been good for that man if he had not been born. ℟. Who, for a certain number of pence, betrayed Christ to the Jews.

LESSON 6   ST. AUGUSTINE, BISHOP ON PSALM 54: 1

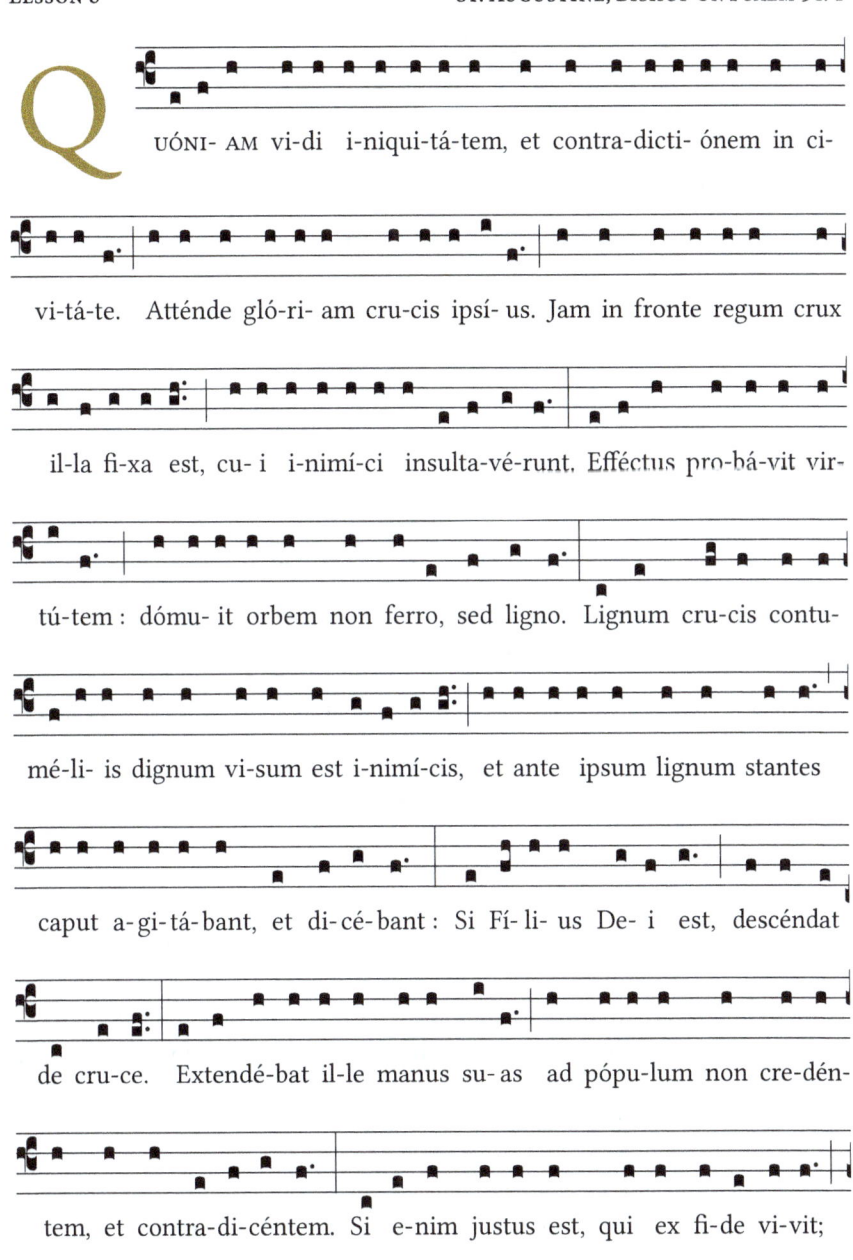

QUÓNI- AM vi-di i-niqui-tá-tem, et contra-dicti- ónem in ci-

vi-tá-te. Atténde gló-ri- am cru-cis ipsí- us. Jam in fronte regum crux

il-la fi-xa est, cu- i i-nimí-ci insulta-vé-runt. Efféctus pro-bá-vit vir-

tú-tem : dómu- it orbem non ferro, sed ligno. Lignum cru-cis contu-

mé-li- is dignum vi-sum est i-nimí-cis, et ante ipsum lignum stantes

caput a-gi-tá-bant, et di-cé-bant : Si Fí- li- us De- i est, descéndat

de cru-ce. Extendé-bat il-le manus su- as ad pópu-lum non cre-dén-

tem, et contra-di-céntem. Si e-nim justus est, qui ex fi-de vi-vit;

i-níquus est, qui non ha-bet fi-dem. Quod ergo hic a- it, i-niqui-tá-

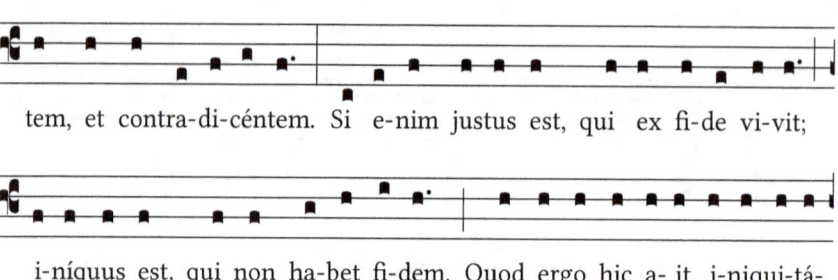

tem, et contra-di-céntem. Si e-nim justus est, qui ex fi-de vi-vit;

i-níquus est, qui non ha-bet fi-dem. Quod ergo hic a- it, i-niqui-tá-

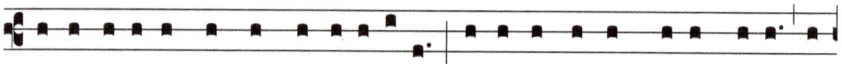

tem : perfí-di- am intél-le-ge. Vi-dé-bat ergo Dómi-nus in ci-vi-tá-te

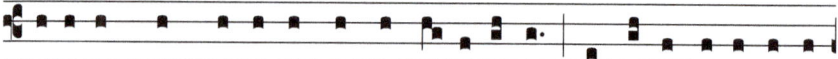

i-niqui-tá-tem et contra-dicti- ónem, et extendé-bat manus su- as ad

pópu-lum non cre-déntem et contra-di-céntem : et tamen et ipsos ex-

spéctans di-cé-bat : Pa-ter, ignósce il-lis, qui- a nésci- unt quid fá-ci- unt.

LESSON 6: We have seen iniquity and strife in the city. Behold, the glory of the Cross. That Cross which was the object of the insults of God's enemies, is established now above the brows of kings. The end hath shown the measure of its power: it hath conquered the world, not by the sword, but by its wood. The enemies of God thought the Cross a meet object of insult and ridicule, yea, they stood before it, wagging their heads and saying: If He be the Son of God, let Him come down from the Cross! And He stretched forth His Hands unto a disobedient and gainsaying people.

If he is just which liveth by faith, he is unjust that hath not faith. Therefore where is written iniquity we may understand unbelief. The Lord therefore saith that He saw iniquity and strife in the city, and that He stretched forth His Hands unto that disobedient and gainsaying people, and, disobedient and gainsaying as they were, He was hungry for their salvation, and said: Father, forgive them, for they know not what they do.

RESPONSORY 6   UNUS EX DISCÍPULIS MEIS

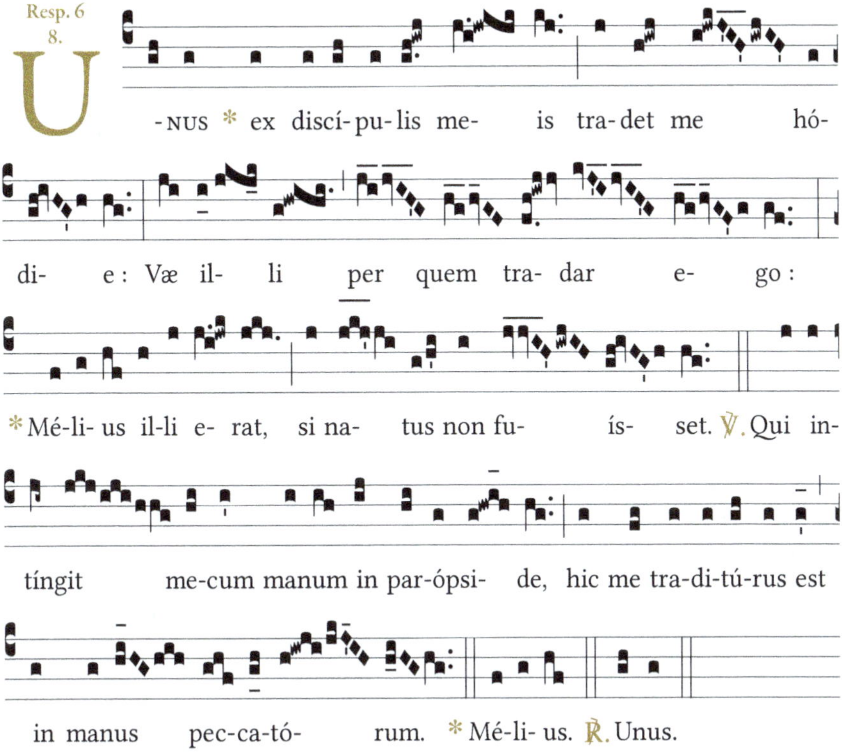

Resp. 6
8.

U -NUS * ex discí-pu-lis me- is tra-det me hó-

di- e : Væ il- li per quem tra- dar e- go :

* Mé-li- us il-li e- rat, si na- tus non fu- ís- set. ℣. Qui in-

tíngit me-cum manum in par-ópsi- de, hic me tra-di-tú-rus est

in manus pec-ca-tó- rum. * Mé-li- us. ℟. Unus.

℟. One of My disciples shall betray Me this night. Woe unto that man by whom I am betrayed! * It had been good for that man if he had not been born. ℣. He that dippeth his hand with Me in the dish, the same shall betray Me into the hands of sinners. ℟. It had been good for that man if he had not been born. ℟. One of My disciples shall betray Me this night. Woe unto that man by whom I am betrayed. * It had been good for that man if he had not been born.

3RD NOCTURN

1. Ant.
7.c

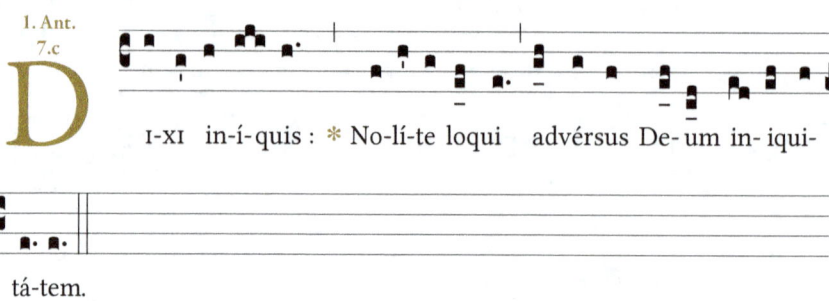

D I-XI in-í-quis : * No-lí-te loqui advérsus De-um in- iqui-

tá-tem.

ANTIPHON: I said unto the wicked: * Speak not wickedness against God.

PSALM 74

1. Confi-té-bimur **ti-** bi, **De-** us : * confi-té-bimur, et invo-cá-bimus

no- men **tu-** um. *Flex :* ex hoc in hoc : †

1. We will praise Thee, O God: * we will praise, and we will call upon Thy name.

2. Narrábimus mirabília **tu**a: * cum accépero tempus, ego justítias **ju**dicábo.

2. We will relate Thy wondrous works: * when I shall take a time, I will judge justices.

3. Liquefácta est terra, et omnes qui hábi**tant** in **ea**: * ego confirmávi co**lúm**nas ejus.

3. The earth is melted, and all that dwell therein: * I have established the pillars thereof.

4. Dixi iníquis: Nolíte iníque ágere: * et delinquéntibus: Nolíte ex- al**tá**re **cor**nu:

4. I said to the wicked: Do not act wickedly: * and to the sinners: Lift not up the horn.

5. Nolíte extóllere in altum **cor**nu **ves**trum: * nolíte loqui advérsus Deum in**i**qui**tá**tem.

5. Lift not up your horn on high: * speak not iniquity against God.

6. Quia neque ab Oriénte, neque ab Occidénte, neque a de**sér**tis **món**tibus: * quóniam **De**us **ju**dex est.

6. For neither from the east, nor from the west, nor from the desert hills: * for God is the judge.

7. Hunc humíliat, et **hunc** exáltat: * quia calix in manu Dómini vini meri **ple**nus **mi**sto.

7. One He putteth down, and another He lifteth up: * for in the hand of the Lord there is a cup of strong wine full of mixture.

8. Et inclinávit ex hoc in hoc: † verúmtamen fæx ejus non est exinaníta: * bibent omnes peccatóres **ter**ræ.

8. And He hath poured it out from this to that: † but the dregs thereof are not emptied: * all the sinners of the earth shall drink.

9. Ego autem annuntiábo in **sǽ**culum: * cantábo **Deo Jacob.**

9. But I will declare for ever: * I will sing to the God of Jacob.

10. Et ómnia córnua peccatórum confríngam: * et exaltabúntur **cór**nua **ju**sti.

10. And I will break all the horns of sinners: * but the horns of the just shall be exalted.

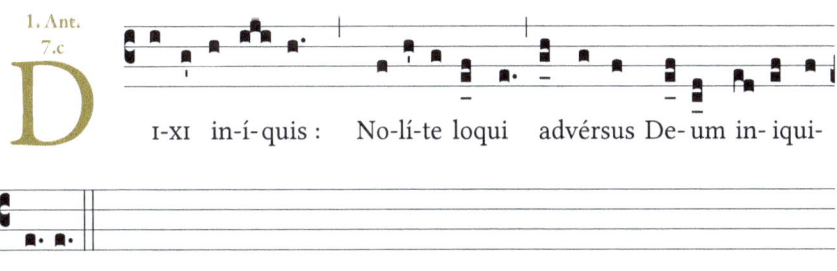

1. Ant.
7.c

DI-XI in-í-quis : No-lí-te loqui advérsus De-um in-iqui-

tá-tem.

The seventh candle is extinguished.

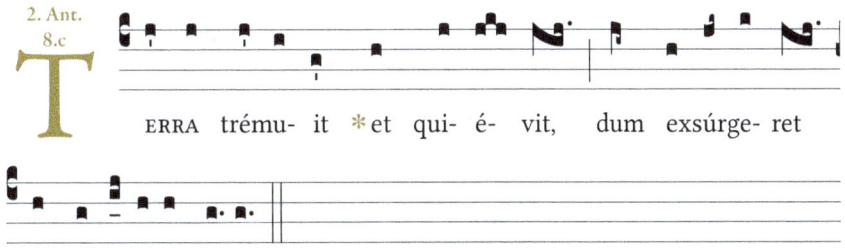

2. Ant.
8.c

TERRA trému-it *et qui-é-vit, dum exsúrge-ret

in ju-dí-ci-o De-us.

ANTIPHON: The earth trembled * and was still, when God arose to judgment.

Psalm 75

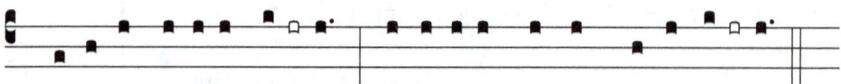

1. No-tus in Judǽ-a **De-** us : * in Isra-ël magnum *nomen* **e-** jus.

1. In Judea God is known: * His name is great in Israel.

2. Et factus est in pace locus **e**jus: * et habitátio e*jus in* **Si**on.

2. And His place is in peace: * and His abode in Sion:

3. Ibi confrégit poténtias **ár**cuum: * scutum, gládi*um, et* **bel**lum.

3. There hath He broken the powers of bows, * the shield, the sword, and the battle.

4. Illúminans tu mirabíliter a móntibus æ**tér**nis: * turbáti sunt omnes insipi*éntes* **cor**de.

4. Thou enlightenest wonderfully from the everlasting hills. * All the foolish of heart were troubled.

5. Dormiérunt somnum **su**um: * et nihil invenérunt omnes viri divi- tiárum in má*nibus* **su**is.

5. They have slept their sleep; * and all the men of riches have found noth- ing in their hands.

6. Ab increpatióne tua, Deus Jacob, * dormitavérunt qui as- cen*dérunt* equos.

6. At Thy rebuke, O God of Jacob, * they have all slumbered that mounted on horseback.

7. Tu terríbilis es, et quis resístet **ti**bi? * ex tunc *ira* **tu**a.

7. Thou art terrible, and who shall resist Thee? * from that time Thy wrath.

8. De cælo audítum fecísti ju**dí**- cium: * terra trémuit *et qui*évit.

8. Thou hast caused judgment to be heard from heaven: * the earth trem- bled and was still,

9. Cum exsúrgeret in judícium **Deus**, * ut salvos fáceret omnes man- su*étos* **ter**ræ.

9. When God arose in judgment, * to save all the meek of the earth.

10. Quóniam cogitátio hóminis confitébitur **ti**bi: * et relíquiæ cogi- tatiónis diem festum *agent* **ti**bi.

10. For the thought of man shall give praise to Thee: * and the remain- ders of the thought shall keep holiday to Thee.

11. Vovéte, et réddite Dómino Deo **ves**tro: * omnes, qui in circúitu ejus af*fértis* **mú**nera.

11. Vow ye, and pay to the Lord your God: * all you that are round about Him bring presents.

12. Terríbili et ei qui aufert spíritum **prín**cipum, * terríbili apud *reges* **ter**ræ.

12. To Him that is terrible, even to Him who taketh away the spirit of princes: * to the terrible with the kings of the earth.

2. Ant.
8.c

TERRA trému- it et qui- é- vit, dum exsúrge- ret

in ju-dí-ci- o De- us.

The eighth candle is extinguished.

3 Ant.
7.a

IN di- e * tri-bu-la- ti- ó-nis me- æ De- um exqui- sí- vi

má-ni-bus me- is.

ANTIPHON: In the day of my trouble * I sought God with my hands.

PSALM 76

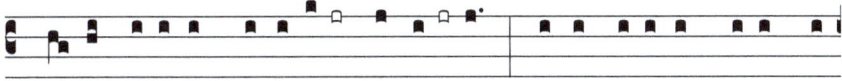

1. Vo-ce me- a ad Dóminum clamá- vi : * vo-ce me- a ad De- um, et

intén-dit mi- hi.   *Flex :* exqui-sí-vi, †

1. I cried to the Lord with my voice; * to God with my voice, and He gave ear to me.

2. In die tribulatiónis meæ Deum exquisívi, † mánibus meis nocte **con**tra eum: * et non **sum** decéptus.

2. In the day of my trouble I sought God, † with my hands lifted up to Him in the night, * and I was not deceived.

3. Rénuit consolári ánima mea: memor fui Dei, et delectátus sum, et exercitátus sum: * et defécit spíritus meus.

4. Anticipavérunt vigílias óculi mei: * turbátus sum, et non sum locútus.

5. Cogitávi dies antíquos: * et annos ætérnos in mente hábui.

6. Et meditátus sum nocte cum corde meo, * et exercitábar, et scopébam spíritum meum.

7. Numquid in ætérnum projíciet Deus: * aut non appónet ut complacítior sit adhuc?

8. Aut in finem misericórdiam suam abscíndet, * a generatióne in generatiónem?

9. Aut obliviscétur miseréri Deus: * aut continébit in ira sua misericórdias suas?

10. Et dixi: Nunc cæpi: * hæc mutátio déxteræ Excélsi.

11. Memor fui óperum Dómini: * quia memor ero ab inítio mirabílium tuórum.

12. Et meditábor in ómnibus opéribus tuis: * et in adinventiónibus tuis exercébor.

13. Deus, in sancto via tua: † quis Deus magnus sicut Deus noster? * tu es Deus qui facis mirabília.

14. Notam fecísti in pópulis virtútem tuam: * redemísti in bráchio tuo pópulum tuum fílios Jacob et Joseph.

15. Vidérunt te aquæ, Deus, vidérunt te aquæ: * et timuérunt et turbátæ sunt abýssi.

3. My soul refused to be comforted: * I remembered God, and was delighted, and was exercised, and my spirit swooned away.

4. My eyes prevented the watches: * I was troubled, and I spoke not.

5. I thought upon the days of old: * and I had in my mind the eternal years.

6. And I meditated in the night with my own heart: * and I was exercised and I swept my spirit.

7. Will God then cast off for ever? * or will He never be more favourable again?

8. Or will He cut off His mercy for ever, * from generation to generation?

9. Or will God forget to shew mercy? * or will He in His anger shut up His mercies?

10. And I said, Now have I begun: * this is the change of the right hand of the most High.

11. I remembered the works of the Lord: * for I will be mindful of Thy wonders from the beginning.

12. And I will meditate on all Thy works: * and will be employed in Thy inventions.

13. Thy way, O God, is in the holy place: † who is the great God like our God? * Thou art the God that dost wonders.

14. Thou hast made Thy power known among the nations: * with Thy arm Thou hast redeemed Thy people the children of Jacob and of Joseph.

15. The waters saw Thee, O God, the waters saw Thee: * and they were afraid, and the depths were troubled.

16. Multitúdo sónitus aquárum: * vocem dedérunt nubes.

16. Great was the noise of the waters: * the clouds sent out a sound.

17. Etenim sagíttæ tuæ tránseunt: * vox tonítrui tui in rota.

17. For Thy arrows pass: * the voice of Thy thunder in a wheel.

18. Illuxérunt coruscatiónes tuæ orbi terræ: * commóta est, et contrémuit terra.

18. Thy lightnings enlightened the world: * the earth shook and trembled.

19. In mari via tua, et sémitæ tuæ in aquis multis: * et vestígia tua non cognoscéntur.

19. Thy way is in the sea, and Thy paths in many waters: * and Thy footsteps shall not be known.

20. Deduxísti sicut oves pópulum tuum, * in manu Móysi et Aaron.

20. Thou hast conducted Thy people like sheep, * by the hand of Moses and Aaron.

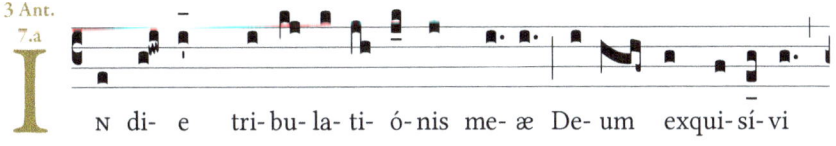

The ninth candle is extinguished.

℣. Exsúrge, Dómi-ne. ℟. Et jú-di-ca causam me- am.

Or:

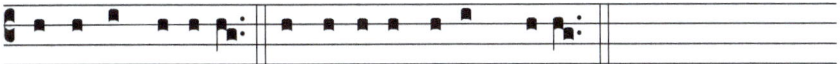

℣. Exsúrge, Dómi-ne. ℟. Et jú-di-ca causam me- am.

℣. Arise, O Lord.
℟. Judge Thou my cause.

The Pater noster *is said silently.*

D E E-písto-la prima be- á-ti Pau-li Apósto-li ad Co-rínthi-

os. Hoc autem præ-cí-pi- o : non laudans quod non in mé-li- us, sed in

de-té-ri- us conve-ní- tis. Primum qui-dem conve-ni- énti-bus vo-bis in

Ecclé-si- am, áudi- o scissú-ras esse inter vos, et ex parte cre-do. Nam

opórtet et hǽ-re-ses esse, ut et qui pro-bá-ti sunt, ma-ni-fésti fi- ant in

vo-bis. Conve-ni- énti-bus ergo vo-bis in unum, jam non est Domí-ni-cam

cenam mandu-cá-re. Unusquísque e-nim su- am cenam præsúmit ad

mandu-cándum. Et á-li- us qui-dem é-su-rit, á-li- us autem ébri- us est.

Numquid domos non ha-bé-tis ad mandu-cándum et bi-béndum? aut Ec-

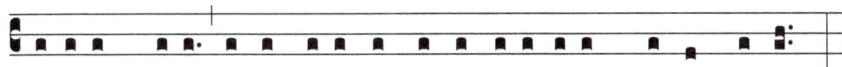

clé-si- am De- i contémni-tis, et confúndi-tis e- os, qui non ha-bent?

Quid di-cam vo-bis? Laudo vos? In hoc non laudo.

From the first letter of the blessed Apostle Paul to Corinthians.

LESSON 7: Now this I ordain: not praising you, that you come together not for the better, but for the worse. For first of all I hear that when you come together in the church, there are schisms among you; and in part I believe it. For there must be also heresies: that they also, who are approved, may be made manifest among you. When you come therefore together into one place, it is not now to eat the Lord's supper. For every one taketh before his own supper to eat. And one indeed is hungry and another is drunk. What, have you not houses to eat and to drink in? Or despise ye the church of God; and put them to shame that have not? What shall I say to you? Do I praise you? In this I praise you not.

RESPONSORY 7   ERAM QUASI AGNUS

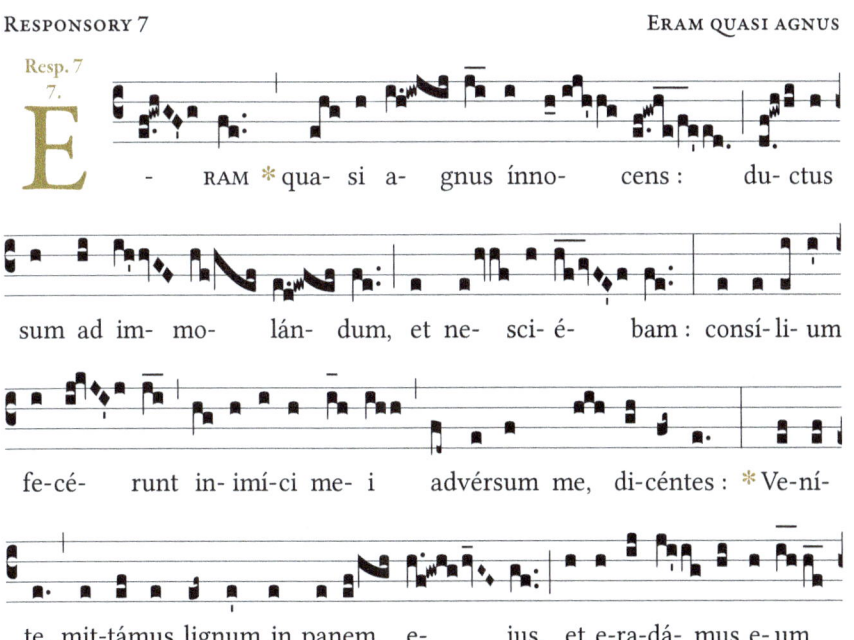

E- RAM *qua- si a- gnus ínno- cens : du- ctus sum ad im- mo- lán- dum, et ne- sci- é- bam : consí-li- um fe-cé- runt in-imí-ci me- i advérsum me, di-céntes : *Ve-ní-te, mit-támus lignum in panem e- jus, et e-ra-dá- mus e- um

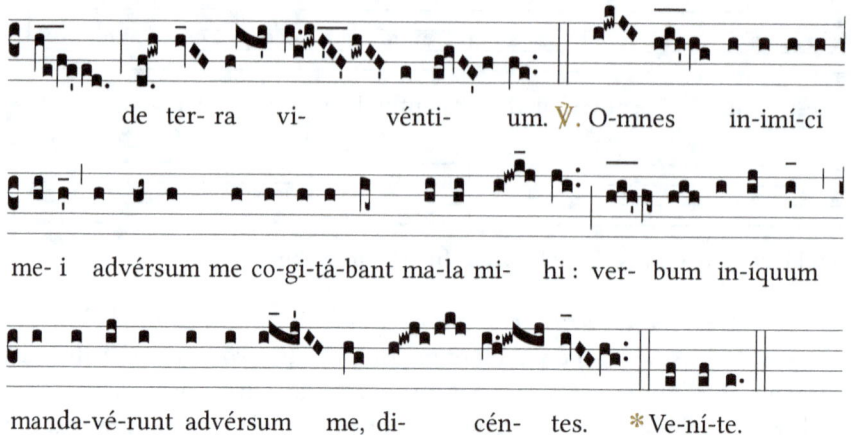

de ter- ra vi- vénti- um. ℣. O-mnes in-imí-ci

me- i advérsum me co-gi-tá-bant ma-la mi- hi : ver- bum in-íquum

manda-vé-runt advérsum me, di- cén- tes. *Ve-ní-te.

℟. I was like a gentle lamb that is brought to the slaughter, and I knew not that Mine enemies had devised devices against Me, saying: * Come, let us put (poison of a deadly) tree into His bread, and let us cut Him off from the land of the living. ℣. All they that hate Me devised my hurt against me: they plotted together to do me evil, saying: ℟. Come, let us put (poison of a deadly) tree into His bread, and let us cut Him off from the land of the living.

LESSON 8   1 CORINTHIANS 11: 23-26

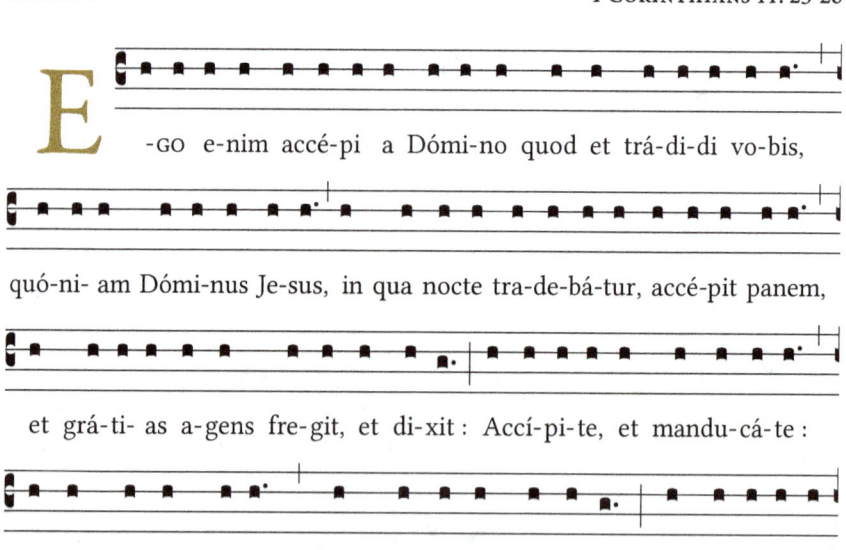

E -GO e-nim accé-pi a Dómi-no quod et trá-di-di vo-bis,

quó-ni- am Dómi-nus Je-sus, in qua nocte trade-bá-tur, accé-pit panem,

et grá-ti- as a-gens fre-git, et di-xit : Accí-pi-te, et mandu-cá-te :

hoc est corpus me- um, quod pro vo-bis tra-dé-tur : hoc fá-ci-te in

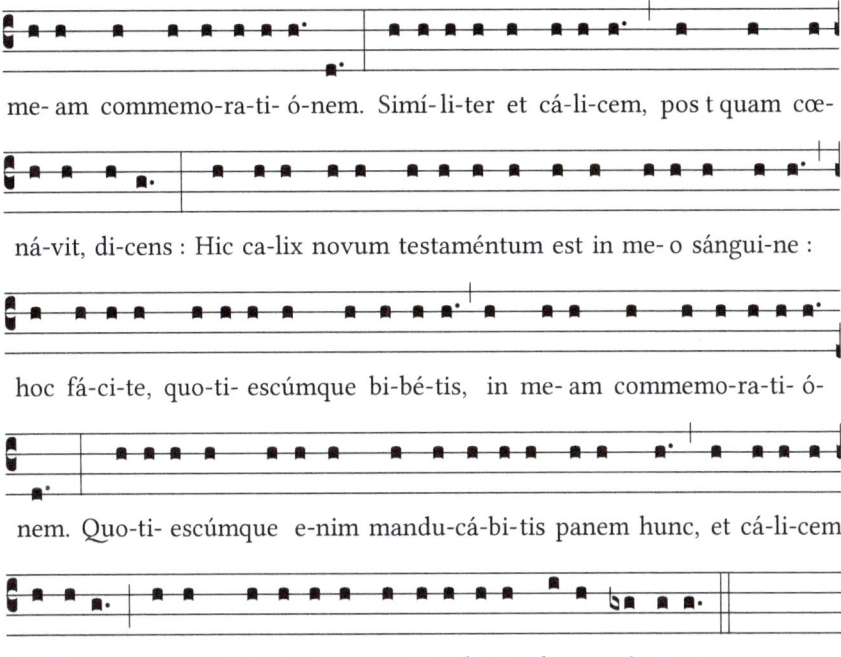

me- am commemo-ra-ti- ó-nem. Simí-li-ter et cá-li-cem, pos t quam cœ-

ná-vit, di-cens : Hic ca-lix novum testaméntum est in me- o sángui-ne :

hoc fá-ci-te, quo-ti- escúmque bi-bé-tis, in me- am commemo-ra-ti- ó-

nem. Quo-ti- escúmque e-nim mandu-cá-bi-tis panem hunc, et cá-li-cem

bi-bé-tis, mortem Dómi-ni annunti- á-bi-tis donec vé-ni- at.

LESSON 8: For I have received of the Lord that which also I delivered unto you, that the Lord Jesus, the same night in which He was betrayed, took bread. And giving thanks, broke, and said: Take ye, and eat: this is My body, which shall be delivered for you: this do for the commemoration of Me. In like manner also the chalice, after He had supped, saying: This chalice is the new testament in My blood: this do ye, as often as you shall drink, for the commemoration of Me. For as often as you shall eat this bread, and drink the chalice, you shall show the death of the Lord, until He come.

RESPONSORY 8   UNA HORA NON POTUÍSTIS

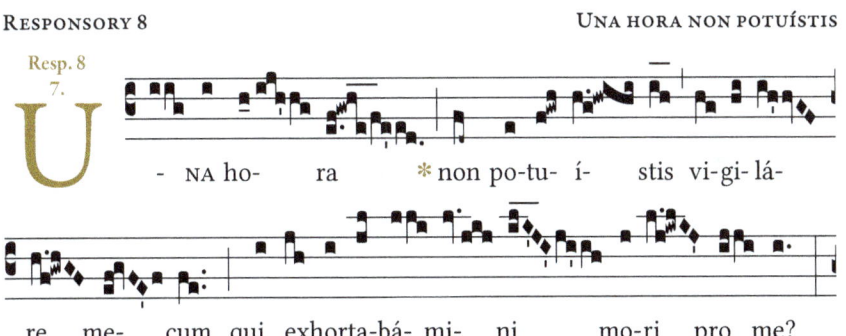

Resp. 8
7.

U - NA ho- ra *non po-tu- í- stis vi-gi-lá-

re me- cum, qui exhorta-bá- mi- ni mo-ri pro me?

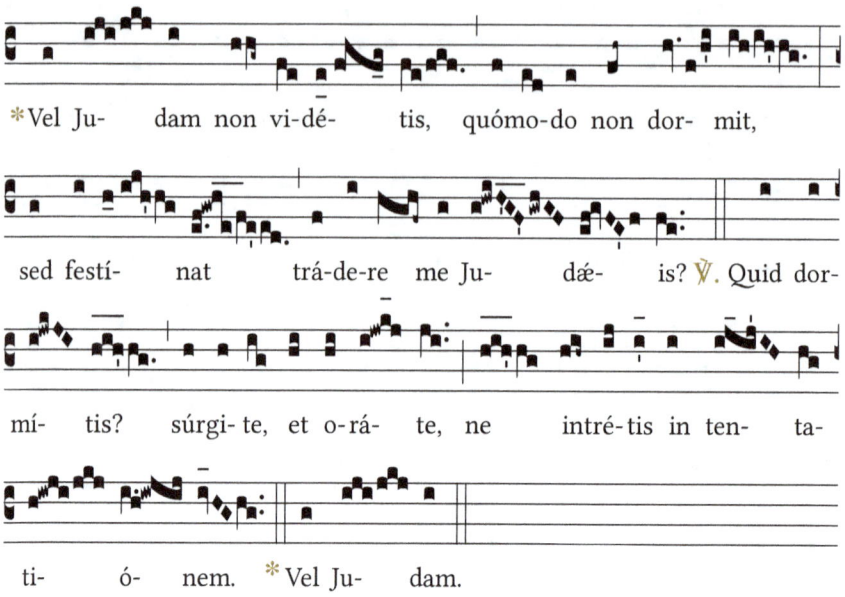

*Vel Ju- dam non vi-dé- tis, quómo-do non dor- mit, sed festí- nat trá-de-re me Ju- dæ- is? ℣. Quid dor- mí- tis? súrgi- te, et o-rá- te, ne intré-tis in ten- ta- ti- ó- nem. *Vel Ju- dam.

℟. Could ye not watch with Me one hour, ye that called one on the other to die for Me? * Or see ye not Judas, how that he sleepeth not, but maketh haste to betray Me to the Jews? ℣. Why sleep ye? Rise, and pray, lest ye enter into temptation. ℟. Or see ye not Judas, how that he sleepeth not, but maketh haste to betray Me to the Jews?

LESSON 9   1 CORINTHIANS 11: 27-34

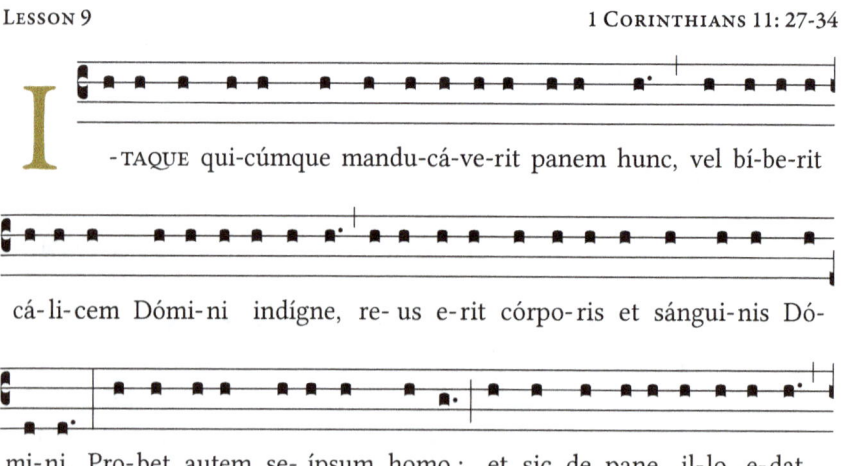

I-TAQUE qui-cúmque mandu-cá-ve-rit panem hunc, vel bí-be-rit cá-li-cem Dómi-ni indígne, re-us e-rit córpo-ris et sángui-nis Dó- mi-ni. Pro-bet autem se- ípsum homo : et sic de pane il-lo e-dat,

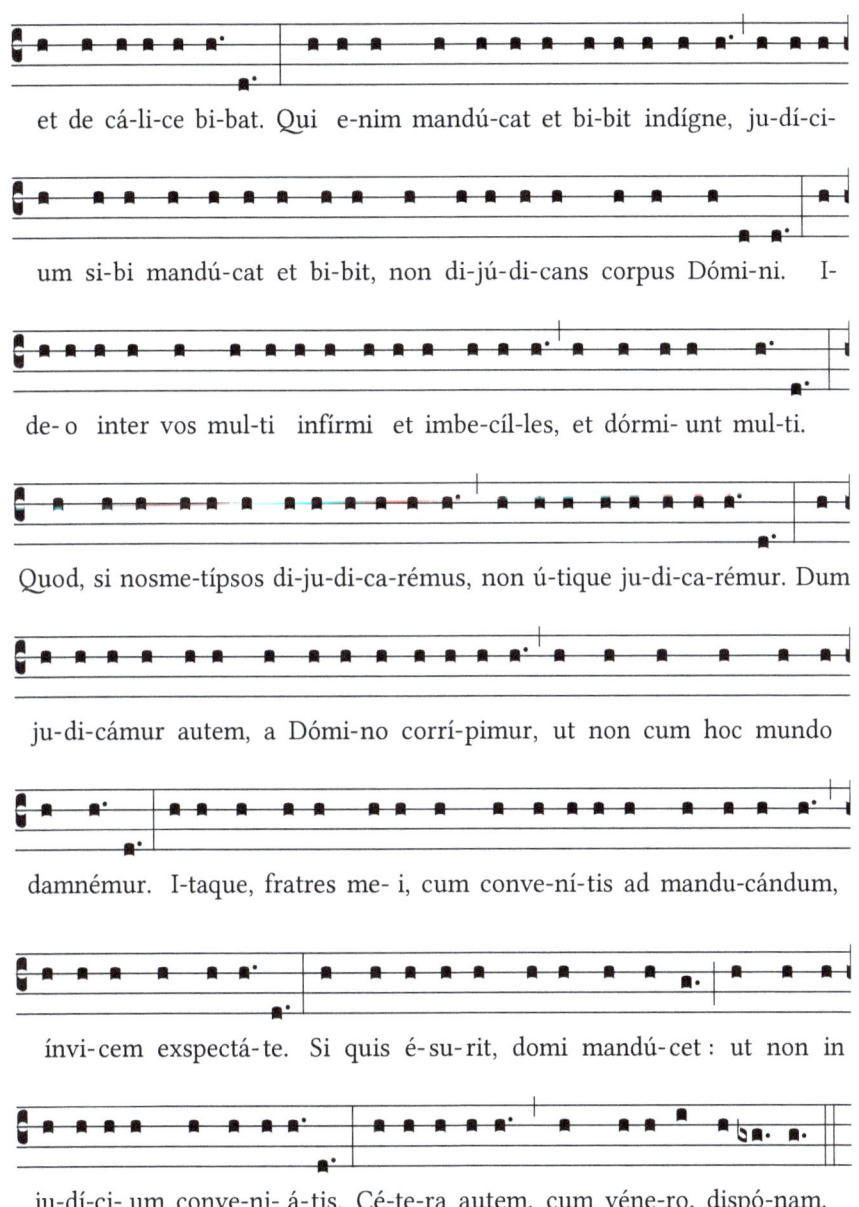

et de cá-li-ce bi-bat. Qui e-nim mandú-cat et bi-bit indígne, ju-dí-ci-

um si-bi mandú-cat et bi-bit, non di-jú-di-cans corpus Dómi-ni.   I-

de- o inter vos mul-ti infírmi et imbe-cíl-les, et dórmi- unt mul-ti.

Quod, si nosme-típsos di-ju-di-ca-rémus, non ú-tique ju-di-ca-rémur. Dum

ju-di-cámur autem, a Dómi-no corrí-pimur, ut non cum hoc mundo

damnémur. I-taque, fratres me- i, cum conve-ní-tis ad mandu-cándum,

ínvi-cem exspectá-te. Si quis é-su-rit, domi mandú-cet : ut non in

ju-dí-ci- um conve-ni- á-tis. Cé-te-ra autem, cum véne-ro, dispó-nam.

LESSON 9: Therefore whosoever shall eat this bread, or drink the chalice of the Lord unworthily, shall be guilty of the body and of the blood of the Lord. But let a man prove himself: and so let him eat of that bread, and drink of the chalice. For he that eateth and drinketh unworthily, eateth and drinketh judgment to himself, not discerning the body of the Lord. Therefore are there many

infirm and weak among you, and many sleep. But if we would judge ourselves, we should not be judged. But whilst we are judged, we are chastised by the Lord, that we be not condemned with this world. Wherefore, my brethren, when you come together to eat, wait for one another. If any man be hungry, let him eat at home; that you come not together unto judgment. And the rest I will set in order, when I come.

RESPONSORY 9   SENIÓRES PÓPULI CONSÍLIUM

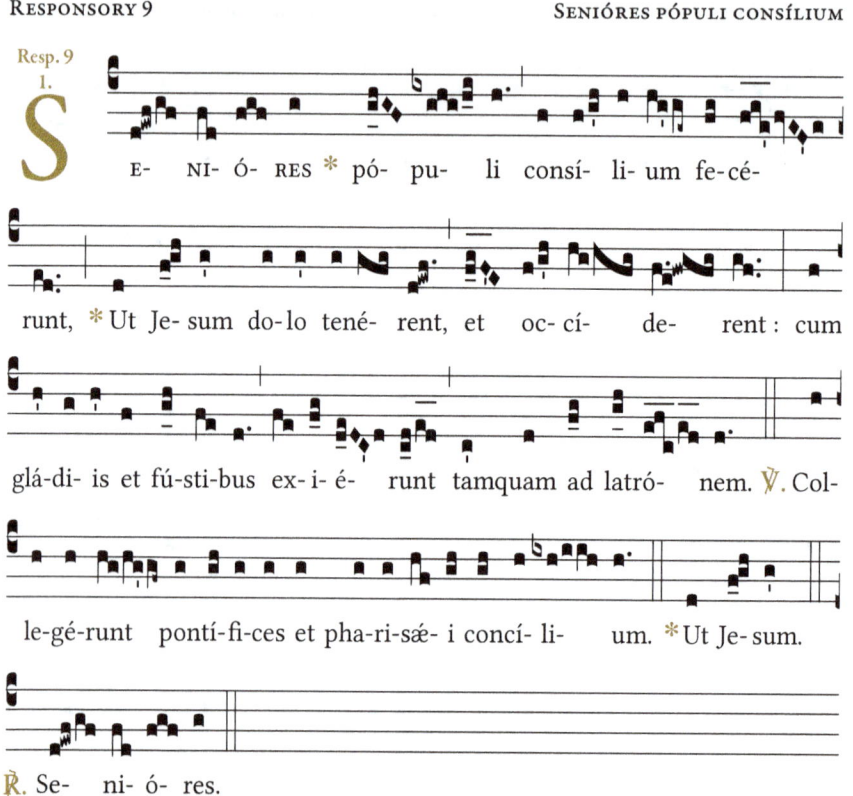

Resp. 9
1.

SE- NI- Ó- RES * pó- pu- li consí- li- um fe- cérunt, * Ut Je- sum do-lo tené- rent, et oc- cí- de- rent : cum
glá-di- is et fú-sti-bus ex-i- é- runt tamquam ad latró- nem. ℣. Col-
le-gé-runt pontí-fi-ces et pha-ri-sǽ- i concí- li- um. * Ut Je-sum.

℟. Se- ni- ó- res.

℟. The elders of the people consulted * That they might take Jesus by subtlety, and kill Him they came out, as against a thief, with swords and staves. ℣. The chief Priests and the Pharisees gathered a council. ℟. That they might take Jesus by subtlety, and kill Him: they came out, as against a thief, with swords and staves. ℟. The elders of the people consulted * That they might take Jesus by subtlety, and kill Him: they came out, as against a thief, with swords and staves.

AT LAUDS

1. Ant.
8.G

Justi- fi- cé- ris, Dómi- ne, * in sermó-ni-bus tu- is, et vincas

cum ju-di-cá-ris.

ANTIPHON: O Lord, Thou shalt be justified * when Thou speakest, and be clear when Thou art judged.

PSALM 50

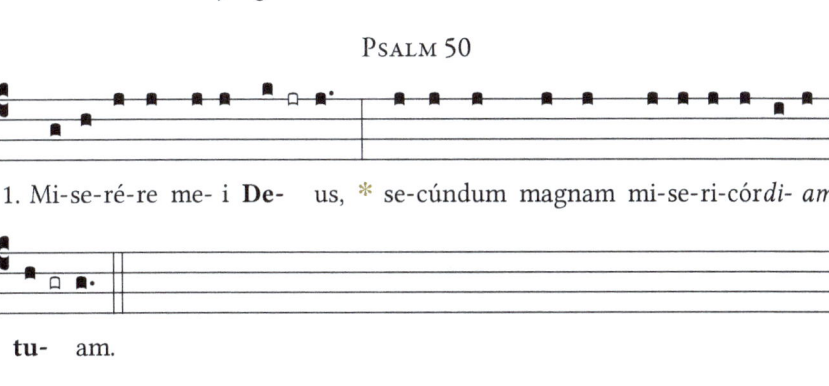

1. Mi-se-ré-re me- i **De-** us, * se-cúndum magnam mi-se-ri-córdi- am

tu- am.

1. Have mercy on me, O God, * according to Thy great mercy.

2. Et secúndum multitúdinem miseratiónum tuárum, * dele iniqui*tátem* **me**am.

2. And according to the multitude of Thy tender mercies * blot out my iniquity.

3. Amplius lava me ab iniquitáte **me**a: * et a peccáto *meo* **mun**da me.

3. Wash me yet more from my iniquity, * and cleanse me from my sin.

4. Quóniam iniquitátem meam ego co**gnó**sco: * et peccátum meum contra *me est* **sem**per.

4. For I know my iniquity, * and my sin is always before me.

5. Tibi soli peccávi, et malum coram te **fe**ci: * ut justificéris in sermónibus tuis, et vincas cum *judi***cá**ris.

5. To Thee only have I sinned, and have done evil before Thee: * that Thou mayst be justified in Thy words, and mayst overcome when Thou art judged.

6. Ecce enim in iniquitátibus con**cé**ptus sum: * et in peccátis concépit me *mater* **me**a.

6. For behold I was conceived in iniquities; * and in sins did my mother conceive me.

7. Ecce enim veritátem dilex*í*sti: * incérta et occúlta sapiéntiæ tuæ mani-fest*ásti* **mi**hi.

7. For behold Thou hast loved truth: * the uncertain and hidden things of Thy wisdom Thou hast made manifest to me.

8. Aspérges me hyssópo, et mun-**dá**bor: * lavábis me, et super nivem *deal***bá**bor.

8. Thou shalt sprinkle me with hys-sop, and I shall be cleansed: * Thou shalt wash me, and I shall be made whiter than snow.

9. Audítui meo dabis gáudium et lætítiam: * et exsultábunt ossa hu-*mili***á**ta.

9. To my hearing Thou shalt give joy and gladness: * and the bones that have been humbled shall rejoice.

10. Avérte fáciem tuam a peccátis **me**is: * et omnes iniquitátes *meas* **de**le.

10. Turn away Thy face from my sins, * and blot out all my iniquities.

11. Cor mundum crea in me, **Deus**: * et spíritum rectum ínnova in visc*éribus* **me**is.

11. Create a clean heart in me, O God: * and renew a right spirit within my bowels.

12. Ne projícias me a fácie **tu**a: * et spíritum sanctum tuum ne áu*feras* **a** me.

12. Cast me not away from Thy face; * and take not Thy holy spirit from me.

13. Redde mihi lætítiam salutáris **tu**i: * et spíritu principá*li* con*fír*ma me.

13. Restore unto me the joy of Thy salvation, * and strengthen me with a perfect spirit.

14. Docébo iníquos vias **tu**as: * et ímpii ad te *conver***tén**tur.

14. I will teach the unjust Thy ways: * and the wicked shall be con-verted to Thee.

15. Líbera me de sanguínibus, Deus, Deus salútis **me**æ: * et exsultábit lin-gua mea just*ítiam* **tu**am.

15. Deliver me from blood, O God, Thou God of my salvation: * and my tongue shall extol Thy justice.

16. Dómine, lábia mea ap*éries*: * et os meum annuntiábit *laudem* **tu**am.

16. O Lord, Thou wilt open my lips: * and my mouth shall declare Thy praise.

17. Quóniam si voluísses sacrifíci-um, dedíssem **úti**que: * holocáustis non *dele***ctá**beris.

17. For if Thou hadst desired sacri-fice, I would indeed have given it: * with burnt offerings Thou wilt not be delighted.

18. Sacrifícium Deo spíritus contribu**lá**tus: * cor contrítum et humiliátum, Deus, *non de***spí**cies.

18. A sacrifice to God is an afflicted spirit: * a contrite and humbled heart, O God, Thou wilt not despise.

19. Benígne fac, Dómine, in bona voluntáte tua **Si**on: * ut ædificéntur m*uri Je***rú**salem.

19. Deal favourably, O Lord, in Thy good will with Sion; * that the walls of Jerusalem may be built up.

20. Tunc acceptábis sacrifícium justítiæ, oblatiónes, et holo**cáu**sta: * tunc impónent super altáre *tuum* **ví**tulos.

20. Then shalt Thou accept the sacrifice of justice, oblations and whole burnt offerings: * then shall they lay calves upon Thy altar.

1. Ant. 8.G

Justi-fi-cé-ris, Dómine, in sermó-ni-bus tu-is, et vincas cum ju-di-cá-ris.

The tenth candle is extinguished.

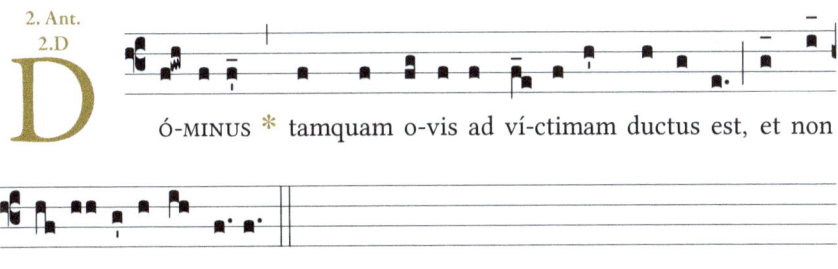

2. Ant. 2.D

Dó-minus * tamquam o-vis ad ví-ctimam ductus est, et non a-pé-ru-it os su-um.

Antiphon: The Lord was brought as a lamb * to the slaughter, and He opened not His mouth.

Psalm 89

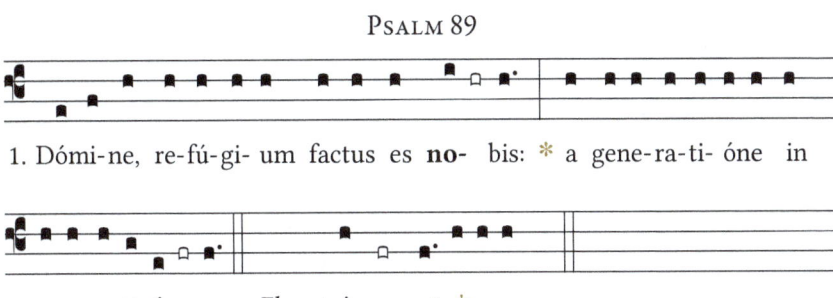

1. Dómi-ne, re-fú-gi-um factus es **no-** bis: * a gene-ra-ti-óne in gene-ra-ti-ó-nem. *Flex:* tránse-at, †

1. Lord, Thou hast been our refuge * from generation to generation.

2. Priúsquam montes fíerent, aut formarétur terra et **orb**is: * a sǽculo et usque in sǽculum tu *es*, **Deus.**

3. Ne avértas hóminem in humilitátem: * et dixísti: Convertímini, fíli*i* **hó**minum.

4. Quóniam mille anni ante óculos **tu**os, * tamquam dies hestérna, quæ *præ*tériit.

5. Et custódia in **no**cte, * quæ pro níhilo habéntur, eórum an*ni* erunt.

6. Mane sicut herba tránseat, † mane flóreat, et **tráns**eat: * véspere décidat, indúret et *a*réscat.

7. Quia defécimus in ira **tu**a, * et in furóre tuo turbá*ti* **su**mus.

8. Posuísti iniquitátes nostras in conspéctu **tu**o: * sǽculum nostrum in illuminatióne vul*tus* **tui.**

9. Quóniam omnes dies nostri defecérunt: * et in ira tua *de*fécimus.

10. Anni nostri sicut aránea meditab**ún**tur: * dies annórum nostrórum in ipsis, septuagín*ta* **an**ni.

11. Si autem in potentátibus, octogínta **an**ni: * et ámplius eórum, labor *et* **do**lor.

12. Quóniam supervénit mansuetúdo: * et corri*pi*émur.

13. Quis novit potestátem iræ **tu**æ: * et præ timóre tuo iram tuam dinu*me*ráre?

14. Déxteram tuam sic **no**tam fac: * et erudítos corde in sa*pi*éntia.

2. Before the mountains were made, or the earth and the world was formed; * from eternity and to eternity Thou art God.

3. Turn not man away to be brought low: * and Thou hast said: Be converted, O ye sons of men.

4. For a thousand years in thy sight * are as yesterday, which is past.

5. And as a watch in the night, * things that are counted nothing, shall their years be.

6. In the morning man shall grow up like grass; † in the morning he shall flourish and pass away: * in the evening he shall fall, grow dry, and wither.

7. For in thy wrath we have fainted away: * and are troubled in thy indignation.

8. Thou hast set our iniquities before thy eyes: * our life in the light of thy countenance.

9. For all our days are spent; * and in thy wrath we have fainted away.

10. Our years shall be considered as a spider: * the days of our years in them are threescore and ten years.

11. But if in the strong they be fourscore years: * and what is more of them is labour and sorrow.

12. For mildness is come upon us: * and we shall be corrected.

13. Who knoweth the power of thy anger, * and for thy fear can number thy wrath?

14. So make thy right hand known: * and men learned in heart, in wisdom.

15. Convértere, Dómine, úsquequo? * et deprecábilis esto super servos tuos.

16. Repléti sumus mane misericórdia tua: * et exsultávimus, et delectáti sumus ómnibus diébus nostris.

17. Lætáti sumus pro diébus, quibus nos humiliásti: * annis, quibus vídimus mala.

18. Réspice in servos tuos, et in ópera tua: * et dírige fílios eórum.

19. Et sit splendor Dómini Dei nostri super nos, † et ópera mánuum nostrárum dírige super nos: * et opus mánuum nostrárum dírige.

15. Return, O Lord, how long? * and be entreated in favour of thy servants.

16. We are filled in the morning with thy mercy: * and we have rejoiced, and are delighted all our days.

17. We have rejoiced for the days in which Thou hast humbled us: * for the years in which we have seen evils.

18. Look upon thy servants and upon their works: * and direct their children.

19. And let the brightness of the Lord our God be upon us: † and direct Thou the works of our hands over us; * yea, the work of our hands do Thou direct.

2. Ant.
2.D

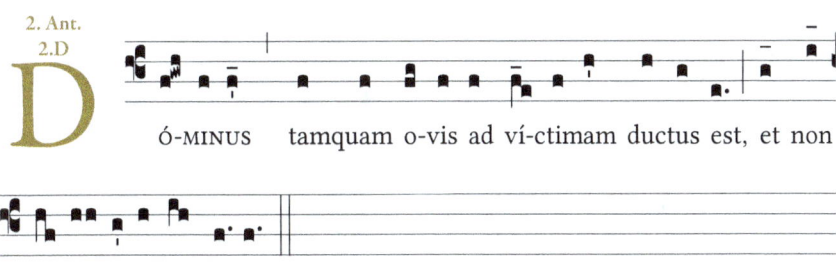

Dó-minus tamquam o-vis ad ví-ctimam ductus est, et non a-pé-ru-it os su-um.

The eleventh candle is extinguished.

3. Ant.
8.G

Contrí-tum est * cor me-um in mé-di-o me-i, contre-mu-é-runt ómni-a ossa me-a.

ANTIPHON: Mine heart is broken within me * all My bones tremble.

Psalm 35

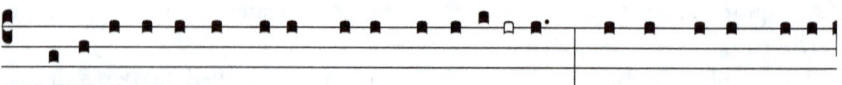

1. Di-xit injústus ut de-línquat in semet-í- pso: * non est timor De- i

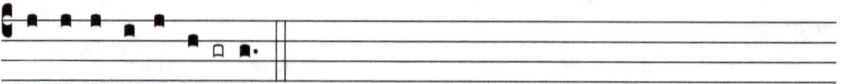

ante ó-*cu-los* e- jus.

1. The unjust hath said within himself, that he would sin: * there is no fear of God before his eyes.

2. Quóniam dolóse egit in conspéctu ejus: * ut inveniátur iníquitas e*jus ad* ódium.

2. For in his sight he hath done deceitfully, * that his iniquity may be found unto hatred.

3. Verba oris ejus iníquitas, et dolus: * nóluit intellígere ut *bene* ágeret.

3. The words of his mouth are iniquity and guile: * he would not understand that he might do well.

4. Iniquitátem meditátus est in cubíli suo: * ástitit omni viæ non bonæ, malítiam autem *non o*dívit.

4. He hath devised iniquity on his bed, * he hath set himself on every way that is not good: but evil he hath not hated.

5. Dómine, in cælo misericórdia tua: * et véritas tua us*que ad* nubes.

5. O Lord, Thy mercy is in heaven, * and Thy truth reacheth even to the clouds.

6. Justítia tua sicut montes Dei: * judícia tua a*býssus* multa.

6. Thy justice is as the mountains of God, * Thy judgments are a great deep.

7. Hómines, et juménta salvábis, Dómine: * quemádmodum multiplicásti misericórdiam *tuam*, Deus,

7. Men and beasts Thou wilt preserve, O Lord: * O how hast Thou multiplied Thy mercy, O God!

8. Fílii autem hóminum, * in tégmine alárum tuá*rum spe*rábunt.

8. But the children of men * shall put their trust under the covert of Thy wings.

9. Inebriabúntur ab ubertáte domus tuæ: * et torrénte voluptátis tuæ po*tábis* eos.

9. They shall be inebriated with the plenty of Thy house; * and Thou shalt make them drink of the torrent of Thy pleasure.

10. Quóniam apud te est fons vitæ: * et in lúmine tuo vidé*bimus* **lu**men.

11. Præténde misericórdiam tuam sciénti**bus** te, * et justítiam tuam his, qui re*cto sunt* **cor**de.

12. Non véniat mihi pes su**pér**biæ: * et manus peccatóris non *móve*-**at** me.

13. Ibi cecidérunt qui operántur iniquitátem: * expúlsi sunt, nec potu*érunt* **sta**re.

10. For with Thee is the fountain of life; * and in Thy light we shall see light.

11. Extend Thy mercy to them that know Thee, * and Thy justice to them that are right in heart.

12. Let not the foot of pride come to me, * and let not the hand of the sinner move me.

13. There the workers of iniquity are fallen, * they are cast out, and could not stand.

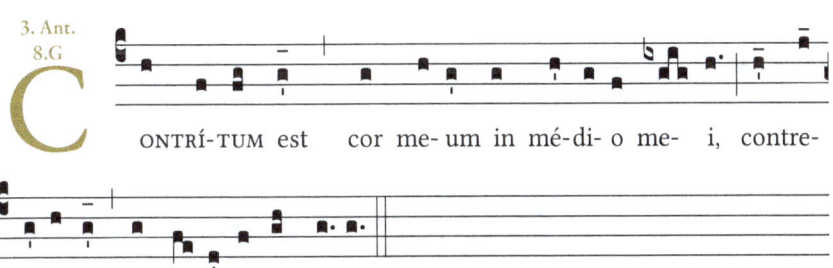

3. Ant. 8.G

CONTRÍ-TUM est cor me- um in mé-di- o me- i, contre-mu- é-runt ómni- a ossa me- a.

The twelfth candle is extinguished.

4. Ant.
4.A*

E XHORTÁTUS es ✷ in virtú-te tú- a, et in re-fecti- ó- ne

sáncta tú- a, Dómi-ne.

ANTIPHON: O Lord, Thou hast spoken unto us * in Thy strength, and in Thy Holy Banquet.

CANTICLE OF MOSES (EXODUS 15: 1-19)

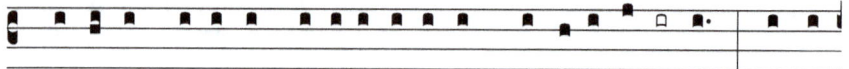

1. Cantémus Dómi-no: glo-ri- ó-se e-nim ma*gni- fi-**cá**-*tus est, * equum

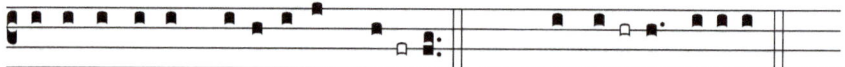

et ascensó-rem de-*jé-cit in* **ma**- re. *Flex :* pugná- tor, †

1. Let us sing to the Lord: for He is gloriously magnified, * the horse and the rider He hath thrown into the sea.

2. Fortitúdo mea, et laus *mea* **Dóminus,** * et factus est mi*hi in* sa*lú*tem.

2. The Lord is my strength and my praise, * and He is become salvation to me:

3. Iste Deus meus, et glorific*ábo* eum: * Deus patris mei, et ex*altábo* eum.

3. He is my God and I will glorify Him: * the God of my father, and I will exalt Him.

4. Dóminus quasi vir pugnátor, † Omnípotens *nomen* ejus. * Currus Pharaónis et exércitum ejus pro*jécit in* **ma**re.

4. The Lord is as a man of war, † Almighty is His name. * Pharao's chariots and His army He hath cast into the sea:

5. Elécti príncipes ejus submér-si sunt in *Mari* **Ru**bro: * abýssi operuérunt eos, descendérunt in profún*dum quasi* **la**pis.

5. His chosen captains are drowned in the Red Sea. * The depths have covered them, they are sunk to the bottom like a stone.

6. Déxtera tua, Dómine, magnificáta est in fortitúdine: † déxtera tua, Dómine, percússit *inimí*cum. * Et in multitúdine glóriæ tuæ deposuísti adver*sários* **tu**os:

7. Misísti iram tuam, quæ devorávit eos *sicut* **stí**pulam. * Et in spíritu furóris tui congre*gátæ sunt* **aquæ**:

8. Stetit *unda* **flu**ens, * congregátæ sunt abýssi in *médio* **ma**ri.

9. Dixit inimícus: Pérsequar et *compre***hén**dam, * dívidam spólia, implébitur *ánima* **me**a:

10. Evaginábo glá*dium* **me**um, * interfíciet e*os manus* **me**a.

11. Flavit spíritus tuus, et opéruit *eos* **ma**re: * submérsi sunt quasi plumbum in a*quis vehe***mén**tibus.

12. Quis símilis tui in fór*tibus*, **Dó**mine? * quis símilis tui, magníficus in sanctitáte, terríbilis atque laudábilis, fáci*ens mira***bí**lia?

13. Extendísti manum tuam, et devorávit *eos* **ter**ra. * Dux fuísti in misericórdia tua pópulo *quem rede***mí**sti:

14. Et portásti eum in fortitú*dine* **tu**a, * ad habitácu*lum sanctum* **tu**um.

15. Ascendérunt pópuli, *et i***rá**ti sunt: * dolóres obtinuérunt habita*tóres Phi***lís**thiim.

16. Tunc conturbáti sunt príncipes Edom, † robústos Moab obtí*nuit* **tre**mor: * obriguérunt omnes habita*tóres* **Chá**naan.

17. Irruat super eos form*ído et* **pa**vor, * in magnitúdine *bráchii* **tu**i:

6. Thy right hand, O Lord, is magnified in strength: † Thy right hand, O Lord, hath slain the enemy. * And in the multitude of Thy glory Thou hast put down Thy adversaries:

7. Thou hast sent Thy wrath, which hath devoured them like stubble. * And with the blast of Thy anger the waters were gathered together:

8. The flowing water stood, * the depths were gathered together in the midst of the sea.

9. The enemy said: I will pursue and overtake, * I will divide the spoils, my soul shall have its fill:

10. I will draw my sword, * my hand shall slay them.

11. Thy wind blew and the sea covered them: * they sunk as lead in the mighty waters.

12. Who is like to Thee, among the strong, O Lord? * who is like to Thee, glorious in holiness, terrible and praiseworthy, doing wonders?

13. Thou stretchedst forth Thy hand, and the earth swallowed them. * In Thy mercy Thou hast been a leader to the people which Thou hast redeemed:

14. And in Thy strength Thou hast carried them * to Thy holy habitation.

15. Nations rose up, and were angry: * sorrows took hold on the inhabitants of Philisthiim.

16. Then were the princes of Edom troubled, † trembling seized on the stout men of Moab: * all the inhabitants of Chanaan became stiff.

17. Let fear and dread fall upon them, * in the greatness of Thy arm:

18. Fiant immóbiles quasi lapis, † donec pertránseat pópulus *tuus*, **Dó**mine, * donec pertránseat pópulus tuus iste, *quem posse***dís**ti.

18. Let them become unmoveable as a stone, until Thy people, O Lord, pass by: * until this Thy people pass by, which Thou hast possessed.

19. Introdúces eos, et plantábis in monte heredi*tátis* **tuæ**, * firmíssimo habitáculo tuo quod oper*átus es*, **Dó**mine:

19. Thou shalt bring them in, and plant them in the mountain of Thy inheritance, * in Thy most firm habitation which Thou hast made, O Lord;

20. Sanctuárium tuum, Dómine, quod firmavérunt *manus* **tuæ**. * Dóminus regnábit in *ætérnum et* **ul**tra.

20. Thy sanctuary, O Lord, which Thy hands have established. * The Lord shall reign for ever and ever.

21. Ingréssus est enim eques Phárao cum cúrribus et equítibus e*jus in* **ma**re: * et redúxit super eos Dómi*nus aquas* **ma**ris:

21. For Pharao went in on horseback with His chariots and horsemen into the sea: * and the Lord brought back upon them the waters of the sea:

22. Fílii autem Israël ambula*vérunt per* **sic**cum * in *médio* **e**jus.

22. But the children of Israel walked on dry ground * in the midst thereof.

4. Ant.
4.A*

EXHORTÁTUS es in virtú-te tú- a, et in re-fecti- ó- ne sáncta tú- a, Dómi-ne.

The thirteenth candle is extinguished.

5. Ant.
2.D

O-BLÁ-TUS est, * qui- a ipse vó-lu- it, et peccá-ta nostra i-pse portá-vit.

ANTIPHON: He was offered up because He willed it * and He bore our sins.

PSALM 146

1. Laudá-te Dómi-num quón-i- am bonus est **psal**-mus : * De- o nostro

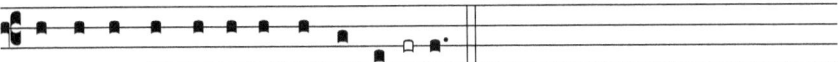

sit ju-cúnda, de-có-raque *laudá*-ti- o.

1. Praise ye the Lord, because psalm is good: * to our God be joyful and comely praise.

2. Ædíficans Jerúsalem **Dó**minus: * dispersiónes Israélis con*gregá*bit.

2. The Lord buildeth up Jerusalem: * He will gather together the dispersed of Israel.

3. Qui sanat contrítos **cor**de: * et álligat contritiónes *eó*rum.

3. Who healeth the broken of heart, * and bindeth up their bruises.

4. Qui númerat multitúdinem stellárum: * et ómnibus eis nómi*na* **vo**cat.

4. Who telleth the number of the stars: * and calleth them all by their names.

5. Magnus Dóminus noster, et magna virtus **e**jus: * et sapiéntiæ ejus non *est* **nú**merus.

5. Great is our Lord, and great is His power: * and of His wisdom there is no number.

6. Suscípiens mansuétos **Dó**minus: * humílians autem peccatóres usque *ad* **ter**ram.

6. The Lord lifteth up the meek, * and bringeth the wicked down even to the ground.

7. Præcínite Dómino in confes-si**ó**ne: * psállite Deo nostro *in* **cí**thara.

7. Sing ye to the Lord with praise: * sing to our God upon the harp.

8. Qui óperit cælum **nú**bibus: * et parat ter*ræ* **plú**viam.

8. Who covereth the heaven with clouds, * and prepareth rain for the earth.

9. Qui prodúcit in móntibus **fæ**num: * et herbam servitú*ti* **hó**mi-num.

9. Who maketh grass to grow on the mountains, * and herbs for the service of men.

10. Qui dat juméntis escam **ip**só*rum: * et pullis corvórum in-vocánt*ibus* eum.

10. Who giveth to beasts their food: * and to the young ravens that call upon Him.

11. Non in fortitúdine equi voluntátem ha**bé**bit: * nec in tíbiis viri beneplácitum *erit* ei.

11. He shall not delight in the strength of the horse: * nor take pleasure in the legs of a man.

12. Beneplácitum est Dómino super timéntes eum: * et in eis, qui sperant super misericórdi*a* ejus.

12. The Lord taketh pleasure in them that fear Him: * and in them that hope in His mercy.

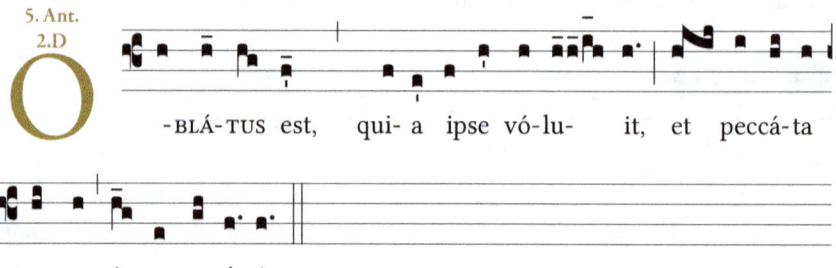

5. Ant.
2.D

O-BLÁ-TUS est, qui- a ipse vó-lu- it, et peccá-ta nostra i-pse portá-vit.

The fourteenth candle is extinguished.

℣. Homo pa-cis me-æ, in quo spe-rá-vi. ℟. Qui e-dé-bat panes me- os, ampli- á-vit advérsum me supplanta-ti- ó-nem.

Or:

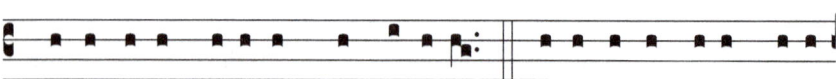

℣. Homo pa-cis me-æ, in quo spe-rá-vi. ℟. Qui e-dé-bat panes me- os,

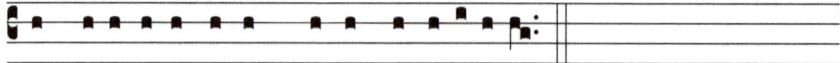

ampli- á-vit advérsum me supplanta-ti- ónem.

℣. Mine own familiar friend, in whom I trusted;
℟. Which did eat of My bread, hath lifted up his heel against Me.

BENEDÍCTUS

At Bened.
1.g

TRÁDI-TOR au-tem * de-dit e- is signum, di-cens : Quem o-scu-

lá-tus fú- e-ro, ipse est, te-né- te e- um.

ANTIPHON: Now he that betrayed Him * gave them a sign, saying: Whomsoever I shall kiss, That Same is He: hold Him fast.

The intonation is sung for every verse.

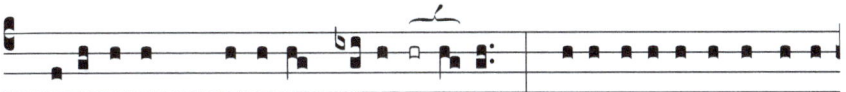

1. Bene-díctus ✠ Dómi-*nus, De- us* **Isra**- ël: * qui- a vi-si-tá-vit, et fe-cit

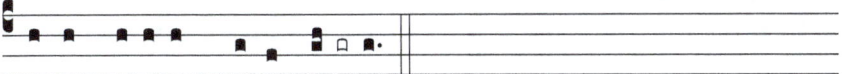

red-empti- ónem *ple-bis* **su**- æ:

1. Blessed be the Lord ✠ God of Israel; * because He hath visited and wrought the redemption of His people:

2. Et eréxit cornu *salútis* **no**bis: * in domo David, pú*eri* **sui.**

2. And hath raised up an horn of salvation to us, * in the house of David His servant:

The first altar candle is extinguished

3. Sicut locútus est *per os san***ctó**rum, * qui a sǽculo sunt, prophe*tárum* ejus:

3. As He spoke by the mouth of His holy Prophets, * who are from the beginning:

4. Salútem ex in*imícis* **no**stris, * et de manu ómnium, *qui o***dé**runt nos.

4. Salvation from our enemies, * and from the hand of all that hate us:

The second altar candle is extinguished

5. Ad faciéndam misericórdiam cum *pátribus* **no**stris: * et memorári testaménti *sui* **san**cti.

5. To perform mercy to our fathers, * and to remember His holy testament,

6. Jusjurándum, quod jurávit ad Abra*ham patrem* **no**strum, * datú*rum se* **no**bis:

6. The oath, which He swore to Abraham our father, * that He would grant to us,

The third altar candle is extinguished

7. Ut sine timóre, de manu inimicórum nostró*rum libe***rá**ti, * servi*ámus* **il**li.

7. That being delivered from the hand of our enemies, * we may serve Him without fear,

8. In sanctitáte, et justíti*a coram* **i**pso, * ómnibus di*ébus* **no**stris.

8. In holiness and justice before Him, * all our days.

The fourth altar candle is extinguished

9. Et tu, puer, Prophéta Altís*simi vo***cá**beris: * præíbis enim ante fáciem Dómini, paráre *vias* **e**jus:

9. And thou, child, shalt be called the prophet of the Highest: * for thou shalt go before the face of the Lord to prepare His ways:

10. Ad dandam sciéntiam salú*tis plebi* **e**jus: * in remissiónem peccat*órum eó*rum:

10. To give knowledge of salvation to His people, * unto the remission of their sins:

The fifth altar candle is extinguished

11. Per víscera misericórdi*æ Dei* **no**stri: * in quibus visitávit nos, óri*ens ex* **al**to:

11. Through the bowels of the mercy of our God, * in which the Orient from on high hath visited us:

12. Illumináre his, qui in ténebris, et in um*bra mortis* **se**dent: * ad dirigéndos pedes nostros in *viam* **pa**cis.

12. To enlighten them that sit in darkness, and in the shadow of death: * to direct our feet into the way of peace.

The sixth altar candle is extinguished

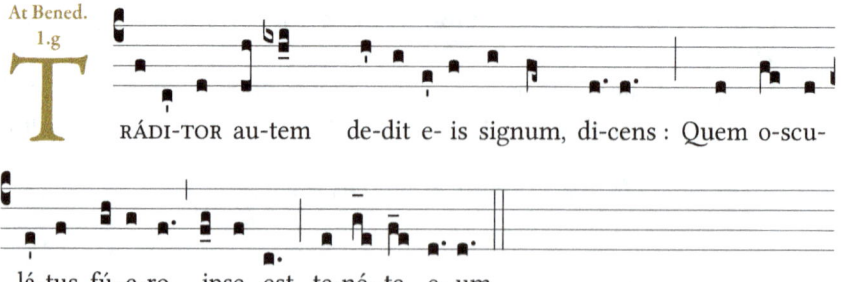

At Bened.
1.g

TRÁDI-TOR au-tem de-dit e- is signum, di-cens : Quem o-scu-lá-tus fú-e-ro, ipse est, te-né- te e- um.

At the conclusion of the antiphon following the Benedíctus, *the remaining candle is removed and "hidden" while all kneel and sing:*

CHRI-STUS * factus est pro no-   bis ob-é-   di- ens

us-que   ad   mor- tem.

ANTIPHON: Christ became obedient for us unto death.

At the conclusion of the antiphon Christus factus est, *the* Pater noster *is said in silence.*

PSALM 50

Recited recto tono

1. Miserére mei, Deus, * secúndum magnam misericórdiam tuam.

2. Et secúndum multitúdinem miseratiónum tuárum, * dele iniquitátem meam.

3. Amplius lava me ab iniquitáte mea: * et a peccáto meo munda me.

4. Quóniam iniquitátem meam ego cognósco: * et peccátum meum contra me est semper.

5. Tibi soli peccávi, et malum coram te feci: * ut justificéris in sermónibus tuis, et vincas cum judicáris.

6. Ecce enim in iniquitátibus concéptus sum: * et in peccátis concépit me mater mea.

1. Have mercy on me, O God, * according to Thy great mercy.

2. And according to the multitude of Thy tender mercies * blot out my iniquity.

3. Wash me yet more from my iniquity, * and cleanse me from my sin.

4. For I know my iniquity, * and my sin is always before me.

5. To Thee only have I sinned, and have done evil before Thee: * that Thou mayst be justified in Thy words, and mayst overcome when Thou art judged.

6. For behold I was conceived in iniquities; * and in sins did my mother conceive me.

7. Ecce enim veritátem dilexísti: *
incérta et occúlta sapiéntiæ tuæ manifestásti mihi.

8. Aspérges me hyssópo, et
mundábor: * lavábis me, et super
nivem dealbábor.

9. Audítui meo dabis gáudium
et lætítiam: * et exsultábunt ossa
humiliáta.

10. Avérte fáciem tuam a peccátis
meis: * et omnes iniquitátes meas dele.

11. Cor mundum crea in me,
Deus: * et spíritum rectum ínnova in
viscéribus meis.

12. Ne projícias me a fácie tua: *
et spíritum sanctum tuum ne áuferas
a me.

13. Redde mihi lætítiam salutáris
tui: * et spíritu principáli confírma
me.

14. Docébo iníquos vias tuas: *
et ímpii ad te converténtur.

15. Líbera me de sanguínibus, Deus,
Deus salútis meæ: * et exsultábit lingua mea justítiam tuam.

16. Dómine, lábia mea apéries: *
et os meum annuntiábit laudem tuam.

17. Quóniam si voluísses sacrifícium, dedíssem útique: * holocáustis
non delectáberis.

18. Sacrifícium Deo spíritus
contribulátus: * cor contrítum et humiliátum, Deus, non despícies.

19. Benígne fac, Dómine, in bona
voluntáte tua Sion: * ut ædificéntur
muri Jerúsalem.

7. For behold Thou hast loved
truth: * the uncertain and hidden
things of Thy wisdom Thou hast made
manifest to me.

8. Thou shalt sprinkle me with hyssop, and I shall be cleansed: * Thou
shalt wash me, and I shall be made
whiter than snow.

9. To my hearing Thou shalt give
joy and gladness: * and the bones that
have been humbled shall rejoice.

10. Turn away Thy face from my
sins, * and blot out all my iniquities.

11. Create a clean heart in me, O
God: * and renew a right spirit within
my bowels.

12. Cast me not away from Thy
face; * and take not Thy holy spirit
from me.

13. Restore unto me the joy of Thy
salvation, * and strengthen me with a
perfect spirit.

14. I will teach the unjust Thy
ways: * and the wicked shall be converted to Thee.

15. Deliver me from blood, O God,
Thou God of my salvation: * and my
tongue shall extol Thy justice.

16. O Lord, Thou wilt open my
lips: * and my mouth shall declare Thy
praise.

17. For if Thou hadst desired sacrifice, I would indeed have given it: *
with burnt offerings Thou wilt not be
delighted.

18. A sacrifice to God is an afflicted
spirit: * a contrite and humbled heart,
O God, Thou wilt not despise.

19. Deal favourably, O Lord, in Thy
good will with Sion; * that the walls of
Jerusalem may be built up.

20. Tunc acceptábis sacrifícium justítiæ, oblatiónes, et holocáusta: * tunc impónent super altáre tuum vítulos.

20. Then shalt Thou accept the sacrifice of justice, oblations and whole burnt offerings: * then shall they lay calves upon Thy altar.

Sung recto tono or to ferial tone without Orémus.

Réspice, quǽsumus, Dómine, super hanc famíliam tuam, pro qua Dóminus noster Jesus Christus non dubitávit mánibus tradi nocéntium, et crucis subíre torméntum:

Look down, we beseech Thee, O Lord, on this Thy family, for which our Lord Jesus Christ did not hesitate to be delivered up into the hands of wicked men, and to suffer the torment of the Cross.

[*Dícitur sub siléntio:* Qui tecum vivit et regnat in unitáte Spíritus Sancti, Deus, per ómnia sǽcula sæculórum. ℟. Amen.]

[*Said in silence:* Who with thee liveth and reigneth, in the unity of the Holy Ghost, God, world without end. ℟. Amen.]

The Strépitus *is begun by the celebrant and continues until the "hidden" candle is brought back out. All then rise and retire in silence.*

THE MASS

PRAYERS AT THE FOOT OF THE ALTAR

The celebrant bows before the altar and makes the sign of the cross saying:

IN NÓMINE Patris, ✠ et Fílii, et Spíritus Sancti. Amen.

℣. Introíbo ad altáre Dei.

℟. Ad Deum, qui lætíficat juventútem meam.

℣. Adjutórium nostrum ✠ in nómine Dómini.

℟. Qui fecit cælum et terram.

IN THE NAME of the Father, ✠ and of the Son, and of the Holy Ghost. Amen.

℣. I will go in to the altar of God.

℟. To God who giveth joy to my youth.

℣. Our help ✠ is in the Name of the Lord.

℟. Who made heaven and earth.

CONFÍTEOR

The celebrant bows low and says:

CONFÍTEOR Deo omnipoténti, beátæ Maríæ semper Vírgini, beáto Michaéli Archángelo, beáto Joánni Baptístæ, sanctis Apóstolis Petro et Paulo, ómnibus Sanctis, et vobis, fratres: quia peccávi nimis cogitatióne, verbo et ópere: **(Pércutit sibi pectus ter, dicens)** mea culpa, mea culpa, mea máxima culpa. Ideo precor beátam Maríam semper Vírginem, beátum Michaélem Archángelum, beátum Joánnem Baptístam, sanctos Apóstolos Petrum et Paulum, omnes Sanctos, et vos, fratres, oráre pro me ad Dóminum, Deum nostrum.

℟. Misereátur tui omnípotens Deus, et, dimíssis peccátis tuis, perdúcat te ad vitam ætérnam.

℣. Amen.

I CONFESS to almighty God, to the blessed Mary ever Virgin, blessed Michael the Archangel, blessed John the Baptist, the holy Apostles Peter and Paul, to all the Saints, and to you, brothers, that I have sinned exceedingly in thought, word, and deed, **(The priest strikes his breast three times, saying:)** through my fault, through my fault, through my most grievous fault. Therefore I beseech the blessed Mary, ever Virgin, blessed Michael the Archangel, blessed John the Baptist, the holy Apostles Peter and Paul, all the Saints, and you, brothers, to pray to the Lord our God for me.

℟. May almighty God be merciful to thee, and forgiving thy sins, bring thee to everlasting life.

℣. Amen

The server bows and says:

CONFÍTEOR Deo omnipoténti, beátæ Maríæ semper Vírgini, beáto Micháéli Archángelo, beáto Joánni Baptístæ, sanctis Apóstolis Petro et Paulo, ómnibus Sanctis, et tibi, pater: quia peccávi nimis cogitatióne, verbo et ópere: (**Pércutit sibi pectus ter, dicens**) mea culpa, mea culpa, mea máxima culpa. Ideo precor beátam Maríam semper Vírginem, beátum Micháélem Archángelum, beátum Joánnem Baptístam, sanctos Apóstolos Petrum et Paulum, omnes Sanctos, et te, pater, oráre pro me ad Dóminum, Deum nostrum.

℣. Misereátur vestri omnípotens Deus, et, dimíssis peccátis vestris, perdúcat vos ad vitam ætérnam.

℟. Amen.

℣. Indulgéntiam, ✠ absolutiónem et remissiónem peccatórum nostrórum tríbuat nobis omnípotens et miséricors Dóminus.

℟. Amen.

The celebrant bows and continues:

℣. Deus, tu convérsus vivificábis nos.

℟. Et plebs tua lætábitur in te.

℣. Osténde nobis, Dómine, misericórdiam tuam.

℟. Et salutáre tuum da nobis.

℣. Dómine, exáudi oratiónem meam.

℟. Et clamor meus ad te véniat.

℣. Dóminus vobíscum.

℟. Et cum spíritu tuo.

ORÉMUS.

I CONFESS to almighty God, to the blessed Mary ever Virgin, blessed Michael the Archangel, blessed John the Baptist, the holy Apostles Peter and Paul, to all the Saints, and to you, Father, that I have sinned exceedingly in thought, word, and deed, (**Now strike your breast three times, saying:**) through my fault, through my fault, through my most grievous fault. Therefore I beseech the blessed Mary, ever Virgin, blessed Michael the Archangel, blessed John the Baptist, the holy Apostles Peter and Paul, all the Saints, and you, Father, to pray to the Lord our God for me.

℣. May almighty God be merciful to thee, and forgiving thy sins, bring thee to everlasting life.

℟. Amen.

℣. May the ✠ almighty and merciful Lord grant us pardon, absolution, and remission of our sins.

℟. Amen.

℣. O God, Thou wilt turn again and quicken us.

℟. And thy people shall rejoice in Thee.

℣. Show us, O Lord, Thy mercy.

℟. And grant us Thy salvation.

℣. O Lord, hear my prayer.

℟. And let my cry come before Thee.

℣. The Lord be with you.

℟. And with thy spirit.

LET US PRAY.

The celebrant ascends to the altar and says silently:

AUFER a nobis, quǽsumus, Dómine, iniquitátes nostras: ut ad Sancta sanctórum puris mereámur méntibus introíre. Per Christum, Dóminum nostrum. Amen.

Orámus te, Dómine, per mérita Sanctórum tuórum, quorum relíquiæ hic sunt, et ómnium Sanctórum: ut indulgére dignéris ómnia peccáta mea. Amen.

TAKE away from us our iniquities, we beseech Thee, O Lord, that we may be worthy to enter with pure minds into the Holy of Holies, through Christ our Lord. Amen.

We beseech Thee, O Lord, by the merits of Thy Saints, whose relics are here, and of all the Saints, that Thou wouldst vouchsafe to forgive me all my sins. Amen.

INTROIT

The celebrant reads the Introit *from the Epistle side of the altar:*

INTROIT   GALATIANS 6: 14

Intr. 4.

Nos au- tem * glo- ri- á- ri opór- tet, in cru- ce Dó- mi-ni no-stri Je- su Chri- sti : in quo est sa-lus, vi- ta, et re- surré-cti- o no- stra : per quem salvá-ti, et li-be-rá- ti su- mus. *Ps.* De- us mi-se-re- á-tur nostri, et be-ne-dí-cat no-bis : * il-lúmi-net vultum su- um super nos, et mi-se-re- á- tur nostri.

Nos au- tem.

Introit: But it behooves us to glory in the cross of Our Lord Jesus Christ: in Whom is our salvation, life, and resurrection; by Whom we are saved and delivered. **Ps. 66:2** May God have mercy on us, and bless us: may He cause the light of His countenance to shine upon us; and may He have mercy on us.

Verses ad Libítum

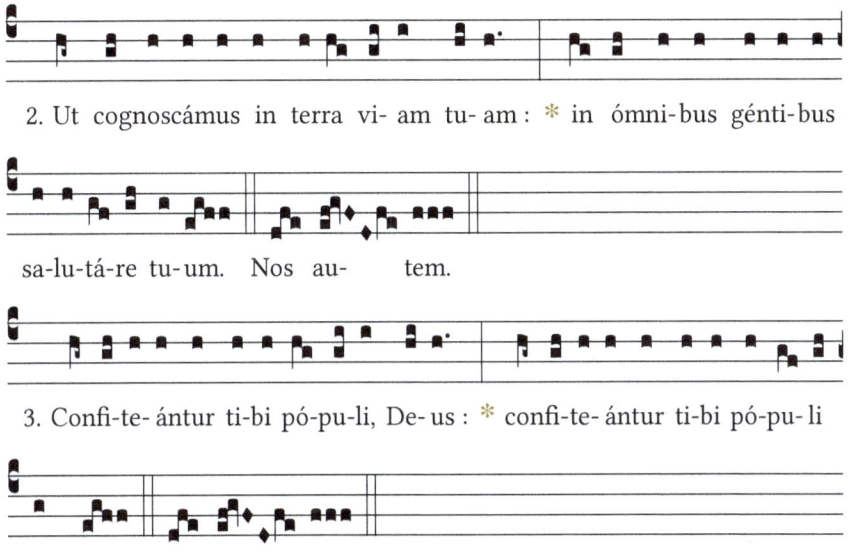

2. Ut cognoscámus in terra vi- am tu- am : * in ómni-bus génti-bus

sa-lu-tá-re tu-um. Nos au- tem.

3. Confi-te- ántur ti-bi pó-pu-li, De- us : * confi-te- ántur ti-bi pó-pu-li

omnes. Nos au- tem.

2. That we may know Thy way upon earth: Thy salvation in all nations.
3. Let people confess to Thee, O God: let all people give praise to Thee.

The celebrant moves to the middle of the altar and alternately recites the Kyrie *with the server.*

Kýrie eléison   IV - Cunctipótens Génitor Deus

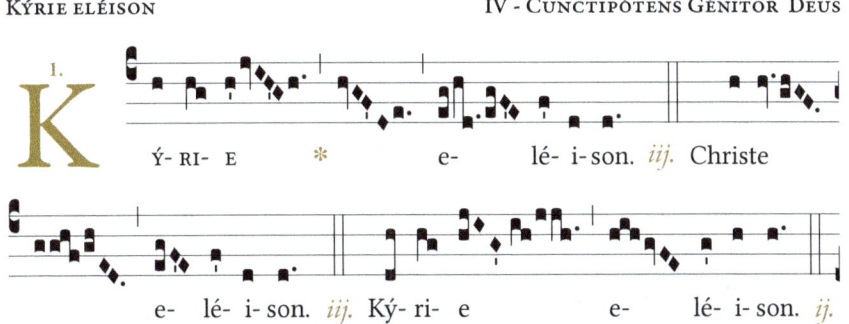

K Ý- RI- E   *   e- lé- i-son. *iij.* Christe

e- lé- i-son. *iij.* Ký- ri- e   e- lé- i-son. *ij.*

Ký-ri- e   *   ** e-   lé- i-son.

KÝRIE: Lord, have mercy. (3x) Christ, have mercy. (3x) Lord, have mercy. (3x)

The bells are rung during the Glória *and the organ may be played during the recitation or until the end of the* Glória, *but are silent until the Easter vigil.*

GLÓRIA IN EXCÉLSIS   IV - CUNCTIPÓTENS GÉNITOR DEUS

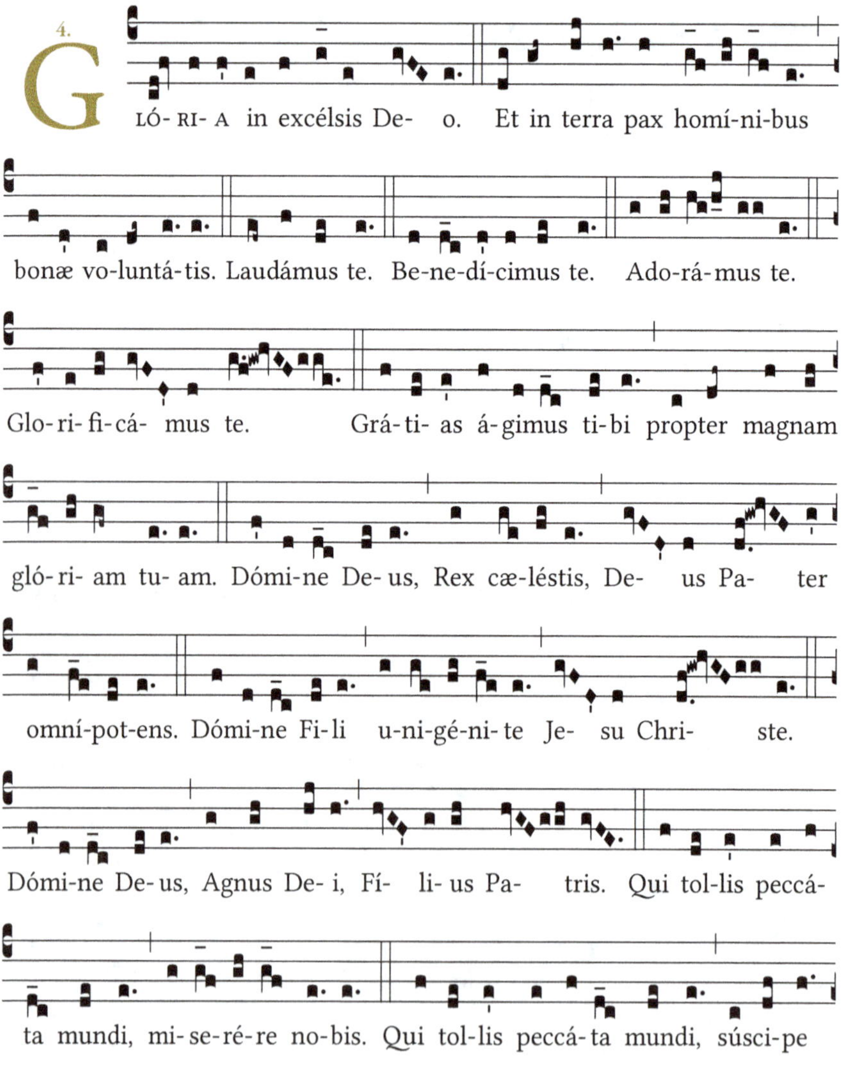

4.

GLÓ- RI- A in excélsis De- o.   Et in terra pax homí-ni-bus

bonæ vo-luntá-tis. Laudámus te. Be-ne-dí-cimus te.   Ado-rá-mus te.

Glo-ri-fi-cá- mus te.   Grá-ti- as á-gimus ti-bi propter magnam

gló-ri- am tu- am. Dómi-ne De- us, Rex cæ-léstis, De- us Pa- ter

omní-pot-ens. Dómi-ne Fi-li u-ni-gé-ni- te Je- su Chri- ste.

Dómi-ne De- us, Agnus De- i, Fí- li-us Pa- tris. Qui tol-lis peccá-

ta mundi, mi-se-ré-re no-bis. Qui tol-lis peccá-ta mundi, súsci-pe

depre-ca-ti-ónem nostram. Qui se-des ad déxte-ram Patris, mi-se-

ré-re no-bis. Quó-ni-am tu so-lus sanctus. Tu so-lus Dómi-nus.

Tu so-lus Altíssimus, Je-su Chri-ste. Cum San-cto Spí-ri-

tu, in gló-ri-a De-i Pa-tris. A-men.

GLORIA: Glory be to God on high, and on earth peace to men of good will. We praise Thee. We bless Thee. We adore Thee. We glorify Thee. We give Thee thanks for Thy great glory. O Lord God, heavenly King, God the Father almighty. O Lord Jesus Christ, the only begotten Son. O Lord God, Lamb of God, Son of the Father. Who takest away the sins of the world, have mercy on us. Who takest away the sins of the world, receive our prayer. Who sittest at the right hand of the Father, have mercy on us. For Thou only art holy. Thou only art the Lord. Thou only art most high, O Jesus Christ. Together with the Holy Ghost ✠ in the glory of God the Father. Amen.

COLLECT

The celebrant turns to the people and says:

℣. Dóminus vobíscum.

℟. Et cum spíritu tuo.

℣. The Lord be with you.

℟. And with thy spirit.

ORÉMUS.

LET US PRAY.

DEUS, a quo et Judas reátus sui pænam, et confessiónis suæ latro prǽmium sumpsit, concéde nobis tuæ propitiatiónis efféctum: ut, sicut in passióne sua Jesus Christus, Dóminus noster, divérsa utrísque íntulit

O GOD, from whom Judas received the punishment of his guilt, and the thief the reward of his confession: grant unto us the full fruit of Thy clemency; that even as in His Passion, our Lord Jesus Christ gave

stipéndia meritórum; ita nobis, abláto vetustátis erróre, resurrectiónis suæ grátiam largiátur: Qui tecum vivit et regnat in unitáte Spíritus Sancti, Deus, per ómnia sǽcula sæculórum.

℟. Amen.

to each a retribution according to his merits, so having taken away our old sins, He may bestow upon us the grace of His Resurrection. Who liveth and reigneth with Thee in the unity of the Holy Ghost, God, world without end.

℟. Amen.

This Collect is the only prayer said here.

The celebrant reads the Lesson from the Epistle side of the altar, or at a Solemn High Mass the subdeacon sings it:

LESSON FROM THE FIRST LETTER OF BLESSED PAUL THE APOSTLE TO THE CORINTHIANS
1 Corinthians 11: 20-32

FRATRES: Conveniéntibus vobis in unum, jam non est Domínicam cœnam manducáre. Unusquísque enim suam cœnam præsúmit ad manducándum. Et alius quidem ésurit: álius autem ébrius est. Numquid domos non habétis ad manducándum et bibéndum? aut ecclésiam Dei contémnitis, et confúnditis eos, qui non habent? Quid dicam vobis? Laudo vos? In hoc non laudo. Ego enim accépi a Dómino quod et trádidi vobis, quóniam Dóminus Jesus, in qua nocte tradebátur, accépit panem, et grátias agens fregit, et dixit: Accípite, et manducáte: hoc est corpus meum, quod pro vobis tradétur: hoc fácite in meam commemoratiónem. Simíliter et cálicem, postquam cænávit, dicens: Hic calix novum Testaméntum est in meo sánguine: hoc fácite, quotiescúmque bibétis, in meam commemoratiónem.

BRETHREN, When you come therefore into one place, it is not now to eat the Lord's supper. For every one taketh before his own supper to eat. And one indeed is hungry and another is drunk. What, have you not houses to eat and to drink in? Or despise ye the church of God and put them to shame that have not? What shall I say to you? Do I praise you? In this I praise you not. For I have received of the Lord that which I also delivered unto you, that the Lord Jesus, the same night in which He was betrayed, took bread, and giving thanks, broke and said: Take ye and eat: This is My Body, which shall be delivered for you. This do for the commemoration of Me. In like manner also the chalice, after He had supped, saying: This chalice is the new testament in My Blood. This do ye, as often as you shall drink, for the

Quotiescúmque enim manducábitis panem hunc et cálicem bibétis: mortem Dómini annuntiábitis, donec véniat.

Itaque quicúmque manducáverit panem hunc vel bíberit cálicem Dómini indígne, reus erit córporis et sánguinis Dómini. Probet autem seípsum homo: et sic de pane illo edat et de cálice bibat. Qui enim mandúcat et bibit indígne, judícium sibi mandúcat et bibit: non dijúdicans corpus Dómini. Ideo inter vos multi infírmi et imbecílles, et dórmiunt multi. Quod si nosmetípsos dijudicarémus, non útique judicarémur. Dum judicámur autem, a Dómino corrípimur, ut non cum hoc mundo damnémur.

commemoration of Me. For as often as you shall eat this bread and drink the chalice, you shall show the death of the Lord, until He come.

Therefore, whosoever shall eat this bread, or drink the chalice of the Lord unworthily, shall be guilty of the Body and the Blood of the Lord. But let a man prove himself; and so let him eat of that bread and drink of the chalice. For he that eateth and drinketh unworthily eateth and drinketh judgment to himself, not discerning the Body of the Lord. Therefore are there many infirm and weak among you: and many sleep. But if we would judge ourselves, we should not be judged. But whilst we are judged, we are chastised by the Lord, that we be not condemned with this world.

℞. Deo grátias.

℞. Thanks be to God.

GRADUAL   PHILIPPIANS 2: 8-9

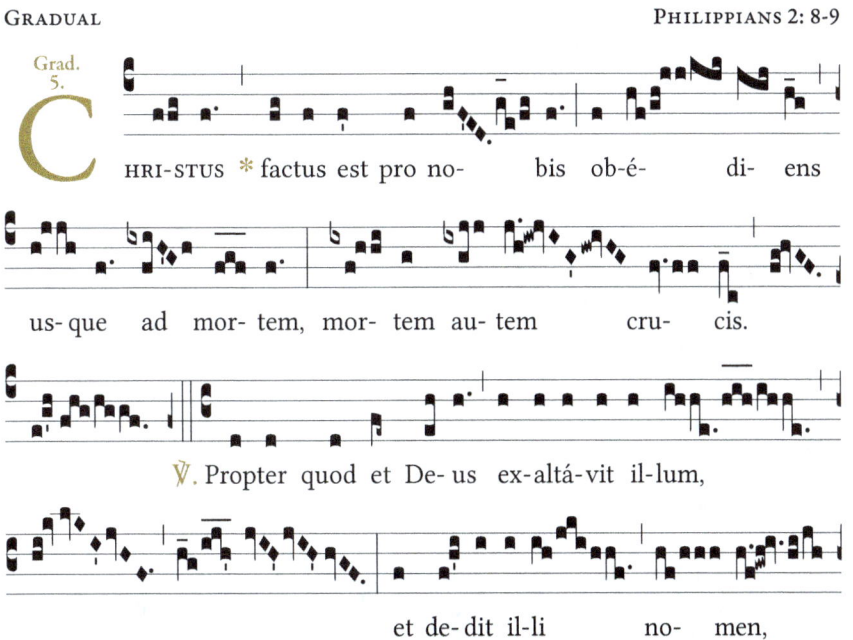

CHRI-STUS * factus est pro no- bis ob-é- di- ens us-que ad mor- tem, mor- tem au- tem cru- cis. ℣. Propter quod et De- us ex-altá-vit il-lum, et de-dit il-li no- men,

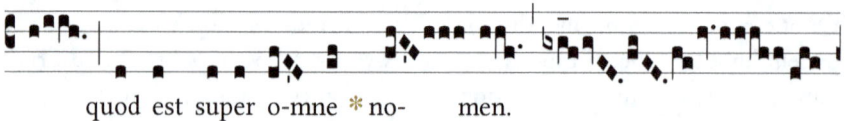

quod est super o-mne * no-   men.

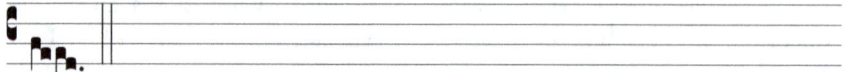

GRADUAL: Christ became obedient for us unto death, even to the death of the cross. ℣. For which cause God also exalted Him and hath given Him a Name which is above all names.

The Missal is transferred to the Gospel side as the celebrant says the Munda cor. *At a Solemn High Mass the deacon kneels and asks the blessing* (Jube, domne) *before singing the Gospel.*

MUNDA cor meum ac lábia mea, omnípotens Deus, qui lábia Isaíæ Prophétæ cálculo mundásti igníto: ita me tua grata miseratióne dignáre mundáre, ut sanctum Evangélium tuum digne váleam nuntiáre. Per Christum, Dóminum nostrum. Amen.

D. Jube, domne, benedícere.

℣. Dóminus sit in corde tuo et in lábiis tuis : ut digne et competénter annúnties Evangélium suum : In nómine Patris, et Fílii, ✠ et Spíritus Sancti. Amen.

CLEANSE my heart and my lips, O almighty God, who didst cleanse the lips of the prophet Isaias with a burning coal, and vouchsafe, through Thy gracious mercy, so to purify me, that I may worthily announce Thy holy Gospel. Through Christ our Lord. Amen.

D. Sir, give me thy blessing.

℣. The Lord be in thy heart and on thy lips, that thou mayst worthily and in a becoming manner, proclaim His holy Gospel. In the name of the Father, and of the Son, ✠ and of the Holy Ghost. Amen.

CONTINUATION ✠ OF THE HOLY GOSPEL ACCORDING TO ST. JOHN
John 13: 1-15

ANTE diem festum Paschæ, sciens Jesus, quia venit hora ejus, ut tránseat ex hoc mundo ad Patrem: cum dilexísset suos, qui erant in mundo, in finem diléxit eos. Et cœna facta, cum diábolus jam misísset in cor, ut tráderet eum Judas Simónis Iscariótæ:

BEFORE the festival-day of the Pasch, Jesus knowing that His hour was come, that He should pass out of this world to the Father, having loved His own who were in the world. He loved them unto the end. And when supper was done the devil

sciens, quia ómnia dedit ei Pater in manus, et quia a Deo exívit, et ad Deum vadit: surgit a cœna et ponit vestiménta sua: et cum accepísset línteum, præcínxit se. Deínde mittit aquam in pelvim, et cæpit laváre pedes discipulórum, et extérgere línteo, quo erat præcínctus. Venit ergo ad Simónem Petrum. Et dicit ei Petrus: Dómine, tu mihi lavas pedes? Respóndit Jesus et dixit ei: Quod ego fácio, tu nescis modo, scies autem póstea. Dicit ei Petrus: Non lavábis mihi pedes in ætérnum. Respóndit ei Jesus: Si non lávero te, non habébis partem mecum. Dicit ei Simon Petrus: Dómine, non tantum pedes meos, sed et manus et caput. Dicit ei Jesus: Qui lotus est, non índiget nisi ut pedes lavet, sed est mundus totus. Et vos mundi estis, sed non omnes. Sciébat enim, quisnam esset, qui tráderet eum: proptérea dixit: Non estis mundi omnes. Postquam ergo lavit pedes eórum et accépit vestiménta sua: cum recubuísset íterum, dixit eis: Scitis, quid fécerim vobis? Vos vocátis me Magíster et Dómine: et bene dícitis: sum étenim. Si ergo ego lavi pedes vestros, Dóminus et Magíster: et vos debétis alter altérius laváre pedes. Exémplum enim dedi vobis, ut, quemádmodum ego feci vobis, ita et vos faciátis.

having now put into the heart of Judas, the son of Simon the Iscariot, to betray Him, knowing that the Father had given Him all things into His hands and that He came from God and goeth to God: He riseth from supper and layeth aside His garments and, having taken a towel, girded Himself. After that, He putteth water into a basin and began to wash the feet of the disciples and to wipe them with the towel wherewith He was girded. He cometh therefore to Simon Peter. And Peter saith to Him: Lord, dost Thou wash my feet? Jesus answered and said to him: What I do, thou knowest not now: but thou shalt know hereafter. Peter saith to Him: Thou shalt never wash my feet. Jesus answered him: If I wash thee not, thou shalt have no part with Me. Simon Peter saith to Him: Lord, not only my feet, but also my hands and my head. Jesus saith to him: He that is washed needeth not but to wash his feet, but is clean wholly. And you are clean, but not all. For He knew who he was that would betray Him; therefore He said: You are not all clean. Then after He had washed their feet and taken His garments, being set down again, He said to them: Know you what I have done to you? You call Me Master and Lord. And you say well; for so I am. If then I being your Lord and Master, have washed your feet, you also ought to wash one another's feet. For I have given you an example, that as I have done to you, so you do also.

CREDO

The celebrant returns to the middle of the altar and says the Credo:

CREDO I

C REDO in unum De- um, Patrem omni-pot-éntem, factó-rem

cæ-li et terræ, vi-si-bí- li- um ómni- um, et invi-si-bí- li- um. Et in

unum Dómi-num Je-sum Christum, Fí-li- um De- i u-ni-gé-ni-tum.

Et ex Patre na-tum ante ómni- a sǽ-cu-la. De-um de De- o, lumen

de lúmi-ne, De-um ve-rum de De- o ve-ro. Gé-ni-tum, non factum,

consubstanti- á-lem Patri : per quem ómni- a facta sunt. Qui propter

nos hómi- nes, et propter nostram sa-lú- tem descéndit de cæ- lis.

Et incarná-tus est de Spí-ri-tu Sancto ex Ma-rí- a Vír-gi-ne :

Alternate chants for the Credo *may be found in the Appendix.*

Et homo factus est. Cru-ci-fí-xus ét-i- am pro no-bis : sub Pónti-

o Pi-lá-to passus, et sepúl-tus est. Et re-surré-xit térti- a di- e,

se-cúndum Scriptú-ras. Et ascéndit in cæ-lum : se-det ad déxte-ram

Patris. Et í-te-rum ventú-rus est cum gló-ri- a, ju-di-cá-re vi-vos

et mórtu- os : cu-jus regni non e-rit fi-nis. Et in Spí-ri-tum Sanctum,

Dómi-num, et vi-vi-fi-cántem : qui ex Patre Fi-li- óque pro-cé-dit.

Qui cum Patre et Fí-li- o simul ado-rá-tur, et conglo-ri- fi-cá-tur :

qui lo-cú-tus est per Prophé-tas. Et unam sanctam cathó-li-cam et

apostó-li-cam Ecclé-si- am. Confí-te- or unum baptísma in remis-

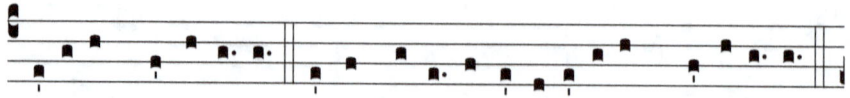

si- ónem pecca-tó-rum. Et exspécto re-surrecti- ónem mortu- ó-rum.

Et vi-tam ventú-ri sæ-cu-li.   A-   men.

CREED: I believe in one God, the Father almighty, Maker of heaven and earth, and of all things, visible and invisible.

And in one Lord Jesus Christ, the only begotten Son of God. And born of the Father, before all ages. God of God: Light of Light: true God of true God. Begotten, not made, consubstantial with the Father, by Whom all things were made. Who, for us men, and for our salvation, came down from heaven. (Kneel down.) And became incarnate by the Holy Ghost of the Virgin Mary: and was made man. He was crucified also for us, suffered under Pontius Pilate, and was buried. And the third day He rose again according to the Scriptures. And ascended into heaven, and sitteth at the right hand of the Father. And He shall come again with glory to judge both the living and the dead, of Whose kingdom there shall be no end.

And in the Holy Ghost, the Lord and Giver of Life, proceeding from the Father and the Son. Who together, with the Father and the Son, is adored and glorified: Who spoke by the prophets. And in one, holy, Catholic and Apostolic Church. I confess one baptism for the remission of sins. And I look for the resurrection of the dead. And the life of the world to come. Amen.

OFFERTORY

The celebrant kisses the altar, turns to the people and says:

℣. Dóminus vobíscum.

℟. Et cum spíritu tuo.

ORÉMUS.

℣. The Lord be with you.

℟. And with thy spirit.

LET US PRAY.

OFFERTORY   Ps 117: 16, 17

ÉXTE- RA Dómi- ni * fe- cit vir- tú- tem, déx- te-ra Dó- mi-ni ex-altá- vit me : non mó-ri- ar, sed vi- vam, et narrábo ó- pe-ra Dómi-ni.

OFFERTORY: The right hand of the Lord hath wrought strength: the right hand of the Lord hath exalted me. I shall not die, but live, and shall declare the works of the Lord.

At Solemn High Mass the subdeacon wearing the Humeral Veil brings the covered chalice to the altar and gives it to the deacon, who then gives the chalice and paten with host to the celebrant. The celebrant then uncovers the chalice and says:

SÚSCIPE, sancte Pater, omnípotens ætérne Deus, hanc immaculátam hóstiam, quam ego indígnus fámulus tuus óffero tibi Deo meo vivo et vero, pro innumerabílibus peccátis, et offensiónibus, et neglegéntiis meis, et pro ómnibus circumstántibus, sed et pro ómnibus fidélibus christiánis vivis atque defúnctis: ut mihi, et illis profíciat ad salútem in vitam ætérnam. Amen.

ACCEPT, O Holy Father, almighty and eternal God, this unspotted host, which I, Thy unworthy servant, offer unto Thee, my living and true God, for my innumerable sins, offenses, and negligences, and for all here present: as also for all faithful Christians, both living and dead, that it may avail both me and them for salvation unto life everlasting. Amen.

DEUS, ✠ qui humánæ substántiæ dignitátem mirabíliter condidísti, et mirabílius reformásti: da nobis per hujus aquæ et vini mystérium, ejus divinitátis esse consórtes, qui humanitátis nostræ fíeri dignátus est párticeps, Jesus Christus, Fílius tuus, Dóminus noster : Qui tecum vivit et regnat in unitáte Spíritus Sancti Deus: per ómnia sǽcula sæculórum. Amen.

O GOD, ✠ who, in creating human nature, didst wonderfully dignify it, and still more wonderfully restore it, grant that, by the Mystery of this water and wine, we may be made partakers of His divine nature, who vouchsafed to be made partaker of our human nature, even Jesus Christ our Lord, Thy Son, who with Thee, liveth and reigneth in the unity of the Holy Ghost, God: world without end. Amen.

OFFÉRIMUS tibi, Dómine, cálicem salutáris, tuam deprecántes cleméntiam: ut in conspéctu divínæ majestátis tuæ, pro nostra et totíus mundi salúte, cum odóre suavitátis ascéndat. Amen.

WE OFFER unto Thee, O Lord, the chalice of salvation, beseeching Thy clemency, that it may ascend before Thy divine Majesty, as a sweet savor, for our salvation, and for that of the whole world. Amen.

IN SPÍRITU humilitátis et in ánimo contríto suscipiámur a te, Dómine: et sic fiat sacrifícium nostrum in conspéctu tuo hódie, ut pláceat tibi, Dómine Deus.

ACCEPT US, O Lord, in the spirit of humility and contrition of heart, and grant that the sacrifice which we offer this day in Thy sight may be pleasing to Thee, O Lord God.

VENI, sanctificátor omnípotens ætérne Deus: et béne✠dic hoc sacrifícium, tuo sancto nómini præparátum.

COME, O almighty and eternal God, the Sanctifier, and bless ✠ this Sacrifice, prepared for the glory of Thy holy Name.

INCENSING

At Solemn High Mass the sacrificial gifts and the altar are incensed respectively, the celebrant first blessing the incense saying:

PER intercessiónem beáti Michaélis Archángeli, stantis a dextris altáris incénsi, et ómnium electórum suórum, incénsum istud dignétur Dóminus bene✠dícere, et in odórem suavitátis accípere. Per Christum, Dóminum nostrum. Amen.

MAY the Lord, by the intercession of blessed Michael the Archangel, who standeth at the right side of the altar of incense, and of all His Elect, vouchsafe to bless ✠ this incense and receive it as an odor of sweetness: through Jesus Christ our Lord. Amen.

The celebrant receives the thurible from the deacon and incenses the sacrificial gifts saying:

INCÉNSUM istud a te benedíctum ascéndat ad te, Dómine: et descéndat super nos misericórdia tua.

MAY THIS incense, which Thou hast blessed, O Lord, ascend to Thee, and may Thy mercy descend upon us.

The celebrant then incenses the altar, reciting from Psalm 140:

DIRIGÁTUR, Dómine, orátio mea, sicut incénsum, in conspéctu tuo: elevátio mánuum meárum sacrifícium vespertínum. Pone, Dómine, custódiam ori meo, et óstium circumstántiæ lábiis meis: ut non declínet cor meum in verba malítiæ, ad excusándas excusatiónes in peccátis.

LET MY prayer, O Lord, be directed as incense in Thy sight: the lifting up of my hands as an evening sacrifice. Set a watch, O Lord, before my mouth, and a door round about my lips. May my heart not incline to evil words, to make excuses for sins.

The celebrant returns the thurible to the deacon saying:

ACCÉNDAT in nobis Dóminus ignem sui amóris, et flammam ætérnæ caritátis. Amen.

MAY THE Lord enkindle within us the fire of His love, and the flame of everlasting charity. Amen.

LAVÁBO

The celebrant then moves to the Epistle side and washes his fingers, reciting from Psalm 25:

LAVÁBO inter innocéntes manus meas: et circúmdabo altáre tuum, Dómine: Ut áudiam vocem laudis, et enárrem univérsa mirabília tua. Dómine, diléxi decórem domus tuæ et locum habitatiónis glóriæ tuæ. Ne perdas cum ímpiis, Deus, ánimam meam, et cum viris sánguinum vitam meam: In quorum mánibus iniquitátes sunt: déxtera eórum repléta est munéribus. Ego autem in innocéntia mea ingréssus sum: rédime me et miserére mei. Pes meus stetit in dirécto: in ecclésiis benedícam te, Dómine.

I WILL WASH my hands among the innocent: and I will compass Thine altar, O Lord That I may hear the voice of praise: and tell of all Thy wonderous works. I have loved, O Lord, the beauty of Thy house and the place where Thy glory dwelleth. Take not away my soul, O God, with the wicked: nor my life with blood-thirsty men. In whose hands are iniquities, their right hand is filled with gifts. But I have walked in my innocence: redeem me, and have mercy on me. My foot hath stood in the direct way, in the churches I will bless Thee, O Lord.

The celebrant returns to the middle of the altar, bows down and prays:

SÚSCIPE, sancta Trínitas, hanc oblatiónem, quam tibi offérimus ob memóriam passiónis, resurrectiónis, et ascensiónis Jesu Christi, Dómini nostri: et in honórem beátæ Maríæ semper Vírginis, et beáti Joannis Baptistæ, et sanctórum Apostolórum Petri et Pauli, et istórum et ómnium Sanctórum: ut illis profíciat ad honórem, nobis autem ad salútem: et illi pro nobis intercédere dignéntur in cælis, quorum memóriam ágimus in terris. Per eúndem Christum, Dóminum nostrum. Amen.

RECEIVE, O holy Trinity, this oblation which we make to Thee, in memory of the Passion, Resurrection and Ascension of our Lord Jesus Christ, and in honor of Blessed Mary, ever Virgin, blessed John the Baptist, the holy Apostles Peter and Paul, and of all the Saints, that it may avail unto their honor and our salvation, and may they vouchsafe to intercede for us in heaven, whose memory we celebrate on earth. Through the same Christ our Lord. Amen.

The celebrant kisses the altar and then turns to the people saying:

℣. ORÁTE, FRATRES: ut meum ac vestrum sacrifícium acceptábile fiat apud Deum Patrem omnipoténtem.

℟. Suscípiat Dóminus sacrifícium de mánibus tuis ad laudem et glóriam nóminis sui, ad utilitátem quoque nostram, totiúsque Ecclésiæ suæ sanctæ.

℣. Amen.

℣. BRETHREN, PRAY that my Sacrifice and yours may be acceptable to God the Father almighty.

℟. May the Lord receive the Sacrifice from thy hands, to the praise and glory of His Name, to our benefit and that of all His holy Church.

℣. Amen.

SECRET

IPSE tibi, quǽsumus, Dómine sancte, Pater omnípotens, ætérne Deus, sacrifícium nostrum reddat accéptum, qui discípulis suis in sui commemoratiónem hoc fíeri hodiérna traditióne monstrávit, Jesus Christus, Fílius tuus, Dóminus noster: Qui tecum vivit et regnat in unitáte Spíritus Sancti Deus per ómnia sǽcula sæculórum.

℟. Amen.

WE beseech Thee, O holy Lord, Father almighty, everlasting God, that He Himself may render our Sacrifice acceptable to Thee, Who, by the tradition of today, taught His disciples to do this in remembrance of Him, Jesus Christ, Thy Son, our Lord, Who livest and reignest with God the Father, in the unity of the Holy Ghost, God, world without end.

℟. Amen.

Preface of the Holy Cross

Per ómnia sæcula sæculórum.
℟. Amen.
℣. Dóminus vobíscum.
℟. Et cum spíritu tuo.
℣. Sursum corda.
℟. Habémus ad Dóminum.

℣. Grátias agámus Dómino Deo nostro.
℟. Dignum et justum est.

Vere dignum et justum est, æquum et salutáre, nos tibi semper et ubíque grátias ágere: Dómine sancte, Pater omnípotens, ætérne Deus: Qui salútem humáni géneris in ligno Crucis constituísti: ut, unde mors oriebátur, inde vita resúrgeret: et, qui in ligno vincébat, in ligno quoque vincerétur: per Christum, Dóminum nostrum. Per quem majestátem tuam laudant Angeli, adórant Dominatiónes, tremunt Potestátes. Cæli cælorúmque Virtútes ac beáta Séraphim sócia exsultatióne concélebrant. Cum quibus et nostras voces ut admítti júbeas, deprecámur, súpplici confessióne dicéntes:

World without end.
℟. Amen.
℣. The Lord be with you.
℟. And with thy spirit.
℣. Lift up your hearts.
℟. We have them lifted up to the Lord.
℣. Let us give thanks to the Lord our God.
℟. It is meet and just.

It is truly meet and just, right and for our salvation, that we should at all times, and in all places, give thanks unto Thee, O holy Lord, Father almighty, everlasting God; Who didst establish the salvation of mankind on the tree of the Cross; that whence death came, thence also life might arise again, and that he, who overcame by the tree, by the tree also might be overcome: Through Christ our Lord. Through whom the Angels praise Thy Majesty, the Dominations worship it, the Powers stand in awe. The Heavens and the heavenly hosts together with the blessed Seraphim in triumphant chorus unite to celebrate it. Together with these we entreat Thee that Thou mayest bid our voices also to be admitted while we say with lowly praise:

Sanctus

IV - Cunctipótens Génitor Deus

San- ctus, * Sanctus, San- ctus Dómi-nus De- us Sá- ba-

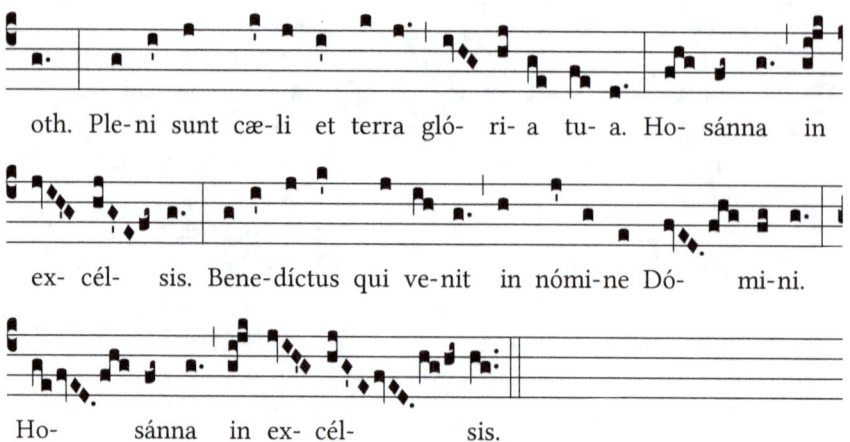

oth. Ple-ni sunt cæ-li et terra gló- ri- a tu- a. Ho- sánna in

ex- cél- sis. Bene-díctus qui ve-nit in nómi-ne Dó- mi-ni.

Ho- sánna in ex- cél- sis.

SANCTUS: Holy, Holy, Holy, Lord God of Sabaoth. Heaven and earth are full of Thy glory. Hosanna in the highest. Blessed is He that cometh in the Name of the Lord. Hosanna in the highest.

Today the celebrant consecrates two hosts, reserving one for the following day when there is no consecration.

The Canon of the Mass

The celebrant joins his hands and bows over the altar, silently praying:

Te ígitur, clementíssime Pater, per Jesum Christum, Fílium tuum, Dóminum nostrum, súpplices rogámus, ac pétimus, uti accépta hábeas et benedícas, hæc ✠ dona, hæc ✠ múnera, hæc ✠ sancta sacrifícia illibáta, in primis, quæ tibi offérimus pro Ecclésia tua sancta cathólica: quam pacificáre, custodíre, adunáre et régere dignéris toto orbe terrárum: una cum fámulo tuo Papa nostro N. et Antístite nostro N. et ómnibus orthodóxis, atque cathólicæ et apostólicæ fídei cultóribus.

Meménto, Dómine, famulórum famularúmque tuarum N. et N. et ómnium circumstántium, quorum tibi fides cógnita est et nota devótio, pro quibus tibi offérimus: vel qui tibi ófferunt hoc sacrifícium laudis, pro se suísque ómnibus: pro redemptióne animárum suárum, pro spe salútis et incolumitátis suæ: tibíque reddunt vota sua ætérno Deo, vivo et vero.

Communicántes et diem sacratíssimum celebrántes, quo Dóminus noster Jesus Christus pro nobis est tráditus: sed et memóriam venerántes, in primis gloriósæ semper Vírginis Maríæ, Genetrícis ejúsdem Dei et Dómini nostri Jesu Christi: sed et beatórum Apostolórum ac Mártyrum tuórum, Petri et Pauli, Andréæ, Jacóbi, Joánnis, Thomæ, Jacóbi, Philíppi, Bartholomǽi, Matthǽi, Simónis

We therefore humbly pray and beseech Thee, most merciful Father, through Jesus Christ; Thy Son, our Lord, that Thou wouldst vouchsafe to accept and bless these ✠ gifts, these ✠ presents, these ✠ holy unspotted Sacrifices, which in the first place we offer Thee for Thy holy Catholic Church to which vouchsafe to grant peace, as also to preserve, unite, and govern it throughout the world, together with Thy servant N., our Pope, and N., our Bishop, and all orthodox believers and professors of the Catholic and Apostolic Faith.

Be mindful, O Lord, of Thy servants and handmaidens, N. and N., and of all here present, whose faith and devotion are known unto Thee, for whom we offer, or who offer up to Thee, this sacrifice of praise for themselves, their families and friends, for the redemption of their souls, for the health and salvation they hope for; and who now pay their vows to Thee, the everlasting, living and true God.

Communicating and celebrating the most sacred day in which our Lord Jesus Christ was betrayed for us: and also honoring in the first place the memory of the glorious and ever Virgin Mary, mother of the same God and Lord Jesus Christ: and of the blessed Apostles and Martyrs Peter and Paul, Andrew, James, John, Thomas, James, Philip, Bartholomew, Matthew, Simon, and Thaddeus;

et Thaddǽi: Lini, Cleti, Cleméntis, Xysti, Cornélii, Cypriáni, Lauréntii, Chrysógoni, Joánnis et Pauli, Cosmæ et Damiáni: et ómnium Sanctórum tuórum; quorum méritis precibúsque concédas, ut in ómnibus protectiónis tuæ muniámur auxílio. Per eúndem Christum, Dóminum nostrum. Amen.

Linus, Cletus, Clement, Xystus, Cornelius, Cyprian, Lawrence, Chrysogonus, John and Paul, Cosmas and Damian, and of all Thy Saints, through whose merits and prayers, grant that we may in all things be defended by the help of Thy protection. Through the same Christ our Lord. Amen.

The bell is rung as the celebrant extends his hands over the oblation and says:

Hanc ígitur oblatiónem servitútis nostræ, sed et cunctæ famíliæ tuæ, quam tibi offérimus ob diem, in qua Dóminus noster Jesus Christus trádidit discípulis suis Córporis et Sánguinis sui mystéria celebránda: quǽsumus, Dómine, ut placátus accípias: diésque nostros in tua pace dispónas, atque ab ætérna damnatióne nos éripi et in electórum tuórum júbeas grege numerári. Per eúndem Christum, Dóminum nostrum. Amen.

We therefore beseech Thee, O Lord, graciously to accept this offering of our service, and that of Thy whole family, which we make to Thee in memory of the day on which our Lord Jesus Christ gave to His disciples the Mysteries of His Body and Blood to be celebrated; and to dispose our days in Thy peace, preserve us from eternal damnation, and rank us in the number of Thine Elect. Through the same Christ our Lord. Amen.

Quam oblatiónem tu, Deus, in ómnibus, quǽsumus, bene✠díctam, adscríp✠tam, ra✠tam, rationábilem acceptabilémque fácere dignéris: ut nobis Cor✠pus, et San✠guis fiat dilectíssimi Fílii tui, Dómini nostri Jesu Christi.

Which oblation do Thou, O God, vouchsafe in all respects, to bless, ✠ approve, ✠ ratify, ✠ make worthy and acceptable; that it may be made for us the Body ✠ and Blood ✠ of Thy most beloved Son Jesus Christ our Lord.

Qui prídie, quam pro nostra omniúmque salúte paterétur, hoc est hódie, accépit panem in sanctas ac venerábiles manus suas, et elevátis óculis in cælum ad te Deum, Patrem suum omnipoténtem, tibi grátias agens, bene✠dixit, fregit, dedítque discípulis suis, dicens: Accípite, et manducáte ex hoc omnes.

Who, the day before He suffered for our salvation and that of all men, that is, on this day, took bread into His most sacred and venerable hands and with His eyes lifted up towards heaven unto Thee, God, His almighty Father, giving thanks to Thee, He blessed ✠ it, broke it and gave it to His disciples saying: Take and eat ye all of this,

Hoc est enim corpus meum.

For this is my body.

The celebrant kneels before the Host and adores. He then elevates the Sacred Host as the bell is rung. The celebrant then uncovers the chalice and says:

Símili modo postquam cenátum est, accípiens et hunc præclárum Cálicem in sanctas ac venerábiles manus suas: item tibi grátias agens, bene✠díxit, dedítque discípulis suis, dicens: Accípite, et bíbite ex eo omnes.

Hic est enim Calix Sánguinis mei, novi et ætérni testaménti; mystérium fidei: qui pro vobis et pro multis effundétur in remissiónem peccatórum.

Hæc quotiescúmque fecéritis, in mei memóriam faciétis.

In like manner, after He had supped, taking also this excellent chalice into His holy and venerable hands He blessed ✠, and gave it to His disciples, saying: Take and drink ye all of this.

For this is the Chalice of my Blood, of the new and eternal testament; the mystery of faith: which shall be shed for you and for many unto the remission of sins.

As often as ye shall do these things, ye shall do them in memory of me.

The celebrant kneels before the Precious Blood and adores. He then elevates the Precious Blood as the bell is rung. Following this the celebrant continues:

Unde et mémores, Dómine, nos servi tui, sed et plebs tua sancta, ejúsdem Christi Fílii tui, Dómini nostri, tam beátæ passiónis, nec non et ab ínferis resurrectiónis, sed et in cælos gloriósæ ascensiónis: offérimus præcláræ majestáti tuæ de tuis donis ac datis, hóstiam ✠ puram, hóstiam ✠ sanctam, hóstiam ✠ immaculátam, Panem ✠ sanctum vitæ ætérnæ, et Cálicem ✠ salútis perpétuæ.

Supra quæ propítio ac seréno vultu respícere dignéris: et accépta habére, sicúti accépta habére dignátus es múnera púeri tui justi Abel, et sacrifícium Patriárchæ nostri Abrahæ: et quod tibi óbtulit summus

Wherefore, O Lord, we Thy servants, as also Thy holy people, calling to mind the blessed Passion of the same Christ, Thy Son, our Lord, and also His Resurrection from the dead and His glorious Ascension into heaven: do offer unto Thy most excellent Majesty of Thine own gifts, bestowed upon us, a pure ✠ Host, a holy ✠ Host, an unspotted ✠ Host, the holy ✠ Bread of eternal life, and the Chalice ✠ of everlasting salvation.

Upon which vouchsafe to look with a propitious and serene countenance, and to accept them, as Thou wert graciously pleased to accept the gifts of Thy just servant Abel, and the sacrifice of our patriarch Abra-

sacérdos tuus Melchísedech, sanctum sacrifícium, immaculátam hóstiam.

SÚPPLICES te rogámus, omnípotens Deus: jube hæc perférri per manus sancti Angeli tui in sublíme altáre tuum, in conspéctu divínæ majestátis tuæ: ut, quotquot ex hac altáris participatióne sacrosánctum Fílii tui Cor✠pus, et Sán✠guinem sumpsérimus, omni benedictióne cælésti et grátia repleámur. Per eúndem Christum, Dóminum nostrum. Amen.

ham, and that which Thy high priest Melchisedech offered to Thee, a holy Sacrifice, and unspotted Victim.

WE MOST humbly beseech Thee, almighty God, command these offerings to be borne by the hands of Thy holy Angel to Thine altar on high, in the sight of Thy divine majesty, that as many as shall partake of the most holy Body ✠ and Blood ✠ of Thy Son at this altar, may be filled with every heavenly grace and blessing. Through the same Christ our Lord. Amen.

The celebrant now commemorates and intercedes for the dead saying:

MEMÉNTO étiam, Dómine, famulórum famularúmque tuárum N. et N., qui nos præcessérunt cum signo fídei, et dórmiunt in somno pacis. Ipsis, Dómine, et ómnibus in Christo quiescéntibus locum refrigérii, lucis, et pacis, ut indúlgeas, deprecámur. Per eúndem Christum, Dóminum nostrum. Amen.

NOBIS quoque peccatóribus fámulis tuis, de multitúdine miseratiónum tuárum sperántibus, partem áliquam et societátem donáre dignéris, cum tuis sanctis Apóstolis et Martýribus: cum Joánne, Stéphano, Matthía, Bárnaba, Ignátio, Alexándro, Marcellíno, Petro, Felicitáte, Perpétua, Agatha, Lúcia, Agnéte, Cæcília, Anastásia, et ómnibus Sanctis tuis: intra quorum nos consórtium, non æstimátor mériti, sed véniæ, quæsumus, largítor admítte. Per Christum, Dóminum nostrum.

REMEMBER also, O Lord, Thy servants and handmaids N. and N., who are gone before us with the sign of faith, and rest in the sleep of peace. To these, O Lord, and to all that rest in Christ, grant, we beseech Thee, a place of refreshment, light, and peace; Through the same Christ our Lord. Amen.

TO US ALSO, Thy sinful servants, confiding in the multitude of Thy mercies, vouchsafe to grant some part and fellowship with Thy holy Apostles and Martyrs, with John, Stephen, Matthias, Barnabas, Ignatius, Alexander, Marcellinus, Peter, Felicitas, Perpetua, Agatha, Lucy, Agnes, Cecilia, Anastasia, and with all Thy Saints, into whose company we beseech Thee to admit us, not weighing our merits, but pardoning our offenses. Through Christ our Lord.

The celebrant reverences the Sacred Host and Chalice and then continues:

PER quem hæc ómnia, Dómine, semper bona creas, sanctí✠ficas, viví✠ficas, bene✠dícis et præstas nobis.

BY Whom, O Lord, Thou dost ever create, sanctify, ✠ quicken, ✠ bless, ✠ and give unto us all these good things.

Per ip✠sum, et cum ip✠so, et in ip✠so, est tibi Deo Patri ✠ omnipoténti, in unitáte Spíritus ✠ Sancti, omnis honor, et glória.

By Him, ✠ and with Him, ✠ and in Him ✠ is to Thee, God the Father ✠ almighty, in the unity of the Holy ✠ Ghost, all honor and glory.

LORD'S PRAYER

PER ómnia sǽcula sæculórum.
℟. Amen.
ORÉMUS: Præcéptis salutáribus móniti, et divína institutióne formáti audémus dícere:

WORLD without end.
℟. Amen.
LET US PRAY. Instructed by Thy saving precepts, and formed by divine institution, we are bold to say:

PATER noster, qui es in cælis, sanctificétur nomen tuum: advéniat regnum tuum: fiat volúntas tua, sicut in cælo et in terra. Panem nostrum quotidiánum da nobis hódie: et dimítte nobis débita nostra, sicut et nos dimíttimus debitóribus nostris: et ne nos indúcas in tentatiónem:
℟. Sed líbera nos a malo.
℣. Amen.

OUR Father, who art in heaven, hallowed be Thy Name; Thy kingdom come; Thy will be done on earth as it is in heaven. Give us this day our daily bread. And forgive us our trespasses, as we forgive those who trespass against us. And lead us not into temptation.
℟. But deliver us from evil.
℣. Amen.

LÍBERA nos, quǽsumus, Dómine, ab ómnibus malis, prætéritis, præséntibus et futúris: et intercedénte beáta et gloriósa semper Vírgine Dei Genetríce María, cum beátis Apóstolis tuis Petro et Paulo, atque Andréa, et ómnibus Sanctis, da propítius pacem in diébus nostris, ut, ope misericórdiæ tuæ adjúti, et a peccáto simus semper líberi et ab omni perturbatióne secúri.

DELIVER us, we beseech Thee, O Lord, from all evils, past, present, and to come; and by the intercession of the Blessed and glorious ever Virgin Mary, Mother of God, and of the holy Apostles, Peter and Paul, and of Andrew, and of all the Saints, mercifully grant peace in our days, that through the assistance of Thy mercy we may be always free from sin, and secure from all disturbance.

Per eúndem Dóminum nostrum Jesum Christum, Fílium tuum. Qui tecum vivit et regnat in unitáte Spíritus Sancti Deus.

Through the same Jesus Christ, Thy Son, our Lord. Who with Thee in the unity of the Holy Ghost liveth and reigneth God,

PER ómnia sǽcula sæculórum.
     ℞. Amen.
    ℣. Pax Dómini sit semper vobíscum.

    ℞. Et cum spíritu tuo.

WORLD without end.
     ℞. Amen.
    ℣. The peace of the Lord be always with you.
    ℞. And with thy spirit.

The celebrant drops a particle of the Sacred Host into the chalice saying:

HÆC commíxtio, et consecrátio Córporis et Sánguinis Dómini nostri Jesu Christi, fiat accipiéntibus nobis in vitam ætérnam. Amen.

MAY this mixture and consecration of the Body and Blood of our Lord Jesus Christ be to us who receive it effectual unto eternal life. Amen.

The celebrant strikes his breast thrice and says:

AGNUS DEI   IV - CUNCTIPÓTENS GÉNITOR DEUS

A-GNUS De- i, * qui tol-lis peccá-ta mundi : mi-se-ré-re no- bis. Agnus De- i, * qui tol-lis peccá-ta mundi : mi-se-ré- re no- bis. Agnus De- i, * qui tol-lis peccá-ta mundi : dona no- bis pa- cem.

AGNUS DEI: Lamb of God, who takest away the sins of the world, have mercy on us. Lamb of God, who takest away the sins of the world, have mercy on us. Lamb of God, who takest away the sins of the world, grant us peace.

The celebrant continues. The Kiss of Peace is omitted today.

DÓMINE Jesu Christe, qui dixísti Apóstolis tuis: Pacem relínquo vobis, pacem meam do vobis: ne respícias peccáta mea, sed fidem Ecclésiæ tuæ; eámque secúndum voluntátem tuam pacificáre et coadunáre dignéris: Qui vivis et regnas Deus per ómnia sæcula sæculórum. Amen.

DÓMINE Jesu Christe, Fili Dei vivi, qui ex voluntáte Patris, cooperánte Spíritu Sancto, per mortem tuam mundum vivificásti: líbera me per hoc sacrosánctum Corpus et Sánguinem tuum ab ómnibus iniquitátibus meis, et univérsis malis: et fac me tuis semper inhærére mandátis, et a te numquam separári permíttas : Qui cum eódem Deo Patre et Spíritu Sancto vivis et regnas Deus in sǽcula sæculórum. Amen.

PERCÉPTIO Córporis tui, Dómine Jesu Christe, quod ego indígnus súmere præsúmo, non mihi provéniat in judícium et condemnatiónem: sed pro tua pietáte prosit mihi ad tutaméntum mentis et córporis, et ad medélam percipiéndam: Qui vivis et regnas cum Deo Patre in unitáte Spíritus Sancti Deus, per ómnia sǽcula sæculórum. Amen.

O LORD Jesus Christ, who saidst to Thine Apostles: Peace I leave you, My peace I give you: regard not my sins, but the faith of Thy Church; and vouchsafe to grant her that peace and unity which is agreeable to Thy will: Who livest and reignest God, world without end. Amen.

O LORD Jesus Christ, Son of the living God, who, according to the will of Thy Father, with the cooperation of the Holy Ghost, hast by Thy death given life to the world; deliver me by this Thy most sacred Body and Blood, from all my iniquities and from all evils; and make me always cleave to Thy commandments, and suffer me never to be separated from Thee, Who livest and reignest, with the same God the Father and the Holy Ghost, God, world without end. Amen.

LET NOT the partaking of Thy Body, O Lord, Jesus Christ, which I, though unworthy, presume to receive, turn to my judgment and condemnation; but let it, through Thy mercy, become a safeguard and remedy, both for soul and body; Who with God the Father, in the unity of the Holy Ghost, livest and reignest God, world without end. Amen.

The celebrant genuflects, rises and then says:

PANEM cæléstem accípiam, et nomen Dómini invocábo.

I WILL take the Bread of heaven, and will call upon the Name of the Lord.

The celebrant strikes his breast and says three times:

DÓMINE, non sum dignus, ut intres sub tectum meum: sed tantum dic verbo, et sanábitur ánima mea.

LORD, I am not worthy that Thou shouldst enter under my roof; say but the word, and my soul shall be healed.

The celebrant makes the Sign of the Cross with the Sacred Host and says:

CORPUS Dómini nostri Jesu Christi custódiat ánimam meam in vitam ætérnam. Amen.

THE BODY of our Lord Jesus Christ preserve my soul unto life everlasting. Amen.

The celebrant consumes the Sacred Host and then purifies the paten saying:

QUID retríbuam Dómino pro ómnibus, quæ retríbuit mihi? Cálicem salutáris accípiam, et nomen Dómini invocábo. Laudans invocábo Dóminum, et ab inimícis meis salvus ero.

WHAT return shall I make to the Lord for all He has given to me? I will take the chalice of salvation, and call upon the Name of the Lord. Praising I will call upon the Lord, and I shall be saved from my enemies.

The celebrant makes the Sign of the Cross with the Chalice saying:

SANGUIS Dómini nostri Jesu Christi custódiat ánimam meam in vitam ætérnam. Amen.

THE BLOOD of our Lord Jesus Christ preserve my soul unto life everlasting. Amen.

The celebrant consumes the Precious Blood as the servers repeat the Confiteor. *At Solemn High Mass this is often chanted:*

CONFÍTEOR Deo omnipoténti, beátæ Maríæ semper Vírgini, beáto Micháéli Archángelo, beáto Joánni Baptístæ, sanctis Apóstolis Petro et Paulo, ómnibus Sanctis, et tibi, pater: quia peccávi nimis cogitatióne, verbo et ópere: (Pércutit sibi pectus ter, dicens) mea culpa, mea culpa, mea máxima culpa.

I CONFESS to almighty God, to the blessed Mary ever Virgin, blessed Michael the Archangel, blessed John the Baptist, the holy Apostles Peter and Paul, to all the Saints, and to you, Father, that I have sinned exceedingly in thought, word, and deed, (Now strike your breast three times, saying:) through my fault, through my fault, through my most grievous fault.

Ideo precor beátam Maríam semper Vírginem, beátum Michaélem Archángelum, beátum Joánnem Baptístam, sanctos Apóstolos Petrum et Paulum, omnes Sanctos, et te, pater, oráre pro me ad Dóminum, Deum nostrum.

℣. Misereátur vestri omnípotens Deus, et, dimíssis peccátis vestris, perdúcat vos ad vitam ætérnam.

℟. Amen.

℣. Indulgéntiam, ✠ absolutiónem et remissiónem peccatórum nostrórum tríbuat nobis omnípotens et miséricors Dóminus.

℟. Amen.

Therefore I beseech the blessed Mary, ever Virgin, blessed Michael the Archangel, blessed John the Baptist, the holy Apostles Peter and Paul, all the Saints, and you, Father, to pray to the Lord our God for me.

℣. May almighty God be merciful to thee, and forgiving thy sins, bring thee to everlasting life.

℟. Amen.

℣. May the ✠ almighty and merciful Lord grant us pardon, absolution, and remission of our sins.

℟. Amen.

The celebrant faces the people holding up one of the Sacred Hosts and says:

Ecce Agnus Dei, ecce qui tollit peccáta mundi.

Behold the Lamb of God, behold Him Who taketh away the sins of the world.

The following is said three times:

Dómine, non sum dignus, ut intres sub tectum meum: sed tantum dic verbo, et sanábitur ánima mea.

Lord, I am not worthy that Thou shouldst enter under my roof; say but the word, and my soul shall be healed.

After distributing Holy Communion the celebrant purifies the sacred vessels. At Solemn High Mass the subdeacon takes the Chalice from the celebrant for purifying as the celebrant says:

Quod ore súmpsimus, Dómine, pura mente capiámus; et de múnere temporáli fiat nobis remédium sempitérnum.

Grant, O Lord, that what we have taken with our mouth, we may receive with a pure mind; and from a temporal gift may it become to us an eternal remedy.

Corpus tuum, Dómine, quod sumpsi, et Sanguis, quem potávi, adhǽreat viscéribus meis: et præsta; ut in me non remáneat scélerum

May Thy Body, O Lord, which I have received, and Thy Blood which I have drunk, cleave to my bowels; and grant that no stain of sin may remain

mácula, quem pura et sancta refecérunt sacraménta: Qui vivis et regnas in sǽcula sæculórum. Amen.

in me, who have been fed with this pure and holy Sacrament; Who livest and reignest for ever and ever. Amen.

The celebrant places the reserved Host into a separate chalice before washing his fingers, and places this chalice in the middle of the altar and covers it with the pall, paten and veil.

The celebrant reads the Communion on the Epistle side of the altar:

 COMMUNION   JOHN 13: 12, 13

Dómi- nus Je-sus, * postquam cœná- vit cum discí-pu-lis su- is, la-vit pe-des e- ó-rum, et a- it il- lis : Sci- tis quid fé-ce-rim vo- bis, e-go Dómi- nus et Ma-gíster? Exémplum de-di vo- bis,

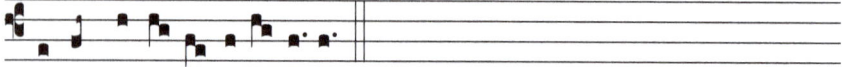

ut et vos i- ta fa-ci- á-tis.

COMMUNION: The Lord Jesus, after He had supped with His disciples, washed their feet, and said to them: Know you what I, your Lord and Master, have done to you? I gave you an example, that you also may do likewise.

POSTCOMMUNION

The celebrant turns to face the people saying:

℣. Dóminus vobíscum.
℟. Et cum spíritu tuo.

℣. The Lord be with you.
℟. And with thy spirit.

<table>
<tr><td>

ORÉMUS.

REFÉCTI vitálibus aliméntis, quǽsumus, Dómine, Deus noster: ut, quod témpore nostræ mortalitátis exséquimur, immortalitátis tuæ múnere consequámur. Per Dóminum nostrum Jesum Christum, Fílium tuum: qui tecum vivit et regnat in unitáte Spíritus Sancti Deus, per ómnia sǽcula sæculórum.

℟. Amen.

</td><td>

LET US PRAY.

STRENGTHENED with life-giving Food, we beseech Thee, O Lord, our God, that what we do in our mortal life may bring us to the reward of life immortal with Thee. Through Jesus Christ, Thy Son our Lord, Who liveth and reigneth with Thee, in the unity of the Holy Ghost, God, world without end.

℟. Amen.

</td></tr>
</table>

CONCLUSION

The celebrant turns to face the people saying:

℣. Dóminus vobíscum.

℟. Et cum spíritu tuo.

℣. The Lord be with you.

℟. And with thy spirit.

At Solemn High Mass the deacon chants the Ite, missa est:

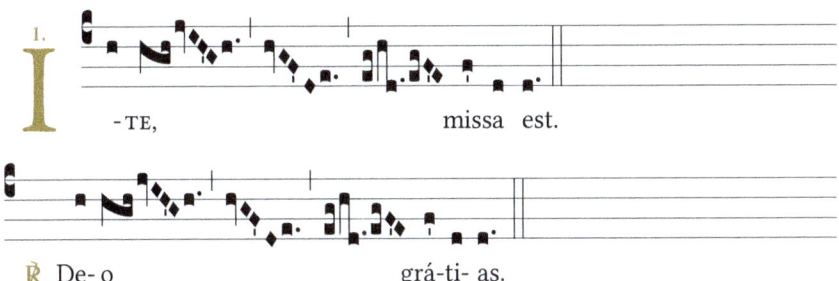

- TE,   missa est.

℟. De- o   grá-ti- as.

ITE MISSA EST: ℣. Go, the Mass is ended. ℟. Thanks be to God.

The celebrant bows over the altar and silently says:

Pláceat tibi, sancta Trínitas, obséquium servitútis meæ: et præsta; ut sacrifícium, quod óculis tuæ majestátis indígnus óbtuli, tibi sit acceptábile, mihíque et ómnibus, pro quibus illud óbtuli, sit, te miseránte, propitiábile. Per Christum, Dóminum nostrum. Amen.

MAY the performance of my homage be pleasing to Thee, O holy Trinity: and grant that the Sacrifice which I, though unworthy, have offered up in the sight of Thy Majesty, may be acceptable to Thee, and through Thy mercy, be a propitiation for me, and for all those for whom I have offered it. Through Christ our Lord. Amen.

The people kneel and the celebrant turns towards them for the blessing saying:

℣. Benedícat vos omnípotens Deus, Pater, et Fílius, ✠ et Spíritus Sanctus.
℟. Amen.

℣. May almighty God the Father, Son, ✠ and Holy Ghost, bless you.
℟. Amen.

The people stand as the celebrant moves to the Gospel side of the altar and reads the Last Gospel:

℣. Dóminus vobíscum.
℟. Et cum spíritu tuo.

℣. The Lord be with you.
℟. And with thy spirit.

THE BEGINNING ✠ OF THE HOLY GOSPEL
ACCORDING TO JOHN
John 1: 1-14

IN princípio erat Verbum, et Verbum erat apud Deum, et Deus erat Verbum. Hoc erat in princípio apud Deum. Omnia per ipsum facta sunt: et sine ipso factum est nihil, quod factum est: in ipso vita erat, et vita erat lux hóminum: et lux in ténebris lucet, et ténebræ eam non comprehendérunt.

IN the beginning was the Word, and the Word was with God, and the Word was God. The same was in the beginning with God. All things were made by Him, and without Him was made nothing that was made: in Him was life, and the life was the Light of men; and the Light shineth in darkness, and the darkness did not comprehend it.

Fuit homo missus a Deo, cui nomen erat Joánnes. Hic venit in testimónium, ut testimónium perhibéret de lúmine, ut omnes créderent per illum. Non erat ille lux, sed ut testimónium perhibéret de lúmine.

Erat lux vera, quæ illúminat omnem hóminem veniéntem in hunc mundum. In mundo erat, et mundus per ipsum factus est, et mundus eum non cognóvit. In própria venit, et sui eum non recepérunt. Quotquot autem recepérunt eum, dedit eis potestátem fílios Dei fíeri, his, qui credunt in nómine ejus : qui non ex sanguínibus, neque ex voluntáte carnis, neque ex voluntáte viri, sed ex Deo nati sunt.

(Genufléctit dicens:)

Et Verbum caro factum est, et habitávit in nobis: et vídimus glóriam ejus, glóriam quasi Unigéniti a Patre, plenum grátiæ et veritátis.

℟. Deo grátias.

There was a man sent from God, whose name was John. This man came for a witness, to testify concerning the Light, that all might believe through Him. He was not the Light, but he was to testify concerning the Light.

That was the true Light, which enlighteneth every man that cometh into this world. He was in the world, and the world was made by Him, and the world knew Him not. He came unto His own, and His own received Him not. But as many as received Him to them He gave power to become sons of God, to them that believe in His Name, who are born not of blood, nor of the will of the flesh, nor of the will of man, but of God.

(Here all kneel.)

And the Word was made flesh, and dwelt among us: and we saw His glory, the glory as of the Only begotten of the Father, full of grace and truth.

℟. Thanks be to God.

THE PROCESSION OF THE BLESSED SACRAMENT

Today a special place in a side chapel or altar is prepared for the Chalice with the reserved Host to be reposed until the following day. The celebrant removes his chasuble and is robed in a white cope for the procession. He carries the Blessed Sacrament which is continually incensed by thurifers until they reach the altar of repose. The hymn Pange lingua *is sung as needed throughout the procession until the deacon places the Chalice on the altar, at which time the verse (5.)* Tantum Ergo *is sung. After* Venerémur cérnui *the celebrant incenses the Blessed Sacrament.*

HYMN   PANGE LINGUA

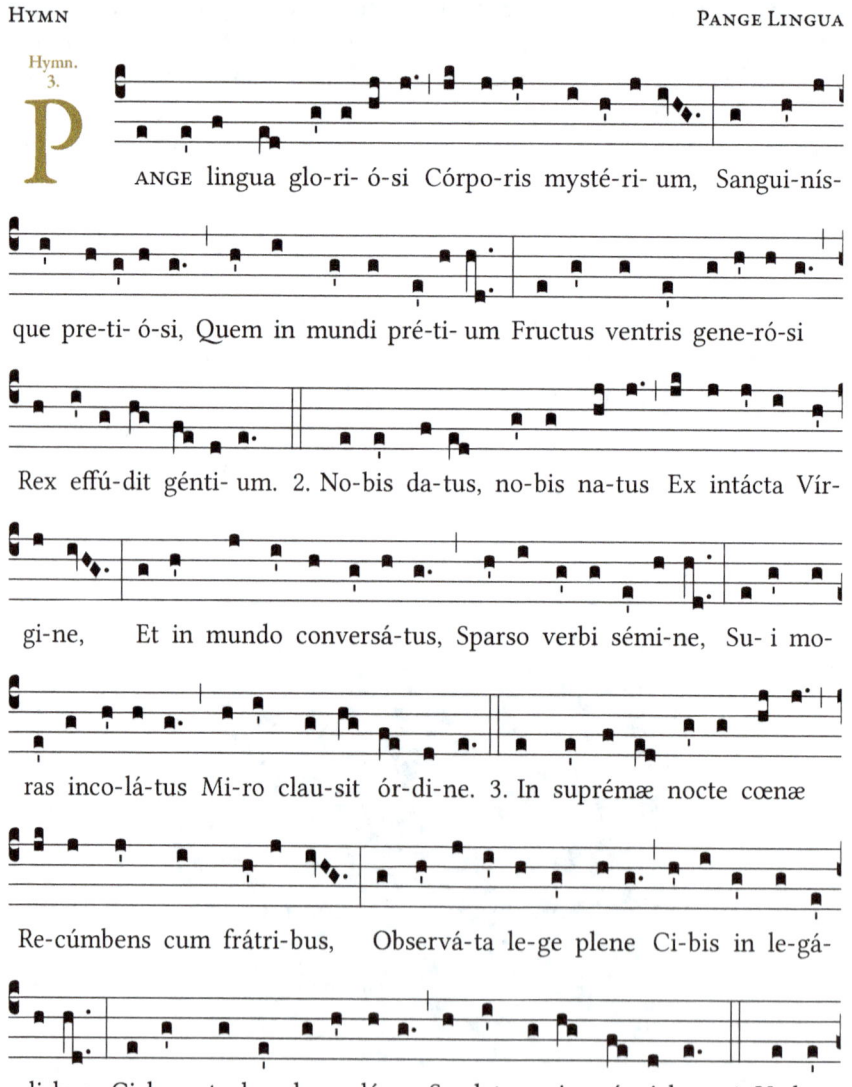

ANGE lingua glo-ri- ó-si Córpo-ris mysté-ri- um, Sangui-nís-

que pre-ti- ó-si, Quem in mundi pré-ti- um Fructus ventris gene-ró-si

Rex effú-dit génti- um. 2. No-bis da-tus, no-bis na-tus Ex intácta Vír-

gi-ne, Et in mundo conversá-tus, Sparso verbi sémi-ne, Su- i mo-

ras inco-lá-tus Mi-ro clau-sit ór-di-ne. 3. In suprémæ nocte cœnæ

Re-cúmbens cum frátri-bus, Observá-ta le-ge plene Ci-bis in le-gá-

li-bus, Ci-bum turbæ du- o-dénæ Se dat su- is má-ni-bus. 4. Verbum

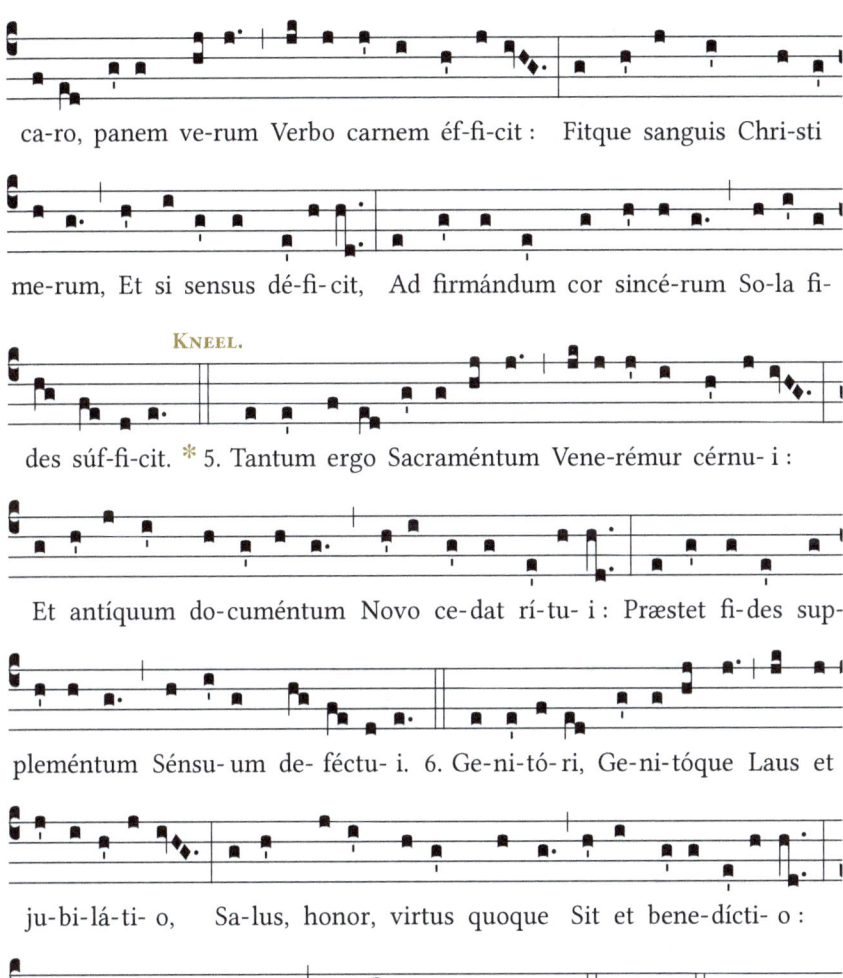

ca-ro, panem ve-rum Verbo carnem éf-fi-cit : Fitque sanguis Chri-sti

me-rum, Et si sensus dé-fi-cit, Ad firmándum cor sincé-rum So-la fi-

Kneel.

des súf-fi-cit. * 5. Tantum ergo Sacraméntum Vene-rémur cérnu- i :

Et antíquum do-cuméntum Novo ce-dat rí-tu- i : Præstet fi-des sup-

pleméntum Sénsu- um de- féctu- i. 6. Ge-ni-tó- ri, Ge-ni-tóque Laus et

ju-bi-lá-ti- o, Sa-lus, honor, virtus quoque Sit et bene-dícti- o :

Pro-ce-dénti ab utróque Compar sit lau-dá- ti- o. A-men.

1. Pange língua, gloriósi	1. Sing, my tongue, the Saviour's glory:
Córporis mystérium,	Of His Flesh the mystery sing
Sanguinísque pretiósi,	Of His Blood all price exceeding.
Quem in mundi prétium	Shed by our immortal King.
Fructus ventris generósi	Destined for the world's redemption
Rex effúdit géntium	From a noble womb to spring.

2. Nobis datus, nobis natus
Ex intácta Vírgine,
Et in mundo conversátus,
Sparso verbi sémine.
Sui moras incolátus.
Miro clausit órdine.

2. Of a pure and spotless Virgin,
Born for us on earth below,
He, as Man with man conversing,
Stayed the seeds of truth to sow,
Then He closed in solemn order
Wondrously His life of woe.

3. In suprémæ nocte cœnæ
Recúmbens cum frátribus,
Observáta lege plene
Cibis in legálibus,
Cibum turbæ duodénæ
Se dat suis mánibus.

3. On the night of His last supper,
Seated with His chosen band,
He, the paschal victim eating,
First fulfills the Law's command;
Then as food to all His brethren
Gives himself with His own hand.

4. Verbum caro, panem verum
Verbo carnem éfficit;
Fitque sanguis Christi merum:
Et si sensus déficit,
Ad firmándum cor sincérum
Sola fides súfficit.

4. Word made Flesh, the bread of nature,
By His words to Flesh He turns;
Wine into His Blood He changes:
What though sense no change discerns,
Only be the heart in earnest,
Faith her lesson quickly learns.

Kneel for Tantum ergo.

5. Tantum ergo Sacraméntum
Venerémur cérnui:
Et antíquum documéntum
Novo cedat rítui:
Præstet fides suppleméntum
Sénsuum deféctui.

5. Down in adoration falling,
Lo, the Sacred Host we hail,
Lo, o'er ancient forms departing
Newer rites of grace prevail;
Faith for all defects supplying,
Where the feeble senses fail.

6. Genitóri, Genitóque
Laus et jubilátio:
Salus, honor, virtus quoque
Sit et benedíctio
Procedénti ab utróque
Compar sit laudátio.

6. To the everlasting Father
And the Son who reigns on high
With the Holy Ghost proceeding
Forth from each eternally,
Be salvation, honor, blessing,
Might and endless majesty.

Amen.

Amen.

Vespers

At Vespers the antiphons and Psalms are recited recto tono *rather than sung.*

The Pater noster *and* Ave María *are said silently.*

Pater noster, qui es in cælis, sanctificétur nomen tuum: advéniat regnum tuum: fiat volúntas tua, sicut in cælo et in terra. Panem nostrum quotidiánum da nobis hódie: et dimítte nobis débita nostra, sicut et nos dimíttimus debitóribus nostris: et ne nos indúcas in tentatiónem: sed líbera nos a malo. Amen.

Our Father, who art in heaven, hallowed be Thy name. Thy kingdom come. Thy will be done on earth as it is in heaven. Give us this day our daily bread. And forgive us our trespasses, as we forgive those who trespass against us. And lead us not into temptation: but deliver us from evil. Amen.

Ave María, grátia plena; Dóminus tecum: benedícta tu in muliéribus, et benedíctus fructus ventris tui Jesus. Sancta María, Mater Dei, ora pro nobis peccatóribus, nunc et in hora mortis nostræ. Amen.

Hail Mary, full of grace; The Lord is with thee; blessed art thou amongst women, and blessed is the fruit of thy womb, Jesus. Holy Mary, Mother of God, pray for us sinners, now and at the hour of our death. Amen.

Antiphon 1: Cálicem * salutáris accípiam et nomen Dómini invocábo.

Antiphon 1: I will take the cup of salvation; * and call upon the Name of the Lord.

Psalm 115

1. Crédidi, propter quod locútus sum : * ego autem humiliátus sum nimis.

1. I have believed, therefore have I spoken; * but I have been humbled exceedingly.

2. Ego dixi in excéssu meo : * Omnis homo mendax.

2. I said in my excess: * Every man is a liar.

3. Quid retríbuam Dómino, * pro ómnibus, quæ retríbuit mihi?

3. What shall I render to the Lord, * for all the things that He hath rendered to me?

4. Cálicem salutáris accípiam : * et nomen Dómini invocábo.

4. I will take the chalice of salvation; * and I will call upon the name of the Lord.

5. Vota mea Dómino reddam coram omni pópulo ejus : * pretiósa in conspéctu Dómini mors sanctórum ejus :

6. O Dómine, quia ego servus tuus : * ego servus tuus, et fílius ancíllæ tuæ.

7. Dirupísti víncula mea : tibi sacrificábo hóstiam laudis, * et nomen Dómini invocábo.

8. Vota mea Dómino reddam in conspéctu omnis pópuli ejus : * in átriis domus Dómini, in médio tui, Jerúsalem.

Antiphon: Cálicem salutáris accípiam et nomen Dómini invocábo.

Antiphon 2: Cum his, * qui odérunt pacem eram pacíficus : dum loquébar illis, impugnábant me gratis.

5. I will pay my vows to the Lord before all his people: * precious in the sight of the Lord is the death of his saints.

6. O Lord, for I am Thy servant: * I am Thy servant, and the son of Thy handmaid.

7. Thou hast broken my bonds: * I will sacrifice to Thee the sacrifice of praise, and I will call upon the name of the Lord.

8. I will pay my vows to the Lord in the sight of all his people: * in the courts of the house of the Lord, in the midst of thee, O Jerusalem.

Antiphon: I will take the cup of salvation; and call upon the Name of the Lord.

Antiphon 2: With them * that hate peace I was peaceable; when I spoke unto them they fought against me without a cause.

Psalm 119

1. Ad Dóminum cum tribulárer clamávi : * et exaudívit me.

2. Dómine, líbera ánimam meam a lábiis iníquis, * et a lingua dolósa.

3. Quid detur tibi, aut quid apponátur tibi * ad linguam dolósam?

4. Sagíttæ poténtis acútæ, * cum carbónibus desolatóriis.

5. Heu mihi! quia incolátus meus prolongátus est : habitávi cum habitántibus Cedar : * multum íncola fuit ánima mea.

1. In my trouble I cried to the Lord: * and he heard me.

2. O Lord, deliver my soul from wicked lips, * and a deceitful tongue.

3. What shall be given to thee, or what shall be added to thee, * to a deceitful tongue?

4. The sharp arrows of the mighty, * with coals that lay waste.

5. Woe is me, that my sojourning is prolonged! I have dwelt with the inhabitants of Cedar: * my soul hath been long a sojourner.

6. Cum his, qui odérunt pacem, eram pacíficus : * cum loquébar illis, impugnábant me gratis.

ANTIPHON: Cum his, qui odérunt pacem eram pacíficus : dum loquébar illis, impugnábant me gratis.

ANTIPHON 3: Ab homínibus * iníquis líbera me, Dómine.

6. With them that hated peace I was peaceable: * when I spoke to them they fought against me without cause.

ANTIPHON: With them that hate peace I was peaceable; when I spoke unto them they fought against me without a cause.

ANTIPHON 3: O Lord, preserve me * from the unjust men.

PSALM 139

1. Éripe me, Dómine, ab hómine malo : * a viro iníquo éripe me.

2. Qui cogitavérunt iniquitátes in corde : * tota die constituébant prælia.

3. Acuérunt linguas suas sicut serpéntis : * venénum áspidum sub lábiis eórum.

4. Custódi me, Dómine, de manu peccatóris : * et ab homínibus iníquis éripe me.

5. Qui cogitavérunt supplantáre gressus meos : * abscondérunt supérbi láqueum mihi :

6. Et funes extendérunt in láqueum : * juxta iter scándalum posuérunt mihi.

7. Dixi Dómino : Deus meus es tu : * exáudi, Dómine, vocem deprecatiónis meæ.

8. Dómine, Dómine, virtus salútis meæ : * obumbrásti super caput meum in die belli.

9. Ne tradas me, Dómine, a desidério meo peccatóri : cogitavérunt contra me, * ne derelínquas me, ne forte exalténtur.

1. Deliver me, O Lord, from the evil man: * rescue me from the unjust man.

2. Who have devised iniquities in their hearts: * all the day long they designed battles.

3. They have sharpened their tongues like a serpent: * the venom of asps is under their lips.

4. Keep me, O Lord, from the hand of the wicked: * and from unjust men deliver me.

5. Who have proposed to supplant my steps: * the proud have hidden a net for me.

6. And they have stretched out cords for a snare: * they have laid for me a stumbling block by the wayside.

7. I said to the Lord: Thou art my God: * hear, O Lord, the voice of my supplication.

8. O Lord, Lord, the strength of my salvation: * Thou hast overshadowed my head in the day of battle.

9. Give me not up, O Lord, from my desire to the wicked: * they have plotted against me; do not Thou forsake me, lest they should triumph.

10. Caput circúitus eórum : * labor labiórum ipsórum opériet eos.

11. Cadent super eos carbónes, in ignem dejícies eos : * in miséri-is non subsístent.

12. Vir linguósus non dirigétur in terra : * virum injústum mala cápi-ent in intéritu.

13. Cognóvi quia fáciet Dóminus judícium ínopis : * et vindíctam páu-perum.

14. Verúmtamen justi confitebún-tur nómini tuo : * et habitábunt recti cum vultu tuo.

ANTIPHON: Ab homínibus iníquis líbera me, Dómine.

ANTIPHON 4: Custódi me * a láqueo, quem statuérunt mihi, et a scándalis operántium iniquitátem.

10. The head of them compassing me about: * the labour of their lips shall overwhelm them.

11. Burning coals shall fall upon them; Thou wilt cast them down into the fire: * in miseries they shall not be able to stand.

12. A man full of tongue shall not be established in the earth: * evil shall catch the unjust man unto destruc-tion.

13. I know that the Lord will do jus-tice to the needy, * and will revenge the poor.

14. But as for the just, they shall give glory to Thy name: * and the upright shall dwell with Thy countenance.

ANTIPHON: O Lord, preserve me from the unjust men.

ANTIPHON 4: Keep me * from the snare which they have laid for me, and the sins of the workers of iniquity.

PSALM 140

1. Dómine, clamávi ad te, exáudi me : * inténde voci meæ, cum clamáve-ro ad te.

2. Dirigátur orátio mea sicut in-cénsum in conspéctu tuo : * elevátio mánuum meárum sacrifícium ves-pertínum.

3. Pone, Dómine, custódi-am ori meo : * et óstium circumstán-tiæ lábiis meis.

4. Non declínes cor meum in ver-ba malítiæ : * ad excusándas excu-satiónes in peccátis.

1. I have cried to Thee, O Lord, hear me: * hearken to my voice, when I cry to thee.

2. Let my prayer be directed as in-cense in Thy sight; * the lifting up of my hands, as evening sacrifice.

3. Set a watch, O Lord, before my mouth: * and a door round about my lips.

4. Incline not my heart to evil words; * to make excuses in sins.

5. Cum homínibus operántibus in- iquitátem : * et non communicábo cum eléctis eórum.

6. Corrípiet me justus in mi- sericórdia, et increpábit me : * óleum autem peccatóris non impínguet ca- put meum.

7. Quóniam adhuc et orátio mea in beneplácitis eórum : * absórpti sunt juncti petræ júdices eórum.

8. Audient verba mea quóniam po- tuérunt : * sicut crassitúdo terræ erúp- ta est super terram.

9. Dissipáta sunt ossa nostra se- cus inférnum : † quia ad te, Dómine, Dómine, óculi mei : * in te sperávi, non áuferas ánimam meam.

10. Custódi me a láqueo, quem statuérunt mihi : * et a scándalis oper- ántium iniquitátem.

11. Cadent in retiáculo ejus pec- catóres : * singuláriter sum ego do- nec tránseam.

ANTIPHON: Custódi me a láqueo, quem statuérunt mihi, et a scándalis operántium iniquitátem.

5. With men that work iniquity: * and I will not communicate with the choicest of them.

6. The just man shall correct me in mercy, and shall reprove me: * but let not the oil of the sinner fatten my head.

7. For my prayer also shall still be against the things with which they are well pleased: * their judges falling upon the rock have been swallowed up.

8. They shall hear my words, for they have prevailed: * as when the thickness of the earth is broken up upon the ground.

9. Our bones are scattered by the side of hell. * But to Thee, O Lord, Lord, are my eyes: in Thee have I put my trust, take not away my soul.

10. Keep me from the snare, which they have laid for me, * and from the stumbling blocks of them that work iniquity.

11. The wicked shall fall in his net: * I am alone until I pass.

ANTIPHON: Keep me from the snare which they have laid for me, and the sins of the workers of iniquity.

ANTIPHON 5: Considerábam * ad déxteram, et vidébam, et non erat qui cognósceret me.

ANTIPHON 5: I looked * on my right hand and beheld: but there was no man that would know me.

PSALM 141

1. Voce mea ad Dóminum clamávi : * voce mea ad Dóminum deprecátus sum :

2. Effúndo in conspéctu ejus oratiónem meam, * et tribulatiónem meam ante ipsum pronúntio.

3. In deficiéndo ex me spíritum meum : * et tu cognovísti sémitas meas.

4. In via hac, qua ambulábam, * abscondérunt láqueum mihi.

5. Considerábam ad déxteram, et vidébam : * et non erat qui cognósceret me.

6. Périit fuga a me : * et non est qui requírat ánimam meam.

7. Clamávi ad te, Dómine, dixi : Tu es spes mea, * pórtio mea in terra vivéntium.

8. Inténde ad deprecatiónem meam : * quia humiliátus sum nimis.

9. Líbera me a persequéntibus me : * quia confortáti sunt super me.

10. Educ de custódia ánimam meam ad confiténdum nómini tuo : * me exspéctant justi, donec retríbuas mihi.

1. I cried to the Lord with my voice: * with my voice I made supplication to the Lord.

2. In His sight I pour out my prayer, * and before Him I declare my trouble:

3. When my spirit failed me, * then Thou knewest my paths.

4. In this way wherein I walked, * they have hidden a snare for me.

5. I looked on my right hand, and beheld, * and there was no one that would know me.

6. Flight hath failed me: * and there is no one that hath regard to my soul.

7. I cried to Thee, O Lord: * I said: Thou art my hope, my portion in the land of the living.

8. Attend to my supplication: * for I am brought very low.

9. Deliver me from my persecutors; * for they are stronger than I.

10. Bring my soul out of prison, that I may praise Thy name: * the just wait for me, until Thou reward me.

ANTIPHON: Considerábam ad déxteram, et vidébam, et non erat qui cognósceret me.

ANTIPHON: I looked on my right hand and beheld: but there was no man that would know me.

Magníficat

Antiphon: Cœnántibus autem illis * accépit Jesus panem, et benedíxit, ac fregit, dedítque discípulis suis.

Antiphon: And, as they were eating * Jesus took bread, and blessed, and broke it, and gave to His disciples.

1. Magníficat ✠ ánima mea Dóminum.

1. My soul ✠ doth magnify the Lord.

2. Et exsultávit spíritus meus : * in Deo, salutári meo.

2. And my spirit hath rejoiced * in God my Saviour.

3. Quia respéxit humilitátem ancíllæ suæ : * ecce enim ex hoc beátam me dicent omnes generatiónes.

3. Because He hath regarded the humility of His handmaid; * for behold from henceforth all generations shall call me blessed.

4. Quia fecit mihi magna qui potens est : * et sanctum nomen ejus.

4. Because He that is mighty, hath done great things to me; * and holy is His name.

5. Et misericórdia ejus a progénie in progénies * timéntibus eum.

5. And His mercy is from generation unto generations, * to them that fear him.

6. Fecit poténtiam in bráchio suo : * dispérsit supérbos mente cordis sui.

6. He hath shewed might in His arm: * he hath scattered the proud in the conceit of their heart.

7. Depósuit poténtes de sede, * et exaltávit húmiles.

7. He hath put down the mighty from their seat, * and hath exalted the humble.

8. Esuriéntes implévit bonis : * et dívites dimísit iná18es.

8. He hath filled the hungry with good things; * and the rich He hath sent empty away.

9. Suscépit Israël púerum suum, * recordátus misericórdiæ suæ.

9. He hath received Israel His servant, * being mindful of His mercy:

10. Sicut locútus est ad patres nostros, * Abraham et sémini ejus in sǽcula.

10. As He spoke to our fathers, * to Abraham and to his seed for ever.

Antiphon: Cœnántibus autem illis accépit Jesus panem, et benedíxit, ac fregit, dedítque discípulis suis.

Antiphon: And, as they were eating Jesus took bread, and blessed, and broke it, and gave to His disciples.

At the conclusion of the antiphon following the Magníficat, *all kneel and say:*

ANTIPHON: Christus factus est pro nobis obédiens usque ad mortem.

ANTIPHON: Christ became obedient for us unto death.

At the conclusion of the antiphon Christus factus est, *the* Pater noster *is said in silence.*

PSALM 50

1. Miserére mei, Deus, * secúndum magnam misericórdiam tuam.

2. Et secúndum multitúdinem miseratiónum tuárum, * dele iniquitátem meam.

3. Amplius lava me ab iniquitáte mea : * et a peccáto meo munda me.

4. Quóniam iniquitátem meam ego cognósco : * et peccátum meum contra me est semper.

5. Tibi soli peccávi, et malum coram te feci : * ut justificéris in sermónibus tuis, et vincas cum judicáris.

6. Ecce enim in iniquitátibus concéptus sum : * et in peccátis concépit me mater mea.

7. Ecce enim veritátem dilexísti : * incérta et occúlta sapiéntiæ tuæ manifestásti mihi.

8. Aspérges me hyssópo, et mundábor : * lavábis me, et super nivem dealbábor.

9. Audítui meo dabis gáudium et lætítiam : * et exsultábunt ossa humiliáta.

10. Avérte fáciem tuam a peccátis meis : * et omnes iniquitátes meas dele.

1: Have mercy on me, O God, * according to Thy great mercy.

2. And according to the multitude of Thy tender mercies * blot out my iniquity.

3. Wash me yet more from my iniquity, * and cleanse me from my sin.

4. For I know my iniquity, * and my sin is always before me.

5. To Thee only have I sinned, and have done evil before Thee: * that Thou mayst be justified in Thy words, and mayst overcome when Thou art judged.

6. For behold I was conceived in iniquities; * and in sins did my mother conceive me.

7. For behold Thou hast loved truth: * the uncertain and hidden things of Thy wisdom Thou hast made manifest to me.

8. Thou shalt sprinkle me with hyssop, and I shall be cleansed: * Thou shalt wash me, and I shall be made whiter than snow.

9. To my hearing Thou shalt give joy and gladness: * and the bones that have been humbled shall rejoice.

10. Turn away Thy face from my sins, * and blot out all my iniquities.

11. Cor mundum crea in me, Deus : * et spíritum rectum ínnova in viscéribus meis.

11. Create a clean heart in me, O God: * and renew a right spirit within my bowels.

12. Ne projícias me a fácie tua : * et spíritum sanctum tuum ne áuferas a me.

12. Cast me not away from Thy face; * and take not Thy holy spirit from me.

13. Redde mihi lætítiam salutáris tui : * et spíritu principáli confírma me.

13. Restore unto me the joy of Thy salvation, * and strengthen me with a perfect spirit.

14. Docébo iníquos vias tuas : * et ímpii ad te converténtur.

14. I will teach the unjust Thy ways: * and the wicked shall be converted to Thee.

15. Líbera me de sanguínibus, Deus, Deus salútis meæ : * et exsultábit lingua mea justítiam tuam.

15. Deliver me from blood, O God, Thou God of my salvation: * and my tongue shall extol Thy justice.

16. Dómine, lábia mea apéries : * et os meum annuntiábit laudem tuam.

16. O Lord, Thou wilt open my lips: * and my mouth shall declare Thy praise.

17. Quóniam si voluísses sacrifícium, dedíssem útique : * holocáustis non delectáberis.

17. For if Thou hadst desired sacrifice, I would indeed have given it: * with burnt offerings Thou wilt not be delighted.

18. Sacrifícium Deo spíritus contribulátus : * cor contrítum et humiliátum, Deus, non despícies.

18. A sacrifice to God is an afflicted spirit: * a contrite and humbled heart, O God, Thou wilt not despise.

19. Benígne fac, Dómine, in bona voluntáte tua Sion : * ut ædificéntur muri Jerúsalem.

19. Deal favourably, O Lord, in Thy good will with Sion; * that the walls of Jerusalem may be built up.

20. Tunc acceptábis sacrifícium justítiæ, oblatiónes, et holocáusta : * tunc impónent super altáre tuum vítulos.

20. Then shalt Thou accept the sacrifice of justice, oblations and whole burnt offerings: * then shall they lay calves upon Thy altar.

RÉSPICE, quǽsumus, Dómine, super hanc famíliam tuam, pro qua Dóminus noster Jesus Christus non dubitávit mánibus tradi nocéntium, et crucis subíre torméntum:

[*Dícitur sub siléntio:* Qui tecum vivit et regnat in unitáte Spíritus Sancti, Deus, per ómnia sǽcula sæculórum. ℟. Amen.]

LOOK down, we beseech Thee, O Lord, on this Thy family, for which our Lord Jesus Christ did not hesitate to be delivered up into the hands of wicked men, and to suffer the torment of the Cross.

[*Said in silence:* Who with thee liveth and reigneth, in the unity of the Holy Ghost, God, world without end. ℟. Amen.]

STRIPPING OF THE ALTAR

Following Vespers the celebrant intones the Antiphon Divisérunt sibi *and then proceeds with the ministers to strip the altar while reciting Psalm 21 in a submissive voice. The choir recites the Psalm following the intonation of the antiphon.*

ANTIPHON: Divisérunt sibi vestiménta mea : et super vestem meam misérunt sortem.

ANTIPHON: They parted My garments amongst them; and upon My vesture they cast lots.

PSALM 21

1. Deus, Deus meus, réspice in me : quare me dereliquísti? * longe a salúte mea verba delictórum meórum.

2. Deus meus, clamábo per diem, et non exáudies : * et nocte, et non ad insipiéntiam mihi.

3. Tu autem in sancto hábitas : * laus Israël.

4. In te speravérunt patres nostri : * speravérunt, et liberásti eos.

5. Ad te clamavérunt, et salvi facti sunt : * in te speravérunt, et non sunt confúsi.

6. Ego autem sum vermis, et non homo : * oppróbrium hóminum, et abjéctio plebis.

1. O God my God, look upon me: † why hast Thou forsaken me? * Far from my salvation are the words of my sins.

2. O my God, I shall cry by day, and Thou wilt not hear: * and by night, and it shall not be reputed as folly in me.

3. But Thou dwellest in the holy place, * the praise of Israel.

4. In Thee have our fathers hoped: * they have hoped, and Thou hast delivered them.

5. They cried to Thee, and they were saved: * they trusted in Thee, and were not confounded.

6. But I am a worm, and no man: * the reproach of men, and the outcast of the people.

7. Omnes vidéntes me derisérunt me : * locúti sunt lábiis, et movérunt caput.

8. Sperávit in Dómino, erípiat eum : * salvum fáciat eum, quóniam vult eum.

9. Quóniam tu es, qui extraxísti me de ventre : * spes mea ab ubéribus matris meæ. In te projéctus sum ex útero.

10. De ventre matris meæ Deus meus es tu, * ne discésseris a me :

11. Quóniam tribulátio próxima est : * quóniam non est qui ádjuvet.

12. Circumdedérunt me vítuli multi : * tauri pingues obsedérunt me.

13. Aperuérunt super me os suum : * sicut leo rápiens et rúgiens.

14. Sicut aqua effúsus sum : * et dispérsa sunt ómnia ossa mea.

15. Factum est cor meum tamquam cera liquéscens : * in médio ventris mei.

16. Aruit tamquam testa virtus mea, † et lingua mea adhǽsit fáucibus meis : * et in púlverem mortis deduxísti me.

17. Quóniam circumdedérunt me canes multi : * concílium malignántium obsédit me.

18. Fodérunt manus meas et pedes meos : * dinumeravérunt ómnia ossa mea.

19. Ipsi vero consideravérunt et inspexérunt me : * divisérunt sibi vestiménta mea, et super vestem meam misérunt sortem.

20. Tu autem, Dómine, ne elongáveris auxílium tuum a me : * ad defensiónem meam cónspice.

7. All they that saw me have laughed me to scorn: * they have spoken with the lips, and wagged the head.

8. He hoped in the Lord, let him deliver him: * let him save him, seeing he delighteth in him.

9. For Thou art he that hast drawn me out of the womb: * my hope from the breasts of my mother. I was cast upon Thee from the womb.

10. From my mother's womb Thou art my God, * depart not from me.

11. For tribulation is very near: * for there is none to help me.

12. Many calves have surrounded me: * fat bulls have besieged me.

13. They have opened their mouths against me, * as a lion ravening and roaring.

14. I am poured out like water; * and all my bones are scattered.

15. My heart is become like wax melting * in the midst of my bowels.

16. My strength is dried up like a potsherd, and my tongue hath cleaved to my jaws: * and Thou hast brought me down into the dust of death.

17. For many dogs have encompassed me: * the council of the malignant hath besieged me.

18. They have dug my hands and feet. * They have numbered all my bones.

19. And they have looked and stared upon me. * They parted my garments amongst them; and upon my vesture they cast lots.

20. But Thou, O Lord, remove not Thy help to a distance from me; * look towards my defense.

21. Erue a frámea, Deus, ánimam meam : * et de manu canis únicam meam.

22. Salva me ex ore leónis : * et a córnibus unicórnium humilitátem meam.

23. Narrábo nomen tuum frátribus meis : * in médio Ecclésiæ laudábo te.

24. Qui timétis Dóminum, laudáte eum : * univérsum semen Jacob, glorificáte eum.

25. Tímeat eum omne semen Israël : * quóniam non sprevit, neque despéxit deprecatiónem páuperis :

26. Nec avértit fáciem suam a me : * et cum clamárem ad eum, exaudívit me.

27. Apud te laus mea in ecclésia magna : * vota mea reddam in conspéctu timéntium eum.

28. Edent páuperes, et saturabúntur : † et laudábunt Dóminum qui requírunt eum : * vivent corda eórum in sǽculum sǽculi.

29. Reminiscéntur et converténtur ad Dóminum * univérsi fines terræ :

30. Et adorábunt in conspéctu ejus * univérsæ família Géntium.

31. Quóniam Dómini est regnum : * et ipse dominábitur Géntium.

32. Manducavérunt et adoravérunt omnes pingues terræ : * in conspéctu ejus cadent omnes qui descéndunt in terram.

33. Et ánima mea illi vivet : * et semen meum sérviet ipsi.

21. Deliver, O God, my soul from the sword: * my only one from the hand of the dog.

22. Save me from the lion's mouth; * and my lowness from the horns of the unicorns.

23. I will declare Thy name to my brethren: * in the midst of the church will I praise Thee.

24. Ye that fear the Lord, praise him: * all ye the seed of Jacob, glorify him.

25. Let all the seed of Israel fear him: * because he hath not slighted nor despised the supplication of the poor man.

26. Neither hath he turned away his face from me: * and when I cried to him he heard me.

27. With Thee is my praise in a great church: * I will pay my vows in the sight of them that fear him.

28. The poor shall eat and shall be filled: † and they shall praise the Lord that seek him: * their hearts shall live for ever and ever.

29. All the ends of the earth * shall remember, and shall be converted to the Lord:

30. And all the kindreds of the Gentiles * shall adore in his sight.

31. For the kingdom is the Lord's; * and he shall have dominion over the nations.

32. All the fat ones of the earth have eaten and have adored: * all they that go down to the earth shall fall before him.

33. And to him my soul shall live: * and my seed shall serve him.

34. Annuntiábitur Dómino generátio ventúra : * et annuntiábunt cæli justítiam ejus pópulo qui nascétur, quem fecit Dóminus.

34. There shall be declared to the Lord a generation to come: * and the heavens shall shew forth his justice to a people that shall be born, which the Lord hath made.

ANTIPHON: Divisérunt sibi vestiménta mea : et super vestem meam misérunt sortem.

ANTIPHON: They parted My garments amongst them; and upon My vesture they cast lots.

WASHING OF THE FEET

The Gospel from the Holy Thursday Mass is again chanted.

℣. Dóminus vobíscum.
℞. Et cum spíritu tuo.

℣. The Lord be with you.
℞. And with thy spirit.

CONTINUATION ✠ OF THE HOLY GOSPEL ACCORDING TO JOHN
John 13: 1-15

ANTE diem festum Paschæ, sciens Jesus, quia venit hora ejus, ut tránseat ex hoc mundo ad Patrem: cum dilexísset suos, qui erant in mundo, in finem diléxit eos. Et cœna facta, cum diábolus jam misísset in cor, ut tráderet eum Judas Simónis Iscariótæ: sciens, quia ómnia dedit ei Pater in manus, et quia a Deo exívit, et ad Deum vadit: surgit a cœna et ponit vestiménta sua: et cum accepísset línteum, præcínxit se. Deínde mittit aquam in pelvim, et cæpit laváre pedes discipulórum, et extérgere línteo, quo erat præcínctus. Venit ergo ad Simónem Petrum. Et dicit ei Petrus: Dómine, tu mihi lavas pedes? Respóndit Jesus et dixit ei: Quod ego fácio, tu nescis modo, scies autem póstea. Dicit ei Petrus: Non lavábis mihi pedes in

BEFORE the festival-day of the Pasch, Jesus knowing that His hour was come, that He should pass out of this world to the Father, having loved His own who were in the world. He loved them unto the end. And when supper was done the devil having now put into the heart of Judas, the son of Simon the Iscariot, to betray Him, knowing that the Father had given Him all things into His hands and that He came from God and goeth to God: He riseth from supper and layeth aside His garments and, having taken a towel, girded Himself. After that, He putteth water into a basin and began to wash the feet of the disciples and to wipe them with the towel wherewith He was girded. He cometh therefore to

ætérnum. Respóndit ei Jesus: Si non lávero te, non habébis partem mecum. Dicit ei Simon Petrus: Dómine, non tantum pedes meos, sed et manus et caput. Dicit ei Jesus: Qui lotus est, non índiget nisi ut pedes lavet, sed est mundus totus. Et vos mundi estis, sed non omnes. Sciébat enim, quisnam esset, qui tráderet eum: proptérea dixit: Non estis mundi omnes. Postquam ergo lavit pedes eórum et accépit vestiménta sua: cum recubuísset íterum, dixit eis: Scitis, quid fécerim vobis? Vos vocátis me Magíster et Dómine: et bene dícitis: sum étenim. Si ergo ego lavi pedes vestros, Dóminus et Magíster: et vos debétis alter altérius laváre pedes. Exémplum enim dedi vobis, ut, quemádmodum ego feci vobis, ita et vos faciátis.

Simon Peter. And Peter saith to Him: Lord, dost Thou wash my feet? Jesus answered and said to him: What I do, thou knowest not now: but thou shalt know hereafter. Peter saith to Him: Thou shalt never wash my feet. Jesus answered him: If I wash thee not, thou shalt have no part with Me. Simon Peter saith to Him: Lord, not only my feet, but also my hands and my head. Jesus saith to him: He that is washed needeth not but to wash his feet, but is clean wholly. And you are clean, but not all. For He knew who he was that would betray Him; therefore He said: You are not all clean. Then after He had washed their feet and taken His garments, being set down again, He said to them: Know you what I have done to you? You call Me Master and Lord. And you say well; for so I am. If then I being your Lord and Master, have washed your feet, you also ought to wash one another's feet. For I have given you an example, that as I have done to you, so you do also.

The celebrant now removes his violet cope, puts on an apron and begins to wash the feet of those appointed, wiping them and kissing the right foot of each person. The choir chants the following antiphons as this is taking place.

The antiphon is sung, followed by a Psalm verse. The antiphon is then repeated. This is the case for all the following antiphons.

ANTIPHON JOHN 13: 34

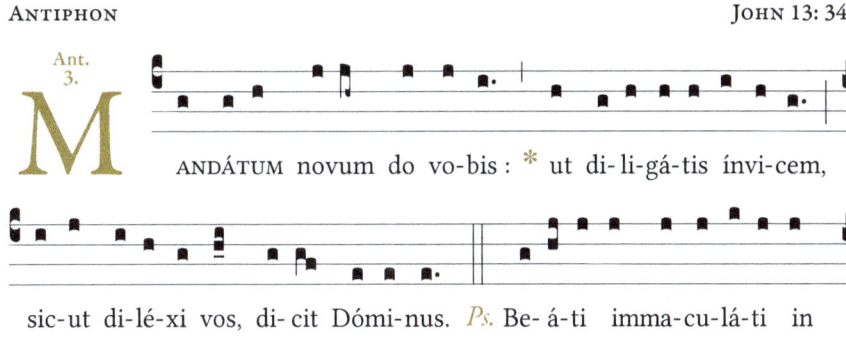

MANDÁTUM novum do vo-bis : * ut di-li-gá-tis ínvi-cem, sic-ut di-lé-xi vos, di- cit Dómi-nus. *Ps.* Be- á-ti imma-cu-lá-ti in vi- a : * qui ámbu-lant in le- ge Dómi-ni. Mandá-tum.

ANTIPHON: A new commandment I give unto you: That you love one another, as I have loved you, saith the Lord. **Ps. 118:1** Blessed are the undefiled in the way: who walk in the law of the Lord.

ANTIPHON JOHN 13: 4, 5, 15

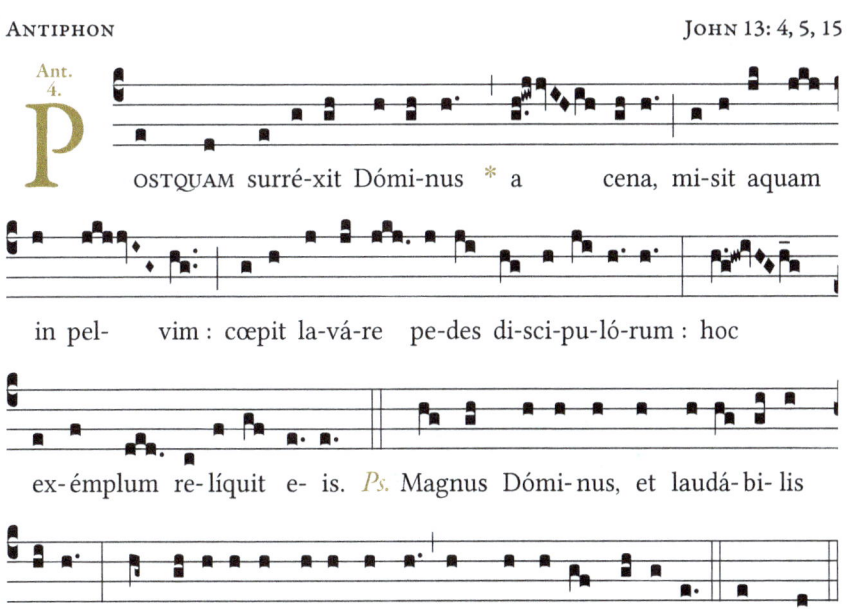

POSTQUAM surré-xit Dómi-nus * a cena, mi-sit aquam in pel- vim : cœpit la-vá-re pe-des di-sci-pu-ló-rum : hoc ex-émplum re-líquit e- is. *Ps.* Magnus Dómi-nus, et laudá-bi- lis nimis : * in ci-vi-tá-te De- i nostri, in monte sancto e-jus. Postquam.

ANTIPHON: After our Lord was risen from supper, He put water into a basin, and began to wash the feet of His disciples: to whom He gave this example. **Ps. 47:2** Great is the Lord, and exceedingly to be praised in the city of our God, in His holy mountain.

ANTIPHON   JOHN 13: 12, 13, 15

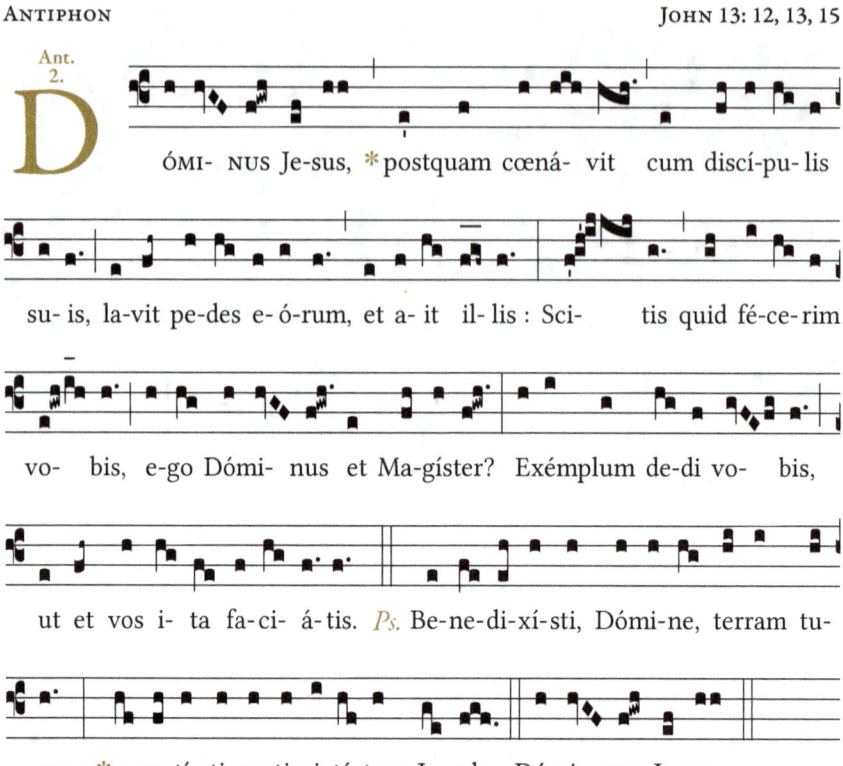

DÓMI- NUS Je-sus, *postquam cœná- vit cum discí-pu- lis su- is, la-vit pe-des e- ó-rum, et a- it il- lis : Sci- tis quid fé-ce- rim vo- bis, e-go Dómi- nus et Ma-gíster? Exémplum de-di vo- bis, ut et vos i- ta fa-ci- á-tis. *Ps.* Be-ne-di-xí-sti, Dómi-ne, terram tu- am : * a-vertí-sti capti-vi- tá-tem Ja-cob. Dómi- nus Je-sus.

ANTIPHON: Our Lord Jesus, after He had supped with His disciples, washed their feet, and said to them: Know you what I your Lord and Master have done to you? I have given you an example, that ye also may do likewise. **Ps. 84:2** Thou hast blessed, O Lord, Thy land; Thou hast turned away the captivity of Jacob.

ANTIPHON   JOHN 13: 12, 13, 15

DÓ-MI-NE, * tu mi-hi la-vas pe-des? Respóndit Je-sus, et di-xit e- i : Si non lá-ve-ro ti- bi pe-des, non ha-bé-bis partem

me-cum. ℣. Ve-nit ergo ad Simónem Petrum, * et di-xit e- i Petrus.

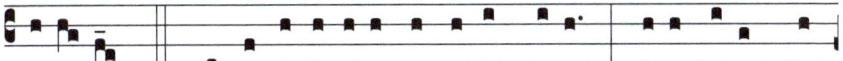

Dómi- ne. ℣. Quod e-go fá-ci- o, tu nescis modo : * sci- es autem póst-

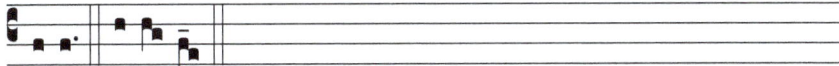

e- a. Dómi- ne.

ANTIPHON: Lord, dost Thou wash my feet? Jesus answered and said to them: If I shall not wash thy feet, thou shalt have no part with Me. ℣. He came to Simon Peter, and Peter said to Him: Lord, dost Thou wash my feet? Jesus answered and said to them: If I shall not wash thy feet, thou shalt have no part with Me. ℣. What I do, thou knowest not now; but thou shalt know hereafter.

ANTIPHON JOHN 13 :14

Ant. 4.

S I e-go Dómi-nus * et Ma-gíster ve- ster la-vi vo-bis pe-des : quanto ma-gis vos de-bé-tis alter al-té-ri- us la-vá- re pe-des? *Ps.* Audí-te hæc, omnes gentes : * áuri-bus percí-pi-te, qui ha-bi-tá- tis orbem. Si e-go.

ANTIPHON: If I your Lord and Master, have washed your feet, how much more ought you to wash one another's feet? **Ps. 48:2** Hear these things, all ye nations: give ear, ye that inhabit the world.

ANTIPHON   JOHN 13:35

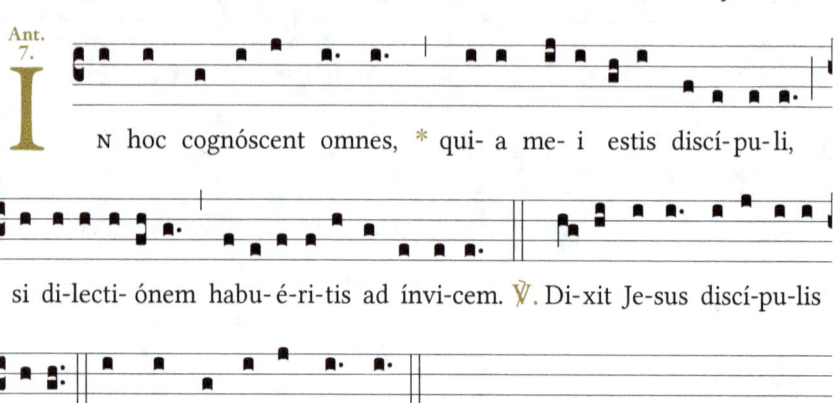

IN hoc cognóscent omnes, * qui- a me- i estis discí-pu-li, si di-lecti- ónem habu- é-ri-tis ad ínvi-cem. ℣. Di-xit Je-sus discí-pu-lis su- is. In hoc cognóscent omnes.

ANTIPHON: By this shall all men know that you are My disciples, if you have love one for another. ℣. Said Jesus to His disciples.

ANTIPHON   1 CORINTHIANS 13: 13

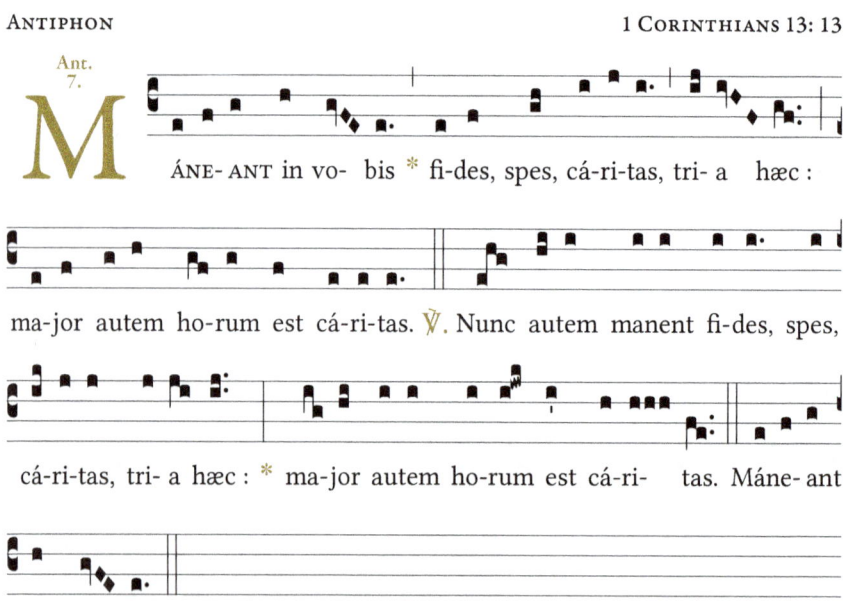

MÁNE- ANT in vo- bis * fi-des, spes, cá-ri-tas, tri- a hæc : ma-jor autem ho-rum est cá-ri-tas. ℣. Nunc autem manent fi-des, spes, cá-ri-tas, tri- a hæc : * ma-jor autem ho-rum est cá-ri- tas. Máne- ant in vo- bis.

ANTIPHON: Let these three, faith, hope and charity, remain in you; but the greatest of these is charity. ℣. And now there remain faith, hope, and charity, these three: but the greatest of these is charity.

Antiphon   Benedícta sit sancta

B ene-dí-cta sit * sancta Trí-ni- tas, atque indi-ví-sa Uni-

tas : confi-té-bi-mur e- i, qui-a fe- cit no-bíscum mi-se-ri-córdi- am su-

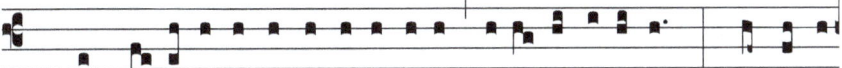

am. ℣. Bene-di-cámus Patrem et Fí-li- um, * cum Sancto Spí-ri-tu.

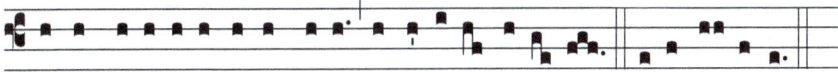

Ps. Quam di- lécta ta-berná-cu-la tu- a, Dómi-ne virtú-tum! * concu-pí-

scit, et dé-fi-cit á-nima me- a   in átri- a Dómi-ni.   Bene-dí-cta sit.

Antiphon: Blessed be the Holy Trinity and undivided Unity: We will give praise to Him, for unto us He hath shown His mercy. ℣. Let us bless the Father, and the Son, and the Holy Ghost. **Ps. 83:2-3** How lovely are Thy tabernacles O ord of Hosts: my soul longeth and fainteth for the courts of the Lord.

Antiphon   1 John 2 :3; 4

U -bi cá-ri-tas et a-mor, De- us i-bi est. ℣. Congre-gá-vit nos

in u-num Chri-sti amor. ℣. Exsultémus, et in i-pso ju-cundémur.

℣. Time- ámus, et amé-mus De- um vi-vum. ℣. Et ex corde di-li-gá-mus

nos sin-cé- ro.

Antiphon: Where charity and love are, there is God. ℣. The love of Christ has gathered us together. ℣. Let us rejoice in Him and be glad. ℣. Let us fear and love the living God. ℣. And let us love one another with a sincere heart.

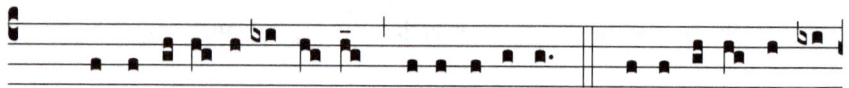

Ant.   U-bi cá- ri- tas et a-mor, De- us i-bi est. ℣. Simul ergo cum in

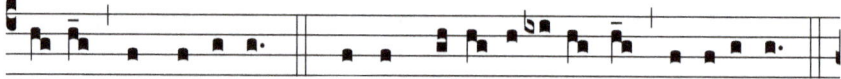

u-num congre-gámur : ℣. Ne nos mente di-vi-dá-mur, ca-ve- ámus.

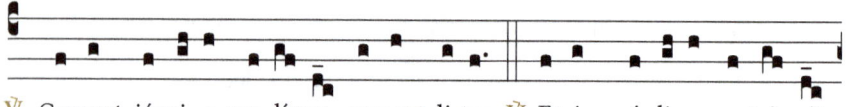

℣. Cessent júrgi- a ma-lígna, cessent li-tes. ℣. Et in mé-di- o nostri sit

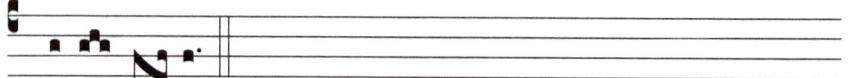

Christus De- us.

Antiphon: Where charity and love are, there is God. ℣. When, therefore, we are assembled together. ℣. Let us take heed, that we be not divided in mind. ℣. Let malicious quarrels and contentions cease. ℣. And let Christ God dwell among us.

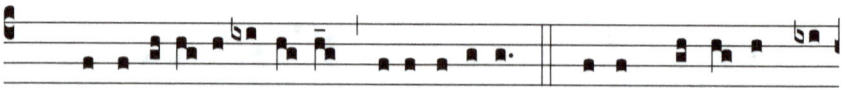

Ant.   U-bi cá- ri- tas et a-mor, De- us i-bi est. ℣. Simul quoque cum be-

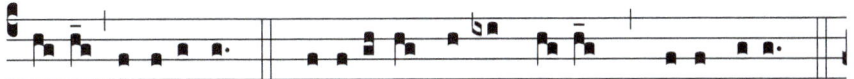

á- tis vi-de-ámus. ℣. Glo-ri- ánter vul-tum tu- um, Christe De-us :

℣. Gáudi- um, quod est imménsum, atque probum. ℣. Sǽcu-la per infi-

ní- ta sæcu- ló- rum. A-men.

Antiphon: Where charity and love are, there is God. ℣. Let us also with the blessed see. ℣. Thy face in glory, O Christ God. ℣. There to possess immeasurable and happy joy. ℣. For infinite ages of ages. Amen.

After completing the washing, the celebrant puts his violet cope back on and begins the Pater noster, *which is said in silence until:*

℣. Et ne nos indúcas in tentatiónem:

℟. Sed líbera nos a malo. Amen.

℣. Tu mandásti mandáta tua, Dómine.

℟. Custodíri nimis.

℣. Tu lavásti pedes discipulórum tuórum.

℟. Opera mánuum tuárum ne despícias.

℣. Dómine, exáudi oratiónem meam.

℟. Et clamor meus ad te véniat.

℣. Dóminus vobíscum.

℟. Et cum spíritu tuo.

℣. And lead us not into temptation:

℟. But deliver us from evil. Amen.

℣. Thou hast commanded Thy commandments, O Lord.

℟. To be exactly observed.

℣. Thou hast washed the feet of Thy disciples.

℟. Despise not the work of Thy hands.

℣. O Lord, hear my prayer.

℟. And let my cry come unto Thee.

℣. The Lord be with you.

℟. And with thy spirit.

Orémus.

Adésto, Dómine, quǽsumus, offício servitútis nostræ: et quia tu discípulis tuis pedes laváre dignátus es, ne despícias ópera mánuum tuárum, quæ nobis retinénda mandásti: ut, sicut hic nobis, et a nobis exterióra abluúntur inquinaménta; sic a te ómnium nostrum interióra lavéntur peccáta. Quod ipse præstáre dignéris, qui vivis et regnas Deus: per ómnia sǽcula sæculórum.

℟. Amen.

Let us pray.

Be present, O Lord, we beseech Thee, at the performance of our service: and since Thou didst vouchsafe to wash the feet of Thy disciples, despise not the work of Thy hands, which Thou hast commanded us to imitate: that as here the outward stains are washed away by us and from us, so the inward sins of us all may be blotted out by Thee. Which do Thou vouchsafe to grant, who livest and reignest God for ever and ever.

℟. Amen.

GOOD FRIDAY

All kneel.

APERI Dómine, os meum ad benedicéndum nomen sanctum tuum: munda quoque cor meum ab ómnibus vanis, pervérsis et aliénis cogitatiónibus; intelléctum illúmina, afféctum inflámma, ut digne, atténte ac devóte hoc Offícium recitáre váleam, et exaudíri mérear ante conspéctum divínæ Majestátis túæ. Per Christum Dóminum nostrum.

℟. Amen.

DÓMINE, in unióne illíus divínæ intentiónis, qua ipse in terris laudes Deo persolvísti, has tibi Horas persólvo.

O LORD, open thou my mouth that I may bless Thy Holy Name. Cleanse my heart from all vain, evil, and wandering thoughts; enlighten my understanding, kindle my affections, that I may pray to, and praise thee with attention and devotion; and may worthily be heard before the presence of Thy Divine Majesty. Through Christ our Lord.

℟. Amen.

LORD, in union with that Divine Intention wherewith Thou didst thyself praise God, whilst Thou wast on earth, I offer these Hours unto Thee.

AT MATINS

The Pater noster, Ave María *and* Credo *are said silently.*

PATER noster, qui es in cælis, sanctificétur nomen tuum: advéniat regnum tuum: fiat volúntas tua, sicut in cælo et in terra. Panem nostrum quotidiánum da nobis hódie: et dimítte nobis débita nostra, sicut et nos dimíttimus debitóribus nostris: et ne nos indúcas in tentatiónem: sed líbera nos a malo. Amen.

OUR Father, who art in heaven, hallowed be Thy name. Thy kingdom come. Thy will be done on earth as it is in heaven. Give us this day our daily bread. And forgive us our trespasses, as we forgive those who trespass against us. And lead us not into temptation: but deliver us from evil. Amen.

AVE María, grátia plena; Dóminus tecum: benedícta tu in muliéribus, et benedíctus fructus ventris tui Jesus. Sancta María, Mater Dei, ora pro nobis peccatóribus, nunc et in hora mortis nostræ. Amen.

CREDO in Deum, Patrem omnipoténtem, Creatórem cæli et terræ.

Et in Jesum Christum, Fílium ejus únicum, Dóminum nostrum: qui concéptus est de Spíritu Sancto, natus ex María Vírgine, passus sub Póntio Piláto, crucifíxus, mórtuus, et sepúltus: descéndit ad ínferos; tértia die resurréxit a mórtuis; ascéndit ad cælos; sedet ad déxteram Dei Patris omnipoténtis: inde ventúrus est judicáre vivos et mórtuos.

Credo in Spíritum Sanctum, sanctam Ecclésiam cathólicam, Sanctórum communiónem, remissiónem peccatórum, carnis resurrectiónem, vitam ætérnam. Amen.

HAIL Mary, full of grace; The Lord is with thee; blessed art thou amongst women, and blessed is the fruit of thy womb, Jesus. Holy Mary, Mother of God, pray for us sinners, now and at the hour of our death. Amen.

I BELIEVE in God, the Father almighty, Creator of heaven and earth.

And in Jesus Christ, His only Son, our Lord; who was conceived by the Holy Ghost, born of the Virgin Mary, suffered under Pontius Pilate, was crucified, died and was buried: He descended into hell; the third day He arose again from the dead; He ascended into heaven; sitteth at the right hand of God the Father almighty: from thence He shall come to judge the living and the dead.

I believe in the Holy Ghost, the holy Catholic Church, the communion of Saints, the forgiveness of sins. The resurrection of the body. And life everlasting. Amen.

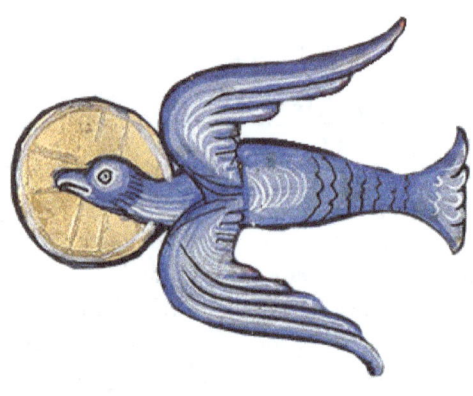

1ST NOCTURN

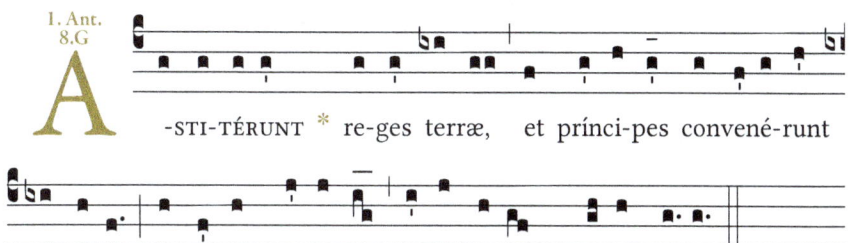

-sti-térunt * re-ges terræ,   et prínci-pes convené-runt

in unum, advérsus Dómi-num, et advérsus Christum e-jus.

ANTIPHON: The kings of the earth set themselves, * and the rulers take counsel together, against the Lord, and against His Anointed.

PSALM 2

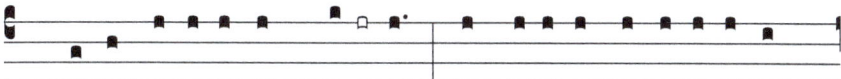

1. Qua- re fremu- é- runt **Gen**- tes: * et pópu- li me- di- tá- ti *sunt*

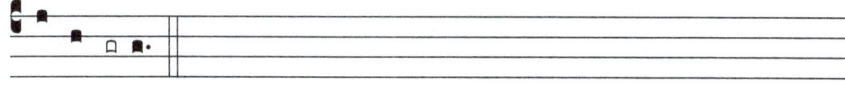

in-**á**-ni- a?

1. Why have the Gentiles raged, * and the people devised vain things?

2. Astitérunt reges terræ, et príncipes convenérunt in **u**num * advérsus Dóminum, et advérsus *Christum* **e**jus.	2. The kings of the earth stood up, and the princes met together, * against the Lord and against His Christ.
3. Dirumpámus víncula e**ó**rum: * et projiciámus a nobis ju*gum i***ps**órum.	3. Let us break their bonds asunder: * and let us cast away their yoke from us.
4. Qui hábitat in cælis, irridébit eos: * et Dóminus subsan*nábit* **e**os.	4. He that dwelleth in heaven shall laugh at them: * and the Lord shall deride them.
5. Tunc loquétur ad eos in ira **su**a, * et in furóre suo contur*bábit* **e**os.	5. Then shall He speak to them in His anger, * and trouble them in His rage.
6. Ego autem constitútus sum Rex ab eo super Sion montem sanctum ejus, * prædicans præ*céptum* **e**jus.	6. But I am appointed king by him over Sion his holy mountain, * preaching his commandment.

7. Dóminus dixit **ad** me: * Fílius meus es tu, ego hódie *génu*i te.

8. Póstula a me, et dabo tibi Gentes hereditátem **tu**am, * et possessiónem tuam tér*minos* **terr**æ.

9. Reges eos in virga **fér**rea, * et tamquam vas fíguli con*frínges* eos.

10. Et nunc, reges, intel**lí**gite: * erudímini, qui judi*cátis* **ter**ram.

11. Servíte Dómino in ti**mó**re: * et exsultáte ei *cum tre***mó**re.

12. Apprehéndite disciplínam, nequándo irascátur **Dó**minus, * et pereátis de *via* **ju**sta.

13. Cum exárserit in brevi ira ejus: * beáti omnes qui confí*dunt in* **e**o.

7. The Lord hath said to me: * Thou art my son, this day have I begotten thee.

8. Ask of me, and I will give thee the Gentiles for thy inheritance, * and the utmost parts of the earth for thy possession.

9. Thou shalt rule them with a rod of iron, * and shalt break them in pieces like a potter's vessel.

10. And now, O ye kings, understand: * receive instruction, you that judge the earth.

11. Serve ye the Lord with fear: * and rejoice unto him with trembling.

12. Embrace discipline, lest at any time the Lord be angry, * and you perish from the just way.

13. When his wrath shall be kindled in a short time, * blessed are all they that trust in him.

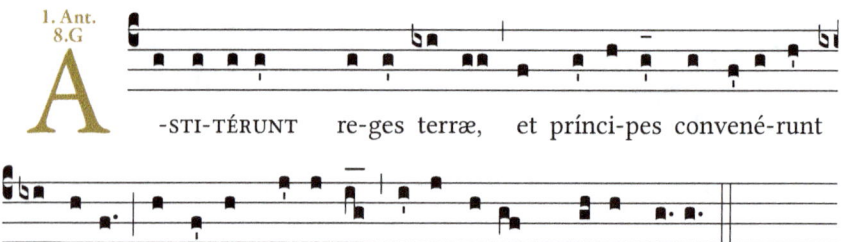

1. Ant. 8.G

A-STI-TÉRUNT re-ges terræ, et prínci-pes convené-runt in unum, advérsus Dómi-num, et advérsus Christum e-jus.

The first candle is extinguished.

2. Ant. 8.G

DI-VI-SÉRUNT si-bi * vestiménta me-a, et super vestem me-am mi-sé-runt sortem.

ANTIPHON: They parted my garments amongst them; and upon my vesture they cast lots.

PSALM 21

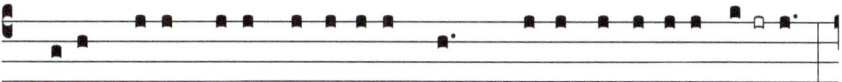

1. De- us, De- us me- us, réspi-ce in me : † qua-re me de-re-li**quí**- sti? *

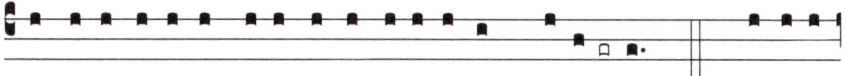

longe a sa-lú-te me- a verba de-lictó-*rum me- **ó**- rum. ℣. 3. Tu autem

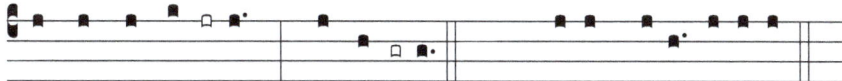

in sancto **há**-bi-tas : * *laus* **Is**ra- ël. *Flex :* virtus me-a †

1. O God my God, look upon me: † why hast thou forsaken me? * Far from my salvation are the words of my sins.

2. Deus meus, clamábo per diem, et non ex**áu**dies: * et nocte, et non ad insipién*tiam* **mi**hi.

2. O my God, I shall cry by day, and Thou wilt not hear: * and by night, and it shall not be reputed as folly in me.

3. Tu autem in sancto **há**bitas: * *laus* **Is**raël.

3. But Thou dwellest in the holy place, * the praise of Israel.

4. In te speravérunt patres **no**stri: * speravérunt, et libe*rásti* **e**os.

4. In Thee have our fathers hoped: * they have hoped, and Thou hast delivered them.

5. Ad te clamavérunt, et salvi **fac**ti sunt: * in te speravérunt, et non *sunt con***fú**si.

5. They cried to Thee, and they were saved: * they trusted in Thee, and were not confounded.

6. Ego autem sum vermis, et non **ho**mo: * oppróbrium hóminum, et abjéc*tio* **ple**bis.

6. But I am a worm, and no man: * the reproach of men, and the outcast of the people.

7. Omnes vidéntes me derisérunt me: * locúti sunt lábiis, et mo*vérunt* **ca**put.

7. All they that saw me have laughed me to scorn: * they have spoken with the lips, and wagged the head.

8. Sperávit in Dómino, erípiat eum: * salvum fáciat eum, quóni*am vult* **e**um.

8. He hoped in the Lord, let Him deliver him: * let Him save him, seeing He delighteth in him.

9. Quóniam tu es, qui extraxísti me de **ven**tre: * spes mea ab ubéribus matris meæ. In te projéctus *sum ex* **ú**tero.

9. For Thou art He that hast drawn me out of the womb: * my hope from the breasts of my mother. I was cast upon Thee from the womb.

10. De ventre matris meæ Deus meus **es** tu, * ne discés*seris* **a** me:

10. From my mother's womb Thou art my God, * depart not from me.

11. Quóniam tribulátio próxi**ma** est: * quóniam non *est qui* **ád**juvet.

11. For tribulation is very near: * for there is none to help me.

12. Circumdedérunt me vítuli **mul**ti: * tauri pingues *obse***dé**runt me.

12. Many calves have surrounded me: * fat bulls have besieged me.

13. Aperuérunt super me os **su**um: * sicut leo rápi*ens et* **rú**giens.

13. They have opened their mouths against me, * as a lion ravening and roaring.

14. Sicut aqua ef**fú**sus sum: * et dispérsa sunt ómnia *ossa* **me**a.

14. I am poured out like water; * and all my bones are scattered.

15. Factum est cor meum tamquam cera li**qué**scens: * in médio *ventris* **me**i.

15. My heart is become like wax melting * in the midst of my bowels.

16. Aruit tamquam testa virtus mea, † et lingua mea adhǽsit fáucibus **me**is: * et in púlverem mortis *dedu***xí**sti me.

16. My strength is dried up like a potsherd, † and my tongue hath cleaved to my jaws: * and Thou hast brought me down into the dust of death.

17. Quóniam circumdedérunt me canes **mul**ti: * concílium malignánti*um ob***sé**dit me.

17. For many dogs have encompassed me: * the council of the malignant hath besieged me.

18. Fodérunt manus meas et pedes **me**os: * dinumeravérunt ómnia *ossa* **me**a.

18. They have dug my hands and feet. * They have numbered all my bones.

19. Ipsi vero consideravérunt et inspe**xé**runt me: * divisérunt sibi vestiménta mea, et super vestem meam mi*sérunt* **sor**tem.

19. And they have looked and stared upon me. * They parted my garments amongst them; and upon my vesture they cast lots.

20. Tu autem, Dómine, ne elongáveris auxílium tuum **a** me: * ad defensiónem *meam* **cón**spice.

20. But Thou, O Lord, remove not Thy help to a distance from me; * look towards my defence.

21. Erue a frámea, Deus, ánimam **me**am: * et de manu canis *ú*nicam **me**am.

21. Deliver, O God, my soul from the sword: * my only one from the hand of the dog.

22. Salva me ex ore leónis: * et a córnibus unicórnium humili*tátem* **me**am.

22. Save me from the lion's mouth; * and my lowness from the horns of the unicorns.

23. Narrábo nomen tuum frátribus **me**is: * in médio Ecclési*æ* *lau***dá**bo te.

24. Qui timétis Dóminum, laudáte eum: * univérsum semen Jacob, glorifi*cáte* eum.

25. Tímeat eum omne semen **Is**raël: * quóniam non sprevit, neque despéxit deprecati*ónem* **páu**peris:

26. Nec avértit fáciem suam **a** me: * et cum clamárem ad eum, *exau***dí**vit me.

27. Apud te laus mea in ecclésia **ma**gna: * vota mea reddam in con- spéctu timén*tium* eum.

28. Edent páuperes, et saturabún- tur: † et laudábunt Dóminum qui requírunt eum: * vivent corda eórum in s*æculum* **sæ**culi.

29. Reminiscéntur et converténtur ad **Dó**minum * univérsi *fines* **ter**ræ:

30. Et adorábunt in conspéctu ejus * univérsæ fam*íliæ* **Gén**tium.

31. Quóniam Dómini est **regnum**: * et ipse domin*ábitur* **Gén**tium.

32. Manducavérunt et adoravérunt omnes pingues **ter**ræ: * in conspéctu ejus cadent omnes qui descén*dunt in* **ter**ram.

33. Et ánima mea illi **vi**vet: * et semen meum sér*viet* **ip**si.

34. Annuntiábitur Dómino generátio ven**tú**ra: * et annuntiábunt cæli justítiam ejus pópulo qui nascé- tur, quem *fecit* **Dó**minus.

23. I will declare Thy name to my brethren: * in the midst of the church will I praise Thee.

24. Ye that fear the Lord, praise Him: * all ye the seed of Jacob, glorify Him.

25. Let all the seed of Israel fear Him: * because He hath not slighted nor despised the supplication of the poor man.

26. Neither hath He turned away His face from me: * and when I cried to Him He heard me.

27. With Thee is my praise in a great church: * I will pay my vows in the sight of them that fear Him.

28. The poor shall eat and shall be filled: and they shall praise the Lord that seek Him: * their hearts shall live for ever and ever.

29. All the ends of the earth * shall remember, and shall be converted to the Lord:

30. And all the kindreds of the Gen- tiles * shall adore in His sight.

31. For the kingdom is the Lord's; * and He shall have dominion over the nations.

32. All the fat ones of the earth have eaten and have adored: * all they that go down to the earth shall fall before Him.

33. And to Him my soul shall live: * and my seed shall serve Him.

34. There shall be declared to the Lord a generation to come: * and the heavens shall shew forth His justice to a people that shall be born, which the Lord hath made.

2. Ant.
8.G

DI-VI-SÉRUNT si-bi　vestiménta me- a,　et super vestem me-

am mi-sé-runt sortem.

The second candle is extinguished.

3. Ant.
8.G

INSURREXÉRUNT in me * testes in-í-qui,　et mentí-ta est in-í-

qui-tas si-bi.

ANTIPHON: False witnesses are risen up against me, * and iniquity hath belied itself.

PSALM 26

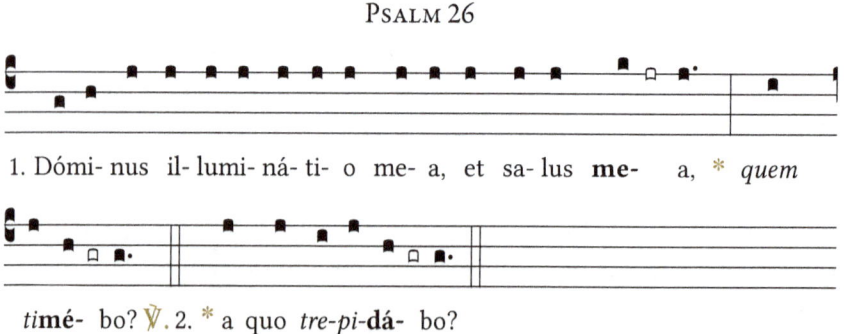

1. Dómi- nus il- lumi- ná- ti- o me- a, et sa- lus **me-**　a, * *quem*

timé- bo? ℣. 2. * a quo *tre-pi-dá-* bo?

1. The Lord is my light and my salvation, * whom shall I fear?

2. Dóminus protéctor vitæ **me**æ, *
a quo *trepi***dá**bo?

2. The Lord is the protector of my
life: * of whom shall I be afraid?

3. Dum apprópiant super me
no**cén**tes, * ut edant *carnes* **me**as:

3. Whilst the wicked draw near
against me, * to eat my flesh.

4. Qui tríbulant me inimíci mei, * ipsi infirmáti sunt et *ceci*dérunt.

5. Si consístant advérsum me ca*stra, * non timé*bit cor me*um.

6. Si exsúrgat advérsum me prǽlium, * in hoc e*go spe*rábo.

7. Unam pétii a Dómino, hanc re*qui*ram, * ut inhábitem in domo Dómini ómnibus diébus *vitæ* me*æ:

8. Ut vídeam voluptátem **Dó**mini, * et vísitem *templum* ejus.

9. Quóniam abscóndit me in tabernáculo **su**o: * in die malórum protéxit me in abscóndito tabernáculi sui.

10. In petra exal**tá**vit me: * et nunc exaltávit caput meum super in*imícos* **me**os.

11. Circuívi et immolávi in tabernáculo ejus hóstiam vociferati**ó**nis: * cantábo et psalmum *dicam* **Dó**mino.

12. Exáudi, Dómine, vocem meam, qua clamávi **ad** te: * miserére mei, *et* *ex*á**u**di me.

13. Tibi dixit cor meum, exquisívit te fácies **me**a: * fáciem tuam, Dómi*ne*, *requí*ram.

14. Ne avértas fáciem tuam **a** me, * ne declínes in ira a *servo* **tu**o.

15. Adjútor meus **e**sto: * ne derelínquas me, neque despícias me, Deus, salu*táris* **me**us.

16. Quóniam pater meus, et mater mea dereli**qué**runt me: * Dóminus au*tem as***sú**mpsit me.

4. My enemies that trouble me, * have themselves been weakened, and have fallen.

5. If armies in camp should stand together against me, * my heart shall not fear.

6. If a battle should rise up against me, * in this will I be confident.

7. One thing I have asked of the Lord, this will I seek after; * that I may dwell in the house of the Lord all the days of my life.

8. That I may see the delight of the Lord, * and may visit His temple.

9. For He hath hidden me in His tabernacle; * in the day of evils, He hath protected me in the secret place of His tabernacle.

10. He hath exalted me upon a rock: * and now He hath lifted up my head above my enemies.

11. I have gone round, and have offered up in His tabernacle a sacrifice of jubilation: * I will sing, and recite a psalm to the Lord.

12. Hear, O Lord, my voice, with which I have cried to Thee: * have mercy on me and hear me.

13. My heart hath said to Thee: My face hath sought Thee: * Thy face, O Lord, will I still seek.

14. Turn not away Thy face from me; * decline not in Thy wrath from Thy servant.

15. Be Thou my helper, * forsake me not; do not Thou despise me, O God my Saviour.

16. For my father and my mother have left me: * but the Lord hath taken me up.

17. Legem pone mihi, Dómine, in via **tua**: * et dírige me in sémitam rectam propter in*mícos* **me**os.

17. Set me, O Lord, a law in Thy way, * and guide me in the right path, because of my enemies.

18. Ne tradíderis me in ánimas tribulántium me: * quóniam insurrexérunt in me testes iníqui, et mentíta est in*íquitas* **si**bi.

18. Deliver me not over to the will of them that trouble me; * for unjust witnesses have risen up against me; and iniquity hath lied to itself.

19. Credo vidére bona **Dó**mini * in ter*ra vivén*tium.

19. I believe to see the good things of the Lord * in the land of the living.

20. Exspécta Dóminum, viríliter **age**: * et confortétur cor tuum, et sús*tine* **Dó**minum.

20. Expect the Lord, do manfully, * and let Thy heart take courage, and wait thou for the Lord.

NSURREXÉRUNT in me   testes in-í-qui,   et mentí-ta est in-í-

qui-tas si-bi.

The third candle is extinguished.

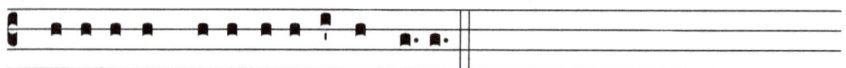

℣. Di-vi-sé-runt si-bi vestiménta me- a.

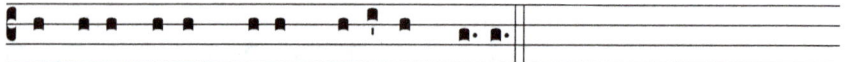

℟. Et super vestem me- am mi-sé-runt sortem.

Or:

℣. Di-vi-sé-runt si-bi vestiménta me- a.

℟. Et super vestem me- am mi-sé-runt sortem.

℣. They part my garments among them.

℟. And cast lots upon my vesture.

The Pater noster *is said silently.*

Lesson 1   Jeremiah 2: 8-11

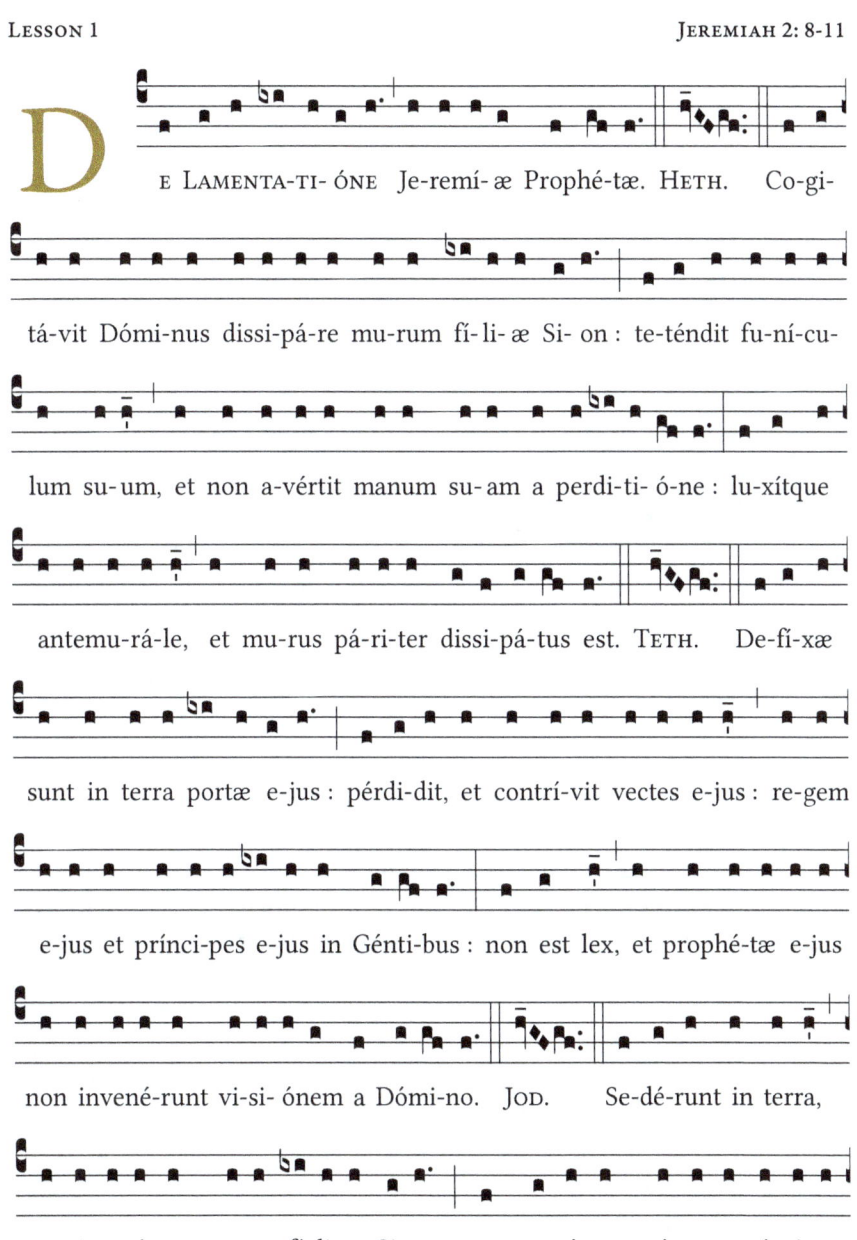

De Lamenta-ti-óne Je-remí-æ Prophé-tæ. Heth.   Co-gi-tá-vit Dómi-nus dissi-pá-re mu-rum fí-li-æ Si-on : te-téndit fu-ní-cu-lum su-um, et non a-vértit manum su-am a perdi-ti-ó-ne : lu-xítque antemu-rá-le, et mu-rus pá-ri-ter dissi-pá-tus est. Teth.   De-fí-xæ sunt in terra portæ e-jus : pérdi-dit, et contrí-vit vectes e-jus : re-gem e-jus et prínci-pes e-jus in Génti-bus : non est lex, et prophé-tæ e-jus non invené-runt vi-si-ónem a Dómi-no. Jod.   Se-dé-runt in terra, conti-cu-é-runt senes fí-li-æ Si-on : conspersé-runt cí-ne-re cá-pi-ta

su- a, accíncti sunt ci-lí-ci- is, abje-cé-runt in terram cá-pi-ta su- a vír-

gi-nes Je-rú-sa-lem. CAPH.   De-fe-cé-runt præ lácrimis ó-cu-li me- i,

conturbá-ta sunt vísce-ra me- a : effú-sum est in terra je-cur me- um

super contri-ti- óne fí-li- æ pópu-li me- i, cum de-fí-ce-ret párvu-lus et

lactens in pla-té- is óppi-di. Je-rú-sa-lem, Je-rú-sa-lem, convérte-re

ad Dómi-num De- um tu- um.

LESSON 1: **HETH.** The Lord hath purposed to destroy the wall of the daughter of Sion: He hath stretched out His line, and hath not withdrawn His hand from destroying: and the bulwark hath mourned, and the wall hath been destroyed together. **TETH.** Her gates are sunk into the ground: He hath destroyed, and broken her bars: her king and her princes are among the Gentiles: the law is no more, and her prophets have found no vision from the Lord. **JOD.** The ancients of the daughter of Sion sit upon the ground, they have held their peace: they have sprinkled their heads with dust, they are girded with haircloth, the virgins of Jerusalem hang down their heads to the ground. **CAPH.** My eyes have failed with weeping, my bowels are troubled: my liver is poured out upon the earth, for the destruction of the daughter of my people, when the children, and the sucklings, fainted away in the streets of the city. *Jerusalem! Jerusalem! Return unto the Lord thy God.*

RESPONSORY 1 OMNES AMÍCI MEI

O- MNES * amí- ci me- i de- re- liqué-

runt me, et præ- va-lu-é- runt insi-di-án- tes mi- hi :

trá-di-dit me quem di-li-gé- bam : *Et terri-bí-li-bus ó- cu-

lis pla- ga crudé- li percu- ti-éntes, a-cé- to po-tá-

bant me. ℣. In- ter in-íquos pro-je-cé-runt me, et non pe-

percé-runt á- nimæ me- æ. * Et terri-bí-li-bus.

℟. All My friends have forsaken Me, and Mine enemies have prevailed against Me; he whom I loved hath betrayed Me. * Mine enemy sharpeneth his eyes upon Me; he breaketh Me with breach upon breach: and in My thirst they gave Me vinegar to drink. ℣. I am numbered with the transgressors; and My life is not spared. ℟. Mine enemy sharpeneth his eyes upon Me; he breaketh Me with breach upon breach; and in My thirst they gave Me vinegar to drink.

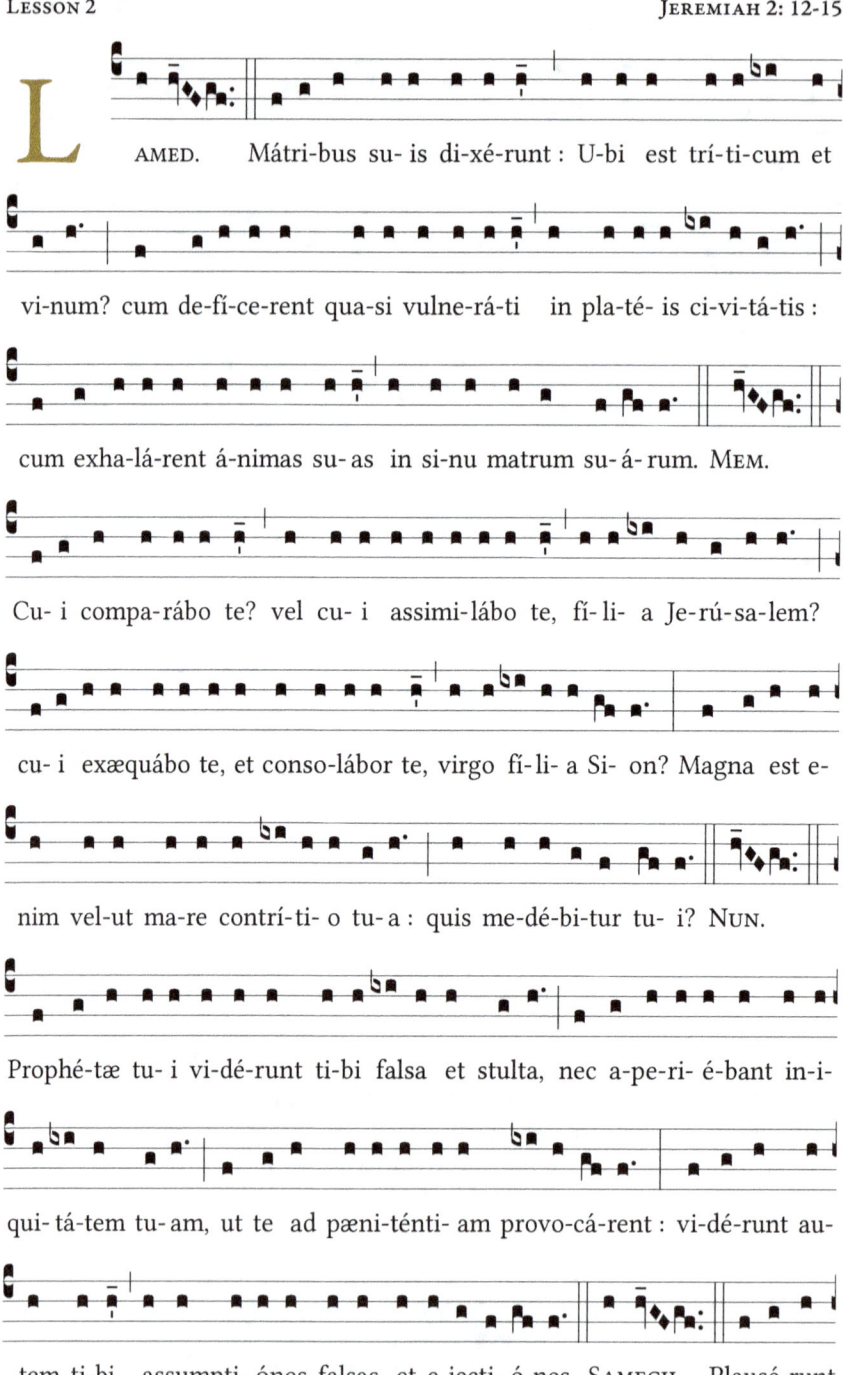

L AMED. Mátri-bus su- is di-xé-runt : U-bi est trí-ti-cum et vi-num? cum de-fí-ce-rent qua-si vulne-rá-ti in pla-té- is ci-vi-tá-tis : cum exha-lá-rent á-nimas su- as in si-nu matrum su- á- rum. MEM.

Cu- i compa-rábo te? vel cu- i assimi-lábo te, fí-li- a Je-rú-sa-lem? cu- i exæquábo te, et conso-lábor te, virgo fí-li- a Si- on? Magna est e- nim vel-ut ma-re contrí-ti- o tu-a : quis me-dé-bi-tur tu- i? NUN.

Prophé-tæ tu- i vi-dé-runt ti-bi falsa et stulta, nec a-pe-ri- é-bant in-i- qui-tá-tem tu- am, ut te ad pæni-ténti- am provo-cá-rent : vi-dé-runt au- tem ti-bi assumpti- ónes falsas, et e-jecti- ó-nes. SAMECH. Plausé-runt

super te má-ni-bus omnes transe- úntes per vi- am : si-bi-la-vé-runt,

et mo-vé-runt caput su- um super fí-li- am Je-rú-sa-lem : Hǽcci-ne

est urbs, di-céntes, per-féci de-có-ris, gáudi- um u-ni-vérsæ terræ?

Je-rú-sa-lem, Je-rú-sa-lem, convérte-re ad Dómi-num De- um tu- um.

Lesson 2: Lamed. They said to their mothers: Where is corn and wine? when they fainted away as the wounded in the streets of the city: when they breathed out their souls in the bosoms of their mothers. **Mem.** To what shall I compare thee? or to what shall I liken thee, O daughter of Jerusalem? to what shall I equal thee, that I may comfort thee, O virgin daughter of Sion? for great as the sea is thy destruction: who shall heal thee? **Nun.** Thy prophets have seen false and foolish things for thee: and they have not laid open thy iniquity, to excite thee to penance: but they have seen for thee false revelations and banishments. **Samech.** All they that passed by the way have clapped their hands at thee: they have hissed, and wagged their heads at the daughter of Jerusalem, saying: Is this the city of perfect beauty, the joy of all the earth? *Jerusalem! Jerusalem! Return unto the Lord thy God.*

RESPONSORY 2   **VELUM TEMPLI SCISSUM**

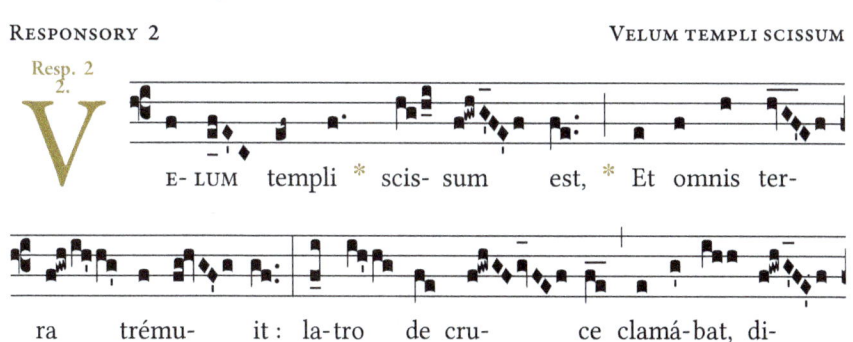

E- LUM templi * scis- sum est, * Et omnis ter-

ra trému- it : la-tro de cru- ce clamá-bat, di-

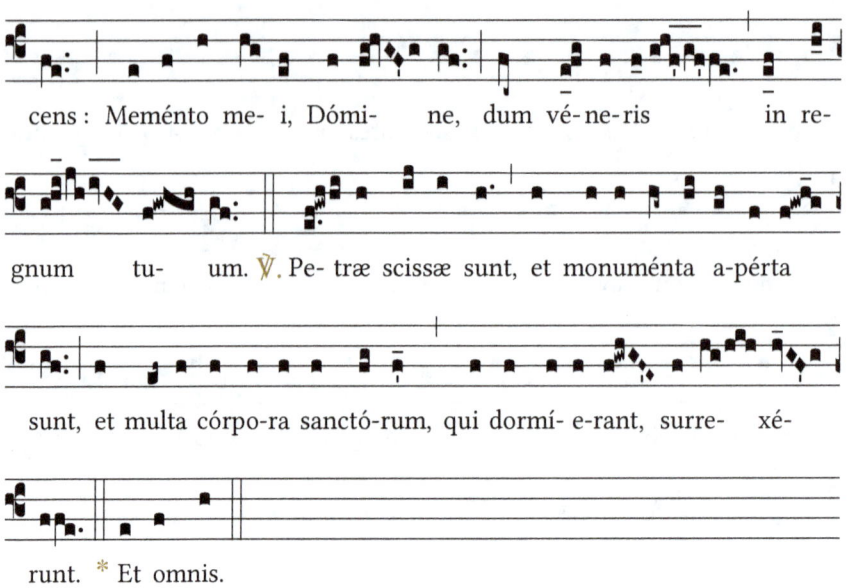

cens : Memento me- i, Domi- ne, dum vé-ne-ris in re-

gnum tu- um. ℣. Pe-træ scissæ sunt, et monuménta a-pérta

sunt, et multa córpo-ra sanctó-rum, qui dormí- e-rant, surre- xé-

runt. * Et omnis.

℟. The veil of the Temple was rent in twain, from the top to the bottom, * And all the earth did quake: the thief on the cross cried, saying: Lord, remember me when Thou comest into Thy kingdom! ℣. The rocks rent, and the graves were opened, and many bodies of the saints, which slept, arose. ℟. And all the earth did quake: the thief on the cross cried, saying: Lord, remember me when thou comest into Thy kingdom.

LESSON 3   LAMENTATIONS 3 :1-9

A -LEPH.   Ego vir vi-dens pauper-tá-tem me- am in virga

indigna-ti- ó-nis e- jus. ALEPH. Me mi-ná-vit, et addú-xit in téne-

bras, et non in lu-cem. ALEPH. Tantum in me vertit, et convértit

manum su- am to-ta di- e. Beth. Ve-tústam fe-cit pel-lem me- am,

et carnem me-am, contrí-vit ossa me- a. Beth. Ædi-fi-cá-vit in

gy-ro me- o, et circúmde-dit me fel-le et la-bó-re. Beth. In te-

nebró-sis collo-cá-vit me, qua-si mórtu- os sempi- térnos. Ghimel.

Circumædi- fi-cá-vit advérsum me, ut non egré-di- ar : aggra-vá-vit

cómpe-dem me- um. Ghimel. Sed et, cum clamá-ve-ro et ro-gá-

ve-ro, exclú-sit o-ra-ti- ónem me- am. Ghimel. Conclú-sit vi- as

me- as la-pí-di-bus quadris, sémi-tas me- as subvér-tit. Je-rú-sa-lem,

Je-rú-sa-lem, convérte-re ad Dómi-num De- um tu- um.

LESSON 3: ALEPH. I am the man that see my poverty by the rod of his indigna-
tion. **ALEPH.** He hath led me, and brought me into darkness, and not into light.
ALEPH. Only against me he hath turned, and turned again his hand all the day.
BETH. My skin and my flesh he hath made old, he hath broken my bones. **BETH.**
He hath built round about me, and he hath compassed me with gall and labour.
BETH. He hath set me in dark places as those that are dead for ever. **GHIMEL.**
He hath built against me round about, that I may not get out: he hath made my
fetters heavy. **GHIMEL.** Yea, and when I cry, and entreat, he hath shut out my
prayer. **GHIMEL.** He hath shut up my ways with square stones, he hath turned
my paths upside down. *Jerusalem! Jerusalem! Return unto the Lord thy God.*

RESPONSORY 3   VÍNEA MEA ELÉCTA

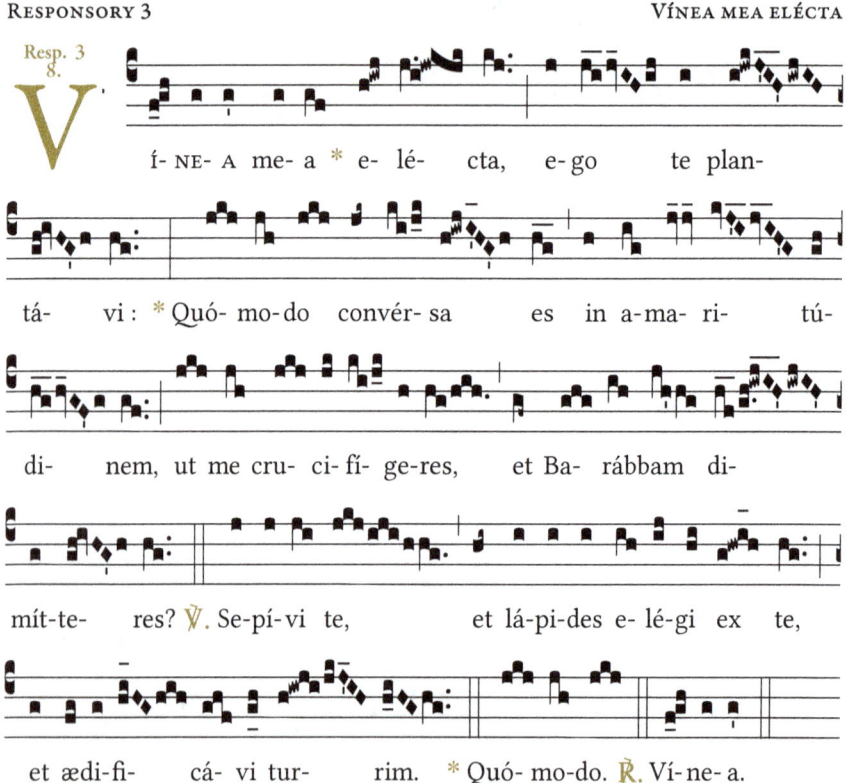

Ví-ne-A me-a * e-lé-cta, e-go te plan-tá-vi: * Quó-mo-do convér-sa es in a-ma-ri-tú-di-nem, ut me cru-ci-fí-ge-res, et Ba-rábbam di-mít-te-res? ℣. Se-pí-vi te, et lá-pi-des e-lé-gi ex te, et ædi-fi-cá-vi tur-rim. * Quó-mo-do. ℟. Ví-ne-a.

℟. I had planted thee a noble vineyard; * How then art thou turned into a
bitterness, that thou shouldst crucify Me, and set Barabbas free? ℣. I fenced
thee, and gathered out the stones from thee, and built a tower in the midst of
the land. ℟. How then art thou turned into a bitterness, that thou shouldst
crucify Me, and set Barabbas free? ℟. I had planted thee a noble vineyard; *
How then art thou turned into a bitterness, that thou shouldst crucify Me, and
set Barabbas free?

2nd Nocturn

ɪᴍ fa-ci- é-bant * qui quæ-ré-bant á-nimam me- am.

Antiphon: They that sought after my life * have used violence again me.

Psalm 37

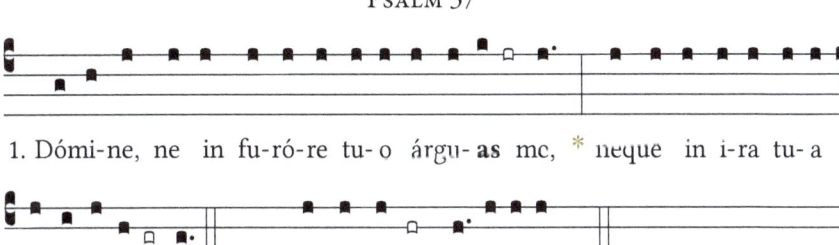

1. Dómi-ne, ne in fu-ró-re tu- o árgu- **as** me, * neque in i-ra tu- a

corrí-pi- **as** me.   *Flex :* conturbá-tum est, †

1. Rebuke me not, O Lord, in thy indignation; * nor chastise me in thy wrath.

2. Quóniam sagíttæ tuæ infíxæ sunt **mi**hi: * et confirmásti super me *manum* **tu**am.

3. Non est sánitas in carne mea a fácie iræ **tuæ**: * non est pax óssibus meis a fácie peccató*rum me*órum.

4. Quóniam iniquitátes meæ supergréssæ sunt caput **me**um: * et sicut onus grave gravá*tæ sunt* **su**per me.

5. Putruérunt et corrúptæ sunt cicatríces **me**æ, * a fácie insipién*tiæ* **me**æ.

6. Miser factus sum, et curvátus sum usque in **fi**nem: * tota die contristátus in*gredi*ébar.

7. Quóniam lumbi mei impléti sunt illusió*ni*bus: * et non est sánitas in *carne* **me**a.

8. Afflíctus sum, et humiliátus sum **ni**mis: * rugiébam a gémitu *cordis* **me**i.

2. For Thy arrows are fastened in me: * and Thy hand hath been strong upon me.

3. There is no health in my flesh, because of Thy wrath: * there is no peace for my bones, because of my sins.

4. For my iniquities are gone over my head: * and as a heavy burden are become heavy upon me.

5. My sores are putrified and corrupted, * because of my foolishness.

6. I am become miserable, and am bowed down even to the end: * I walked sorrowful all the day long.

7. For my loins are filled with illusions; * and there is no health in my flesh.

8. I am afflicted and humbled exceedingly: * I roared with the groaning of my heart.

9. Dómine, ante te omne desidérium **me**um: * et gémitus meus a te non *est abscón*ditus.

10. Cor meum conturbátum est, † derelíquit me virtus **me**a: * et lumen oculórum meórum, et ipsum *non est* **me**cum.

11. Amíci mei, et próximi **mei** * advérsum me appropinquavérunt, *et ste*térunt.

12. Et qui juxta me erant, de longe stetérunt: * et vim faciébant qui quærébant *ánimam* **me**am.

13. Et qui inquirébant mala mihi, locúti sunt vani**tát**es: * et dolos tota die me*dita*bántur.

14. Ego autem tamquam surdus non audiébam: * et sicut mutus non apéri*ens os* **su**um.

15. Et factus sum sicut homo non **áu**diens: * et non habens in ore suo redar*guti*ónes.

16. Quóniam in te, Dómine, sperávi: * tu exáudies me, Dómine, *Deus* **me**us.

17. Quia dixi: Nequándo supergáudeant mihi inimíci **mei**: * et dum commovéntur pedes mei, super me ma*gna lo***cú**ti sunt.

18. Quóniam ego in flagélla pa**rá**tus sum: * et dolor meus in conspéctu *meo* **sem**per.

19. Quóniam iniquitátem meam annuntiábo: * et cogitábo pro pec**cá**to **me**o.

20. Inimíci autem mei vivunt, et confirmáti sunt **su**per me: * et multiplicáti sunt qui odérunt *me* *in***í**que.

21. Qui retríbuunt mala pro bonis, detrahébant **mi**hi: * quóniam sequébar *boni***tá**tem.

9. Lord, all my desire is before Thee, * and my groaning is not hidden from Thee.

10. My heart is troubled, † my strength hath left me, * and the light of my eyes itself is not with me.

11. My friends and my neighbours * have drawn near, and stood against me.

12. And they that were near me stood afar off: * and they that sought my soul used violence.

13. And they that sought evils to me spoke vain things, * and studied deceits all the day long.

14. But I, as a deaf man, heard not: * and as a dumb man not opening his mouth.

15. And I became as a man that heareth not: * and that hath no reproofs in his mouth.

16. For in Thee, O Lord, have I hoped: * Thou wilt hear me, O Lord my God.

17. For I said: Lest at any time my enemies rejoice over me: * and whilst my feet are moved, they speak great things against me.

18. For I am ready for scourges: * and my sorrow is continually before me.

19. For I will declare my iniquity: * and I will think for my sin.

20. But my enemies live, and are stronger than I: * and they that hate me wrongfully are multiplied.

21. They that render evil for good, have detracted me, * because I followed goodness.

22. Ne derelínquas me, Dómine, Deus **me**us: * ne discés*seris* **a** me.

22. Forsake me not, O Lord my God: * do not Thou depart from me.

23. Inténde in adjutórium **me**um, * Dómine, Deus, sa*lútis* **me**æ.

23. Attend unto my help, * O Lord, the God of my salvation.

1. Ant.
8.G

Vim fa-ci- é-bant   qui quæ-ré-bant á-nimam me- am.

The fourth candle is extinguished.

2. Ant.
4.A*

Confundántur * et re-ve-re- ántur, qui quæ-runt á-nimam me- am, ut áufe-rant e- am.

Antiphon: Let them be ashamed and confounded * together that seek after my soul, to destroy it.

Psalm 39

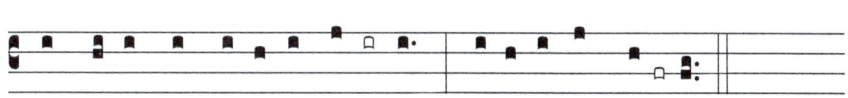

1. Exspéctans exspe*ctá-vi* **Dó**mi-num, * et *inténdit* **mi**- hi.

1. With expectation I have waited for the Lord, * and He was attentive to me.

2. Et exaudívit *preces* **me**as: * et edúxit me de lacu misériæ, et *de luto* **fæ**cis.

2. And He heard my prayers, * and brought me out of the pit of misery and the mire of dregs.

3. Et státuit super petram *pedes* **me**os: * et diré*xit gressus* **me**os.

3. And He set my feet upon a rock, * and directed my steps.

4. Et immísit in os meum cán*ticum* **no**vum * car*men Deo* **no**stro.

4. And He put a new canticle into my mouth, * a song to our God.

5. Vidébunt multi, *et ti***mé**bunt: * et spe*rábunt in* **Dó**mino.

5. Many shall see, and shall fear: * and they shall hope in the Lord.

6. Beátus vir, cujus est nomen Dóm*ini spes* ejus * et non respéxit in vanitátes et in*sánias* **fal**sas.

6. Blessed is the man whose trust is in the name of the Lord; * and who hath not had regard to vanities, and lying follies.

7. Multa fecísti tu, Dómine, Deus meus, mirab*ília* **tu**a: * et cogitatiónibus tuis non est qui sí*milis sit* **ti**bi.

7. Thou hast multiplied Thy wonderful works, O Lord my God: * and in Thy thoughts there is no one like to Thee.

8. Annuntiávi *et lo*cú*tus* sum: * multiplicáti *sunt super* **nú**merum.

8. I have declared and I have spoken * they are multiplied above number.

9. Sacrifícium et oblatiónem *nolu*ísti: * aures autem per*fecísti* **mi**hi.

9. Sacrifice and oblation Thou didst not desire; * but Thou hast pierced ears for me.

10. Holocáustum et pro peccáto non *postu*lásti: * tunc di*xi: Ecce* **vé**nio.

10. Burnt offering and sin offering Thou didst not require: * then said I, Behold I come.

11. In cápite libri scriptum est de me ut fácerem volun*tátem* **tu**am: * Deus meus, vólui, et legem tuam in médi*o* *cordis* **me**i.

11. In the head of the book it is written of me that I should do Thy will: * O my God, I have desired it, and Thy law in the midst of my heart.

12. Annuntiávi justítiam tuam in ecclé*sia* **ma**gna, * ecce lábia mea non prohibébo: Dó*mine, tu* **sci**sti.

12. I have declared Thy justice in a great church, * lo, I will not restrain my lips: O Lord, Thou knowest it.

13. Justítiam tuam non abscóndi in *corde* **me**o: * veritátem tuam et salutá*re tuum* **di**xi.

13. I have not hid Thy justice within my heart: * I have declared Thy truth and Thy salvation.

14. Non abscóndi misericórdiam tuam et veri*tátem* **tu**am * a con*cílio* **mul**to.

14. I have not concealed Thy mercy and Thy truth * from a great council.

15. Tu autem, Dómine, ne longe fácias miseratiónes *tuas* **a** me: * misericórdia tua et véritas tua sem*per* *susce***pé**runt me.

15. Withhold not Thou, O Lord, Thy tender mercies from me: * Thy mercy and Thy truth have always upheld me.

16. Quóniam circumdedérunt me mala, quorum *non est* **nú**merus: * comprehendérunt me iniquitátes meæ, et non pótu*i ut vi***dé**rem.

16. For evils without number have surrounded me; * my iniquities have overtaken me, and I was not able to see.

17. Multiplicátæ sunt super capíllos cá*pitis* **me**i: * et cor me*um dere*lí**quit me.

17. They are multiplied above the hairs of my head: * and my heart hath forsaken me.

18. Compláceat tibi, Dómine, ut *éru*as me: * Dómine, ad adju*vándum* *me* ré*spice.

19. Confundántur et revereántur simul, qui quærunt á*nimam* me*am, * ut *áuferant* e*am.

20. Convertántur retrórsum et reve*reán*tur: * qui vo*lunt mihi* ma*la.

21. Ferant conféstim confusi*ónem* su*am: * qui dicunt mi*hi*: *Euge,* eu*ge.

22. Exsúltent et læténtur super te om*nes quærén*tes te: * et dicant semper: Magnificétur Dóminus: qui díligunt sa*lutáre* tu*um.

23. Ego autem mendícus sum, *et* pau*per: * Dóminus sollí*citus est* me*i.

24. Adjútor meus et protéctor *meus* tu* es: * Deus me*us, ne tar*dá*veris.

18. Be pleased, O Lord to deliver me: * look down, O Lord, to help me.

19. Let them be confounded and ashamed together, that seek after my soul * to take it away.

20. Let them be turned backward and be ashamed * that desire evils to me.

21. Let them immediately bear their confusion, * that say to me: 'Tis well, 'tis well.

22. Let all that seek Thee rejoice and be glad in Thee: * and let such as love Thy salvation say always: The Lord be magnified.

23. But I am a beggar and poor: * the Lord is careful for me.

24. Thou art my helper and my protector: * O my God, be not slack.

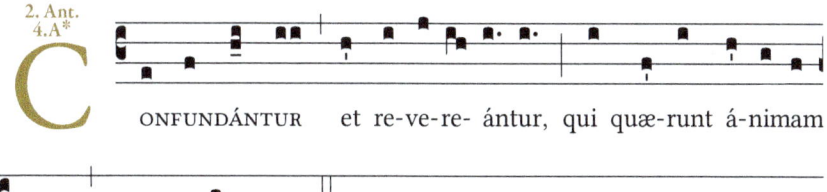

2. Ant.
4. A*

CONFUNDÁNTUR et re-ve-re- ántur, qui quæ-runt á-nimam

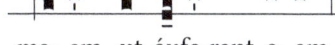

me- am, ut áufe-rant e- am.

The fifth candle is extinguished.

3. Ant.
4.A*

A - LI- ÉNI * insurre-xé-runt in me, et fortes quæ-si- é- runt

á-nimam me- am.

ANTIPHON: Strangers are risen up against me, * and oppressors seek after my soul.

PSALM 53

1. De- us, in nómi-ne tu- o *salvum* **me** fac: * et in virtú-te tu- *a jú-di-*

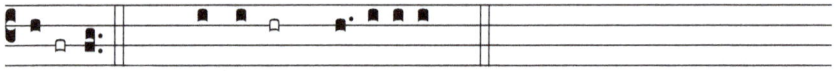

ca me. *Flex :* advérsum me, †

1. Save me, O God, by thy name, * and judge me in thy strength.

2. Deus, exáudi orati*ónem* **me**am: * áuribus pércipe ver*ba oris* **mei**.

2. O God, hear my prayer: * give ear to the words of my mouth.

3. Quóniam aliéni insurrexérunt advérsum me, † et fortes quæsiérunt *ánimam* **me**am: * et non proposuérunt Deum ante *conspéctum* **su**um.

3. For strangers have risen up against me; † and the mighty have sought after my soul: * and they have not set God before their eyes.

4. Ecce enim Deus *ádju*vat me: * et Dóminus suscéptor est *ánimæ* **meæ**.

4. For behold God is my helper: * and the Lord is the protector of my soul.

5. Avérte mala inimícis **me**is: * et in veritáte tua *dispérde* **illos**.

5. Turn back the evils upon my enemies; * and cut them off in thy truth.

6. Voluntárie sacrific*ábo* **ti**bi, * et confitébor nómini tuo, Dómine: *quóniam* **bo**num est:

6. I will freely sacrifice to thee, * and will give praise, O God, to thy name: because it is good:

7. Quóniam ex omni tribulatióne *eripu*ísti me: * et super inimícos meos despéxit *óculus* **me**us.

7. For thou hast delivered me out of all trouble: * and my eye hath looked down upon my enemies.

3. Ant.
4. A*

A - LI- ÉNI   insurre-xé-runt in me,   et fortes quæ-si- é- runt

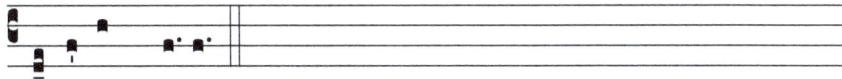

á-nimam me- am.

The sixth candle is extinguished.

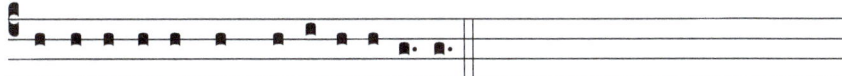

℣. Insurre-xé-runt in me testes in-íqui.

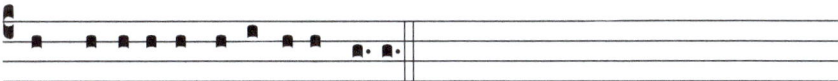

℟. Et mentí-ta est in-íqui-tas si-bi.

Or:

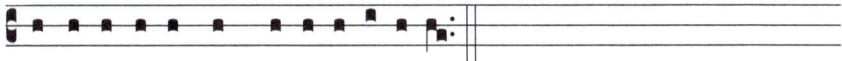

℣. Insurre-xé-runt in me testes in-íqui.

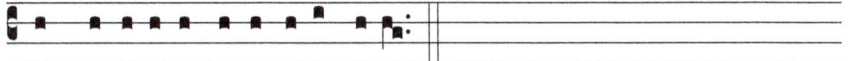

℟. Et mentí-ta est in-íqui-tas si-bi.

℣. False witnesses are risen up against me.
℟. And iniquity hath belied itself.

The Pater noster *is said silently.*

Lesson 4   St. Augustine, Bishop on Psalm 63 :2

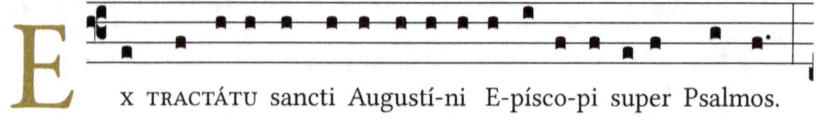

Ex tractátu sancti Augustí-ni E-písco-pi super Psalmos.

Pro-te-xí-sti me, De- us, a convéntu ma-lignánti- um, a mul-ti-tú-di-

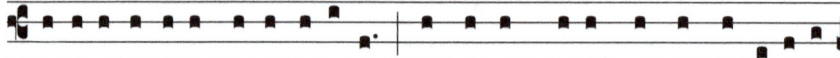

ne ope-ránti- um i-niqui-tá-tem. Jam ipsum caput nostrum intu- e- á-

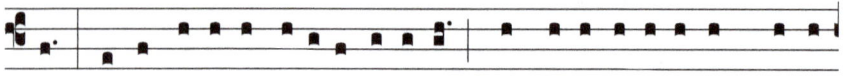

mur. Mul-ti Márty-res tá-li- a passi sunt, sed ni-hil sic e-lú-cet, quómo-

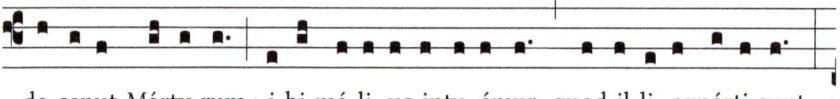

do caput Márty-rum : i-bi mé-li- us intu- émur, quod il-li expérti sunt.

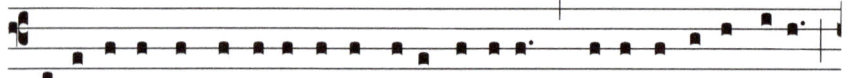

Pro-téctus est a mul-ti-tú-di-ne ma-lignánti- um, pro-te-génte se De- o,

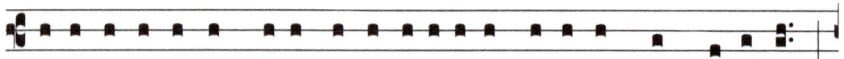

pro-te-génte carnem su- am ipso Fí-li- o, et hómi-ne, quem ge-ré-bat :

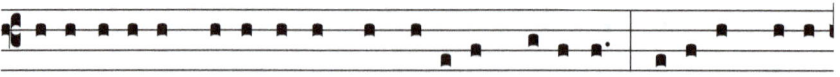

qui- a fí- li- us hómi- nis est, et Fí- li- us De- i est. Fí- li- us De- i,

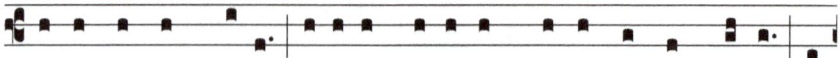

propter formam De- i : fí- li- us hómi-nis, propter formam servi, ha-

bens in po-testá-te póne-re á-nimam su- am, et re-cí-pe-re e- am.

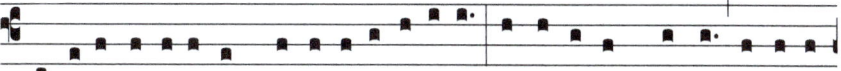

Quid e- i po-tu- é-runt fá-ce-re i-nimí-ci? Occi-dé-runt corpus, á-nimam

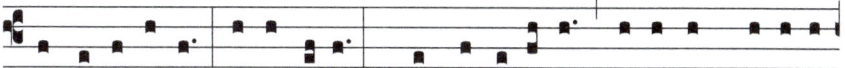

non occi-dé-runt. Inténdi-te. Pa-rum ergo e-rat, Dómi-num hortá-ri

Márty-res verbo, ni-si firmá-ret e-xémplo.

From the Treatise of St. Augustine, Bishop, Upon the Psalms.

LESSON 4: Thou hast hidden me from the secret counsel of the wicked, from the insurrection of the workers of iniquity. Now let us fix our eyes upon our Head. Many martyrs have suffered such things as He suffered, but God's hiding of His suffering servants is not so well seen in the Martyrs, as it is in the Captain of the Martyrs. And it is in Him that we best see how it fared with them. He was hidden from the secret counsel of the wicked; hidden by God, being Himself God; hidden, as touching the Manhood, by God the Son, and the very Manhood, Which is taken into God the Son; because He is the Son of man, and He is the Son of God; Son of God, as being in the form of God; Son of man, as having taken upon Him the form of a servant, Whose life no man taketh from Him, but Who layeth it down of Himself. He hath power to lay it down, and He hath power to take it again, What then was all that they which hated Him could do? They could kill the body, but they were not able to kill the soul. Consider this very earnestly. It had been a small thing for the Lord to preach to the Martyrs by His word, if He had not also nerved them by His example.

RESPONSORY 4   TAMQUAM AD LATRÓNEM

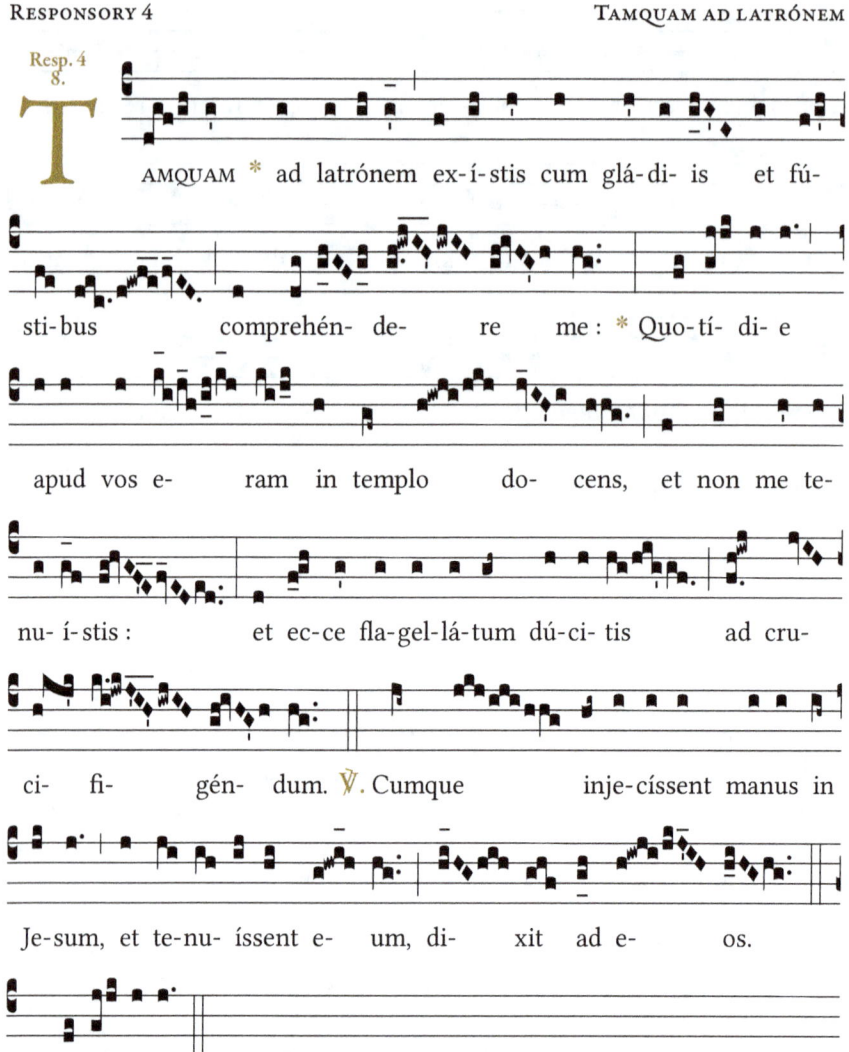

Resp. 4
8.

TAMQUAM * ad latrónem ex-í-stis cum glá-di- is et fú-sti-bus comprehén- de- re me : * Quo-tí- di- e apud vos e- ram in templo do- cens, et non me te-nu- í-stis : et ec-ce fla-gel-lá-tum dú-ci- tis ad cru-ci- fi- gén- dum. ℣. Cumque inje-císsent manus in Je-sum, et te-nu- íssent e- um, di- xit ad e- os.

* Quo-tí- di- e.

℟. Are ye come out, as against a thief, with swords and staves, for to take Me? * I sat daily with you, teaching in the Temple, and ye laid no hold on Me; and, now when ye have scourged Me, ye lead Me away to crucify Me! ℣. And when they had laid hands on Jesus, and taken Him, He said unto them: ℟. I sat daily with you, teaching in the Temple, and ye laid no hold on Me; and now, when ye have scourged Me, ye lead Me away to crucify Me!

Lesson 5   St. Augustine, Bishop on Psalm 63 :2

N ostis qui convéntus e-rat ma-lignánti- um Judæ- ó-rum,

et quæ mul-ti-túdo e-rat ope-ránti- um i-niqui-tá-tem. Quam i-niqui-

tá-tem? Qui- a vo-lu- é-runt occí-de-re Dómi-num Je-sum Christum.

Tanta ópe-ra bona, inquit, osténdi vo-bis : propter quod ho-rum me vul-

tis occí-de-re? Pértu-lit omnes infírmos e- ó-rum, cu-rá-vit omnes lán-

gui-dos e- ó-rum, prædi-cá-vit regnum cæ-ló-rum, non tá-cu- it ví-ti- a

e- ó-rum, ut ipsa pó-ti- us e- is displi-cé-rent, non mé-di-cus, a quo sa-

na-bántur. His ómni-bus cu-ra-ti- ó-ni-bus e-ius ingrá-ti, tamquam mul-

ta febre phrené-ti-ci, insa-ni- éntes in mé-di-cum, qui véne-rat cu-rá-

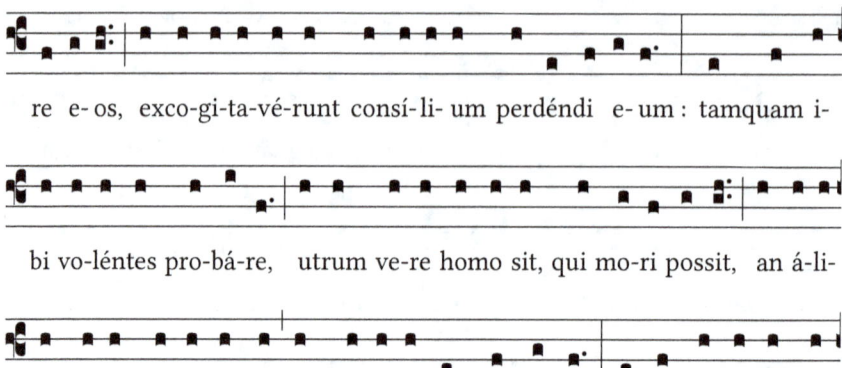

re e- os, exco-gi-ta-vé-runt consí-li- um perdéndi e- um : tamquam i-

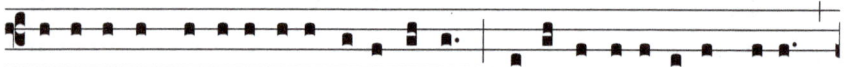

bi vo-léntes pro-bá-re,   utrum ve-re homo sit, qui mo-ri possit,   an á-li-

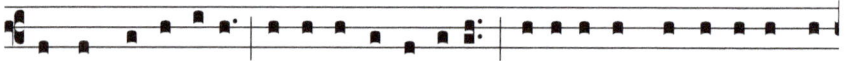

quid super hómi-nes sit, et mo-ri se non permít-tat. Verbum ipsó-rum a-

gnóscimus in Sa-pi- énti- a Sa-lomó-nis : Morte turpíssima, ínqui- unt,

condemnémus e- um. Interro-gémus e- um : e-rit e-nim respéctus in ser-

mó-ni-bus il-lí- us. Si e-nim ve-re Fí-li- us De- i est, lí-be-ret e- um.

LESSON 5: We know what secret counsel was that of the wicked Jews, and what insurrection was that of the workers of iniquity. Of what iniquity were they the workers? The murder of our Lord Jesus Christ. Many good works, saith He, have I showed you: for which of those works go ye about to kill Me? He had borne with all their weaknesses: He had healed all their diseases: He had preached unto them the kingdom of heaven: He had discovered to them their iniquities, that they might rather hate them, than the Physician that came to cure them. And now at last, without gratitude for all the tenderness of His healing love, like men raging in a high delirium, throwing themselves madly on the Physician, Who had come to cure them, they took counsel together how they might kill Him, as if to see if He were a Man and could die, or something more than a man, and that would not let Himself die. In the Wisdom of Solomon we recognize their words. Let us condemn Him with a shameful death. Let us examine Him; for, by His own saying, He shall be respected. If He be the Son of God, let Him help Him.

RESPONSORY 5 TÉNEBRÆ FACTÆ SUNT

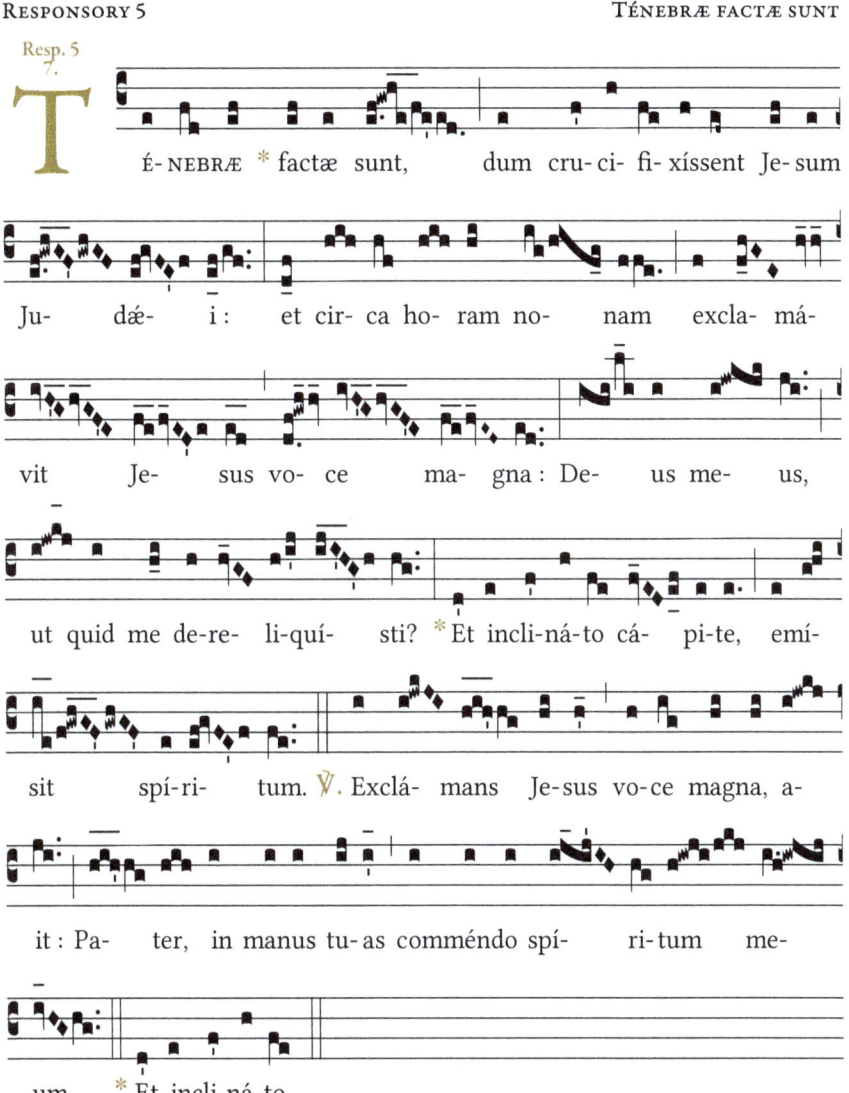

Té-NEBRÆ * factæ sunt, dum cru-ci-fi-xíssent Je-sum Ju-dǽ-i: et cir-ca ho-ram no-nam excla-má-vit Je-sus vo-ce ma-gna: De-us me-us, ut quid me de-re-li-quí-sti? * Et incli-ná-to cá-pi-te, emí-sit spí-ri-tum. ℣. Exclá-mans Je-sus vo-ce magna, a-it: Pa-ter, in manus tu-as comméndo spí-ri-tum me-um. * Et incli-ná-to.

℟. The Jews crucified Jesus: and there was darkness (over all the land, unto the ninth hour): and about the ninth hour Jesus cried with a loud voice, (saying): My God, (My God,) why hast Thou forsaken Me? * And He bowed His Head, and gave up the Ghost. ℣. When Jesus had cried with a loud voice, He said: Father, into Thy hands I commend My Spirit. ℟. And He bowed His Head, and gave up the Ghost.

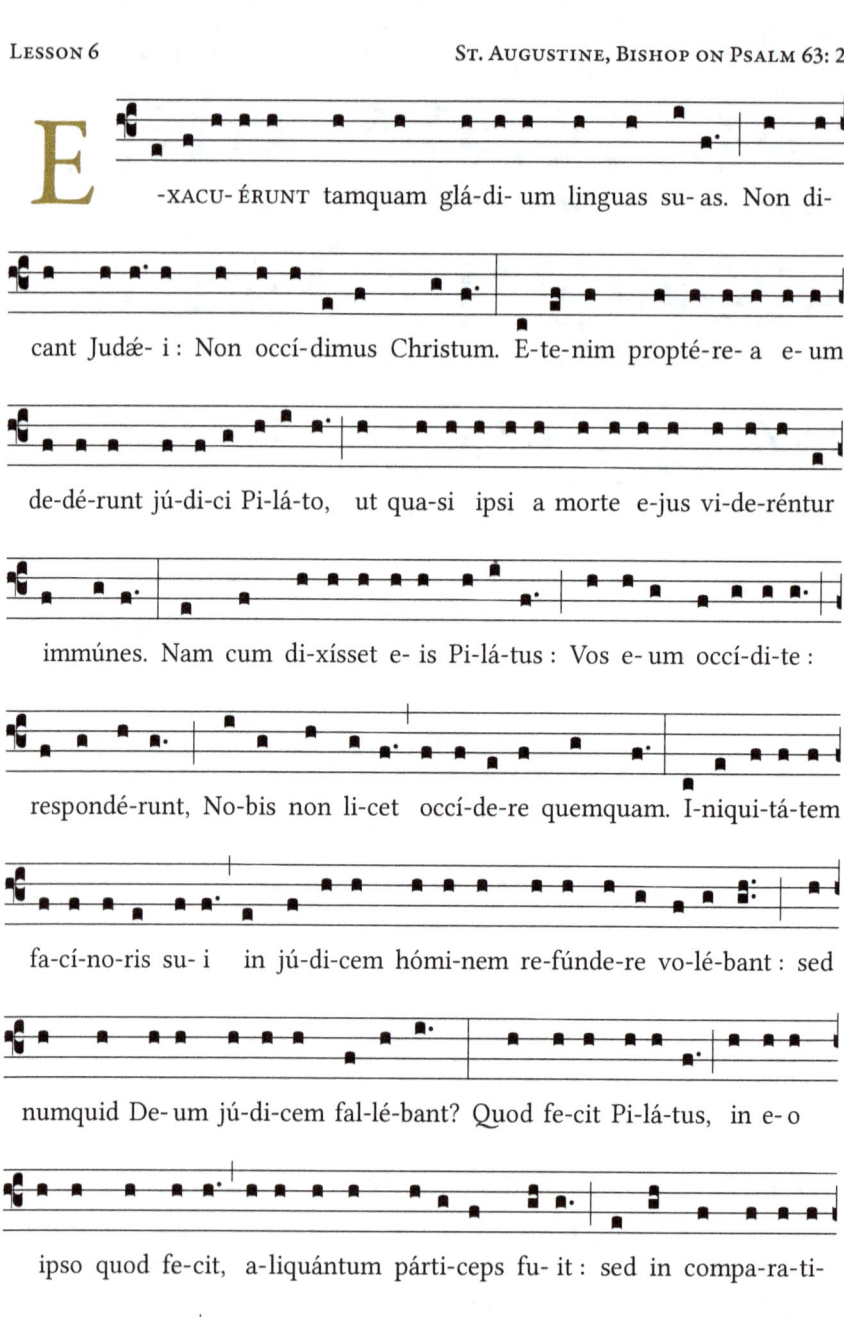

E-XACU-ÉRUNT tamquam glá-di-um linguas su-as. Non di-

cant Judǽ-i : Non occí-dimus Christum. E-te-nim propté-re-a e-um

de-dé-runt jú-di-ci Pi-lá-to, ut qua-si ipsi a morte e-jus vi-de-réntur

immúnes. Nam cum di-xísset e-is Pi-lá-tus : Vos e-um occí-di-te :

respondé-runt, No-bis non li-cet occí-de-re quemquam. I-niqui-tá-tem

fa-cí-no-ris su-i in jú-di-cem hómi-nem re-fúnde-re vo-lé-bant : sed

numquid De-um jú-di-cem fal-lé-bant? Quod fe-cit Pi-lá-tus, in e-o

ipso quod fe-cit, a-liquántum párti-ceps fu-it : sed in compa-ra-ti-

óne il-ló-rum multo ipse inno-cénti-or. Insti-tit e-nim quantum

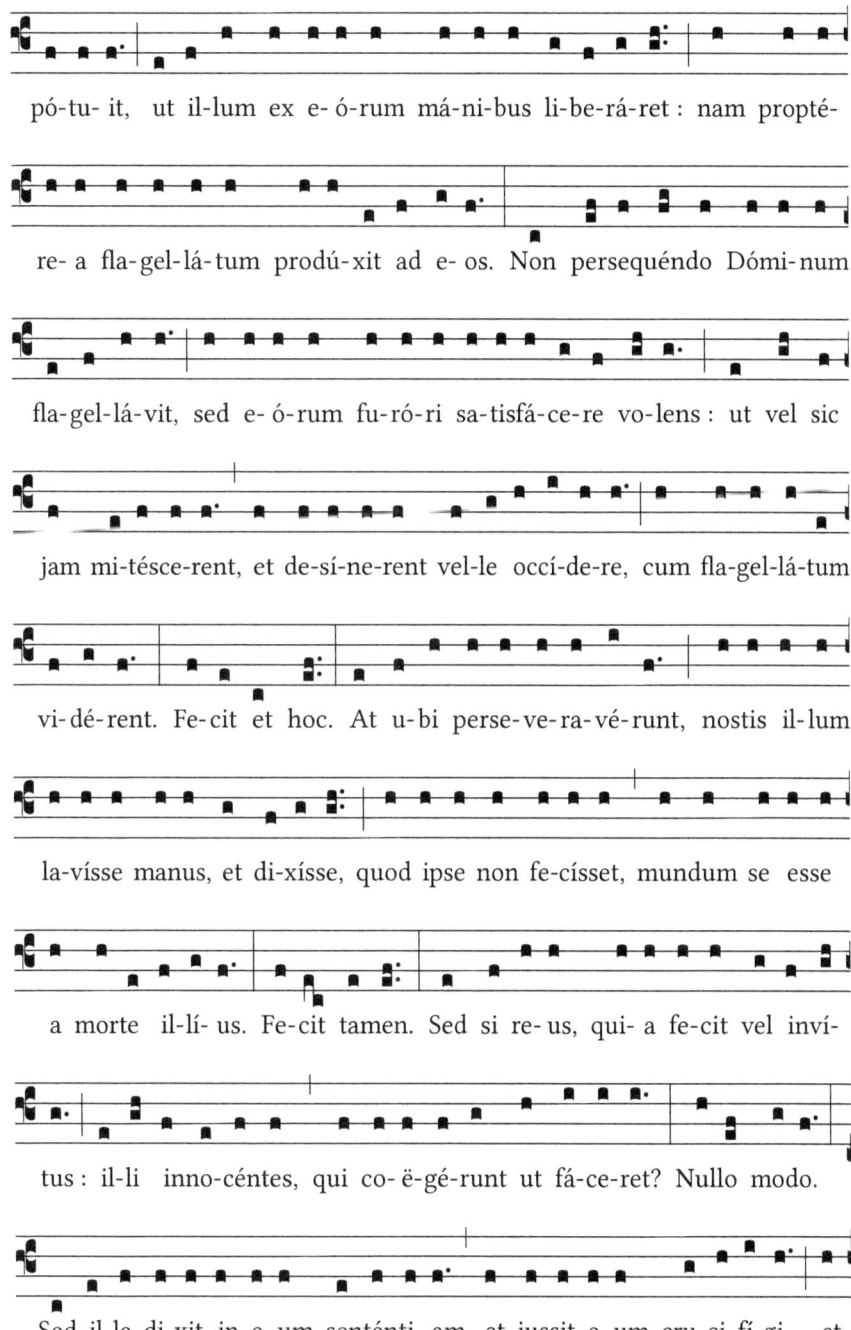

pó-tu- it, ut il-lum ex e- ó-rum má-ni-bus li-be-rá-ret : nam propté-

re- a fla-gel-lá-tum prodú-xit ad e- os.   Non persequéndo Dómi-num

fla-gel-lá-vit, sed e- ó-rum fu-ró-ri sa-tisfá-ce-re vo-lens : ut vel sic

jam mi-tésce-rent, et de-sí-ne-rent vel-le occí-de-re, cum fla-gel-lá-tum

vi- dé-rent. Fe-cit et hoc. At u- bi perse-ve-ra-vé-runt, nostis il-lum

la-vísse manus, et di-xísse, quod ipse non fe-císset, mundum se esse

a morte il-lí- us. Fe-cit tamen. Sed si re- us, qui- a fe-cit vel invi-

tus : il-li inno-céntes, qui co- ë-gé-runt ut fá-ce-ret? Nullo modo.

Sed il-le di-xit in e- um senténti- am, et jussit e- um cru-ci-fí-gi,   et

qua-si ipse occí-dit : et vos, o Judǽ- i, occi-dí-stis. Unde occi-dí-stis?

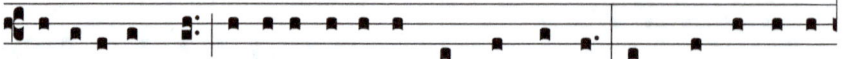

Glá-di- o linguæ : a-cu- í-stis e-nim linguas vestras. Et quando percus-

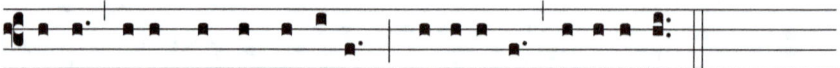

sí-stis, ni-si quando clamástis : Cru-ci-fí-ge, cru-ci-fí-ge?

LESSON 6: They whetted their tongue like a sword. The Jews cannot say: We did not murder Christ, albeit they gave Him over to Pilate His judge, that they themselves might seem free of His death. For when Pilate said unto them, Take ye Him: and kill Him, they answered, It is not lawful for us to put any man to death. They could throw the blame of their sin upon a human judge: but did they deceive God, the Great Judge? In that which Pilate did, he was their accomplice, but in comparison with them, he had far the lesser sin. Pilate strove, as far as he could, to deliver Him out of their hands; for the which reason also he scourged Him, and brought Him forth to them. He scourged not the Lord for cruelty's sake, but in the hope that he might so slake their wild thirst for blood: that, perchance, even they might be touched with compassion, and cease to lust for His death, when they saw what He was after the flagellation. Even this effort he made! But when Pilate saw that he could not prevail, but that rather a tumult was made, ye know how that he took water, and washed his hands before the multitude, saying: I am innocent of the blood of this Just Person. And yet he delivered Him to be crucified! But if he were guilty who did it against his will, were they innocent who goaded him on to it? No. Pilate gave sentence against Him and commanded Him to be crucified. But ye, O ye Jews, ye also are His murderers! Wherewith? With your tongue, whetted like a sword. And when? But when ye cried, Crucify Him! Crucify Him!

Responsory 6   Animam meam diléctam

A-nimam me- am * di-lé- ctam trá-di- di in ma- nus in-

iquó- rum, et facta est mi- hi he-ré-di- tas me- a

sic- ut le- o in sil-va : de-dit contra me vo-ces adver-sá-

ri- us, di-cens : Congre-gá- mi-ni, et pro-pe-rá-

te ad de-vo-rán- dum il-lum : po-su- é-runt me in de- sér-

to so-li- tú-di- nis, et lu- xit super me omnis ter- ra :

*Qui- a non est invéntus qui me agnó- sce- ret, et fá- ce-

ret be- ne. ℣. Insurre-xé-runt in me vi-ri absque mi-se-ri-

córdi- a, et non pe-percé-runt á- ni-mæ me- æ.

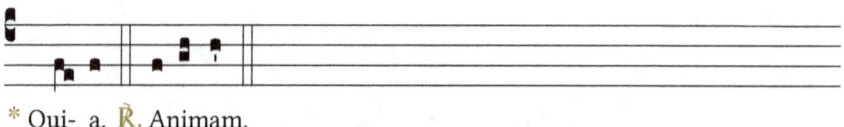

* Qui- a. ℟. Animam.

℟. I have given the dearly-beloved of My soul into the hand of her enemies and Mine heritage is become unto Me as a lion in the forest; the enemy crieth out against Me, saying: Assemble yourselves together, hasten to devour Him: they have made My portion a desolate wilderness, and the whole land mourneth unto Me: * Because there is none found that will know Me, nor do well. ℣. There be risen up against me such as breathe out cruelty, and they have not spared my soul. ℟. Because there is none found that will know Me, nor do well. ℟. I have given the dearly-beloved of My soul into the hand of her enemies, and Mine heritage is become unto Me as a lion in the forest: the enemy crieth out against Me, saying: Assemble yourselves together, hasten to devour Him: they have made My portion a desolate wilderness, and the whole land mourneth unto me: * Because there is none found that will know Me, nor do well.

3RD NOCTURN

1. Ant.
1.f

B insurgénti-bus in me * lí-be-ra me, Dómi-ne, qui- a

occupa-vé-runt á-nimam me- am.

ANTIPHON: O Lord, defend me from them that rise up against me, * for they lie in wait for my life.

PSALM 58

1. E-ri-pe me de in-imí-cis me- is, **De-** us **me-** us: * et ab insurgén-

ti-bus in me *lí-be-***ra** me. *Flex :* o-re su- o, †

1. Deliver me from my enemies, O my God; * and defend me from them that rise up against me.

2. Eripe me de operántibus iniquitátem : * et de viris sán*guinum* **sal**va me.

2. Deliver me from them that work iniquity, * and save me from bloody men.

3. Quia ecce cepérunt **á**nimam **me**am : * irruérunt *in me* **for**tes.

3. For behold they have caught my soul: * the mighty have rushed in upon me:

4. Neque iníquitas mea, neque peccátum **me**um, **Dó**mine : * sine iniquitáte cucúrri, *et di***ré**xi.

4. Neither is it my iniquity, nor my sin, O Lord: * without iniquity have I run, and directed my steps.

5. Exsúrge in occúrsum **me**um, et **vi**de : * et tu, Dómine, Deus virtútum, *Deus* **Is**raël.

5. Rise up Thou to meet me, and behold: * even Thou, O Lord, the God of hosts, the God of Israel.

6. Inténde ad visitándas **o**mnes **Gen**tes : * non misereáris ómnibus, qui operántur in*iqui***tá**tem.

6. Attend to visit all the nations: * have no mercy on all them that work iniquity.

7. Converténtur ad vésperam : et famem patién**tur** ut **ca**nes : * et circuíbunt *civi***tá**tem.

7. They shall return at evening, and shall suffer hunger like dogs: * and shall go round about the city.

8. Ecce loquéntur in ore suo, † et gládius in lábi**is** e**ó**rum : * quóniam *quis au***dí**vit?

8. Behold they shall speak with their mouth, † and a sword is in their lips: * for who, say they, hath heard us?

9. Et tu, Dómine, deri**dé**bis eos : * ad níhilum dedúces *omnes* **Gen**tes.

9. But Thou, O Lord, shalt laugh at them: * Thou shalt bring all the nations to nothing.

10. Fortitúdinem meam ad te custódiam, † quia, Deus, sus**cé**ptor **me**us es : * Deus meus, misericórdia ejus præ*véni***et** me.

10. I will keep my strength to Thee: for Thou art my protector: * my God, His mercy shall prevent me.

11. Deus osténdet mihi super inimícos meos, ne occídas eos : * nequándo obliviscántur pópuli mei.

12. Dispérge illos in virtúte tua : * et depóne eos, protéctor meus, Dómine :

13. Delíctum oris eórum, sermónem labiórum ipsórum : * et comprehendántur in supérbia sua.

14. Et de exsecratióne et mendácio annuntiabúntur in consummatióne: * in ira consummatiónis, et non erunt.

15. Et scient quia Deus dominábitur Jacob : * et fínium terræ.

16. Converténtur ad vésperam : et famem patiéntur ut canes, * et circuíbunt civitátem.

17. Ipsi dispergéntur ad manducándum : * si vero non fúerint saturáti, et murmurábunt.

18. Ego autem cantábo fortitúdinem tuam : * et exsultábo mane misericórdiam tuam.

19. Quia factus es suscéptor meus, * et refúgium meum, in die tribulatiónis meæ.

20. Adjútor meus, tibi psallam, † quia, Deus, suscéptor meus es : * Deus meus, misericórdia mea.

11. God shall let me see over my enemies: slay them not, * lest at any time my people forget.

12. And scatter them by Thy power; * and bring them down, O Lord, my protector:

13. For the sin of their mouth, and the word of their lips: * and let them be taken in their pride.

14. And for their cursing and lying they shall be talked of, when they are consumed: * when they are consumed by Thy wrath, and they shall be no more.

15. And they shall know that God will rule Jacob, * and all the ends of the earth.

16. They shall return at evening and shall suffer hunger like dogs: * and shall go round about the city.

17. They shall be scattered abroad to eat, * and shall murmur if they be not filled.

18. But I will sing Thy strength: * and will extol Thy mercy in the morning.

19. For Thou art become my support, * and my refuge, in the day of my trouble.

20. Unto Thee, O my helper, will I sing, † for Thou art God my defence: * my God my mercy.

1. Ant.
1.f

AB insurgénti-bus in me lí-be-ra me, Dómi-ne, qui- a occupa-vé-runt á-nimam me- am.

The seventh candle is extinguished.

2. Ant.
8.G

Longe fe-cí-sti * no-tos me- os a me : trá-di-tus sum, et non

egre-di- é-bar.

ANTIPHON: Thou hast put away mine acquaintance far from me; * I am shut up, and cannot come forth.

PSALM 87

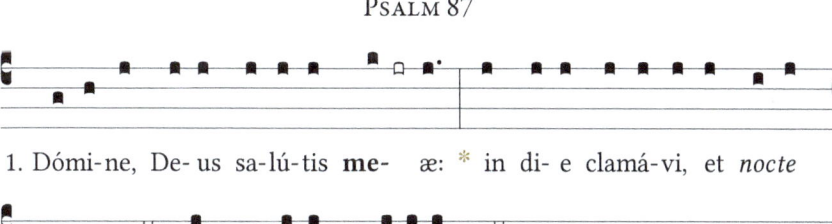

1. Dómi-ne, De- us sa-lú-tis me- æ: * in di- e clamá-vi, et *nocte*

co-ram te.   *Flex :* in sepúlcris, †

1. Lord, the God of my salvation: * I have cried in the day, and in the night before Thee.

2. Intret in conspéctu tuo orátio **me**a : * inclína aurem tuam ad *precem* **me**am :

2. Let my prayer come in before Thee : * incline Thy ear to my petition.

3. Quia repléta est malis ánima **me**a : * et vita mea inférno ap*propin***quá**vit.

3. For my soul is filled with evils : * and my life hath drawn nigh to hell.

4. Æstimátus sum cum descendénti-bus in **lacum** : * factus sum sicut homo sine adjutório, inter mór*tuos* **li**ber.

4. I am counted among them that go down to the pit : * I am become as a man without help, free among the dead.

5. Sicut vulneráti dormiéntes in sepúlcris, † quorum non es memor **ám**plius : * et ipsi de manu tu*a* re**púl**si sunt.

5. Like the slain sleeping in the sepulchres, † whom Thou remember-est no more : * and they are cast off from Thy hand.

6. Posuérunt me in lacu inferióri : * in tenebrósis, et in *umbra* **mor**tis.

6. They have laid me in the lower pit: * in the dark places, and in the shadow of death.

7. Super me confirmátus est furor **tu**us : * et omnes fluctus tuos indu*xísti* **su**per me.

7. Thy wrath is strong over me: * and all Thy waves Thou hast brought in upon me.

8. Longe fecísti notos meos **a** me : * posuérunt me abominati*ónem* **si**bi.

8. Thou hast put away my acquaintance far from me: * they have set me an abomination to themselves.

9. Tráditus sum, et non egrediébar : * óculi mei languérunt *præ in*ó*pia.

9. I was delivered up, and came not forth: * my eyes languished through poverty.

10. Clamávi ad te, Dómine, tota **die** : * expándi ad te *manus* **me**as.

10. All the day I cried to Thee, O Lord: * I stretched out my hands to Thee.

11. Numquid mórtuis fácies mira**bí**lia : * aut médici suscitábunt, et confite*búntur* **ti**bi?

11. Wilt Thou shew wonders to the dead? * or shall physicians raise to life, and give praise to Thee?

12. Numquid narrábit áliquis in sepúlcro misericórdiam **tu**am, * et veritátem tuam in per*diti*ó*ne?

12. Shall any one in the sepulchre declare Thy mercy: * and Thy truth in destruction?

13. Numquid cognoscéntur in ténebris mirabília **tu**a, * et justítia tua in terra ob*livi*ó*nis?

13. Shall Thy wonders be known in the dark; * and Thy justice in the land of forgetfulness?

14. Et ego ad te, Dómine, clam**á**vi : * et mane orátio mea præ*véni*et te.

14. But I, O Lord, have cried to Thee: * and in the morning my prayer shall prevent Thee.

15. Ut quid, Dómine, repéllis oratiónem **me**am : * avértis fáciem *tuam* **a** me?

15. Lord, why castest Thou off my prayer: * why turnest Thou away Thy face from me?

16. Pauper sum ego, et in labóribus a juventúte **me**a : * exaltátus autem, humiliátus sum et *contur***bá**tus.

16. I am poor, and in labours from my youth: * and being exalted have been humbled and troubled.

17. In me transiérunt iræ **tu**æ : * et terróres tui con*turba***vé**runt me.

17. Thy wrath hath come upon me: * and Thy terrors have troubled me.

18. Circumdedérunt me sicut aqua tota **die** : * circumdedé*runt me* **si**mul.

18. They have come round about me like water all the day: * they have compassed me about together.

19. Elongásti a me amícum et **pró**ximum : * et notos meos *a mis*éria.

19. Friend and neighbour Thou hast put far from me: * and my acquaintance, because of misery.

2. Ant.
8.G

Longe fe-cí-sti no-tos me- os a me : trá-di-tus sum, et non egre-di- é-bar.

The eighth candle is extinguished.

3. Ant.
8.G

Captábunt * in á-nimam ju-sti, et sángui-nem inno-céntem condemná-bunt.

ANTIPHON: They will hunt after the soul of the Just; * and will condemn innocent blood.

Psalm 93

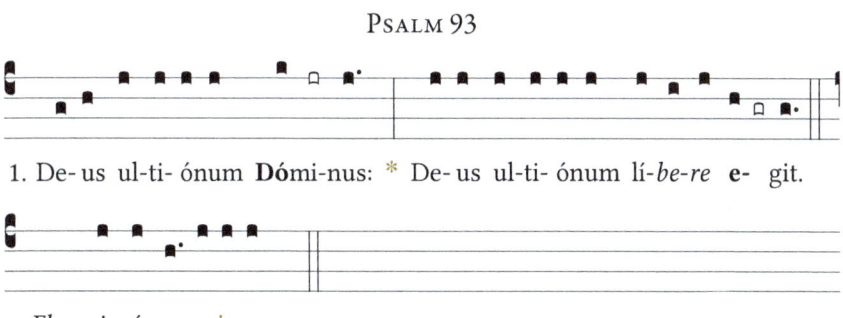

1. De- us ul-ti- ónum **Dó**mi-nus: * De- us ul-ti- ónum lí-*be-re* **e**- git.

Flex : ipsó-rum: †

1. The Lord is the God to Whom revenge belongeth: * the God of revenge hath acted freely.

2. Exaltáre, qui júdicas **ter**ram : *
redde retributió*nem su***pér**bis.

3. Usquequo peccatóres, **Dó**mine : *
úsquequo peccatóres glor*ia***bún**tur :

4. Effabúntur et loquéntur
iniqui**tá**tem : * loquéntur omnes, qui
operántur *inju***stí**tiam?

5. Pópulum tuum, Dómine,
humiliavérunt : * et hereditátem tuam
*vexa***vé**runt.

6. Víduam et ádvenam inter-
fecérunt : * et pupíllos *occi***dé**runt.

7. Et dixérunt : Non vidébit **Dó**mi-
nus : * nec intélliget *Deus* **Ja**cob.

8. Intellígite, insipiéntes in
pópulo : * et stulti, ali*quándo* **sá**pite.

9. Qui plantávit aurem, non
áudiet? * aut qui finxit óculum, *non*
*con***sí**derat?

10. Qui córripit Gentes, non
árguet : * qui docet hómi*nem*
*sci***én**tiam?

11. Dóminus scit cogitatiónes
hóminum, * quóni*am* **va**næ sunt.

12. Beátus homo, quem tu erudíeris,
Dómine, * et de lege tua docú*eris* eum.

13. Ut mítiges ei a diébus **ma**lis : *
donec fodiátur pecca*tóri* **fó**vea.

14. Quia non repéllet Dóminus
plebem **su**am : * et hereditátem suam
non *dere***lín**quet.

15. Quoadúsque justítia convertátur in ju**dí**cium : * et qui juxta illam
omnes qui re*cto sunt* **cor**de.

2. Lift up Thyself, Thou that judg-
est the earth: * render a reward to the
proud.

3. How long shall sinners, O Lord: *
how long shall sinners glory?

4. Shall they utter, and speak iniquity: * shall all speak who work injus-
tice?

5. Thy people, O Lord, they have
brought low: * and they have afflicted
Thy inheritance.

6. They have slain the widow and
the stranger: * and they have murdered the fatherless.

7. And they have said: The Lord
shall not see: * neither shall the God
of Jacob understand.

8. Understand, ye senseless among
the people: * and, you fools, be wise
at last.

9. He that planted the ear, shall He
not hear? * or He that formed the eye,
doth He not consider?

10. He that chastiseth nations, shall
He not rebuke: * He that teacheth
man knowledge?

11. The Lord knoweth the thoughts
of men, * that they are vain.

12. Blessed is the man whom Thou
shalt instruct, O Lord: * and shalt
teach him out of Thy law.

13. That Thou mayst give him rest
from the evil days: * till a pit be dug
for the wicked.

14. For the Lord will not cast off
His people: * neither will He forsake
His own inheritance.

15. Until justice be turned into
judgment: * and they that are near it
are all the upright in heart.

16. Quis consúrget mihi advérsus malignántes? * aut quis stabit mecum advérsus operántes in*iqui*tátem?

16. Who shall rise up for me against the evildoers? * or who shall stand with me against the workers of iniquity?

17. Nisi quia Dóminus ad**jú**vit me : * paulo minus habitásset in inférno á*nima* **me**a.

17. Unless the Lord had been my helper, * my soul had almost dwelt in hell.

18. Si dicébam : Motus est pes **me**us : * misericórdia tua, Dómine, *adju***vá**bat me.

18. If I said: My foot is moved: * Thy mercy, O Lord, assisted me.

19. Secúndum multitúdinem dolórum meórum in corde **me**o : * consolatiónes tuæ lætificavérunt á*nimam* **me**am.

19. According to the multitude of my sorrows in my heart, * Thy comforts have given joy to my soul.

20. Numquid adhǽret tibi sedes iniqui**tá**tis : * qui fingis labórem *in præ***cé**pto?

20. Doth the seat of iniquity stick to thee, * who framest labour in commandment?

21. Captábunt in ánimam **ju**sti : * et sánguinem innocéntem *condem***ná**bunt.

21. They will hunt after the soul of the just, * and will condemn innocent blood.

22. Et factus est mihi Dóminus in re**fú**gium : * et Deus meus in adjutórium *spei* **me**æ.

22. But the Lord is my refuge: * and my God the help of my hope.

23. Et reddet illis iniquitátem ipsórum : † et in malítia eórum dispérdet **e**os : * dispérdet illos Dóminus *Deus* **no**ster.

23. And He will render them their iniquity: † and in their malice He will destroy them: * the Lord our God will destroy them.

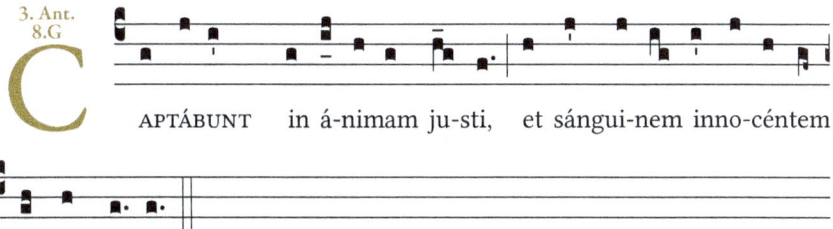

3. Ant.
8.G

CAPTÁBUNT in á-nimam ju-sti, et sángui-nem inno-céntem

condemná-bunt.

The ninth candle is extinguished.

℣. Lo-cú-ti sunt advérsum me lingua do-ló-sa. ℟. Et sermó-ni-bus ó-di- i

circumde-dé-runt me, et expugna-vé-runt me gra-tis.

Or:

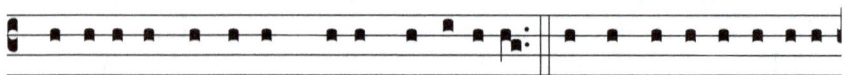

℣. Lo-cú-ti sunt advérsum me lingua do-ló-sa. ℟. Et sermó-ni-bus ó-di- i

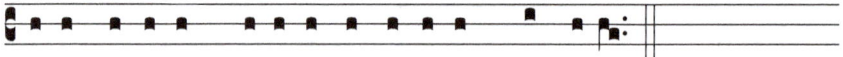

circumde-dé-runt me, et expugna-vé-runt me gra-tis.

℣. They have spoken against me with a lying tongue.

℟. They compassed me about also with words of hatred, and fought against me without a cause.

The Pater noster *is said silently.*

LESSON 7   HEBREWS 4: 11-15

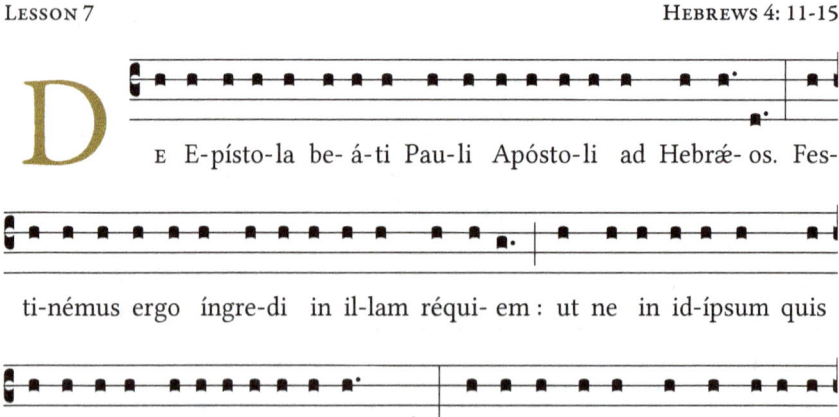

D E E-písto-la be- á-ti Pau-li Apósto-li ad Hebræ- os. Fes-

ti-némus ergo íngre-di in il-lam réqui- em : ut ne in id-ípsum quis

ínci-dat incredu-li-tá-tis ex-émplum. Vi-vus est e-nim sermo De- i, et

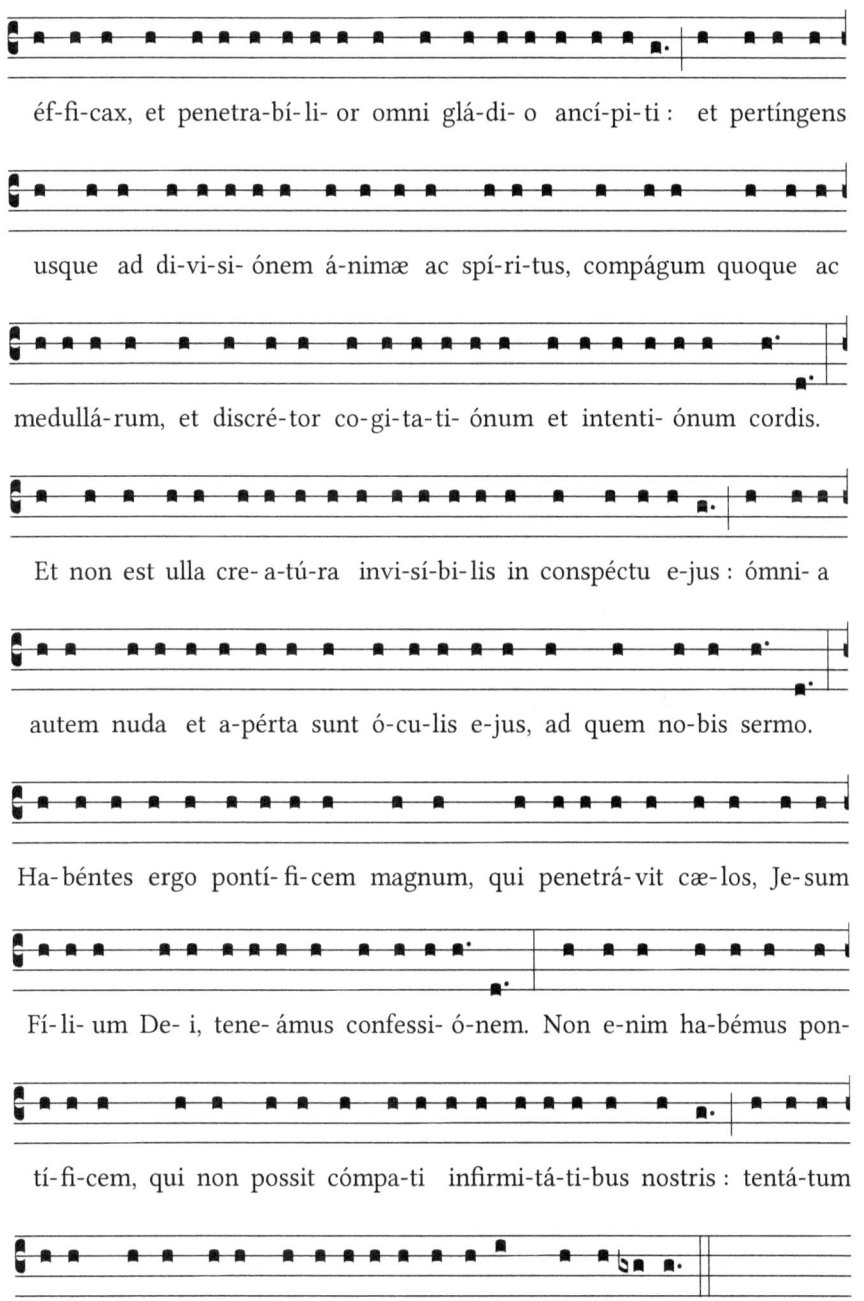

éf-fi-cax, et penetra-bí- li- or omni glá-di- o ancí-pi-ti : et pertíngens

usque ad di-vi-si- ónem á-nimæ ac spí-ri-tus, compágum quoque ac

medullá-rum, et discré-tor co-gi-ta-ti- ónum et intenti- ónum cordis.

Et non est ulla cre- a-tú-ra invi-sí-bi-lis in conspéctu e-jus : ómni- a

autem nuda et a-pérta sunt ó-cu-lis e-jus, ad quem no-bis sermo.

Ha-béntes ergo pontí- fi-cem magnum, qui penetrá-vit cæ-los, Je-sum

Fí-li- um De- i, tene- ámus confessi- ó-nem. Non e-nim ha-bémus pon-

tí-fi-cem, qui non possit cómpa-ti infirmi-tá-ti-bus nostris : tentá-tum

autem per ómni- a pro simi-li-tú-di-ne absque peccá-to.

From the letter of the blessed Apostle Paul to the Hebrews.

LESSON 7: Let us hasten therefore to enter into that rest; lest any man fall into the same example of unbelief. For the word of God is living and effectual, and more piercing than any two edged sword; and reaching unto the division of the soul and the spirit, of the joints also and the marrow, and is a discerner of the thoughts and intents of the heart. Neither is there any creature invisible in His sight: but all things are naked and open to His eyes, to whom our speech is. Having therefore a great high priest that hath passed into the heavens, Jesus the Son of God: let us hold fast our confession. For we have not a high priest, who cannot have compassion on our infirmities: but One tempted in all things like as we are, without sin.

RESPONSORY 7　　　　　　　　　　　　　　　TRADIDÉRUNT ME IN MANUS

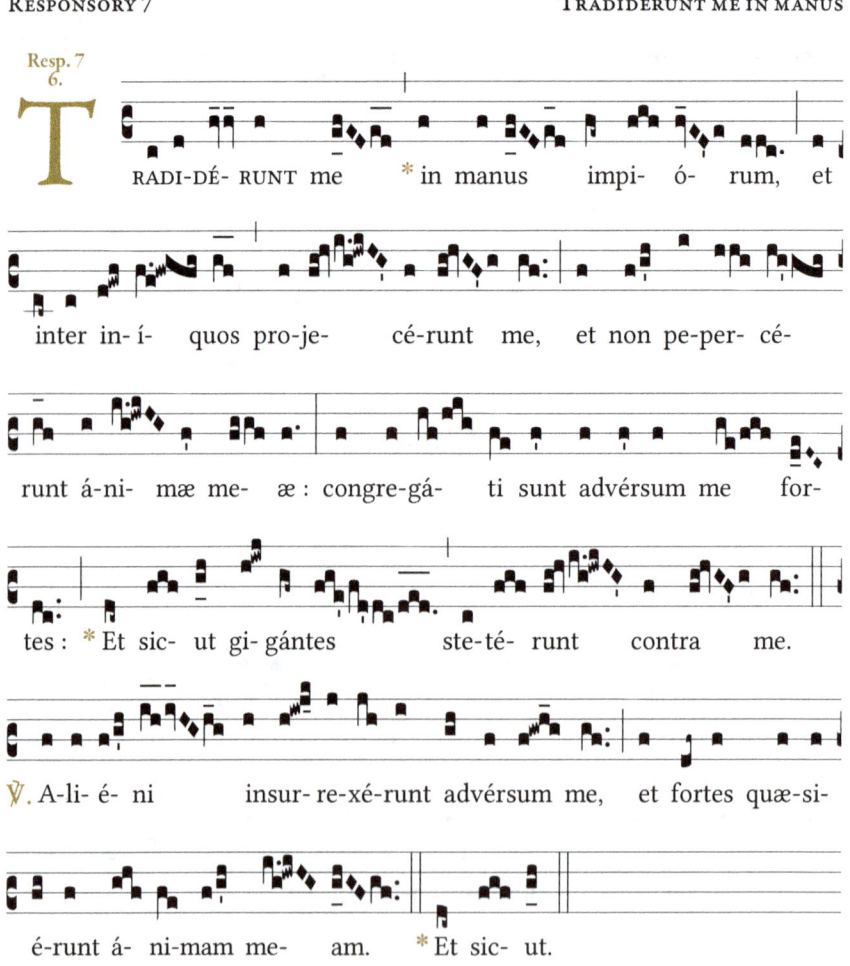

RADI-DÉ-RUNT me *in manus impi-ó-rum, et inter in-í-quos pro-je-cé-runt me, et non pe-per-cé-runt á-ni-mæ me-æ: congre-gá-ti sunt advérsum me for-tes: *Et sic-ut gi-gántes ste-té-runt contra me.

℣. A-li-é-ni insur-re-xé-runt advérsum me, et fortes quæ-si-é-runt á-ni-mam me-am. *Et sic-ut.

℟. They have turned me over into the hands of the wicked: they also have numbered me with the transgressors, neither have they spared my life: the mighty are gathered together against me; * And stand up against me like giants. ℣. Strangers are risen up against me, and oppressors seek after my soul. ℟. And stand up against me like giants.

LESSON 8   HEBREWS 4: 16; 5: 1-3

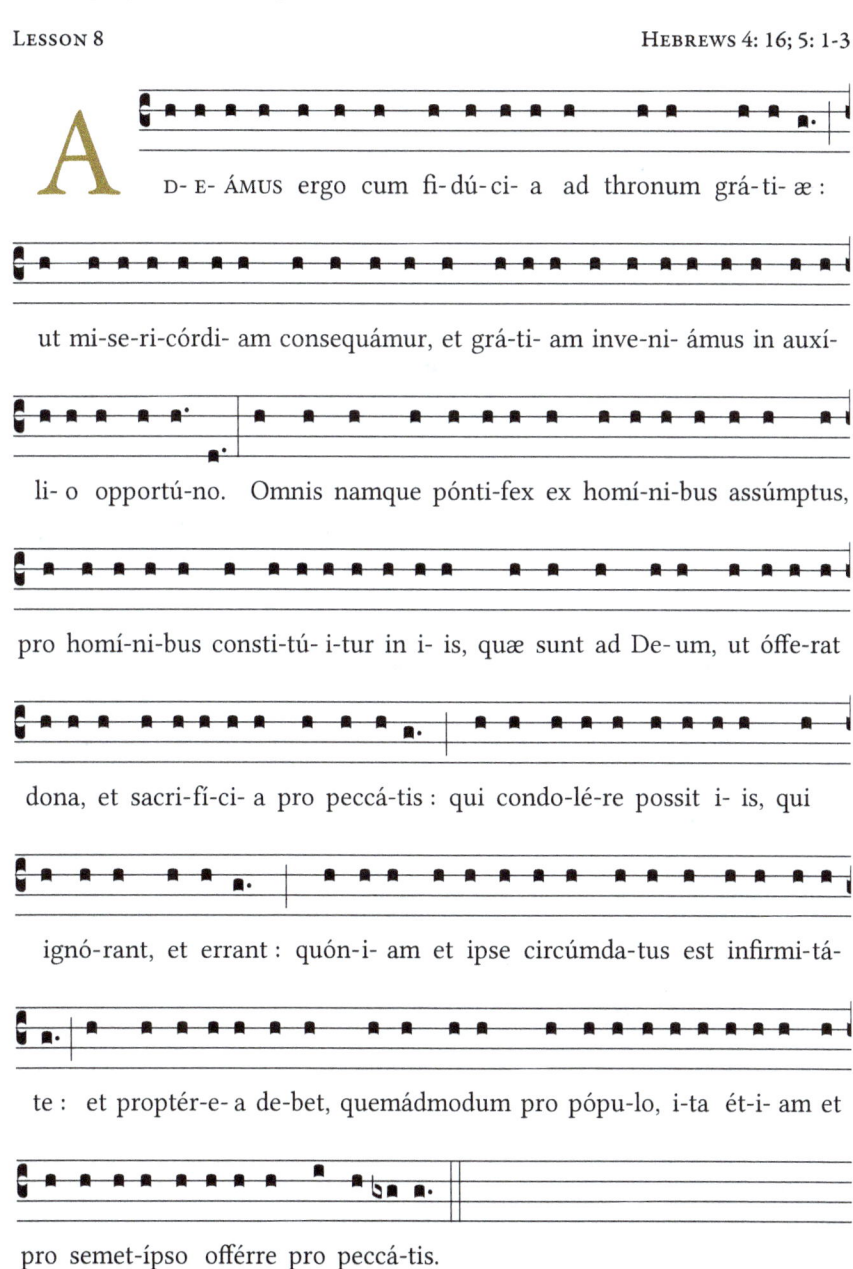

A-de-e-ámus ergo cum fi-dú-ci- a ad thronum grá-ti- æ :

ut mi-se-ri-córdi- am consequámur, et grá-ti- am inve-ni- ámus in auxí-

li- o opportú-no. Omnis namque pónti-fex ex homí-ni-bus assúmptus,

pro homí-ni-bus consti-tú- i-tur in i- is, quæ sunt ad De- um, ut óffe-rat

dona, et sacri-fí-ci- a pro peccá-tis : qui condo-lé-re possit i- is, qui

ignó-rant, et errant : quón-i- am et ipse circúmda-tus est infirmi-tá-

te : et proptér-e- a de-bet, quemádmodum pro pópu-lo, i-ta ét-i- am et

pro semet-ípso offérre pro peccá-tis.

LESSON 8: Let us go therefore with confidence to the throne of grace: that we may obtain mercy, and find grace in seasonable aid. For every high priest taken from among men, is ordained for men in the things that appertain to God, that he may offer up gifts and sacrifices for sins: Who can have compassion on them that are ignorant and that err: because he himself also is compassed with infirmity. And therefore he ought, as for the people, so also for himself, to offer for sins.

RESPONSORY 8   JESUM TRÁDIDIT ÍMPIUS

J E-SUM   * trá- di-dit   ímpi- us summis princí-pi-bus sa-cerdó- tum, et se-ni- ó- ri-bus pópu- li : * Petrus au- tem seque-bá-tur e- um a lon- ge, ut vi-dé-ret fi- nem. ℣. Addu-xé-runt autem e- um ad Cá- ipham prínci-pem sa-cerdó- tum, u-bi scri-bæ et pha-ri-sǽ- i convé-ne- rant. * Petrus.

℞. That wicked one betrayed Jesus to the chief-priests and elders of the people. * But Peter followed Him afar off, to see the end. ℣. And they led Him away to Caiaphas the High Priest, where the Scribes and Pharisees were assembled. ℞. But Peter followed Him afar off, to see the end.

Nec quisquam sumit si-bi honó-rem, sed qui vo-cá-tur a De-

o, tamquam A-a-ron. Sic et Christus non semet-ípsum cla-ri-fi-cá-vit

ut pónti-fex fí- e-ret : sed qui lo-cú-tus est ad e- um : Fí-li- us me-us es

tu, e-go hó-di- e génu- i te. Quemádmodum et in á-li- o lo-co di-cit :

Tu es sa-cérdos in æ-térnum, se-cúndum órdi-nem Melchí-se-dech. Qui

in di- é-bus carnis su-æ pre-ces, suppli-ca-ti- onésque ad e- um, qui pos-

sit il-lum salvum fá-ce-re a morte, cum clamó-re vá-li-do, et lácrymis

óffe-rens, exaudí-tus est pro su- a re-ve-rénti- a. Et qui-dem cum esset

Fí-li- us De- i, dí-di-cit ex i- is, quæ passus est, ob-e-di- énti- am : et con-

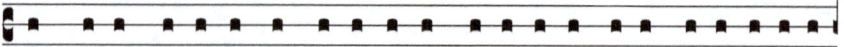

summá-tus, factus est ómni-bus obtempe-ránti-bus si-bi, causa sa-lú-tis

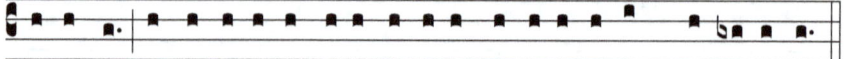

æ-térnæ, appel-lá-tus a De-o pónti-fex juxta órdi-nem Melchí-se-dech.

LESSON 9: Neither doth any man take the honour to himself, but He that is called by God, as Aaron was. So Christ also did not glorify Himself, that He might be made a high priest: but He that said unto Him: Thou art my Son, this day have I begotten Thee. As He saith also in another place: Thou art a priest for ever, according to the order of Melchisedech. Who in the days of His flesh, with a strong cry and tears, offering up prayers and supplications to Him that was able to save Him from death, was heard for His reverence. And whereas indeed He was the Son of God, He learned obedience by the things which He suffered: And being consummated, He became, to all that obey Him, the cause of eternal salvation: called by God a high priest according to the order of Melchisedech.

RESPONSORY 9   CALIGAVÉRUNT ÓCULI MEI

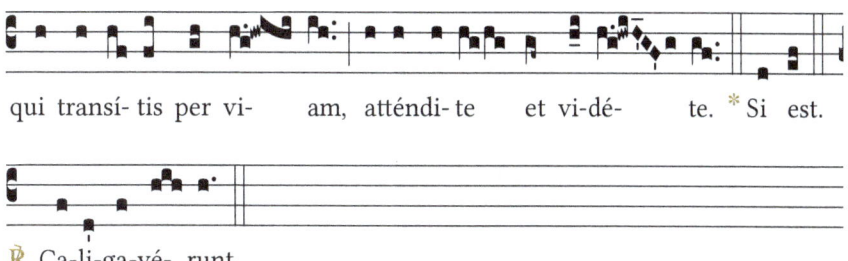

qui transí- tis per vi-   am, atténdi- te   et vi-dé-   te. * Si est.

Ⱳ. Ca-li-ga-vé- runt.

Ⱳ. Mine eyes do fail with tears, because the one that should comfort Me is far from Me. Behold, O all ye nations * If there be any sorrow like unto My sorrow. Ꝟ. O all ye that pass by, behold, and see Ⱳ. If there be any sorrow like unto My sorrow. Ⱳ. Mine eyes do fail with tears, because the one that should comfort Me is far from Me. Behold, O all ye nations, * If there be any sorrow like unto My sorrow.

AT LAUDS

1. Ant. 7.c

Próri- o * Fí- li- o su- o non pe- pér- cit De- us,

sed pro no-bis ómni-bus trá-di-dit il-lum.

ANTIPHON: God spared not His Own Son * but delivered Him up for us all.

PSALM 50

1. Mi-se-ré-re **me-** i De- *us, * se-cúndum magnam mi-se-ri-**cór**di- am

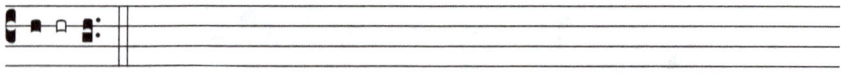

tu- am.

1. Have mercy on me, O God, * according to Thy great mercy.

2. Et secúndum multitúdinem miseratiónum tuárum, * dele iniquitátem **me**am.

2. And according to the multitude of Thy tender mercies * blot out my iniquity.

3. Amplius lava me ab iniquitáte **me**a : * et a peccáto **me**o **mun**da me.

3. Wash me yet more from my iniquity, * and cleanse me from my sin.

4. Quóniam iniquitátem meam **ego** co**gnós**co : * et peccátum meum contra **me** est **sem**per.

4. For I know my iniquity, * and my sin is always before me.

5. Tibi soli peccávi, et malum **co**ram te **fe**ci : * ut justificéris in sermónibus tuis, et vincas cum **ju**di**cá**ris.

5. To Thee only have I sinned, and have done evil before Thee: * that Thou mayst be justified in Thy words, and mayst overcome when Thou art judged.

6. Ecce enim in iniquitátibus concéptus sum : * et in peccátis concépit me **mater me**a.

7. Ecce enim veritátem di**lexí**sti : * incérta et occúlta sapiéntiæ tuæ manife**stá**sti **mi**hi.

8. Aspérges me hyssópo, **et** mun**dá**bor : * lavábis me, et super nivem de**al**b**á**bor.

9. Audítui meo dabis gáudium **et** læ**tí**tiam : * et exsultábunt ossa hu**mi**li**á**ta.

10. Avérte fáciem tuam a peccátis **me**is : * et omnes iniquitátes **me**as **de**le.

11. Cor mundum crea **in** me, **D**eus : * et spíritum rectum ínnova in vi**scé**ri**bus me**is.

12. Ne projícias me a **fá**cie **tu**a : * et spíritum sanctum tuum ne **áu**feras **a** me.

13. Redde mihi lætítiam salu**tá**ris **tu**i : * et spíritu princi**pá**li con**fír**ma me.

14. Docébo iníquos **vi**as **tu**as : * et ímpii ad te **con**ver**tén**tur.

15. Líbera me de sanguínibus, Deus, Deus sa**lú**tis **me**æ : * et exsultábit lingua mea ju**stí**tiam **tu**am.

16. Dómine, lábia **me**a a**pé**ries : * et os meum annuntiábit **lau**dem **tu**am.

17. Quóniam si voluísses sacrifícium, de**dís**sem **úti**que : * holocáustis non de**lectá**beris.

6. For behold I was conceived in iniquities; * and in sins did my mother conceive me.

7. For behold Thou hast loved truth: * the uncertain and hidden things of Thy wisdom Thou hast made manifest to me.

8. Thou shalt sprinkle me with hyssop, and I shall be cleansed: * Thou shalt wash me, and I shall be made whiter than snow.

9. To my hearing Thou shalt give joy and gladness: * and the bones that have been humbled shall rejoice.

10. Turn away Thy face from my sins, * and blot out all my iniquities.

11. Create a clean heart in me, O God: * and renew a right spirit within my bowels.

12. Cast me not away from Thy face; * and take not Thy holy spirit from me.

13. Restore unto me the joy of Thy salvation, * and strengthen me with a perfect spirit.

14. I will teach the unjust Thy ways: * and the wicked shall be converted to Thee.

15. Deliver me from blood, O God, Thou God of my salvation: * and my tongue shall extol Thy justice.

16. O Lord, Thou wilt open my lips: * and my mouth shall declare Thy praise.

17. For if Thou hadst desired sacrifice, I would indeed have given it: * with burnt offerings Thou wilt not be delighted.

18. Sacrifícium Deo spíritus con-**tribulátus** : * cor contrítum et humiliátum, Deus, **non** despícies.

19. Benígne fac, Dómine, in bona voluntáte **tu**a **Si**on : * ut ædificéntur **mu**ri Jerúsalem.

20. Tunc acceptábis sacrifícium justítiæ, oblatiónes, et **holocáu**sta : * tunc impónent super altáre **tu**um vítulos.

18. A sacrifice to God is an afflicted spirit: * a contrite and humbled heart, O God, Thou wilt not despise.

19. Deal favourably, O Lord, in Thy good will with Sion; * that the walls of Jerusalem may be built up.

20. Then shalt Thou accept the sacrifice of justice, oblations and whole burnt offerings: * then shall they lay calves upon Thy altar.

1. Ant.
7.c

P RÓPRI- O   Fí- li- o su- o   non pe-pér- cit De- us,

sed pro no-bis ómni-bus trá-di-dit il-lum.

The tenth candle is extinguished.

2. Ant.
4.E

A NXI- ÁTUS est in me * spí- ri-tus me- us : in me turbá- tum

est cor me- um.

ANTIPHON: My spirit is overwhelmed within me; * my heart within me is troubled.

PSALM 142

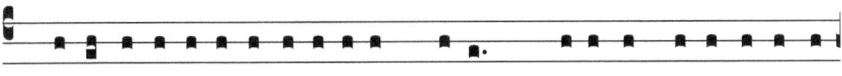

1. Dómi-ne, exáudi o-ra-ti- ónem me- am : † áuri-bus pérci-pe obse-

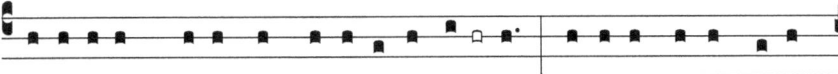

cra-ti- ónem me- am in ve-ri-*tá- te* **tu-** a : * exáudi me in *tu- a*

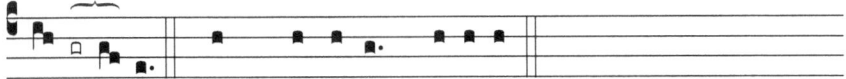

justí- **ti-** a. *Flex :* antiquó-rum, †

1. Hear, O Lord, my prayer: † give ear to my supplication in Thy truth: * hear me in Thy justice.

2. Et non intres in judícium cum *servo* **tuo** : * quia non justificábitur in conspéctu tu*o omnis* **vivens.**

2. And enter not into judgment with Thy servant: * for in Thy sight no man living shall be justified.

3. Quia persecútus est inimícus *ánimam* **me**am : * humiliávit in ter*ra vitam* **me**am.

3. For the enemy hath persecuted my soul: * he hath brought down my life to the earth.

4. Collocávit me in obscúris si-cut mórtuos sǽculi : † et anxiátus est super me sp*íritus* **me**us, * in me turbá*tum est cor* **me**um.

4. He hath made me to dwell in darkness as those that have been dead of old: * and my spirit is in anguish within me: my heart within me is troubled.

5. Memor fui diérum antiquórum, † meditátus sum in ómnibus opé*ribus* **tu**is : * in factis mánuum tuá*rum med-i**tá**bar.

5. I remembered the days of old, † I meditated on all Thy works: * I med-itated upon the works of Thy hands.

6. Expándi manus *meas* **ad** te : * ánima mea sicut terra s*ine aqua* **ti**bi.

6. I stretched forth my hands to Thee: * my soul is as earth without water unto Thee.

7. Velóciter exáu*di me*, **Dó**mine : * defécit sp*íritus* **me**us.

7. Hear me speedily, O Lord: * my spirit hath fainted away.

8. Non avértas fáciem *tuam* **a** me : * et símilis ero descendén*tibus in* **la**cum.

8. Turn not away Thy face from me, * lest I be like unto them that go down into the pit.

9. Audítam fac mihi mane misericór*diam* **tu**am : * quia *in te sper*ávi.

9. Cause me to hear Thy mercy in the morning; * for in Thee have I hoped.

10. Notam fac mihi viam, *in qua* **ám**bulem : * quia ad te levávi *ánimam* **me**am.

10. Make the way known to me, wherein I should walk: * for I have lifted up my soul to Thee.

11. Eripe me de inimícis meis, Dómine, ad *te con*f**ú**gi : * doce me fácere voluntátem tuam, quia De*us meus* **es** tu.

11. Deliver me from my enemies, O Lord, to Thee have I fled: * teach me to do Thy will, for Thou art my God.

12. Spíritus tuus bonus dedúcet me in *terram* **re**ctam : * propter nomen tuum, Dómine, vivificábis me, in *æquitáte* **tu**a.

12. Thy good spirit shall lead me into the right land: * for Thy name's sake, O Lord, Thou wilt quicken me in Thy justice.

13. Edúces de tribulatióne *ánimam* **me**am : * et in misericórdia tua dispérdes in*imícos* **me**os.

13. Thou wilt bring my soul out of trouble: * and in Thy mercy Thou wilt destroy my enemies.

14. Et perdes omnes, qui tríbulant *ánimam* **me**am, * quóniam e*go servus* **tuus** sum.

14. And Thou wilt cut off all them that afflict my soul: * for I am Thy servant.

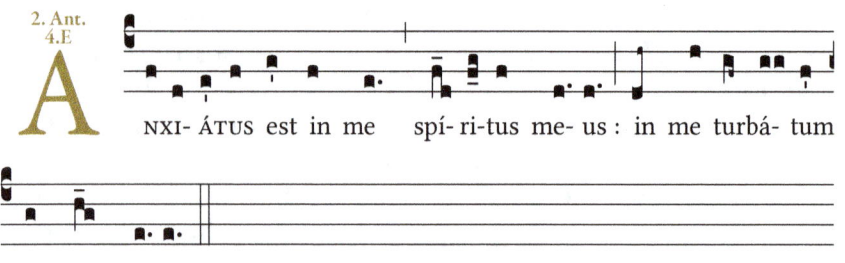

2. Ant.
4.E

A NXI- ÁTUS est in me spí- ri-tus me- us : in me turbá- tum

est cor me- um.

The eleventh candle is extinguished.

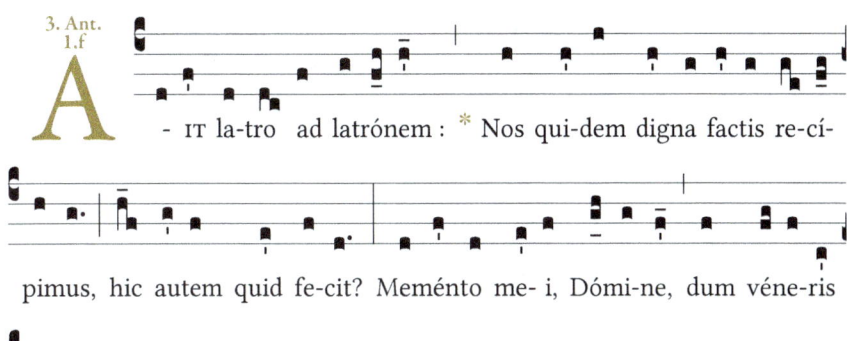

3. Ant.
1.f

A - IT la-tro ad latrónem : * Nos qui-dem digna factis re-cí-pimus, hic autem quid fe-cit? Meménto me- i, Dómi-ne, dum véne-ris in regnum tu- um.

ANTIPHON: One thief said unto the other: * We indeed receive the due reward of our deeds, but what hath this man done? Lord, remember me, when thou comest into thy kingdom.

PSALM 84

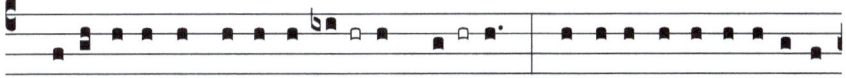

1. Bene-di-xí-sti, Dómi-ne, **ter**- ram **tu**- am: * a-vertís-ti capti-vi-*tá-tem*

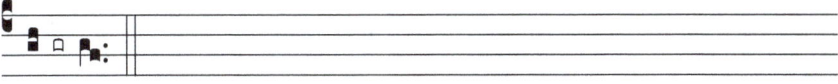

Ja- cob.

1. Lord, Thou hast blessed Thy land: * Thou hast turned away the captivity of Jacob.

2. Remisísti iniquitátem **ple**bis **tu**æ : * operuísti ómnia peccá*ta* e**ó**rum.

3. Mitigásti omnem **i**ram **tu**am : * avertísti ab ira indignati*ónis* **tu**æ.

4. Convérte nos, Deus, salutáris **no**ster : * et avérte iram tu*am a* **no**bis.

5. Numquid in ætérnum irascéris **no**bis? * aut exténdes iram tuam a generatióne in gener*ati***ó**nem?

2. Thou hast forgiven the iniquity of Thy people: * Thou hast covered all their sins.

3. Thou hast mitigated all Thy anger: * Thou hast turned away from the wrath of Thy indignation.

4. Convert us, O God our saviour: * and turn off Thy anger from us.

5. Wilt Thou be angry with us for ever: * or wilt Thou extend Thy wrath from generation to generation?

6. Deus, tu convérsus vivificábis nos : * et plebs tua lætábitur **in** te.

6. Thou wilt turn, O God, and bring us to life: * and Thy people shall rejoice in Thee.

7. Osténde nobis, Dómine, misericórdiam **tu**am : * et salutáre tu*um da* **no**bis.

7. Show us, O Lord, Thy mercy; * and grant us Thy salvation.

8. Audiam quid loquátur in me **Dóminus Deus** : * quóniam loquétur pacem in *plebem* **su**am.

8. I will hear what the Lord God will speak in me: * for He will speak peace unto His people:

9. Et super **san**ctos **su**os : * et in eos, qui conver*túntur* **ad** cor.

9. And unto His saints: * and unto them that are converted to the heart.

10. Verúmtamen prope timéntes eum salu**tá**re ip**sí**us : * ut inhábitet glória in *terra* **no**stra.

10. Surely His salvation is near to them that fear Him: * that glory may dwell in our land.

11. Misericórdia, et véritas obviavérunt **si**bi : * justítia, et pax *oscu*látæ sunt.

11. Mercy and truth have met each other: * justice and peace have kissed.

12. Véritas de **ter**ra **or**ta est : * et justítia de c*ælo pro*spéxit.

12. Truth is sprung out of the earth: * and justice hath looked down from heaven.

13. Etenim Dóminus dabit benignitátem : * et terra nostra dabit *fructum* **su**um.

13. For the Lord will give goodness: * and our earth shall yield her fruit.

14. Justítia ante eum **am**bulábit : * et ponet in via *gressus* **su**os.

14. Justice shall walk before Him: * and shall set His steps in the way.

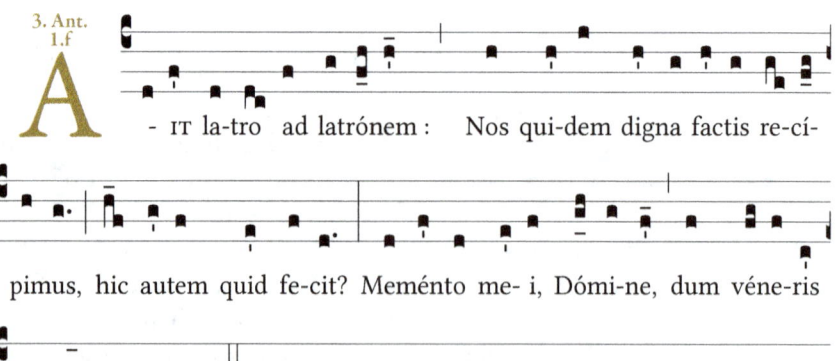

3. Ant.
1.f

A- it la-tro ad latrónem : Nos qui-dem digna factis recí-pimus, hic autem quid fe-cit? Memén-to me- i, Dómi-ne, dum véne-ris in regnum tu- um.

The twelfth candle is extinguished.

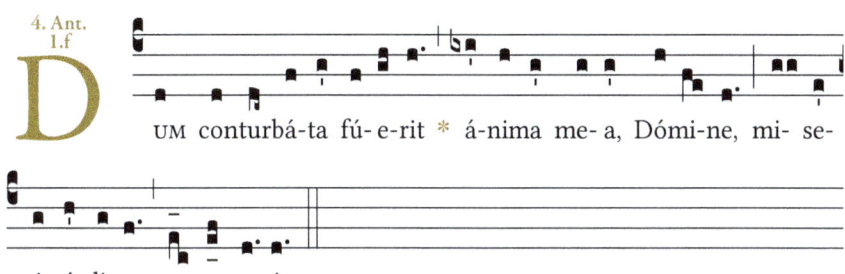

um conturbá-ta fú- e- rit * á-nima me- a, Dómi-ne, mi- se-

ri-córdi- æ memor e-ris.

ANTIPHON: Lord, when my soul is troubled, * Thou wilt remember mercy.

CANTICLE OF HABACUC

1. Dómi- ne, audí- vi audi- ti- ó- nem tu-   am, * *et* **tímu**- i.

Flex : terræ : †   *Ending of* ℣. 2 : vi-ví-*fi-ca* **il**- lud :

1. O Lord, I have heard Thy hearing, * and was afraid.

2. Dómine, **o**pus **tu**um, * in médio annórum viví*fica* **ill**ud :

2. O Lord, Thy work, * in the midst of the years bring it to life:

3. In médio annórum **no**tum **fá**cies : * cum irátus fúeris, misericórdiæ *recor***dá**beris.

3. In the midst of the years Thou shalt make it known: * when Thou art angry, Thou wilt remember mercy.

4. Deus ab **Au**stro **vé**niet, * et sanctus de *monte* **Pha**ran :

4. God will come from the south, * and the holy one from mount Pharan:

5. Opéruit cælos **gló**ria **e**jus : * et laudis ejus ple*na est* **ter**ra.

5. His glory covered the heavens, * and the earth is full of His praise.

6. Splendor ejus **ut** lux **e**rit : * córnua in má*nibus* **e**jus :

6. His brightness shall be as the light: * horns are in His hands:

7. Ibi abscóndita est forti**tú**do **e**jus : * ante fáciem *ejus* **i**bit mors.

7. There is His strength hid: * Death shall go before His face.

8. Et egrediétur diábolus ante **pe**des **e**jus. * Stetit, et men*sus est* **ter**ram.

8. And the devil shall go forth before His feet. * He stood and measured the earth.

9. Aspéxit, et dissólvit **gen**tes : *
et contríti sunt *montes* **sǽ**culi.

10. Incurváti sunt **colles mun**di, *
ab itinéribus æterni*tátis* **e**jus.

11. Pro iniquitáte vidi tentória
Æthi**ó**piæ, * turbabúntur pelles *terræ*
Mádian.

12. Numquid in flumínibus i**rá**tus
es, **Dó**mine? * aut in flumínibus furor
tuus? vel in mari indigná*tio* **tu**a?

13. Qui ascéndes super equos
tuos : * et quadrígæ tu*æ sal***vá**tio.

14. Súscitans suscitábis **ar**cum
tuum : * juraménta tríbubus *quæ*
*lo***cú**tus es.

15. Flúvios scindes terræ : † vidérunt
te, et doluérunt **mon**tes : * gurges
a*quárum* **tráns**iit.

16. Dedit abýssus **vo**cem **su**am : *
altitúdo manus su*as le***vá**vit.

17. Sol, et luna stetérunt in habi**tá**-
culo **su**o, * in luce sagittárum tuárum,
ibunt in splendóre fulgurántis *hastæ*
tuæ.

18. In frémitu conculcábis **ter**ram : *
et in furóre obstupefá*cies* **gen**tes.

19. Egréssus es in salútem **pó**puli
tui : * in salútem cum *Christo* **tu**o.

20. Percussísti caput de **do**mo
ímpii : * denudásti fundaméntum ejus
us*que ad* **col**lum.

21. Maledixísti sceptris ejus, † cápiti
bella**tó**rum **e**jus, * veniéntibus ut
turbo ad *dispe***gén**dum me.

22. Exsultá**tio** e**ó**rum * sicut ejus,
qui dévorat páuperem *in abs***cón**dito.

9. He beheld, and melted the nations: * and the ancient mountains
were crushed to pieces.

10. The hills of the world were
bowed down * by the journeys of His
eternity.

11. I saw the tents of Ethiopia for
their iniquity, * the curtains of the
land of Madian shall be troubled.

12. Wast Thou angry, O Lord, with
the rivers? * or was Thy wrath upon
the rivers? or Thy indignation in the
sea?

13. Who will ride upon Thy horses: *
and Thy chariots are salvation.

14. Thou wilt surely take up Thy
bow: * according to the oaths which
Thou hast spoken to the tribes.

15. Thou wilt divide the rivers of the
earth. † The mountains saw Thee, and
were grieved: * the great body of waters passed away.

16. The deep put forth its voice: *
the deep lifted up its hands.

17. The sun and the moon stood
still in their habitation, * in the light
of Thy arrows, they shall go in the
brightness of Thy glittering spear.

18. In Thy anger Thou wilt tread the
earth under foot: * in Thy wrath Thou
wilt astonish the nations.

19. Thou wentest forth for the salvation of Thy people: * for salvation
with Thy Christ.

20. Thou struckest the head of the
house of the wicked: * Thou hast laid
bare his foundation even to the neck.

21. Thou hast cursed his sceptres, †
the head of his warriors, * them that
came out as a whirlwind to scatter me.

22. Their joy * was like that of him
that devoureth the poor man in secret.

23. Viam fecísti in mari equis tuis, * in luto aquárum multárum.

23. Thou madest a way in the sea for Thy horses, * in the mud of many waters.

24. Audívi, et conturbátus est venter meus : * a voce contremuérunt lábia mea.

24. I have heard and my bowels were troubled: * my lips trembled at the voice.

25. Ingrediátur putrédo in óssibus meis, * et subter me scáteat.

25. Let rottenness enter into my bones, * and swarm under me.

26. Ut requiéscam in die tribulatiónis : * ut ascéndam ad pópulum accínctum nostrum.

26. That I may rest in the day of tribulation: * that I may go up to our people that are girded.

27. Ficus enim non florébit : * et non erit germen in víneis.

27. For the fig tree shall not blossom: * and there shall be no spring in the vines.

28. Mentiétur opus olívæ : * et arva non áfferent cibum.

28. The labour of the olive tree shall fail: * and the fields shall yield no food:

29. Abscindétur de ovíli pecus : * et non erit arméntum in præsépibus.

29. The flock shall be cut off from the fold, * and there shall be no herd in the stalls.

30. Ego autem in Dómino gaudébo : * et exsultábo in Deo Jesu meo.

30. But I will rejoice in the Lord: * and I will joy in God my Jesus.

31. Deus Dóminus fortitúdo mea : * et ponet pedes meos quasi cervórum.

31. The Lord God is my strength: * and He will make my feet like the feet of harts:

32. Et super excélsa mea dedúcet me victor * in psalmis canéntem.

32. And He the conqueror will lead me upon my high places * singing psalms.

4. Ant.
1.f

Dum conturbáta fúerit ánima mea, Dómine, miseri-córdiæ memor eris.

The thirteenth candle is extinguished.

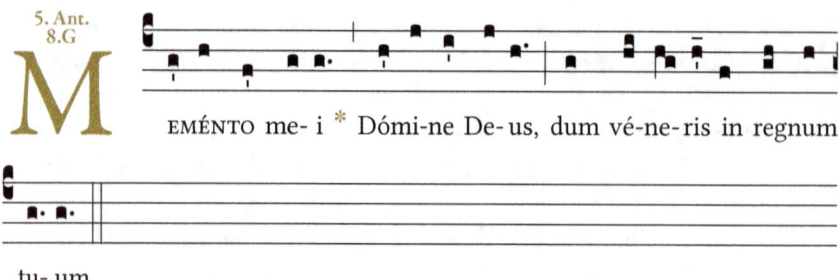

5. Ant.
8.G

MEMÉNTO me-i * Dómi-ne De-us, dum vé-ne-ris in regnum

tu-um.

ANTIPHON: Lord, remember me * when thou comest into thy kingdom.

Psalm 147

1. Lauda, Je-rú-sa-lem, **Dómi-num** : * lauda De-um *tu-um*, **Si-** on.

1. Praise the Lord, O Jerusalem: * praise thy God, O Sion.

2. Quóniam confortávit seras portárum tuárum : * benedíxit fíliis *tuis* **in** te.

2. Because He hath strengthened the bolts of thy gates * He hath blessed thy children within thee.

3. Qui pósuit fines tuos **pa**cem : * et ádipe fruménti *sáti*at te.

3. Who hath placed peace in thy borders: * and filleth thee with the fat of corn.

4. Qui emíttit elóquium suum **terræ** : * velóciter currit *sermo* ejus.

4. Who sendeth forth His speech to the earth: * His word runneth swiftly.

5. Qui dat nivem sicut **la**nam : * nébulam sicut *cínerem* **sparg**it.

5. Who giveth snow like wool: * scattereth mists like ashes.

6. Mittit crystállum suam sicut buc-**cél**las : * ante fáciem frígoris ejus quis *susti*né**bit**?

6. He sendeth His crystal like morsels: * who shall stand before the face of His cold?

7. Emíttet verbum suum, et lique-fáciet **ea** : * flabit spíritus ejus, et *flu*ent aquæ.

7. He shall send out His word, and shall melt them: * His wind shall blow, and the waters shall run.

8. Qui annúntiat verbum suum Jacob : * justítias, et judícia *sua* **Is**raël.

8. Who declareth His word to Jacob: * His justices and His judgments to Israel.

9. Non fecit táliter omni natióni : * et judícia sua non manife*stávit* eis.

9. He hath not done in like manner to every nation: * and His judgments He hath not made manifest to them.

5. Ant.
8.G

MEMÉNTO me-i Dómi-ne De-us, dum vé-ne-ris in regnum

tu-um.

The fourteenth candle is extinguished.

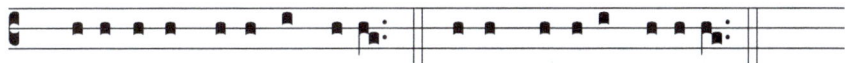

℣. Collo-cá-vit me in obscú-ris. ℟. Si-cut mórtu-os sǽcu-li.

Or:

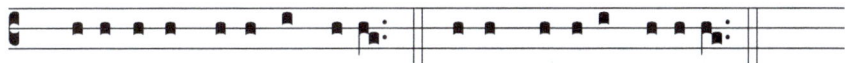

℣. Collo-cá-vit me in obscú-ris. ℟. Si-cut mórtu-os sǽcu-li.

℣. He hath set me in dark places.
℟. As they that be dead of old.

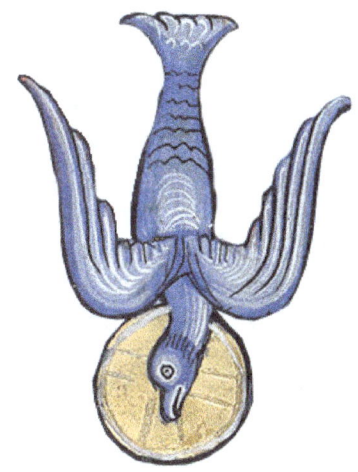

BENEDÍCTUS

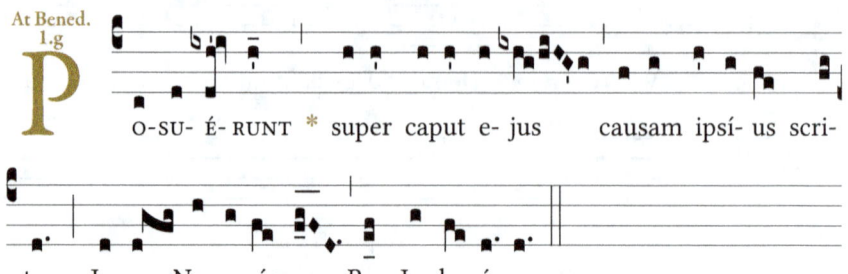

PO-SU- É- RUNT * super caput e- jus   causam ipsí- us scri-

ptam : Je-sus Na-za-ré-nus,   Rex Ju-dæ- ó-rum.

ANTIPHON: They set up over His head his accusation written: * Jesus of Nazareth, King of the Jews.

The intonation is sung for every verse.

1. Bene-díctus ✠ Dómi-*nus, De- us* **Isra**- ël: * qui- a vi-si-tá-vit, et fe-cit

red-empti- ónem *ple-bis* **su**- æ:

1. Blessed be the Lord ✠ God of Israel; * because He hath visited and wrought the redemption of His people:

2. Et eréxit cornu *salútis* **no**bis: * in domo David, pú*eri* **su**i.

2. And hath raised up an horn of salvation to us, * in the house of David His servant:

The first altar candle is extinguished

3. Sicut locútus est *per os* **sanct**órum, * qui a sǽculo sunt, prophe*tárum* ejus:

3. As He spoke by the mouth of His holy Prophets, * who are from the beginning:

4. Salútem ex in*imícis* **no**stris, * et de manu ómnium, *qui o*dérunt nos.

4. Salvation from our enemies, * and from the hand of all that hate us:

The second altar candle is extinguished

5. Ad faciéndam misericórdiam cum *pátribus* **no**stris: * et memorári testaménti *sui* **san**cti.

5. To perform mercy to our fathers, * and to remember His holy testament,

6. Jusjurándum, quod jurávit ad Abra*ham patrem* **no**strum, * datú*rum se* **no**bis:

6. The oath, which He swore to Abraham our father, * that He would grant to us,

The third altar candle is extinguished

7. Ut sine timóre, de manu inimicórum nostró*rum libe*ráti, * servi*ámus* **il**li.

7. That being delivered from the hand of our enemies, * we may serve Him without fear,

8. In sanctitáte, et justíti*a coram* **i**pso, * ómnibus di*ébus* **no**stris.

8. In holiness and justice before Him, * all our days.

The fourth altar candle is extinguished

9. Et tu, puer, Prophéta Altís*simi* vo**cáb**eris: * præíbis enim ante fáciem Dómini, paráre *vias* **e**jus:

9. And thou, child, shalt be called the prophet of the Highest: * for thou shalt go before the face of the Lord to prepare His ways:

10. Ad dandam sciéntiam salú*tis* **plebi** **e**jus: * in remissiónem peccató*rum e***ó**rum:

10. To give knowledge of salvation to His people, * unto the remission of their sins:

The fifth altar candle is extinguished

11. Per víscera misericórdi*æ Dei* **no**stri: * in quibus visitávit nos, óri*ens ex* **al**to:

11. Through the bowels of the mercy of our God, * in which the Orient from on high hath visited us:

12. Illumináre his, qui in ténebris, et in um*bra mortis* **se**dent: * ad dirigéndos pedes nostros in *viam* **pa**cis.

12. To enlighten them that sit in darkness, and in the shadow of death: * to direct our feet into the way of peace.

The sixth altar candle is extinguished

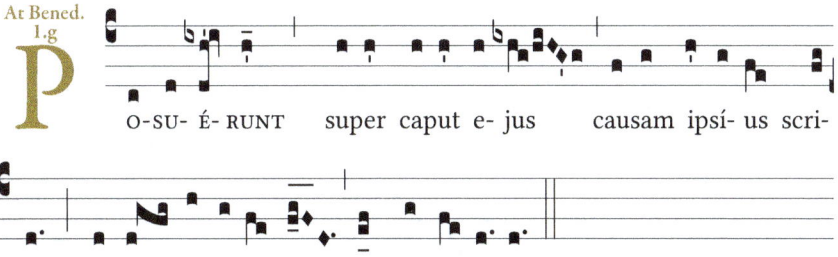

At Bened.
1.g

PO-SU- É- RUNT super caput e- jus causam ipsí- us scri-

ptam : Je-sus Na-za-ré-nus, Rex Ju-dæ- ó-rum.

At the conclusion of the antiphon following the Benedíctus, *the remaining candle is removed and "hidden" while all kneel and sing:*

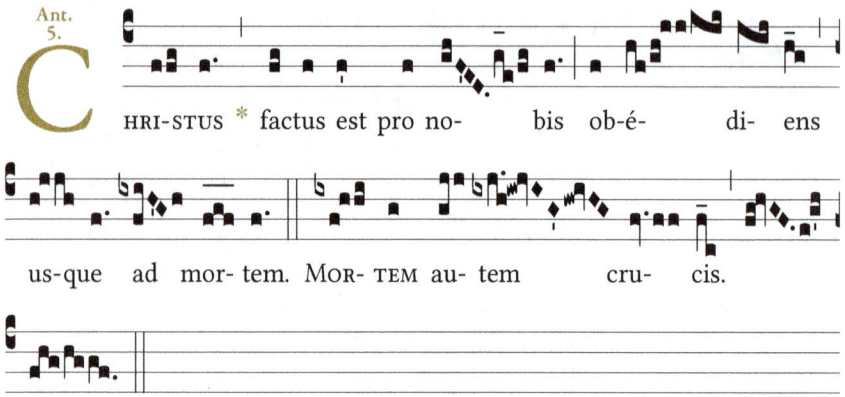

ANTIPHON: Christ became obedient for us unto death, even to the death of the cross.

At the conclusion of the antiphon Christus factus est, *the* Pater noster *is said in silence.*

PSALM 50

Recited recto tono

1. Miserére mei, Deus, * secúndum magnam misericórdiam tuam.

2. Et secúndum multitúdinem miseratiónum tuárum, * dele iniquitátem meam.

3. Amplius lava me ab iniquitáte mea : * et a peccáto meo munda me.

4. Quóniam iniquitátem meam ego cognósco : * et peccátum meum contra me est semper.

5. Tibi soli peccávi, et malum coram te feci : * ut justificéris in sermónibus tuis, et vincas cum judicáris.

1. Have mercy on me, O God, * according to Thy great mercy.

2. And according to the multitude of Thy tender mercies * blot out my iniquity.

3. Wash me yet more from my iniquity, * and cleanse me from my sin.

4. For I know my iniquity, * and my sin is always before me.

5. To Thee only have I sinned, and have done evil before Thee: * that Thou mayst be justified in Thy words, and mayst overcome when Thou art judged.

6. Ecce enim in iniquitátibus concéptus sum : * et in peccátis concépit
me mater mea.

7. Ecce enim veritátem dilexísti : *
incérta et occúlta sapiéntiæ tuæ manifestásti mihi.

8. Aspérges me hyssópo, et
mundábor : * lavábis me, et super
nivem dealbábor.

9. Audítui meo dabis gáudium et
lætítiam : * et exsultábunt ossa humiliáta.

10. Avérte fáciem tuam a peccátis
meis : * et omnes iniquitátes meas
dele.

11. Cor mundum crea in me,
Deus : * et spíritum rectum ínnova in
viscéribus meis.

12. Ne projícias me a fácie tua : *
et spíritum sanctum tuum ne áuferas
a me.

13. Redde mihi lætítiam salutáris
tui : * et spíritu principáli confírma
me.

14. Docébo iníquos vias tuas : *
et ímpii ad te converténtur.

15. Líbera me de sanguínibus, Deus,
Deus salútis meæ : * et exsultábit lingua mea justítiam tuam.

16. Dómine, lábia mea apéries : *
et os meum annuntiábit laudem tuam.

17. Quóniam si voluísses sacrifícium, dedíssem útique : * holocáustis
non delectáberis.

6. For behold I was conceived in iniquities; * and in sins did my mother
conceive me.

7. For behold Thou hast loved
truth: * the uncertain and hidden
things of Thy wisdom Thou hast made
manifest to me.

8. Thou shalt sprinkle me with hyssop, and I shall be cleansed: * Thou
shalt wash me, and I shall be made
whiter than snow.

9. To my hearing Thou shalt give
joy and gladness: * and the bones that
have been humbled shall rejoice.

10. Turn away Thy face from my
sins, * and blot out all my iniquities.

11. Create a clean heart in me,
O God: * and renew a right spirit
within my bowels.

12. Cast me not away from Thy
face; * and take not Thy holy spirit
from me.

13. Restore unto me the joy of Thy
salvation, * and strengthen me with a
perfect spirit.

14. I will teach the unjust Thy
ways: * and the wicked shall be converted to Thee.

15. Deliver me from blood, O God,
Thou God of my salvation: * and my
tongue shall extol Thy justice.

16. O Lord, Thou wilt open my
lips: * and my mouth shall declare Thy
praise.

17. For if Thou hadst desired sacrifice, I would indeed have given it: *
with burnt offerings Thou wilt not be
delighted.

18. Sacrifícium Deo spíritus con-tribulátus : * cor contrítum et hu-miliátum, Deus, non despícies.

18. A sacrifice to God is an afflicted spirit: * a contrite and humbled heart, O God, Thou wilt not despise.

19. Benígne fac, Dómine, in bona voluntáte tua Sion : * ut ædificéntur muri Jerúsalem.

19. Deal favourably, O Lord, in Thy good will with Sion; * that the walls of Jerusalem may be built up.

20. Tunc acceptábis sacrifícium justítiæ, oblatiónes, et holocáusta : * tunc impónent super altáre tuum vítu-los.

20. Then shalt Thou accept the sac-rifice of justice, oblations and whole burnt offerings: * then shall they lay calves upon Thy altar.

Sung recto tono or to ferial tone without Orémus.

Réspice, quǽsumus, Dómine, su-per hanc famíliam tuam, pro qua Dóminus noster Jesus Christus non dubitávit mánibus tradi nocéntium, et crucis subíre torméntum:

Look down, we beseech Thee, O Lord, on this Thy family, for which our Lord Jesus Christ did not hesitate to be delivered up into the hands of wicked men, and to suffer the torment of the Cross.

[*Dícitur sub siléntio:* Qui tecum vivit et regnat in unitáte Spíritus Sanc-ti, Deus, per ómnia sǽcula sæculórum. ℟. Amen.]

[*Said in silence:* Who with thee liveth and reigneth, in the unity of the Holy Ghost, God, world without end. ℟. Amen.]

The Strépitus *is begun by the celebrant and continues until the "hidden" candle is brought back out. All then rise and retire in silence.*

CESVS ABEL RVIT·ET ROSEVS
FLVIT IN HAC E SANGVIS·
ENEVS IN CRVCE·VVLNERE
PRO TRVCE TENDITVR ANGVIS·

THE MASS OF THE PRESANCTIFIED

LESSONS

The priests and his ministers, dressed in black vestments, go up to the altar without lights or incense and prostate themselves before it while the acolytes cover the altar with a single linen cloth. A lector then reads from the Epistle side:

FIRST LESSON — OSEE 6: 1-6

HÆC dicit Dóminus: In tribulatióne sua mane consúrgent ad me: Veníte, et revertámur ad Dóminum: quia ipse cepit, et sanábit nos: percútiet, et curábit nos. Vivificábit nos post duos dies: in die tértia suscitábit nos, et vivémus in conspéctu ejus. Sciémus, sequemúrque, ut cognoscámus Dóminum: quasi dilúculum præparátus est egréssus ejus, et véniet quasi imber nobis temporáneus et serótinus terræ. Quid fáciam tibi, Ephraim? Quid fáciam tibi, Juda? misericórdia vestra quasi nubes matutína: et quasi ros mane pertránsiens. Propter hoc dolávi in prophétis, occídi eos in verbis oris mei: et judícia tua quasi lux egrediéntur. Quia misericórdiam vólui, et non sacrifícium, et sciéntiam Dei, plus quam holocáusta.

THUS saith the Lord: In their affliction they will rise early to Me: Come, and let us return to the Lord, for He hath taken us, and He will heal us, He will strike, and He will cure us. He will revive us after two days: on the third day He will raise us up and we shall live in His sight. We shall know and we shall follow on, that we may know the Lord. His going forth is prepared as the morning light and He will come to us as the early and the latter rain to the earth. What shall I do to thee, O Ephraim? What shall I do to thee, O Juda? Your mercy is as a morning cloud and as the dew that goeth away in the morning. For this reason have I hewed them by the Prophets, I have slain them by the words of my mouth: and thy judgements shall go forth as the light. For I desired mercy and not sacrifice: and the knowledge of God more than holocausts.

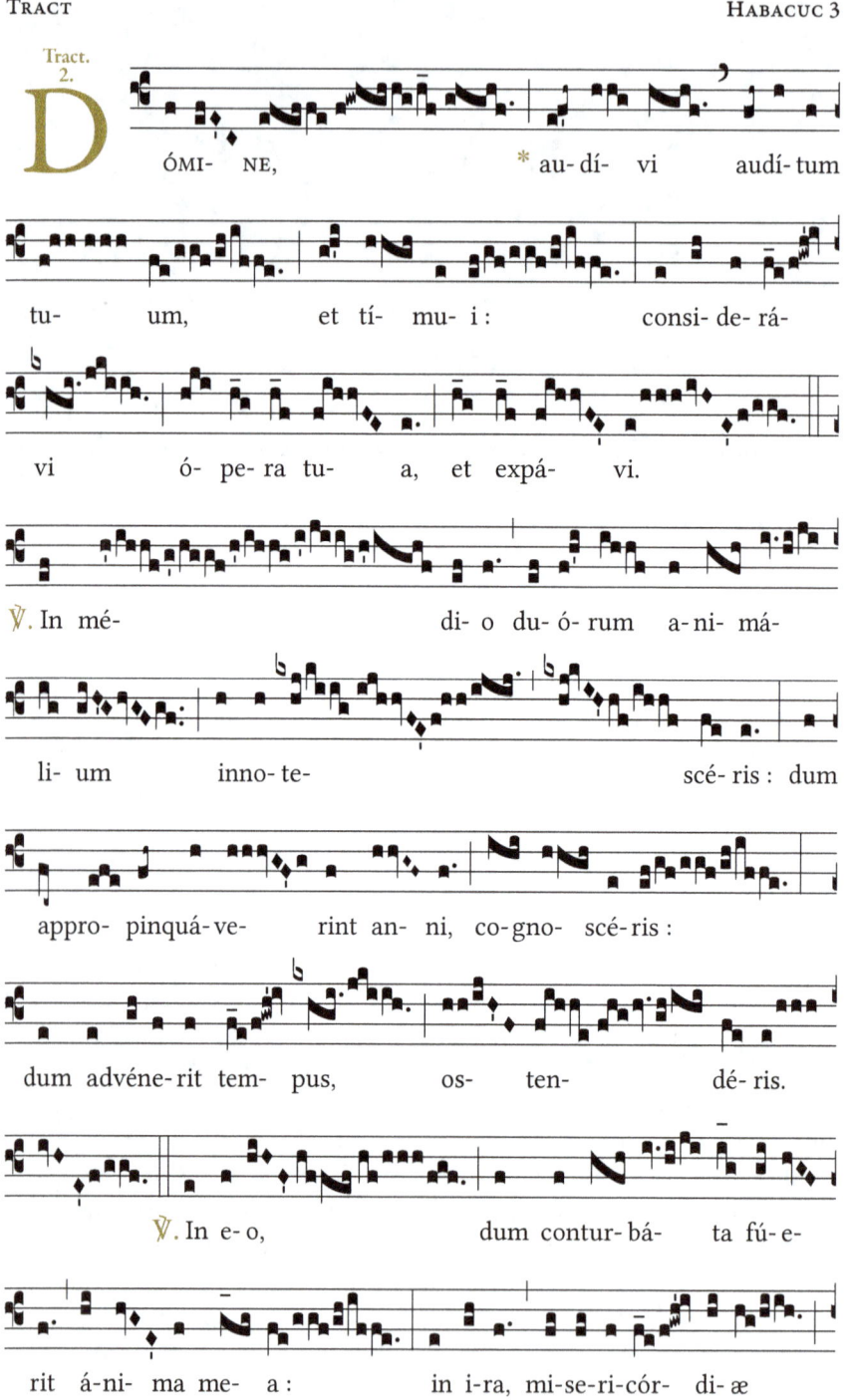

D ÓMI- NE, * au- dí- vi audí- tum
tu- um, et tí- mu- i: consi- de- rá-
vi ó- pe- ra tu- a, et expá- vi.

℣. In mé- di- o du- ó- rum a- ni- má-
li- um inno- te- scé- ris : dum
appro- pinquá- ve- rint an- ni, co-gno- scé- ris :
dum advéne- rit tem- pus, os- ten- dé- ris.

℣. In e- o, dum contur- bá- ta fú- e-
rit á- ni- ma me- a : in i-ra, mi-se-ri-cór- di- æ

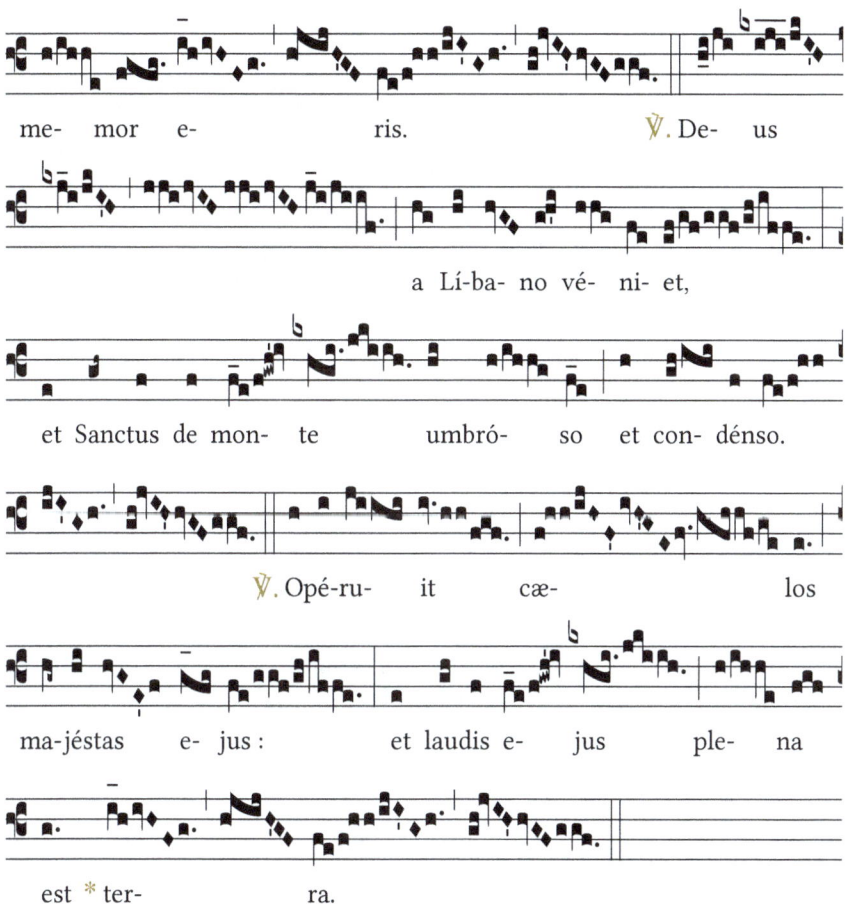

me- mor e- ris. ℣. De- us

a Lí-ba- no vé- ni- et,

et Sanctus de mon- te umbró- so et con- dénso.

℣. Opé-ru- it cæ- los

ma-jéstas e- jus : et laudis e- jus ple- na

est * ter- ra.

Tract: O Lord, I have heard Thy hearing and was afraid: I have considered Thy works and trembled. ℣. In the midst of two animals Thou shalt be made known: when the years shall draw nigh Thou shalt be known: when the time shall come, Thou shalt be manifested. ℣. When my soul shall be in trouble, Thou wilt remember mercy, even in Thy wrath. ℣. God will come from Libanus, and the Holy One from the shady and thickly covered mountain. ℣. His majesty covered the heavens: and the earth is full of His praise.

<table>
<tr><td>Orémus.</td><td>Let us pray.</td></tr>
</table>

Orémus.

℣. Flectámus genua. ℟. Leváte.

Let us pray.

℣. Let us kneel. ℟. Arise.

Deus, a quo et Judas reátus sui poenam, et confessiónis suæ latro præmium sumpsit, concéde nobis tuæ propitiatiónis efféctum: ut, sicut

O God, from whom Judas received the punishment of his guilt, and the thief the reward of his confession: grant unto us the full fruit

in passióne sua Jesus Christus, Dóminus noster, divérsa utrísque íntulit
stipéndia meritórum; ita nobis, abláto
vetustátis erróre, resurrectiónis suæ
grátiam largiátur: Qui tecum vivit et
regnat in unitáte Spíritus Sancti Deus
per ómnia sǽcula sæculórum.

℟. Amen.

of Thy clemency; that even as in His
Passion, our Lord Jesus Christ gave
to each a retribution according to his
merits, so having taken away our old
sins, He may bestow upon us the grace
of His Resurrection. Who with Thee
liveth and reigneth in the unity of the
Holy Ghost, God, world without end.

℟. Amen.

The subdeacon sings the following lesson:

SECOND LESSON — EXODUS 12: 1-11

IN diébus illis: Dixit Dóminus ad
Móysen et Aaron in terra Ægýpti:
Mensis iste vobis princípium ménsium primus erit in ménsibus anni.
Loquímini ad univérsum cœtum
filiórum Israël, et dícite eis: Décima
die mensis hujus tollat unusquísque
agnum per famílias et domos suas. Sin
autem minor est númerus, ut suffícere
possit ad vescéndum agnum, assúmet
vicínum suum, qui junctus est dómui
suæ, juxta númerum animárum, quæ
suffícere possunt ad esum agni. Erit
autem agnus absque mácula, másculus, annículus: juxta quem ritum
tollétis et hædum. Et servábitis eum
usque ad quartam décimam diem
mensis hujus: immolabítque eum
univérsa multitúdo filiórum Israël ad
vésperam. Et sument de sánguine ejus,
ac ponent super utrúmque postem
et in superlimináribus domórum,
in quibus cómedent illum. Et edent
carnes nocte illa assas igni, et ázymos
panes cum lactúcis agréstibus. Non
comedétis ex eo crudum quid nec
coctum aqua, sed tantum assum igni:

IN those days the Lord said to Moses
and Aaron in the land of Egypt:
This month shall be to you the beginning of months: it shall be the first in
the months of the year. Speak ye to the
whole assembly of the children of Israel, and say to them: On the tenth day of
this month let every man take a lamb
by their families and houses. But if the
number be less than may suffice to eat
the lamb, he shall take unto him his
neighbor that joineth to his house, according to the number of souls which
may be enough to eat the lamb. And
it shall be a lamb without blemish, a
male, of one year: according to which
rite also you shall take a kid. And you
shall keep it until the fourteenth day of
this month: and the whole multitude
of the children of Israel shall sacrifice
it in the evening. And they shall take
of the blood thereof, and put it upon
both the side posts, and on the upper
door posts of the houses, wherein
they shall eat it. And they shall eat the
flesh that night roasted at the fire: and
unleavened bread with wild lettuce.

caput cum pédibus ejus et intestínis vorábitis. Nec remanébit quidquam ex eo usque mane. Si quid resíduum fúerit, igne comburétis. Sic autem comedétis illum: Renes vestros accingétis, et calceaménta habébitis in pédibus, tenéntes báculos in mánibus, et comedétis festinánter: est enim Phase – id est tránsitus – Dómini.

You shall not eat thereof any thing raw, nor boiled in water, but only roasted at the fire. You shall eat the head with the feet and entrails thereof. Neither shall there remain any thing of it until morning. If there be any thing left, you shall burn it with fire. And thus you shall eat it: You shall gird your reins, and you shall have shoes on your feet, holding staves in your hands, and you shall eat in haste; for it is the Phase (that is, the Passage) of the Lord.

TRACT   PSALM 139: 2-10; 14

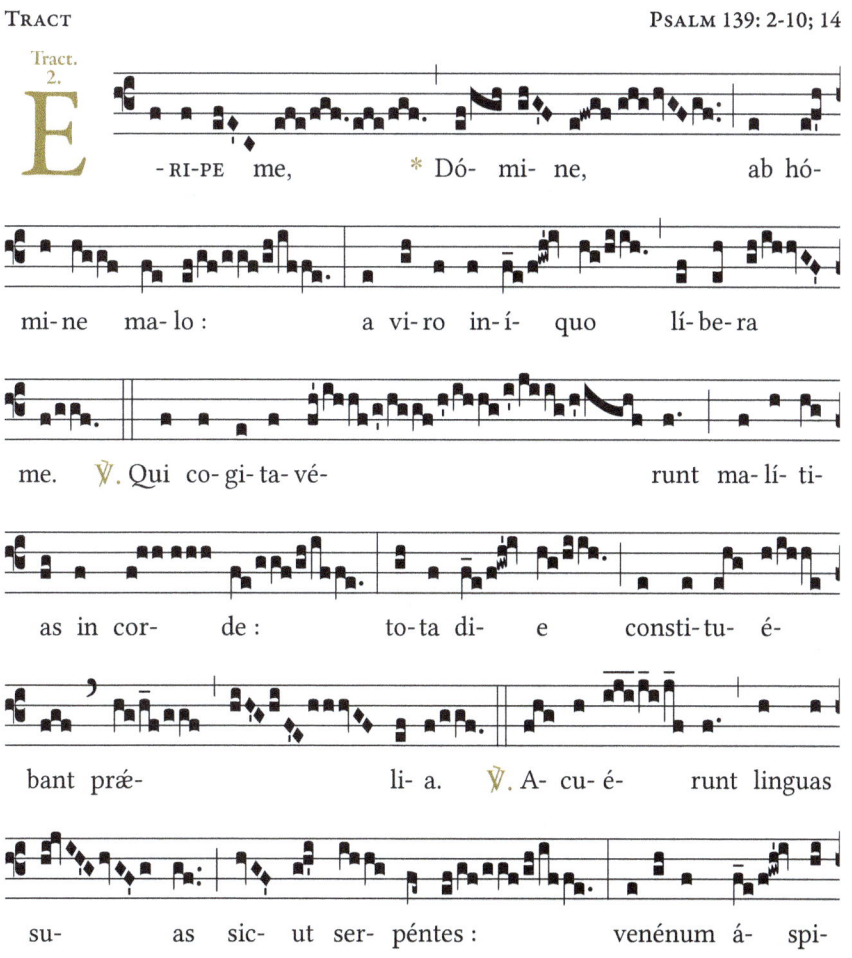

E-RI-PE me, * Dó- mi- ne, ab hó- mi-ne ma- lo : a vi-ro in-í- quo lí- be- ra me. ℣. Qui co-gi-ta-vé- runt ma-lí- ti-as in cor- de : to-ta di- e consti-tu- é- bant præ- li- a. ℣. A- cu- é- runt linguas su- as sic- ut ser- péntes : venénum á- spi-

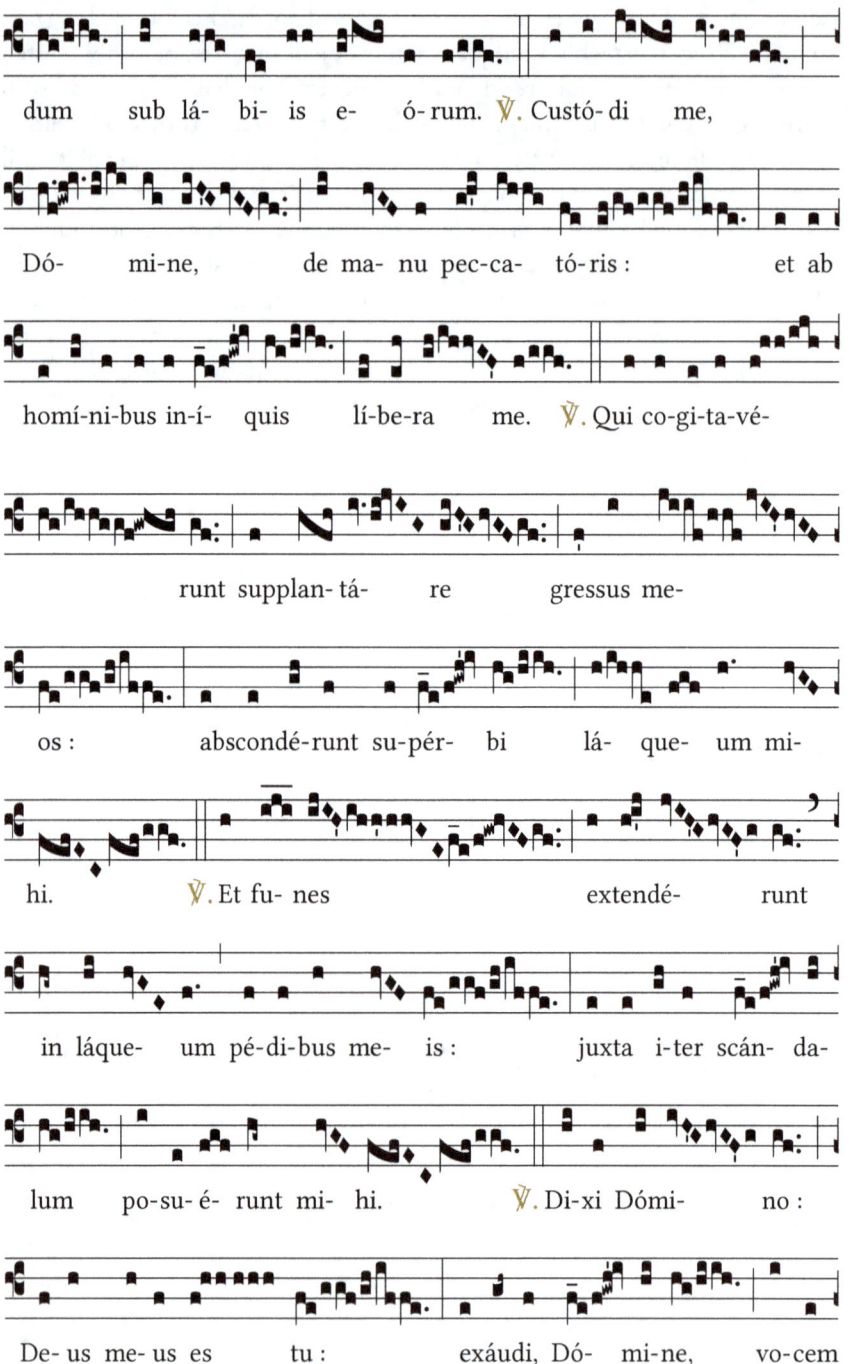

dum sub lá- bi- is e- ó- rum. ℣. Custó- di me,

Dó- mi-ne, de ma- nu pec-ca- tó-ris : et ab

homí-ni-bus in-í- quis lí-be-ra me. ℣. Qui co-gi-ta-vé-

runt supplan- tá- re gressus me-

os : abscondé-runt su-pér- bi lá- que- um mi-

hi. ℣. Et fu- nes extendé- runt

in láque- um pé-di-bus me- is : juxta i-ter scán- da-

lum po-su-é- runt mi- hi. ℣. Di-xi Dómi- no :

De- us me- us es tu : exáudi, Dó- mi-ne, vo-cem

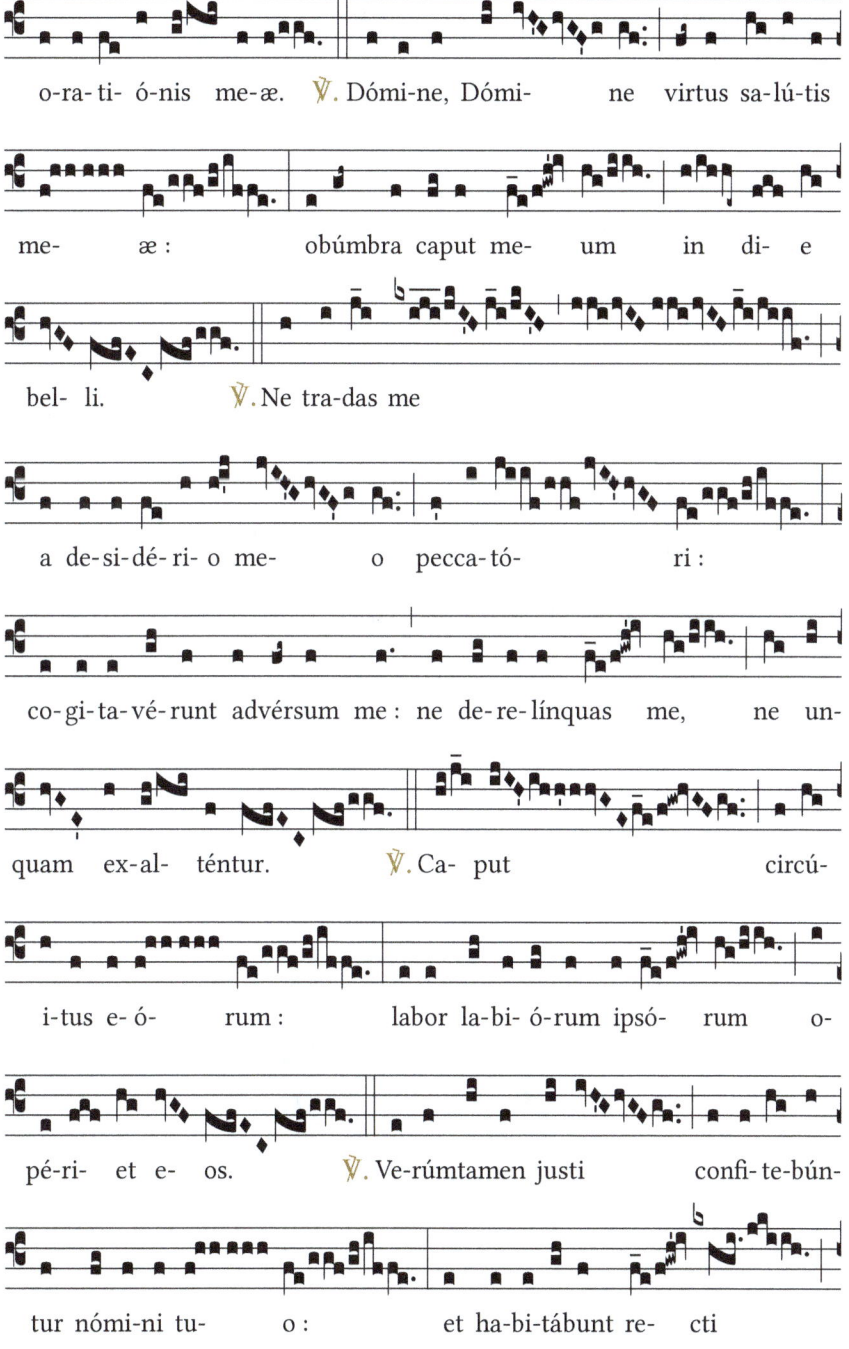

o-ra-ti- ó-nis me-æ. ℣. Dómi-ne, Dómi- ne virtus sa-lú-tis

me- æ: obúmbra caput me- um in di- e

bel- li. ℣. Ne tra-das me

a de-si-dé- ri- o me- o pecca-tó- ri :

co-gi-ta-vé-runt advérsum me : ne de-re-línquas me, ne un-

quam ex-al- téntur. ℣. Ca- put circú-

i-tus e- ó- rum : labor la-bi- ó-rum ipsó- rum o-

pé-ri- et e- os. ℣. Ve-rúmtamen justi confi- te-bún-

tur nómi-ni tu- o : et ha-bi-tábunt re- cti

cum   vul- tu   * tu-   o.

TRACT: Deliver me, O Lord, from the evil man: rescue me from the unjust man. ℣. Who have devised iniquities in their hearts: all the day long they designed battles. ℣. They have sharpened their tongues like a serpent; the venom of asps is under their lips. ℣. Keep me, O Lord, from the hand of the wicked: and from unjust men deliver me. ℣. Who have proposed to supplant my steps. The proud have hidden a net for me. ℣. And they have stretched out cords for a snare for my feet; they have laid for me a stumbling-block by the wayside. ℣. I said to the Lord: Thou art my God. Hear, O Lord, the voice of my supplication. ℣. O Lord, Lord, the strength of my salvation: overshadow my head in the day of battle. ℣. Give me not up from my desire to the wicked: they have plotted against me. Do not Thou forsake me, lest at any time they should triumph. ℣. The head of them compassing me about: the labor of their lips shall overwhelm them. ℣. But the just shall give glory to Thy Name: and the upright shall dwell with Thy countenance.

PASSION

THE PASSION ✠ OF OUR LORD JESUS CHRIST ACCORDING TO ST. JOHN
John 18: 1-40; 19: 1-42

J: Our Lord Jesus Christ | C: Narrator | *S: Other speaker(s)*

IN illo témpore: Egréssus est Jesus cum discípulis suis trans torréntem Cedron, ubi erat hortus, in quem introívit ipse et discípuli ejus. Sciébat autem et Judas, qui tradébat eum, locum: quia frequénter Jesus convénerat illuc cum discípulis suis. Judas ergo cum accepísset cohórtem, et a pontifícibus et pharisǽis minístros, venit illuc cum latérnis et fácibus et armis.

Jesus ítaque sciens ómnia, quæ ventúra erant super eum, procéssit, et dixit eis:

J. Quem quǽritis?
C. Respondérunt ei:
S. Jesum Nazarénum.
C. Dicit eis Jesus:
J. Ego sum.
C. Stabat autem et Judas, qui tradébat eum, cum ipsis. Ut ergo dixit eis: Ego sum: abiérunt retrórsum, et cecidérunt in terram. Iterum ergo interrogávit eos:

J. Quem quǽritis?
C. Illi autem dixérunt:
S. Jesum Nazarénum.
C. Respóndit Jesus:
J. Dixi vobis, quia ego sum: si ergo me quǽritis, sínite hos abíre.

AT that time Jesus went forth with His disciples over the brook Cedron, where there was a garden, into which He entered with His disciples. And Judas also, who betrayed Him, knew the place: because Jesus had often resorted thither together with His disciples. Judas therefore having received a band of soldiers and servants from the chief priests and the Pharisees, cometh thither with lanterns and torches and weapons.

Jesus therefore, knowing that all things that should come upon Him, went forth and said to them:

J. Whom seek ye?
C. They answered Him:
S. Jesus of Nazareth.
C. Jesus saith to them:
J. I am He.
C. And Judas also, who betrayed Him, stood with them. As soon therefore as He had said to them: I am He; they went backward and fell to the ground. Again therefore He asked them:

J. Whom seek ye?
C. And they said:
S. Jesus of Nazareth.
C. Jesus answered:
J. I have told you that I am He. If therefore you seek Me, let these go their way;

C. Ut implerétur sermo, quem dixit: Quia quos dedísti mihi, non pérdidi ex eis quemquam.

Simon ergo Petrus habens gládium edúxit eum: et percússit pontíficis servum: et abscídit aurículam ejus déxteram. Erat autem nomen servo Malchus. Dixit ergo Jesus Petro:

J. Mitte gládium tuum in vagínam. Cálicem, quem dedit mihi Pater, non bibam illum?

C. Cohors ergo et tribúnus et minístri Judæórum comprehendérunt Jesum, et ligavérunt eum: et adduxérunt eum ad Annam primum, erat enim socer Cáiphæ, qui erat póntifex anni illíus. Erat autem Cáiphas, qui consílium déderat Judæis: Quia éxpedit, unum hóminem mori pro pópulo.

Sequebátur autem Jesum Simon Petrus et álius discípulus. Discípulus autem ille erat notus pontífici, et intróivit cum Jesu in átrium pontíficis. Petrus autem stabat ad óstium foris. Exívit ergo discípulus álius, qui erat notus pontífici, et dixit ostiáriæ: et introdúxit Petrum. Dicit ergo Petro ancílla ostiária:

S. Numquid et tu ex discípulis es hóminis istíus?

C. Dicit ille:

S. Non sum.

C. Stabant autem servi et minístri ad prunas, quia frigus erat, et calefaciébant se: erat autem cum eis et Petrus stans et calefáciens se.

C. That the word might be fulfilled which He said: Of them whom Thou hast given Me, I have not lost anyone.

Then Simon Peter, having a sword, drew it and struck the servant of the high priest and cut off his right ear. And the name of the servant was Malchus. Jesus therefore said to Peter:

J. Put up thy sword in the scabbard. The chalice which My Father hath given Me, shall I not drink it?

C. Then the band and the tribune and the servants of the Jews took Jesus, and bound Him. And they led Him away to Annas first, for he was father-in-law to Caiphas, who was the high priest that year. Now Caiphas was he who had given the counsel to the Jews: that it was expedient that one man should die for the people.

And Simon Peter followed Jesus: and so did another disciple. And that disciple was known to the high priest and went in with Jesus into the court of the high priest. But Peter stood at the door without. The other disciple therefore, who was known to the high priest, went out and spoke to the portress and brought in Peter. The maid therefore that was portress saith to Peter:

S. Art not thou also one of this man's disciples?

C. He saith:

S. I am not.

C. Now the servants and ministers stood at a fire of coals, because it was cold, and warmed themselves. And with them was Peter, also, standing and warming himself.

Póntifex ergo interrogávit Jesum de discípulis suis et de doctrína ejus. Respóndit ei Jesus:

J. Ego palam locútus sum mundo: ego semper dócui in synagóga et in templo, quo omnes Judǽi convéniunt: et in occúlto locútus sum nihil. Quid me intérrogas? Intérroga eos, qui audiérunt, quid locútus sum ipsis: ecce, hi sciunt, quæ díxerim ego.

C. Hæc autem cum dixísset, unus assístens ministrórum dedit álapam Jesu, dicens:

S. Sic respóndes pontífici?

C. Respóndit ei Jesus:

J. Si male locútus sum, testimónium pérhibe de malo: si autem bene, quid me cædis?

C. Et misit eum Annas ligátum ad Cáipham pontíficem. Erat autem Simon Petrus stans et calefáciens se. Dixérunt ergo ei:

S. Numquid et tu ex discípulis ejus es?

C. Negávit ille et dixit:

S. Non sum.

C. Dicit ei unus ex servis pontíficis, cognátus ejus, cujus abscídit Petrus aurículam:

S. Nonne ego te vidi in horto cum illo?

C. Iterum ergo negávit Petrus: et statim gallus cantávit.

Addúcunt ergo Jesum a Cáipha in prætórium. Erat autem mane: et ipsi non introiérunt in prætórium, ut non contaminaréntur, sed ut manducárent pascha. Exívit ergo Pilátus ad eos foras et dixit:

The high priest therefore asked Jesus of His disciples and of His doctrine. Jesus answered him:

J. I have spoken openly to the world. I have always taught in the synagogue and in the temple, whither all the Jews resort: and in secret I have spoken nothing. Why asketh thou Me? Ask them who have heard what I have spoken unto them. Behold they know what things I have said.

C. And when He had said these things, one of the servants, standing by, gave Jesus a blow, saying:

S. Answerest Thou the high priest so?

C. Jesus answered him:

J. If I have spoken evil, give testimony of the evil; but if well, why strikest thou Me?

C. And Annas sent Him bound to Caiphas the high priest. And Simon Peter was standing and warming himself. They said therefore to him:

S. Art not thou also one of His disciples?

C. He denied it and said:

S. I am not.

C. One of the servants of the high priest (a kinsman to him whose ear Peter cut off) saith to him:

S. Did I not see thee in the garden with Him?

C. Again therefore Peter denied; and immediately the cock crew.

Then they led Jesus from Caiphas to the governor's hall. And it was morning; and they went not into the hall, that they might not be defiled, but that they might eat the Pasch. Pilate therefore went out to them, and said:

S. *Quam accusatiónem affértis ad-*
vérsus hóminem hunc?

C. Respondérunt et dixérunt ei:

S. *Si non esset hic malefáctor, non*
tibi tradidissémus eum.

C. Dixit ergo eis Pilátus:

S. *Accípite eum vos, et secúndum*
legem vestram judicáte eum.

C. Dixérunt ergo ei Judǽi:

S. *Nobis non licet interfícere quem-*
quam.

C. Ut sermo Jesu implerétur, quem
dixit, signíficans, qua morte esset
moritúrus.

Introívit ergo íterum in prætórium
Pilátus, et vocávit Jesum et dixit ei:

S. *Tu es Rex Judæórum?*

C. Respóndit Jesus:

J. A temetípso hoc dicis, an álii
dixérunt tibi de me?

C. Respóndit Pilátus:

S. *Numquid ego Judǽus sum? Gens*
tua et pontífices tradidérunt te mihi:
quid fecísti?

C. Respóndit Jesus:

J. Regnum meum non est de hoc
mundo. Si ex hoc mundo esset regnum meum, minístri mei útique
decertárent, ut non tráderer Judǽis:
nunc autem regnum meum non est
hinc.

C. Dixit ítaque ei Pilátus:

S. *Ergo Rex es tu?*

C. Respóndit Jesus:

J. Tu dicis, quia Rex sum ego.
Ego in hoc natus sum et ad hoc veni
in mundum, ut testimónium per-
híbeam veritáti: omnis, qui est ex
veritáte, audit vocem meam.

S. *What accusation bring you*
against this man?

C. They answered and said to him:

S. *If He were not a malefactor, we*
would not have delivered Him up to
thee.

C. Pilate therefore said to them:

S. *Take Him you, and judge Him*
according to your law.

C. The Jews therefore said to him:

S. *It is not lawful for us to put any*
man to death.

C. That the word of Jesus might be
fulfilled, which He said, signifying
what death He should die.

Pilate therefore went into the hall
again and called Jesus and said to
Him:

S. *Art Thou the King of the Jews?*

C. Jesus answered:

J. Sayest thou this thing of thyself,
or have others told it thee of Me?

C. Pilate answered:

S. *Am I a Jew? Thine own nation*
and the chief priests have delivered
Thee up to me. What hast Thou done?

C. Jesus answered:

J. My kingdom is not of this
world. If My kingdom were of this
world, My servants would certainly
strive that I should not be delivered
to the Jews: but now My kingdom is
not from hence.

C. Pilate therefore said to Him:

S. *Art Thou a King then?*

C. Jesus answered:

J. Thou sayest I am a king. For this
was I born, and for this came I into
the world; that I should give testimony of the truth. Every one that is
of the truth heareth My voice.

C. Dicit ei Pilátus:

S. *Quid est véritas?*

C. Et cum hoc dixísset, íterum exívit ad Judǽos, et dicit eis:

S. *Ego nullam invénio in eo causam. Est autem consuetúdo vobis, ut unum dimíttam vobis in Pascha: vultis ergo dimíttam vobis Regem Judæórum?*

C. Clamavérunt ergo rursum omnes, dicéntes:

S. *Non hunc, sed Barábbam.*

C. Erat autem Barábbas latro. Tunc ergo apprehéndit Pilátus Jesum et flagellávit. Et mílites plecténtes corónam de spinis, imposuérunt cápiti ejus: et veste purpúrea circumdedérunt eum. Et veniébant ad eum, et dicébant:

S. *Ave, Rex Judæórum.*

C. Et dabant ei álapas.

Exívit ergo íterum Pilátus foras et dicit eis:

S. *Ecce, addúco vobis eum foras, ut cognoscátis, quia nullam invénio in eo causam.*

C. Exívit ergo Jesus portans corónam spíneam et purpúreum vestiméntum. Et dicit eis:

S. *Ecce homo.*

C. Cum ergo vidíssent eum pontífices et minístri, clamábant, dicéntes:

S. *Crucifíge, crucifíge eum.*

C. Dicit eis Pilátus:

S. *Accípite eum vos et crucifígite: ego enim non invénio in eo causam.*

C. Respondérunt ei Judǽi:

C. Pilate saith to Him:

S. *What is truth?*

C. And when he had said this, he went out again to the Jews and saith to them:

S. *I find no cause in Him. But you have a custom that I should release one unto you at the Pasch. Will you, therefore, that I release unto you the King of the Jews?*

C. Then cried they all again, saying:

S. *Not this man, but Barabbas.*

C. Now Barabbas was a robber. Then therefore Pilate took Jesus and scourged Him. And the soldiers platting a crown of thorns, put it upon His head; and they put on Him a purple garment. And they came to Him and said:

S. *Hail, King of the Jews.*

C. And they gave Him blows. Pilate therefore went forth again and saith to them:

S. *Behold, I bring Him forth unto you, that you may know that I find no cause in Him.*

C. Jesus therefore came forth, bearing the crown of thorns and the purple garment. And he saith to them:

S. *Behold the man.*

C. When the chief priests, therefore, and the servants had seen Him, they cried out, saying:

S. *Crucify Him, crucify Him.*

C. Pilate saith to them:

S. *Take Him you, and crucify Him; for I find no cause in Him.*

C. The Jews answered him:

S. *Nos legem habémus, et secúndum legem debet mori, quia Fílium Dei se fecit.*

C. Cum ergo audísset Pilátus hunc sermónem, magis tímuit.

Et ingréssus est prætórium íterum: et dixit ad Jesum:

S. *Unde es tu?*

C. Jesus autem respónsum non dedit ei. Dicit ergo ei Pilátus:

S. *Mihi non lóqueris? Nescis, quia potestátem hábeo crucifígere te, et potestátem hábeo dimíttere te?*

C. Respóndit Jesus:

J. Non habéres potestátem advérsum me ullam, nisi tibi datum esset désuper. Proptérea, qui me trádidit tibi, majus peccátum habet.

C. Et exínde quærébat Pilátus dimíttere eum. Judǽi autem clamábant, dicéntes:

S. *Si hunc dimíttis, non es amícus Cǽsaris. Omnis enim, qui se regem facit, contradícit Cǽsari.*

C. Pilátus autem cum audísset hos sermónes, addúxit foras Jesum, et sedit pro tribunáli, in loco, qui dícitur Lithóstrotos, hebráice autem Gábbatha. Erat autem Parascéve Paschæ, hora quasi sexta, et dicit Judǽis:

S. *Ecce Rex vester.*

C. Illi autem clamábant:

S. *Tolle, tolle, crucifíge eum.*

C. Dicit eis Pilátus:

S. *Regem vestrum crucifígam?*

C. Respondérunt pontífices:

S. *We have a law, and according to the law He ought to die, because He made Himself the Son of God.*

C. When Pilate, therefore, had heard this saying, he feared the more.

And he entered into the hall again; and he said to Jesus:

S. *Whence art Thou?*

C. But Jesus gave him no answer. Pilate therefore saith to Him:

S. *Speakest Thou not to me? Knowest Thou not that I have power to crucify Thee, and I have power to release Thee?*

C. Jesus answered:

J. Thou shouldst not have any power against Me, unless it were given thee from above. Therefore, he that hath delivered Me to thee hath a greater sin.

C. And from henceforth Pilate sought to release Him. But the Jews cried out, saying:

S. *If thou release this Man, thou art not Caesar's friend. For whosoever maketh himself a king speaketh against Caesar.*

C. Now when Pilate had heard these words, he brought Jesus forth and sat down in the judgment seat, in the place that is called Lithostrotos, and in Hebrew Gabbatha. And it was Parasceve of the Pasch, about the sixth hour; and he saith to the Jews:

S. *Behold your King.*

C. But they cried out:

S. *Away with Him. Away with Him: Crucify Him.*

C. Pilate saith to them:

S. *Shall I crucify your King?*

C. The chief priests answered:

S. Non habémus regem nisi Cǽsarem.

C. Tunc ergo trádidit eis illum, ut crucifigerétur.

Suscepérunt autem Jesum et eduxérunt. Et bájulans sibi crucem, exívit in eum, qui dícitur Calváriæ, locum, hebráice autem Gólgotha: ubi crucifixérunt eum, et cum eo álios duos, hinc et hinc, médium autem Jesum.

Scripsit autem et títulum Pilátus: et pósuit super crucem. Erat autem scriptum: Jesus Nazarénus, Rex Judæórum. Hunc ergo títulum multi Judæórum legérunt, quia prope civitátem erat locus, ubi crucifíxus est Jesus. Et erat scriptum hebráice, grǽce et latíne. Dicébant ergo Piláto pontífices Judæórum:

S. Noli scríbere Rex Judæórum, sed quia ipse dixit: Rex sum Judæórum.

C. Respóndit Pilátus:

S. Quod scripsi, scripsi.

C. Mílites ergo cum crucifixíssent eum, accepérunt vestiménta ejus et fecérunt quátuor partes: unicuíque míliti partem, et túnicam. Erat autem túnica inconsútilis, désuper contéxta per totum. Dixérunt ergo ad ínvicem:

S. Non scindámus eam, sed sortiámur de illa, cujus sit.

C. Ut Scriptúra implerétur, dicens: Partíti sunt vestiménta mea sibi: et in vestem meam misérunt sortem. Et mílites quidem hæc fecérunt.

Stabant autem juxta crucem Jesu Mater ejus et soror Matris ejus, María

---

S. We have no king but Caesar.

C. Then, therefore, he delivered Him to them to be crucified.

And they took Jesus and led Him forth. And bearing His cross, He went forth to that place which is called Calvary but in Hebrew Golgotha, where they crucified Him, and with Him two others, one on each side and Jesus in the midst.

And Pilate wrote a title also: and he put it upon the cross. And the writing was: Jesus of Nazareth, the King of the Jews. This title therefore many of the Jews did read: because the place where Jesus was crucified was nigh to the city. And it was written in Hebrew, Greek, and in Latin. Then the chief priests of the Jews said to Pilate:

S. Write not: The King of the Jews; but that He said: I am the King of the Jews.

C. Pilate answered:

S. What I have written, I have written.

C. The soldiers therefore, when they had crucified Him, took His garments and they made four parts, to every soldier a part and also His coat. Now the coat was without seam, woven from the top throughout. They said then one to another:

S. Let us not cut it, but let us cast lots for it, whose it shall be:

C. That the Scripture might be fulfilled which saith: They have parted My garments among them, and upon My vesture they have cast lots. And the soldiers indeed did these things.

Now there stood by the cross of Jesus His Mother, and His Mother's

Cléophæ, et María Magdaléne. Cum vidísset ergo Jesus Matrem et discípulum stantem, quem diligébat, dicit Matri suæ:

J. Múlier, ecce fílius tuus.

C. Deínde dicit discípulo:

J. Ecce mater tua.

C. Et ex illa hora accépit eam discípulus in sua.

Póstea sciens Jesus, quia ómnia consummáta sunt, ut consummarétur Scriptúra, dixit:

J. Sítio.

C. Vas ergo erat pósitum acéto plenum. Illi autem spóngiam plenam acéto, hyssópo circumponéntes, obtulérunt ori ejus. Cum ergo accepísset Jesus acétum, dixit:

J. Consummátum est.

C. Et inclináto cápite trádidit spíritum.

sister, Mary of Cleophas, and Mary Magdalen. When Jesus therefore had seen His Mother and the disciple standing whom He loved, He saith to His Mother:

J. Woman, behold thy son.

C. After that, He saith to the disciple:

J. Behold thy mother.

C. And from that hour, the disciple took her to his own.

Afterwards, Jesus, knowing that all things were now accomplished, that the Scripture might be fulfilled, said:

J. I thirst.

C. Now there was a vessel set there, full of vinegar. And they, putting a sponge full of vinegar about hyssop, put it to His mouth. Jesus therefore, when He had taken the vinegar, said:

J. It is consummated.

C. And bowing His head, He gave up the ghost.

Here all kneel and pause a few moments.

JUDÆI ergo, quóniam Parascéve erat, ut non remanérent in cruce córpora sábbato (erat enim magnus dies ille sábbati), rogavérunt Pilátum, ut frangeréntur eórum crura et tolleréntur. Venérunt ergo mílites: et primi quidem fregérunt crura et altérius, qui crucifíxus est cum eo. Ad Jesum autem cum veníssent, ut vidérunt eum jam mórtuum, non fregérunt ejus crura, sed unus mílitum láncea latus ejus apéruit, et contínuo exívit sanguis et aqua. Et qui vidit, testimónium perhíbuit: et verum est testimónium ejus. Et ille scit, quia vera dicit: ut et vos credátis. Facta sunt enim hæc, ut Scriptúra implerétur:

THEN the Jews, because it was the Parasceve, that the bodies might not remain upon the cross on the Sabbath day (for that was a great Sabbath day), besought Pilate that their legs might be broken and that they might be taken away. The soldiers therefore came, and they broke the legs of the first, and of the other that was crucified with Him. But after they were come to Jesus, when they saw that He was already dead, they did not break His legs. But one of the soldiers with a spear opened His side, and immediately there came out blood and water. And he that saw it hath given testimony: and his testimony is true.

Os non comminuétis ex eo. Et íterum ália Scriptúra dicit: Vidébunt in quem transfixérunt.

And he knoweth that he saith true: that you also may believe. For these things were done that the Scripture might be fulfilled: you shall not break a bone of Him. And again another Scripture saith: They shall look on Him whom they pierced.

Here Munda cor meum *is said, but the deacon does not ask the celebrant's blessing. The lights are not carried; nor does the celebrant kiss the book at the end.*

MUNDA cor meum ac lábia mea, omnípotens Deus, qui lábia Isaíæ Prophétæ cálculo mundásti igníto: ita me tua grata miseratióne dignáre mundáre, ut sanctum Evangélium tuum digne váleam nuntiáre. Per Christum, Dóminum nostrum. Amen.

CLEANSE my heart and my lips, O almighty God, who didst cleanse the lips of the prophet Isaias with a burning coal, and vouchsafe, through Thy gracious mercy, so to purify me, that I may worthily announce Thy holy Gospel. Through Christ our Lord. Amen.

The deacon concludes:

POST hæc autem rogávit Pilátum Joseph ab Arimathæa, eo quod esset discípulus Jesu, occúltus autem propter metum Judæórum, ut tólleret corpus Jesu. Et permísit Pilátus. Venit ergo et tulit corpus Jesu. Venit autem et Nicodémus, qui vénerat ad Jesum nocte primum, ferens mixtúram myrrhæ et áloës, quasi libras centum. Accepérunt ergo corpus Jesu, et ligavérunt illud línteis cum aromátibus, sicut mos est Judæis sepelíre. Erat autem in loco, ubi crucifíxus est, hortus: et in horto monuméntum novum, in quo nondum quisquam pósitus erat. Ibi ergo propter Parascéven Judæórum, quia juxta erat monuméntum, posuérunt Jesum.

AND after these things, Joseph of Arimathea—because he was a disciple of Jesus, but secretly for fear of the Jews—besought Pilate that he might take away the Body of Jesus. And Pilate gave leave. He came therefore and took away the Body of Jesus. And Nicodemus also came—he who at the first came to Jesus by night—bringing a mixture of myrrh and aloes, about a hundred pound weight. They took therefore the Body of Jesus and bound it in linen cloths, with the spices, as the manner of the Jews is to bury. Now there was in the place where He was crucified a garden: and in the garden a new sepulchre, wherein no man yet had been laid. There, therefore, because of the Parasceve of the Jews, they laid Jesus, because the sepulchre was nigh at hand.

THE GREAT INTERCESSIONS

Then the celebrant standing at the epistle corner sings the following Collects:

FOR THE CHURCH

ORÉMUS, dilectíssimi nobis, pro Ecclésia sancta Dei: ut eam Deus et Dóminus noster pacificáre, adunáre, et custodíre dignétur toto orbe terrárum: subjíciens ei principátus et potestátes: detque nobis quiétam et tranquíllam vitam degéntibus, glorificáre Deum, Patrem omnipoténtem.

ORÉMUS.
℣. Flectámus genua. ℟. Leváte.

OMNÍPOTENS sempitérne Deus, qui glóriam tuam ómnibus in Christo géntibus revelásti: custódi ópera misericórdiæ tuæ; ut Ecclésia tua, toto orbe diffúsa, stábili fide in confessióne tui nóminis persevéret. Per eúndem Dóminum nostrum Jesum Christum Fílium tuum, qui tecum vivit et regnat in unitáte Spíritus Sancti, Deus, per ómnia sǽcula sæculórum.
℟. Amen.

LET us pray, dearly beloved, for the holy Church of God: that our Lord and God may deign to give it peace, keep it in unity, and guard it throughout the world, subjecting to it principalities and powers: and may grant unto us that, leading a peaceful and quiet life, we may glorify God, the Father almighty.

LET US PRAY.
℣. Let us kneel. ℟. Arise.

ALMIGHTY and everlasting God, Who in Christ hast revealed Thy glory to all nations: guard the works of Thy mercy; that Thy Church, spread over the whole world, may with steadfast faith persevere in the confession of Thy Name. Through the same Jesus Christ, thy Son, Our Lord, Who liveth and reigneth with Thee in the unity of the Holy Ghost, God, world without end.
℟. Amen.

FOR THE POPE

ORÉMUS et pro beatíssimo Papa nostro **N.,** ut Deus et Dóminus noster, qui elégit eum in órdine episcopátus, salvum atque incólumem custódiat Ecclésiæ suæ sanctæ, ad regéndum pópulum sanctum Dei.

LET us pray for our most holy Father Pope **N.,** that our Lord and God, Who chose him to the order of the Episcopate, may keep him in health and safety for His holy Church to govern the holy people of God.

Orémus.
℣. Flectámus genua. ℟. Leváte.

Deus, cujus judício univérsa fundántur: réspice propítius ad preces nostras, et eléctum nobis Antístitem tua pietáte consérva; ut christiána plebs, quæ te gubernátur auctóre, sub tanto Pontífice, credulitátis suæ méritis augeátur. Per Dóminum nostrum Jesum Christum, Fílium tuum: qui tecum vivit et regnat in unitáte Spíritus Sancti Deus, per ómnia sǽcula sæculórum.

℟. Amen.

Let us pray.
℣. Let us kneel. ℟. Arise.

Almighty and everlasting God, by Whose judgement all things are established, mercifully regard our prayers, and in Thy goodness preserve the Bishop chosen for us: that the Christian people who are ruled by Thine authority, may under so great a Pontiff, be increased in the merits of faith. Through Jesus Christ, Thy Son our Lord, Who liveth and reigneth with Thee, in the unity of the Holy Ghost, God, world without end.

℟. Amen.

FOR THE CLERGY AND THE PEOPLE

Orémus et pro ómnibus Epíscopis, Presbýteris, Diacónibus, Subdiacónibus, Acólythis, Exorcístis, Lectóribus, Ostiáriis, Confessóribus, Virgínibus, Víduis: et pro omni pópulo sancto Dei.

Let us pray also for all Bishops, Priests, Deacons, Subdeacons, Acolytes, Exorcists, Readers, Porters, Confessors, Virgins, Widows, and for all the holy people of God.

Orémus.
℣. Flectámus genua. ℟. Leváte.

Omnípotens sempitérne Deus, cujus Spíritu totum corpus Ecclésiæ sanctificátur et régitur: exáudi nos pro univérsis ordínibus supplicántes; ut, grátiæ tuæ múnere, ab ómnibus tibi grádibus fidéliter serviátur. Per Dóminum nostrum Jesum Christum, Fílium tuum: qui tecum vivit et regnat in unitáte Spíritus Sancti Deus, per ómnia sǽcula sæculórum.

℟. Amen.

Let us pray.
℣. Let us kneel. ℟. Arise.

Almighty and everlasting God, by Whose Spirit the whole body of the Church is sanctified and ruled, hear our humble pleading for all the orders thereof; that, by the gift of Thy grace, all in their several degrees may faithfully serve Thee. Through Jesus Christ, Thy Son our Lord, Who liveth and reigneth with Thee, in the unity of the Holy Ghost, God, world without end.

℟. Amen.

FOR THE EMPEROR

ORÉMUS et pro Christianíssimo Imperatóre nostro **N.** ut Deus, et Dóminus noster súbditas illi fáciat omnes bárbaras natiónes, ad nostram perpétuam pacem.

LET us pray also for our most Christian Emperor **N.,** that our Lord and God may subject to him all the barbarous nations, to our perpetual peace.

ORÉMUS.
℣. Flectámus genua. ℟. Leváte.

LET US PRAY.
℣. Let us kneel. ℟. Arise.

OMNÍPOTENS sempitérne Deus, in cujus manu sunt ómnium potestátes, et ómnium jura regnórum: réspice ad Románum benígnus Impérium; ut gentes, quæ in sua feritáte confídunt, poténtiæ tuæ déxtera comprimántur. Per Dóminum nostrum Jesum Christum, Fílium tuum: qui tecum vivit et regnat in unitáte Spíritus Sancti Deus, per ómnia sæcula sæculórum.
℟. Amen.

ALMIGHTY and everlasting God, in Whose hands are the powers of all men and the rights of all kingdoms; graciously look down upon the Roman Empire, that the nations that confide in their fierceness may be repressed by the power of Thy right hand. Through Jesus Christ, Thy Son our Lord, Who liveth and reigneth with Thee, in the unity of the Holy Ghost, God, world without end.
℟. Amen.

FOR THE CATECHUMENS

ORÉMUS et pro catechúmenis nostris: ut Deus et Dóminus noster adapériat aures præcordiórum ipsórum januámque misericórdiæ; ut, per lavácrum regeneratiónis accépta remissióne ómnium peccatórum, et ipsi inveniántur in Christo Jesu, Dómino nostro.

LET us pray also for our Catechumens: that our Lord and God would open the ears of their hearts, and the gate of mercy; that, having received by the font of regeneration the remission of all their sins, they also may be found in Christ Jesus our Lord.

ORÉMUS.
℣. Flectámus genua. ℟. Leváte.

LET US PRAY.
℣. Let us kneel. ℟. Arise.

OMNÍPOTENS sempitérne Deus, qui Ecclésiam tuam nova semper prole fecúndas: auge fidem et intelléctum catechúmenis nostris; ut, renáti fonte baptísmatis, adoptiónis

ALMIGHTY and everlasting God, who dost ever make Thy Church fruitful with new offspring: increase the faith and understanding of our Catechumens; that being born again

tuæ fíliis aggregéntur. Per Dóminum nostrum Jesum Christum, Fílium tuum: qui tecum vivit et regnat in unitáte Spíritus Sancti Deus, per ómnia sǽcula sæculórum.

℟. Amen.

in the font of Baptism, they may be associated with the children of Thine adoption. Through Jesus Christ, Thy Son our Lord, Who liveth and reigneth with Thee, in the unity of the Holy Ghost, God, world without end.

℟. Amen.

AGAINST ERRORS

Orémus, dilectíssimi nobis, Deum Patrem omnipoténtem, ut cunctis mundum purget erróribus: morbos áuferat: famem depéllat: apériat cárceres: víncula dissólvat: peregrinántibus réditum: infirmántibus sanitátem: navigántibus portum salútis indúlgeat.

Let us pray, dearly beloved, to God the Father almighty, that He would cleanse the world of all errors: take away diseases, drive away famine, open prisons, break chains, grant a sure return to travellers, health to the sick, and a safe haven to those at sea.

ORÉMUS.
℣. Flectámus genua. ℟. Leváte.

LET US PRAY.
℣. Let us kneel. ℟. Arise.

Omnípotens sempitérne Deus, mæstórum consolátio, laborántium fortitúdo: pervéniant ad te preces de quacúmque tribulatióne clamántium; ut omnes sibi in necessitátibus suis misericórdiam tuam gáudeant affuísse. Per Dóminum nostrum Jesum Christum, Fílium tuum: qui tecum vivit et regnat in unitáte Spíritus Sancti Deus, per ómnia sǽcula sæculórum.

℟. Amen.

Almighty and everlasting God, the comfort of the sorrowful, let the prayers of those who call upon Thee in any trouble be heard by Thee; that all may rejoice that in their necessities Thy mercy has helped them. Through Jesus Christ, Thy Son our Lord, Who liveth and reigneth with Thee, in the unity of the Holy Ghost, God, world without end.

℟. Amen.

FOR HERETICS AND SCHISMATICS

Orémus et pro hæréticis et schismáticis: ut Deus et Dóminus noster éruat eos ab erróribus univérsis; et ad sanctam matrem Ecclésiam Cathólicam atque Apostólicam revocáre dignétur.

Let us pray also for heretics and schismatics: that our Lord God would be pleased to rescue them from all their errors; and recall them to our holy mother the Catholic and Apostolic Church.

Orémus.

℣. Flectámus genua. ℟. Leváte.

Omnípotens sempitérne Deus, qui salvas omnes, et néminem vis períre: réspice ad ánimas diabólica fraude decéptas; ut, omni hærética pravitáte depósita, errántium corda resipíscant, et ad veritátis tuæ rédeant unitátem. Per Dóminum nostrum Jesum Christum, Fílium tuum: qui tecum vivit et regnat in unitáte Spíritus Sancti Deus, per ómnia sǽcula sæculórum.

℟. Amen.

Let us pray.

℣. Let us kneel. ℟. Arise.

Almighty and everlasting God, who savest all, and wouldst that no one should perish: look on the souls that are led astray by the deceit of the devil: that having set aside all heretical evil, the hearts of those that err may repent, and return to the unity of Thy truth. Through Jesus Christ, Thy Son our Lord, Who liveth and reigneth with Thee, in the unity of the Holy Ghost, God, world without end.

℟. Amen.

FOR THE JEWS

Orémus et pro pérfidis Judǽis: ut Deus et Dóminus noster áuferat velámen de córdibus eórum; ut et ipsi agnóscant Jesum Christum, Dóminum nostrum.

Omnípotens sempitérne Deus, qui étiam judáicam perfídiam a tua misericórdia non repéllis: exáudi preces nostras, quas pro illíus pópuli obcæcatióne deférimus; ut, ágnita veritátis tuæ luce, quæ Christus est, a suis ténebris eruántur. Per eúndem Dóminum nostrum Jesum Christum Fílium tuum, qui tecum vivit et regnat in unitáte Spíritus Sancti Deus, per ómnia sǽcula sæculórum.

℟. Amen.

Let us pray also for the perfidious Jews: that our God and Lord would remove the veil from their hearts: that they also may acknowledge our Lord Jesus Christ.

Almighty and everlasting God, who drivest not away from Thy mercy even the perfidious Jews: hear our prayers, which we offer for the blindness of that people: that, acknowledging the light of Thy truth, which is Christ, they may be rescued from their darkness. Through the same Jesus Christ, thy Son, Our Lord, Who liveth and reigneth with Thee in the unity of the Holy Ghost, God, world without end.

℟. Amen.

FOR THE PAGANS

Orémus et pro págánis: ut Deus omnípotens áuferat iniquitátem a córdibus eórum; ut, relíctis idólis

Let us pray also for the pagans: that almighty God would remove iniquity from their hearts: that,

suis, convertántur ad Deum vivum et verum, et únicum Fílium ejus Jesum Christum, Deum et Dóminum nostrum.

putting aside their idols, they may be converted to the true and living God, and His only Son, Jesus Christ our God and Lord.

ORÉMUS.

℣. Flectámus genua. ℟. Leváte.

LET US PRAY.

℣. Let us kneel. ℟. Arise.

OMNÍPOTENS sempitérne Deus, qui non mortem peccatórum, sed vitam semper inquíris: súscipe propítius oratiónem nostram, et líbera eos ab idolórum cultúra; et ággrega Ecclésiæ tuæ sanctæ, ad laudem et glóriam nóminis tui. Per Dóminum nostrum Jesum Christum, Fílium tuum: qui tecum vivit et regnat in unitáte Spíritus Sancti Deus, per ómnia sæcula sæculórum.

℟. Amen.

ALMIGHTY and everlasting God, who ever seekest not the death, but the life of sinners: mercifully hear our prayer, and deliver them from the worship of idols: and join them to Thy holy Church for the praise and glory of Thy Name. Through Jesus Christ, Thy Son our Lord, Who liveth and reigneth with Thee, in the unity of the Holy Ghost, God, world without end.

℟. Amen.

ADORATION OF THE CROSS

After these Collects, the celebrant lays aside his chasuble and goes to the Epistle corner of the altar, where he receives from the deacon the veiled Cross, which has been previously arranged on the altar. Then turning towards the people, he uncovers first the upper portion of the veiled Cross and intones the verse:

Ant. 6.

Ec-ce li-gnum Cru- cis, in quo sa-lus mun-di pe-pén- dit. ℟. Ve-ní-te, ad-o-ré- mus.

℣. Behold the wood of the Cross, on which hung the Saviour of the world.
℟. Come, let us adore.

When the choir sings these words, all kneel, except the celebrant. The celebrant then advances to the Epistle corner, and uncovers the right arm; elevating the Crucifix a little, he sings on a higher tone than before:

℣. Behold the wood of the Cross, on which hung the Saviour of the world.
℟. Come, let us adore.

Then at the middle of the altar the Celebrant uncovers the whole Cross, and, lifting it up, begins still higher, the ministers and choir continuing as before:

℣. Behold the wood of the Cross, on which hung the Saviour of the world.
℟. Come, let us adore.

The celebrant carries the Cross to the place prepared for it in front of the altar, and kneeling, lays it on a cushion. After which he takes off his shoes and chasuble. Then the celebrant, his ministers, and the rest of the clergy, and the laity double genuflect thrice and adore the Cross in turn. During the adoration of the Cross, the Impropéria or Reproaches are sung, while the celebrant, sitting, recites them with his ministers.

IMPROPÉRIA

P ÓPU-LE me-us, quid fe- ci ti-bi? Aut in quo contri-
stá-vi te? Respón-de mi-hi. ℣. Qui- a e-dú- xi te de ter-ra
Ægýpti : pa-rá- sti Cru-cem Salva-tó- ri tu- o.

℣. O my people, what have I done to thee? or wherein have I afflicted thee? Answer me. ℣. Because I led thee out of the land of Egypt, thou hast prepared a cross for thy Saviour.

The two choirs then sing alternately:

℟. O holy God! ℟. O holy God!

℟. O holy strong One! ℟. O holy strong One!

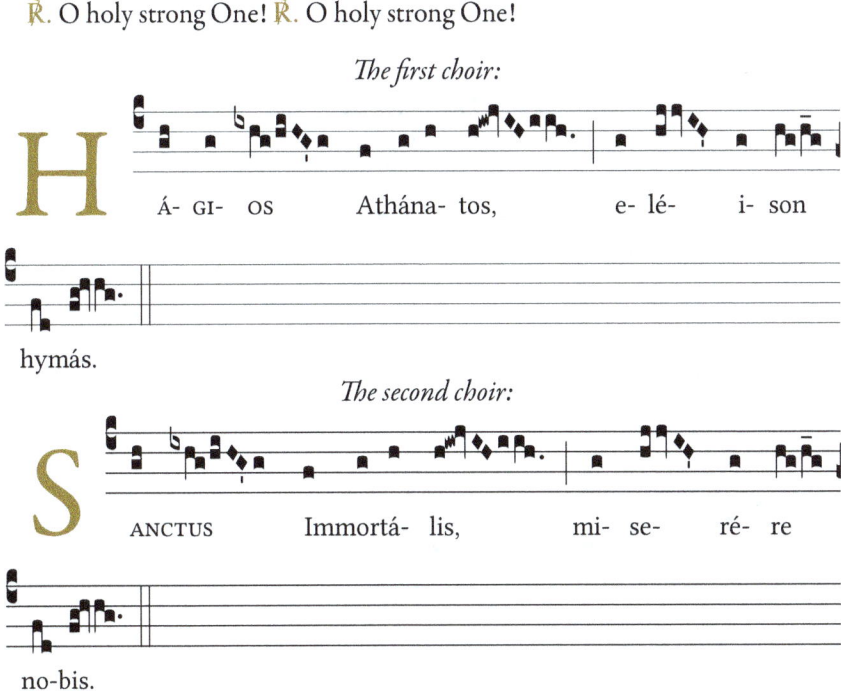

℟. O holy immortal One, have mercy on us. ℟. O holy immortal One, have mercy on us.

Two Cantors:

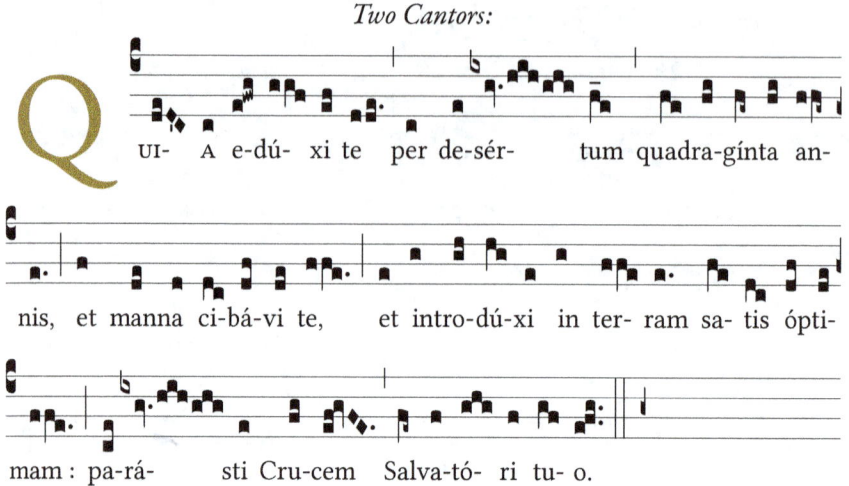

QUI- A e-dú- xi te per de-sér- tum quadra-gínta an-

nis, et manna ci-bá-vi te, et intro-dú-xi in ter- ram sa-tis ópti-

mam : pa-rá- sti Cru-cem Salva-tó- ri tu- o.

℣. Because I led thee out through the desert forty years: and fed thee with manna, and brought thee into a land exceeding good, thou hast prepared a Cross for thy Saviour.

The two choirs alternately repeat **Hágios o Theós,** *etc.*

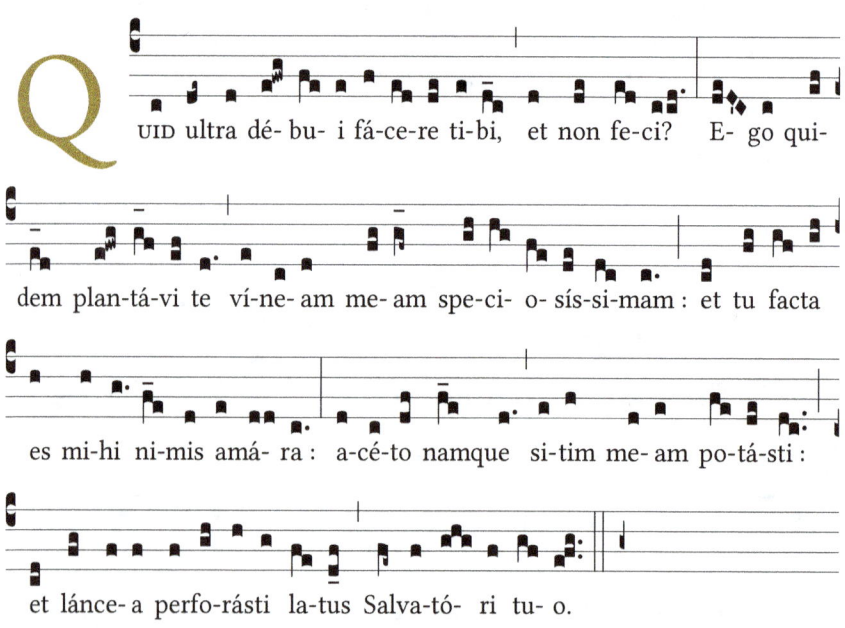

QUID ultra dé-bu- i fá-ce-re ti-bi, et non fe-ci? E- go qui-

dem plan-tá-vi te ví-ne- am me- am spe-ci- o- sís-si-mam : et tu facta

es mi-hi ni-mis amá- ra : a-cé-to namque si-tim me- am po-tá-sti :

et lánce- a perfo-rásti la-tus Salva-tó- ri tu- o.

℣. What more ought I have done for thee, that I have not done? I planted thee, indeed, My most beautiful vineyard: and thou hast become exceeding bitter to Me: for in My thirst thou gavest Me vinegar to drink: and with a lance thou hast pierced the side of thy Saviour.

The two choirs alternately repeat **Hágios o Theós,** *etc. The verses of the following Reproaches are sung alternately, and the choirs respond with* **Pópule meus** *after each verse, as far as the verse* **Quia edúxi te.**

Two Cantors:

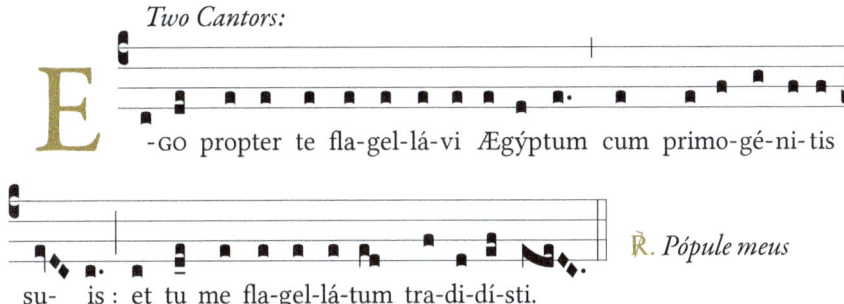

-GO propter te fla-gel-lá-vi Ægýptum cum primo-gé-ni-tis

su- is : et tu me fla-gel-lá-tum tra-di-dí-sti. ℟. *Pópule meus*

℣. For thy sake I scourged Egypt with its first-born: and thou hast scourged Me and delivered Me up.

First choir:

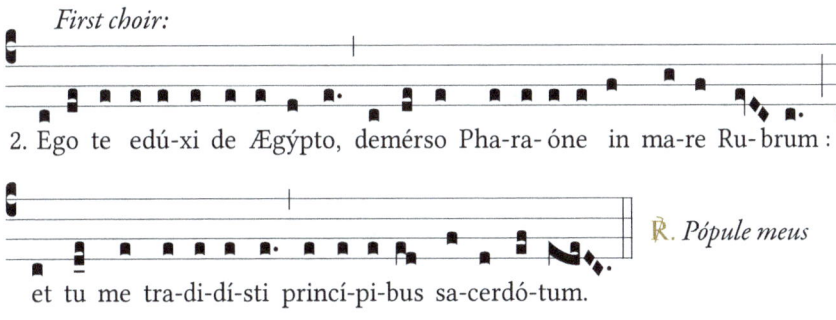

2. Ego te edú-xi de Ægýpto, demérso Pha-ra-óne in ma-re Ru-brum :

et tu me tra-di-dí-sti princí-pi-bus sa-cerdó-tum. ℟. *Pópule meus*

℣. I led thee out of Egypt having drowned Pharaoh in the Red Sea: and thou hast delivered Me to the chief priests.

Second choir:

3. Ego ante te a-pé-ru-i ma- re : et tu a-pe-ru-í-sti lánce-a la-tus

me-um. ℟. *Pópule meus*

℣. I opened the sea before thee: and thou with a spear hast opened My side.

First choir:

4. Ego ante te præ- í-vi   in co-lúmna nu- bis : et tu me du-xí-sti

ad præ-tó-ri- um Pi-lá-ti.

℟. *Pópule meus*

℣. I went before thee in a pillar of cloud: and thou hast led Me to the judgement hall of Pilate.

Second choir:

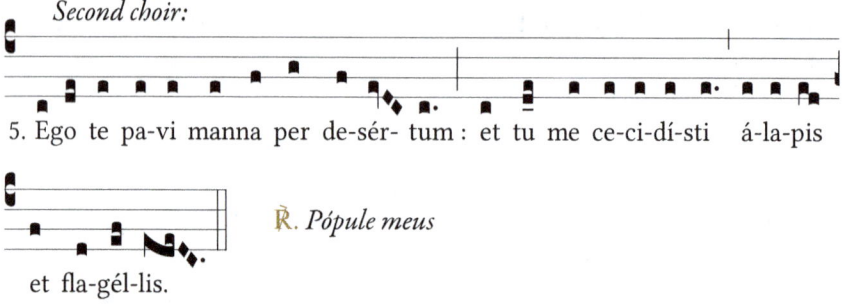

5. Ego te pa-vi manna per de-sér- tum : et tu me ce-ci-dí-sti   á-la-pis

et fla-gél-lis.

℟. *Pópule meus*

℣. I fed thee with manna in the desert; and thou hast beaten Me with whips and scourges.

First choir:

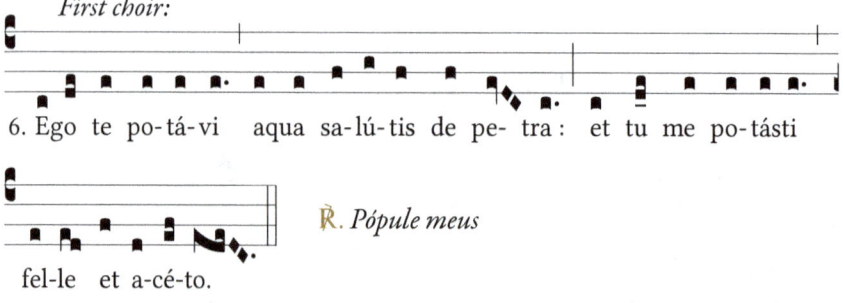

6. Ego te po-tá-vi   aqua sa-lú-tis de pe- tra : et tu me po-tásti

fel-le   et a-cé-to.

℟. *Pópule meus*

℣. I gave thee the water of salvation from the rock to drink: and thou hast given Me gall and vinegar.

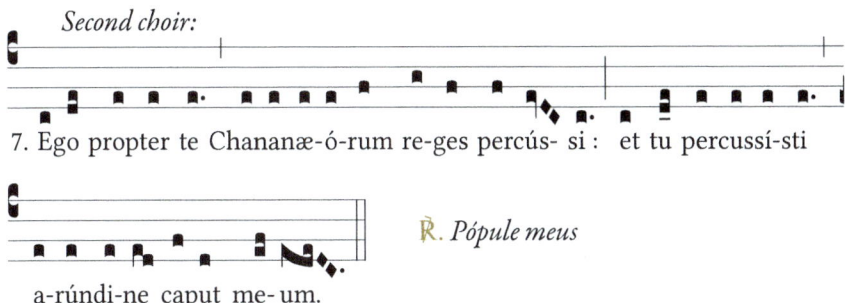

7. Ego propter te Chananæ-ó-rum re-ges percús- si : et tu percussí-sti

℟. Pópule meus

a-rúndi-ne caput me- um.

℣. For thy sake I struck the kings of the Chanaanites: and thou hast struck My head with a reed.

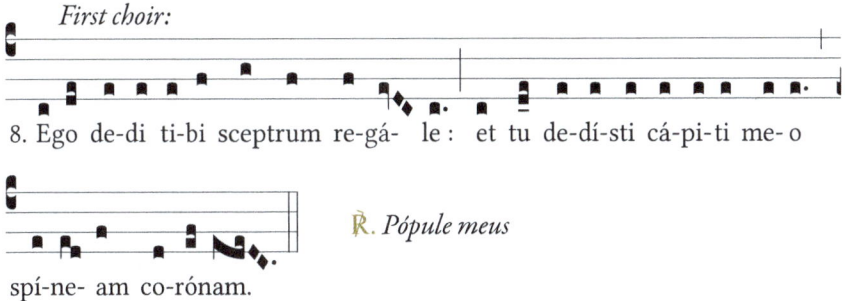

8. Ego de-di ti-bi sceptrum re-gá- le : et tu de-dí-sti cá-pi-ti me- o

℟. Pópule meus

spí-ne- am co-rónam.

℣. I gave thee a royal sceptre: and thou hast given to My head a crown of thorns.

9. Ego te ex-altá-vi magna virtú- te : et tu me suspendí-sti in pa-

℟. Pópule meus

tí-bu-lo Cru-cis.

℣. I exalted thee with great strength: and thou hast hanged Me on the gibbet of the Cross.

The following antiphon is then sung:

CRUCEM tu-am * ado-rámus, Dó-mi-ne : et sanctam re-surre-

cti- ónem tu-am laudámus et glo-ri- fi-cámus : ecce e-nim propter li-

gnum ve- nit gáudi- um in u-ni-vérso mundo. *Ps.* De- us mi-se-re-á-

tur nostri, et be-ne-dí-cat no-bis : * il-lúmi-net vultum su-um super

repeat Antiphon: *Crucem tuam*

nos, et mi-se-re- á- tur nostri.

ANTIPHON: We adore Thy Cross, O Lord: and we praise and glorify Thy holy Resurrection: for behold by the wood of the Cross joy has come into the whole world. **Ps. 66:2** May God have mercy on us, and bless us: May He cause the light of His countenance to shine upon us, and have mercy on us. ℟. We adore Thy Cross, O Lord: and we praise and glorify Thy holy Resurrection: for behold by the wood of the Cross joy has come into the whole world.

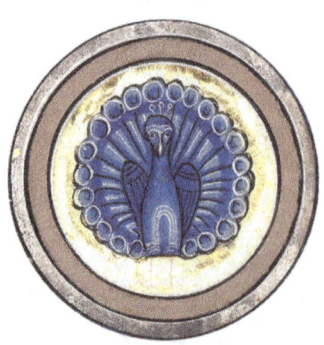

Crux fidélis *is then sung followed by the hymn* Pange lingua, gloriósi. *After the first stanza of the hymn, the* ℣. Crux fidélis *is repeated as far as* Dulce lignum; *after the second stanza,* Dulce lignum *as follows:*

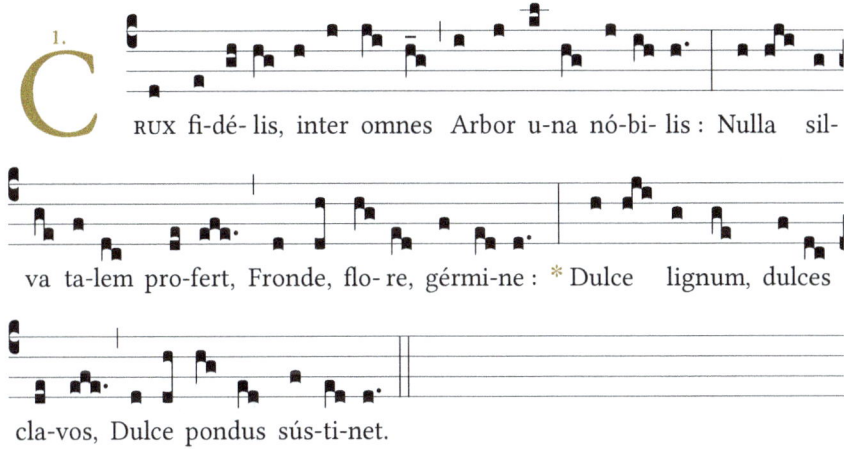

CRUX fi-dé- lis, inter omnes Arbor u-na nó-bi- lis : Nulla sil-va ta-lem pro-fert, Fronde, flo- re, gérmi-ne : * Dulce lignum, dulces cla-vos, Dulce pondus sús-ti-net.

Faithful Cross! above all other, One and only noble Tree! None in foliage, none in blossom, None in fruit thy peer may be; * Sweetest wood and sweetest iron, Sweetest weight is hung on thee.

ANGE, lingua, glo-ri- ó- si Láure- am certá-mi-nis, Et su- per Cru-cis trophǽ-o Dic tri- úmphum nó-bi- lem : Quá-li- ter Red-émptor orbis Immo-lá- tus ví-ce- rit.

Crux fidélis.

SING, my tongue, the glorious battle! | With completed victory rife! | And above the Cross's trophy | Tell the triumph of the strife: | How the world's Redeemer conquer'd | By the offering of His life.

℣. 2. De pa-réntis pro-toplá-sti Fraude Factor cóndo-lens, Quando pomi

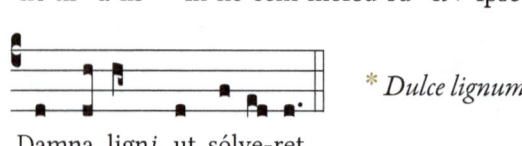

no-xi- á-lis   In ne-cem morsu ru- it : Ipse   lignum tunc no-tá-vit,

* *Dulce lignum.*

Damna ligni, ut sólve-ret.

℣. 2. God, his Maker, sorely grieving, | That the first-made Adam fell, |
When he ate the fruit of sorrow, | Whose reward was death and hell, |
Noted then this Wood the ruin, | Of the ancient wood to quell.

℣. 3. Hoc opus nostræ sa-lú- tis Ordo de-po-pósce-rat : Mul-ti- fórmis

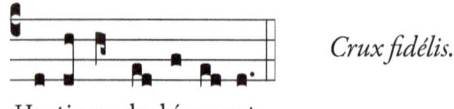

pro-di- tó-ris   Ars ut artem fál-le-ret : Et me- dé-lam ferret inde,

Crux fidélis.

Hostis unde læ-se-rat.

℣. 3. For this work of our salvation | Needs must have its order so, |
And the manifold deceiver's | Art by art would overthrow, |
And from thence would bring the healing, | Whence the insult of the foe.

℣. 4. Quando ve-nit ergo sa-cri Ple-ni-tú-do témpo-ris, Missus est ab

arce Patris Na-tus, orbis Cóndi-tor, Atque ventre vir-gi-ná-li

* *Dulce lignum.*

Carne a-mí-ctus pród-i- it.

℣. 4. Wherefore when th' appointed fullness | Of the holy time was come, |
He was sent who maketh all things | From th' eternal Father's home, |
And proceeded, God Incarnate, | Offspring of the Virgin's womb.

℣. 5. Va-git infans inter arcta Cóndi-tus præ-sé-pi- a : Membra pannis

invo-lú-ta Virgo Ma- ter ál-li-gat : Et De- i ma-nus pe-désque

Crux fidélis.

Stricta cingit fásci- a.

℣. 5. Weeps the Infant in the manger | That in Bethlehem's stable stands: |
And His Limbs the Virgin Mother | Doth compose in swaddling bands, |
Meetly thus in linen folding | Of her God the feet and hands.

℣. 6. Lustra sex qui jam per-é- git, Tempus implens córpo-ris, Sponte lí-be-ra Red-émptor Passi- ó- ni dé-di-tus, Agnus in Cru-cis le-vá-tur Immo-lándus stí-pi- te.

Dulce lignum.

℣. 6. Thirty years among us dwelling, | His appointed time fulfilled, |
Born for this, He meets His Passion, | For that this He freely willed: |
On the Cross the Lamb is lifted, | Where His life-blood shall be spilled.

℣. 7. Fel-le po-tus ecce languet : Spi-na, cla-vi lánce- a, Mi-te corpus per-fo-rá-runt, Unda ma-nat et cru- or : Terra, pontus, astra, mun-dus, Quo la-vántur flúmi-ne!

Crux fidélis.

℣. 7. He endured the nails, the spitting, | Vinegar, and spear, and reed; |
From that holy Body broken | Blood and water forth proceed: |
Earth, and stars, and sky, and ocean, | By that flood from stain are freed.

℣. 8. Flecte ramos, arbor al- ta, Tensa la-xa vísce-ra, Et ri- gor lenté-

scat il-le, Quem de-dit na-tí-vi-tas : Et su- pérni membra Re-gis

* *Dulce lignum.*

Tende mi- ti stí-pi- te.

℣. 8. Bend thy boughs, O Tree of glory! | Thy relaxing sinews bend; |
For awhile the ancient rigor, | That thy birth bestowed, suspend: |
And the King of heavenly beauty | On thy bosom gently tend!

℣. 9. So-la digna tu fu- í- sti Ferre mundi ví-cti-mam : Atque portum

præ-pa-rá-re Arca mundo náufra-go : Quam sa- cer cru- or per-ún-

Crux fidélis.

xit, Fu-sus Agni córpo-re.

℣. 9. Thou alone wast counted worthy | This world's ransom to uphold; |
For a shipwrecked race preparing | Harbor, like the Ark of old; |
With the sacred Blood anointed | From the smitten Lamb that rolled.

The conclusion is never omitted:

℣. 10. Sempi-térna sit be- á- tæ Tri-ni-tá- ti gló- ri- a : Æqua Pa-tri

Fi- li- óque; Par de-cus Pa-rá-cli- to : Uní- us Tri-níque nomen

Laudet u- ni-vér-si- tas. A-men.   * *Dulce lignum.*

℣. 10. To the Trinity be glory | Everlasting, as is meet: |
Equal to the Father, equal | To the Son, and Paraclete: |
Trinal Unity, Whose praises | All created things repeat. Amen.

When the adoration of the Cross is ended, the candles are lighted on the altar; and the Cross having been replaced, a procession to the Altar of Repose takes place; the celebrant and his ministers with the clergy go to the place where the Blessed Sacrament has reposed since the previous day. The Sacred Host is incensed and then It is taken from the tabernacle and is solemnly borne back to the High Altar. During the procession is sung the Vexílla Regis.

**Hymn.
1.**

E-XÍLLA Re- gis pró- de-unt : Fulget Cru-cis mysté-ri- um,

Qua vi-ta mor-tem pér-tu- lit, Et mor- te vi-tam pró-tu-lit. 2. Quæ vul-

ne-rá- ta lán-ce-æ Mucróne di-ro, crími-num Ut nos la-vá-ret sór-di-

bus, Ma-ná- vit unda et sángui-ne. 3. Implé-ta sunt quæ cón-ci-nit

Da-vid fi-dé- li cármi-ne, Di-céndo na- ti- ó- ni-bus : Regná- vit a li-

gno De- us. 4. Arbor de-có- ra et fúl- gi-da, Orná-ta Re-gis púrpu-ra,

E-lécta digno stí- pi- te Tam san- cta membra tánge-re. 5. Be- á- ta,

cu- jus brá-chi- is Prétium pe-péndit sǽcu-li : Sta-té-ra facta córpo-

ris, Tu- lít- que præ-dam tárta-ri. 6. O Crux ave, spes ú- ni-ca,

Hoc Passi- ó-nis témpo-re Pi- is adáuge grá- ti- am, Re- ís- que de-le

crími-na. 7. Te, fons sa-lú- tis Trí- ni- tas, Colláudet omnis spí-ri-tus :

Qui-bus Cru-cis victó- ri- am Largí- ris, adde prǽmi- um. A-men.

1. Vexílla Regis pródeunt;
Fulget crucis mystérium,
Qua vita mortem pértulit,
Et morte vitam prótulit.

1. The royal banners forward go
The Cross shines forth in mystic glow,
Where life Himself our death endured,
And by His death our life procured.

2. Quæ vulneráta lánceæ
Mucróne diro, críminum
Ut nos laváret sórdibus,
Manávit unda et sánguine.

2. Where deep for us the spear was dyed,
Life's torrent rushing from His side,
To wash us in that precious flood,
Where mingled water flowed, and blood.

3. Impléta sunt quæ cóncinit
David fidéli cármine,
Dicéndo natiónibus :
Regnávit a ligno Deus.

3. Fulfill'd is all that David told
In true prophetic song of old
To all the nations: "God," saith he,
"Hath reigned and triumphed from the Tree."

4. Arbor decóra et fúlgida,
Ornáta regis púrpura,
Elécta digno stípite
Tam sancta membra tángere.

4. O Tree of beauty, Tree of light,
O Tree with royal purple dight,
Elect on whose triumphal breast
These holy limbs should find their rest;

5. Beáta, cujus bráchiis
Prétium pepéndit sǽculi,
Statéra facta córporis,
Tulítque prædam tártari.

5. On whose dear arms, so widely flung,
The weight of this world's ransom hung;
The price of humankind to pay,
And spoil the spoiler of his prey.

6. O CRUX, AVE, SPES ÚNICA,
Hoc Passiónis témpore!
Piis adáuge grátiam,
Reísque dele crímina.

6. O CROSS, OUR ONE RELIANCE, HAIL!
This holy Passiontide avail
To give new virtue to the saint,
And pardon to the penitent.

7. Te, fons salútis, Trínitas,
Colláudet omnis spíritus :
Quibus crucis victóriam
Largíris, adde prǽmium.

7. To Thee, eternal Three in One,
Let homage meet by all be done;
As by the Cross Thou dost restore,
So rule and guide us evermore.

Amen.

Amen.

MASS OF THE PRESANCTIFIED

Having arrived at the altar, the celebrant incenses the Blessed Sacrament, places the Host on the corporal, and, having received wine and water, he incenses again the oblation and the altar as at High Mass, saying:

℣. Incénsum istud, a te bene✠díctum, ascéndat ad te, Dómine: et descéndat super nos misericórdia tua.

May this incense, ✠ which Thou hast blessed, O Lord, ascend to Thee, and may Thy mercy descend upon us.

Then he incenses the altar, saying:

PSALM 140: 2-4

Dirigátur, Dómine, orátio mea, sicut incénsum in conspéctu tuo: elevátio mánuum meárum sacrifícium vespertínum. Pone, Dómine, custódiam ori meo, et óstium circumstántiæ lábiis meis: ut non declínet cor meum in verba malítiæ, ad excusándas excusatiónes in peccátis.

Let my prayer, O Lord, be directed as incense in Thy sight: the lifting up of my hands as an evening sacrifice. Set a watch, O Lord, before my mouth, and a door round about my lips. May my heart not incline to evil words, to make excuses for sins.

Giving the censer to the deacon, he says:

Accéndat in nobis Dóminus ignem sui amóris, et flammam ætérnæ caritátis. Amen.

May the Lord enkindle within us the fire of His love, and the flame of everlasting charity. Amen.

The celebrant is not incensed, and having washed his hands in silence, bows down before the altar and says:

In spíritu humilitátis et in ánimo contríto suscipiámur a te, Dómine: et sic fiat sacrifícium nostrum in conspéctu tuo hódie, ut pláceat tibi, Dómine Deus.

Accept us, O Lord, in the spirit of humility and contrition of heart, and grant that this sacrifice which we offer this day in Thy sight may be pleasing to Thee, O Lord God.

He now turns to the people, saying the Oráte Fratres, *as usual:*

Oráte, fratres, ut meum ac vestrum sacrifícium acceptábile fiat apud Deum Patrem omnipoténtem.

Brethren, pray that my Sacrifice and yours may be acceptable to God the Father almighty.

No answer is made, but the celebrant immediately sings:

Orémus: Præcéptis salutáribus móniti, et divína institutióne formáti, audémus dícere:

Let us pray. Instructed by Thy saving precepts, and formed by Thy divine institution, we are bold to say:

Pater noster, qui es in cælis, sanctificétur nomen tuum: advéniat regnum tuum: fiat volúntas tua, sicut in cælo et in terra. Panem nostrum quotidiánum da nobis hódie: et dimítte nobis débita nostra, sicut et nos dimíttimus debitóribus nostris: et ne nos indúcas in tentatiónem:

℟. Sed líbera nos a malo.

Our Father, who art in heaven, hallowed be Thy Name; Thy kingdom come; Thy will be done on earth as it is in heaven. Give us this day our daily bread. And forgive us our trespasses, as we forgive those who trespass against us. And lead us not into temptation.

℟. But deliver us from evil.

The celebrant says Amen in a low voice, and continues aloud:

Líbera nos, quǽsumus, Dómine, ab ómnibus malis, prætéritis, præséntibus et futúris: et intercedénte beáta et gloriósa semper Vírgine Dei Genetríce María, cum beátis Apóstolis tuis Petro et Paulo, atque Andréa, et ómnibus Sanctis, da propítius pacem in diébus nostris: ut, ope misericórdiæ tuæ adjúti, et a peccáto simus semper líberi et ab omni perturbatióne secúri. Per eúndem Dóminum nostrum Jesum Christum, Fílium tuum: Qui tecum vivit et regnat in unitáte Spíritus Sancti Deus, per ómnia sǽcula sæculórum.

℟. Amen.

Deliver us, we beseech Thee, O Lord, from all evils, past, present, and to come; and by the intercession of the blessed and glorious ever Virgin Mary, Mother of God, and of the Holy Apostles, Peter and Paul, and of Andrew, and of all the Saints, mercifully grant peace in our days, that through the assistance of Thy mercy we may be always free from sin, and secure from all disturbance. Through the same Jesus Christ, Thy Son, our Lord, Who with Thee in the unity of the Holy Ghost liveth and reigneth God, world without end.

℟. Amen.

The Host is elevated, then divided into three parts, the last being put into the chalice. The celebrant then continues with the following prayer:

Percéptio Córporis tui, Dómine Jesu Christe, quod ego indígnus súmere præsúmo, non mihi provéniat in judícium et condemnatiónem:

Let not the partaking of Thy Body, O Lord Jesus Christ, which I, though unworthy, presume to receive, turn to my judgment and

sed pro tua pietáte prosit mihi ad tutaméntum mentis et córporis, et ad medélam percipiéndam: Qui vivis et regnas cum Deo Patre in unitáte Spíritus Sancti Deus, per ómnia sǽcula sæculórum. Amen.

condemnation; but let it, through Thy mercy, become a safeguard and remedy, both for soul and body; Who with God the Father, in the unity of the Holy Ghost, livest and reignest God, for ever and ever. Amen.

Then he kneels and takes the paten with the Body of Christ and says:

PANEM cæléstem accípiam, et nomen Dómini invocábo.

I WILL take the Bread of heaven, and will call upon the Name of the Lord.

He strikes his breast and says three times devoutly and humbly:

DÓMINE, non sum dignus, ut intres sub tectum meum: sed tantum dic verbo, et sanábitur ánima mea.

LORD, I am not worthy that Thou shouldst enter under my roof; say but the word, and my soul shall be healed.

Then, with his right hand making the Sign of the Cross with the Host over the paten, he says:

CORPUS Dómini nostri Jesu Christi custódiat ánimam meam in vitam ætérnam. Amen.

MAY the body of our Lord Jesus Christ preserve my soul unto life everlasting. Amen.

He receives the Sacred Host and drinks from the chalice the wine with the consecrated particle, and having received the ablution, with bowed head and hands joined, he says:

QUOD ore súmpsimus, Dómine, pura mente capiámus: et de múnere temporáli fiat nobis remédium sempitérnum.

GRANT, O Lord, that what we have taken with our mouth, we may receive with a pure mind; and from a temporal gift may it become to us an eternal remedy.

Then the celebrant and his ministers, having bowed before the altar, depart in silence.

Vespers

At Vespers the antiphons and Psalms are recited recto tono *rather than sung.*

The Pater noster *and* Ave María *are said silently.*

PATER noster, qui es in cælis, sanctificétur nomen tuum: advéniat regnum tuum: fiat volúntas tua, sicut in cælo et in terra. Panem nostrum quotidiánum da nobis hódie: et dimítte nobis débita nostra, sicut et nos dimíttimus debitóribus nostris: et ne nos indúcas in tentatiónem: sed líbera nos a malo. Amen.

OUR Father, who art in heaven, hallowed be Thy name. Thy kingdom come. Thy will be done on earth as it is in heaven. Give us this day our daily bread. And forgive us our trespasses, as we forgive those who trespass against us. And lead us not into temptation: but deliver us from evil. Amen.

AVE María, grátia plena; Dóminus tecum: benedícta tu in muliéribus, et benedíctus fructus ventris tui Jesus. Sancta María, Mater Dei, ora pro nobis peccatóribus, nunc et in hora mortis nostræ. Amen.

HAIL Mary, full of grace; The Lord is with thee; blessed art thou amongst women, and blessed is the fruit of thy womb, Jesus. Holy Mary, Mother of God, pray for us sinners, now and at the hour of our death. Amen.

Antiphon 1: Cálicem * salutáris accípiam et nomen Dómini invocábo.

Antiphon 1: I will take the cup of salvation; * and call upon the Name of the Lord.

Psalm 115

1. Crédidi, propter quod locútus sum : * ego autem humiliátus sum nimis.

2. Ego dixi in excéssu meo : * Omnis homo mendax.

3. Quid retríbuam Dómino, * pro ómnibus, quæ retríbuit mihi?

4. Cálicem salutáris accípiam : * et nomen Dómini invocábo.

1. I have believed, therefore have I spoken; * but I have been humbled exceedingly.

2. I said in my excess: * Every man is a liar.

3. What shall I render to the Lord, * for all the things that He hath rendered to me?

4. I will take the chalice of salvation; * and I will call upon the name of the Lord.

5. Vota mea Dómino reddam coram omni pópulo ejus : * pretiósa in conspéctu Dómini mors sanctórum ejus :

5. I will pay my vows to the Lord before all His people: * precious in the sight of the Lord is the death of His saints.

6. O Dómine, quia ego servus tuus : * ego servus tuus, et fílius ancíllæ tuæ.

6. O Lord, for I am Thy servant: * I am Thy servant, and the son of Thy handmaid.

7. Dirupísti víncula mea : tibi sacrificábo hóstiam laudis, * et nomen Dómini invocábo.

7. Thou hast broken my bonds: * I will sacrifice to Thee the sacrifice of praise, and I will call upon the name of the Lord.

8. Vota mea Dómino reddam in conspéctu omnis pópuli ejus : * in átriis domus Dómini, in médio tui, Jerúsalem.

8. I will pay my vows to the Lord in the sight of all His people: * in the courts of the house of the Lord, in the midst of thee, O Jerusalem.

Antiphon: Cálicem salutáris accípiam et nomen Dómini invocábo.

Antiphon: I will take the cup of salvation; and call upon the Name of the Lord.

Antiphon 2: Cum his, * qui odérunt pacem eram pacíficus : dum loquébar illis, impugnábant me gratis.

Antiphon 2: With them * that hate peace I was peaceable; when I spoke unto them they fought against me without a cause.

Psalm 119

1. Ad Dóminum cum tribulárer clamávi : * et exaudívit me.

1. In my trouble I cried to the Lord: * and He heard me.

2. Dómine, líbera ánimam meam a lábiis iníquis, * et a lingua dolósa.

2. O Lord, deliver my soul from wicked lips, * and a deceitful tongue.

3. Quid detur tibi, aut quid apponátur tibi * ad linguam dolósam?

3. What shall be given to thee, or what shall be added to thee, * to a deceitful tongue?

4. Sagíttæ poténtis acútæ, * cum carbónibus desolatóriis.

4. The sharp arrows of the mighty, * with coals that lay waste.

5. Heu mihi! quia incolátus meus prolongátus est : habitávi cum habitántibus Cedar : * multum íncola fuit ánima mea.

5. Woe is me, that my sojourning is prolonged! I have dwelt with the inhabitants of Cedar: * my soul hath been long a sojourner.

6. Cum his, qui odérunt pacem, eram pacíficus : * cum loquébar illis, impugnábant me gratis.

Antiphon: Cum his, qui odérunt pacem eram pacíficus : dum loquébar illis, impugnábant me gratis.

Antiphon 3: Ab homínibus * iníquis líbera me, Dómine.

6. With them that hated peace I was peaceable: * when I spoke to them they fought against me without cause.

Antiphon: With them that hate peace I was peaceable; when I spoke unto them they fought against me without a cause.

Antiphon 3: O Lord, preserve me * from the wicked man.

Psalm 139

1. Éripe me, Dómine, ab hómine malo : * a viro iníquo éripe me.

2. Qui cogitavérunt iniquitátes in corde : * tota die constituébant prǽlia.

3. Acuérunt linguas suas sicut serpéntis : * venénum áspidum sub lábiis eórum.

4. Custódi me, Dómine, de manu peccatóris : * et ab homínibus iníquis éripe me.

5. Qui cogitavérunt supplantáre gressus meos : * abscondérunt supérbi láqueum mihi :

6. Et funes extendérunt in láqueum : * juxta iter scándalum posuérunt mihi.

7. Dixi Dómino : Deus meus es tu : * exáudi, Dómine, vocem deprecatiónis meæ.

8. Dómine, Dómine, virtus salútis meæ : * obumbrásti super caput meum in die belli.

9. Ne tradas me, Dómine, a desidério meo peccatóri : † cogitavérunt contra me, * ne derelínquas me, ne forte exalténtur.

1. Deliver me, O Lord, from the evil man: * rescue me from the unjust man.

2. Who have devised iniquities in their hearts: * all the day long they designed battles.

3. They have sharpened their tongues like a serpent: * the venom of asps is under their lips.

4. Keep me, O Lord, from the hand of the wicked: * and from unjust men deliver me.

5. Who have proposed to supplant my steps: * the proud have hidden a net for me.

6. And they have stretched out cords for a snare: * they have laid for me a stumbling block by the wayside.

7. I said to the Lord: Thou art my God: * hear, O Lord, the voice of my supplication.

8. O Lord, Lord, the strength of my salvation: * Thou hast overshadowed my head in the day of battle.

9. Give me not up, O Lord, from my desire to the wicked: * they have plotted against me; do not Thou forsake me, lest they should triumph.

10. Caput circúitus eórum : * labor labiórum ipsórum opériet eos.

11. Cadent super eos carbónes, † in ignem dejícies eos : * in misériis non subsístent.

12. Vir linguósus non dirigétur in terra : * virum injústum mala cápient in intéritu.

13. Cognóvi quia fáciet Dóminus judícium ínopis : * et vindíctam páuperum.

14. Verúmtamen justi confitebúntur nómini tuo : * et habitábunt recti cum vultu tuo.

ANTIPHON: Ab homínibus iníquis líbera me, Dómine.

ANTIPHON 4: Custódi me * a láqueo, quem statuérunt mihi, et a scándalis operántium iniquitátem.

10. The head of them compassing me about: * the labour of their lips shall overwhelm them.

11. Burning coals shall fall upon them; Thou wilt cast them down into the fire: * in miseries they shall not be able to stand.

12. A man full of tongue shall not be established in the earth: * evil shall catch the unjust man unto destruction.

13. I know that the Lord will do justice to the needy, * and will revenge the poor.

14. But as for the just, they shall give glory to Thy name: * and the upright shall dwell with Thy countenance.

ANTIPHON: O Lord, preserve me from the wicked man.

ANTIPHON 4: Keep me * from the snare which they have laid for me, and the sins of the workers of iniquity.

Psalm 140

1. Dómine, clamávi ad te, exáudi me : * inténde voci meæ, cum clamávero ad te.

2. Dirigátur orátio mea sicut incénsum in conspéctu tuo : * elevátio mánuum meárum sacrifícium vespertínum.

3. Pone, Dómine, custódiam ori meo : * et óstium circumstántiæ lábiis meis.

4. Non declínes cor meum in verba malítiæ : * ad excusándas excusatiónes in peccátis.

1. I have cried to Thee, O Lord, hear me: * hearken to my voice, when I cry to Thee.

2. Let my prayer be directed as incense in Thy sight; * the lifting up of my hands, as evening sacrifice.

3. Set a watch, O Lord, before my mouth: * and a door round about my lips.

4. Incline not my heart to evil words; * to make excuses in sins.

5. Cum homínibus operántibus iniquitátem : * et non communicábo cum eléctis eórum.

6. Corrípiet me justus in misericórdia, et increpábit me : * óleum autem peccatóris non impínguet caput meum.

7. Quóniam adhuc et orátio mea in beneplácitis eórum : * absórpti sunt juncti petræ júdices eórum.

8. Audient verba mea quóniam potuérunt : * sicut crassitúdo terræ erúpta est super terram.

9. Dissipáta sunt ossa nostra secus inférnum : † quia ad te, Dómine, Dómine, óculi mei : * in te sperávi, non áuferas ánimam meam.

10. Custódi me a láqueo, quem statuérunt mihi : * et a scándalis operántium iniquitátem.

11. Cadent in retiáculo ejus peccatóres : * singuláriter sum ego donec tránseam.

ANTIPHON: Custódi me a láqueo, quem statuérunt mihi, et a scándalis operántium iniquitátem.

5. With men that work iniquity: * and I will not communicate with the choicest of them.

6. The just man shall correct me in mercy, and shall reprove me: * but let not the oil of the sinner fatten my head.

7. For my prayer also shall still be against the things with which they are well pleased: * their judges falling upon the rock have been swallowed up.

8. They shall hear my words, for they have prevailed: * as when the thickness of the earth is broken up upon the ground.

9. Our bones are scattered by the side of hell. * But to Thee, O Lord, Lord, are my eyes: in Thee have I put my trust, take not away my soul.

10. Keep me from the snare, which they have laid for me, * and from the stumbling blocks of them that work iniquity.

11. The wicked shall fall in his net: * I am alone until I pass.

ANTIPHON: Keep me from the snare which they have laid for me, and the sins of the workers of iniquity.

Antiphon 5: Considerábam * ad déxteram, et vidébam, et non erat qui cognósceret me.

Antiphon 5: I looked * on my right hand and beheld: but there was no man that would know me.

Psalm 141

1. Voce mea ad Dóminum clamávi : * voce mea ad Dóminum deprecátus sum :

2. Effúndo in conspéctu ejus oratiónem meam, * et tribulatiónem meam ante ipsum pronúntio.

3. In deficiéndo ex me spíritum meum : * et tu cognovísti sémitas meas.

4. In via hac, qua ambulábam, * abscondérunt láqueum mihi.

5. Considerábam ad déxteram, et vidébam : * et non erat qui cognósceret me.

6. Périit fuga a me : * et non est qui requírat ánimam meam.

7. Clamávi ad te, Dómine, † dixi : Tu es spes mea, * pórtio mea in terra vivéntium.

8. Inténde ad deprecatiónem meam : * quia humiliátus sum nimis.

9. Líbera me a persequéntibus me : * quia confortáti sunt super me.

10. Educ de custódia ánimam meam ad confiténdum nómini tuo : * me exspéctant justi, donec retríbuas mihi.

1. I cried to the Lord with my voice: * with my voice I made supplication to the Lord.

2. In His sight I pour out my prayer, * and before Him I declare my trouble:

3. When my spirit failed me, * then Thou knewest my paths.

4. In this way wherein I walked, * they have hidden a snare for me.

5. I looked on my right hand, and beheld, * and there was no one that would know me.

6. Flight hath failed me: * and there is no one that hath regard to my soul.

7. I cried to Thee, O Lord: * I said: Thou art my hope, my portion in the land of the living.

8. Attend to my supplication: * for I am brought very low.

9. Deliver me from my persecutors; * for they are stronger than I.

10. Bring my soul out of prison, that I may praise Thy name: * the just wait for me, until Thou reward me.

Antiphon: Considerábam ad déxteram, et vidébam, et non erat qui cognósceret me.

Antiphon: I looked on my right hand and beheld: but there was no man that would know me.

Magníficat

Antiphon: Cum accepísset acétum, * dixit : Consummátum est : et inclináto cápite, emísit spíritum.

Antiphon: When He had received the vinegar, * He said: It is finished! and He bowed his Head, and gave up the Ghost.

1. Magníficat ✠ ánima mea Dóminum.

1. My soul ✠ doth magnify the Lord.

2. Et exsultávit spíritus meus : * in Deo, salutári meo.

2. And my spirit hath rejoiced * in God my Saviour.

3. Quia respéxit humilitátem ancíllæ suæ : * ecce enim ex hoc beátam me dicent omnes generatiónes.

3. Because He hath regarded the humility of His handmaid; * for behold from henceforth all generations shall call me blessed.

4. Quia fecit mihi magna qui potens est : * et sanctum nomen ejus.

4. Because He that is mighty, hath done great things to me; * and holy is His name.

5. Et misericórdia ejus a progénie in progénies * timéntibus eum.

5. And His mercy is from generation unto generations, * to them that fear him.

6. Fecit poténtiam in bráchio suo : * dispérsit supérbos mente cordis sui.

6. He hath showed might in His arm: * He hath scattered the proud in the conceit of their heart.

7. Depósuit poténtes de sede, * et exaltávit húmiles.

7. He hath put down the mighty from their seat, * and hath exalted the humble.

8. Esuriéntes implévit bonis : * et dívites dimísit inánes.

8. He hath filled the hungry with good things; * and the rich He hath sent empty away.

9. Suscépit Israël púerum suum, * recordátus misericórdiæ suæ.

9. He hath received Israel His servant, * being mindful of His mercy:

10. Sicut locútus est ad patres nostros, * Abraham et sémini ejus in sǽcula.

10. As He spoke to our fathers, * to Abraham and to His seed for ever.

Antiphon: Cum accepísset acétum, dixit : Consummátum est : et inclináto cápite, emísit spíritum.

Antiphon: When He had received the vinegar, He said: It is finished! and He bowed his Head, and gave up the Ghost.

At the conclusion of the antiphon following the Magnificat, *all kneel and say:*

Antiphon: Christus factus est pro nobis obédiens usque ad mortem, mortem autem crucis.

Antiphon: Christ became obedient for us unto death, even to the death of the cross.

At the conclusion of the antiphon Christus factus est, the Pater noster is said in silence.

Psalm 50

1. Miserére mei, Deus, * secúndum magnam misericórdiam tuam.

2. Et secúndum multitúdinem miseratiónum tuárum, * dele iniquitátem meam.

3. Amplius lava me ab iniquitáte mea : * et a peccáto meo munda me.

4. Quóniam iniquitátem meam ego cognósco : * et peccátum meum contra me est semper.

5. Tibi soli peccávi, et malum coram te feci : * ut justificéris in sermónibus tuis, et vincas cum judicáris.

6. Ecce enim in iniquitátibus concéptus sum : * et in peccátis concépit me mater mea.

7. Ecce enim veritátem dilexísti : * incérta et occúlta sapiéntiæ tuæ manifestásti mihi.

8. Aspérges me hyssópo, et mundábor : * lavábis me, et super nivem dealbábor.

9. Audítui meo dabis gáudium et lætítiam : * et exsultábunt ossa humiliáta.

1. Have mercy on me, O God, * according to Thy great mercy.

2. And according to the multitude of Thy tender mercies * blot out my iniquity.

3. Wash me yet more from my iniquity, * and cleanse me from my sin.

4. For I know my iniquity, * and my sin is always before me.

5. To Thee only have I sinned, and have done evil before Thee: * that Thou mayst be justified in Thy words, and mayst overcome when Thou art judged.

6. For behold I was conceived in iniquities; * and in sins did my mother conceive me.

7. For behold Thou hast loved truth: * the uncertain and hidden things of Thy wisdom Thou hast made manifest to me.

8. Thou shalt sprinkle me with hyssop, and I shall be cleansed: * Thou shalt wash me, and I shall be made whiter than snow.

9. To my hearing Thou shalt give joy and gladness: * and the bones that have been humbled shall rejoice.

10. Avérte fáciem tuam a peccátis meis : * et omnes iniquitátes meas dele.

11. Cor mundum crea in me, Deus : * et spíritum rectum ínnova in viscéribus meis.

12. Ne projícias me a fácie tua : * et spíritum sanctum tuum ne áuferas a me.

13. Redde mihi lætítiam salutáris tui : * et spíritu principáli confírma me.

14. Docébo iníquos vias tuas : * et ímpii ad te converténtur.

15. Líbera me de sanguínibus, Deus, Deus salútis meæ : * et exsultábit lingua mea justítiam tuam.

16. Dómine, lábia mea apéries : * et os meum annuntiábit laudem tuam.

17. Quóniam si voluísses sacrifícium, dedíssem útique : * holocáustis non delectáberis.

18. Sacrifícium Deo spíritus contribulátus : * cor contrítum et humiliátum, Deus, non despícies.

19. Benígne fac, Dómine, in bona voluntáte tua Sion : * ut ædificéntur muri Jerúsalem.

20. Tunc acceptábis sacrifícium justítiæ, oblatiónes, et holocáusta : * tunc impónent super altáre tuum vítulos.

10. Turn away Thy face from my sins, * and blot out all my iniquities.

11. Create a clean heart in me, O God: * and renew a right spirit within my bowels.

12. Cast me not away from Thy face; * and take not Thy Holy Ghost from me.

13. Restore unto me the joy of Thy salvation, * and strengthen me with a perfect spirit.

14. I will teach the unjust Thy ways: * and the wicked shall be converted to Thee.

15. Deliver me from blood, O God, Thou God of my salvation: * and my tongue shall extol Thy justice.

16. O Lord, Thou wilt open my lips: * and my mouth shall declare Thy praise.

17. For if Thou hadst desired sacrifice, I would indeed have given it: * with burnt offerings Thou wilt not be delighted.

18. A sacrifice to God is an afflicted spirit: * a contrite and humbled heart, O God, Thou wilt not despise.

19. Deal favourably, O Lord, in Thy good will with Sion; * that the walls of Jerusalem may be built up.

20. Then shalt Thou accept the sacrifice of justice, oblations and whole burnt offerings: * then shall they lay calves upon Thy altar.

Réspice, quæsumus, Dómine, super hanc famíliam tuam, pro qua Dóminus noster Jesus Christus non dubitávit mánibus tradi nocéntium, et crucis subíre torméntum:

[*Dícitur sub siléntio:* Qui tecum vivit et regnat in unitáte Spíritus Sancti, Deus, per ómnia sǽcula sæculórum. ℟. Amen.]

Look down, we beseech Thee, O Lord, on this Thy family, for which our Lord Jesus Christ did not hesitate to be delivered up into the hands of wicked men, and to suffer the torment of the Cross.

[*Said in silence:* Who with thee liveth and reigneth, in the unity of the Holy Ghost, God, world without end. ℟. Amen.]

Holy Saturday

All kneel.

Aperi Dómine, os meum ad benedicéndum nomen sanctum tuum: munda quoque cor meum ab ómnibus vanis, pervérsis et aliénis cogitatiónibus; intelléctum illúmina, afféctum inflámma, ut digne, atténte ac devóte hoc Offícium recitáre váleam, et exaudíri mérear ante conspéctum divínæ Majestátis túæ. Per Christum Dóminum nostrum.

℟. Amen.

Dómine, in unióne illíus divínæ intentiónis, qua ipse in terris laudes Deo persolvísti, has tibi Horas persólvo.

O Lord, open thou my mouth that I may bless Thy Holy Name. Cleanse my heart from all vain, evil, and wandering thoughts; enlighten my understanding, kindle my affections, that I may pray to, and praise Thee with attention and devotion; and may worthily be heard before the presence of Thy Divine Majesty. Through Christ our Lord.

℟. Amen.

Lord, in union with that Divine Intention wherewith Thou didst Thyself praise God, whilst Thou wast on earth, I offer these Hours unto Thee.

At Matins

The Pater noster, Ave María *and* Credo *are said silently.*

Pater noster, qui es in cælis, sanctificétur nomen tuum: advéniat regnum tuum: fiat volúntas tua, sicut in cælo et in terra. Panem nostrum quotidiánum da nobis hódie: et dimítte nobis débita nostra, sicut et nos dimíttimus debitóribus nostris: et ne nos indúcas in tentatiónem: sed líbera nos a malo. Amen.

Our Father, who art in heaven, hallowed be Thy name. Thy kingdom come. Thy will be done on earth as it is in heaven. Give us this day our daily bread. And forgive us our trespasses, as we forgive those who trespass against us. And lead us not into temptation: but deliver us from evil. Amen.

AVE María, grátia plena; Dómi-nus tecum: benedícta tu in muliéribus, et benedíctus fructus ventris tui Jesus. Sancta María, Mater Dei, ora pro nobis peccatóribus, nunc et in hora mortis nostræ. Amen.

CREDO in Deum, Patrem omnipoténtem, Creatórem cæli et terræ.

Et in Jesum Christum, Fílium ejus únicum, Dóminum nostrum: qui concéptus est de Spíritu Sancto, natus ex María Vírgine, passus sub Póntio Piláto, crucifíxus, mórtuus, et sepúltus: descéndit ad ínferos; tértia die resurréxit a mórtuis; ascéndit ad cælos; sedet ad déxteram Dei Patris omnipoténtis: inde ventúrus est judicáre vivos et mórtuos.

Credo in Spíritum Sanctum, sanctam Ecclésiam cathólicam, Sanctórum communiónem, remissiónem peccatórum, carnis resurrectiónem, vitam ætérnam. Amen.

HAIL Mary, full of grace; The Lord is with thee; blessed art thou amongst women, and blessed is the fruit of thy womb, Jesus. Holy Mary, Mother of God, pray for us sinners, now and at the hour of our death. Amen.

I BELIEVE in God, the Father almighty, Creator of heaven and earth.

And in Jesus Christ, His only Son, our Lord; who was conceived by the Holy Ghost, born of the Virgin Mary, suffered under Pontius Pilate, was crucified, died and was buried: He descended into hell; the third day He arose again from the dead; He ascended into heaven; sitteth at the right hand of God the Father almighty: from thence He shall come to judge the living and the dead.

I believe in the Holy Ghost, the holy Catholic Church, the communion of Saints, the forgiveness of sins. The resurrection of the body. And life everlasting. Amen.

1ST NOCTURN

IN pa-ce * in id- í-psum, dórmi- am et requi- éscam.

ANTIPHON: I will both lay me down in peace, * and sleep.

PSALM 4

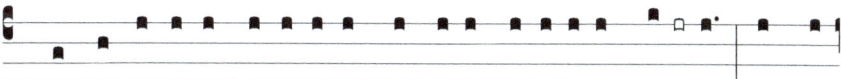

1. Cum invo-cá-rem exaudí-vit me De- us justí-ti- æ **me-**   æ: * in tri-

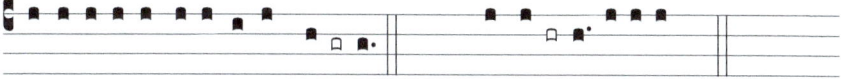

bu-la-ti- óne di-la-*tásti* **mi-** hi.   *Flex :* peccá- re: †

1. When I called upon Him, the God of my justice heard me: * when I was in distress, Thou hast enlarged me.

2. Miserére **mei**, * et exáudi oratiónem **me**am.

2. Have mercy on me: * and hear my prayer.

3. Fílii hóminum, úsquequo gravi **cor**de? * ut quid dilígitis vanitátem et quǽri*tis men***dá**cium?

3. O ye sons of men, how long will you be dull of heart? * Why do you love vanity, and seek after lying?

4. Et scitóte quóniam mirificávit Dóminus sanctum **su**um: * Dóminus exáudiet me cum clamáve*ro ad* **e**um.

4. Know ye also that the Lord hath made His holy one wonderful: * the Lord will hear me when I shall cry unto Him.

5. Irascímini, et nolíte peccáre: † quæ dícitis in córdibus **ve**stris, * in cubílibus vestris *compun***gí**mini.

5. Be ye angry, and sin not: † the things you say in your hearts, * be sorry for them upon your beds.

6. Sacrificáte sacrifícium justítiæ, † et speráte in **Dó**mino. * Multi dicunt: quis osténdit *nobis* **bo**na?

6. Offer up the sacrifice of justice, † and trust in the Lord: * many say, Who sheweth us good things?

7. Signátum est super nos lumen vultus tui, **Dó**mine: * dedísti lætítiam in *corde* **me**o.

7. The light of Thy countenance, O Lord, is signed upon us: * Thou hast given gladness in my heart.

8. A fructu fruménti, vini et ólei **sui** * mul*tiplic*áti sunt.

8. By the fruit of their corn, their wine, and oil, * they are multiplied.

9. In pace in id*í*psum * dórmiam et *requié*scam;

9. In peace in the selfsame * I will sleep, and I will rest:

10. Quóniam tu, Dómine, singuláriter **in** spe * con*stitu*ísti me.

10. For Thou, O Lord, singularly * hast settled me in hope.

1. Ant.
8.G

IN pa-ce   in id- í-psum, dórmi- am et requi- éscam.

The first candle is extinguished.

2. Ant.
4.E

HA- BI-TÁ-BIT * in ta-berná-cu-lo tu- o, requi- é-scet in mon- te sancto tu- o.

Antiphon: He shall abide in Thy tabernacle: * he shall dwell in Thy holy hill.

PSALM 14

1. Dómi-ne, quis ha-bi-tá-bit in ta-berná-*cu-lo* **tu-** o? * aut quis requi- éscet in mon*te sancto* **tu-** o? ℣. 7. *Qui* **fa-**cit hæc: *

1. Lord, who shall dwell in Thy tabernacle? * or who shall rest in Thy holy hill?

2. Qui ingréditur *sine* **mác**ula, * et oper*átur ju*st*íti*am:

2. He that walketh without blemish, * and worketh justice:

3. Qui lóquitur veritátem in *corde* **su**o, * qui non egit dolum *in lingua* **su**a:

3. He that speaketh truth in his heart, * who hath not used deceit in his tongue:

4. Nec fecit próximo *suo* **ma**lum, *
et oppróbrium non accépit advérsus
próximos **su**os.

4. Nor hath done evil to his neighbour: * nor taken up a reproach
against his neighbours.

5. Ad níhilum dedúctus est in
conspéctu e*jus ma*lígnus: * timéntes
autem Dó*minum glo*rí**fi**cat:

5. In his sight the malignant is
brought to nothing: * but he glorifi-
eth them that fear the Lord:

6. Qui jurat próximo suo, *et non*
décipit, * qui pecúniam suam non
dedit ad usúram, et múnera super
innocén*tem non ac*cépit.

6. He that sweareth to his neighbour, and deceiveth not; * He that
hath not put out his money to usury,
nor taken bribes against the innocent:

7. *Qui* **fa**cit hæc: * non movébi*tur*
*in æ*tér*num.

7. He that doth these things, * shall
not be moved for ever.

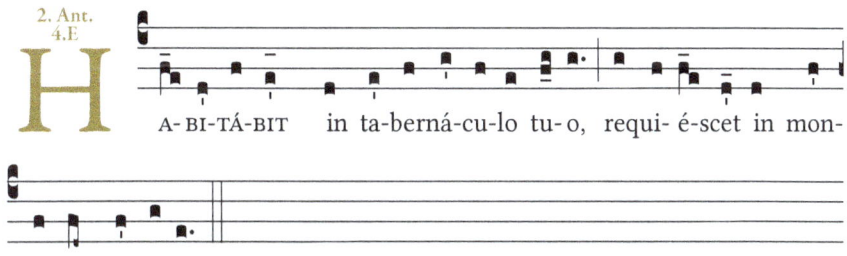

2. Ant.
4.E

HA- BI-TÁ-BIT   in ta-berná-cu-lo tu- o,   requi- é-scet in mon-

te sancto tu- o.

The second candle is extinguished.

3. Ant.
7.c

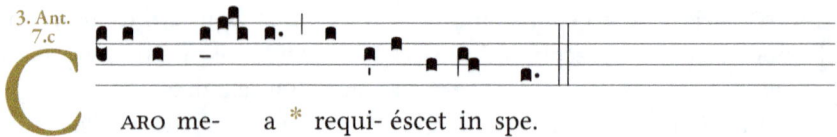

C aro me- a * requi- éscet in spe.

Antiphon: My flesh * shall rest in hope.

Psalm 15

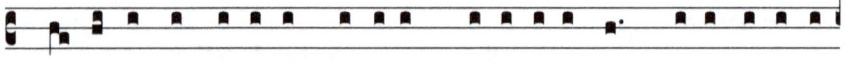

1. Consérva me, Dómi-ne, quón-i- am spe-rá-vi in te: † Di-xi Dómi-no:

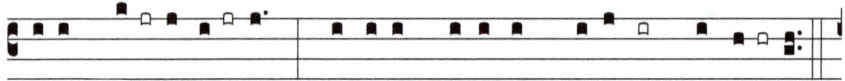

De-us **me-** us **es** tu, * quón-i- am bonó-rum me- **ó**-rum non e- ges.

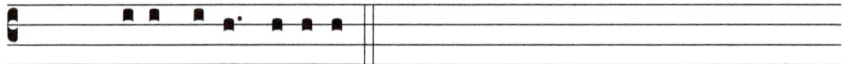

Flex : vi- as vi-tæ, †

1. Preserve me, O Lord, for I have put my trust in thee. * I have said to the Lord, thou art my God, for thou hast no need of my goods.

2. Sanctis, qui sunt in **ter**ra ejus, * mirificávit omnes voluntátes **me**as in eis.

2. To the saints, who are in his land, * he hath made wonderful all my desires in them.

3. Multiplicátæ sunt infirmitátes eórum: * póstea accelera**vé**runt.

3. Their infirmities were multiplied: * afterwards they made haste.

4. Non congregábo conventícula eórum **de** san**guí**nibus, * nec memor ero nóminum eórum per **lá**bia **me**a.

4. I will not gather together their meetings for blood offerings: * nor will I be mindful of their names by my lips.

5. Dóminus pars hereditátis meæ, et **cá**licis mei: * tu es, qui restítues hereditátem **me**am **mi**hi.

5. The Lord is the portion of my inheritance and of my cup: * it is thou that wilt restore my inheritance to me.

6. Funes cecidérunt mihi **in** præ**clá**ris: * étenim heréditas mea præ**clá**ra est **mi**hi.

6. The lines are fallen unto me in goodly places: * for my inheritance is goodly to me.

7. Benedícam Dóminum, qui tríbuit mihi **intelléctum:** * ínsuper et usque ad noctem increpuérunt me **renes mei.**

8. Providébam Dóminum in con-spéctu **meo semper:** * quóniam a dex-tris est mihi, **ne commóvear.**

9. Propter hoc lætátum est cor meum, et exsultávit **lingua mea:** * ínsuper et caro mea requiéscet **in spe.**

10. Quóniam non derelínques án-imam meam **in inférno:** * nec dabis sanctum tuum vidére cor**rupti**ónem.

11. Notas mihi fecísti vias vitæ, † adimplébis me lætítia cum **vultu tuo:** * delectatiónes in déxtera tua **us**que in **fi**nem.

7. I will bless the Lord, who hath given me understanding: * moreover my reins also have corrected me even till night.

8. I set the Lord always in my sight: * for he is at my right hand, that I be not moved.

9. Therefore my heart hath been glad, and my tongue hath rejoiced: * more-over my flesh also shall rest in hope.

10. Because thou wilt not leave my soul in hell; * nor wilt thou give thy holy one to see corruption.

11. Thou hast made known to me the ways of life, † thou shalt fill me with joy with thy countenance: * at thy right hand are delights even to the end.

3. Ant.
7.c

CARO me- a requi- éscet in spe.

The third candle is extinguished.

℣. In pa-ce in i-dípsum. ℟. Dórmi- am et requi- éscam.

Or:

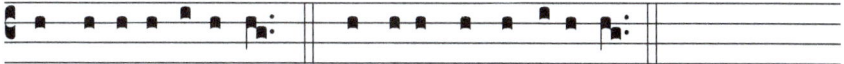

℣. In pa-ce in i-dípsum. ℟. Dórmi- am et requi- éscam.

℣. I will both lay me down in peace. ℟. And sleep.

The Pater noster *is said silently.*

Lesson 1   Lamentations 3: 22-30

De Lamenta-ti-óne Je-remí-æ Prophé-tæ. Heth. Mi-se-ri-córdi-æ Dómi-ni qui- a non sumus consúmpti : qui- a non de-fe-cé-runt mi-se-ra-ti-ónes e-jus. Heth. No-vi di-lú-cu-lo, multa est fi-des tu- a. Heth. Pars me-a Dómi-nus, di-xit á-nima me-a : proptér-e-a exspectábo e-um. Teth. Bonus est Dómi-nus spe-rán-ti-bus in e-um, á-nimæ quæ-rénti il-lum. Teth. Bonum est præ-sto-lá-ri cum si-lénti-o sa-lu-tá-re De-i. Teth. Bonum est vi-ro, cum por-tá-ve-rit jugum ab ado-lescénti-a su-a. Jod. Se-dé-bit so-li-tá-ri-us, et ta-cé-bit : qui-a le-vá-vit su-per se. Jod. Ponet in

púlve-re os su-um, si forte sit spes. JOD.   Da-bit percu-ti- énti

se ma-xíl-lam, sa-tu-rá-bi-tur oppróbri- is. Je-rú-sa-lem, Je-rú-sa-lem,

convérte-re ad Dómi-num De- um tu- um.

LESSON 1: **HETH.** The mercies of the Lord that we are not consumed: because his commiserations have not failed. **HETH.** They are new every morning,
great is thy faithfulness. **HETH.** The Lord is my portion, said my soul: therefore
will I wait for him. **TETH.** The Lord is good to them that hope in him, to the
soul that seeketh him. **TETH.** It is good to wait with silence for the salvation of
God. **TETH.** It is good for a man, when he hath borne the yoke from his youth.
JOD. He shall sit solitary, and hold his peace: because he hath taken it up upon
himself. **JOD.** He shall put his mouth in the dust, if so be there may be hope.
JOD. He shall give his cheek to him that striketh him, he shall be filled with
reproaches. *Jerusalem! Jerusalem! Return unto the Lord thy God.*

RESPONSORY 1   SICUT OVIS AD OCCISIÓNEM

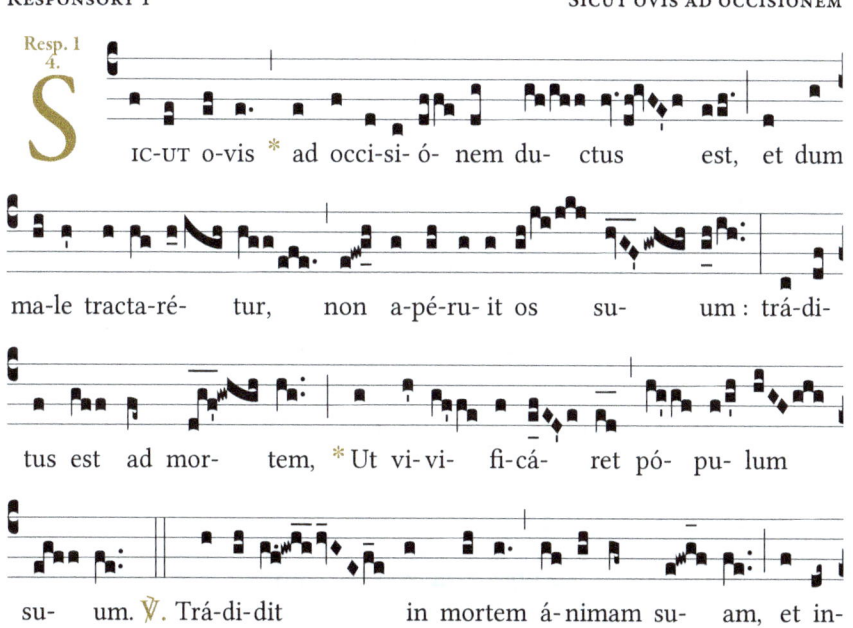

Resp. 1
4.

SIC-UT o-vis * ad occi-si- ó- nem du- ctus   est, et dum

ma-le tracta-ré- tur,   non a-pé-ru- it os   su- um : trá-di-

tus est ad mor- tem, *Ut vi-vi- fi-cá- ret pó- pu- lum

su- um. ℣. Trá-di-dit   in mortem á-nimam su- am, et in-

ter sce-le-rá-tos re- pu-tá- tus est. * Ut vi-vi- fi-cá- ret.

℟. He hath been brought as a lamb to the slaughter, and while He was evilly treated He opened not His mouth: He was delivered up to death * That He might quicken His people. ℣. He hath poured out His soul unto death, and He was numbered with the transgressors. ℟. That He might quicken His people.

LESSON 2   LAMENTATIONS 4: 1-6

A -LEPH. Quómodo obscu-rá-tum est aurum, mu-tá-tus est

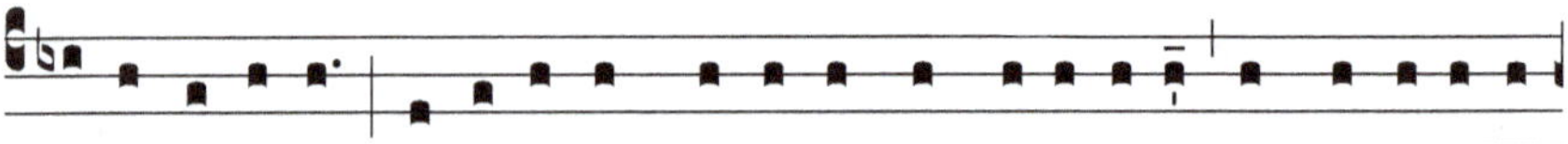

co-lor óptimus, dispérsi sunt lá-pi-des sanctu-á-ri- i in cá-pi-te ó-

mni- um pla-te-á- rum? BETH. Fí-li- i Si- on íncly-ti, et amícti auro

primo : quómodo repu-tá-ti sunt in va-sa téste- a, opus mánu- um fí-gu-

li? GHIMEL. Sed et lámi- æ nuda-vé-runt mammam, lacta-vé-runt

cá-tu-los su- os : fí- li- a pópu-li me- i crudé-lis, qua-si strúthi- o in

de-sér-to. DA-LETH. Adhǽ-sit lingua lacténtis ad pa-lá-tum e-jus in

si-ti : párvu-li pe-ti- é-runt panem, et non e-rat qui fránge-ret e- is.

HE. Qui vesce-bántur vo-luptu- ó-se, inter-i- é-runt in vi- is :

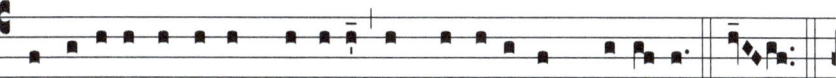

qui nutri- e-bántur in cró-ce- is, ample-xá-ti sunt stérco-ra. VAU.

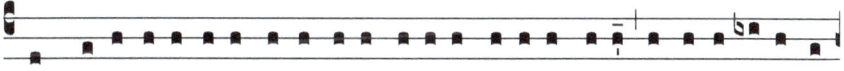

Et ma-jor effécta est in-íqui-tas fí-li- æ pópu-li me- i peccá-to Sodomó-

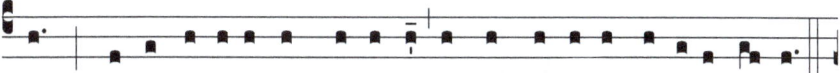

rum, quæ subvérsa est in moménto, et non ce-pé-runt in e- a ma-nus.

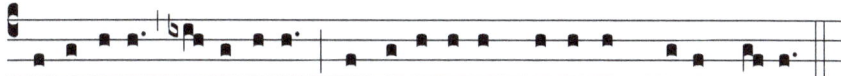

Je-rú-sa-lem, Je-rú-sa-lem, convérte-re ad Dómi-num De- um tu- um.

LESSON 2: ALEPH. How is the gold become dim, the finest colour is changed, the stones of the sanctuary are scattered in the top of every street? **BETH.** The noble sons of Sion, and they that were clothed with the best gold: how are they esteemed as earthen vessels, the work of the potter's hands? **GHIMEL.** Even the sea monsters have drawn out the breast, they have given suck to their young: the daughter of my people is cruel, like the ostrich in the desert. **DALETH.** The tongue of the sucking child hath stuck to the roof of his mouth for thirst: the little ones have asked for bread, and there was none to break it unto them. **HE.** They that were fed delicately have died in the streets; they that were brought up in scarlet have embraced the dung. **VAU.** And the iniquity of the daughter of my people is made greater than the sin of Sodom, which was overthrown in a moment, and hands took nothing in her. *Jerusalem! Jerusalem! Return unto the Lord thy God.*

RESPONSORY 2 — JERÚSALEM, SURGE

Resp. 2
5.

JERÚ-SA-LEM, * sur- ge, et éx-u-e te vé-sti- bus ju-cun-

di- tá- tis : indú-e-re cí-ne-re et ci-lí- ci- o,

* Qui-a in te oc-cí- sus est Salvá- tor Isra- ël.

℣. Deduc qua-si torréntem lácrimas per di-em et no- ctem, et non

tá-ce-at pu-píl-la ó- cu-li tu- i. * Qui- a.

℟. Arise, O Jerusalem, and put off thy garments of rejoicing: cover thee with sackcloth and ashes. * For the Saviour of Israel hath been slain in the midst of thee. ℣. Let thy tears run down like a river day and night, and let not the apple of thine eye cease. ℟. For the Saviour of Israel hath been slain in the midst of thee.

LESSON 3 — LAMENTATIONS 5: 1-11

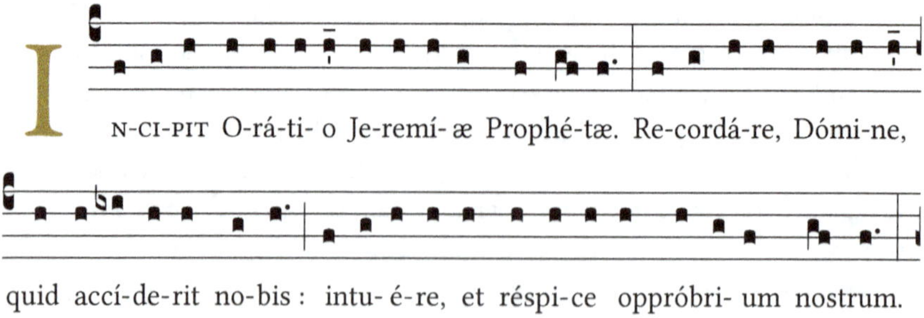

INCIPIT O-rá-ti-o Je-remí-æ Prophé-tæ. Re-cordá-re, Dómi-ne,

quid accí-de-rit no-bis : intu-é-re, et réspi-ce oppróbri-um nostrum.

He-ré-di-tas nostra versa est ad a-li- énos : domus nostræ ad extrá-ne-

os. Pu-píl-li facti sumus absque patre, matres nostræ qua-si ví-du- æ.

Aquam nostram pe-cú-ni- a bí-bimus : ligna nostra pré-ti- o compa-rá-

vimus. Cerví-ci-bus nostris mi-na-bámur, lassis non da-bá-tur réqui-

es. Ægýpto dé-dimus manum, et Assý-ri- is, ut sa-tu-ra-rémur pa-ne.

Patres nostri pecca-vé-runt, et non sunt : et nos in-iqui-tá-tes e- ó-rum

portá-vimus. Servi domi-ná-ti sunt nostri : non fu- it qui re-díme-ret

de manu e- ó- rum. In a-nimábus nostris affe-re-bámus panem no-bis,

a fá-ci- e glá-di- i in de-sér-to. Pel-lis nostra qua-si clí-ba-nus ex-ústa

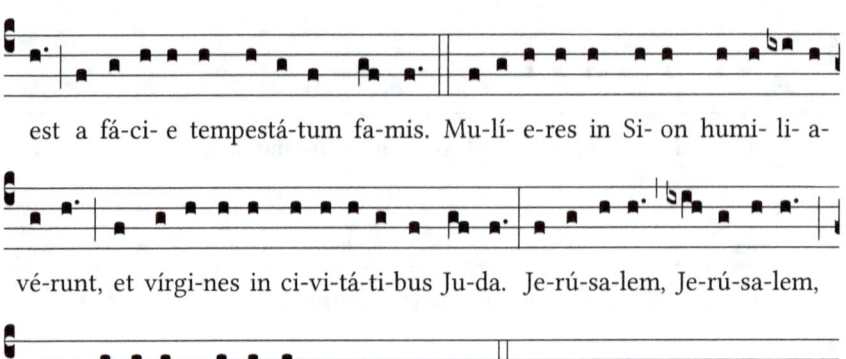

est a fá-ci- e tempestá-tum fa-mis. Mu-lí- e-res in Si- on humi- li- a-

vé-runt, et vírgi-nes in ci-vi-tá-ti-bus Ju-da. Je-rú-sa-lem, Je-rú-sa-lem,

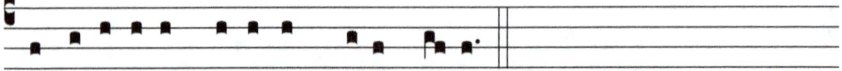

convérte-re ad Dómi-num De-um tu- um.

LESSON 3: Remember, O Lord, what is come upon us: consider and behold our reproach. Our inheritance is turned to aliens: our houses to strangers. We are become orphans without a father: our mothers are as widows. We have drunk our water for money: we have bought our wood. We were dragged by the necks, we were weary and no rest was given us. We have given our hand to Egypt, and to the Assyrians, that we might be satisfied with bread. Our fathers have sinned, and are not: and we have borne their iniquities. Servants have ruled over us: there was none to redeem us out of their hand. We fetched our bread at the peril of our lives, because of the sword in the desert. Our skin was burnt as an oven, by reason of the violence of the famine. They oppressed the women in Sion, and the virgins in the cities of Juda. *Jerusalem! Jerusalem! Return unto the Lord thy God.*

RESPONSORY 3   PLANGE QUASI VIRGO

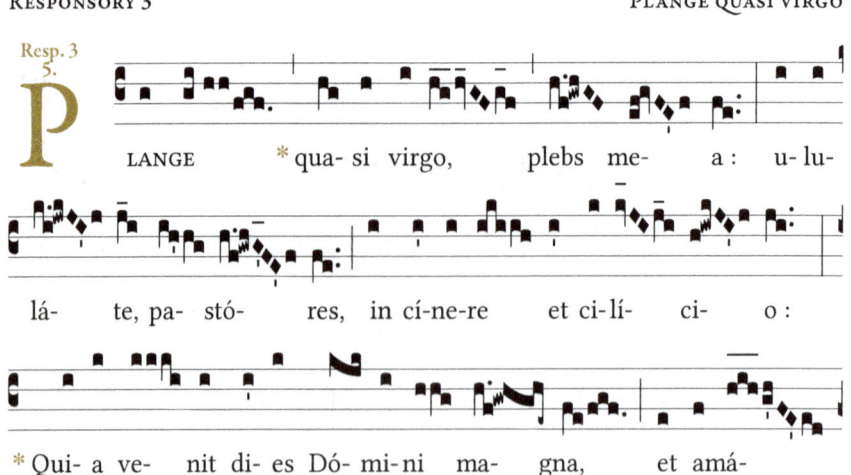

LANGE * qua- si virgo, plebs me- a: u- lu-

lá- te, pa- stó- res, in cí-ne-re et ci-lí- ci- o:

* Qui- a ve- nit di- es Dó- mi-ni ma- gna, et amá-

ra val- de. ℣. Accíngi-te vos, sa-cerdó-tes, et plángi-te,

mi-nístri al-tá- ris, aspérgi-te vos cí-ne- re. * Qui- a.

℟. Plange.

℟. O my people! lament, like a virgin, howl, ye shepherds, in sack-cloth and ashes * For the day of the Lord is at hand, and it is great and very terrible. ℣. Gird yourselves, ye Priests, and wail, ye ministers of the altar: cast up ashes upon you. ℟. For the day of the Lord is at hand, and it is great and very terrible. ℟. O my people! lament, like a virgin, howl, ye shepherds, in sack-cloth and ashes * For the day of the Lord is at hand, and it is great and very terrible.

2ND NOCTURN

1. Ant.
5.a

E- LEVÁMI-NI, * portæ æ-terná-les, et intro- í- bit Rex

gló-ri- æ.

ANTIPHON: Be ye lifted up, * ye everlasting doors, and the King of glory shall come in.

PSALM 23

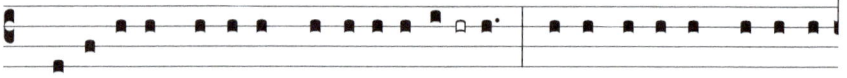

1. Dómi-ni est terra, et ple-ni-túdo e- jus: * orbis terrá-rum, et u-ni-

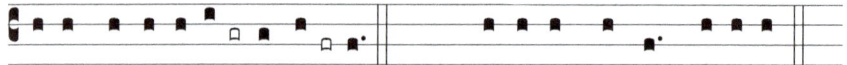

vérsi qui há-bi-**tant** in e- o. *Flex :* prínci-pes, vestras, †

1. The earth is the Lord's and the fulness thereof: * the world, and all they that dwell therein.

2. Quia ipse super mária fundávit eum: * et super flúmina præparávit eum.

2. For He hath founded it upon the seas; * and hath prepared it upon the rivers.

3. Quis ascéndet in montem Dómini? * aut quis stabit in loco sancto ejus?

3. Who shall ascend into the mountain of the Lord: * or who shall stand in His holy place?

4. Innocens mánibus et mundo corde, * qui non accépit in vano ánimam suam, nec jurávit in dolo próximo suo.

4. The innocent in hands, and clean of heart, * who hath not taken His soul in vain, nor sworn deceitfully to His neighbour.

5. Hic accípiet benedictiónem a Dómino: * et misericórdiam a Deo, salutári suo.

5. He shall receive a blessing from the Lord, * and mercy from God His Saviour.

6. Hæc est generátio quæréntium eum, * quæréntium fáciem **Dei Jacob.**

7. Attóllite portas, príncipes, vestras, † et elevámini, portæ æternáles: * et introíbit Rex **glóriæ.**

8. Quis est iste Rex **glóriæ**? * Dóminus fortis et potens: Dóminus **pot**ens in **præ**lio.

9. Attóllite portas, príncipes, vestras, † et elevámini, portæ æternáles: * et introíbit Rex **glóriæ.**

10. Quis est iste Rex **glóri**æ? * Dóminus virtútum ipse **est** Rex **glóriæ.**

6. This is the generation of them that seek Him, * of them that seek the face of the God of Jacob.

7. Lift up your gates, O ye princes, † and be ye lifted up, O eternal gates: * and the King of Glory shall enter in.

8. Who is this King of Glory? * the Lord who is strong and mighty: the Lord mighty in battle.

9. Lift up your gates, O ye princes, † and be ye lifted up, O eternal gates: * and the King of Glory shall enter in.

10. Who is this King of Glory? * the Lord of hosts, He is the King of Glory.

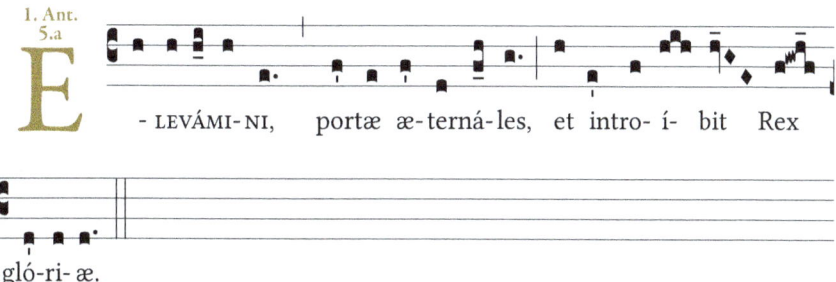

1. Ant.
5.a

E - LEVÁMI-NI, portæ æ-ternáles, et intro-í-bit Rex

glóri-æ.

The fourth candle is extinguished.

2. Ant.
4.E

CREDO vi-dé-re * bona Dómi-ni in terra vi-vénti- um.

Antiphon: I believe that I shall yet see * the goodness of the Lord in the land of the living.

Psalm 26

1. Dómi- nus il- lumi- ná- ti- o me- a, et *sa- lus* **me**- a, * *quem*

ti- **mé**-bo? ℣.2. * a *quo tre-pi-* **dá**-bo?

1. The Lord is my light and my salvation, * whom shall I fear?

2. Dóminus protéctor *vitæ* **meæ**, * a *quo trepi***dá**bo?

2. The Lord is the protector of my life: * of whom shall I be afraid?

3. Dum apprópiant super *me* *no***cén**tes, * ut e*dant carnes* **me**as:

3. Whilst the wicked draw near against me, * to eat my flesh.

4. Qui tríbulant me ini*míci* **mei**, * ipsi infirmáti sunt *et ceci***dé**runt.

4. My enemies that trouble me, * have themselves been weakened, and have fallen.

5. Si consístant advér*sum* *me* **ca**stra, * non ti*mébit cor* **me**um.

5. If armies in camp should stand together against me, * my heart shall not fear.

6. Si exsúrgat advér*sum* *me* **præ**lium, * in hoc *ego spe***rá**bo.

6. If a battle should rise up against me, * in this will I be confident.

7. Unam pétii a Dómino, *hanc* requí*ram*, * ut inhábitem in domo Dómini ómnibus dié*bus vitæ* **meæ**:

7. One thing I have asked of the Lord, this will I seek after; * that I may dwell in the house of the Lord all the days of my life.

8. Ut vídeam volu*ptátem* **Dó**mini, * et ví*sitem templum* **e**jus.

8. That I may see the delight of the Lord, * and may visit His temple.

9. Quóniam abscóndit me in taber*náculo* **suo**: * in die malórum protéxit me in abscóndito taber*náculi* **su**i.

9. For He hath hidden me in His tabernacle; * in the day of evils, He hath protected me in the secret place of His tabernacle.

10. In petra *exal***tá**vit me: * et nunc exaltávit caput meum super in*imícos* **me**os.

11. Circuívi et immolávi in taber-náculo ejus hóstiam vocif*eratió*nis: * cantábo et psal*mum dicam* **Dómi**no.

12. Exáudi, Dómine, vocem meam, qua cla*mávi* **ad** te: * miserére me*i, et* *ex***áudi** me.

13. Tibi dixit cor meum, exquisívit te f*ácies* **me**a: * fáciem tuam, Dó*mine,* *re***quí**ram.

14. Ne avértas fáciem *tuam* **a** me, * ne declínes in ira *a servo* **tu**o.

15. Adjútor *meus* **esto**: * ne derelín-quas me, neque despícias me, Deus, sa*lutáris* **me**us.

16. Quóniam pater meus, et mater mea de*reli***qué**runt me: * Dóminus *autem as***súmpsit** me.

17. Legem pone mihi, Dómine, in *via* **tu**a: * et dírige me in sémitam rectam propter in*imícos* **me**os.

18. Ne tradíderis me in ánimas tribu*lánti***um** me: * quóniam insur-rexérunt in me testes iníqui, et mentí-ta est in*íquitas* **si**bi.

19. Credo vidére *bona* **Dó**mini * in *terra viv***énti**um.

20. Exspécta Dóminum, vir*íliter* **age**: * et confortétur cor tuum, et *sústine* **Dómi**num.

10. He hath exalted me upon a rock: * and now He hath lifted up my head above my enemies.

11. I have gone round, and have of-fered up in His tabernacle a sacrifice of jubilation: * I will sing, and recite a psalm to the Lord.

12. Hear, O Lord, my voice, with which I have cried to Thee: * have mercy on me and hear me.

13. My heart hath said to Thee: My face hath sought Thee: * Thy face, O Lord, will I still seek.

14. Turn not away Thy face from me; * decline not in Thy wrath from Thy servant.

15. Be Thou my helper, * forsake me not; do not Thou despise me, O God my Saviour.

16. For my father and my mother have left me: * but the Lord hath tak-en me up.

17. Set me, O Lord, a law in Thy way, * and guide me in the right path, because of my enemies.

18. Deliver me not over to the will of them that trouble me; * for unjust witnesses have risen up against me; and iniquity hath lied to itself.

19. I believe to see the good things of the Lord * in the land of the living.

20. Expect the Lord, do manfully, * and let Thy heart take courage, and wait Thou for the Lord.

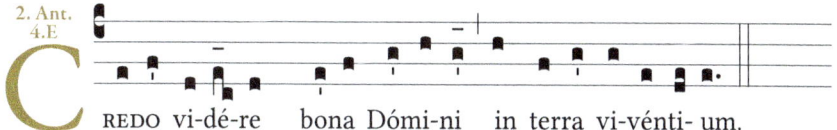

2. Ant.
4.E

CREDO vi-dé-re bona Dómi-ni in terra vi-vénti-um.

The fifth candle is extinguished.

3. Ant.
8.G

Dómine, * abstra-xí-sti ab ín-fe-ris á-nimam me- am.

ANTIPHON: O Lord, Thou hast brought up * my soul from the grave.

PSALM 29

1. Exaltábo te, Dómi-ne, quón-i- am susce-**pí**sti me: * nec de-lectásti

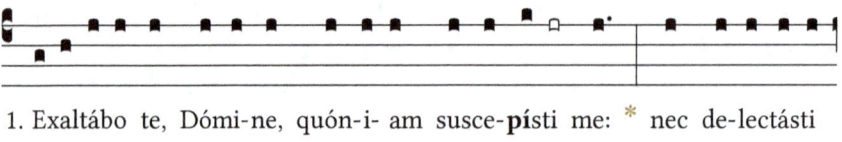

in-imí-cos *me- os* **su**per me. ℣. 2. * *et sa***ná**sti me.

1. I will extol Thee, O Lord, for Thou hast upheld me: * and hast not made my enemies to rejoice over me.

2. Dómine, Deus meus, clamávi **ad** te, * *et sa***ná**sti me.

2. O Lord my God, I have cried to Thee, * and Thou hast healed me.

3. Dómine, eduxísti ab inférno ánimam **me**am: * salvásti me a de-scendénti*bus in* **la**cum.

3. Thou hast brought forth, O Lord, my soul from hell: * Thou hast saved me from them that go down into the pit.

4. Psállite Dómino, sancti **e**jus: * et confitémini memóriæ sancti*tátis* **e**jus.

4. Sing to the Lord, O ye His saints: * and give praise to the memory of His holiness.

5. Quóniam ira in indignatióne **e**jus: * et vita in volun*táte* **e**jus.

5. For wrath is in His indignation; * and life in His good will.

6. Ad vésperum demorábitur **fle**tus: * et ad matutí*num læ***tí**tia.

6. In the evening weeping shall have place, * and in the morning gladness.

7. Ego autem dixi in abundántia **me**a: * Non movébor *in æ***tér**num.

7. And in my abundance I said: * I shall never be moved.

8. Dómine, in voluntáte **tu**a, * præstitísti decóri me*o vir***tú**tem.

8. O Lord, in Thy favour, * Thou gavest strength to my beauty.

9. Avertísti fáciem tuam **a** me, * et factus sum *contur***bá**tus.

9. Thou turnedst away Thy face from me, * and I became troubled.

10. Ad te, Dómine, clamábo: * et ad Deum meum *depre***cá**bor.

10. To Thee, O Lord, will I cry: * and I will make supplication to my God.

11. Quæ utílitas in sánguine **me**o, * dum descéndo in corr*uptió*nem?

11. What profit is there in my blood, * whilst I go down to corruption?

12. Numquid confitébitur tibi **pul**vis, * aut annuntiábit veri*tátem* **tu**am?

12. Shall dust confess to Thee, * or declare Thy truth?

13. Audívit Dóminus, et misértus est **mei**: * Dóminus factus est ad*jútor* **me**us.

13. The Lord hath heard, and hath had mercy on me: * the Lord became my helper.

14. Convertísti planctum meum in gáudium **mi**hi: * conscidísti saccum meum, et circumdedísti *me læ*tí*ti*a:

14. Thou hast turned for me my mourning into joy: * Thou hast cut my sackcloth, and hast compassed me with gladness:

15. Ut cantet tibi glória mea, et non com**pún**gar: * Dómine, Deus meus, in ætérnum confi*tébor* **ti**bi.

15. To the end that my glory may sing to Thee, and I may not regret: * O Lord my God, I will give praise to Thee for ever.

3. Ant.
8.G

DÓMINE, abstra-xí-sti ab ín-fe-ris á-nimam me- am.

The sixth candle is extinguished.

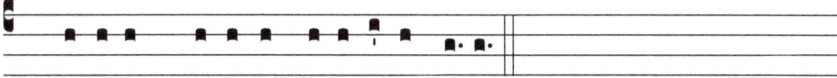

℣. Tu autem, Dómi-ne, mi-se-ré-re me- i.

℟. Et re-súsci-ta me, et retrí-bu- am e- is.

Or:

℣. Tu autem, Dómi-ne, mi-se-ré-re me- i.

℟. Et re-súsci-ta me, et retrí-bu- am e- is.

℣. But Thou, O Lord, be merciful unto me.
℟. And raise me up; and I will requite them.

The Pater noster *is said silently.*

LESSON 4   ST. AUGUSTINE, BISHOP ON PSALM 63: 7

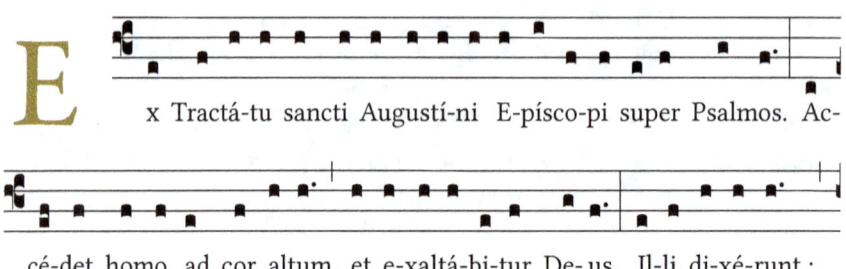

E x Tractá-tu sancti Augustí-ni E-písco-pi super Psalmos. Ac-

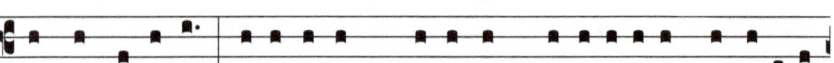

cé-det homo ad cor altum, et e-xaltá-bi-tur De- us. Il-li di-xé-runt :

Quis nos vi-dé-bit? De-fe-cé-runt scru-tántes scru-ta-ti- ónes, consí-li- a

ma-la. Accéssit homo ad ipsa consí-li- a, passus est se tené-ri ut ho-

mo. Non e-nim tene-ré-tur ni-si homo, aut vi-de-ré-tur ni-si homo,

aut cæde-ré-tur ni-si homo, aut cru-ci-fi-ge-ré-tur, aut mo-re-ré-

tur ni-si homo. Accéssit ergo homo ad il-las omnes passi- ónes,

quæ in il-lo ni-hil va-lé-rent, ni-si esset homo. Sed si il-le non es-

set homo, non li-be-ra-ré-tur homo. Accéssit homo ad cor altum,

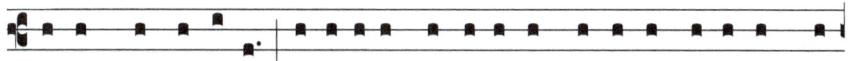

id est, cor secré-tum, objí-ci- ens aspécti-bus humá-nis hómi-nem, ser-

vans intus De- um : ce-lans formam De- i, in qua æquá-lis est Patri,

et óffe-rens formam servi, qua mi-nor est Patre.

From the Treatise of St. Augustine, Bishop, Upon the Psalms.

LESSON 4: Man shall come to the deep heart, and God shall be exalted. They said: "Who will see us?" They failed in making diligent search for wicked designs. Christ, as Man, came to those designs, and suffered himself to be seized on as man. For He could not be seized if he were not man, nor seen if He were not man, nor scourged if He were not man, nor crucified if He were not man. As man, therefore, he came to all these sufferings, which could have no effect on him if he were not man. But if He had not been man, man could not have been redeemed. Man came to the deep heart, that is, the secret heart, exposing His humanity to human view, but hiding His divinity: concealing the form of God, by which He is equal to the Father; and offering the form of the servant, by which he is inferior to the Father.

RESPONSORY 4   RECÉSSIT PASTOR NOSTER

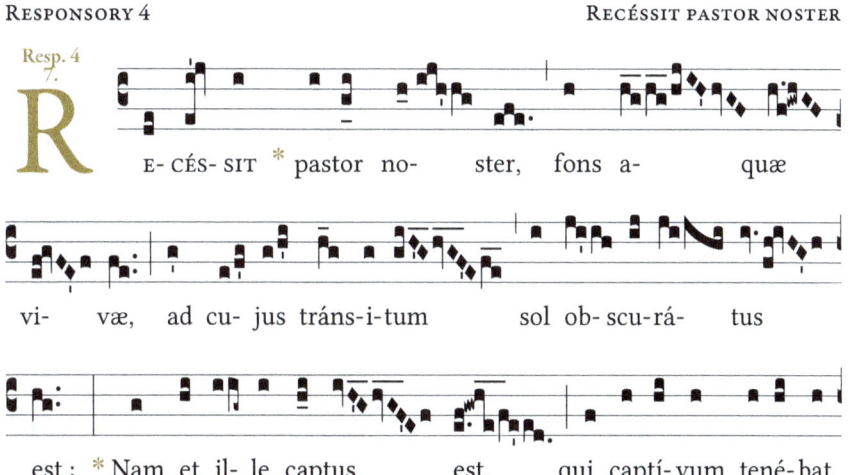

RE- CÉS- SIT * pastor no- ster, fons a- quæ vi- væ, ad cu- jus tráns-i-tum sol ob-scu-rá- tus est : *Nam et il- le captus est, qui captí-vum tené-bat

pri- mum hómi- nem : hó-di- e por- tas mor-

tis et se- ras pá- ri-ter Salvá-tor no- ster dis- rú- pit.

℣. Destrú- xit qui-dem claustra infér- ni, et sub-vértit pot-énti-

as di- á- bo- li. * Nam et il- le.

℟. Our Shepherd, even the Fountain of living waters, is gone from us; He passed away, and the sun was darkened. * For now hath our Saviour bound captive the one who bound the first man captive; this day hath He burst the gates and bars of death. ℣. The bands of hell He hath utterly abolished, and hath done away the power of the devil. ℟. For now hath our Saviour bound captive the one who bound the first man captive; this day hath He burst the gates and bars of death.

LESSON 5   ST. AUGUSTINE, BISHOP ON PSALM 63: 7

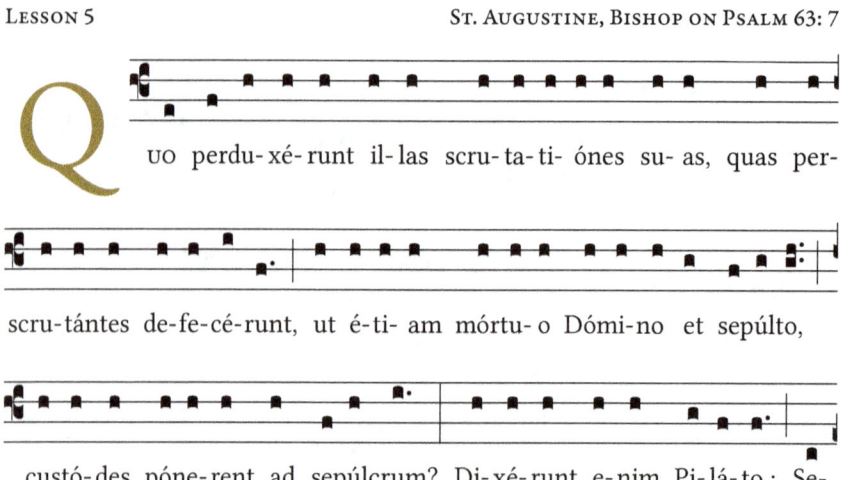

Q uo perdu-xé-runt il-las scru-ta-ti- ónes su- as, quas per-

scru-tántes de-fe-cé-runt, ut é-ti- am mórtu- o Dómi-no et sepúlto,

custó-des póne-rent ad sepúlcrum? Di-xé-runt e-nim Pi-lá-to: Se-

dúctor il-le : hoc appel-la-bá-tur nómi-ne Dómi-nus Je-sus Christus,

ad so-lá-ti- um servó-rum su- ó-rum, quando di-cúntur seductó-res :

ergo il-li Pi-lá-to : Sedúctor il-le, ínqui- unt, di-xit adhuc vi-vens :

Post tres di- es re-súrgam. Jube í-taque custo-dí-ri sepúlcrum usque

in di- em térti- um, ne forte vé-ni- ant discí-pu-li e-jus, et fu-réntur

e- um, et di-cant ple-bi : Surré-xit a mórtu- is : et e-rit no-víssimus

error pe-jor pri- ó-re. A- it il-lis Pi-lá-tus : Ha-bé-tis custó-di- am,

i-te, custo-dí-te si-cut sci-tis. Il-li autem a-be- úntes, mu-ni- é-runt

sepúlcrum, signántes lá-pi-dem cum custó-di-bus.

LESSON 5: How far did they carry this, their diligent search, in which they failed so much, that, when our Lord was dead and buried, they placed guards at the sepulcher? For they said to Pilate: "This seducer"; by which name our Lord Jesus Christ was called, for the comfort of his servants, when they are called seducers. "This seducer", say they to Pilate, "whilst he was yet alive, said: After three days I will rise again. Command, therefore, the sepulcher to be guarded until the third day; lest his disciples come and steal him away, and say to the people: He is risen from the dead: so shall the last error be worse than the first." Pilate said to them: "You have a guard, go and guard it as you know." And they, departing, made the sepulcher sure with guards, sealing up the stone.

RESPONSORY 5   O VOS OMNES

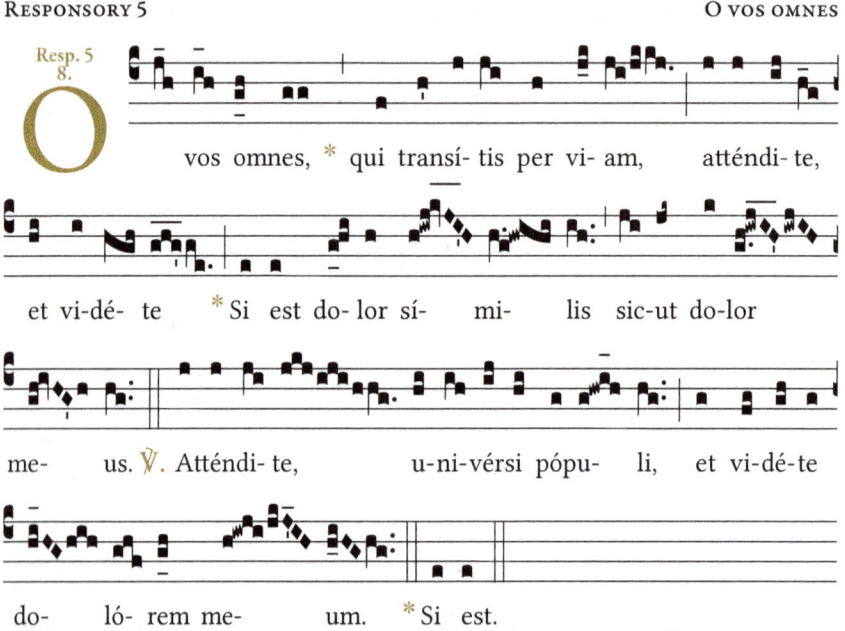

O vos omnes, * qui transí- tis per vi- am, atténdi- te, et vi-dé- te *Si est do-lor sí- mi- lis sic-ut do-lor me- us. ℣. Atténdi- te, u-ni-vérsi pópu- li, et vi-dé-te do- ló- rem me- um. * Si est.

℟. O all ye that pass by, behold and see; * If there be any sorrow like unto My sorrow. ℣. O all ye nations, behold, and see My sorrow, ℟. If there be any sorrow like unto My sorrow.

Lesson 6 St. Augustine, Bishop on Psalm 63: 7

P o-su- érunt custó- des mí- li-tes ad sepúlcrum. Concússa

terra Dómi-nus re-surré-xit : mi-rá-cu-la facta sunt tá-li- a circa sepúl-

crum, ut et ipsi mí-li-tes, qui custó-des advéne-rant, testes fí- e-rent,

si vel-lent ve-ra nunti- á-re. Sed a-va-rí-ti- a il-la, quæ capti-vá-vit

discí-pu-lum cómi-tem Chri-sti, capti-vá-vit et mí- li-tem custó-dem

sepúlcri. Damus, ínqui- unt, vo-bis pe-cú-ni- am : et dí-ci-te, qui- a vo-

bis dormi- énti-bus vené-runt discí-pu-li e-jus, et abstu-lé-runt e- um.

Ve-re de-fe-cé-runt scru-tántes scru-ta-ti- ónes. Quid est quod di-xí-

sti, o infé-lix astú-ti- a? Tantúmne dé-se-ris lu-cem consí- li- i pi- e-

tá-tis, et in pro-fúnda versú-ti- æ demérge-ris, ut hoc di-cas : Dí-ci-te

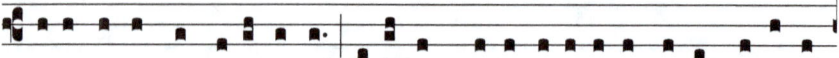

qui- a vo-bis dormi- énti-bus vené-runt discí-pu-li e-jus, et abstu-lé-runt

e- um? Dormi- éntes testes ádhi-bes : ve-re tu ipse obdormí-sti, qui

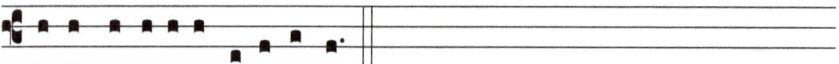

scru-tándo tá-li- a de-fe-cí-sti.

Lesson 6: They placed soldiers to guard the sepulcher. The earth shook, and the Lord rose again: such miracles were done at the sepulcher, that the very soldiers who came as guards, might be witnesses of it, if they would declare the truth. But that covetousness, which possessed the disciple who was the companion of Christ, blinded also the soldiers who were the guards of His sepulcher. "We will give you money", said they: "and say, that whilst you were asleep, his disciples came and took him away;" they truly failed in making diligent search. What is it thou hast said, O wretched craft? Dost thou shut thy eyes against the light of prudence and piety, and plunge thyself so deep in cunning, as to say this: "say, that whilst you were asleep, his disciples came and took them away"? Dost thou produce sleeping witnesses? Certainly thou thyself sleepest who failest in making search after such things.

RESPONSORY 6   ECCE QUÓMODO MÓRITUR

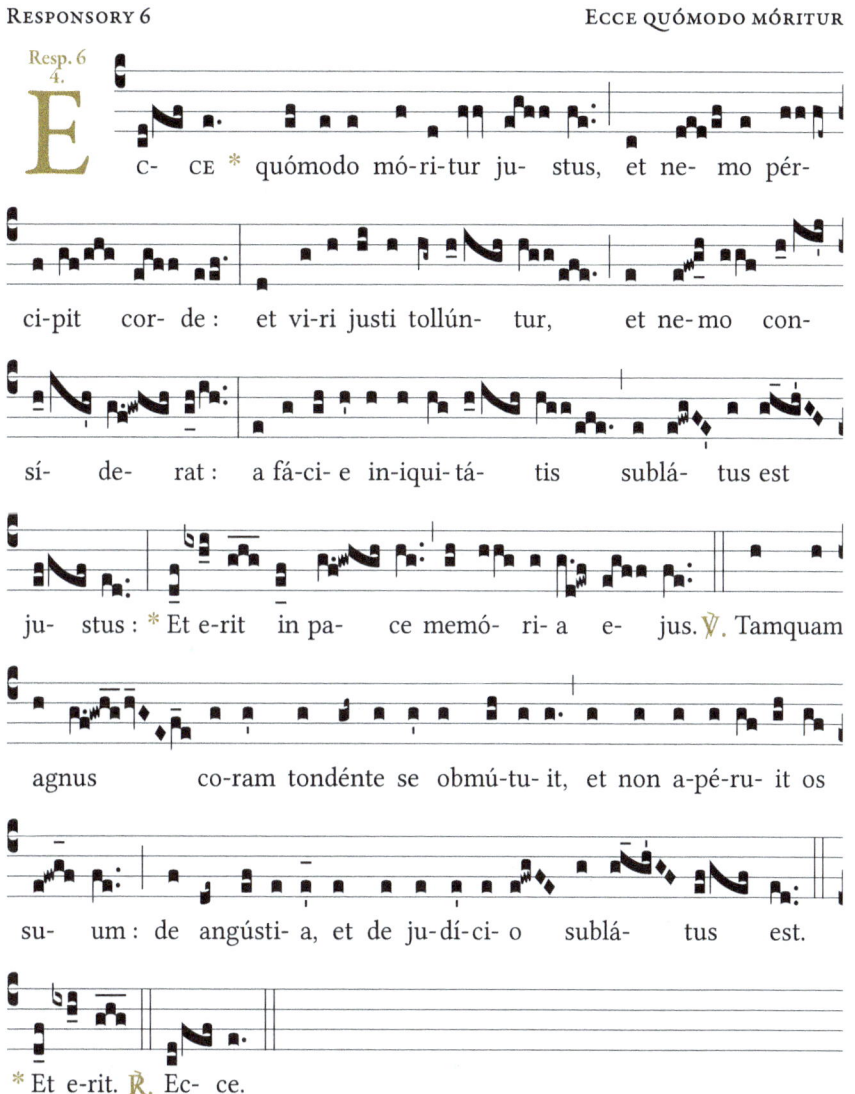

E-ce * quómodo mó-ri-tur ju- stus, et ne- mo pér-ci-pit cor- de : et vi-ri justi tollún- tur, et ne-mo con-sí- de- rat : a fá-ci- e in-iqui-tá- tis sublá- tus est ju- stus : * Et e-rit in pa- ce memó- ri- a e- jus. ℣. Tamquam agnus co-ram tondénte se obmú-tu- it, et non a-pé-ru- it os su- um : de angústi- a, et de ju-dí-ci- o sublá- tus est.

* Et e-rit. ℟. Ec- ce.

℟. Behold how the righteous dieth, and no man taketh it to heart; and the just are taken away, and none considereth. From the midst of sinners is the righteous translated; * And his memory is in peace. ℣. As a lamb before his shearers is dumb, so He opened not His mouth; He was taken from prison and from judgment. ℟. And his memory is in peace. ℟. Behold how the righteous dieth, and no man taketh it to heart; and the just are taken away, and none considereth. From the midst of sinners is the righteous translated; * And his memory is in peace.

3RD NOCTURN

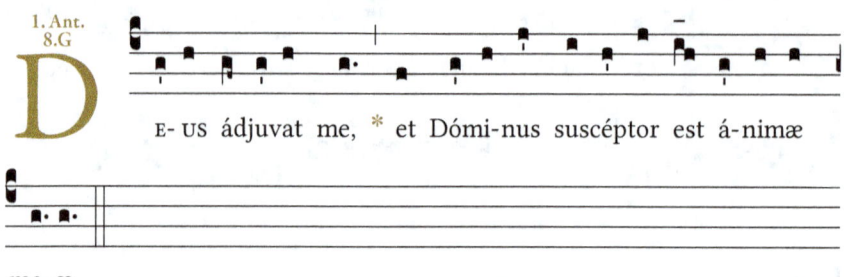

1. Ant.
8.G

D E- US ádjuvat me, * et Dómi-nus suscéptor est á-nimæ

me- æ.

ANTIPHON: God is my helper, * and the Lord upholdeth my soul.

PSALM 53

1. De- us, in nómi-ne tu- o salvum **me**   fac : * et in virtú-te tu- a

jú-di-**ca**   me.   *Flex :* advérsum me, †

1. Save me, O God, by Thy name, * and judge me in Thy strength.

2. Deus, exáudi oratiónem **me**am: * áuribus pércipe verba *oris* **me**i.

3. Quóniam aliéni insurrexérunt advérsum me, † et fortes quæsiérunt ánimam **me**am: * et non proposuérunt Deum ante con*spéctum* **su**um.

4. Ecce enim Deus ádju**vat** me: * et Dóminus suscéptor est á*nimæ* **me**æ.

5. Avérte mala inimícis **me**is: * et in veritáte tua dis*pérde* **il**los.

6. Voluntárie sacrificábo **ti**bi, * et confitébor nómini tuo, Dómine: quón*iam* **bo**num est:

2. O God, hear my prayer: * give ear to the words of my mouth.

3. For strangers have risen up against me; † and the mighty have sought after my soul: * and they have not set God before their eyes.

4. For behold God is my helper: * and the Lord is the protector of my soul.

5. Turn back the evils upon my enemies; * and cut them off in Thy truth.

6. I will freely sacrifice to Thee, * and will give praise, O God, to Thy name: because it is good:

7. Quóniam ex omni tribulatióne eripuísti me: * et super inimícos meos despéxit *óculus* **me**us.

7. For Thou hast delivered me out of all trouble: * and my eye hath looked down upon my enemies.

1. Ant.
8.G

D e- us ádjuvat me, et Dómi-nus suscéptor est á-nimæ

me- æ.

The seventh candle is extinguished.

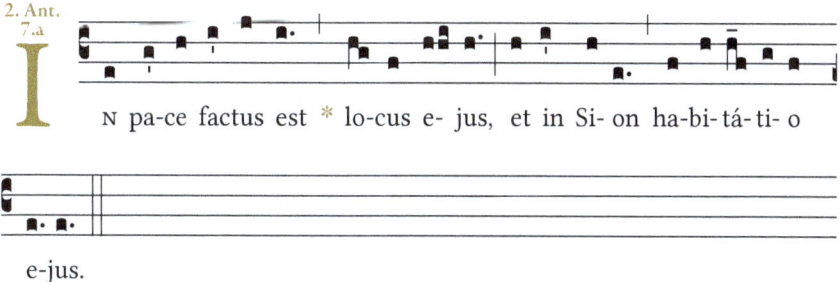

2. Ant.
7.a

I n pa-ce factus est * lo-cus e- jus, et in Si- on ha-bi-tá-ti- o

e-jus.

ANTIPHON: His place is in peace * and His dwelling-place in Zion.

PSALM 75

1. No-tus in Judǽ- a De- us : * in Isra- ël magnum **no**- men e- jus.

1. In Judea God is known: * His name is great in Israel.

2. Et factus est in pace **lo**cus ejus: * et habitátio ejus in **Si**on.

2. And His place is in peace: * and His abode in Sion:

3. Ibi confrégit poténtias **árc**uum: * scutum, gládi**um**, et **bel**lum.

3. There hath He broken the powers of bows, * the shield, the sword, and the battle.

4. Illúminans tu mirabíliter a mónti**bus** æt**érn**is: * turbáti sunt omnes insipi**én**tes **cor**de.

4. Thou enlightenest wonderfully from the everlasting hills. * All the foolish of heart were troubled.

5. Dormiérunt **somnum suu**m: * et nihil invenérunt omnes viri divitiárum in **mán**ibus **su**is.

6. Ab increpatióne tua, **Deus Ja**cob, * dormitavérunt qui ascen**dé**runt equos.

7. Tu terríbilis es, et quis resístet **ti**bi? * ex tunc **ira tu**a.

8. De cælo audítum fecísti ju**dí**cium: * terra trémuit **et** quiévit.

9. Cum exsúrgeret in ju**dí**cium **Deus**, * ut salvos fáceret omnes mansuétos **ter**ræ.

10. Quóniam cogitátio hóminis confitébitur **ti**bi: * et relíquiæ cogitatiónis diem festum **agent ti**bi.

11. Vovéte, et réddite Dómino **Deo ve**stro: * omnes, qui in circúitu ejus af**fér**tis **mú**nera.

12. Terríbili et ei qui aufert **spí**ritum **prín**cipum, * terríbili apud **reges ter**ræ.

5. They have slept their sleep; * and all the men of riches have found nothing in their hands.

6. At Thy rebuke, O God of Jacob, * they have all slumbered that mounted on horseback.

7. Thou art terrible, and who shall resist Thee? * from that time Thy wrath.

8. Thou hast caused judgment to be heard from heaven: * the earth trembled and was still,

9. When God arose in judgment, * to save all the meek of the earth.

10. For the thought of man shall give praise to Thee: * and the remainders of the thought shall keep holiday to Thee.

11. Vow ye, and pay to the Lord your God: * all you that are round about Him bring presents.

12. To Him that is terrible, even to Him who taketh away the spirit of princes: * to the terrible with the kings of the earth.

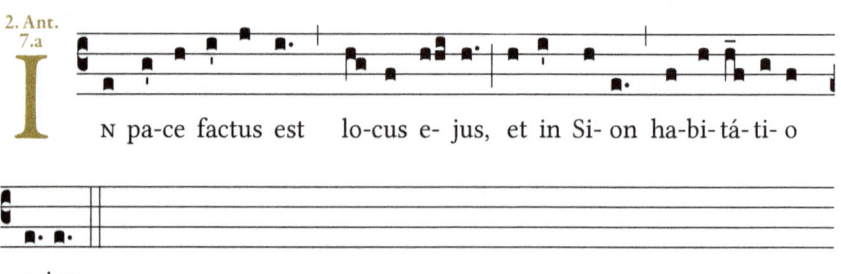

2. Ant.
7.a

IN pa-ce factus est lo-cus e- jus, et in Si- on ha-bi-tá-ti-o

e-jus.

The eighth candle is extinguished.

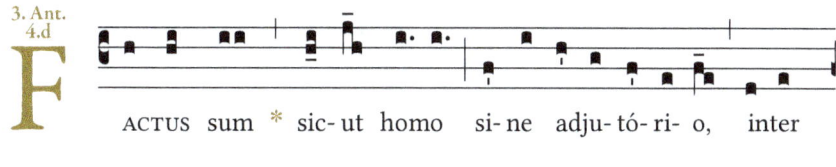

3. Ant.
4.d

F ACTUS sum * sic- ut homo si- ne adju- tó- ri- o, inter

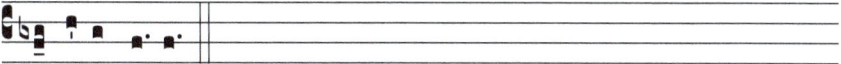

mórtu- os li-ber.

ANTIPHON: I am become as a man without help, * free among the dead.

PSALM 87

1. Dómi-ne, De- us sa-*lú-tis* **me**- æ : * in di- e clamá-vi, *et nocte*

co-ram te. *Flex :* sepúlcris, †

1. Lord, the God of my salvation: * I have cried in the day, and in the night before Thee.

2. Intret in conspéctu tuo orá*tio* **me**a: * inclína aurem tuam *ad precem* **me**am:

2. Let my prayer come in before Thee: * incline Thy ear to my petition.

3. Quia repléta est malis á*nima* **me**a: * et vita mea inférno *appropin-* **quá**vit.

3. For my soul is filled with evils: * and my life hath drawn nigh to hell.

4. Æstimátus sum cum descendénti-*bus in* **la**cum: * factus sum sicut homo sine adjutório, inter *mórtuos* **li**ber.

4. I am counted among them that go down to the pit: * I am become as a man without help, free among the dead.

5. Sicut vulneráti dormiéntes in sepúlcris, † quorum non es *memor* **á**mplius: * et ipsi de manu *tua re***púl**si sunt.

5. Like the slain sleeping in the sepulchres, † whom Thou remember-est no more: * and they are cast off from Thy hand.

6. Posuérunt me in lacu in*feri***ó**ri: * in tenebrósis, et *in umbra* **mor**tis.

6. They have laid me in the lower pit: * in the dark places, and in the shadow of death.

7. Super me confirmátus est *furor tu*us: * et omnes fluctus tuos in*duxísti* super me.

8. Longe fecísti notos *meos* **a** me: * posuérunt me abomina*tiónem* **si**bi.

9. Tráditus sum, et non e*gredié*bar: * óculi mei langué*runt præ in*ópia.

10. Clamávi ad te, Dómine, *tota* **die**: * expándi ad *te manus* **me**as.

11. Numquid mórtuis fácies *mira*bília: * aut médici suscitábunt, et confi*tebúntur* **ti**bi?

12. Numquid narrábit áliquis in sepúlcro misericór*diam* **tu**am, * et veritátem tuam in *perditi*óne?

13. Numquid cognoscéntur in ténebris mirabí*lia* **tu**a, * et justítia tua in terra oblivi*ó*nis?

14. Et ego ad te, Dómine, *cla*mávi: * et mane orátio mea *prævéni*et te.

15. Ut quid, Dómine, repéllis orati*ónem* **me**am: * avértis fáci*em* *tuam* **a** me?

16. Pauper sum ego, et in labóribus a juven*túte* **me**a: * exaltátus autem, humiliátus sum *et contur*bátus.

17. In me transiérunt *iræ* **tu**æ: * et terróres tui *conturba*vérunt me.

18. Circumdedérunt me sicut aqua *tota* **die**: * circumde*dérunt me* **si**mul.

19. Elongásti a me amí*cum et* **pró**ximum: * et notos me*os a mi*sé*ria.

7. Thy wrath is strong over me: * and all Thy waves Thou hast brought in upon me.

8. Thou hast put away my acquaintance far from me: * they have set me an abomination to themselves.

9. I was delivered up, and came not forth: * my eyes languished through poverty.

10. All the day I cried to Thee, O Lord: * I stretched out my hands to Thee.

11. Wilt Thou shew wonders to the dead? * or shall physicians raise to life, and give praise to Thee?

12. Shall any one in the sepulchre declare Thy mercy: * and Thy truth in destruction?

13. Shall Thy wonders be known in the dark; * and Thy justice in the land of forgetfulness?

14. But I, O Lord, have cried to Thee: * and in the morning my prayer shall prevent Thee.

15. Lord, why castest Thou off my prayer: * why turnest Thou away Thy face from me?

16. I am poor, and in labours from my youth: * and being exalted have been humbled and troubled.

17. Thy wrath hath come upon me: * and Thy terrors have troubled me.

18. They have come round about me like water all the day: * they have compassed me about together.

19. Friend and neighbour Thou hast put far from me: * and my acquaintance, because of misery.

3. Ant.
4.d

F actus sum sic- ut homo si- ne adju- tó- ri- o, inter

mórtu- os li-ber.

The ninth candle is extinguished.

℣. In pa-ce factus est lo-cus e-jus. ℟. Et in Si- on ha-bi-tá-ti- o e-jus.

Or:

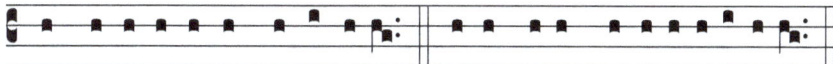

℣. In pa-ce factus est lo-cus e-jus. ℟. Et in Si- on ha-bi-tá-ti- o e-jus.

℣. His place is in peace. ℟. And His dwelling-place in Zion.

The Pater noster *is said silently.*

Lesson 7   Hebrews 9: 11-14

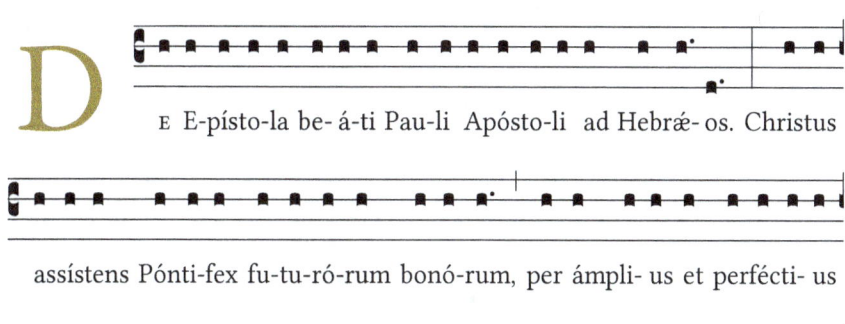

D e E-písto-la be- á-ti Pau-li Apósto-li ad Hebræ- os. Christus

assístens Pónti-fex fu-tu-ró-rum bonó-rum, per ámpli- us et perfécti- us

ta-berná-cu-lum non manu-fáctum, id est, non hu-jus cre- a-ti- ó-nis:

neque per sángui-nem hircó-rum, aut vi-tu-ló-rum, sed per própri-

um sángui-nem intro- í-vit semel in Sancta, æ-térna re-dempti- óne

invénta. Si e-nim sanguis hircó-rum, et tauró-rum, et ci-nis ví-tu-

læ aspérsus inqui-ná-tos sanctí-fi-cat ad emunda-ti- ónem carnis:

quanto ma-gis sanguis Chri-sti, qui per Spí-ri-tum Sanctum seme-típsum

óbtu-lit imma-cu-lá-tum De- o, emundá-bit consci- énti- am nostram

ab opé-ri-bus mórtu- is, ad servi- éndum De- o vi-vénti?

From the letter of the blessed Apostle Paul to the Hebrews.

LESSON 7: But Christ, being come a high priest of the good things to come, by a greater and more perfect tabernacle not made by hand, that is, not of this creation: Neither by the blood of goats, nor of calves, but by His own blood, entered once into the holies, having obtained eternal redemption. For if the blood of goats and of oxen, and the ashes of a heifer being sprinkled, sanctify such as are defiled, to the cleansing of the flesh: How much more shall the blood of Christ, who by the Holy Ghost offered himself unspotted unto God, cleanse our conscience from dead works, to serve the living God?

RESPONSORY 7 ASTITÉRUNT REGES TERRÆ

Resp. 7
4.

A-STI- TÉ- RUNT * re- ges terræ, et prín- ci- pes

conve- né- runt in u- num, * Ad- vér- sus Dó- mi-

num, et advér- sus Chri- stum e- jus. ℣. Qua-

re fremu- é-runt gen- tes, et pópu-li me-di-tá-ti sunt in- á-

ni- a? * Ad- vér- sus.

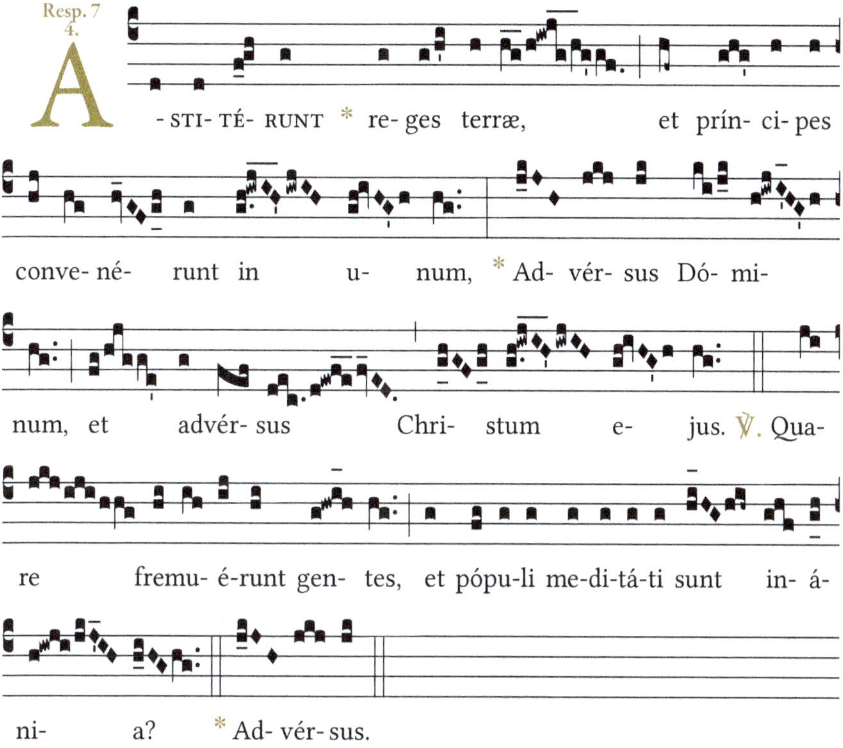

℟. The kings of the earth set themselves, and the rulers take counsel together *
Against the Lord, and against His Anointed. ℣. Why do the heathen rage? and
the people imagine a vain thing, ℟. Against the Lord, and against His Anointed?

LESSON 8 HEBREWS 9: 15-18

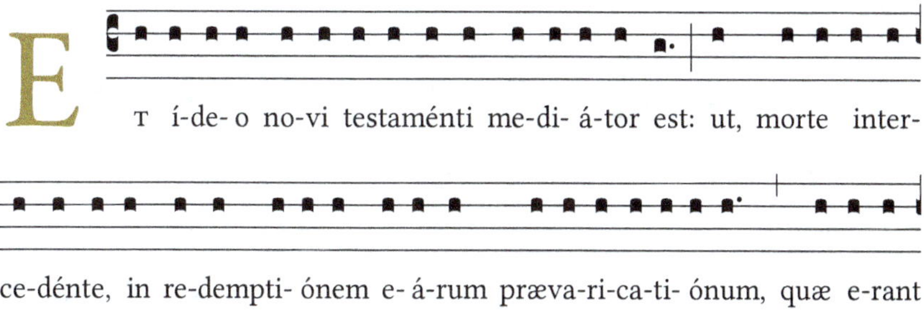

E T í-de- o no-vi testaménti me-di- á-tor est: ut, morte inter-

ce-dénte, in re-dempti- ónem e- á-rum præva-ri-ca-ti- ónum, quæ e-rant

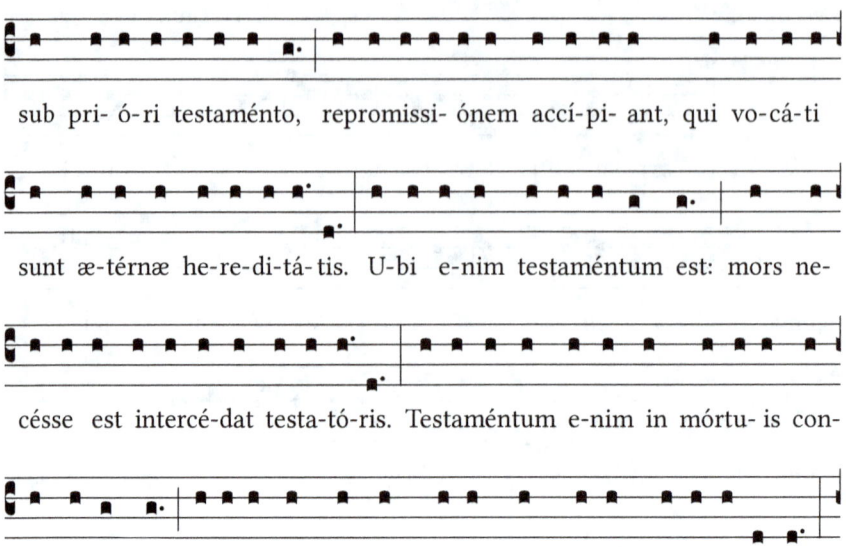

sub pri- ó-ri testaménto, repromissi- ónem accí-pi- ant, qui vo-cá-ti

sunt æ-térnæ he-re-di-tá- tis. U-bi e-nim testaméntum est: mors ne-

césse est intercé-dat testa-tó-ris. Testaméntum e-nim in mórtu- is con-

firmá-tum est: a-li- óquin nondum va-let, dum vi-vit qui testá-tus est.

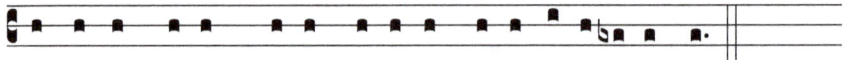

Unde nec primum qui-dem si-ne sángui-ne de-di-cá-tum est.

LESSON 8: And therefore He is the mediator of the new testament: that by means of His death, for the redemption of those transgressions, which were under the former testament, they that are called may receive the promise of eternal inheritance. For where there is a testament, the death of the testator must of necessity come in. For a testament is of force, after men are dead: otherwise it is as yet of no strength, whilst the testator liveth. Whereupon neither was the first indeed dedicated without blood.

RESPONSORY 8   **ÆSTIMÁTUS SUM CUM DESCENDÉNTIBUS**

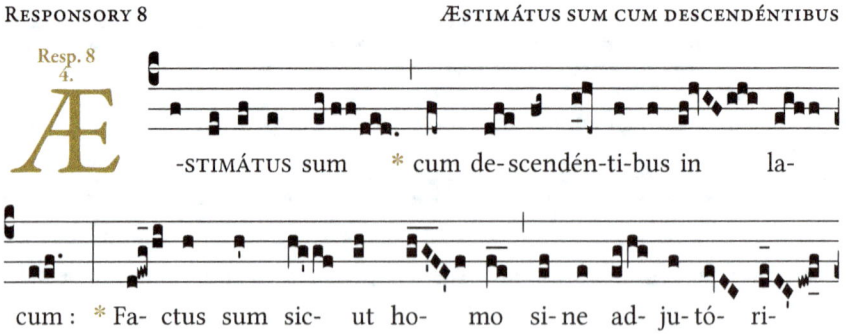

Resp. 8
4.

-STIMÁTUS sum   * cum de-scendén-ti-bus in   la-

cum : * Fa- ctus sum sic- ut ho- mo si- ne ad- ju-tó- ri-

o, inter mór- tu- os li- ber. ℣. Po-su- é-runt me

in la-cu infe-ri- ó- ri, in tenebró-sis, et in umbra mor-

tis. * Fa- ctus.

℟. I am counted with them that go down into the pit. * I am become as a man without help, free among the dead. ℣. They have laid me in the lowest pit, in darkness, and in the shadow of death. ℟. I am become as a man without help, free among the dead.

LESSON 9   HEBREWS 9: 19-22

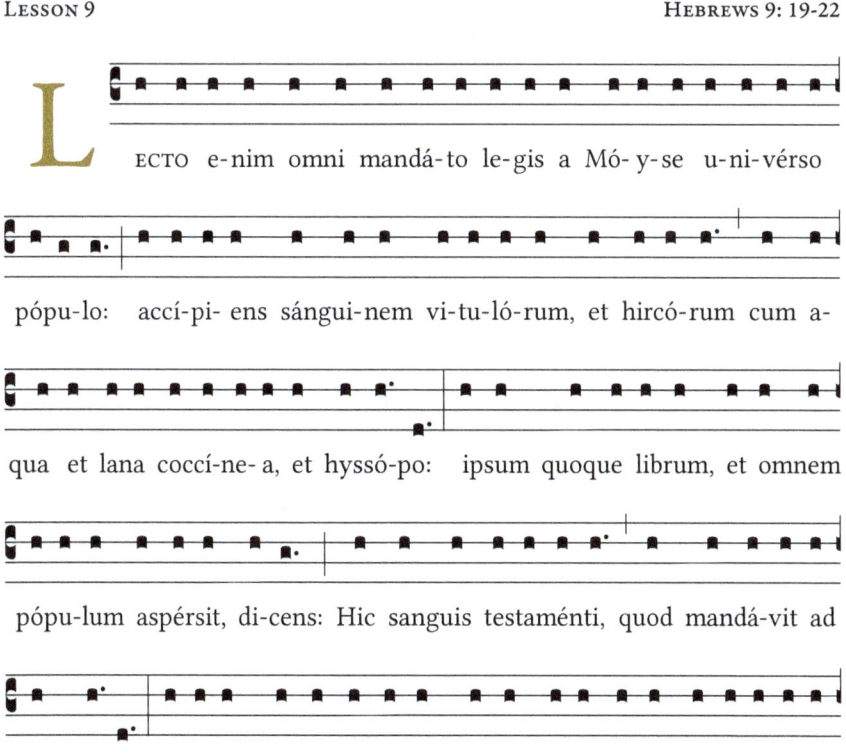

L ECTO e-nim omni mandá-to le-gis a Mó- y-se u-ni-vérso

pópu-lo: accí-pi- ens sángui-nem vi-tu-ló-rum, et hircó-rum cum a-

qua et lana coccí-ne- a, et hyssó-po: ipsum quoque librum, et omnem

pópu-lum aspérsit, di-cens: Hic sanguis testaménti, quod mandá-vit ad

vos De- us. E-ti- am ta-berná-cu-lum, et ómni- a va-sa mi-nisté-ri- i

sángui-ne simí-li-ter aspérsit: et ómni- a pene in sángui-ne se-cúndum

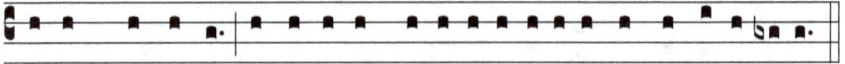

le-gem mundántur: et si-ne sángui-nis effu-si- óne non fit remís-si- o.

LESSON 9: For when every commandment of the law had been read by Moses to all the people, he took the blood of calves and goats, with water, and scarlet wool and hyssop, and sprinkled both the book itself and all the people, Saying: This is the blood of the testament, which God hath enjoined unto you. The tabernacle also and all the vessels of the ministry, in like manner, he sprinkled with blood. And almost all things, according to the law, are cleansed with blood: and without shedding of blood there is no remission [of sin].

RESPONSORY 9   SEPÚLTO DÓMINO

Resp. 9

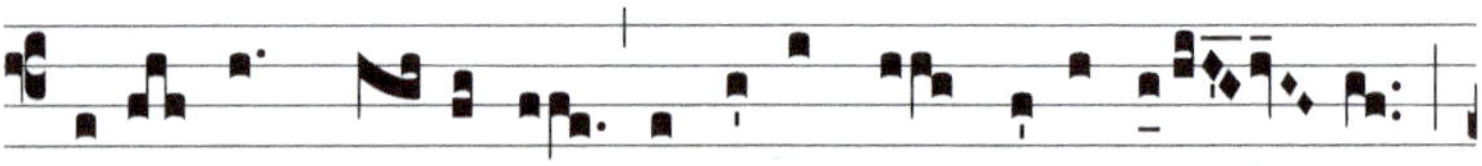

EPÚL-TO * Dó- mi-no,   signá-tum est monumén-   tum,

volvén- tes lá-pi-   dem ad ósti- um monumén-   ti : * Po-nén-

tes mí-li-   tes, qui custo-dí- rent   il-   lum. ℣. Acce-dén- tes

prínci-pes sa-cerdó-tum ad Pi-lá-   tum, pe-ti-   é-runt   il-   lum.

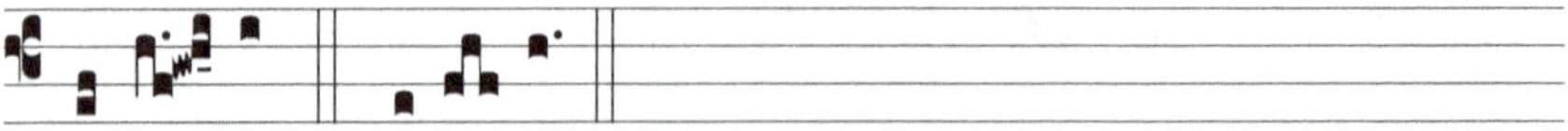

* Po-nén- tes. ℟. Sepúl- to.

℟. After the Lord was buried, they sealed the sepulchre, rolling a stone to the door of the sepulchre * Setting a watch to keep Him. ℣. The chief priests came together unto Pilate, and made that request unto him. ℟. Setting a watch to keep Him. ℟. After the Lord was buried, they sealed the sepulchre, rolling a stone to the door of the sepulchre, * Setting a watch to keep Him.

At Lauds

1. Ant.
4.c

O mors, * e-ro mors tu- a : morsus tu- us   e-ro, inférne.

ANTIPHON: O death, I will be thy death; * O grave, I will be thy destruction.

Psalm 50

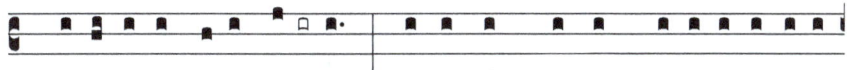

1. Mi-se-ré-re *me- i* **De-**   us, * se-cúndum magnam mi-se-ri-córdi- am

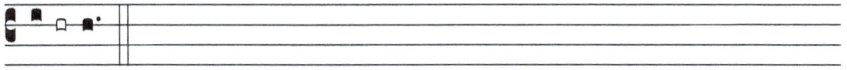

tu-   am.

1. Have mercy on me, O God, * according to Thy great mercy.

2. Et secúndum multitúdinem miseratió*num tu*árum, * dele ini-quitátem **me**am.

2. And according to the multitude of Thy tender mercies * blot out my iniquity.

3. Amplius lava me ab ini-qui*táte* **me**a: * et a peccáto meo **mun**-da me.

3. Wash me yet more from my iniquity, * and cleanse me from my sin.

4. Quóniam iniquitátem meam *ego co*gnósco: * et peccátum meum contra me est **sem**per.

4. For I know my iniquity, * and my sin is always before me.

5. Tibi soli peccávi, et malum co*ram te* **fe**ci: * ut justificéris in ser-mónibus tuis, et vincas cum judi**cá**ris.

5. To Thee only have I sinned, and have done evil before Thee: * that Thou mayst be justified in Thy words, and mayst overcome when Thou art judged.

6. Ecce enim in iniquitátibus concéptus sum: * et in peccátis concépit me mater mea.

7. Ecce enim veritátem dilexísti: * incérta et occúlta sapiéntiæ tuæ manifestásti mihi.

8. Aspérges me hyssópo, et mundábor: * lavábis me, et super nivem dealbábor.

9. Audítui meo dabis gáudium et lætítiam: * et exsultábunt ossa humiliáta.

10. Avérte fáciem tuam a peccátis meis: * et omnes iniquitátes meas dele.

11. Cor mundum crea in me, Deus: * et spíritum rectum ínnova in viscéribus meis.

12. Ne projícias me a fácie tua: * et spíritum sanctum tuum ne áuferas a me.

13. Redde mihi lætítiam salutáris tui: * et spíritu principáli confírma me.

14. Docébo iníquos vias tuas: * et ímpii ad te converténtur.

15. Líbera me de sanguínibus, Deus, Deus salútis meæ: * et exsultábit lingua mea justítiam tuam.

16. Dómine, lábia mea apéries: * et os meum annuntiábit laudem tuam.

17. Quóniam si voluísses sacrifícium, dedíssem útique: * holocáustis non delectáberis.

18. Sacrifícium Deo spíritus contribulátus: * cor contrítum et humiliátum, Deus, non despícies.

6. For behold I was conceived in iniquities; * and in sins did my mother conceive me.

7. For behold Thou hast loved truth: * the uncertain and hidden things of Thy wisdom Thou hast made manifest to me.

8. Thou shalt sprinkle me with hyssop, and I shall be cleansed: * Thou shalt wash me, and I shall be made whiter than snow.

9. To my hearing Thou shalt give joy and gladness: * and the bones that have been humbled shall rejoice.

10. Turn away Thy face from my sins, * and blot out all my iniquities.

11. Create a clean heart in me, O God: * and renew a right spirit within my bowels.

12. Cast me not away from Thy face; * and take not Thy holy spirit from me.

13. Restore unto me the joy of Thy salvation, * and strengthen me with a perfect spirit.

14. I will teach the unjust Thy ways: * and the wicked shall be converted to Thee.

15. Deliver me from blood, O God, Thou God of my salvation: * and my tongue shall extol Thy justice.

16. O Lord, Thou wilt open my lips: * and my mouth shall declare Thy praise.

17. For if Thou hadst desired sacrifice, I would indeed have given it: * with burnt offerings Thou wilt not be delighted.

18. A sacrifice to God is an afflicted spirit: * a contrite and humbled heart, O God, Thou wilt not despise.

19. Benígne fac, Dómine, in bona voluntáte *tua* **Si**on: * ut ædificéntur muri Jer**ú**salem.

19. Deal favourably, O Lord, in Thy good will with Sion; * that the walls of Jerusalem may be built up.

20. Tunc acceptábis sacrifícium justítiæ, oblatiónes, et *holo*cáusta: * tunc impónent super altáre tuum vítulos.

20. Then shalt Thou accept the sacrifice of justice, oblations and whole burnt offerings: * then shall they lay calves upon Thy altar.

1. Ant.
4.c

O mors, e-ro mors tu- a : morsus tu- us e-ro, inférne.

The tenth candle is extinguished.

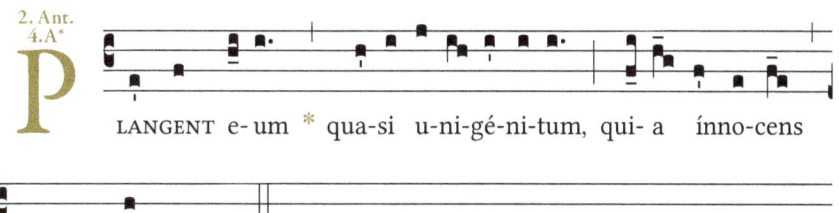

2. Ant.
4.A*

P LANGENT e- um * qua-si u-ni-gé-ni-tum, qui- a ínno-cens

Dómi-nus occí-sus est.

ANTIPHON: They shall mourn for Him * as one mourneth for an only son, for the innocent Lord hath been put to death.

PSALM 91

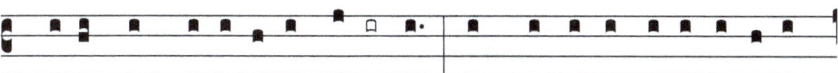

1. Bonum est confi- té- ri **Dó**mi- no: * et psál- le- re nómi- ni *tu- o,*

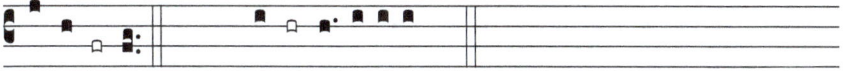

Al**tís**sime.   *Flex :* Dómi-ne, †

1. It is good to give praise to the Lord: * and to sing to Thy name, O most High.

2. Ad annuntiándum mane misericórdiam tuam: * et veritátem tuam per noctem.

3. In decachórdo, psaltério: * cum cántico, in cíthara.

4. Quia delectásti me, Dómine, in factúra tua: * et in opéribus mánuum tuárum exsultábo.

5. Quam magnificáta sunt ópera tua, Dómine! * nimis profúndæ factæ sunt cogitatiónes tuæ.

6. Vir insípiens non cognóscet: * et stultus non intélliget hæc.

7. Cum exórti fúerint peccatóres sicut fænum: * et apparúerint omnes, qui operántur iniquitátem.

8. Ut intéreant in sæculum sæculi: * tu autem Altíssimus in ætérnum, Dómine.

9. Quóniam ecce inimíci tui, Dómine, † quóniam ecce inimíci tui períbunt: * et dispergéntur omnes, qui operántur iniquitátem.

10. Et exaltábitur sicut unicórnis cornu meum: * et senéctus mea in misericórdia úberi.

11. Et despéxit óculus meus inimícos meos: * et in insurgéntibus in me malignántibus áudiet auris mea.

12. Justus, ut palma florébit: * sicut cedrus Líbani multiplicábitur.

13. Plantáti in domo Dómini, * in átriis domus Dei nostri florébunt.

14. Adhuc multiplicabúntur in senécta úberi: * et bene patiéntes erunt, ut annúntient:

2. To show forth Thy mercy in the morning, * and Thy truth in the night:

3. Upon an instrument of ten strings, upon the psaltery: * with a canticle upon the harp.

4. For Thou hast given me, O Lord, a delight in Thy doings: * and in the works of Thy hands I shall rejoice.

5. O Lord, how great are Thy works! * Thy thoughts are exceeding deep.

6. The senseless man shall not know: * nor will the fool understand these things.

7. When the wicked shall spring up as grass: * and all the workers of iniquity shall appear:

8. That they may perish for ever and ever: * but Thou, O Lord, art most high for evermore.

9. For behold Thy enemies, O Lord, † for behold Thy enemies shall perish: * and all the workers of iniquity shall be scattered.

10. But my horn shall be exalted like that of the unicorn: * and my old age in plentiful mercy.

11. My eye also hath looked down upon my enemies: * and my ear shall hear of the downfall of the malignant that rise up against me.

12. The just shall flourish like the palm tree: * he shall grow up like the cedar of Libanus.

13. They that are planted in the house of the Lord * shall flourish in the courts of the house of our God.

14. They shall still increase in a fruitful old age: * and shall be well treated, that they may show,

15. Quóniam rectus Dóminus, *Deus* **no**ster: * et non est in*íquitas in* **e**o.

15. That the Lord our God is righteous, * and there is no iniquity in Him.

LANGENT e- um qua-si u-ni-gé-ni-tum, qui- a ínno-cens

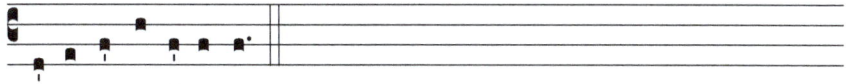

Dómi-nus occí-sus est.

The eleventh candle is extinguished.

T-TÉN-DI-TE * u-ni-vérsi pópu-li, et vi-dé- te do-ló-rem

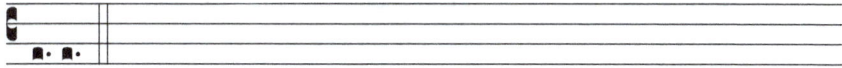

me- um.

ANTIPHON: O all ye nations, behold * and see my sorrow.

PSALM 63

1. Exáudi, De- us, o-ra-ti- ónem **me-** am cum **dé**pre-cor : * a timó-re

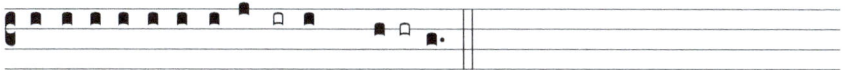

in-imí-ci é-ri-pe á-nimam **me-** am.

1. Hear, O God, my prayer, when I make supplication to Thee: * deliver my soul from the fear of the enemy.

2. Protexísti me a convéntu **ma-lignán**tium: * a multitúdine operántium in**i**quit**á**tem.

3. Quia exacuérunt ut gládium **lin**guas **su**as: * intendérunt arcum rem amáram, ut sagíttent in occúltis im**maculá**tum.

4. Súbito sagittábunt eum, et **non** ti**mé**bunt: * firmavérunt sibi ser**mó**nem **ne**quam.

5. Narravérunt ut abs**cón**derent **lá**queos: * dixérunt: Quis vi**dé**bit eos?

6. Scrutáti sunt in**i**quit**á**tes: * defecérunt scru**tán**tes scru**tí**nio.

7. Accédet homo **ad** cor **al**tum: * et exalt**á**bitur **De**us.

8. Sagíttæ parvulórum factæ sunt **plagæ** e**ó**rum: * et infirmátæ sunt contra eos **linguæ** e**ó**rum.

9. Conturbáti sunt omnes qui vi**dé**bant eos: * et tímuit **om**nis **ho**mo.

10. Et annuntiavérunt **ó**pera **Dei**, * et facta ejus in**tel**lexé**runt.

11. Lætábitur justus in Dómino, et sper**á**bit in **e**o: * et laudabúntur omnes **rec**ti **cor**de.

2. Thou hast protected me from the assembly of the malignant; * from the multitude of the workers of iniquity.

3. For they have whetted their tongues like a sword; * they have bent their bow a bitter thing, to shoot in secret the undefiled.

4. They will shoot at him on a sudden, and will not fear: * they are resolute in wickedness.

5. They have talked of hiding snares; * they have said: Who shall see them?

6. They have searched after iniquities: * they have failed in their search.

7. Man shall come to a deep heart: * and God shall be exalted.

8. The arrows of children are their wounds: * and their tongues against them are made weak.

9. All that saw them were troubled; * and every man was afraid.

10. And they declared the works of God: * and understood His doings.

11. The just shall rejoice in the Lord, and shall hope in Him: * and all the upright in heart shall be praised.

3. Ant. 7.b

A-T-TÉN-DI-TE u-ni-vérsi pópu-li, et vi-dé- te do-ló-rem

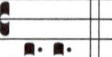

me- um.

The twelfth candle is extinguished.

4. Ant.
2.D

A por-ta ínfe-ri * é-ru- e, Dómi-ne, á-nimam me- am.

Antiphon: O Lord, deliver my soul * from the gates of the grave.

Canticle of Ezechias

1. Ego di-xi: In dimí-di- o di- é-rum me- **ó**- rum * va-dam ad por*tas*

ínfe-ri. *Flex :* vi-ta me- a: †

1. I said: In the midst of my days * I shall go to the gates of hell:

2. Quæsívi resíduum annórum meórum. * Dixi: Non vidébo Dóminum Deum in terra *vivén*tium.

3. Non aspíciam hóminem **ul**tra, * et habitatórem *qui*étis.

4. Generátio mea abláta est, et convolúta est **a** me, * quasi tabernáculum *pa***st**órum.

5. Præcísa est velut a texénte, vita mea: † dum adhuc ordírer, suc**cí**dit me: * de mane usque ad vésperam fí*ni*es me.

6. Sperábam usque ad **ma**ne, * quasi leo sic contrívit ómnia os*sa* **me**a:

7. De mane usque ad vésperam fínies me: sicut pullus hirúndinis sic clamábo, * meditábor ut *co***lúm**ba:

8. Attenuáti sunt óculi **mei**, * suspiciéntes in *ex***cél**sum.

2. I sought for the residue of my years. * I said: I shall not see the Lord God in the land of the living.

3. I shall behold man no more, * nor the inhabitant of rest.

4. My generation is at an end, and it is rolled away from me, * as a shepherd's tent.

5. My life is cut off, as by a weaver: † whilst I was yet but beginning, He cut me off: * from morning even to night Thou wilt make an end of me.

6. I hoped till morning, * as a lion so hath He broken all my bones:

7. From morning even to night Thou wilt make an end of me. * I will cry like a young swallow, I will meditate like a dove:

8. My eyes are weakened * looking upward:

9. Dómine, vim pátior, respónde **pro** me. * Quid dicam, aut quid respondébit mihi, cum *ipse* **fé**cerit?

10. Recogitábo tibi omnes annos **me**os * in amaritúdine ánim*æ* me*æ*.

11. Dómine, si sic vívitur, et in tálibus vita spíritus mei, † corrípies me, et vivifi**cá**bis me. * Ecce, in pace amaritúdo mea a*mar*í*s*sima:

12. Tu autem eruísti ánimam meam ut non períret: * projecísti post tergum tuum ómnia peccá*ta* **me**a.

13. Quia non inférnus confitébitur tibi, † neque mors lau**dá**bit te: * non exspectábunt qui descéndunt in lacum, veritá*tem* **tu**am.

14. Vivens vivens ipse confitébitur tibi, sicut et ego **hó**die: * pater fíliis notam fáciet veritá*tem* **tu**am.

15. Dómine, salvum **me** fac * et psalmos nostros cantábimus cunctis diébus vitæ nostræ in do*mo* **Dó**mini.

9. Lord, I suffer violence, answer Thou for me. * What shall I say, or what shall He answer for me, whereas He Himself hath done it?

10. I will recount to Thee all my years * in the bitterness of my soul.

11. O Lord, if man's life be such, and the life of my spirit be in such things as these, † Thou shalt correct me, and make me to live. * Behold in peace is my bitterness most bitter:

12. But Thou hast delivered my soul that it should not perish, * Thou hast cast all my sins behind Thy back.

13. For hell shall not confess to Thee, † neither shall death praise Thee: * nor shall they that go down into the pit, look for Thy truth.

14. The living, the living, he shall give praise to Thee, as I do this day: * the father shall make Thy truth known to the children.

15. O Lord, save me, and we will sing our psalms all the days of our life * in the house of the Lord.

4. Ant.
2.D

A por-ta ínfe-ri é-ru-e, Dómi-ne, á-nimam me-am.

The thirteenth candle is extinguished.

5. Ant.
8.c

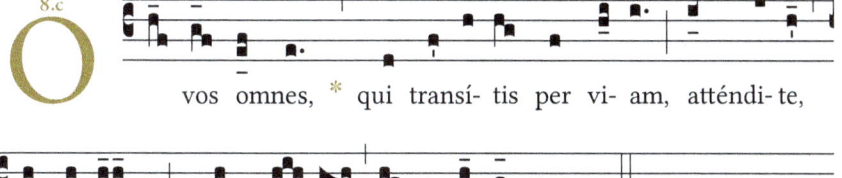

vos omnes, * qui transí- tis per vi- am, atténdi- te,

et vi-dé- te si est do- lor   sic-ut do- lor me- us.

ANTIPHON: O all ye that pass by * behold, and see if there be any sorrow like unto my sorrow.

PSALM 150

1. Laudá-te Dómi-num in sanctis **e-** jus : * laudá-te e- um in firmamén-

to vir*tú-tis* **e-** jus. *Flex:* bene-sonánti-bus : †

1. Praise ye the Lord in His holy places: * praise ye Him in the firmament of His power.

2. Laudáte eum in virtútibus **ejus:** * laudáte eum secúndum multitúdinem magnitú*dinis* **ejus.**

2. Praise ye Him for His mighty acts: * praise ye Him according to the multitude of His greatness.

3. Laudáte eum in sono **tubæ:** * laudáte eum in psaltério, *et* **cí**thara.

3. Praise Him with sound of trumpet: * praise Him with psaltery and harp.

4. Laudáte eum in týmpano, et **cho**ro: * laudáte eum in chor*dis,* *et* **ór**gano.

4. Praise Him with timbrel and choir: * praise Him with strings and organs.

5. Laudáte eum in cýmbalis benesonántibus: † laudáte eum in cýmbalis jubilatiónis: * omnis spíritus *laudet* **Dó**minum.

5. Praise Him on high sounding cymbals: † praise Him on cymbals of joy: * let every spirit praise the Lord.

5. Ant.
8.c

O vos omnes, qui transí- tis per vi- am, atténdi- te,

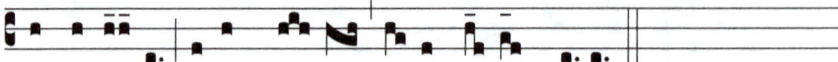

et vi-dé- te si est do- lor sic-ut do- lor me- us.

The fourteenth candle is extinguished.

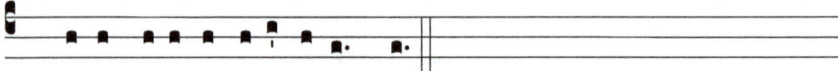

℣. Ca-ro me- a requi- éscet in spe.

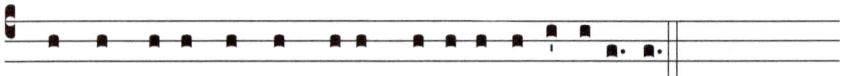

℟. Et non da-bis Sanctum tu-um vi-dé-re corrupti- ó-nem.

Or:

℣. Ca-ro me- a requi- éscet in spe.

℟. Et non da-bis Sanctum tu-um vi-dé-re corrupti- ónem.

℣. My flesh shall rest in hope.
℟. Neither wilt Thou suffer thine Holy One to see corruption.

BENEDÍCTUS

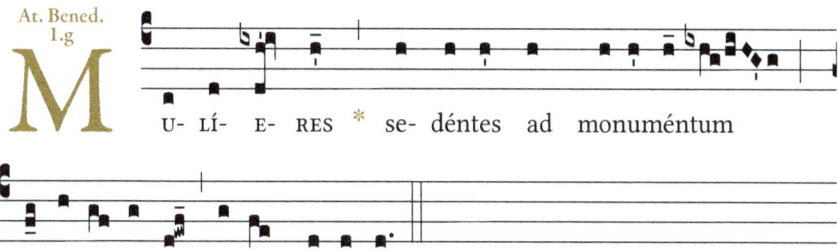

U- LÍ- E- RES * se- déntes ad monuméntum

lamenta-bántur, flentes Dómi-num.

ANTIPHON: There were women sitting over against the sepulchre * weeping, and making lamentation for the Lord.

1. Bene-díctus ✠ Dómi-*nus, De- us* **Isra**- ël: * qui- a vi-si-tá-vit, et fe-cit

red-empti- ónem *ple-bis* **su**- æ:

1. Blessed be the Lord ✠ God of Israel; * because He hath visited and wrought the redemption of His people:

2. Et eréxit cornu *salútis* **no**bis: * in domo David, pú*eri* **sui**.

2. And hath raised up an horn of salvation to us, * in the house of David His servant:

The first altar candle is extinguished

3. Sicut locútus est *per os sanct*ó*rum,* * qui a sǽculo sunt, prophet*árum* **e**jus:

3. As He spoke by the mouth of His holy Prophets, * who are from the beginning:

4. Salútem ex in*imícis* **no**stris, * et de manu ómnium, *qui o*dé*r*unt nos.

4. Salvation from our enemies, * and from the hand of all that hate us:

The second altar candle is extinguished

5. Ad faciéndam misericórdiam cum *pátribus* **no**stris: * et memorári testaménti *sui* **san**cti.

5. To perform mercy to our fathers, * and to remember His holy testament,

6. Jusjurándum, quod jurávit ad Abra*ham patrem* **no**strum, * datú*rum se* **no**bis:

6. The oath, which He swore to Abraham our father, * that He would grant to us,

The third altar candle is extinguished

7. Ut sine timóre, de manu in- imicórum nostró*rum* *libe***rá**ti, * servi*ámus* **ill**i.

7. That being delivered from the hand of our enemies, * we may serve Him without fear,

8. In sanctitáte, et justíti*a coram* **ip**so, * ómnibus di*ébus* **no**stris.

8. In holiness and justice before Him, * all our days.

The fourth altar candle is extinguished

9. Et tu, puer, Prophéta Altíss*imi* *vo***cáb**eris: * præíbis enim ante fáciem Dómini, paráre *vias* **e**jus:

9. And thou, child, shalt be called the prophet of the Highest: * for thou shalt go before the face of the Lord to prepare His ways:

10. Ad dandam sciéntiam salú*tis ple-* bi **e**jus: * in remissiónem peccató*rum e***ó**rum:

10. To give knowledge of salvation to His people, * unto the remission of their sins:

The fifth altar candle is extinguished

11. Per víscera misericórdi*æ Dei* **no**stri: * in quibus visitávit nos, óri*ens ex* **al**to:

11. Through the bowels of the mer- cy of our God, * in which the Orient from on high hath visited us:

12. Illumináre his, qui in ténebris, et in um*bra mortis* **se**dent: * ad dirigén- dos pedes nostros in *viam* **pa**cis.

12. To enlighten them that sit in darkness, and in the shadow of death: * to direct our feet into the way of peace.

The sixth altar candle is extinguished

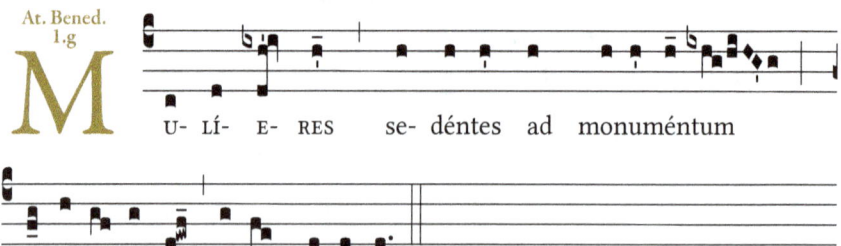

At. Bened.
1.g

MU- LÍ- E- RES se- déntes ad monuméntum

lamenta-bántur, flentes Dómi-num.

At the conclusion of the antiphon following the Benedictus, *the remaining candle is removed and "hidden" while all kneel and sing:*

ANTIPHON: Christ became obedient for us unto death, even to the death of the cross. For which cause God also hath exalted Him, and hath given Him a name which is above all names.

At the conclusion of the antiphon Christus factus est, *the* Pater noster *is said in silence.*

Psalm 50

Recited recto tono

1. Miserére mei, Deus, * secúndum magnam misericórdiam tuam.

2. Et secúndum multitúdinem miseratiónum tuárum, * dele iniquitátem meam.

3. Amplius lava me ab iniquitáte mea : * et a peccáto meo munda me.

4. Quóniam iniquitátem meam ego cognósco : * et peccátum meum contra me est semper.

5. Tibi soli peccávi, et malum coram te feci : * ut justificéris in sermónibus tuis, et vincas cum judicáris.

6. Ecce enim in iniquitátibus concéptus sum : * et in peccátis concépit me mater mea.

7. Ecce enim veritátem dilexísti : * incérta et occúlta sapiéntiæ tuæ manifestásti mihi.

8. Aspérges me hyssópo, et mundábor : * lavábis me, et super nivem dealbábor.

9. Audítui meo dabis gáudium et lætítiam : * et exsultábunt ossa humiliáta.

10. Avérte fáciem tuam a peccátis meis : * et omnes iniquitátes meas dele.

11. Cor mundum crea in me, Deus : * et spíritum rectum ínnova in viscéribus meis.

12. Ne projícias me a fácie tua : * et spíritum sanctum tuum ne áuferas a me.

1: Have mercy on me, O God, * according to thy great mercy.

2. And according to the multitude of Thy tender mercies * blot out my iniquity.

3. Wash me yet more from my iniquity, * and cleanse me from my sin.

4. For I know my iniquity, * and my sin is always before me.

5. To Thee only have I sinned, and have done evil before Thee: * that Thou mayst be justified in Thy words, and mayst overcome when Thou art judged.

6. For behold I was conceived in iniquities; * and in sins did my mother conceive me.

7. For behold Thou hast loved truth: * the uncertain and hidden things of Thy wisdom Thou hast made manifest to me.

8. Thou shalt sprinkle me with hyssop, and I shall be cleansed: * Thou shalt wash me, and I shall be made whiter than snow.

9. To my hearing Thou shalt give joy and gladness: * and the bones that have been humbled shall rejoice.

10. Turn away Thy face from my sins, * and blot out all my iniquities.

11. Create a clean heart in me, O God: * and renew a right spirit within my bowels.

12. Cast me not away from Thy face; * and take not Thy holy spirit from me.

13. Redde mihi lætítiam salutáris tui : * et spíritu principáli confírma me.

14. Docébo iníquos vias tuas : * et ímpii ad te converténtur.

15. Líbera me de sanguínibus, Deus, Deus salútis meæ : * et exsultábit lingua mea justítiam tuam.

16. Dómine, lábia mea apéries : * et os meum annuntiábit laudem tuam.

17. Quóniam si voluísses sacrifícium, dedíssem útique : * holocáustis non delectáberis.

18. Sacrifícium Deo spíritus contribulátus : * cor contrítum et humiliátum, Deus, non despícies.

19. Benígne fac, Dómine, in bona voluntáte tua Sion : * ut ædificéntur muri Jerúsalem.

20. Tunc acceptábis sacrifícium justítiæ, oblatiónes, et holocáusta : * tunc impónent super altáre tuum vítulos.

13. Restore unto me the joy of Thy salvation, * and strengthen me with a perfect spirit.

14. I will teach the unjust Thy ways: * and the wicked shall be converted to Thee.

15. Deliver me from blood, O God, Thou God of my salvation: * and my tongue shall extol Thy justice.

16. O Lord, Thou wilt open my lips: * and my mouth shall declare Thy praise.

17. For if Thou hadst desired sacrifice, I would indeed have given it: * with burnt offerings Thou wilt not be delighted.

18. A sacrifice to God is an afflicted spirit: * a contrite and humbled heart, O God, Thou wilt not despise.

19. Deal favourably, O Lord, in Thy good will with Sion; * that the walls of Jerusalem may be built up.

20. Then shalt Thou accept the sacrifice of justice, oblations and whole burnt offerings: * then shall they lay calves upon Thy altar.

Sung recto tono or to ferial tone without Orémus.

RÉSPICE, quǽsumus, Dómine, super hanc famíliam tuam, pro qua Dóminus noster Jesus Christus non dubitávit mánibus tradi nocéntium, et crucis subíre torméntum:

[*Dícitur sub siléntio:* Qui tecum vivit et regnat in unitáte Spíritus Sancti, Deus, per ómnia sǽcula sæculórum. ℟. Amen.]

LOOK down, we beseech Thee, O Lord, on this Thy family, for which our Lord Jesus Christ did not hesitate to be delivered up into the hands of wicked men, and to suffer the torment of the Cross.

[*Said in silence:* Who with thee liveth and reigneth, in the unity of the Holy Ghost, God, world without end. ℟. Amen.]

The Strépitus *is begun by the celebrant and continues until the "hidden" candle is brought back out. All then rise and retire in silence.*

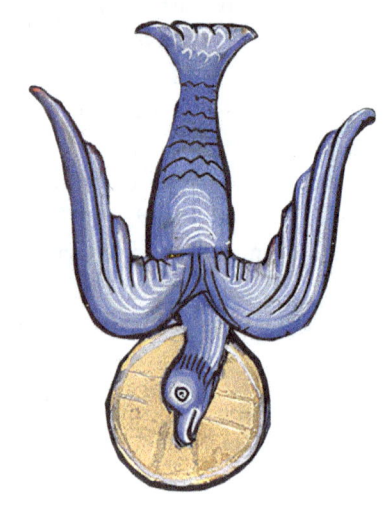

EASTER VIGIL

THE BLESSING OF THE FIRE

At a convenient time, the altar is prepared, and the Hours are recited in choir, but the candles are not lighted until the beginning of Mass. Meanwhile fire is struck from a flint outside the church and coals are kindled from it. Near at hand lies a vessel containing five large grains of incense to be set in the paschal candle. The celebrant wearing amice, alb, girdle, stole and violet cope, goes to the church door accompanied by his ministers with the processional cross, holy water and incense, and blesses the new fire. The celebrant first blesses the new fire, saying:

℣. Dóminus vobíscum.
℟. Et cum spíritu tuo.

℣. The Lord be with you.
℟. And with thy spirit.

ORÉMUS.

LET US PRAY.

DEUS, qui per Fílium tuum, angulárem scílicet lápidem, claritátis tuæ ignem fidélibus contulísti: prodúctum e sílice, nostris profutúrum úsibus, novum hunc ignem sanctí✠fica: et concéde nobis, ita per hæc festa paschália cæléstibus desidériis inflammári; ut ad perpétuæ claritátis, puris méntibus, valeámus festa pertíngere. Per eúndem Christum Dóminum nostrum.
℟. Amen.

O GOD, Who hast bestowed on the faithful the fire of Thy brightness by Thy Son, Who is the Corner-stone, hallow ✠ this new fire produced from a flint that it may be profitable to us: and grant that during this Paschal festival we may be so inflamed with heavenly desires, that with pure minds we may come to the solemnity of perpetual light. Through the same Christ our Lord.
℟. Amen.

ORÉMUS.

ORÉMUS.

Dómine Deus, Pater omnípotens, lumen indefíciens, qui es cónditor ómnium lúminum: béne✠dic hoc lumen, quod a te sanctificátum atque benedíctum est, qui illuminásti omnem mundum: ut ab eo lúmine accendámur, atque illuminémur igne claritátis tuæ: et sicut illuminásti Móysen exeúntem de Ægýpto, ita illúmines corda, et sensus nostros; ut ad vitam et lucem ætérnam perveníre mereámur. Per Christum, Dóminum nostrum.

℟. Amen.

LET US PRAY.

O Lord God, almighty Father, never-failing Light, Who art the Creator of all lights, bless this light that is blessed ✠ and sanctified by Thee, Who hast enlightened the whole world: that we may be inflamed with that light and enlightened by the fire of Thy brightness: and as Thou didst give light to Moses when he went out of Egypt, so enlighten our hearts and senses, that we may be found worthy to arrive at light and life everlasting. Through Christ our Lord.

℟. Amen.

ORÉMUS.

Dómine sancte, Pater omnípotens, ætérne Deus: benedicéntibus nobis hunc ignem in nómine tuo, et unigéniti Fílii tui, Dei ac Dómini nostri Jesu Christi, et Spíritus Sancti, cooperári dignéris; et ádjuva nos contra igníta tela inimíci, et illústra grátia cælésti: Qui vivis et regnas cum eódem Unigénito tuo, et Spíritu Sancto, Deus: per ómnia sæcula sæculórum.

℟. Amen.

LET US PRAY.

O Holy Lord, almighty Father, everlasting God: vouchsafe to co-operate with us, who bless this fire in Thy Name, and in that of Thine only-begotten Son Jesus Christ our Lord and God, and of the Holy Ghost: help us against the fiery darts of the enemy, and illumine us with Thy heavenly grace. Who livest and reignest with the same Thine only-begotten Son and the Holy Ghost, one God, for ever and ever.

℟. Amen.

He then blesses the five grains of incense to be placed in the paschal candle, saying the following prayer:

Véniat, quǽsumus, omnípotens Deus, super hoc incénsum larga tuæ bene✠dictiónis infúsio: et hunc noctúrnum splendórem invisíbilis regenerátor accénde; ut non solum sacrifícium, quod hac nocte litátum est,

May the abundant outpouring of Thy ✠ blessing, we beseech Thee, almighty God, descend upon this incense: and do Thou, O invisible Regenerator, lighten this nocturnal brightness, that not only the sacrifice

arcána lúminis tui admixtióne refúl-geat; sed in quocúmque loco ex hujus sanctificatiónis mystério aliquid fúerit deportátum, expúlsa diabólicæ fraudis nequítia, virtus tuæ majestátis assístat. Per Christum, Dóminum nostrum.

R̃. Amen.

that is offered this night may shine by the secret mixture of Thy light: but also into whatever place anything of this mysterious sanctification shall be brought, there the power of Thy Majesty may be present and all the malicious artifices of Satan may be defeated. Through Christ our Lord.

R̃. Amen.

During this prayer an acolyte fills the thurible with coals from the blessed fire. The celebrant then puts incense into the thurible, blessing it in the usual manner: he sprinkles the grains of incense and the new fire thrice with holy water, saying the Asperges Me, *without the psalm, and thrice incenses them. All the lamps in the church are extinguished, that they may afterward be lighted from the blessed fire. The deacon, vested in a white dalmatic, now takes up a reed with a triple candle fixed on the top: and all enter the church. The thurifer goes first, with an acolyte carrying in a dish the five grains of incense; the subdeacon follows with the cross, and the clergy in order; then the deacon with the reed and after him the officiating celebrant. When the deacon has entered the church, he lowers the reed, and an acolyte, bringing a taper lighted from the new fire, lights one of the three candles set on the top; and the deacon, raising the reed, kneels down, as do all the rest, except the subdeacon who carries the cross, and sings:*

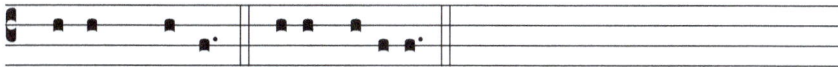

V̌. Lumen Chri-sti. R̃. De- o grá-ti- as.

V̌. The light of Christ. R̃. Thanks be to God.

In the middle of the church the second branch of the candle is lighted, with the same ceremonies; and the third branch is lighted in the sanctuary, the deacon each time singing Lumen Christi *on a higher tone.*

THE BLESSING OF THE PASCHAL CANDLE

The celebrant goes up to the epistle corner and the deacon takes the book and asks the celebrant's blessing as at the Gospel. The blessing is given in the following words:

DÓMINUS sit in corde tuo et in lábiis tuis: ut digne et competénter annúnties suum paschále præcónium: In nómine Patris, et Fílii, ✠ et Spíritus Sancti.
℟. Amen.

MAY THE LORD be in thy heart and on thy lips, that thou mayest worthily and fitly proclaim His Paschal praise. In the Name of the Father, and of the Son, ✠ and of the Holy Ghost.
℟. Amen.

Then the deacon goes up to the lectern, puts the book on it and incenses it. At his right hand stands the subdeacon with the cross, and the thurifer, at his left two acolytes holding the reed and the grains of incense which are to be fixed in the candle. All rise and stand and the deacon sings:

EXSULTET

Exsúltet jam Angélica turba cælórum: exsúltent divína mystéria: et pro tanti Regis victória tuba ínsonet salutáris. Gáudeat et tellus tantis irradiáta fulgóribus: et ætérni Regis splendóre illustráta, totíus orbis se séntiat amisísse calíginem. Lætétur et mater Ecclésia, tanti lúminis adornáta fulgóribus: et magnis populórum vócibus hæc aula resúltet. Quaprópter astántes vos, fratres caríssimi, ad tam miram hujus sancti lúminis claritátem, una mecum, quæso, Dei omnipoténtis misericórdiam invocáte. Ut, qui me non meis méritis intra Levitárum númerum dignatus est aggregáre: lúminis sui claritátem infúndens, Cérei hujus laudem implére perfíciat. Per Dominum nostrum Jesum Christum, Fílium suum: qui cum eo vivit et regnat in unitáte Spíritus Sancti Deus :

Let the angelic choirs of Heaven now rejoice; let the divine Mysteries rejoice; and let the trumpet of salvation sound forth the victory of so great a King. Let the earth also rejoice, made radiant by such splendor; and, enlightened with the brightness of the eternal King, let it know that the darkness of the whole world is scattered. Let our mother the Church also rejoice, adorned with the brightness of so great a light; and let this temple resound with the loud acclamations of the people. Wherefore I beseech you, most beloved brethren, who are here present in the wondrous brightness of this holy light, to invoke wtih me the mercy of almighty God. That He who has vouchsafed to admit me among the Levites, without any merits of mine, would pour forth the brightness of His light upon me, and

Per omnia sǽcula sæculórum.
℟. Amen.
℣. Dóminus vobíscum.
℟. Et cum Spíritu tuo.
℣. Sursum corda.
℟. Habémus ad Dóminum.

℣. Grátias agámus Dómino Deo nostro.
℟. Dignum et justum est.

Vere dignum et justum est invisíbilem Deum Patrem omnipoténtem Filiúmque ejus unigénitum, Dóminum nostrum Jesum Christum, toto cordis ac mentis afféctu et vocis ministério personáre. Qui pro nobis ætérno Patri Adæ débitum solvit: et véteris piáculi cautiónem pio cruóre detérsit. Hæc sunt enim festa paschália, in quibus verus ille Agnus occíditur, cujus sánguine postes fidélium consecrántur. Hæc nox est, in qua primum patres nostros, fílios Israël edúctos de Ægýpto, Mare Rubrum sicco vestígio transíre fecísti. Hæc ígitur nox est, quæ peccatórum ténebras colúmnæ illuminatióne purgávit. Hæc nox est, quæ hódie per univérsum mundum in Christo credéntes, a vítiis sǽculi et calígine peccatórum segregátos, reddit grátiæ, sóciat sanctitáti. Hæc nox est, in qua, destrúctis vínculis mortis, Christus ab ínferis victor ascéndit. Nihil enim nobis nasci prófuit, nisi rédimi profuísset.

enable me to perfect the praise of this wax candle. Through our Lord Jesus Christ His Son, Who with Him and the Holy Ghost liveth and reigneth one God:

World without end.
℟. Amen.
℣. The Lord be with you.
℟. And with thy spirit.
℣. Lift up your hearts.
℟. We have them lifted up to the Lord.
℣. Let us give thanks to the Lord our God.
℟. It is meet and just.

It is truly meet and right to proclaim with all our heart and all the affection of our mind, and with the ministry of our voices, the invisible God, the Father almighty, and His only-begotten Son our Lord Jesus Christ, who repaid for us to His eternal Father the debt of Adam, and by the merciful shedding of His Blood, cancelled the debt incurred by original sin. For this is the Paschal Festival; in which that true Lamb is slain, with Whose Blood the doorposts of the faithful are consecrated. This is the night in which Thou didst formerly cause our forefathers, the children of Israel, when brought out of Egypt, to pass through the Red Sea with dry foot. This, therefore, is the night which dissipated the darkness of sinners by the light of the pillar. This is the night which at this time throughout the world restores to grace and unites in sanctity those that believe in Christ, and are separated from the vices of the world and

O mira circa nos tuæ pietátis dignátio! O inæstimábilis diléctio caritátis: ut servum redímeres, Fílium tradidísti! O certe necessárium Adæ peccátum, quod Christi morte delétum est! O felix culpa, quæ talem ac tantum méruit habére Redemptórem! O vere beáta nox, quæ sola méruit scire tempus et horam, in qua Christus ab ínferis resurréxit! Hæc nox est, de qua scriptum est: Et nox sicut dies illuminábitur: Et nox illuminátio mea in delíciis meis. Hujus ígitur sanctificátio noctis fugat scélera, culpas lavat: et reddit innocéntiam lapsis et mæstis lætítiam. Fugat ódia, concórdiam parat et curvat impéria.

the darkness of sinners. This is the night in which, destroying the chains of death, Christ arose victorious from the grave. For it would have profited us nothing to have been born, unless redemption had also been bestowed upon us. O wondrous condescension of Thy mercy towards us! O inestimable affection of love: that Thou mightest redeem a slave, Thou didst deliver up Thy Son! O truly needful sin of Adam, which was blotted out by the death of Christ! O happy fault, that merited to possess such and so great a Redeemer! O truly blessed night, which alone deserved to know the time and hour when Christ rose again from hell! This is the night of which it is written: And the night shall be as clear as the day; and the night is my light in my delights. Therefore the hallowing of this night puts to flight all wickedness, cleanses sins, and restores innocence to the fallen, and gladness to the sorrowful. It drives forth hatreds, it prepares concord, and brings down haughtiness.

Here the deacon fixes the five blessed grains of incense in the paschal candle in the form of a cross.

IN hujus ígitur noctis grátia, súscipe, sancte Pater, incénsi hujus sacrifícium vespertínum: quod tibi in hac Cérei oblatióne sollémni, per ministrórum manus de opéribus apum, sacro sancta reddit Ecclésia. Sed jam colúmnæ hujus præcónia nóvimus, quam in honórem Dei rútilans ignis accéndit.

WHEREFORE, in this sacred night, receive, O holy Father, the evening sacrifice of this incense, which holy Church renders to Thee by the hands of Thy ministers in the solemn offering of this wax candle, made out the work of bees. Now also we know the praises of this pillar, which the shining fire enkindles to the honor of God.

Here the deacon lights the paschal candle with one of the three candles on the reed.

QUI licet sit divísus in partes, mutuáti tamen lúminis detriménta non novit. Alitur enim liquántibus ceris, quas in substántiam pretiósæ hujus lámpadis, apis mater edúxit.

WHICH fire, although divided into parts, suffers no loss from its light being borrowed. For it is nourished by the melting wax, which the mother bee produced for the substance of this precious light.

Here the lamps are lighted.

O VERE beáta nox, quæ exspoliávit Ægýptios, ditávit Hebræos! Nox, in qua terrénis cæléstia, humánis divína jungúntur. Orámus ergo te, Dómine : ut Céreus iste in honórem tui nóminis consecrátus, ad noctis hujus calíginem destruéndam, indefíciens persevéret. Et in odórem suavitátis accéptus, supérnis lumináribus misceátur. Flammas ejus lúcifer matutínus invéniat. Ille, inquam, lúcifer, qui nescit occásum. Ille, qui regréssus ab ínferis, humáno géneri serénus illúxit. Precámur ergo te, Dómine : ut nos fámulos tuos, omnémque clerum, et devotíssimum pópulum: una cum beatíssimo Papa nostro **N.** et Antístite nostro **N.** quiéte témporum concéssa, in his paschálibus gáudiis, assídua protectióne régere, gubernáre et conserváre dignéris. Per eúndem Dóminum nostrum Jesum Christum, Fílium tuum: Qui tecum vivit et regnat in unitáte Spíritus Sancti Deus: per ómnia sæcula sæculórum.

O TRULY blessed night, which plundered the Egyptians and enriched the Hebrews! A night in which heavenly things are united to those of earth, and things divine to those which are of man. We beseech Thee, therefore, O Lord, that this wax candle hallowed in honor of Thy Name, may continue to burn to dissipate the darkness of this night. And being accepted as a sweet savor, may be united with the heavenly lights. Let the morning star find its flame alight. That star, I mean, which knows no setting. He Who returning from hell, serenely shone forth upon mankind. We beseech Thee therefore, O Lord, that Thou wouldst grant peaceful times during this Paschal Festival, and vouchsafe to rule, govern, and keep with Thy constant protection us Thy servants, and all the clergy, and the devout people, together with our most holy Father, Pope **N.** and our Bishop **N.** Through the same Jesus Christ, Thy Son, our Lord, who with Thee and the Holy Ghost liveth and reigneth one God for ever and ever.

℟. Amen.

℟. Amen.

THE PROPHECIES

After the blessing of the paschal candle the deacon lays aside his white dalmatic and puts on a violet one, and the officiating celebrant takes off his violet cope and puts on a violet chasuble. The prophecies are then chanted without any title, while the celebrant, standing at the epistle corner, reads them in a low voice.

FIRST PROPHECY
Genesis 1: 1-31; 2: 1-2

IN princípio creávit Deus cælum et terram. Terra autem erat inánis et vácua, et ténebræ erant super fáciem abýssi: et Spíritus Dei ferebátur super aquas. Dixítque Deus: Fiat lux. Et facta est lux. Et vidit Deus lucem, quod esset bona: et divísit lucem a ténebris. Appellavítque lucem Diem, et ténebras Noctem: factúmque est véspere et mane, dies unus.

Dixit quoque Deus: Fiat firmaméntum in médio aquárum: et dívidat aquas ab aquis. Et fecit Deus firmaméntum, divisítque aquas, quæ erant sub firmaménto, ab his, quæ erant super firmaméntum. Et factum est ita. Vocavítque Deus firmaméntum, Cælum: et factum est véspere et mane, dies secúndus.

Dixit vero Deus: Congregéntur aquæ, quæ sub cælo sunt, in locum unum: et appáreat árida. Et factum est ita. Et vocávit Deus áridam, Terram: congregationésque aquárum appellávit Mária. Et vidit Deus, quod esset bonum. Et ait: Gérminet terra herbam viréntem et faciéntem semen, et lignum pomíferum fáciens fructum

IN the beginning, God created heaven and earth. And the earth was void and empty, and darkness was upon the face of the deep: and the Spirit of God moved over the water. And God said: Be light made. And light was made. And God saw the light, that it was good: and He divided the light from the darkness. And He called the light Day, and the darkness Night: and there was evening and morning, one day.

And God said: Let there be a firmament made amidst the waters: and let it divide the waters from the waters. And God made a firmament, and divided the waters that were under the firmament from those that were above the firmament. And it was so. And God called the firmament Heaven: and the evening and morning were the second day.

God also said: Let the waters that are under the heaven be gathered together into one place; and let the dry land appear. And it was so done. And God called the dry land Earth: and the gathering together of the waters He called Seas. And God saw that it was good. And He said: Let the earth bring forth his green herb, after its

juxta genus suum, cujus semen in se-metípso sit super terram. Et factum est ita. Et prótulit terra herbam viréntem et faciéntem semen juxta genus suum, lignúmque fáciens fructum, et habens unumquódque seméntem secúndum spéciem suam. Et vidit Deus, quod esset bonum. Et factum est véspere et mane, dies tértius.

Dixit autem Deus: Fiant luminária in firmaménto cæli, et dívidant diem ac noctem, et sint in signa et témpo-ra et dies et annos: ut lúceant in fir-maménto cæli, et illúminent terram. Et factum est ita. Fecítque Deus duo luminária magna: lumináre majus, ut præésset diéi: et lumináre minus, ut præésset nocti: et stellas. Et pósuit eas in firmaménto cæli, ut lucérent super terram, et præéssent diéi ac nocti, et divíderent lucem ac ténebras. Et vidit Deus, quod esset bonum. Et factum est véspere et mane, dies quartus.

Dixit étiam Deus: Prodúcant aquæ réptile ánimæ vivéntis, et volátile super terram sub firmaménto cæli. Creavítque Deus cete grándia, et omnem ánimam vivéntem atque motábilem, quam prodúxerant aquæ in spécies suas, et omne volátile secún-dum genus suum. Et vidit Deus, quod esset bonum. Benedixítque eis, dicens: Créscite et multiplicámini, et repléte aquas maris: avésque multiplicéntur super terram. Et factum est véspere et mane, dies quintus.

kind, which may have seed in itself upon the earth. And it was so done. And the earth brought forth the green herb, and such as yieldeth seed according to its kind. And God saw that it was good. And the evening and morning were the third day.

And God said: Let there be lights made in the firmament of heaven to divide the day and the night, and let them be for signs, and for seasons, and for days and years: to shine in the fir-mament of heaven and to give light to the earth. And it was so done. And God made two great lights: a great-er light to rule the day; and a lesser light to rule the night: and the stars. And He set them in the firmament of heaven, to shine upon the earth, and to rule the day and the night, and to divide the light and the darkness. And God saw that it was good. And the evening and morning were the fourth day.

God also said: Let the waters bring forth the creeping creature having life, and the fowl that may fly over the earth under the firmament of heaven. And God created the great whales, and every living thing and moving creature which the waters brought forth, according to their kinds, and ev-ery winged fowl according to its kind. And God saw that it was good. And He blessed them, saying: Increase and multiply, and fill the waters of the sea: and let the birds be multiplied upon the earth. And the evening and the morning were the fifth day.

Dixit quoque Deus: Prodúcat terra ánimam vivéntem in génere suo: juménta et reptília, et béstias terræ secúndum spécies suas. Factúmque est ita. Et fecit Deus béstias terræ juxta spécies suas, et juménta, et omne réptile terræ in génere suo. Et vidit Deus, quod esset bonum, et ait: Faciámus hóminem ad imáginem et similitúdinem nostram: et præsit píscibus maris et volatílibus cæli, et béstiis universǽque terræ, omníque réptili, quod movétur in terra. Et creávit Deus hóminem ad imáginem suam: ad imáginem Dei creávit illum, másculum et féminam creávit eos. Benedixítque illis Deus, et ait: Créscite et multiplicámini, et repléte terram, et subjícite eam, et dominámini píscibus maris et volatílibus cæli, et univérsis animántibus, quæ movéntur super terram. Dixítque Deus: Ecce, dedi vobis omnem herbam afferéntem semen super terram, et univérsa ligna, quæ habent in semetípsis seméntem géneris sui, ut sint vobis in escam: et cunctis animántibus terræ, omníque vólucri cæli, et univérsis, quæ movéntur in terra, et in quibus est ánima vivens, ut hábeant ad vescéndum. Et factum est ita. Vidítque Deus cuncta, quæ fécerat: et erant valde bona. Et factum est véspere et mane, dies sextus.

Igitur perfécti sunt cæli et terra, et omnis ornátus eórum. Complevítque Deus die séptimo opus suum, quod fécerat: et requiévit die séptimo ab univérso ópere, quod patrárat.

And God said: Let the earth bring forth the living creature in its kind, cattle, and creeping things, and beasts of the earth according to their kinds. And it was so done. And God made the beasts of the earth according to their kinds, and cattle, and every thing that creepeth on the earth after its kind. And God saw that it was good. And He said: Let us make man to Our own image and likeness: and let him have dominion over the fishes of the sea, and the fowls of the air, and the beasts, and the whole earth, and every creeping creature that moveth upon the earth. And God created man to His own image: to the image of God He created him, male and female He created them. And God blessed them, saying: Increase and multiply, and fill the earth, and subdue it, and rule over the fishes of the sea, and the fowls of the air, and all living creatures that move upon the earth. And God said: Behold, I have given you every herb-bearing seed upon the earth, and all trees that have in themselves seed of their own kind to be your meat: and to all the beasts of the earth, and to every fowl of the air, and to all that move upon the earth, and wherein there is life, that they may have to feed upon. And it was so done. And God saw all the things that He had made, and they were very good. And the evening and morning were the sixth day.

So the heavens and the earth were finished, and all the furniture of them. And on the seventh day God ended His work which He had made: and He rested on the seventh day from all His work which He had done.

ORÉMUS.
℣. Flectámus génua. ℟. Leváte.

LET US PRAY.
℣. Let us kneel. ℟. Arise.

DEUS, qui mirabíliter creásti hóminem et mirabílius redemísti: da nobis, quǽsumus, contra oblectaménta peccáti, mentis ratióne persístere; ut mereámur ad ætérna gáudia perveníre. Per Dóminum nostrum Jesum Christum, Fílium tuum: qui tecum vivit et regnat in unitáte Spíritus Sancti Deus, per ómnia sǽcula sæculórum.
℟. Amen.

O GOD, who hast wonderfully created man, and more wonderfully restored him: grant us, we beseech Thee, to stand firm with strong minds against the allurements of sin, that we may deserve to arrive at everlasting joys. Through Jesus Christ, Thy Son our Lord, Who liveth and reigneth with Thee, in the unity of the Holy Ghost, God, world without end.
℟. Amen.

SECOND PROPHECY
Genesis 5: 31; 6; 7; 8: 1-21

NOË vero cum quingentórum esset annórum, génuit Sem, Cham et Japheth. Cumque cæpíssent hómines multiplicári super terram et fílias procreássent, vidéntes fílii Dei fílias hóminum, quod essent pulchræ, accepérunt sibi uxóres ex ómnibus, quas elégerant. Dixítque Deus: Non permanébit spíritus meus in hómine in ætérnum, quia caro est: erúntque dies illíus centum vigínti annórum. Gigántes autem erant super terram in diébus illis. Postquam enim ingréssi sunt fílii Dei ad fílias hóminum illǽque genuérunt, isti sunt poténtes a sǽculo viri famósi. Videns autem Deus, quod multa malítia hóminum esset in terra, et cuncta cogitátio cordis inténta esset ad malum omni témpore, pǽnituit eum, quod hóminem fecísset in terra. Et tactus dolóre cordis intrínsecus: Delébo, inquit, hóminem, quem creávi, a fácie terræ, ab hómine usque ad animántia, a réptili

NOE, when he was five hundred years old, begot Sem, Cham, and Japheth. And after that men began to be multiplied upon the earth, and daughters were born to them, the sons of God seeing the daughters of men, that they were fair, took to themselves wives of all, which they chose. And God said: My Spirit shall not remain in man for ever, because he is flesh: and his days shall be a hundred and twenty years. Now giants were upon the earth in those days. For after the sons of God went in to the daughters of men, and they brought forth children, those are the mighty men of old, men of renown. And God seeing that the wickedness of men was great on the earth, and that all the thought of their heart was bent upon evil at all times, it repented Him that He had made man on the earth. And being touched inwardly with sorrow of heart, He said: I will destroy man,

usque ad vólucres cæli; pǽnitet enim me fecísse eos.

Noë vero invénit grátiam coram Dómino. Hæ sunt generatiónes Noë: Noë vir justus atque perféctus fuit in generatiónibus suis, cum Deo ambulávit. Et génuit tres fílios, Sem, Cham et Japheth.

Corrúpta est autem terra coram Deo et repléta est iniquitáte. Cumque vidísset Deus terram esse corrúptam, dixit ad Noë: Finis univérsæ carnis venit coram me: repléta est terra iniquitáte a fácie eórum, et ego dispérdam eos cum terra. Fac tibi arcam de lignis lævigátis: mansiúnculas in arca fácies, et bitúmine línies intrínsecus et extrínsecus. Et sic fácies eam: Trecentórum cubitórum erit longitúdo arcæ, quinquagínta cubitórum latitúdo, et trigínta cubilórum altitúdo illíus. Fenéstram in arca fácies, et in cúbito consummábis summitátem ejus: óstium autem arcæ pones ex látere: deórsum cenácula et trístega fácies in ea.

Ecce, ego addúcam aquas dilúvii super terram, ut interfíciam omnem carnem, in qua spíritus vitæ est subter cælum. Univérsa, quæ in terra sunt, consuméntur. Ponámque fœdus meum tecum: et ingrédiens arcam tu et fílii tui, uxor tua et uxóres filiórum tuórum tecum. Et ex cunctis animántibus univérsæ carnis bina indúces in arcam, ut vivant tecum: masculíni

whom I have created, from the face of the earth, from man even to beasts, from the creeping thing even to the fowls of the air; for it repenteth Me that I have made them.

But Noe found grace before the Lord. These are the generations of Noe: Noe was a just and perfect man in his generations, he walked with God. And he begot three sons, Sem, Cham, and Japheth.

And the earth was corrupted before God, and was filled with iniquity. And when God had seen that the earth was corrupted, He said to Noe: The end of all flesh is come before Me: the earth is filled with iniquity through them, and I will destroy them with the earth. Make thee an ark of timber planks: thou shalt make little rooms in the ark, and thou shalt pitch it within and without. And thus shalt thou make it: The length of the ark shall be three hundred cubits, the breadth of it fifty cubits, and the height of it thirty cubits. Thou shalt make a window in the ark, and in a cubit shall thou finish the top of it: and the door of the ark thou shalt set in the side; with lower, middle chambers and third stories shalt thou make it.

Behold I will bring the waters of a great flood upon the earth, to destroy all flesh, wherein is the breath of life, under heaven. All things that are in the earth shall be consumed, and I will establish My covenant with thee: and thou shalt enter into the ark, thou and thy sons, and thy wife, and the wives of thy sons with thee. And of every living creature of all flesh, thou shalt

sexus et feminíni. De volúcribus juxta genus suum, et de juméntis in génere suo, et ex omni réptili terræ secúndum genus suum: bina de ómnibus ingrediántur tecum, ut possint vívere. Tolles ígitur tecum ex ómnibus escis, quæ mandi possunt, et comportábis apud te: et erunt tam tibi quam illis in cibum.

Fecit ígitur Noë ómnia, quæ præcéperat illi Deus. Erátque sexcentórum annórum, quando dilúvii aquæ inundavérunt super terram. Rupti sunt omnes fontes abýssi magnæ, et cataráctæ cæli apértæ sunt: et facta est plúvia super terram quadragínta diébus et quadragínta nóctibus.

In artículo diéi illíus ingréssus est Noë, et Sem et Cham et Japheth, fílii ejus, uxor illíus et tres uxóres filiórum ejus cum eis in arcam: ipsi, et omne ánimal secúndum genus suum, univérsaque juménta in génere suo, et omne, quod movétur super terram in génere suo, cunctúmque volátile secúndum genus suum. Porro arca ferebátur super aquas. Et aquæ prævaluérunt nimis super terram: opertíque sunt omnes montes excélsi sub univérso cælo. Quíndecim cúbitis áltior fuit aqua super montes, quos operúerat.

Consúmptaque est omnis caro, quæ movebátur super terram, vólucrum, animántium, bestiárum, omniúmque reptílium, quæ reptant super terram. Remánsit autem solus Noë, et qui cum eo erant in arca. Obtinuerúntque aquæ terram centum quinquagínta diébus.

Recordátus autem Deus Noë, cunctorúmque animántium et ómnium

bring two of a sort into the ark, that they may live with thee: of the male sex, and the female. Of fowls according to their kind: two of every sort shall go in with thee, that they may live. Thou shalt take unto thee of all food that may be eaten, and thou shalt lay it up with thee: and it shall be food for thee and them.

And Noe did all things which God commanded Him. And he was six hundred years old when the waters of the flood overflowed the earth. All the fountains of the great deep were broken up, and the flood-gates of heaven were opened; and the rain fell upon the earth forty days and forty nights.

In the self-same day, Noe, and Shem, and Cham, and Japheth, his sons, his wife, and the three wives of his sons with them, went into the ark: they and every beast according to its kind, and all the cattle in their kind, and every thing that moveth upon the earth according to its kind. And the ark was carried upon the waters. And the waters prevailed beyond measure upon the earth: and all the high mountains under the whole heaven were covered. The water was fifteen cubits higher than the mountains which it covered.

And all flesh was destroyed that moved upon the earth, both of fowl, and of cattle, and of beasts, and of all creeping things that creep upon the earth. And Noe only remained, and they that were with him in the ark. And the waters prevailed upon the earth a hundred and fifty days.

And God remembered Noe, and all the living creatures and all the cattle

jumentórum, quæ erant cum eo in arca, addúxit spíritum super terram, et imminútæ sunt aquæ. Et clausi sunt fontes abýssi et cataráctæ cæli: et prohíbitæ sunt plúviæ de cælo. Reversǽque sunt aquæ de terra eúntes et redeúntes: et cæpérunt mínui post centum quinquagínta dies.

Cumque transíssent quadragínta dies, apériens Noë fenéstram arcæ, quam fécerat, dimísit corvum, qui egrediebátur, et non revertebátur, donec siccaréntur aquæ super terram. Emísit quoque colúmbam post eum, ut vidéret, si jam cessássent aquæ super fáciem terræ. Quæ cum non invenísset, ubi requiésceret pes ejus, revérsa est ad eum in arcam: aquæ enim erant super univérsam terram: extendítque manum et apprehénsam íntulit in arcam. Exspectátis autem ultra septem diébus áliis, rursum dimísit colúmbam ex arca. At illa venit ad eum ad vésperam, portans ramum olívæ viréntibus fóliis in ore suo. Intelléxit ergo Noë, quod cessássent aquæ super terram. Exspectavítque nihilóminus septem álios dies: et emísit colúmbam, quæ non est revérsa ultra ad eum.

Locútus est autem Deus ad Noë, dicens: Egrédere de arca, tu et uxor tua, fílii tui et uxóres filiórum tuórum tecum. Cuncta animántia, quæ sunt apud te, ex omni carne, tam in volatílibus quam in béstiis et univérsis reptílibus, quæ reptant super terram, educ tecum, et ingredímini super ter-

which were with him in the ark, and brought a wind upon the earth, and the waters were abated. The fountains also of the deep, and the flood-gates of heaven were shut up: and the rain from heaven was restrained. And the waters returned from off the earth, going and coming: and they began to be abated after a hundred and fifty days.

And after that forty days were passed, Noë, opening the window of the ark which he had made, sent forth a raven, which went forth and did not return, till the waters were dried up upon the earth. He sent forth also a dove after him, to see if the waters had now ceased upon the face of the earth. But she not finding where her foot might rest, returned to him into the ark: for the waters were upon the whole earth: and he put forth his hand, and caught her, and brought her into the ark. And having waited yet seven other days, he again sent forth the dove out of the ark. And she came to him in the evening, carrying a bough of an olive tree with green leaves in her mouth. Noe therefore understood that the waters were ceased upon the earth. And he stayed yet another seven days: and he sent forth the dove, which returned not any more unto him.

And God spoke to Noe, saying: Go out of the ark, thou and thy wife, thy sons, and the wives of thy sons with thee. All living things that are with thee of all flesh, as well in fowls as in beasts, and all creeping things that creep upon the earth, bring out with thee, and go ye upon the earth: in-

ram: créscite et multiplicámini super eam. Egréssus est ergo Noë et fílii ejus, uxor illíus et uxóres filiórum ejus cum eo. Sed et ómnia animántia, juménta et reptília, quæ reptant super terram, secúndum genus suum, egréssa sunt de arca. Ædificávit autem Noë altáre Dómino: et tollens de cunctis pecóribus et volúcribus mundis, óbtulit holocáusta super altáre. Odoratúsque est Dóminus odórem suavitátis.

crease and multiply upon it. So Noe went out, he and his sons, his wife, and the wives of his sons with him. And all living things, and cattle, and creeping things that creep upon the earth, according to their kinds, went out of the ark. And Noe built an altar unto the Lord, and taking of all cattle and fowls that were clean, offered holocausts upon the altar. And the Lord smelled a sweet savor.

ORÉMUS.
℣. Flectámus génua. ℟. Leváte.

DEUS, incommutábilis virtus et lumen ætérnum: réspice propítius ad totíus Ecclésiæ tuæ mirábile sacraméntum, et opus salútis humánæ, perpétuæ dispositiónis efféctu, tranquíllius operáre; totúsque mundus experiátur et vídeat, dejécta érigi, inveteráta renovári, et per ipsum redíre ómnia in íntegrum, a quo sumpsére princípium: Dóminum nostrum Jesum Christum, Fílium tuum: Qui tecum vivit et regnat in unitáte Spíritus Sancti Deus per ómnia sǽcula sæculórum.

℟. Amen.

LET US PRAY.
℣. Let us kneel. ℟. Arise.

O GOD, unchangeable power and light everlasting: mercifully regard the wonderful Mystery of Thy whole Church, and peacefully effect by Thine everlasting decree the work of man's salvation: and may the whole world experience and see that what was cast down is raised up, what was old is renewed, and all things are returning to perfection, through Him from whom they received their first being, our Lord Jesus Christ Thy Son: Who livest and reignest with God the Father, in the unity of the Holy Ghost, God, world without end.

℟. Amen.

THIRD PROPHECY
Genesis 22: 1-19

IN diébus illis: Tentávit Deus Abra-ham, et dixit ad eum: Abraham, Abraham. At ille respóndit: Adsum. Ait illi: Tolle fílium tuum unigéni-tum, quem díligis, Isaac, et vade in ter-ram visiónis: atque ibi ófferes eum in holocáustum super unum móntium, quem monstrávero tibi.

Igitur Abraham de nocte consúr-gens, stravit ásinum suum: ducens secum duos júvenes et Isaac, fílium suum. Cumque concidísset ligna in holocáustum, ábiit ad locum, quem præcéperat ei Deus. Die autem tértio, elevátis óculis, vidit locum procul: dixítque ad púeros suos: Exspectáte hic cum ásino: ego et puer illuc usque properántes, postquam adoravérimus, revertémur ad vos. Tulit quoque ligna holocáusti, et impósuit super Isaac, fílium suum: ipse vero portábat in mánibus ignem et gládium.

Cumque duo pérgerent simul, dixit Isaac patri suo: Pater mi. At ille respóndit: Quid vis, fili? Ecce, inquit, ignis et ligna: ubi est víctima ho-locáusti? Dixit autem Abraham: Deus providébit sibi víctimam holocáusti, fili mi.

Pergébant ergo páriter: et venérunt ad locum, quem osténderat ei Deus, in quo ædificávit altáre et désuper ligna compósuit: cumque alligásset Isaac, fílium suum, pósuit eum in altáre su-per struem lignórum. Extendítque

IN those days God tempted Abra-ham, and said to him: Abraham, Abraham. And he answered: Here I am. He said to him: Take thine on-ly-begotten son, Isaac, whom thou lovest, and go into the land of vision: and there thou shalt offer him for a holocaust upon one of the mountains which I will show thee.

So Abraham, rising up in the night, saddled his ass: and took with him two young men, and Isaac his son. And when he had cut wood for the holocaust, he went his way to the place which God had commanded him. And on the third day, lifting up his eyes, he saw the place afar off; and he said to his young men: Stay you here with the ass: I and the boy will go with speed as far as yonder, and after we have worshipped will return to you. And he took the wood for the holocaust and laid it upon Isaac his son: and he himself carried in his hands fire and a sword.

And as they two were on togeth-er, Isaac said to his father: My father. And he answered: What wilt thou, son? Behold, saith he, fire and wood: where is the victim for the holocaust? And Abraham said: God will provide Himself a victim for a holocaust, my son.

So they went on together; and they came to the place which God had shown him, where he built an al-tar and laid the wood in order upon it; and when he had bound Isaac, his son, he laid him upon the altar upon

manum et arrípuit gládium, ut immoláret fílium suum. Et ecce, Angelus Dómini de cælo clamávit, dicens: Abraham, Abraham. Qui respóndit: Adsum. Dixítque ei: Non exténdas manum tuam super púerum neque fácias illi quidquam: nunc cognóvi, quod times Deum, et non pepercísti unigénito fílio tuo propter me.

Levávit Abraham óculos suos, vidítque post tergum aríetem inter vepres hæréntem córnibus, quem assúmens óbtulit holocáustum pro fílio. Appellavítque nomen loci illíus, Dóminus videt. Unde usque hódie dícitur: In monte Dóminus vidébit.

Vocávit autem Angelus Dómini Abraham secúndo de cælo, dicens: Per memetípsum jurávi, dicit Dóminus: quia fecísti hanc rem, et non pepercísti fílio tuo unigénito propter me: benedícam tibi, et multiplicábo semen tuum sicut stellas cæli et velut arénam, quæ est in lítore maris: possidébit semen tuum portas inimicórum suórum, et benedicéntur in sémine tuo omnes gentes terræ, quia obedísti voci meæ. Revérsus est Abraham ad púeros suos, abierúntque Bersabée simul, et habitávit ibi.

the pile of wood. And he put forth his hand, and took the sword to sacrifice his son. And behold an angel of the Lord from heaven called to him, saying: Abraham, Abraham. And he answered: Here I am. And he said to him: Lay not thy hand upon the boy, neither do thou any thing to him: now I know that thou fearest God, and hast not spared thine only-begotten son for My sake.

Abraham lifted up his eyes and saw behind his back a ram amongst the briers, sticking fast by the horns, which he took and offered for a holocaust instead of his son. And he called the name of that place, the Lord seeth. Whereupon even to this day it is said: In the mountain the Lord will see.

And the angel of the Lord called to Abraham a second time from heaven, saying: By My own self have I sworn, saith the Lord: because Thou hast done this thing, and hast not spared thine only-begotten son for My sake; I will bless thee, and I will multiply thy seed as the stars of heaven, and as the sand that is by the sea shore: thy seed shall possess the gates of their enemies, and in thy seed shall all the nations of the earth be blessed, because thou hast obeyed my voice. Abraham returned to his young men, and they went to Bersabee together, and he dwelt there.

ORÉMUS.

℣. Flectámus génua. ℟. Leváte.

DEUS, fidélium Pater summe, qui in toto orbe terrárum, promissiónis tuæ fílios diffúsa adoptiónis grátia multíplicas: et per

LET US PRAY.

℣. Let us kneel. ℟. Arise.

O GOD, the supreme Father of all the faithful, who all over the world dost multiply the children of Thy promise by diffusing the grace of

paschále sacraméntum, Abraham púerum tuum universárum, sicut jurásti, géntium éfficis patrem; da pópulis tuis digne ad grátiam tuæ vocatiónis introíre. Per Dóminum nostrum Jesum Christum, Fílium tuum: qui tecum vivit et regnat in unitáte Spíritus Sancti Deus, per ómnia sǽcula sæculórum.

℟. Amen.

Thine adoption: and by this Paschal Sacrament dost make Thy servant Abraham, according to Thine oath, the father of all nations: grant that Thy people may worthily enter into the grace of Thy vocation. Through Jesus Christ, Thy Son our Lord, Who liveth and reigneth with Thee, in the unity of the Holy Ghost, God, world without end.

℟. Amen.

FOURTH PROPHECY
Exodus 14: 24; 15: 1

IN diébus illis: Factum est in vigília matutína, et ecce, respíciens Dóminus super castra Ægyptiórum per colúmnam ignis et nubis, interfécit exércitum eórum: et subvértit rotas cúrruum, ferebantúrque in profúndum. Dixérunt ergo Ægýptii: Fugiámus Israélem: Dóminus enim pugnat pro eis contra nos. Et ait Dóminus ad Móysen: Exténde manum tuam super mare, ut revertántur aquæ ad Ægýptios super currus et équites eórum.

Cumque extendísset Móyses manum contra mare, revérsum est primo dilúculo ad priórem locum: fugientibúsque Ægýptiis occurrérunt aquæ, et invólvit eos Dóminus in médiis flúctibus. Reversǽque sunt aquæ, et operuérunt currus, et équites cuncti exércitus Pharaónis, qui sequéntes ingréssi fúerant mare: nec unus quidem supérfuit ex eis. Fílii autem Israël perrexérunt per médium sicci maris, et aquæ eis erant quasi pro muro a dextris

IN those days, it came to pass in the morning watch, and behold the Lord looking upon the Egyptian army through the pillar of fire, and of the cloud, slew their host: and overthrew the wheels of the chariots, and they were carried into the deep. And the Egyptians said: Let us flee from Israel: for the Lord fighteth for them against us. And the Lord said to Moses: Stretch forth thy hand over the sea, that the waters may come again upon the Egyptians, upon their chariots and horsemen.

And when Moses had stretched forth his hand towards the sea, it returned at the first break of day to the former place: and as the Egyptians were fleeing away the waters came upon them, and the Lord shut them up in the middle of the waves. And the waters returned, and covered the chariots and the horsemen of all the army of Pharao, who had come into the sea after them: neither did there so much as one of them remain. But the

et a sinístris: liberavítque Dóminus in die illa Israël de manu Ægyptiórum. Et vidérunt Ægýptios mórtuos super litus maris, et manum magnam, quam exercúerat Dóminus contra eos: timuítque pópulus Dóminum, et credidérunt Dómino et Móysi, servo ejus.

children of Israel marched through the midst of the sea upon dry land, and the waters were to them as a wall on the right hand and the left: and the Lord delivered Israel on that day out of the hand of the Egyptians. And they saw the Egyptians dead upon the sea shore, and the mighty hand that the Lord had used against them: and the people feared the Lord, and they believed the Lord, and Moses His servant.

Tunc cécinit Móyses et fílii Israël carmen hoc Dómino, et dixérunt:

Then Moses and the children of Israel sung this canticle to the Lord, and said:

TRACT

EXODUS 15: 1-2

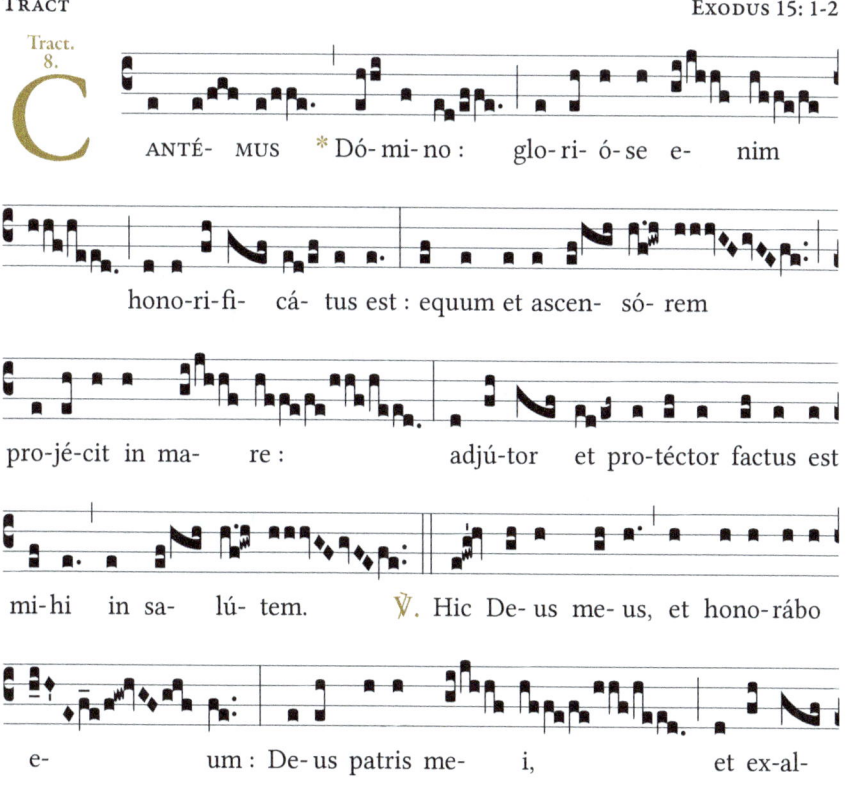

Tract. 8.

CANTÉMUS * Dómino: glorióse enim honorificátus est: equum et ascensórem projécit in mare: adjútor et protéctor factus est mihi in salútem. ℣. Hic Deus meus, et honorábo eum: Deus patris mei, et exal-

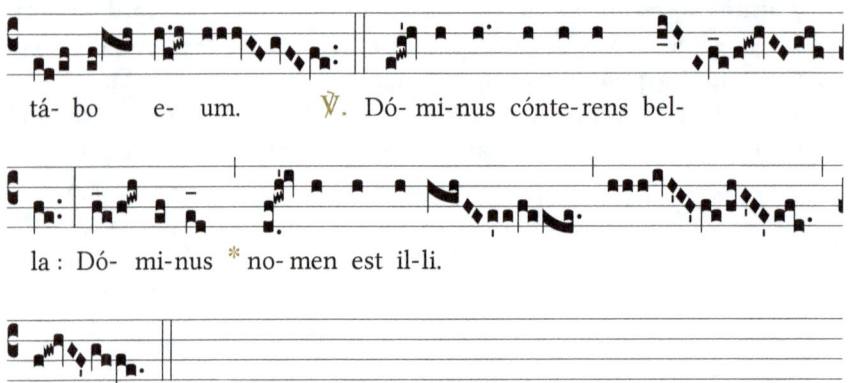

tá- bo e- um. ℣. Dó- mi-nus cónte-rens bel-

la: Dó- mi-nus * no- men est il-li.

TRACT: Let us sing to the Lord, for He is gloriously honored: the horse and the rider He hath thrown into the sea: He has become my Helper and Protector unto salvation. ℣. He is my God, and I will honor Him: the God of my father, and I will extol Him. ℣. He is the Lord that destroys wars: the Lord is His Name.

<table>
<tr><td>ORÉMUS.</td><td>LET US PRAY.</td></tr>
<tr><td>℣. Flectámus génua. ℟. Leváte.</td><td>℣. Let us kneel. ℟. Arise.</td></tr>
</table>

DEUS, cujus antíqua mirácula étiam nostris sǽculis coruscáre sentímus: dum, quod uni pópulo, a persecutióne Ægyptíaca liberándo, déxteræ tuæ poténtia contulísti, id in salútem géntium per aquam regeneratiónis operáris: præsta; ut in Abrahæ fílios et in Israëlíticam dignitátem, totíus mundi tránseat plenitúdo. Per Dóminum nostrum Jesum Christum, Fílium tuum: qui tecum vivit et regnat in unitáte Spíritus Sancti Deus, per ómnia sǽcula sæculórum.

℟. Amen.

O GOD, Whose ancient miracles we see shining also in our days, whilst by the water of regeneration Thou dost operate for the salvation of the Gentiles, that which by the power of Thy right hand Thou didst confer upon one people, by delivering them from the Egyptian persecution: grant that all the nations of the world may become the children of Abraham, and partake of the dignity of the people of Israel. Through Jesus Christ, Thy Son our Lord, Who liveth and reigneth with Thee, in the unity of the Holy Ghost, God, world without end.

℟. Amen.

FIFTH PROPHECY
Isaiah 54: 17; 55: 1-11

HÆC est heréditas servórum Dómini: et justítia eórum apud me, dicit Dóminus. Omnes sitiéntes, veníte ad aquas: et qui non habétis argéntum, properáte, émite et comédite: veníte, émite absque argénto et absque ulla commutatióne vinum et lac. Quare appénditis argéntum non in pánibus, et labórem vestrum non in saturitáte? Audíte audiéntes me, et comédite bonum, et delectábitur in crassitúdine ánima vestra. Inclináte aurem vestram, et veníte ad me: audíte, et vivet ánima vestra, et fériam vobíscum pactum sempitérnum, misericórdias David fidéles. Ecce, testem pópulis dedi eum, ducem ac præceptórem géntibus.

Ecce, gentem, quam nesciébas, vocábis: et gentes, quæ te non cognovérunt, ad te current propter Dóminum, Deum tuum, et sanctum Israël, quia glorificávit te. Quǽrite Dóminum, dum inveníri potest: invocáte eum, dum prope est. Derelínquat ímpius viam suam et vir iníquus cogitatiónes suas, et revertátur ad Dóminum, et miserébitur ejus, et ad Deum nostrum: quóniam multus est ad ignoscéndum.

Non enim cogitatiónes meæ cogitatiónes vestræ: neque viæ vestræ viæ meæ, dicit Dóminus. Quia sicut exaltántur cæli a terra, sic exaltátæ sunt viæ meæ a viis vestris, et cogitatiónes

THIS is the inheritance of the servants of the Lord, and their justice with Me, saith the Lord. All you that thirst, come to the waters: and you that have no money make haste, buy, and eat: come ye, buy wine and milk without money, and without any price. Why do you spend money for that which is not bread, and your labour for that which doth not satisfy you? Hearken diligently to Me, and eat that which is good, and your soul shall be delighted in fatness. Incline your ear and come to Me: hear and your soul shall live, and I will make an everlasting covenant with you, the faithful mercies of David. Behold I have given him for a witness to the people, for a leader and a master to the Gentiles.

Behold thou shalt call a nation, which thou knewest not: and the nations that knew not thee shall run to thee, because of the Lord thy God, and for the Holy One of Israel, for He hath glorified thee. Seek ye the Lord, while He may be found: call upon Him, while He is near. Let the wicked forsake his way, and the unjust man his thoughts, and let him return to the Lord, and He will have mercy on him, and to our God: for He is bountiful to forgive.

For My thoughts are not your thoughts: nor your ways My ways, saith the Lord. For as the heavens are exalted above the earth, so are My ways exalted above your ways, and My

meæ a cogitatiónibus vestris. Et quómodo descéndit imber et nix de cælo, et illuc ultra non revértitur, sed inébriat terram, et infúndit eam, et germináre eam facit, et dat semen serénti et panem comedénti: sic erit verbum meum, quod egrediátur de ore meo: non revertátur ad me vácuum, sed fáciet, quæcúmque vólui, et prosperábitur in his, ad quæ misi illud: dicit Dóminus omnípotens.

thoughts above your thoughts. And as the rain and the snow come down from heaven, and return no more thither, but soak the earth, and water it, and make it to spring, and give seed to the sower, and bread to the eater: So shall My word be, which shall go forth from My mouth: it shall not return to Me void, but it shall do whatsoever I please, and shall prosper in the things for which I sent it.

ORÉMUS.

℣. Flectámus génua. ℟. Leváte.

Omnípotens sempitérne Deus, multíplica in honórem nóminis tui, quod patrum fídei spopondísti: et promissiónis fílios sacra adoptióne diláta; ut, quod prióres Sancti non dubitavérunt futúrum, Ecclésia tua magna jam ex parte cognóscat implétum. Per Dóminum nostrum Jesum Christum, Fílium tuum: qui tecum vivit et regnat in unitáte Spíritus Sancti Deus, per ómnia sǽcula sæculórum.

℟. Amen.

LET US PRAY.

℣. Let us kneel. ℟. Arise.

O Almighty and everlasting God, for the glory of thy name, enlarge the promise which thou madest to the faith of our forefathers, and by the grace of thy adoption, multiply the children of promise, that what the saints of old did not doubt would be, thy Church may find even now in great part fulfilled. Through Jesus Christ, Thy Son our Lord, Who liveth and reigneth with Thee, in the unity of the Holy Ghost, God, world without end.

℟. Amen.

SIXTH PROPHECY
Baruch 3: 9-38

Audi, Israël, mandáta vitæ: áuribus pércipe, ut scias prudéntiam. Quid est, Israël, quod in terra inimicórum es? Inveterásti in terra aliéna, coinquinátus es cum mórtuis: deputátus es cum descendéntibus in inférnum. Dereliquísti fontem sapiéntiæ. Nam si in via Dei ambulásses, habitásses útique in pace sempitérna.

Hear, O Israel, the commandments of life: give ear, that thou mayst learn wisdom. How happeneth it, O Israel, that thou art in thy enemies land? Thou art grown old in a strange country, thou art defiled with the dead: thou art counted with them that go down into hell. Thou hast forsaken the fountain of wisdom: For if

thou hadst walked in the way of God, thou hadst surely dwelt in peace for ever.

Disce, ubi sit prudéntia, ubi sit virtus, ubi sit intelléctus: ut scias simul, ubi sit longitúrnitas vitæ et victus, ubi sit lumen oculórum et pax. Quis invénit locum ejus? et quis intrávit in thesáuros ejus? Ubi sunt príncipes géntium, et qui dominántur super béstias, quæ sunt super terram? qui in ávibus cæli ludunt, qui argéntum thesaurízant et aurum, in quo confídunt hómines, et non est finis acquisitiónis eórum? qui argéntum fábricant, et sollíciti sunt, nec est invéntio óperum illórum? Extermináti sunt, et ad ínferos descendérunt, et álii loco eórum surrexérunt.

Learn where is wisdom, where is strength, where is understanding: that thou mayst know also where is length of days and life, where is the light of the eyes, and peace. Who hath found out her place? and who hath gone in to her treasures? Where are the princes of the nations, and they that rule over the beasts that are upon the earth? That take their diversion with the birds of the air. That hoard up silver and gold, wherein men trust, and there is no end of their getting? who work in silver and are solicitous, and their works are unsearchable. They are cut off, and are gone down to hell, and others are risen up in their place.

Júvenes vidérunt lumen, et habitavérunt super terram: viam autem disciplínæ ignoravérunt, neque intellexérunt sémitas ejus, neque fílii eórum suscepérunt eam, a fácie ipsórum longe facta est: non est audíta in terra Chánaan, neque visa est in Theman. Fílii quoque Agar, qui exquírunt prudéntiam, quæ de terra est, negotiatóres Merrhæ et Theman, et fabulatóres, et exquisitóres prudéntiæ et intellegéntias: viam autem sapiéntiæ nesciérunt, neque commemoráti sunt sémitas ejus.

Young men have seen the light, and dwelt upon the earth: but the way of knowledge they have not known, Nor have they understood the paths thereof, neither have their children received it, it is far from their face. It hath not been heard of in the land of Chanaan, neither hath it been seen in Theman. The children of Agar also, that search after the wisdom that is of the earth, the merchants of Merrha, and of Theman, and the tellers of fables, and searchers of prudence and understanding: but the way of wisdom they have not known, neither have they remembered her paths.

O Israël, quam magna est domus Dei et ingens locus possessiónis ejus! Magnus est et non habet finem: excélsus et imménsus. Ibi fuérunt gigántes nomináti illi, qui ab inítio fuérunt,

O Israel, how great is the house of God, and how vast is the place of his possession! It is great, and hath no end: it is high and immense. There were the giants, those renowned men

statúra magna, sciéntes bellum. Non hos elégit Dóminus, neque viam disciplínæ invenérunt: proptérea periérunt. Et quóniam non habuérunt sapiéntiam, interiérunt propter suam insipiéntiam.

Quis ascéndit in cælum, et accépit eam et edúxit eam de núbibus? Quis transfretávit mare, et invénit illam? et áttulit illam super aurum eléctum? Non est, qui possit scire vias ejus neque qui exquírat sémitas ejus: sed qui scit univérsa, novit eam et adinvénit eam prudéntia sua: qui præparávit terram in ætérno témpore, et replévit eam pecúdibus et quadrupédibus: qui emíttit lumen, et vadit: et vocávit illud, et obédit illi in tremóre. Stellæ autem dedérunt lumen in custódiis suis, et lætátæ sunt: vocátæ sunt, et dixérunt: Adsumus: et luxérunt ei cum jucunditáte, qui fecit illas.

Hic est Deus noster, et non æstimábitur álius advérsus eum. Hic adinvénit omnem viam disciplínæ, et trádidit illam Jacob púero suo et Israël dilécto suo. Post hæc in terris visus est, et cum homínibus conversátus est.

that were from the beginning, of great stature, expert in war. The Lord chose not them, neither did they find the way of knowledge: therefore did they perish. And because they had not wisdom, they perished through their folly.

Who hath gone up into heaven, and taken her, and brought her down from the clouds? Who hath passed over the sea, and found her, and brought her preferably to chosen gold? here is none that is able to know her ways, nor that can search out her paths: But he that knoweth all things, knoweth her, and hath found her out with his understanding: he that prepared the earth for evermore, and filled it with cattle and four-footed beasts: He that sendeth forth light, and it goeth: and hath called it, and it obeyeth him with trembling. And the stars have given light in their watches, and rejoiced: They were called, and they said: Here we are: and with cheerfulness they have shined forth to him that made them.

This is our God, and there shall no other be accounted of in comparison of him. He found out all the way of knowledge, and gave it to Jacob his servant, and to Israel his beloved. Afterwards he was seen upon earth, and conversed with men.

ORÉMUS.

℣. Flectámus génua. ℟. Leváte.

DEUS, qui Ecclésiam tuam semper géntium vocatióne multíplicas: concéde propítius; ut, quos aqua baptísmatis ábluis, contínua protectióne tueáris. Per Dóminum nostrum Jesum Christum, Fílium tuum: qui tecum vivit et regnat in unitáte Spíritus Sancti Deus, per ómnia sǽcula sæculórum.

℟. Amen.

LET US PRAY.

℣. Let us kneel. ℟. Arise.

O GOD, who by thy calling of the nations dost increase thy Church, mercifully grant, that all those whom thou cleansest in the waters of baptism may have thy continual protection. Through Jesus Christ, Thy Son our Lord, Who liveth and reigneth with Thee, in the unity of the Holy Ghost, God, world without end.

℟. Amen.

SEVENTH PROPHECY
Ezechiel 37: 1-14

IN diébus illis: Facta est super me manus Dómini, et edúxit me in spíritu Dómini: et dimísit me in médio campi, qui erat plenus óssibus: et circumdúxit me per ea in gyro: erant autem multa valde super fáciem campi síccaque veheménter. Et dixit ad me: Fili hóminis, putásne vivent ossa ista? Et dixi: Dómine Deus, tu nosti. Et dixit ad me: Vaticináre de óssibus istis: et dices eis: Ossa árida, audíte verbum Dómini. Hæc dicit Dóminus Deus óssibus his: Ecce, ego intromíttam in vos spíritum, et vivétis. Et dabo super vos nervos, et succréscere fáciam super vos carnes, et superexténdam in vobis cutem: et dabo vobis spíritum, et vivétis, et sciétis, quia ego Dóminus.

THE hand of the Lord was upon me, and brought me forth in the spirit of the Lord: and set me down in the midst of a plain that was full of bones. And He led me about through them on every side: now they were very many upon the face of the plain, and they were exceeding dry. And He said to me: Son of man, dost thou think these bones shall live? And I answered: O Lord God, Thou knowest. And he said to me: Prophesy concerning these bones; and say to them: Ye dry bones, hear the word of the Lord. Thus saith the Lord God to these bones: Behold, I will send spirit into you, and you shall live. And I will lay sinews upon you, and will cause flesh to grow over you, and will cover you with skin: and I will give you spirit and you shall live, and you shall know that I am the Lord.

Et prophetávi, sicut præcéperat mihi: factus est autem sónitus prophetánte me, et ecce commótio:

And I prophesied as he had commanded me: and as I prophesied there was a noise, and behold a commotion:

et accessérunt ossa ad ossa, unum-quódque ad junctúram suam. Et vidi, et ecce, super ea nervi et carnes as-cendérunt: et exténta est in eis cutis désuper, et spíritum non habébant.

Et dixit ad me: Vaticináre ad spíritum, vaticináre, fili hóminis, et dices ad spíritum: Hæc dicit Dóminus Deus: A quátuor ventis veni, spíri-tus, et insúffla super interféctos istos, et revivíscant. Et prophetávi, sicut præcéperat mihi: et ingréssus est in ea spíritus, et vixérunt: steterúntque su-per pedes suos exércitus grandis nimis valde.

Et dixit ad me: Fili hóminis, ossa hæc univérsa, domus Israël est: ipsi dicunt: Aruérunt ossa nostra, et pé-riit spes nostra, et abscíssi sumus. Proptérea vaticináre, et dices ad eos: Hæc dicit Dóminus Deus: Ecce, ego apériam túmulos vestros, et edú-cam vos de sepúlcris vestris, pópulus meus: et indúcam vos in terram Israël. Et sciétis, quia ego Dóminus, cum aperúero sepúlcra vestra et edúxero vos de túmulis vestris, pópule meus: et dédero spíritum meum in vobis, et vixéritis, et requiéscere vos fáciam su-per humum vestram: dicit Dóminus omnípotens.

and the bones came together, each one to its joint. And I saw, and behold the sinews, and the flesh came up upon them: and the skin was stretched out over them, but there was no spirit in them.

And He said to me: Prophesy to the spirit, prophesy, O son of man, and say to the spirit: Thus saith the Lord God: Come, spirit, from the four winds, and blow upon these slain, and let them live again. And I prophesied as He had commanded me: and the spirit came into them, and they lived: and they stood up upon their feet, an exceeding great army.

And He said to me: Son of man: All these bones are the house of Isra-el: they say: Our bones are dried up, and our hope is lost, and we are cut off. Therefore prophesy, and say to them: Thus saith the Lord God: Be-hold I will open your graves, and will bring you out of your sepulchres, O my people: and will bring you into the land of Israel. And you shall know that I am the Lord, when I shall have opened your sepulchres, and shall have brought you out of your graves, O My people: And shall have put my spirit in you, and you shall live, and I shall make you rest upon your own land: and you shall know that I the Lord have spoken, and done it, saith the Lord God.

ORÉMUS.

℣. Flectámus génua. ℟. Leváte.

DEUS, qui nos ad celebrándum paschále sacraméntum utriúsque Testaménti páginis ínstruis: da nobis intellégere misericórdiam tuam; ut ex perceptióne præséntium múnerum firma sit exspectátio futurórum. Per Dóminum nostrum Jesum Christum, Fílium tuum: qui tecum vivit et regnat in unitáte Spíritus Sancti Deus, per ómnia sǽcula sæculórum.

℟. Amen.

LET US PRAY.

℣. Let us kneel. ℟. Arise.

O GOD, who teaches us by the pages of both testaments to celebrate the paschal mystery, grant us such understanding of thy mercy, that we, receiving thy gifts of this present time, may have a firm hope for those times that are to come. Through Jesus Christ, Thy Son our Lord, Who liveth and reigneth with Thee, in the unity of the Holy Ghost, God, world without end.

℟. Amen.

EIGHTH PROPHECY
Isaiah 4: 1-6

APPREHÉNDENT septem mulíeres virum unum in die illa, dicéntes: Panem nostrum comedémus et vestiméntis nostris operiémur: tantúmmodo invocétur nomen tuum super nos, aufer opróbrium nostrum. In die illa erit germen Dómini in magnificéntia et glória, et fructus terræ súblimis, et exsultátio his, qui salváti fúerint de Israël. Et erit: Omnis, qui relíctus fúerit in Sion et resíduus in Jerúsalem, sanctus vocábitur, omnis, qui scriptus est in vita in Jerúsalem. Si ablúerit Dóminus sordes filiárum Sion, et sánguinem Jerúsalem láverit de médio ejus, in spíritu judícii et spíritu ardóris.

Et creábit Dóminus super omnem locum montis Sion, et ubi invocátus est, nubem per diem, et fumum et splendórem ignis flammántis in nocte: super omnem enim glóriam protéctio.

AND in that day seven women shall take hold of one man, saying: We will eat our own bread, and wear our own apparel: only let us be called by thy name, take away our reproach. In that day the bud of the Lord shall be in magnificence and glory, and the fruit of the earth shall be high, and a great joy to them that shall have escaped of Israel. And it shall come to pass, that every one that shall be left in Sion, and that shall remain in Jerusalem, shall be called holy, every one that is written in life in Jerusalem. If the Lord shall wash away the filth of the daughters of Sion, and shall wash away the blood of Jerusalem out of the midst thereof, by the spirit of judgment, and by the spirit of burning.

And the Lord will create upon every place of mount Sion, and where He is called upon, a cloud by day, and a smoke and the brightness of a flaming fire in the night: for over all the

Et tabernáculum erit in umbráculum diéi ab æstu, et in securitátem et absconsiónem a túrbine et a plúvia.

glory shall be a protection. And there shall be a tabernacle for a shade in the daytime from the heat, and for a security and covert from the whirlwind, and from rain.

TRACT   ISAIAH 5: 1-2

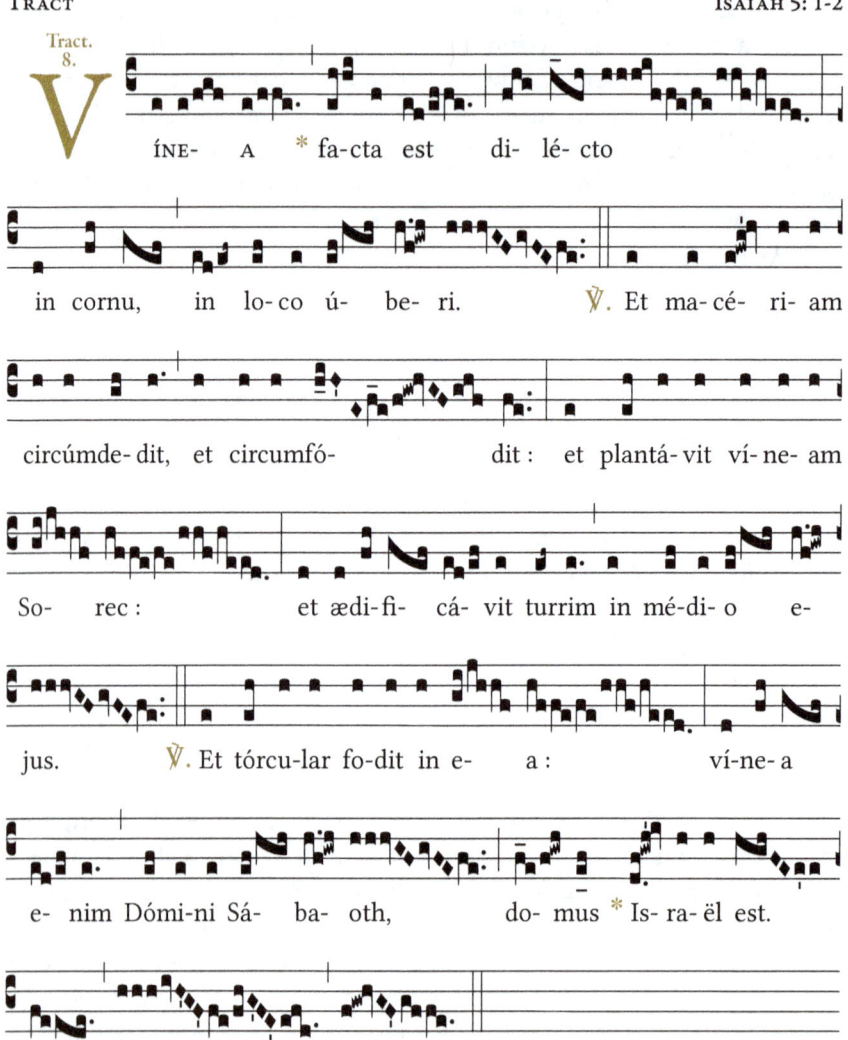

VÍNEA * facta est di-lé-cto in cornu, in lo-co ú-be-ri. ℣. Et ma-cé-ri-am circúmde-dit, et circumfó-dit: et plantá-vit ví-ne-am Sorec: et ædi-fi-cá-vit turrim in mé-di-o e-jus. ℣. Et tórcu-lar fo-dit in e-a: ví-ne-a e-nim Dómi-ni Sá-ba-oth, do-mus * Is-ra-ël est.

TRACT: My beloved had a vineyard on a hill in a fruitful place. ℣. And he fenced it in, and picked the stones out of it, and planted it with the choicest vines, and built a tower in the midst thereof, ℣. and set up a winepress therein: for the vineyard of the Lord of hosts is the house of Israel.

<table>
<tr><td>

ORÉMUS.
℣. Flectámus génua. ℟. Leváte.

</td><td>

LET US PRAY.
℣. Let us kneel. ℟. Arise.

</td></tr>
</table>

D EUS, qui in ómnibus Ecclésiæ tuæ fíliis, sanctórum Prophetárum voce manifestásti, in omni loco dominatiónis tuæ, satórem te bonórum séminum, et electórum pálmitum esse cultórem: tríbue pópulis tuis, qui et vineárum apud te nómine censéntur et ségetum; ut, spinárum et tribulórum squalóre resecáto, digna efficiántur fruge fecúndi. Per Dóminum nostrum Jesum Christum, Fílium tuum: qui tecum vivit et regnat in unitáte Spíritus Sancti Deus, per ómnia sǽcula sæculórum.

℟. Amen.

O GOD, who by the voice of Thy holy prophets hast made manifest to all the children of Thy Church, that through the whole extent of Thy empire Thou art the sower of good seed, and the cultivator of chosen branches: grant to Thy people who are called by the name of the vines and harvests, that they may root out all thorns and briers, and bring forth good fruit in abundance. Through Jesus Christ, Thy Son our Lord, Who liveth and reigneth with Thee, in the unity of the Holy Ghost, God, world without end.

℟. Amen.

NINTH PROPHECY
Exodus 12: 1-11

I N diébus illis: Dixit Dóminus ad Móysen et Aaron in terra Ægýpti: Mensis iste vobis princípium ménsium: primus erit in ménsibus anni. Loquímini ad univérsum cœtum filiórum Israël, et dícite eis: Décima die mensis hujus tollat unusquísque agnum per famílias et domos suas. Sin autem minor est númerus, ut suffícere possit ad vescéndum agnum, assúmet vicínum suum, qui junctus est dómui suæ, juxta númerum animárum, quæ suffícere possunt ad esum agni. Erit autem agnus absque mácula, másculus, annículus: juxta quem ritum tollétis et hædum.

A ND the Lord said to Moses and Aaron in the land of Egypt: This month shall be to you the beginning of months: it shall be the first in the months of the year. Speak ye to the whole assembly of the children of Israel, and say to them: On the tenth day of this month let every man take a lamb by their families and houses. But if the number be less than may suffice to eat the lamb, he shall take unto him his neighbour that joineth to his house, according to the number of souls which may be enough to eat the lamb. And it shall be a lamb without blemish, a male, of one year: according to which rite also you shall take a kid.

Et servábitis eum usque ad quartam décimam diem mensis hujus: immolabítque eum univérsa multitúdo filiórum Israël ad vésperam. Et sument de sánguine ejus, ac ponent super utrúmque postem et in superlimináribus domórum, in quibus cómedent illum. Et edent carnes nocte illa assas igni, et ázymos panes cum lactúcis agréstibus. Non comedétis ex eo crudum quid nec coctum aqua, sed tantum assum igni: caput cum pédibus ejus et intestínis vorábitis. Nec remanébit quidquam ex eo usque mane. Si quid resíduum fúerit, igne comburétis.

Sic autem comedétis illum: Renes vestros accingétis, et calceaménta habébitis in pédibus, tenéntes báculos in mánibus, et comedétis festinánter: est enim Phase (id est tránsitus) Dómini.

And you shall keep it until the fourteenth day of this month: and the whole multitude of the children of Israel shall sacrifice it in the evening. And they shall take of the blood thereof, and put it upon both the side posts, and on the upper door posts of the houses, wherein they shall eat it. And they shall eat the flesh that night roasted at the fire, and unleavened bread with wild lettuce. You shall not eat thereof any thing raw, nor boiled in water, but only roasted at the fire: you shall eat the head with the feet and entrails thereof. Neither shall there remain any thing of it until morning. If there be any thing left, you shall burn it with fire.

And thus you shall eat it: you shall gird your reins, and you shall have shoes on your feet, holding staves in your hands, and you shall eat in haste: for it is the Phase (that is, the Passage) of the Lord.

ORÉMUS.
℣. Flectámus génua. ℟. Leváte.

O MNÍPOTENS sempitérne Deus, qui in ómnium óperum tuórum dispensatióne mirábilis es: intéllegant redémpti tui, non fuísse excelléntius, quod inítio factus est mundus, quam quod in fine sæculórum Pascha nostrum immolátus est Christus: Qui tecum vivit et regnat in unitáte Spíritus Sancti Deus per ómnia sǽcula sæculórum.
℟. Amen.

LET US PRAY.
℣. Let us kneel. ℟. Arise.

O ALMIGHTY everlasting God, who art wonderful in the ordering of all thy works, let thy redeemed understand that the creation of the world at the beginning was not a greater work than the immolation, in the fullness of time, of Christ, our passover. Who livest and reignest with Thee in the unity of the Holy Ghost, God, world without end.
℟. Amen.

Tenth Prophecy
Jonae 3: 1-10

In diébus illis: Factum est verbum Dómini ad Jonam Prophétam secúndo, dicens: Surge, et vade in Níniven civitátem magnam: et prǽdica in ea prædicatiónem, quam ego loquor ad te. Et surréxit Jonas, et ábiit in Níniven juxta verbum Dómini. Et Nínive erat cívitas magna itínere trium diérum. Et cæpit Jonas introíre in civitátem itínere diéi uníus: et clamávit et dixit: Adhuc quadragínta dies, et Nínive subvertétur.

Et credidérunt viri Ninivítæ in Deum: et prædicavérunt jejúnium, et vestíti sunt saccis a majóre usque ad minórem. Et pervénit verbum ad regem Nínive: et surréxit de sólio suo, et abjécit vestiméntum suum a se, et indútus est sacco, et sedit in cínere. Et clamávit et dixit in Nínive ex ore regis et príncipum ejus, dicens: Hómines et juménta et boves et pécora non gustent quidquam: nec pascántur, et aquam non bibant. Et operiántur saccis hómines et juménta, et clament ad Dóminum in fortitúdine, et convertatur vir a via sua mala, et ab iniquitáte, quæ est in mánibus eórum. Quis scit, si convertátur et ignóscat Deus: et revertátur a furóre iræ suæ, et non períbimus?

Et vidit Deus ópera eórum, quia convérsi sunt de via sua mala: et misértus est pópulo suo, Dóminus, Deus noster.

And the word of the Lord came to Jonas the second time, saying: Arise, and go to Ninive the great city: and preach in it the preaching that I bid thee. And Jonas arose, and went to Ninive, according to the word of the Lord: now Ninive was a great city of three days' journey. And Jonas began to enter into the city one day's journey: and he cried, and said: Yet forty days, and Ninive shall be destroyed.

And the men of Ninive believed in God: and they proclaimed a fast, and put on sackcloth from the greatest to the least. And the word came to the king of Ninive; and he rose up out of his throne, and cast away his robe from him, and was clothed with sackcloth, and sat in ashes. And he caused it to be proclaimed and published in Ninive from the mouth of the king and of his princes, saying: Let neither men nor beasts, oxen nor sheep, taste any thing: let them not feed, nor drink water. And let men and beasts be covered with sackcloth, and cry to the Lord with all their strength, and let them turn every one from his evil way, and from the iniquity that is in their hands. Who can tell if God will turn, and forgive: and will turn away from His fierce anger, and we shall not perish?

And God saw their works, that they were turned from their evil way: and the Lord our God had mercy on His people.

ORÉMUS.

℣. Flectámus génua. ℟. Leváte.

DEUS, qui diversitátem géntium in confessióne tui nóminis adunásti: da nobis et velle et posse, quæ præcipis; ut, pópulo ad æternitátem vocáto, una sit fides méntium et píetas actiónum. Per Dóminum nostrum Jesum Christum, Fílium tuum: qui tecum vivit et regnat in unitáte Spíritus Sancti Deus, per ómnia sǽcula sæculórum.

℟. Amen.

LET US PRAY.

℣. Let us kneel. ℟. Arise.

O GOD, who hast gathered together the diverse nations of earth in the confession of thy name, grant us both the will and the power to keep thy commandments, that all those whom thou hast called to everlasting life, may be one in faith of mind and in goodness of conduct. Through Jesus Christ, Thy Son our Lord, Who liveth and reigneth with Thee, in the unity of the Holy Ghost, God, world without end.

℟. Amen.

ELEVENTH PROPHECY
Deuteronomy 31: 22-30

IN diébus illis: Scripsit Móyses cánticum, et dócuit fílios Israël. Præcepítque Dóminus Jósue, fílio Nun, et ait: Confortáre, et esto robústus: tu enim introdúces fílios Israël in terram, quam pollícitus sum, et ego ero tecum.

Postquam ergo scripsit Móyses verba legis hujus in volúmine, atque complévit: præcépit Levítis, qui portábant arcam fœderis Dómini, dicens: Tóllite librum istum, et pónite eum in látere arcæ fœderis Dómini, Dei vestri: ut sit ibi contra te in testimónium. Ego enim scio contentiónem tuam et cérvicem tuam duríssimam. Adhuc vivénte me et ingrediénte vobíscum, semper contentióse egístis contra Dóminum: quanto magis, cum mórtuus fúero? Congregáte ad me omnes majóres natu per tribus vestras, atque

MOSES therefore wrote the canticle and taught it to the children of Israel. And the Lord commanded Josue the son of Nun, and said: Take courage, and be valiant: for thou shalt bring the children of Israel into the land which I have promised, and I will be with thee.

Therefore after Moses had wrote the words of this law in a volume, and finished it: He commanded the Levites, who carried the ark of the covenant of the Lord. saying: Take this book, and put it in the side of the ark of the covenant of the Lord your God: that it may be there for a testimony against thee. For I know thy obstinacy, and thy most stiff neck. While I am yet living, and going in with you, you have always been rebellious against the Lord: how much more when I shall be dead? Gather unto me all the ancients

doctóres, et loquar audiéntibus eis sermónes istos, et invocábo contra eos cælum et terram. Novi enim, quod post mortem meam iníque agétis et declinábitis cito de via, quam præcépi vobis: et occúrrent vobis mala in extrémo témpore, quando fecéritis malum in conspéctu Dómini, ut irritétis eum per ópera mánuum vestrárum.

of your tribes, and your doctors, and I will speak these words in their hearing, and will call heaven and earth to witness against them. For I know that, after my death, you will do wickedly, and will quickly turn aside from the way that I have commanded you: and evils shall come upon you in the latter times, when you shall do evil in the sight of the Lord, to provoke him by the works of your hands.

Locútus est ergo Móyses, audiénte univérso cœtu Israël, verba cárminis hujus, et ad finem usque complévit.

Moses therefore spoke, in the hearing of the whole assembly of Israel, the words of this canticle, and finished it even to the end.

Tract   Deuteronomy 32: 1-4

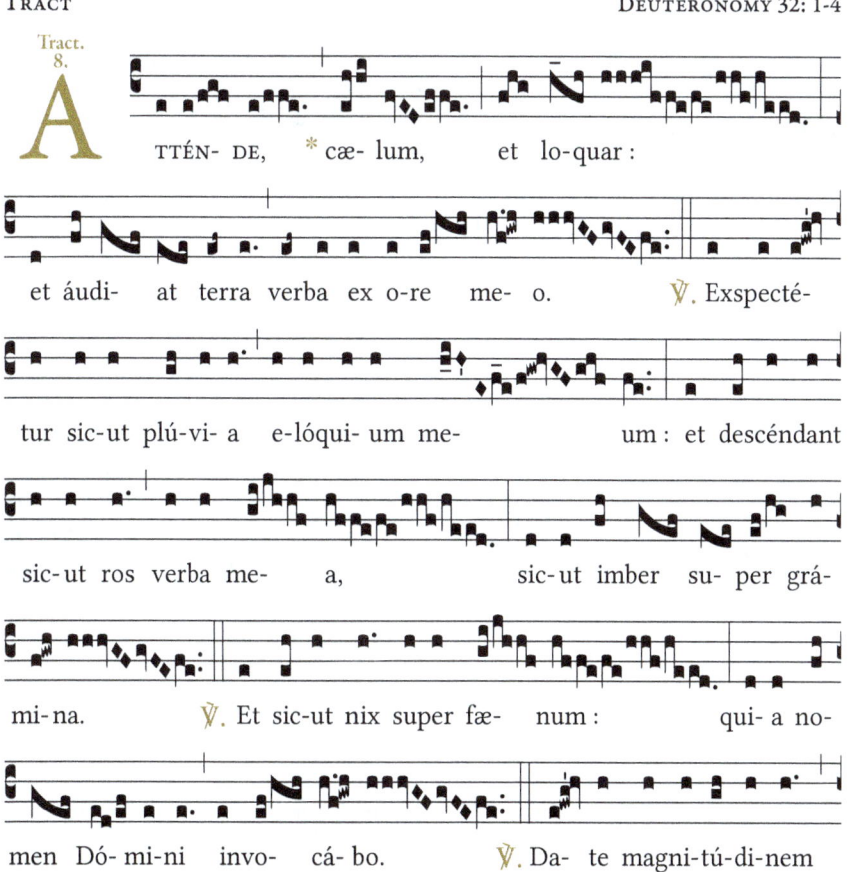

Tract. 8.

Atténde, *cælum, et loquar: et áudiat terra verba ex ore meo. ℣. Exspectétur sicut plúvia elóquium meum: et descéndant sicut ros verba mea, sicut imber super grámina. ℣. Et sicut nix super fænum: quia nomen Dómini invocábo. ℣. Date magnitúdinem

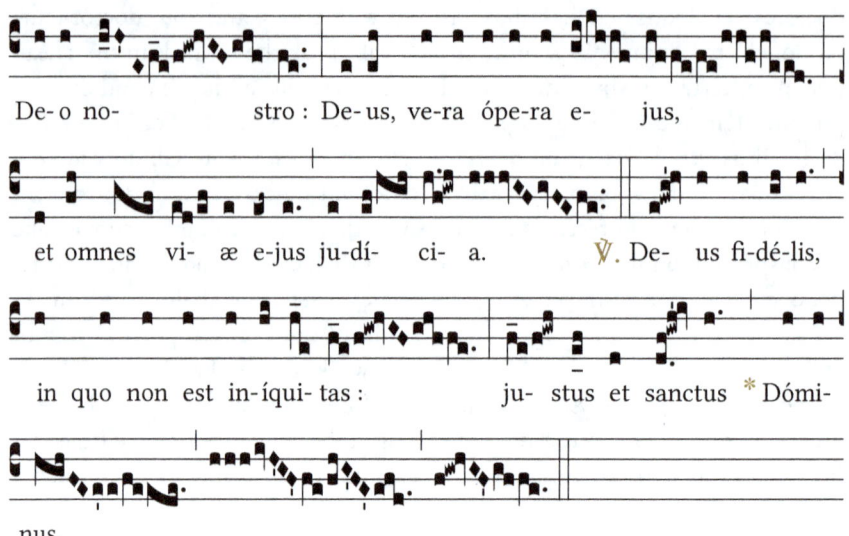

De- o no- stro : De- us, ve-ra ópe-ra e- jus, et omnes vi- æ e-jus ju-dí- ci- a. ℣. De- us fi-dé-lis, in quo non est in-íqui- tas : ju- stus et sanctus * Dómi- nus.

TRACT: Hear, O ye heavens, the things I speak, let the earth give ear to the words of my mouth. ℣. Let my doctrine gather as the rain, let my speech distil as the dew, ℣. As a shower upon the herb, and as drops upon the grass. Because I will invoke the name of the Lord: ℣. Give ye magnificence to our God. The works of God are perfect, and all his ways are judgments: ℣. God is faithful and without any iniquity, he is just and right.

ORÉMUS.

℣. Flectámus génua. ℟. Leváte.

Deus, celsitúdo humílium et fortitúdo rectórum, qui per sanctum Móysen, púerum tuum, ita erudíre pópulum tuum sacri cárminis tui decantatióne voluísti, ut illa legis iterátio fíeret étiam nostra diréctio: éxcita in omnem justificatárum géntium plenitúdinem poténtiam tuam, et da lætítiam, mitigándo terrórem; ut, ómnium peccátis tua remissióne delétis, quod denuntiátum est in ultiónem, tránseat in salútem. Per Dóminum nostrum Jesum Christum,

LET US PRAY.

℣. Let us kneel. ℟. Arise.

O GOD, greatness of the humble and the strength of the righteous, who was pleased by thy holy servant Moses so to instruct thy people with the singing of thy sacred canticle that his repeating of the law should be also for our guiding, stir up thy might upon all the multitude of peoples that are justified before thee, quiet their fear and make them to rejoice; that all their sins being blotted out by thy remission, the threatenings of thy vengeance may turn to their salvation.

Fílium tuum: qui tecum vivit et regnat in unitáte Spíritus Sancti Deus, per ómnia sǽcula sæculórum.

℟. Amen.

Through Jesus Christ, Thy Son our Lord, Who liveth and reigneth with Thee, in the unity of the Holy Ghost, God, world without end.

℟. Amen.

TWELFTH PROPHECY
Daniel 3: 1-24

In diébus illis: Nabuchodónosor rex fecit státuam áuream, altitúdine cubitórum sexagínta, latitúdine cubitórum sex, et státuit eam in campo Dura provínciæ Babylónis. Itaque Nabuchodónosor rex misit ad congregándos sátrapas, magistrátus, et júdices, duces, et tyránnos, et præféctos, omnésque príncipes regiónum, ut convenírent ad dedicatiónem státuæ, quam eréxerat Nabuchodónosor rex. Tunc congregáti sunt sátrapæ, magistrátus, et júdices, duces, et tyránni, et optimátes, qui erant in potestátibus constitúti, et univérsi príncipes regiónum, ut convenírent ad dedicatiónem státuæ, quam eréxerat Nabuchodónosor rex. Stabant autem in conspéctu státuæ, quam posúerat Nabuchodónosor rex, et præco clamábat valénter:

Vobis dícitur pópulis, tríbubus et linguis: In hora, qua audiéritis sónitum tubæ, et fístulæ, et cítharæ, sambúcæ, et psaltérii, et symphóniæ, et univérsi géneris musicórum, cadéntes adoráte státuam áuream, quam constítuit Nabuchodónosor rex. Si quis autem non prostrátus adoráverit, eádem hora mittétur in fornácem ignis ardéntis. Post hæc ígitur statim ut audiérunt omnes pópuli sónitum

King Nabuchodonosor made a statue of gold, of sixty cubits high, and six cubits broad, and he set it up in the plain of Dura of the province of Babylon. Then Nabuchodonosor the king sent to call together the nobles, the magistrates, and the judges, the captains, the rulers, and governors, and all the chief men of the provinces, to come to the dedication of the statue which king Nabuchodonosor had set up. Then the nobles, the magistrates, and the judges, the captains, and rulers, and the great men that were placed in authority, and all the princes of the provinces, were gathered together to come to the dedication of the statue, which king Nabuchodonosor had set up. And they stood before the statue which king Nabuchodonosor had set up. Then a herald cried with a strong voice:

To you it is commanded, O nations, tribes, and languages: That in the hour that you shall hear the sound of the trumpet, and of the flute, and of the harp, of the sackbut, and of the psaltery, and of the symphony, and of all kind of music; ye fall down and adore the golden statue which king Nabuchodonosor hath set up. But if any man shall not fall down and adore, he shall the same hour be cast into a fur-

tubæ, fístulæ, et cítharæ, sambúcæ, et psaltérii, et symphóniæ, et omnis géneris musicórum, cadéntes omnes pópuli, tribus et linguæ adoravérunt státuam áuream, quam constitúerat Nabuchodónosor rex.

Statímque in ipso témpore accedéntes viri Chaldǽi accusavérunt Judǽos, dixerúntque Nabuchodónosor regi: Rex, in ætérnum vive: tu, rex, posuísti decrétum, ut omnis homo, qui audíerit sónitum tubæ, fístulæ, et cítharæ, sambúcæ, et psaltérii, et symphóniæ, et univérsi géneris musicórum, prostérnat se et adóret státuam áuream: si quis autem non prócidens adoráverit, mittátur in fornácem ignis ardéntis. Sunt ergo viri Judǽi, quos constituísti super ópera regiónis Babylónis, Sidrach, Misach et Abdénago: viri isti contempsérunt, rex, decrétum tuum: deos tuos non colunt, et státuam áuream, quam erexísti, non adórant.

Tunc Nabuchodónosor in furóre et in ira præcépit, ut adduceréntur Sidrach, Misach et Abdénago: qui conféstim addúcti sunt in conspéctu regis. Pronuntiánsque Nabuchodónosor rex, ait eis: Veréne, Sidrach, Misach et Abdénago, deos meos non cólitis, et státuam áuream, quam constítui, non adorátis? Nunc ergo si estis paráti, quacúmque hora audiéritis sónitum tubæ, fístulæ, cítharæ, sambúcæ, et psaltérii, et symphóniæ,

nace of burning fire. Upon this therefore, at the time when all the people heard the sound of the trumpet, the flute, and the harp, of the sackbut, and the psaltery, of the symphony, and of all kind of music: all the nations, tribes, and languages fell down and adored the golden statue which king Nabuchodonosor had set up.

And presently at that very time some Chaldeans came and accused the Jews, and said to king Nabuchodonosor: O king, live for ever: Thou, O king, hast made a decree that every man that shall hear the sound of the trumpet, the flute, and the harp, of the sackbut, and the psaltery, of the symphony, and of all kind of music, shall prostrate himself, and adore the golden statue: And that if any man shall not fall down and adore, he should be cast into a furnace of burning fire. Now there are certain Jews whom thou hast set over the works of the province of Babylon, Sidrach, Misach, and Abdenago: these men, O king, have slighted thy decree: they worship not thy gods, nor do they adore the golden statue which thou hast set up.

Then Nabuchodonosor in fury, and in wrath, commanded that Sidrach, Misach, and Abdenago should be brought: who immediately were brought before the king. And Nabuchodonosor the king spoke to them, and said: Is it true, O Sidrach, Misach, and Abdenago, that you do not worship my gods, nor adore the golden statue that I have set up? Now therefore if you be ready at what hour soever you shall hear the sound of the

omnísque géneris musicórum, prostérnite vos et adoráte státuam, quam feci: quod si non adoravéritis, eádem hora mittémini in fornácem ignis ardéntis; et quis est Deus, qui erípiet vos de manu mea?

Respondéntes Sidrach, Misach et Abdénago, dixérunt regi Nabuchodónosor: Non opórtet nos de hac re respóndere tibi. Ecce enim, Deus noster, quem cólimus, potest erípere nos de camíno ignis ardéntis, et de mánibus tuis, o rex, liberáre. Quod si nolúerit, notum sit tibi; rex, quia deos tuos non cólimus et státuam áuream, quam erexísti, non adorámus.

Tunc Nabuchodónosor replétus est furóre, et aspéctus faciéi illíus immutátus est super Sidrach, Misach et Abdénago, et præcépit, ut succenderétur fornax séptuplum, quam succéndi consuéverat. Et viris fortíssimis de exércitu suo jussit, ut, ligátis pédibus Sidrach, Misach et Abdénago, mítterent eos in fornácem ignis ardéntis. Et conféstim viri illi vincti, cum braccis suis et tiáris et calceaméntis et véstibus, missi sunt in médium fornácis ignis ardéntis: nam jússio regis urgébat: fornax autem succénsa erat nimis. Porro viros illos, qui míserant Sidrach, Misach et Abdénago, interfécit flamma ignis.

trumpet, flute, harp, sackbut, and psaltery, and symphony, and of all kind of music, prostrate yourselves, and adore the statue which I have made: but if you do not adore, you shall be cast the same hour into the furnace of burning fire: and who is the God that shall deliver you out of my hand?

Sidrach, Misach, and Abdenago answered and said to king Nabuchodonosor: We have no occasion to answer thee concerning this matter. For behold our God, whom we worship, is able to save us from the furnace of burning fire, and to deliver us out of thy hands, O king. But if He will not, be it known to thee, O king, that we will not worship thy gods, nor adore the golden statue which thou hast set up.

Then was Nabuchodonosor filled with fury: and the countenance of his face was changed against Sidrach, Misach, and Abdenago, and he commanded that the furnace should be heated seven times more than it had been accustomed to be heated. And he commanded the strongest men that were in his army, to bind the feet of Sidrach, Misach, and Abdenago, and to cast them into the furnace of burning fire. And immediately these men were bound and were cast into the furnace of burning fire, with their coats, and their caps, and their shoes, and their garments. For the king's commandment was urgent, and the furnace was heated exceedingly. And the flame of the fire slew those men that had cast in Sidrach, Misach, and Abdenago.

Viri autem hi tres, id est, Sidrach, Misach et Abdénago, cecidérunt in médio camíno ignis ardéntis colligáti. Et ambulábant in médio flammæ laudántes Deum, et benedicéntes Dómino.

But these three men, that is, Sidrach, Misach, and Abdenago, fell down bound in the midst of the furnace of burning fire. And they walked in the midst of the flame, praising God and blessing the Lord.

Orémus.

Let us pray.

O mnípotens sempitérne Deus, spes única mundi, qui Prophetárum tuórum præcónio præséntium témporum declarásti mystéria: auge pópuli tui vota placátus; quia in nullo fidélium, nisi ex tua inspiratióne, provéniunt quarúmlibet increménta virtútum. Per Dóminum nostrum Jesum Christum, Fílium tuum: qui tecum vivit et regnat in unitáte Spíritus Sancti Deus, per ómnia sǽcula sæculórum.

℟. Amen.

O almighty and everlasting God, the only hope of the world who by the voice of thy prophets didst foretell the mysteries of this present time, graciously strengthen the desires of thy people: for no increase of virtue shall be given to any of them save only by thy holy inspiration. Through Jesus Christ, Thy Son our Lord, Who liveth and reigneth with Thee, in the unity of the Holy Ghost, God, world without end.

℟. Amen.

The Blessing of the Baptismal Water

In churches that have a baptismal font, the blessing of the baptismal water now takes place. The celebrant with ministers carrying the cross, the candles and the lighted paschal candle, proceeds to the baptistery, while the following tract is chanted:

Tract   Psalm 41: 2-4

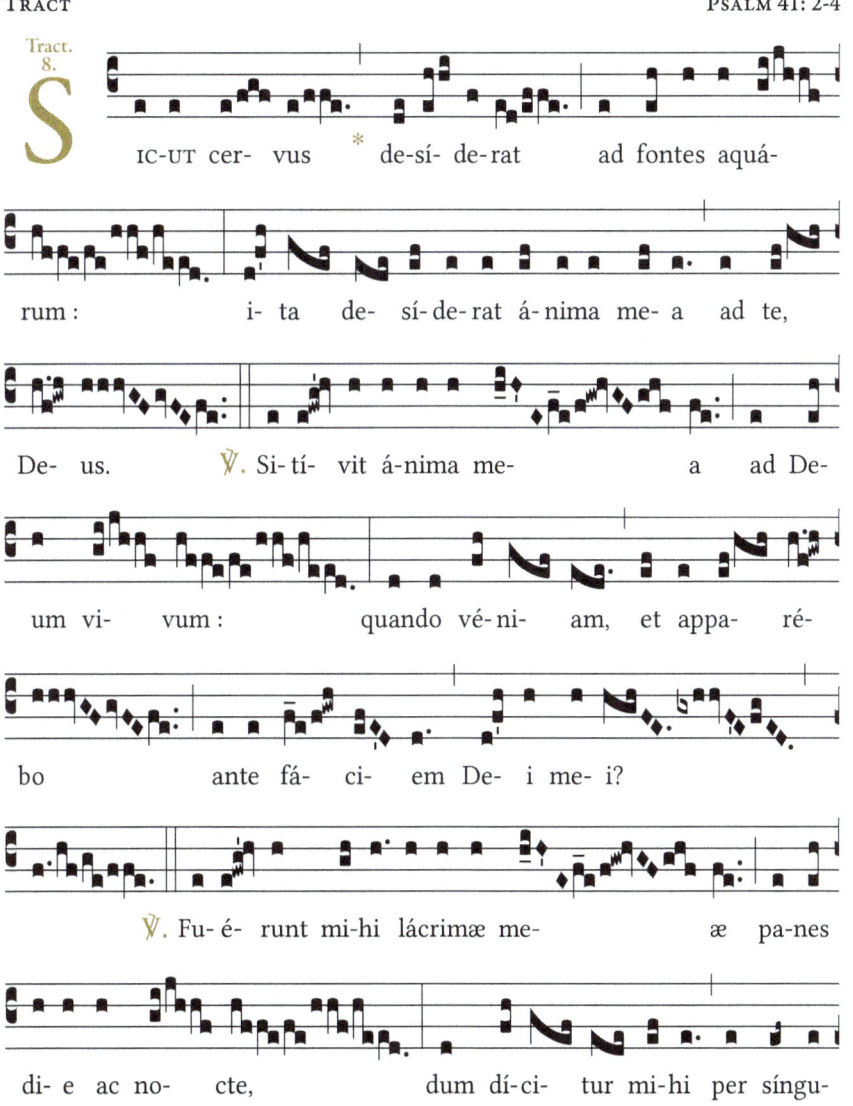

Tract.
8.

S IC-UT cer- vus * de-sí- de-rat ad fontes aquá-

rum : i- ta de- sí-de-rat á-nima me- a ad te,

De- us. ℣. Si-tí- vit á-nima me- a ad De-

um vi- vum : quando vé-ni- am, et appa- ré-

bo ante fá- ci- em De- i me- i?

℣. Fu- é- runt mi-hi lácrimæ me- æ pa-nes

di- e ac no- cte, dum dí-ci- tur mi-hi per síngu-

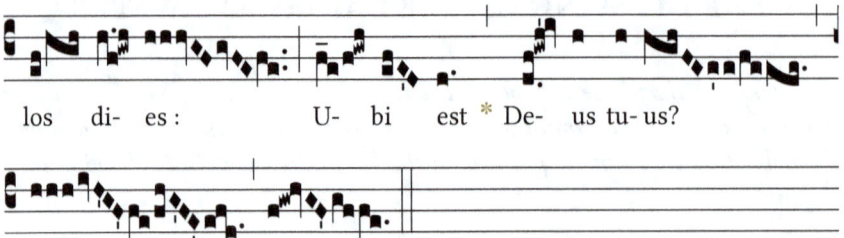

los   di- es: U- bi   est * De- us tu- us?

TRACT: As the hart panteth after the fountains of water; so my soul panteth after Thee, O God. ℣. My soul hath thirsted after the strong living God; when shall I come and appear before the face of God? ℣. My tears have been my bread day and night, whilst it is said to me daily: Where is thy God?

Before the celebrant enters the baptistery, the following prayer is said:

℣. Dóminus vobíscum.

℟. Et cum spíritu tuo.

℣. The Lord be with you.

℟. And with thy spirit.

ORÉMUS.

LET US PRAY.

Omnípotens sempitérne Deus, réspice propítius ad devotiónem pópuli renascéntis, qui, sicut cervus, aquárum tuárum éxpetit fontem: et concéde propítius; ut fídei ipsíus sitis, baptísmatis mystério, ánimam corpúsque sanctíficet. Per Dóminum nostrum Jesum Christum, Fílium tuum: qui tecum vivit et regnat in unitáte Spíritus Sancti Deus, per ómnia sǽcula sæculórum.

O almighty and everlasting God, look mercifully on the devotion of Thy people about to be reborn, who like the hart pant after the fountain of Thy waters: and mercifully grant that the thirst of their faith may, by the Sacrament of Baptism, hallow their souls and bodies. Through Jesus Christ, Thy Son our Lord, Who liveth and reigneth with Thee, in the unity of the Holy Ghost, God, world without end.

℟. Amen.

℟. Amen.

When the celebrant enters the baptistery, the blessing is performed as follows:

℣. Dóminus vobíscum.

℟. Et cum spíritu tuo.

℣. The Lord be with you.

℟. And with thy spirit.

ORÉMUS.   LET US PRAY.

O MNÍPOTENS sempitérne Deus, adésto magnæ pietátis tuæ mystériis, adésto sacraméntis: et ad recreándos novos pópulos, quos tibi fons baptísmatis párturit, spíritum adoptiónis emítte; ut, quod nostræ humilitátis geréndum est ministério, virtútis tuæ impleátur efféctu. Per Dóminum nostrum Jesum Christum, Fílium tuum: qui tecum vivit et regnat in unitáte Spíritus Sancti Deus, per ómnia sǽcula sæculórum.

℟. Amen.

P ER omnia sǽcula sæculórum.
     ℟. Amen.
    ℣. Dóminus vobíscum.
    ℟. Et cum Spíritu tuo.
    ℣. Sursum corda.
    ℟. Habémus ad Dóminum.

    ℣. Grátias agámus Dómino Deo nostro.
    ℟. Dignum et justum est.

V ERE dignum et justum est, æquum et salutáre, nos tibi semper et ubíque grátias ágere, Dómine sancte, Pater omnípotens, ætérne Deus: Qui invisíbili poténtia sacramentórum tuórum mirabíliter operáris efféctum: Et licet nos tantis mystériis exsequéndis simus indígni: Tu tamen grátiæ tuæ dona non déserens, étiam ad nostras preces aures tuæ pietátis inclínas. Deus, cujus Spíritus super aquas inter ipsa mundi primórdia

O ALMIGHTY and eternal God, be present at these mysteries, be present at these sacraments of thy great goodness: and send forth the spirit of thy adoption to regenerate the new people, whom the font of baptism bringeth forth: that what is to be done by the ministry of us thy servants, may be accomplished by the effect of thy power. Through Jesus Christ, Thy Son our Lord, Who liveth and reigneth with Thee, in the unity of the Holy Ghost, God, world without end.
℟. Amen.

W ORLD without end.
     ℟. Amen.
    ℣. The Lord be with you.
    ℟. And with thy spirit.
    ℣. Lift up thy hearts.
    ℟. We have them lifted up to the Lord.
    ℣. Let us give thanks to the Lord our God.
    ℟. It is meet and just.

I T is truly meet and just, right and availing unto salvation, to give Thee thanks always and in all places, O holy Lord, almighty Father, everlasting God, Who, by Thine ineffable power dost wonderfully produce the effect of Thy Sacraments: and though we are unworthy to perform such great mysteries: yet, as Thou dost not abandon the gifts of Thy grace, so Thou inclinest the ears of Thy goodness, even to our prayers. O God, Whose Spirit

ferebátur: ut jam tunc virtútem sanctificatiónis aquárum natúra concíperet.
Deus, qui, nocéntis mundi crímina per
aquas ábluens, regeneratiónis spéciem
in ipsa dilúvii effusióne signásti: ut,
uníus ejusdémque eleménti mystério,
et finis esset vítiis et orígo virtútibus.
Réspice, Dómine, in fáciem Ecclésiæ
tuæ, et multíplica in ea regeneratiónes
tuas, qui grátiæ tuæ affluéntis ímpetu
lætíficas civitátem tuam: fontémque
baptísmatis áperis toto orbe terrárum
géntibus innovándis: ut, tuæ majestátis império, sumat Unigéniti tui grátiam de Spíritu Sancto.

in the very beginning of the world
moved over the waters, that even then
the nature of water might receive the
virtue of sanctification. O God, Who
by water didst wash away the crimes
of the guilty world, and by the pouring out of the deluge didst give a figure of regeneration, that one and the
same element might in a mystery be
the end of vice and the beginning of
virtue. Look, O Lord, on the face of
Thy Church, and multiply in her Thy
regenerations, who by the streams of
Thine abundant grace fillest Thy city
with joy, and openest the font of Baptism all over the world for the renewal
of the Gentiles: that by the command
of Thy Majesty she may receive the
grace of Thine only Son from the
Holy Ghost.

Here the celebrant, with outstretched hand, divides the water in the form of a cross, and wiping his hand with a towel, says:

Qui hanc aquam, regenerán-
dis homínibus præparátam,
arcána sui núminis admixtióne fecúndet: ut, sanctificatióne concépta, ab
immaculáto divíni fontis útero, in
novam renáta creatúram, progénies
cæléstis emérgat: Et quos aut sexus in
córpore aut ætas discérnit in témpore,
omnes in unam páriat grátia mater
infántiam. Procul ergo hinc, jubénte
te, Dómine, omnis spíritus immún-
dus abscédat: procul tota nequítia
diabólicæ fraudis absístat. Nihil hic
loci hábeat contráriæ virtútis admíx-
tio: non insidiándo circúmvolet: non
laténdo subrépat: non inficiéndo cor-
rúmpat.

May He by a secret mixture of
His divine virtue render this
water fruitful for the regeneration of
men, to the end that a heavenly offspring, conceived by sanctification,
may emerge from the immaculate
womb of this divine font, reborn a
new creature: and may all, however
distinguished either by sex in body, or
by age in time, be brought forth to the
same infancy by grace, their mother.
Therefore may all unclean spirits, by
Thy command, O Lord, depart far
from hence: may the whole malice of
diabolical deceit be entirely banished:
may no power of the enemy prevail
here: let him not fly about to lay his
snares; may he not creep in by stealth:
may he not corrupt with his poison.

He touches the water with his hand:

S IT hæc sancta et ínnocens creatúra líbera ab omni impugnatóris incúrsu, et totíus nequítiæ purgáta discéssu. Sit fons vivus, aqua regénerans, unda puríficans: ut omnes hoc lavácro salutífero diluéndi, operánte in eis Spíritu Sancto, perféctæ purgatiónis indulgéntiam consequántur.

M AY this holy and innocent creature be free from all the assaults of the enemy, and purified by the destruction of all his wickedness. May it be a living fountain, a regenerating water, a purifying stream: that all those that are to be washed in this saving bath may obtain, by the operation of the Holy Ghost, the grace of a perfect cleansing.

He makes the Sign of the Cross over the water three times, and continues:

U NDE benedíco te, creatúra aquæ, per Deum ✠ vivum, per Deum ✠ verum, per Deum ✠ sanctum: per Deum, qui te in princípio verbo separávit ab árida: cujus Spíritus super te ferebátur.

T HEREFORE, I bless thee, O creature of water, by the living ✠ God, by the true ✠ God, by the holy ✠ God: by that God Who, in the beginning, separated thee by His Word from the dry land, Whose Spirit moved over thee.

Here he divides the water and casts some toward the four corners of the earth, saying:

Q UI te de paradísi fonte manáre fecit, et in quátuor flumínibus totam terram rigáre præcépit. Qui te in desérto amáram, suavitáte indíta, fecit esse potábilem, et sitiénti pópulo de petra prodúxit. Be✠nedíco te et per Jesum Christum, Fílium ejus únicum, Dominum nostrum: qui te in Cana Galilǽæ signo admirábili sua poténtia convértit in vinum. Qui pédibus super te ambulávit: et a Joánne in Jordáne in te baptizátus est. Qui te una cum sánguine de látere suo prodúxit: et discípulis suis jussit, ut credéntes baptizaréntur in te, dicens: Ite, docéte omnes gentes, baptizántes eos in nómine Patris, et Fílii, et Spíritu Sancti.

W HO made thee flow from the fountain of paradise and commanded thee to water the whole earth with thy four rivers. Who, changing thy bitterness in the desert into sweetness made thee fit to drink, and produced thee out of a rock to quench the thirsty people. I bless ✠ thee also by our Lord Jesus Christ, His only Son: Who in Cana of Galilee changed thee into wine by a wonderful miracle of His power. Who walked upon thee with dry foot, and was baptized in thee by John in the Jordan. Who made thee flow out of His side together with His Blood, and commanded His disciples that such as believed should be

baptised in thee, saying: Go, teach all nations, baptizing them in the Name of the Father, and of the Son, and of the Holy Ghost.

Hæc nobis præcépta servántibus, tu, Deus omnípotens, clemens adésto: tu benígnus aspíra.

Do thou, almighty God, mercifully assist us who observe this commandment: do Thou graciously inspire us.

He breathes on the water three times in the shape of the Cross.

Tu has símplices aquas tuo ore benedícito: ut præter naturálem emundatiónem, quam lavándis possunt adhibére corpóribus, sint étiam purificándis méntibus efficáces.

Do Thou with Thy mouth bless these clear waters: that besides their natural virtue of cleansing the body, they may also prove efficacious for the purifying of the soul.

He lowers the Paschal candle into the water three times, saying each time:

Descéndat in hanc plenitúdinem fontis virtus Spíritus Sancti.

May the virtue of the Holy Ghost descend into all the water of this font.

Breathing thrice upoin the water, he says:

Totámque hujus aquæ substántiam regenerándi fecúndet efféctu.

And make the whole substance of this water fruitful for regeneration.

Here the Paschal candle is taken out of the water, and he continues:

Hic ómnium peccatórum máculæ deleántur: hic natúra ad imáginem tuam cóndita, et ad honórem sua reformáta princípii, cunctis vetustátis squalóribus emundétur: ut omnis homo, sacraméntum hoc regeneratiónis ingréssus, in veræ innocéntiæ novam infántiam renascátur.

Here may the stains of all sins be washed out; here may human nature, created in Thine image, and reformed to the honor of its Author, be cleansed from all the filth of the old man: that all who receive the Sacrament of regeneration, may be born again new children of true innocence.

Per Dominum nostrum Jesum Christum, Fílium tuum: Qui ventúrus est judicáre vivos et mórtuos, et sǽculum per ignem.

Through our Lord Jesus Christ, Thy Son: Who shall come to judge the living and the dead, and the world by fire.

The people are then sprinkled with the blessed water, some of which is distributed for use in the homes of the faithful.

The celebrant pours some of the oil of cathechumens into the water in the form of cross saying:

SANCTIFICÉTUR ✠ et fecundétur fons iste Oleo salútis renascéntibus ex eo, in vitam ætérnam.

℟. Amen.

MAY THIS font be sanctified ✠ and made fruitful with the oil of salvation for all them who shall be born anew of its waters unto life everlasting. ℟. Amen.

In the same manner pouring in chrism he says:

INFÚSIO Chrísmatis Dómini nostri Jesu Christi, et Spíritus Sancti Parácliti, fiat in nómine sanctæ Trinitátis.

℟. Amen.

MAY THIS pouring in the chrism of our Lord Jesus Christ, and the Holy Ghost, the comforter, be made in the name of the Holy Trinity.

℟. Amen.

Pouring the oil and the chrism together into the water in the form of cross saying:

COMMÍXTIO Chrísmatis sanctificatiónis, et Olei unctiónis, et Aquæ baptísmatis, páriter fiat in nómine Pa✠tris, et Fí✠lii, et Spíritus ✠ Sancti.

℟. Amen.

LET THIS mingling of the chrism of sanctification, with the oil of unction, and of the water of Baptism, be likewise made in the name of the Father ✠ and of the Son ✠ and of the Holy ✠ Ghost.

℟. Amen.

He mingles the oil itself with the water and with his hands spreads it through the whole font. If there be any to receive baptism, he baptizes them.

THE LITANY OF THE SAINTS

The celebrant lays aside the chasuble or cope and returns to the altar, where he and his ministers lie prostrate before it. The rest kneel, and the Litany is sung by two cantors in the middle of the choir. They sing each petition and response, which is repeated by the others.

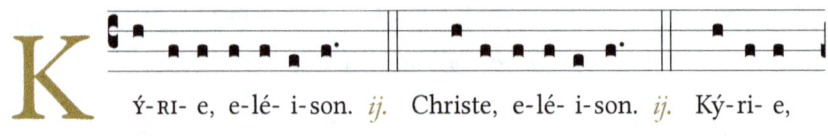

Ý-RI- e, e-lé- i-son. *ij.* Christe, e-lé- i-son. *ij.* Ký-ri- e,

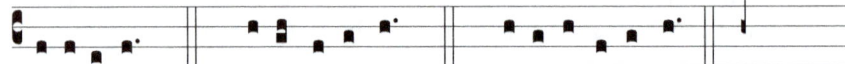

e-lé- i-son. *ij.* Christe, audi nos. *ij.* Christe, exáudi nos. *ij.*

Lord, have mercy. Christ, have mercy. Lord, have mercy.
Christ hear us. Christ graciously hear us.

Pa-ter de cǽ-lis,   **De**-us, mi-se-*ré-re* no-bis.

God the Father of heaven, have mercy on us.

Fili, Redémptor mundi, **D**eus, miser*ére* **no**bis.	God the Son, Redeemer of the world, have mercy on us.
Spíritus Sancte, **D**eus, miser*ére* **no**bis.	God the Holy Ghost, have mercy on us.
Sancta Trínitas, unus **D**eus, miser*ére* **no**bis.	Holy Trinity, one God, have mercy on us.

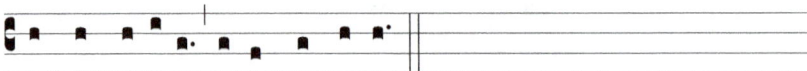

Sancta Mar-í- a,   o-*ra pro* **no**-bis.

Holy Mary, pray for us.

Sancta Dei **G**énetrix, *ora pro* **no**bis.	Holy Mother of God, pray for us.
Sancta Virgo **vír**ginum, *ora pro* **no**bis.	Holy Virgin of virgins, pray for us.
Sancte **Mí**chaël, *ora pro* **no**bis.	Saint Michael, pray for us.
Sancte **Gá**briel, *ora pro* **no**bis.	Saint Gabriel, pray for us.
Sancte **Rá**phaël, *ora pro* **no**bis.	Saint Raphael, pray for us.

Omnes sancti Ange- li et Archánge- li, o- rá- *te pro* **no-** bis.

All ye holy Angels and Archangels, pray for us.

Omnes sancti beatórum Spirítuum **ór**dines, orá*te pro* **no**bis.	All ye holy orders of blessed Spirits, pray for us.
Sancte Joánnes Bapt**ís**ta, *ora pro* **no**bis.	Saint John the Baptist, pray for us.
Sancte **Jos**eph, *ora pro* **no**bis.	Saint Joseph, pray for us.
Omnes sancti Patriárchæ et Pro**phét**æ, orá*te pro* **no**bis.	All ye holy Patriarchs and Prophets, pray for us.

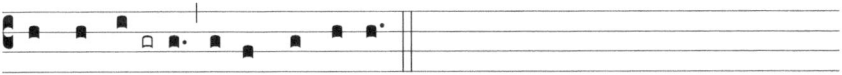

Sancte **Pe-** tre, o-*ra pro* **no**-bis.

Saint Peter, pray for us.

Sancte **Pau**le, *ora pro* **no**bis.	Saint Paul, pray for us.
Sancte An**dré**a, *ora pro* **no**bis.	Saint Andrew, pray for us.
Sancte Joán**nes**, *ora pro* **no**bis.	Saint John, pray for us.
Omnes sancti Apóstoli et Evange**lís**tæ, orá*te pro* **no**bis.	All ye holy Apostles and Evangelists, pray for us.
Omnes sancti Discípuli **Dó**mini, orá*te pro* **no**bis.	All ye holy Disciples of the Lord, pray for us.
Sancte **Sté**phane, *ora pro* **no**bis.	Saint Stephen, pray for us.
Sancte Lau**rén**ti, *ora pro* **no**bis.	Saint Lawrence, pray for us.
Sancte Vin**cén**ti, *ora pro* **no**bis.	Saint Vincent, pray for us.
Omnes sancti **Már**tyres, orá*te.*	All ye holy Martyrs, pray for us.
Sancte Sil**ves**ter, *ora pro* **no**bis.	Saint Silvester, pray for us.
Sancte Gre**gó**ri, *ora pro* **no**bis.	Saint Gregory, pray for us.
Sancte Augus**tí**ne, *ora pro* **no**bis.	Saint Augustine, pray for us.
Omnes sancti Pontífices et Confess**ó**res, orá*te pro* **no**bis.	All ye holy Bishops and Confessors, pray for us.
Omnes sancti Doc**tó**res, orá*te.*	All ye holy Doctors, pray for us.
Sancte An**tó**ni, *ora pro* **no**bis.	Saint Anthony, pray for us.
Sancte Bene**dí**cte, *ora pro* **no**bis.	Saint Benedict, pray for us.
Sancte Do**mí**nice, *ora pro* **no**bis.	Saint Dominic, pray for us.
Sancte Fran**cí**sce, *ora pro* **no**bis.	Saint Francis, pray for us.
Omnes sancti Sacerdótes et Le**ví**tæ, orá*te pro* **no**bis.	All ye holy Priests and Deacons, pray for us.

Omnes sancti Mónachi et Eremítæ, orá*te pro* **no**bis.	All ye holy Monks and Hermits, pray for us.
Sancta María Magdaléna, o*ra pro* **no**bis.	Saint Mary Magdalen, pray for us.
Sancta **Agnes**, o*ra pro* **no**bis.	Saint Agnes, pray for us.
Sancta Cæcília, o*ra pro* **no**bis.	Saint Cecilia, pray for us.
Sancta **Agatha**, o*ra pro* **no**bis.	Saint Agatha, pray for us.
Sancta Ana**stá**sia, o*ra pro* **no**bis.	Saint Anastasia, pray for us.
Omnes sanctæ Vírgines et **Ví**duæ, orá*te pro* **no**bis.	All ye holy Virgins and Widows, pray for us.
Omnes Sancti et Sanctæ **Dei**, intercédi*te pro* **no**bis.	All ye holy Saints of God, intercede for us.

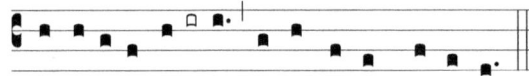

Pro-pí-*ti- us* **es**- to, parce no-bis Dómi-ne.

Be merciful, spare us, O Lord.

Prop*ítius* **es**to, exáudi nos, Dómine.	Be merciful, graciously hear us, O Lord.
Ab *omni* **ma**lo, libera nos, Dómine.	From all evil, deliver us, O Lord.
Ab *omni pec***cá**to, líbera nos, Dómine.	From all sin, deliver us, O Lord.
A mor*te per***pé**tua, líbera nos, Dómine.	From everlasting death, deliver us, O Lord.
Per mystérium sanctæ incarnati*ónis* **tu**æ, líbera nos, Dómine.	Through the mystery of Thy holy incarnation, deliver us, O Lord.
Per ad*véntum* **tu**um, líbera nos, Dómine.	Through Thy coming, deliver us, O Lord.
Per nativi*tátem* **tu**am, líbera nos, Dómine.	Through Thy Nativity, deliver us, O Lord.
Per baptísmum et sanctum jejú*nium* **tu**um, líbera nos, Dómine.	Through Thy Baptism and holy fasting, deliver us, O Lord.
Per crucem et passi*ónem* **tu**am, líbera nos, Dómine.	Through Thy Cross and Passion, deliver us, O Lord.
Per mortem et sepul*túram* **tu**am, líbera nos, Dómine.	Through Thy Death and Burial, deliver us, O Lord.
Per sanctam resurrecti*ónem* **tu**am, líbera nos, Dómine.	Through Thy holy Resurrection, deliver us, O Lord.
Per admirábilem ascensi*ónem* **tu**am, líbera nos, Dómine.	Through Thy wonderful Ascension, deliver us, O Lord.

Per advéntum Spíritus San*cti*
  *Pa***rá**cliti, líbera nos, Dómine.

In d*ie ju***dí**cii,
  líbera nos, Dómine.

Through the coming of the
  Holy Ghost, the Paraclete,
  deliver us, O Lord.

In the day of judgement,
  deliver us, O Lord.

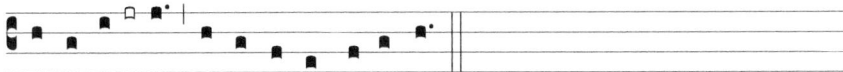

Pec*ca*-**tó**- res, te ro-gámus audi nos.

We sinners, beseech Thee to hear us.

Ut n*obis* **par**cas, te rogámus, audi nos.

That Thou wouldst spare us, we beseech Thee to hear us.

Ut Ecclésiam tuam sanctam régere et conserváre *di***gné**ris, te rogámus, audi nos.

That Thou wouldst vouchsafe to govern and preserve Thy holy Church, we beseech Thee to hear us.

Ut domnum apostólicum et omnes ecclesiásticos órdines ' in sancta religióne conserváre *di***gné**ris, te rogámus, audi nos.

That Thou wouldst vouchsafe to preserve our Apostolic Prelate, and all orders of the Church in holy religion, we beseech Thee to hear us.

Ut inimícos sanctæ Ecclésiæ ' humiliáre *di***gné**ris, te rogámus, audi nos.

That Thou wouldst vouchsafe to humble the enemies of holy Church, we beseech Thee to hear us.

Ut régibus et princípibus christiánis pacem et veram concórdiam donáre *di***gné**ris, te rogámus, audi nos.

That Thou wouldst vouchsafe to give peace and true concord to Christian kings and princes, we beseech Thee to hear us.

Ut nosmetípsos in tuo sancto servítio confortáre et conserváre *di***gné**ris, te rogámus, audi nos.

That Thou wouldst vouchsafe to confirm and preserve us in Thy holy service, we beseech Thee to hear us.

Ut ómnibus benefactóribus nostris sempitérna bona *re***trí**buas, te rogámus, audi nos.

That Thou wouldst render eternal blessings to all our benefactors, we beseech Thee to hear us.

Ut fructus terræ dare et conserváre *di***gné**ris, te rogámus, audi nos.

That Thou wouldst vouchsafe to give and preserve the fruits of the earth, we beseech Thee to hear us.

Ut ómnibus fidélibus defúnctis réquiem ætérnam donáre *di***gné**ris, te rogámus, audi nos.

That Thou wouldst vouchsafe to grant eternal rest to all the faithful departed, we beseech Thee to hear us.

Ut nos exaudíre *di***gné**ris, te rogámus, audi nos.

That Thou wouldst vouchsafe to hear us, we beseech Thee to hear us.

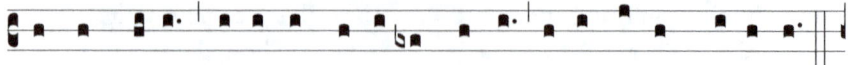

Agnus De- i, qui tol-lis peccá- ta mundi, parce no-bis, Dómi-ne.

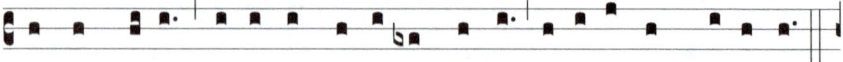

Agnus De- i, qui tol-lis peccá- ta mundi, exáudi nos, Dómi-ne.

Agnus De- i, qui tol-lis peccá-ta mundi, mi-se-ré-re no-bis. Christe,

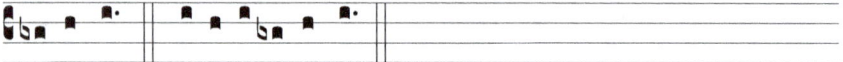

audi nos. Christe, exáudi nos.

Lamb of God, who takest away the sins of the world, spare us, O Lord. Lamb of God, who takest away the sins of the world, graciously hear us, O Lord. Lamb of God, who takest away the sins of the world, have mercy on us. Christ, hear us. Christ, graciously hear us.

THE MASS

The chanters now solemnly sing the Kýrie.

KÝRIE ELÉISON   I- LUX ET ORÍGO

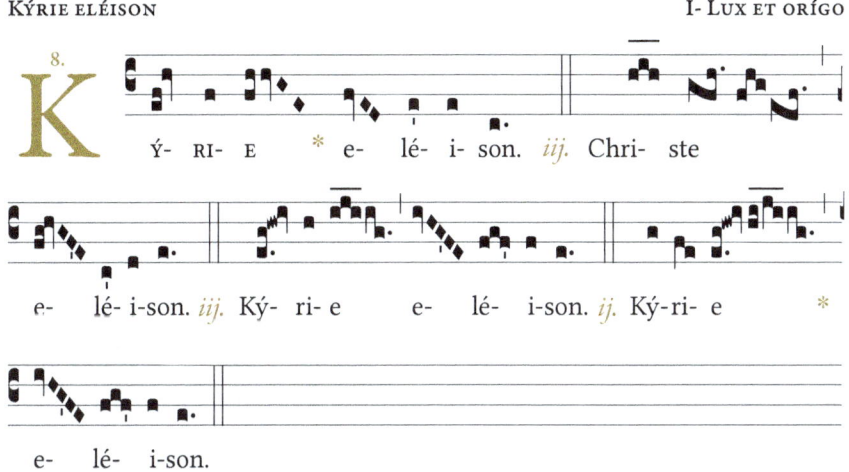

Ký- RI- E * e- lé- i- son. *iij.* Chri- ste

e- lé- i-son. *iij.* Ký- ri- e e- lé- i- son. *ij.* Ký-ri- e *

e- lé- i-son.

KÝRIE: Lord, have mercy. (3x) Christ, have mercy. (3x) Lord, have mercy. (3x)

PRAYERS AT THE FOOT OF THE ALTAR

The celebrant bows before the altar and makes the sign of the cross saying:

IN nómine Patris, ✠ et Fílii, et Spíritus Sancti.
Amen.

V̦. Introíbo ad altáre Dei.
R̦. Ad Deum, qui lætíficat juventútem meam.

V̦. Júdica me, Deus, et discérne causam meam de gente non sancta: ab hómine iníquo et dolóso érue me.

R̦. Quia tu es, Deus, fortitúdo mea: quare me reppulísti, et quare tristis incédo, dum afflígit me inimícus?

IN the Name of the Father, ✠ and of the Son, and of the Holy Ghost.
Amen.

V̦. I will go in to the altar of God.
R̦. To God who giveth joy to my youth.

V̦. Judge me, O God, and distinguish my cause from the nation which is not holy: deliver me from the unjust and deceitful man.

R̦. For Thou, O God, art my strength: why hast Thou cast me off? and why go I sorrowful whilst the enemy afflicteth me?

℣. Emítte lucem tuam et veritátem tuam: ipsa me deduxérunt, et adduxérunt in montem sanctum tuum et in tabernácula tua.

℟. Et introíbo ad altáre Dei: ad Deum, qui lætíficat juventútem meam.

℣. Confitébor tibi in cíthara, Deus, Deus meus: quare tristis es, ánima mea, et quare contúrbas me?

℟. Spera in Deo, quóniam adhuc confitébor illi: salutáre vultus mei, et Deus meus.

℣. Glória Patri, et Fílio, et Spirítui Sancto.

℟. Sicut erat in princípio, et nunc, et semper: et in sǽcula sæculórum. Amen.

℣. Introíbo ad altáre Dei.

℟. Ad Deum, qui lætíficat juventútem meam.

℣. Adjutórium nostrum ✠ in nómine Dómini.

℟. Qui fecit cælum et terram.

℣. Send forth Thy light and Thy truth: they have conducted me and brought me unto Thy holy mount, and into Thy tabernacles.

℟. And I will go in to the altar of God: to God who giveth joy to my youth.

℣. To Thee, O God, my God, I will give praise upon the harp; why art thou sad, O my soul, and why dost thou disquiet me?

℟. Hope in God, for I will still give praise to Him: the salvation of my countenance and my God.

℣. Glory be to the Father, and to the Son, and to the Holy Ghost.

℟. As it was in the beginning, is now, and ever shall be, world without end. Amen.

℣. I will go in to the altar of God.

℟. To God who giveth joy to my youth.

℣. Our help ✠ is in the Name of the Lord.

℟. Who made heaven and earth.

CONFÍTEOR

The celebrant bows low and says:

CONFÍTEOR Deo omnipoténti, beátæ Maríæ semper Vírgini, beáto Michaéli Archángelo, beáto Joánni Baptístæ, sanctis Apóstolis Petro et Paulo, ómnibus Sanctis, et vobis, fratres: quia peccávi nimis cogitatióne, verbo et ópere: (**Pércutit sibi pectus ter, dicens**) mea culpa, mea culpa, mea máxima culpa. Ideo precor beátam Maríam semper Vírginem,

I CONFESS to almighty God, to the blessed Mary ever Virgin, blessed Michael the Archangel, blessed John the Baptist, the holy Apostles Peter and Paul, to all the Saints, and to you, brothers, that I have sinned exceedingly in thought, word, and deed, (**The priest strikes his breast three times, saying:**) through my fault, through my fault, through my most grievous fault.

beátum Michaélem Archángelum, beátum Joánnem Baptístam, sanctos Apóstolos Petrum et Paulum, omnes Sanctos, et vos, fratres, oráre pro me ad Dóminum, Deum nostrum.

℟. Misereátur tui omnípotens Deus, et, dimíssis peccátis tuis, perdúcat te ad vitam ætérnam.

℣. Amen.

The server bows and says:

CONFÍTEOR Deo omnipoténti, beátæ Maríæ semper Vírgini, beáto Michaéli Archángelo, beáto Joánni Baptístæ, sanctis Apóstolis Petro et Paulo, ómnibus Sanctis, et tibi, pater: quia peccávi nimis cogitatióne, verbo et ópere: (**Pércutit sibi pectus ter, dicens**) mea culpa, mea culpa, mea máxima culpa. Ideo precor beátam Maríam semper Vírginem, beátum Michaélem Archángelum, beátum Joánnem Baptístam, sanctos Apóstolos Petrum et Paulum, omnes Sanctos, et te, pater, oráre pro me ad Dóminum, Deum nostrum.

℣. Misereátur vestri omnípotens Deus, et, dimíssis peccátis vestris, perdúcat vos ad vitam ætérnam.

℟. Amen.

℣. Indulgéntiam, ✠ absolutiónem et remissiónem peccatórum nostrórum tríbuat nobis omnípotens et miséricors Dóminus.

℟. Amen.

Therefore I beseech the blessed Mary, ever Virgin, blessed Michael the Archangel, blessed John the Baptist, the holy Apostles Peter and Paul, all the Saints, and you, brothers, to pray to the Lord our God for me.

℟. May almighty God be merciful to thee, and forgiving thy sins, bring thee to everlasting life.

℣. Amen.

I CONFESS to almighty God, to the blessed Mary ever Virgin, blessed Michael the Archangel, blessed John the Baptist, the holy Apostles Peter and Paul, to all the Saints, and to you, Father, that I have sinned exceedingly in thought, word, and deed, (**Now strike your breast three times, saying:**) through my fault, through my fault, through my most grievous fault. Therefore I beseech the blessed Mary, ever Virgin, blessed Michael the Archangel, blessed John the Baptist, the holy Apostles Peter and Paul, all the Saints, and you, Father, to pray to the Lord our God for me.

℣. May almighty God be merciful to thee, and forgiving thy sins, bring thee to everlasting life.

℟. Amen.

℣. May the ✠ almighty and merciful Lord grant us pardon, absolution, and remission of our sins.

℟. Amen.

The celebrant bows and continues:

℣. Deus, tu convérsus vivificábis nos.

℟. Et plebs tua lætábitur in te.

℣. Osténde nobis, Dómine, misericórdiam tuam.

℟. Et salutáre tuum da nobis.

℣. Dómine, exáudi oratiónem meam.

℟. Et clamor meus ad te véniat.

℣. Dóminus vobíscum.

℟. Et cum spíritu tuo.

℣. O God, Thou wilt turn again and quicken us.

℟. And thy people shall rejoice in Thee.

℣. Show us, O Lord, Thy mercy.

℟. And grant us Thy salvation.

℣. O Lord, hear my prayer.

℟. And let my cry come before Thee.

℣. The Lord be with you.

℟. And with thy spirit.

ORÉMUS.   LET US PRAY.

The celebrant ascends to the altar and says silently:

AUFER a nobis, quǽsumus, Dómine, iniquitátes nostras: ut ad Sancta sanctórum puris mereámur méntibus introíre. Per Christum, Dóminum nostrum. Amen.

Orámus te, Dómine, per mérita Sanctórum tuórum, quorum relíquiæ hic sunt, et ómnium Sanctórum: ut indulgére dignéris ómnia peccáta mea. Amen.

TAKE away from us our iniquities, we beseech Thee, O Lord, that we may be worthy to enter with pure minds into the Holy of Holies, through Christ our Lord. Amen.

We beseech Thee, O Lord, by the merits of Thy Saints, whose relics are here, and of all the Saints, that Thou wouldst vouchsafe to forgive me all my sins. Amen.

The celebrant kisses the altar and intones the Glória, *during which bells are rung.*

GLÓRIA   I- LUX ET ORÍGO

GLÓRI- A in excélsis De- o. Et in ter- ra pax homí-ni-bus bo-næ vo-luntá- tis. Laudámus te. Bene-dí-ci- mus te. Ado-rámus te. Glo-ri-fi-cá-mus te. Grá-ti- as á-gimus ti- bi propter magnam gló-ri- am tu- am. Dó-mi-ne De- us, Rex cæ-lé-stis, De- us Pa- ter o-mní-pot-ens. Dómi-ne Fi- li u-ni-gé-ni-te Je- su Chri-ste. Dó- mi-ne De- us, Agnus De- i, Fí- li- us Pa-tris. Qui tol-lis peccá-ta mun-di, mi-se-ré-re no- bis. Qui tol-lis peccá-ta mundi, súsci-pe depre-ca- ti- ó-nem nostram. Qui se-des ad déx- te-ram Pa-tris, mi-se-ré-re no- bis. Quó-ni- am tu so-lus sanctus. Tu so-lus Dó- mi-nus. Tu so-lus Altíssi-

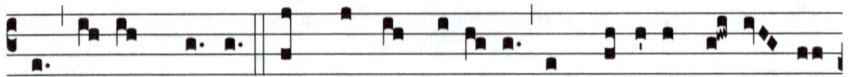

mus, Je- su Chri- ste. Cum Sancto Spí- ri- tu, in gló- ri- a De- i Pa-

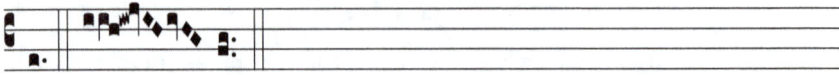

tris. A- men.

GLORIA: Glory be to God on high, and on earth peace to men of good will. We praise Thee. We bless Thee. We adore Thee. We glorify Thee. We give Thee thanks for Thy great glory. O Lord God, heavenly King, God the Father almighty. O Lord Jesus Christ, the only begotten Son. O Lord God, Lamb of God, Son of the Father. Who takest away the sins of the world, have mercy on us. Who takest away the sins of the world, receive our prayer. Who sittest at the right hand of the Father, have mercy on us. For Thou only are holy. Thou only art the Lord. Thou only art most high, O Jesus Christ. Together with the Holy Ghost ✠ in the glory of God the Father. Amen.

COLLECT

The celebrant turns to the people and says:

℣. Dóminus vobíscum.

℞. Et cum spíritu tuo.

ORÉMUS.

DEUS, qui hanc sacratíssimam noctem glória Domínicæ Resurrectiónis illústras: consérva in nova famíliæ tuæ progénie adoptiónis spíritum, quem dedísti; ut, córpore et mente renováti, puram tibi exhíbeant servitútem. Per eúndem Dóminum nostrum Jesum Christum Fílium tuum, qui tecum vivit et regnat in unitáte Spíritus Sancti, Deus, per ómnia sǽcula sæculórum.

℞. Amen.

℣. The Lord be with you.

℞. And with thy spirit.

LET US PRAY.

O GOD, who dost illuminate this most holy night by the glory of the Lord's Resurrection, preserve in the new children of Thy family the spirit of adoption which Thou hast given; that renewed in body and mind, they may render to Thee a pure service. Through the same Jesus Christ, thy Son, Our Lord, Who liveth and reigneth with Thee in the unity of the Holy Ghost, God, world without end.

℞. Amen.

The celebrant reads the Lesson from the Epistle side of the altar, or at a Solemn High Mass the subdeacon sings it:

LESSON FROM THE EPISTLE OF BLESSED PAUL THE APOSTLE TO THE COLOSSIANS
Colossians 3: 1-4

FRATRES: Si consurrexístis cum Christo, quæ sursum sunt quǽrite, ubi Christus est in déxtera Dei sedens: quæ sursum sunt sápite, non quæ super terram. Mórtui enim estis, et vita vestra est abscóndita cum Christo in Deo. Cum Christus apparúerit, vita vestra: tunc et vos apparébitis cum ipso in glória.

BRETHREN, if you be risen with Christ, seek the things that are above, where Christ is sitting at the right hand of God: mind the things that are above, not the things that are upon the earth. For you are dead, and your life is hid with Christ in God. When Christ should appear, who is your life, then you also shall appear with Him in glory.

After the Epistle all rise and the celebrant sings the Allelúia *three times.*

A-LE- LÚ- ia.

After the third time, the choir sings:

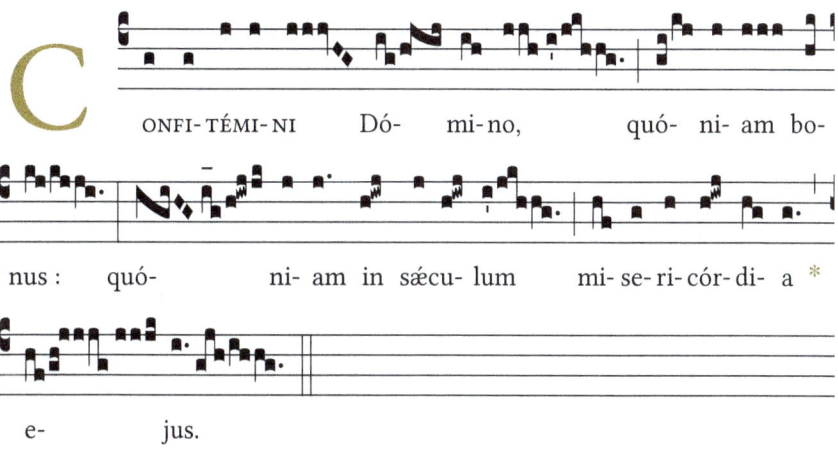

CONFI- TÉMI- NI Dó- mi-no, quó- ni- am bonus: quó- ni- am in sǽcu- lum mi- se- ri- cór-di- a * e- jus.

PSALM 117:1 Give praise to the Lord for He is good: for His mercy endureth forever.

TRACT   PSALM 116: 1-2

LAUDÁ- TE   * Dó- mi- num   omnes gentes : et collau- dá- te   e- um   o- mnes pó- pu-li. ℣. Quó-ni- am confirmá- ta est su- per nos mi-se- ri-cór-di- a e- jus :   et vé-ri- tas Dó- mi- ni   ma- net * in æ-tér- num.

TRACT: O praise the Lord, all ye nations, and praise Him all ye people. ℣. For His mercy is confirmed upon us: and the truth of the Lord remaineth forever.

The Missal is transferred to the Gospel side as the celebrant says the Munda cor. *At a Solemn High Mass the deacon kneels and asks the blessing* (Jube, domne) *before singing the Gospel.*

MUNDA cor meum ac lábia mea, omnípotens Deus, qui lábia Isaíæ Prophétæ cálculo mundásti igníto: ita me tua grata miseratióne dignáre mundáre, ut sanctum Evangélium tuum digne váleam nuntiáre. Per Christum, Dóminum nostrum. Amen.

CLEANSE my heart and my lips, O almighty God, who didst cleanse the lips of the prophet Isaias with a burning coal, and vouchsafe, through Thy gracious mercy, so to purify me, that I may worthily announce Thy holy Gospel. Through Christ our Lord. Amen.

D. Jube, domne, benedícere.

℣. Dóminus sit in corde tuo et in lábiis tuis: ut digne et competénter annúnties Evangélium suum: In nómine Patris, et Fílii, ✠ et Spíritus Sancti.

Amen.

℣. Dóminus vobíscum.
℟. Et cum spíritu tuo.

D. Sir, give me thy blessing.

℣. The Lord be in thy heart and on thy lips, that thou mayst worthily and in a becoming manner, proclaim His holy Gospel. In the name of the Father, and of the Son, ✠ and of the Holy Ghost. Amen.

℣. The Lord be with you.
℟. And with thy spirit.

CONTINUATION ✠ OF THE HOLY GOSPEL ACCORDING TO ST. MATTHEW
Matthew 28:1-7

VÉSPERE autem sábbati, quæ lucéscit in prima sábbati, venit María Magdaléne et áltera María vidére sepúlcrum. Et ecce, terræmótus factus est magnus. Angelus enim Dómini descéndit de cælo: et accédens revólvit lápidem, et sedébat super eum: erat autem aspéctus ejus sicut fulgur: et vestiméntum ejus sicut nix. Præ timóre autem ejus extérriti sunt custódes, et facti sunt velut mórtui. Respóndens autem Angelus, dixit muliéribus: Nolíte timére vos: scio enim, quod Jesum, qui crucifíxus est, quǽritis: non est hic: surréxit enim, sicut dixit. Veníte, et vidéte locum, ubi pósitus erat Dóminus. Et cito eúntes, dícite discípulis ejus, quia surréxit: et ecce, præcédit vos in Galilǽam: ibi eum vidébitis. Ecce, prædíxi vobis.

AND in the end of the Sabbath, when it began to dawn toward the first day of the week, came Mary Magdalen and the other Mary to see the sepulchre. And behold there was a great earthquake. For an Angel of the Lord descended from heaven, and coming, rolled back the stone and sat upon it: and his countenance was as lightning and his raiment as snow. And for fear of him the guards were struck with terror and became as dead men. And the Angel answering, said to the women: Fear not you: for I know that you seek Jesus who was crucified: He is not here: for He is risen, as He said. Come and see the place where the Lord was laid. And going quickly, tell ye His disciples that He is risen: and behold He will go before you into Galilee: there you shall see Him. Lo, I have foretold it to you.

The Creed is not said nor is there an Offertory verse. The celebrant continues:

℣. Dóminus vobíscum.

℟. Et cum spíritu tuo.

℣. The Lord be with you.

℟. And with thy spirit.

Orémus.

Let us pray.

Súscipe, sancte Pater, omnípotens ætérne Deus, hanc immaculátam hóstiam, quam ego indígnus fámulus tuus óffero tibi Deo meo vivo et vero, pro innumerabílibus peccátis, et offensiónibus, et neglegéntiis meis, et pro ómnibus circumstántibus, sed et pro ómnibus fidélibus christiánis vivis atque defúnctis: ut mihi, et illis profíciat ad salútem in vitam ætérnam. Amen.

Accept, O Holy Father, almighty and eternal God, this unspotted host, which I, Thy unworthy servant, offer unto Thee, my living and true God, for my innumerable sins, offenses, and negligences, and for all here present: as also for all faithful Christians, both living and dead, that it may avail both me and them for salvation unto life everlasting. Amen.

Deus, ✠ qui humánæ substántiæ dignitátem mirabíliter condidísti, et mirabílius reformásti: da nobis per hujus aquæ et vini mystérium, ejus divinitátis esse consórtes, qui humanitátis nostræ fíeri dignátus est párticeps, Jesus Christus, Fílius tuus, Dóminus noster: Qui tecum vivit et regnat in unitáte Spíritus Sancti Deus: per ómnia sǽcula sæculórum. Amen.

O God, ✠ who, in creating human nature, didst wonderfully dignify it, and still more wonderfully restore it, grant that, by the Mystery of this water and wine, we may be made partakers of His divine nature, who vouchsafed to be made partaker of our human nature, even Jesus Christ our Lord, Thy Son, who with Thee, liveth and reigneth in the unity of the Holy Ghost, God: world without end. Amen.

Offérimus tibi, Dómine, cálicem salutáris, tuam deprecántes cleméntiam: ut in conspéctu divínæ majestátis tuæ, pro nostra et totíus mundi salúte, cum odóre suavitátis ascéndat. Amen.

We offer unto Thee, O Lord, the chalice of salvation, beseeching Thy clemency, that it may ascend before Thy divine Majesty, as a sweet savor, for our salvation, and for that of the whole world. Amen.

In spíritu humilitátis et in ánimo contríto suscipiámur a te, Dómine: et sic fiat sacrifícium nostrum in conspéctu tuo hódie, ut pláceat tibi, Dómine Deus.

Accept us, O Lord, in the spirit of humility and contrition of heart, and grant that the sacrifice which we offer this day in Thy sight may be pleasing to Thee, O Lord God.

VENI, sanctificátor omnípotens ætérne Deus: et béne✠dic hoc sacrifícium, tuo sancto nómini præparátum.

COME, O almighty and eternal God, the Sanctifier, and bless ✠ this Sacrifice, prepared for the glory of Thy holy Name.

INCENSING

At Solemn High Mass the sacrificial gifts and the altar are incensed respectively, the celebrant first blessing the incense saying:

PER intercessiónem beáti Michaélis Archángeli, stantis a dextris altáris incénsi, et ómnium electórum suórum, incénsum istud dignétur Dóminus bene✠dícere, et in odórem suavitátis accípere. Per Christum, Dóminum nostrum. Amen.

MAY THE Lord, by the intercession of blessed Michael the Archangel, who standeth at the right side of the altar of incense, and of all His Elect, vouchsafe to bless ✠ this incense and receive it as an odor of sweetness: through Jesus Christ our Lord. Amen.

The celebrant receives the thurible from the deacon and incenses the sacrificial gifts saying:

INCÉNSUM istud a te benedíctum ascéndat ad te, Dómine: et descéndat super nos misericórdia tua.

MAY THIS incense, which Thou hast blessed, O Lord, ascend to Thee, and may Thy mercy descend upon us.

The celebrant then incenses the altar, reciting from Psalm 140:

DIRIGÁTUR, Dómine, orátio mea, sicut incénsum, in conspéctu tuo: elevátio mánuum meárum sacrifícium vespertínum. Pone, Dómine, custódiam ori meo, et óstium circumstántiæ lábiis meis: ut non declínet cor meum in verba malítiæ, ad excusándas excusatiónes in peccátis.

LET MY prayer, O Lord, be directed as incense in Thy sight: the lifting up of my hands as an evening sacrifice. Set a watch, O Lord, before my mouth, and a door round about my lips. May my heart not incline to evil words, to make excuses for sins.

The celebrant returns the thurible to the deacon saying:

ACCÉNDAT in nobis Dóminus ignem sui amóris, et flammam ætérnæ caritátis. Amen.

MAY THE Lord enkindle within us the fire of His love, and the flame of everlasting charity. Amen.

LAVÁBO

The celebrant then moves to the Epistle side and washes his fingers, reciting from Psalm 25:

LAVÁBO inter innocéntes manus meas: et circúmdabo altáre tuum, Dómine: Ut áudiam vocem laudis, et enárrem univérsa mirabília tua. Dómine, diléxi decórem domus tuæ et locum habitatiónis glóriæ tuæ. Ne perdas cum ímpiis, Deus, ánimam meam, et cum viris sánguinum vitam meam: In quorum mánibus iniquitátes sunt: déxtera eórum repléta est munéribus. Ego autem in innocéntia mea ingréssus sum: rédime me et miserére mei. Pes meus stetit in dirécto: in ecclésiis benedícam te, Dómine.

℣. Glória Patri, et Fílio, et Spirítui Sancto.

℟. Sicut erat in princípio, et nunc, et semper, et in sǽcula sæculórum. Amen.

I WILL wash my hands among the innocent: and I will compass Thine altar, O Lord That I may hear the voice of praise: and tell of all Thy wonderous works. I have loved, O Lord, the beauty of Thy house and the place where Thy glory dwelleth. Take not away my soul, O God, with the wicked: nor my life with blood-thirsty men. In whose hands are iniquities, their right hand is filled with gifts. But I have walked in my innocence: redeem me, and have mercy on me. My foot hath stood in the direct way, in the churches I will bless Thee, O Lord.

℣. Glory be to the Father, and to the Son, and to the Holy Ghost.

℟. As it was in the beginning, is now, and ever shall be, world without end. Amen.

The celebrant returns to the middle of the altar, bows down and prays:

SÚSCIPE, sancta Trínitas, hanc oblatiónem, quam tibi offérimus ob memóriam passiónis, resurrectiónis, et ascensiónis Jesu Christi, Dómini nostri: et in honórem beátæ Maríæ semper Vírginis, et beáti Joannis Baptístæ, et sanctórum Apostolórum Petri et Pauli, et istórum et ómnium Sanctórum: ut illis profíciat ad honórem, nobis autem ad salútem: et illi pro nobis intercédere dignéntur in cælis, quorum memóriam ágimus in terris. Per eúndem Christum, Dóminum nostrum. Amen.

RECEIVE, O holy Trinity, this oblation which we make to Thee, in memory of the Passion, Resurrection and Ascension of our Lord Jesus Christ, and in honor of Blessed Mary, ever Virgin, blessed John the Baptist, the holy Apostles Peter and Paul, and of all the Saints, that it may avail unto their honor and our salvation, and may they vouchsafe to intercede for us in heaven, whose memory we celebrate on earth. Through the same Christ our Lord.

Amen.

The celebrant kisses the altar and then turns to the people saying:

℣. ORÁTE, FRATRES: ut meum ac vestrum sacrifícium acceptábile fiat apud Deum Patrem omnipoténtem.

℟. Suscípiat Dóminus sacrifícium de mánibus tuis ad laudem et glóriam nominis sui, ad utilitátem quoque nostram, totiúsque Ecclésiæ suæ sanctæ.

℣. Amen.

℣. BRETHREN, PRAY that my Sacrifice and yours may be acceptable to God the Father almighty.

℟. May the Lord receive the Sacrifice from thy hands, to the praise and glory of His Name, to our benefit and that of all His holy Church.

℣. Amen.

SECRET & PREFACE

SÚSCIPE, quǽsumus, Dómine, preces pópuli tui, cum oblatiónibus hostiárum: ut paschálibus initiátam mystériis, ad æternitátis nobis medélam, te operánte, profíciant. Per Dóminum nostrum Jesum Christum, Fílium tuum: qui tecum vivit et regnat in unitáte Spíritus Sancti Deus:

ACCEPT, we beseech Thee, O Lord, the prayers of Thy people together with the sacrifice they offer: that what has begun by the Paschal Mysteries, may by Thine arrangement result in our eternal healing. Through Jesus Christ, Thy Son our Lord, Who liveth and reigneth with Thee, in the unity of the Holy Ghost, God:

PER ómnia sǽcula sæculórum.
℟. Amen.
℣. Dóminus vobíscum.
℟. Et cum spíritu tuo.
℣. Sursum corda.
℟. Habémus ad Dóminum.

℣. Grátias agámus Dómino, Deo nostro.
℟. Dignum et justum est.

WORLD without end.
℟. Amen.
℣. The Lord be with you.
℟. And with thy spirit.
℣. Lift up your hearts.
℟. We have lifted them up to the Lord.

℣. Let us give thanks to the Lord our God.
℟. It is meet and just.

PREFACE FOR EASTER

VERE dignum et justum est, æquum et salutáre: Te quidem, Dómine, omni témpore, sed in hac potíssimum nocte gloriósius prædicáre, cum Pascha nostrum immolátus est Christus.

IT is truly meet and just, right and for our salvation, at all times to praise Thee, O Lord, but more gloriously especially this night when Christ our Pasch was sacrificed.

Ipse enim verus est Agnus, qui ábstulit peccáta mundi. Qui mortem nostram moriéndo destrúxit et vitam resurgéndo reparávit. Et ídeo cum Angelis et Archángelis, cum Thronis et Dominatiónibus cumque omni milítia cæléstis exércitus hymnum glóriæ tuæ cánimus, sine fine dicéntes:

For He is the Lamb Who hath taken away the sins of the world: Who by dying hath destroyed our death: and by rising again hath restored us to life. And therefore with Angels and Archangels, with Thrones and Dominations, and with all the hosts of the heavenly army, we sing the hymn of Thy glory, evermore saying:

SANCTUS   I- LUX ET ORÍGO

SANCTUS, * Sanctus, Sanctus Dómi-nus De- us Sá-ba- oth. Ple-ni sunt cæ- li et terra gló- ri-a tu-a. Ho-sánna in ex-cél-sis. Be-ne-díctus qui ve-nit in nó-mi-ne Dómi-ni. Ho- sánna in excél- sis.

SANCTUS: Holy, Holy, Holy, Lord God of Sabaoth. Heaven and earth are full of Thy glory. Hosanna in the highest. Blessed is He that cometh in the Name of the Lord. Hosanna in the highest.

THE CANON OF THE MASS

The celebrant joins his hands and bows over the altar, silently praying:

TE ígitur, clementíssime Pater, per Jesum Christum, Fílium tuum, Dóminum nostrum, súpplices rogámus, ac pétimus, uti accépta hábeas et benedícas, hæc ✠ dona, hæc ✠ múnera, hæc ✠ sancta sacrifícia illibáta, in primis, quæ tibi offérimus pro Ecclésia tua sancta cathólica: quam pacificáre, custodíre, adunáre et régere dignéris toto orbe terrárum: una cum fámulo tuo Papa nostro **N.** et Antístite nostro **N.** et ómnibus orthodóxis, atque cathólicæ et apostólicæ fídei cultóribus.

MEMÉNTO, Dómine, famulórum famularúmque tuarum **N.** et **N.** et ómnium circumstántium, quorum tibi fides cógnita est et nota devótio, pro quibus tibi offérimus: vel qui tibi ófferunt hoc sacrifícium laudis, pro se suísque ómnibus: pro redemptióne animárum suárum, pro spe salútis et incolumitátis suæ: tibíque reddunt vota sua ætérno Deo, vivo et vero.

COMMUNICÁNTES, et noctem sacratíssimam celebrántes Resurrectiónis Dómini nostri Jesu Christi secúndum carnem: sed et memóriam venerántes, in primis gloriósæ semper Vírginis Maríæ, Genetrícis ejúsdem Dei et Dómini nostri Jesu Christi: sed et beatórum Apostolórum ac Mártyrum tuórum, Petri et Pauli, Andréæ, Jacóbi, Joánnis, Thomæ, Jacóbi, Philíppi, Bartholomǽi, Matthǽi, Simónis et Thaddǽi: Lini, Cleti,

WE therefore, humbly pray and beseech Thee, most merciful Father, through Jesus Christ; Thy Son, our Lord, that Thou wouldst vouchsafe to accept and bless these ✠ gifts, these ✠ presents, these ✠ holy unspotted Sacrifices, which in the first place we offer Thee for Thy holy Catholic Church to which vouchsafe to grant peace, as also to preserve, unite, and govern it throughout the world, together with Thy servant **N.,** our Pope, and **N.,** our Bishop, and all orthodox believers and professors of the Catholic and Apostolic Faith.

BE MINDFUL, O Lord, of Thy servants and handmaidens, **N.** and **N.,** and of all here present, whose faith and devotion are known unto Thee, for whom we offer, or who offer up to Thee, this sacrifice of praise for themselves, their families and friends, for the redemption of their souls, for the health and salvation they hope for; and who now pay their vows to Thee, the everlasting, living and true God.

COMMUNICATING, and keeping this most holy night of the Resurrection of our Lord Jesus Christ according to the flesh; and also reverencing the memory, first, of the glorious Mary, ever Virgin, Mother of the same our God and Lord Jesus Christ: as also of the blessed Apostles and Martyrs Peter and Paul, Andrew, James, John, Thomas, James, Philip, Bartholomew, Matthew, Simon, and Thaddeus; Linus, Cletus, Clement,

Cleméntis, Xysti, Cornélii, Cypriáni, Lauréntii, Chrysógoni, Joánnis et Pauli, Cosmæ et Damiáni: et ómnium Sanctórum tuórum; quorum méritis precibúsque concédas, ut in ómnibus protectiónis tuæ muniámur auxílio. Per eúndem Christum, Dóminum nostrum. Amen.

Xystus, Cornelius, Cyprian, Lawrence, Chrysogonus, John and Paul, Cosmas and Damian, and of all Thy Saints, through whose merits and prayers, grant that we may in all things be defended by the help of Thy protection. Through the same Christ our Lord. Amen.

The bell is rung as the celebrant extends his hands over the oblation and says:

HANC ígitur oblatiónem servitútis nostræ, sed et cunctæ famíliæ tuæ, quam tibi offérimus pro his quoque, quos regeneráre dignátus es ex aqua et Spíritu Sancto, tríbuens eis remissiónem ómnium peccatórum, quǽsumus, Dómine, ut placátus accípias: diésque nostros in tua pace dispónas, atque ab ætérna damnatióne nos éripi, et in electórum tuórum júbeas grege numerári. Per eúndem Christum, Dóminum nostrum. Amen.

WE therefore beseech Thee, O Lord, graciously to accept this oblation of our service, as also of Thy whole family, which we make unto Thee on behalf of these whom Thou hast vouchsafed to bring to a new birth by water and the Holy Ghost, granting them remission of all their sins: and to dispose our days in Thy peace, preserve us from final damnation and rank us in the number of Thine Elect. Through the same Christ our Lord. Amen.

QUAM oblatiónem tu, Deus, in ómnibus, quǽsumus, bene✠díctam, adscríp✠tam, ra✠tam, rationábilem acceptabilémque fácere dignéris: ut nobis Cor✠pus, et San✠guis fiat dilectíssimi Fílii tui, Dómini nostri Jesu Christi.

WHICH oblation do Thou, O God, vouchsafe in all respects, to bless, ✠ approve, ✠ ratify, ✠ make worthy and acceptable; that it may be made for us the Body ✠ and Blood ✠ of Thy most beloved Son Jesus Christ our Lord.

QUI prídie, quam pro nostra omniúmque salúte paterétur, hoc est hódie, accépit panem in sanctas ac venerábiles manus suas, et elevátis óculis in cælum ad te Deum, Patrem suum omnipoténtem, tibi grátias agens, bene✠dixit, fregit, dedítque discípulis suis, dicens: Accípite, et manducáte ex hoc omnes.

WHO, the day before He suffered for our salvation and that of all men, that is, on this day, took bread into His most sacred and venerable hands and with His eyes lifted up towards heaven unto Thee, God, His almighty Father, giving thanks to Thee, He blessed ✠ it, broke it and gave it to His disciples saying: Take and eat ye all of this,

Hoc est enim corpus meum.

For this is my body.

The celebrant kneels before the Host and adores. He then elevates the Sacred Host as the bell is rung. The celebrant then uncovers the chalice and says:

Símili modo postquam cenátum est, accípiens et hunc præclárum Cálicem in sanctas ac venerábiles manus suas: item tibi grátias agens, bene✠díxit, dedítque discípulis suis, dicens: Accípite, et bíbite ex eo omnes.

In like manner, after He had supped, taking also this excellent chalice into His holy and venerable hands He blessed ✠, and gave it to His disciples, saying: Take and drink ye all of this.

Hic est enim Calix Sánguinis mei, novi et ætérni testaménti; mystérium fidei: qui pro vobis et pro multis effundétur in remissiónem peccatórum.

For this is the Chalice of my Blood, of the new and eternal testament; the mystery of faith: which shall be shed for you and for many unto the remission of sins.

Hæc quotiescúmque fecéritis, in mei memóriam faciétis.

As often as ye shall do these things, ye shall do them in memory of me.

The celebrant kneels before the Precious Blood and adores. He then elevates the Precious Blood as the bell is rung. Following this the celebrant continues:

Unde et mémores, Dómine, nos servi tui, sed et plebs tua sancta, ejúsdem Christi Fílii tui, Dómini nostri, tam beátæ passiónis, nec non et ab ínferis resurrectiónis, sed et in cælos gloriósæ ascensiónis: offérimus præclárae majestáti tuæ de tuis donis ac datis, hóstiam ✠ puram, hóstiam ✠ sanctam, hóstiam ✠ immaculátam, Panem ✠ sanctum vitæ ætérnæ, et Cálicem ✠ salútis perpétuæ.

Wherefore, O Lord, we Thy servants, as also Thy holy people, calling to mind the blessed Passion of the same Christ, Thy Son, our Lord, and also His Resurrection from the dead and His glorious Ascension into heaven: do offer unto Thy most excellent Majesty of Thine own gifts, bestowed upon us, a pure ✠ Host, a holy ✠ Host, an unspotted ✠ Host, the holy ✠ Bread of eternal life, and the Chalice ✠ of everlasting salvation.

Supra quæ propítio ac seréno vultu respícere dignéris: et accépta habére, sicúti accépta habére dignátus es múnera púeri tui justi Abel, et sacrifícium Patriárchæ nostri Abrahæ:

Upon which vouchsafe to look with a propitious and serene countenance, and to accept them, as Thou wert graciously pleased to accept the gifts of Thy just servant Abel, and

et quod tibi óbtulit summus sacérdos tuus Melchísedech, sanctum sacrifícium, immaculátam hóstiam.

Súpplices te rogámus, omnípotens Deus: jube hæc perférri per manus sancti Angeli tui in sublíme altáre tuum, in conspéctu divínæ majestátis tuæ: ut, quotquot ex hac altáris participatióne sacrosánctum Fílii tui Cor✠pus, et Sán✠guinem sumpsérimus, omni benedictióne cælésti et grátia repleámur. Per eúndem Christum, Dóminum nostrum. Amen.

the sacrifice of our patriarch Abraham, and that which Thy high priest Melchisedech offered to Thee, a holy Sacrifice, and unspotted Victim.

We most humbly beseech Thee, almighty God, command these offerings to be borne by the hands of Thy holy Angel to Thine altar on high, in the sight of Thy divine majesty, that as many as shall partake of the most holy Body ✠ and Blood ✠ of Thy Son at this altar, may be filled with every heavenly grace and blessing. Through the same Christ our Lord. Amen.

The celebrant now commemorates and intercedes for the dead saying:

MEMÉNTO étiam, Dómine, famulórum famularúmque tuárum **N.** et **N.,** qui nos præcessérunt cum signo fídei, et dórmiunt in somno pacis. Ipsis, Dómine, et ómnibus in Christo quiescéntibus locum refrigérii, lucis, et pacis, ut indúlgeas, deprecámur. Per eúndem Christum, Dóminum nostrum. Amen.

Nobis quoque peccatóribus fámulis tuis, de multitúdine miseratiónum tuárum sperántibus, partem áliquam et societátem donáre dignéris, cum tuis sanctis Apóstolis et Martýribus: cum Joánne, Stéphano, Matthía, Bárnaba, Ignátio, Alexándro, Marcellíno, Petro, Felicitáte, Perpétua, Agatha, Lúcia, Agnéte, Cæcília, Anastásia, et ómnibus Sanctis tuis: intra quorum nos consórtium, non æstimátor mériti, sed véniæ, quǽsumus, largítor admítte. Per Christum, Dóminum nostrum.

REMEMBER also, O Lord, Thy servants and handmaids **N.** and **N.,** who are gone before us with the sign of faith, and rest in the sleep of peace. To these, O Lord, and to all that rest in Christ, grant, we beseech Thee, a place of refreshment, light, and peace; Through the same Christ our Lord. Amen.

To us also, Thy sinful servants, confiding in the multitude of Thy mercies, vouchsafe to grant some part and fellowship with Thy holy Apostles and Martyrs, with John, Stephen, Matthias, Barnabas, Ignatius, Alexander, Marcellinus, Peter, Felicitas, Perpetua, Agatha, Lucy, Agnes, Cecilia, Anastasia, and with all Thy Saints, into whose company we beseech Thee to admit us, not weighing our merits, but pardoning our offenses. Through Christ our Lord.

The celebrant reverences the Sacred Host and Chalice and then continues:

PER quem hæc ómnia, Dómine, semper bona creas, sanctí✠ficas, viví✠ficas, bene✠dícis et præstas nobis.

BY Whom, O Lord, Thou dost ever create, sanctify, ✠ quicken, ✠ bless, ✠ and give unto us all these good things.

Per ip✠sum, et cum ip✠so, et in ip✠so, est tibi Deo Patri ✠ omnipoténti, in unitáte Spíritus ✠ Sancti, omnis honor, et glória.

By Him, ✠ and with Him, ✠ and in Him ✠ is to Thee, God the Father ✠ almighty, in the unity of the Holy ✠ Ghost, all honor and glory.

LORD'S PRAYER

PER ómnia sæcula sæculórum.
℟. Amen.

ORÉMUS: Præcéptis salutáribus móniti, et divína institutióne formáti audémus dícere:

WORLD without end.
℟. Amen.

LET US PRAY. Instructed by Thy saving precepts, and formed by Thy divine institution, we are bold to say:

PATER noster, qui es in cælis, sanctificétur nomen tuum: advéniat regnum tuum: fiat volúntas tua, sicut in cælo et in terra. Panem nostrum quotidiánum da nobis hódie: et dimítte nobis débita nostra, sicut et nos dimíttimus debitóribus nostris: et ne nos indúcas in tentatiónem:
℟. Sed líbera nos a malo
℣. Amen.

OUR Father, who art in heaven, hallowed be Thy Name; Thy kingdom come; Thy will be done on earth as it is in heaven. Give us this day our daily bread. And forgive us our trespasses, as we forgive those who trespass against us. And lead us not into temptation.
℟. But deliver us from evil.
℣. Amen.

LÍBERA nos, quǽsumus, Dómine, ab ómnibus malis, prætéritis, præséntibus et futúris: et intercedénte beáta et gloriósa semper Vírgine Dei Genetríce María, cum beátis Apóstolis tuis Petro et Paulo, atque Andréa, et ómnibus Sanctis, da propítius pacem in diébus nostris, ut, ope misericórdiæ tuæ adjúti, et a peccáto simus semper

DELIVER us, we beseech Thee, O Lord, from all evils, past, present, and to come; and by the intercession of the Blessed and glorious ever Virgin Mary, Mother of God, and of the holy Apostles, Peter and Paul, and of Andrew, and of all the Saints, mercifully grant peace in our days, that through the assistance of Thy mercy we may be

líberi et ab omni perturbatióne secúri. Per eúndem Dóminum nostrum Jesum Christum, Fílium tuum. Qui tecum vivit et regnat in unitáte Spíritus Sancti Deus.

always free from sin, and secure from all disturbance. Through the same Jesus Christ, Thy Son, our Lord. Who with Thee in the unity of the Holy Ghost liveth and reigneth God,

P ER ómnia sǽcula sæculórum.
     ℟. Amen.
     ℣. Pax Dómini sit semper vobíscum.

     ℟. Et cum spíritu tuo.

W ORLD without end.
     ℟. Amen.
     ℣. The peace of the Lord be always with you.

     ℟. And with thy spirit.

The celebrant drops a particle of the Sacred Host into the chalice saying:

H ÆC commíxtio, et consecrátio Córporis et Sánguinis Dómini nostri Jesu Christi, fiat accipiéntibus nobis in vitam ætérnam. Amen.

M AY this mixture and consecration of the Body and Blood of our Lord Jesus Christ be to us who receive it effectual unto eternal life. Amen.

The celebrant continues. The Kiss of Peace and the Agnus Dei are omitted today.

D ÓMINE Jesu Christe, qui dixísti Apóstolis tuis: Pacem relínquo vobis, pacem meam do vobis: ne respícias peccáta mea, sed fidem Ecclésiæ tuæ; eámque secúndum voluntátem tuam pacificáre et coadunáre dignéris: Qui vivis et regnas Deus per ómnia sǽcula sæculórum. Amen.

DÓMINE Jesu Christe, Fili Dei vivi, qui ex voluntáte Patris, cooperánte Spíritu Sancto, per mortem tuam mundum vivificásti: líbera me per hoc sacrosánctum Corpus et Sánguinem tuum ab ómnibus iniquitátibus meis, et univérsis malis: et fac me tuis semper inhærére mandátis, et a te numquam separári permíttas: Qui cum eódem Deo Patre et Spíritu Sancto vivis et regnas Deus in sǽcula sæculórum. Amen.

O LORD Jesus Christ, who saidst to Thine Apostles: Peace I leave you, My peace I give you: regard not my sins, but the faith of Thy Church; and vouchsafe to grant her that peace and unity which is agreeable to Thy will: Who livest and reignest God, world without end. Amen.

O LORD Jesus Christ, Son of the living God, who, according to the will of Thy Father, with the cooperation of the Holy Ghost, hast by Thy death given life to the world; deliver me by this Thy most sacred Body and Blood, from all my iniquities and from all evils; and make me always cleave to Thy commandments, and suffer me never to be separated from Thee, Who livest and reignest, with the same God the Father and the Holy Ghost, God, world without end. Amen.

PERCÉPTIO Córporis tui, Dómine Jesu Christe, quod ego indígnus súmere præsúmo, non mihi provéniat in judícium et condemnatiónem: sed pro tua pietáte prosit mihi ad tutaméntum mentis et córporis, et ad medélam percipiéndam: Qui vivis et regnas cum Deo Patre in unitáte Spíritus Sancti Deus, per ómnia sǽcula sæculórum. Amen.

LET NOT the partaking of Thy Body, O Lord, Jesus Christ, which I, though unworthy, presume to receive, turn to my judgment and condemnation; but let it, through Thy mercy, become a safeguard and remedy, both for soul and body; Who with God the Father, in the unity of the Holy Ghost, livest and reignest God, world without end. Amen.

The celebrant genuflects, rises and then says:

P ANEM cæléstem accípiam, et nomen Dómini invocábo.

I WILL TAKE the Bread of heaven, and will call upon the Name of the Lord.

The celebrant strikes his breast and says three times:

DÓMINE, non sum dignus, ut intres sub tectum meum: sed tantum dic verbo, et sanábitur ánima mea.

LORD, I am not worthy that Thou shouldst enter under my roof; say but the word, and my soul shall be healed.

The celebrant makes the Sign of the Cross with the Sacred Host and says:

CORPUS Dómini nostri Jesu Christi custódiat ánimam meam in vitam ætérnam. Amen.

THE BODY of our Lord Jesus Christ preserve my soul unto life everlasting. Amen.

The celebrant consumes the Sacred Host and then purifies the paten saying:

QUID retríbuam Dómino pro ómnibus, quæ retríbuit mihi? Cálicem salutáris accípiam, et nomen Dómini invocábo. Laudans invocábo Dóminum, et ab inimícis meis salvus ero.

WHAT return shall I make to the Lord for all He has given to me? I will take the chalice of salvation, and call upon the Name of the Lord. Praising I will call upon the Lord, and I shall be saved from my enemies.

The celebrant makes the Sign of the Cross with the Chalice saying:

SANGUIS Dómini nostri Jesu Christi custódiat ánimam meam in vitam ætérnam. Amen.

THE BLOOD of our Lord Jesus Christ preserve my soul unto life everlasting. Amen.

The celebrant consumes the Precious Blood as the servers repeat the Confíteor. *At Solemn High Mass this is often chanted:*

CONFÍTEOR Deo omnipoténti, beátæ Maríæ semper Vírgini, beáto Michaéli Archángelo, beáto Joánni Baptístæ, sanctis Apóstolis Petro et Paulo, ómnibus Sanctis, et tibi, pater: quia peccávi nimis cogitatióne, verbo et ópere: (**Pércutit sibi pectus ter, dicens**) mea culpa, mea culpa, mea máxima culpa. Ideo precor beátam Maríam semper Vírginem, beátum Michaélem Archángelum, beátum Joánnem Baptístam, sanctos Apóstolos Petrum et Paulum, omnes Sanctos, et te, pater, oráre pro me ad Dóminum, Deum nostrum.

℣. Misereátur vestri omnípotens Deus, et, dimíssis peccátis vestris, perdúcat vos ad vitam ætérnam.

℟. Amen.

℣. Indulgéntiam, ✠ absolutiónem et remissiónem peccatórum nostrórum tríbuat nobis omnípotens et miséricors Dóminus.

℟. Amen.

I CONFESS to almighty God, to the blessed Mary ever Virgin, blessed Michael the Archangel, blessed John the Baptist, the holy Apostles Peter and Paul, to all the Saints, and to you, Father, that I have sinned exceedingly in thought, word, and deed, (**Now strike your breast three times, saying:**) through my fault, through my fault, through my most grievous fault. Therefore I beseech the blessed Mary, ever Virgin, blessed Michael the Archangel, blessed John the Baptist, the holy Apostles Peter and Paul, all the Saints, and you, Father, to pray to the Lord our God for me.

℣. May almighty God be merciful to thee, and forgiving thy sins, bring thee to everlasting life.

℟. Amen.

℣. May the ✠ almighty and merciful Lord grant us pardon, absolution, and remission of our sins.

℟. Amen.

The celebrant faces the people holding up one of the Sacred Hosts and says:

ECCE Agnus Dei, ecce qui tollit peccáta mundi.

BEHOLD the Lamb of God, behold Him Who taketh away the sins of the world.

The following is said three times:

DÓMINE, non sum dignus, ut intres sub tectum meum: sed tantum dic verbo, et sanábitur ánima mea.

LORD, I am not worthy that Thou shouldst enter under my roof; say but the word, and my soul shall be healed.

After distributing Holy Communion the celebrant purifies the sacred vessels. At Solemn High Mass the subdeacon takes the Chalice from the celebrant for purifying as the celebrant says:

QUOD ore súmpsimus, Dómine, pura mente capiámus; et de múnere temporáli fiat nobis remédium sempitérnum.

GRANT, O Lord, that what we have taken with our mouth, we may receive with a pure mind; and from a temporal gift may it become to us an eternal remedy.

CORPUS tuum, Dómine, quod sumpsi, et Sanguis, quem potávi, adhǽreat viscéribus meis: et præsta; ut in me non remáneat scélerum mácula, quem pura et sancta refecérunt sacraménta: Qui vivis et regnas in sǽcula sæculórum. Amen.

MAY THY Body, O Lord, which I have received, and Thy Blood which I have drunk, cleave to my bowels; and grant that no stain of sin may remain in me, who have been fed with this pure and holy Sacrament; Who livest and reignest for ever and ever. Amen.

VESPERS

Vespers begins with the following antiphon:

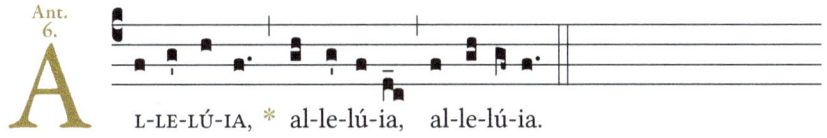

Ant. 6.

AL-LE-LÚ-IA, * al-le-lú-ia, al-le-lú-ia.

PSALM 116

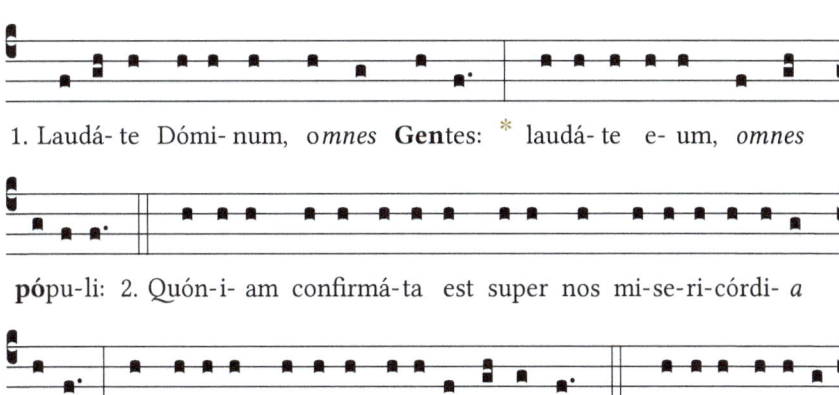

1. Laudá- te Dómi- num, o*mnes* **Gen**tes: * laudá- te e- um, *omnes*

pópu-li: 2. Quón-i- am confirmá-ta est super nos mi-se-ri-córdi- *a*

e-jus: * et vé-ri-tas Dómi-ni manet *in* æ-**tér**num. 3. Gló-ri- a Patri, *et*

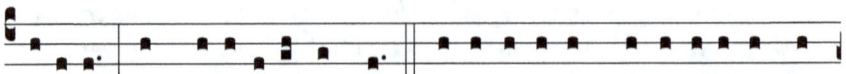

Fí-li- o, * et Spi-rí-*tu- i* **San**cto. 4. Sic-ut e-rat in princí-pi- o, et nunc,

et **sem**per, * et in sǽcu-la sæcu-*ló-rum.* Amen.

1. Praise the Lord all ye nations: * praise him, all ye people.

2. For his mercy is confirmed upon us: * and the truth of the Lord remaineth for ever.

3. Glory be to the Father, and to the Son, * and to the Holy Ghost.

4. As it was in the beginning, is now, * and ever shall be, world without end. Amen.

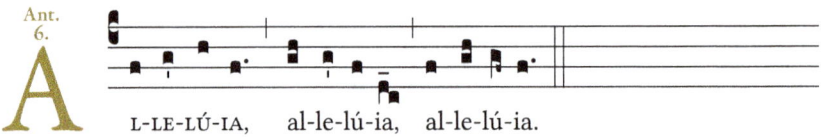

L-LE-LÚ-IA,   al-le-lú-ia,   al-le-lú-ia.

The celebrant then intones the antiphon at the Magníficat:

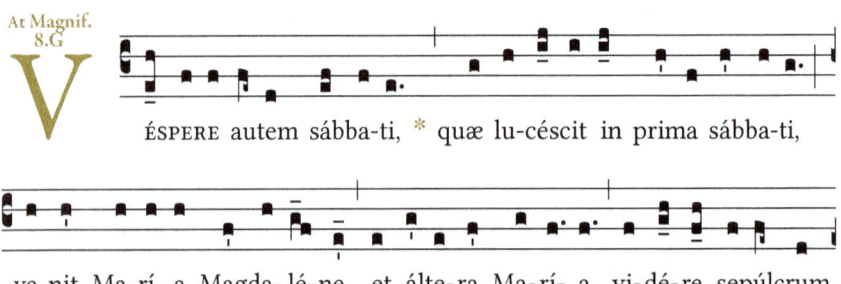

ÉSPERE autem sábba-ti, * quæ lu-céscit in prima sábba-ti,

ve-nit Ma-rí- a Magda-lé-ne, et álte-ra Ma-rí- a, vi-dé-re sepúlcrum,

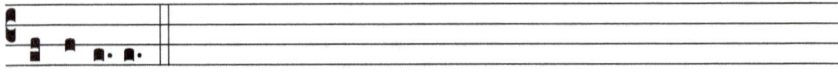

al-le-lú-ia.

ANTIPHON: And in the end of the sabbath, when it began to dawn towards the first day of the week, came Mary Magdalen and the other Mary, to see the sepulchre, alleluia.

MAGNÍFICAT

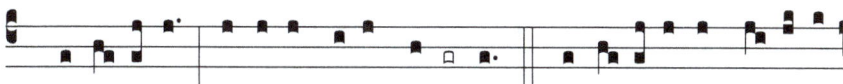

1. Magní- fi-cat ✠ á-nima *me- a* **Dó**mi-num. 2. Et exsultá-vit *spí- ri-tus*

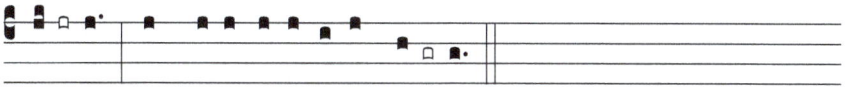

me- us * in De- o sa-lu-*tá-ri* **me**- o.

1. My soul ✠ doth magnify the Lord.
2. And my spirit hath rejoiced * in God my Saviour.

3. Quia respéxit humilitátem *ancíllæ* **su**æ: * ecce enim ex hoc beátam me dicent omnes gene*ratió*nes.

3. Because he hath regarded the humility of his handmaid; * for behold from henceforth all generations shall call me blessed.

4. Quia fecit mihi *magna qui* **po**tens est: * et sanctum *nomen* ejus.

4. Because he that is mighty, hath done great things to me; * and holy is his name.

5. Et misericórdia ejus a progénie *in prog*é*nies* * timén*ti-bus* eum.

5. And his mercy is from generation unto generations, * to them that fear him.

6. Fecit poténtiam in *bráchio* **su**o: * dispérsit supérbos mente *cordis* **su**i.

6. He hath showed might in his arm: * he hath scattered the proud in the conceit of their heart.

7. Depósuit pot*éntes de* **se**de, * et exal*távit* **hú**miles.

7. He hath put down the mighty from their seat, * and hath exalted the humble.

8. Esuriéntes *implévit* **bo**nis: * et dívites dim*ísit in*ánes.

8. He hath filled the hungry with good things; * and the rich he hath sent empty away.

9. Suscépit Israël *púerum* **su**um, * recordátus misericór*diæ* **su**æ.

9. He hath received Israel his servant, * being mindful of his mercy:

10. Sicut locútus est *ad patres* **no**stros, * Abraham et sémini e*jus in* **sǽ**cula.

10. As he spoke to our fathers, * to Abraham and to his seed for ever.

11. Glória *Patri, et* **Fí**lio, * et Spirí-*tui* **San**cto.

11. Glory be to the Father, and to the Son, * and to the Holy Ghost.

12. Sicut erat in princípio, *et nunc, et* **sem**per, * et in sǽcula sæcu*lórum.* **A**men.

12. As it was in the beginning, is now, * and ever shall be, world without end. Amen.

At Magnif.
8.G

Véspere autem sábba-ti,   quæ lu-céscit in prima sábba-ti,

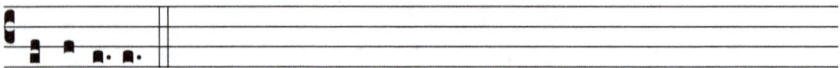

ve-nit Ma-rí- a Magda-lé-ne, et álte-ra Ma-rí- a, vi-dé-re sepúlcrum,

al-le-lú-ia.

The celebrant turns to the people and says:

℣. Dóminus vobíscum.   ℣. The Lord be with you.

℟. Et cum spíritu tuo.   ℟. And with thy spirit.

ORÉMUS.   LET US PRAY.

SPÍRITUM nobis, Dómine, tuæ caritátis infúnde: ut, quos sacraméntis paschálibus satiásti, tua fácias pietáte concórdes. Per Dóminum nostrum Jesum Christum, Fílium tuum: qui tecum vivit et regnat in unitáte ejúsdem Spíritus Sancti Deus, per ómnia sǽcula sæculórum.

POUR forth, O Lord, we beseech thee, the Spirit of thy love into our hearts, and by thy mercy make all them to be of one mind to whom Thou hast given to eat of thy mystic Passover. Through Jesus Christ, Thy Son our Lord, Who liveth and reigneth with Thee, in the unity of the same Holy Ghost, God, world without end.

℟. Amen.   ℟. Amen.

The celebrant turns to the people and says:

℣. Dóminus vobíscum.   ℣. The Lord be with you.

℟. Et cum spíritu tuo.   ℟. And with thy spirit.

At Solemn High Mass the deacon chants the Ite, Missa est:

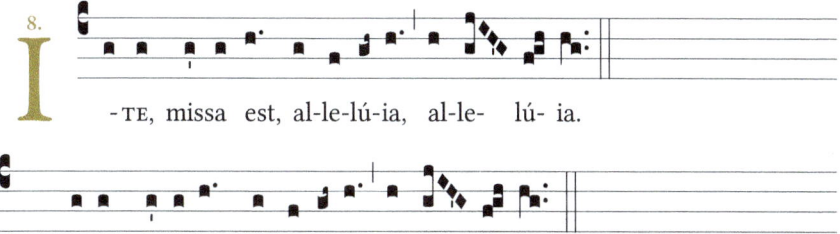

-TE, missa est, al-le-lú-ia, al-le- lú- ia.

℟. De- o grá-ti- as, al-le-lú-ia, al-le- lú- ia.

Ite Missa Est: Go, the Mass is ended, alleluia, alleluia. ℟. Thanks be to God, allelúia, allelúia.

The celebrant bows over the altar and silently says:

Pláceat tibi, sancta Trínitas, obséquium servitútis meæ: et præsta; ut sacrifícium, quod óculis tuæ majestátis indígnus óbtuli, tibi sit acceptábile, mihíque et ómnibus, pro quibus illud óbtuli, sit, te miseránte, propitiábile. Per Christum, Dóminum nostrum. Amen.

May the performance of my homage be pleasing to Thee, O holy Trinity: and grant that the Sacrifice which I, though unworthy, have offered up in the sight of Thy Majesty, may be acceptable to Thee, and through Thy mercy, be a propitiation for me, and for all those for whom I have offered it. Through Christ our Lord. Amen.

The people kneel and the celebrant turns towards them for the blessing saying:

℣. Benedícat vos omnípotens Deus, Pater, et Fílius, ✠ et Spíritus Sanctus.
℟. Amen.

℣. May almighty God the Father, Son, ✠ and Holy Ghost, bless you.
℟. Amen.

The people stand as the celebrant moves to the Gospel side of the altar and reads the Last Gospel:

℣. Dóminus vobíscum.
℟. Et cum spíritu tuo.

℣. The Lord be with you.
℟. And with thy spirit.

THE BEGINNING ✠ OF THE HOLY GOSPEL
ACCORDING TO JOHN
John 1: 1-14

IN princípio erat Verbum, et Verbum erat apud Deum, et Deus erat Verbum. Hoc erat in princípio apud Deum. Omnia per ipsum facta sunt: et sine ipso factum est nihil, quod factum est: in ipso vita erat, et vita erat lux hóminum: et lux in ténebris lucet, et ténebræ eam non comprehendérunt.

Fuit homo missus a Deo, cui nomen erat Joánnes. Hic venit in testimónium, ut testimónium perhibéret de lúmine, ut omnes créderent per illum. Non erat ille lux, sed ut testimónium perhibéret de lúmine.

Erat lux vera, quæ illúminat omnem hóminem veniéntem in hunc mundum. In mundo erat, et mundus per ipsum factus est, et mundus eum non cognóvit. In própria venit, et sui eum non recepérunt. Quotquot autem recepérunt eum, dedit eis potestátem fílios Dei fíeri, his, qui credunt in nómine ejus: qui non ex sanguínibus, neque ex voluntáte carnis, neque ex voluntáte viri, sed ex Deo nati sunt.

(**Genufléctit dicens:**)

ET VERBUM CARO FACTUM EST, et habitávit in nobis: et vídimus glóriam ejus, glóriam quasi Unigéniti a Patre, plenum grátiæ et veritátis.

℟. Deo grátias.

IN the beginning was the Word, and the Word was with God, and the Word was God. The same was in the beginning with God. All things were made by Him, and without Him was made nothing that was made: in Him was life, and the life was the Light of men; and the Light shineth in darkness, and the darkness did not comprehend it.

There was a man sent from God, whose name was John. This man came for a witness, to testify concerning the Light, that all might believe through Him. He was not the Light, but he was to testify concerning the Light.

That was the true Light, which enlighteneth every man that cometh into this world. He was in the world, and the world was made by Him, and the world knew Him not. He came unto His own, and His own received Him not. But as many as received Him to them He gave power to become sons of God, to them that believe in His Name, who are born not of blood, nor of the will of the flesh, nor of the will of man, but of God.

(**Here all kneel.**)

AND THE WORD WAS MADE FLESH, and dwelt among us: and we saw His glory, the glory as of the Only begotten of the Father, full of grace and truth.

℟. Thanks be to God.

APPENDIX

ALTERNATE CHANTS- LAMENTATIONS

MOZARIBIC

HOLY THURSDAY - MATINS   LECTIO 1

IN-CI-PIT lamentá-ti- o Je-remí- æ Prophé-tæ. ALEPH.

Quómodo se-det so-la cí-vi-tas plena pópu- lo: facta est qua-si ví-

du- a dómi-na Génti- um: princeps pro-vinci- á- rum facta est sub

tri-bú-to. BETH. Plo-rans plo-rá-vit in nocte, et lácrimæ é-jus

in ma-xíl-lis é- jus. Non est qui conso-lé-tur e- am ex ómni-bus

ca-ris é-jus. Omnes amí-ci é-jus spre-vé-runt e- am, et facti sunt

e- i i-ni-mí-ci. Ghimel. Migrá-vit Júdas propter afflicti- ónem

et mul-ti-tú-di-nem servi-tú-tis : ha-bi-tá-vit inter gentes, nec invé-

nit réqui- em. Omnes perse-cu-tó-res é-jus apprehendé-runt e- am

in-ter angú-sti- as. Da-leth. Vi- æ Si- on lugent, e- o quod non

sint qui vé-ni- ant ad so-lemni-tá-tem : omnes portæ é-jus destrúctæ,

sa-cerdó-tes é-jus geméntes : vírgi-nes é-jus s quá-lidæ, et ipsa opprés-

sa a-ma-ri-tú-di-ne. He. Facti sunt hostes é-jus in cá-pi-te,

i-nimí-ci é-jus lo-cuple-tá-ti sunt : qui- a Dómi-nus lo-cú-tus est

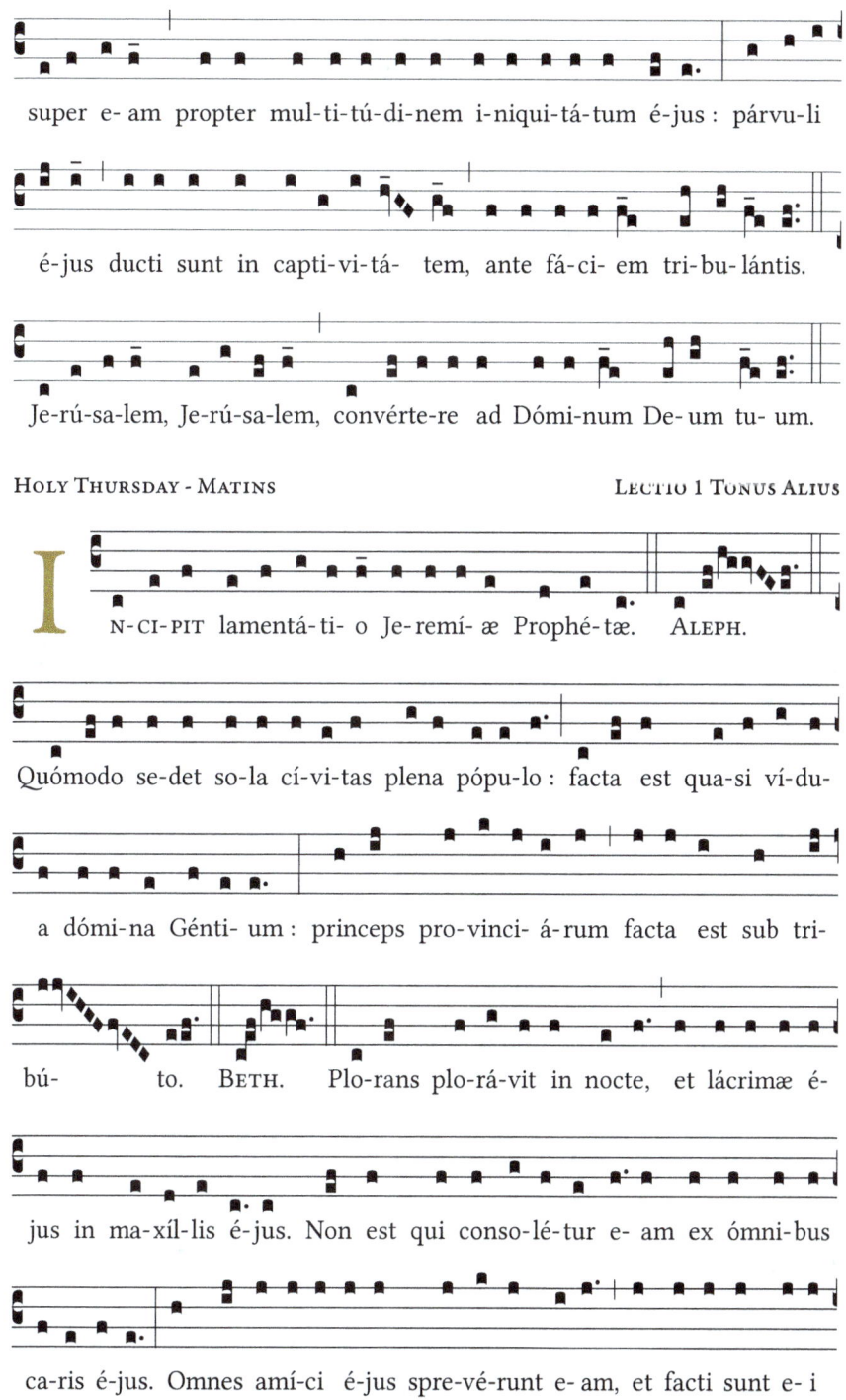

super e- am propter mul-ti-tú-di-nem i-niqui-tá-tum é-jus : párvu-li

é-jus ducti sunt in capti-vi-tá- tem, ante fá-ci- em tri-bu-lántis.

Je-rú-sa-lem, Je-rú-sa-lem, convérte-re ad Dómi-num De- um tu- um.

HOLY THURSDAY - MATINS   LECTIO 1 TONUS ALIUS

IN-CI-PIT lamentá-ti- o Je-remí- æ Prophé-tæ.   ALEPH.

Quómodo se-det so-la cí-vi-tas plena pópu-lo : facta est qua-si ví-du-

a dómi-na Génti- um : princeps pro-vinci- á-rum facta est sub tri-

bú-   to.   BETH.   Plo-rans plo-rá-vit in nocte, et lácrimæ é-

jus in ma-xíl-lis é-jus. Non est qui conso-lé-tur e- am ex ómni-bus

ca-ris é-jus. Omnes amí-ci é-jus spre-vé-runt e- am, et facti sunt e- i

in-imí-ci. GHIMEL. Migrá-vit Júdas propter afflicti- ónem

et mul-ti-tú-di-nem servi-tú-tis : ha-bi-tá-vit inter gentes, nec invé-nit

réqui- em. Omnes perse-cu-tó-res é-jus apprehendé-runt e- am inter an-

gústi- as. DA-LETH. Vi- æ Si- on lugent, e- o quod non sint

qui vé-ni- ant ad so-lemni-tá-tem : omnes portæ é-jus destrúctæ, sa-cer-

dó-tes é-jus geméntes : vírgi-nes é-jus s quá-lidæ, et ipsa oppréssa a-

ma-ri-tú-di-ne. HE. Facti sunt hostes é-jus in cá-pi-te, i-nimí-ci

é-jus lo-cuple-tá-ti sunt : qui- a Dómi-nus lo-cú-tus est super e- am

propter mul-ti-tú-di-nem i-niqui-tá-tum é-jus : párvu-li é-jus ducti sunt

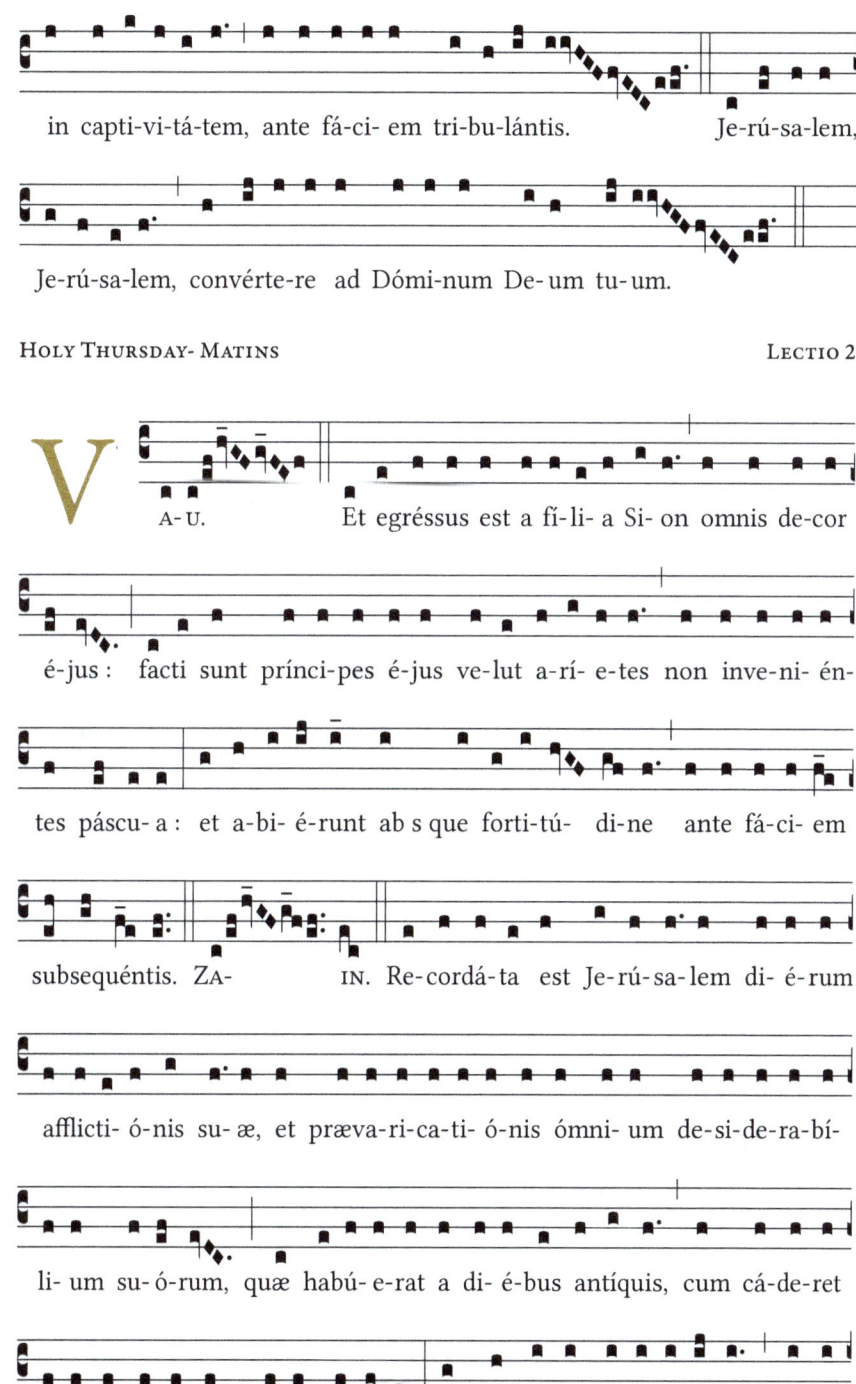

in capti-vi-tá-tem, ante fá-ci- em tri-bu-lántis.   Je-rú-sa-lem,

Je-rú-sa-lem, convérte-re ad Dómi-num De-um tu-um.

Holy Thursday- Matins   Lectio 2

A- U.   Et egréssus est a fí-li- a Si- on omnis de-cor

é-jus :   facti sunt prínci-pes é-jus ve-lut a-rí- e-tes non inve-ni- én-

tes páscu- a : et a-bi- é-runt ab s que forti-tú- di-ne   ante fá-ci- em

subsequéntis. Za-   in. Re-cordá-ta est Je-rú-sa-lem di- é-rum

afflicti- ó-nis su- æ, et præva-ri-ca-ti- ó-nis ómni- um de-si-de-ra-bí-

li- um su-ó-rum, quæ habú- e-rat a di- é-bus antíquis, cum cá-de-ret

pópu-lus é-jus in manu hostí- li,   et non esset auxi- li- á-tor : vi-dé-

runt e- am ho- stes, et de-ri-sé-runt sábba-ta é- jus. HETH.

Peccá-tum peccá-vit Je-rú-sa-lem, propté-re- a instá-bi-lis facta   est :

omnes, qui glo-ri-fi-cá-bant e- am, spre-vé-runt il-lam, qui- a vi-dé-runt

ignomí-ni- am é-jus : ípsa autem ge- mens convérsa est re-trórsum.

TETH.   Sordes é-jus in pé-di-bus é-jus, nec re-cordá-ta est fi-nis

su- i : depó-si-ta est veheménter, non ha-bens conso-la-tó-rem : vi-de,

Dómi-ne, afflicti- ónem me- am, quó-ni- am e-réctus est i-ni-mí-cus.

Je-rú-sa-lem, Je-rú-sa-lem, convérte-re ad Dómi-num De- um tu- um.

A- U.   Et egréssus est a fí-li- a Si- on omnis de-cor

é-jus : facti sunt prínci-pes é-jus ve-lut a- rí- e-tes non inve-ni- éntes

pá-scu- a : et a-bi- é-runt ab s que forti-tú-di-ne ante fá-ci- em subse-

quén- tis. ZA- IN.   Re-cordá-ta est Je-rú-sa-lem dié-rum afflicti- ó-

nis su- æ, et præva-ri-ca-ti- ó-nis ómni- um de-si-de-ra-bí-li- um su-ó-

rum, quæ habú- e-rat a di- é-bus antí- quis, cum cá-de-ret pópu-lus é-jus

in manu hostí-li, et non esset auxi-li- á-tor : vi-dé-runt e- am hostes,

et de-ri-sé-runt sábba-ta é- jus. HETH.   Peccá-tum peccá-vit Je-

rú-sa-lem, propté-re- a instá-bi-lis fa- cta est : omnes, qui glo-ri-fi-cá-

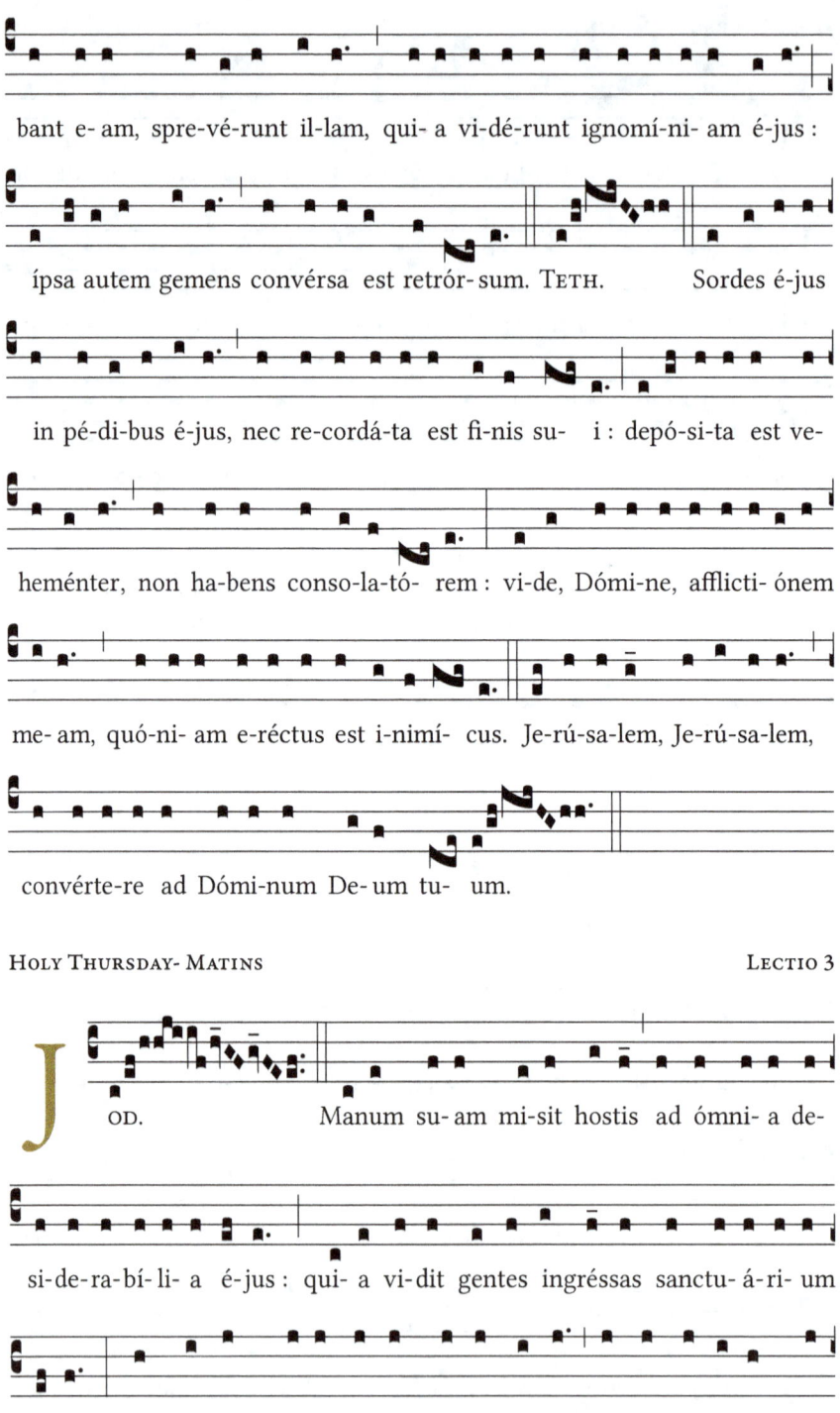

bant e- am, spre-vé-runt il-lam, qui- a vi-dé-runt ignomí-ni- am é-jus :

ípsa autem gemens convérsa est retrór- sum. TETH. Sordes é-jus

in pé-di-bus é-jus, nec re-cordá-ta est fi-nis su- i : depó-si-ta est ve-

heménter, non ha-bens conso-la-tó- rem : vi-de, Dómi-ne, afflicti- ónem

me- am, quó-ni- am e-réctus est i-nimí- cus. Je-rú-sa-lem, Je-rú-sa-lem,

convérte-re ad Dómi-num De- um tu- um.

HOLY THURSDAY- MATINS   LECTIO 3

J OD.   Manum su- am mi-sit hostis ad ómni- a de-

si-de-ra-bí- li- a é-jus : qui- a vi-dit gentes ingréssas sanctu- á-ri- um

su- um, de qui-bus præcé-pe-ras ne intrá-rent in ecclé- si- am tu-

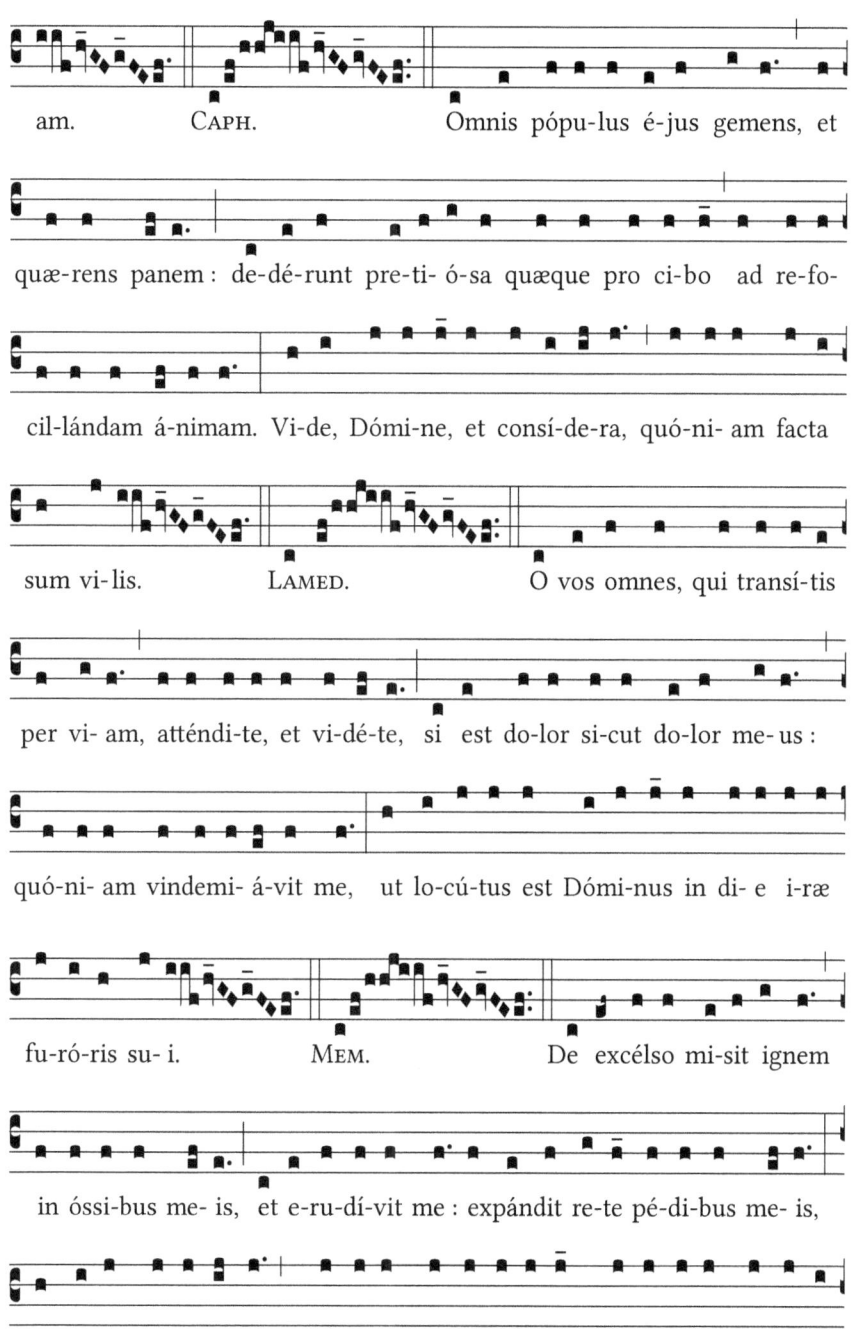

am. CAPH. Omnis pópu-lus é-jus gemens, et

quæ-rens panem : de-dé-runt pre-ti- ó-sa quæque pro ci-bo ad re-fo-

cil-lándam á-nimam. Vi-de, Dómi-ne, et consí-de-ra, quó-ni- am facta

sum vi- lis. LAMED. O vos omnes, qui transí-tis

per vi- am, atténdi-te, et vi-dé-te, si est do-lor si-cut do-lor me- us :

quó-ni- am vindemi- á-vit me, ut lo-cú-tus est Dómi-nus in di- e i-ræ

fu-ró-ris su- i. MEM. De excélso mi-sit ignem

in óssi-bus me- is, et e-ru-dí-vit me : expándit re-te pé-di-bus me- is,

convértit me retrórsum : pó-su- it me de-so-lá-tam, to-ta di- e mæ-ró-re

conféctam.   NUN.   Vi-gi-lá-vit iugum i-niqui-tá-

tum me- á-rum : in manu é-jus convo-lú-tæ sunt, et impó-si-tæ collo

me- o : infirmá-ta est virtus me- a : de-dit me Dómi-nus in manu,

de qua non pó-te-ro súrge-re.   Je-rú-sa-lem, Je-rú-sa-lem,

convérte-re ad Dómi-num De- um tu- um.

GOOD FRIDAY- MATINS   LECTIO 1

D E Lamenta- ti- óne Je- remí- æ Prophé- tæ HETH.

Co-gi-tá-vit Dómi-nus dissi-pá-re mu-rum fí- li- æ Si- on :

te-téndit fu-ní-cu-lum su- um, et non a-vértit manum su- am a per-

di- ti- óne : lu-xítque antemu-rá-le, et mu-rus pá-ri-ter dissi-pá-tus

est.   Teth.   De-fí-xæ sunt in terra portæ é-jus :

pérdi-dit, et contrí-vit vectes é-jus : re-gem é-jus et prínci-pes é-jus in

génti-bus : non est lex, et prophé-tæ é-jus non invené-runt vi-si- ónem

a Dómi-no.   Jod.   Se-dé-runt in terra, conti-

cu- é-runt senes fí-li- æ Si- on : conspersé-runt cí-ne-re cá-pi-ta su- a,

accíncti sunt ci- lí-ci- is, a-bi- e-cé-runt in terram cá-pi-ta su- a

vírgi-nes Je-rú-sa-lem.   Caph.   De-fe-cé-runt præ

lácrimis ó-cu-li me- i, conturbá-ta sunt vísce-ra me- a : effú-sum est in

terra je-cur me-um super contri-ti- óne fí-li- æ pópu-li me- i, cum de-

fí-ce-ret párvu-lus et lactens in pla-té- is óppi-di.   Je-rú-sa-

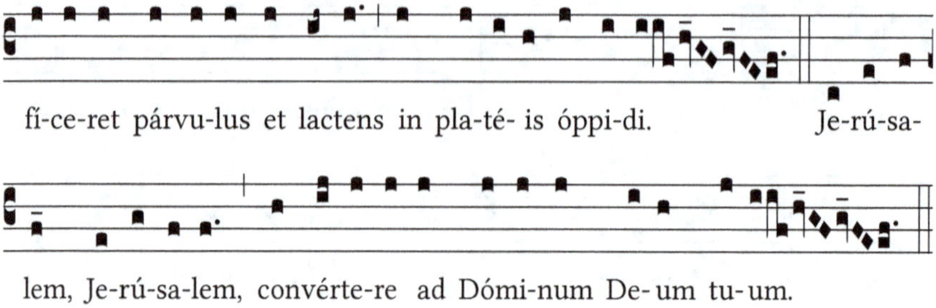

lem, Je-rú-sa-lem, convérte-re ad Dómi-num De- um tu- um.

Good Friday- Matins   Lectio 2

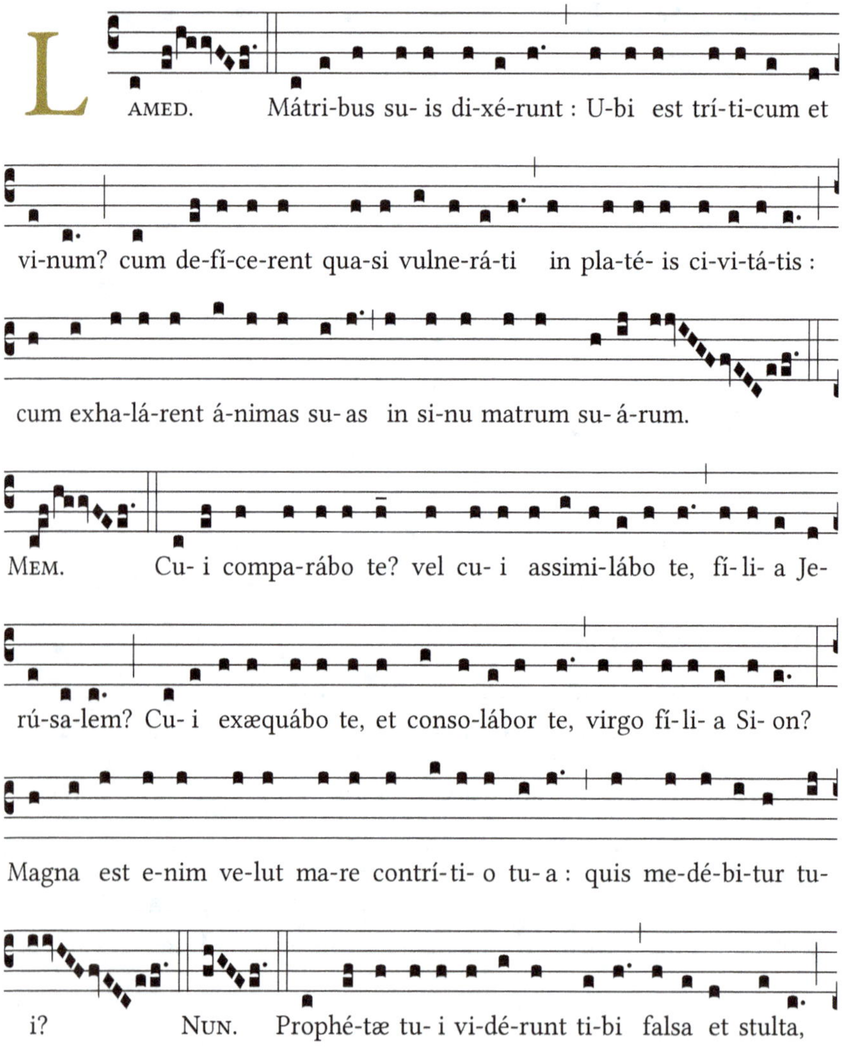

L AMED.   Mátri-bus su- is di-xé-runt : U-bi est trí-ti-cum et

vi-num? cum de-fí-ce-rent qua-si vulne-rá-ti in pla-té- is ci-vi-tá-tis :

cum exha-lá-rent á-nimas su- as in si-nu matrum su- á-rum.

Mem.   Cu- i compa-rábo te? vel cu- i assimi-lábo te, fí- li- a Je-

rú-sa-lem? Cu- i exæquábo te, et conso-lábor te, virgo fí-li- a Si- on?

Magna est e-nim ve-lut ma-re contrí-ti- o tu- a : quis me-dé-bi-tur tu-

i?   Nun.   Prophé-tæ tu- i vi-dé-runt ti-bi falsa et stulta,

nec a-pe-ri- é-bant i-niqui-tá-tem tu- am, ut te ad pœni-ténti- am pro-

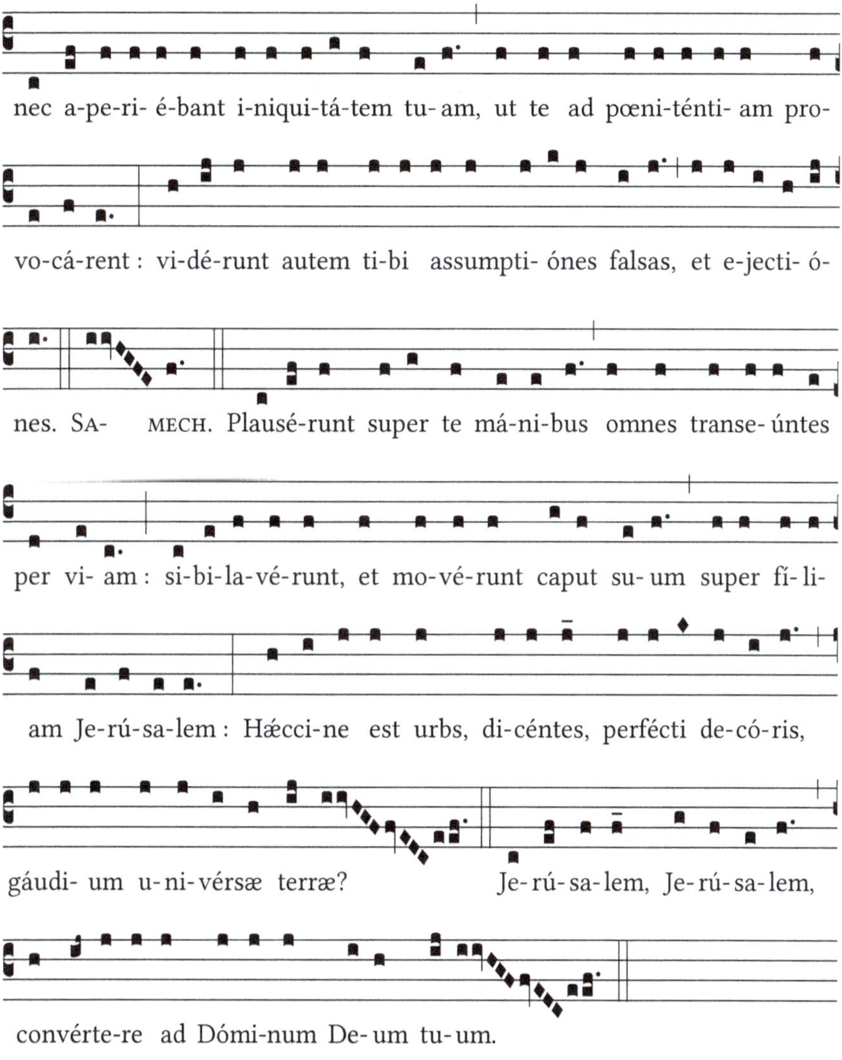

vo-cá-rent : vi-dé-runt autem ti-bi assumpti- ónes falsas, et e-jecti- ó-

nes. SA- MECH. Plausé-runt super te má-ni-bus omnes transe-úntes

per vi- am : si-bi-la-vé-runt, et mo-vé-runt caput su- um super fí-li-

am Je-rú-sa-lem : Hǽcci-ne est urbs, di-céntes, perfécti de-có-ris,

gáudi- um u-ni-vérsæ terræ? Je-rú-sa-lem, Je-rú-sa-lem,

convérte-re ad Dómi-num De- um tu- um.

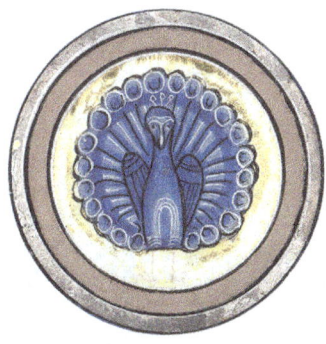

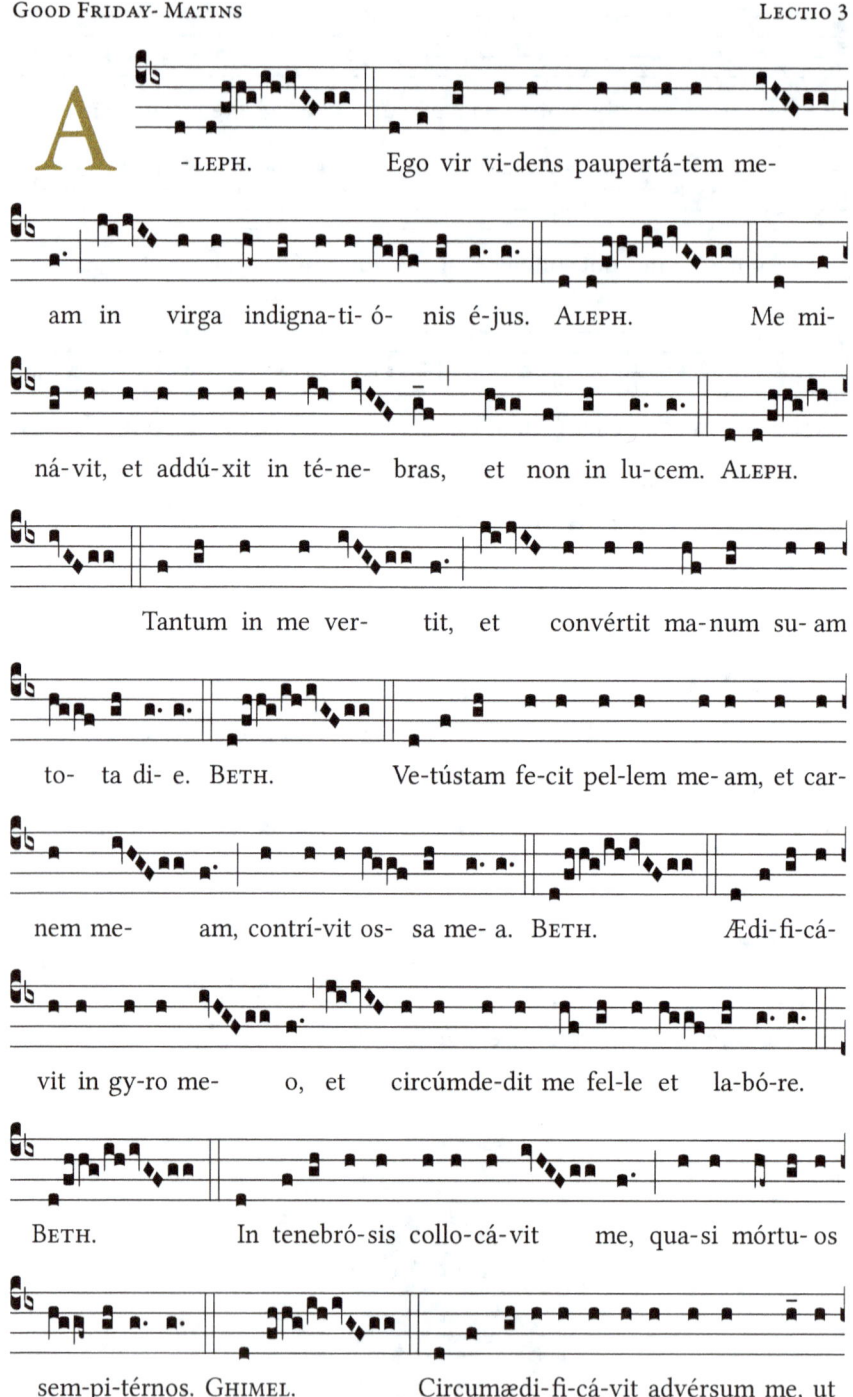

A -ʟᴇᴘʜ. Ego vir vi-dens paupertá-tem me-

am in virga indigna-ti- ó- nis é-jus. Aʟᴇᴘʜ. Me mi-

ná-vit, et addú-xit in té-ne- bras, et non in lu-cem. Aʟᴇᴘʜ.

Tantum in me ver- tit, et convértit ma-num su- am

to- ta di- e. Bᴇᴛʜ. Ve-tústam fe-cit pel-lem me- am, et car-

nem me- am, contrí-vit os- sa me- a. Bᴇᴛʜ. Ædi-fi-cá-

vit in gy-ro me- o, et circúmde-dit me fel-le et la-bó-re.

Bᴇᴛʜ. In tenebró-sis collo-cá-vit me, qua-si mórtu- os

sem-pi-térnos. Gʜɪᴍᴇʟ. Circumædi-fi-cá-vit advérsum me, ut

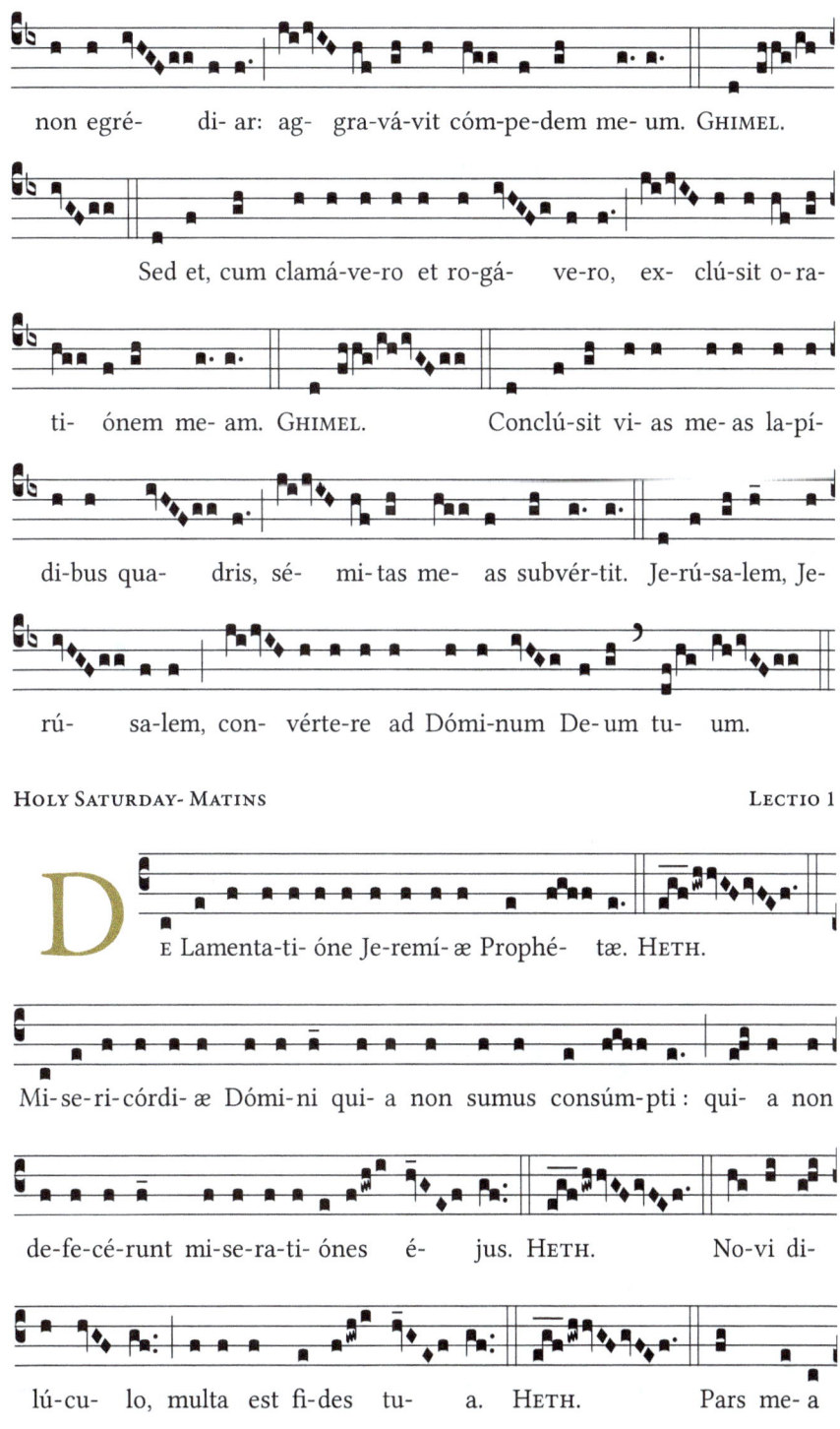

non egré- di- ar: ag- gra-vá-vit cóm-pe-dem me- um. GHIMEL.

Sed et, cum clamá-ve-ro et ro-gá- ve-ro, ex- clú-sit o-ra-

ti- ónem me- am. GHIMEL. Conclú-sit vi- as me- as la-pí-

di-bus qua- dris, sé- mi-tas me- as subvér-tit. Je-rú-sa-lem, Je-

rú- sa-lem, con- vér-te-re ad Dómi-num De-um tu- um.

HOLY SATURDAY- MATINS   LECTIO 1

D E Lamenta-ti- óne Je-remí- æ Prophé- tæ. HETH.

Mi-se-ri-córdi- æ Dómi-ni qui- a non sumus consúm-pti : qui- a non

de-fe-cé-runt mi-se-ra-ti- ónes é- jus. HETH. No-vi di-

lú-cu- lo, multa est fi-des tu- a. HETH. Pars me-a

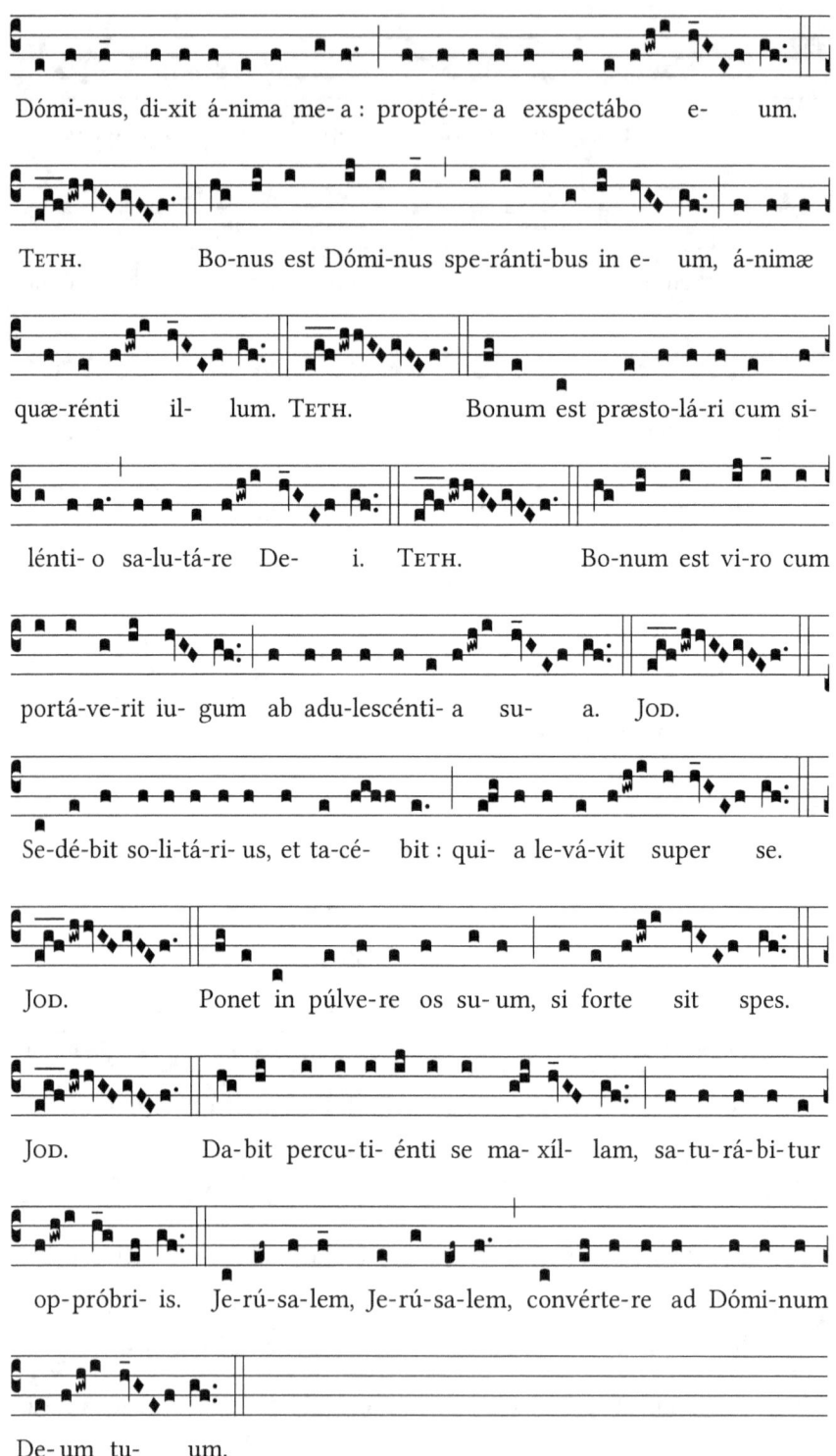

Dómi-nus, di-xit á-nima me- a : propté-re- a exspectábo e- um.

TETH. Bo-nus est Dómi-nus spe-ránti-bus in e- um, á-nimæ

quæ-rénti il- lum. TETH. Bonum est præsto-lá-ri cum si-

lénti- o sa-lu-tá-re De- i. TETH. Bo-num est vi-ro cum

portá-ve-rit iu- gum ab adu-lescénti- a su- a. JOD.

Se-dé-bit so-li-tá-ri- us, et ta-cé- bit : qui- a le-vá-vit super se.

JOD. Ponet in púlve-re os su- um, si forte sit spes.

JOD. Da-bit percu-ti- énti se ma-xíl- lam, sa-tu-rá-bi-tur

op-próbri- is. Je-rú-sa-lem, Je-rú-sa-lem, convérte-re ad Dómi-num

De-um tu- um.

A -LEPH. Quómodo obscu-rá-tum est au- rum, mu-tá-tus est co-lor óp- timus, dispérsi sunt lá-pi-des sanctu- á-ri- i in cá-pi-te ómni- um pla-te- á-rum? BETH. Fí-li- i Si- on íncli- ti, et amícti auro pri- mo: quómodo repu-tá-ti sunt in va-sa téste- a, opus mánu-um fí- gu-li? GHIMEL. Sed et lámi- æ nuda-vé-runt mam- mam, lacta-vé-runt cá-tu-los su- os: fí-li- a pópu-li me- i crudé- lis, qua-si strúthi- o in de- sér-to. DA-LETH. Adhǽ-sit lingua lactén- tis ad pa-lá-tum é-jus in si- ti: párvu-li pe-ti- é-runt pa- nem, et non e-rat qui frán-ge-ret

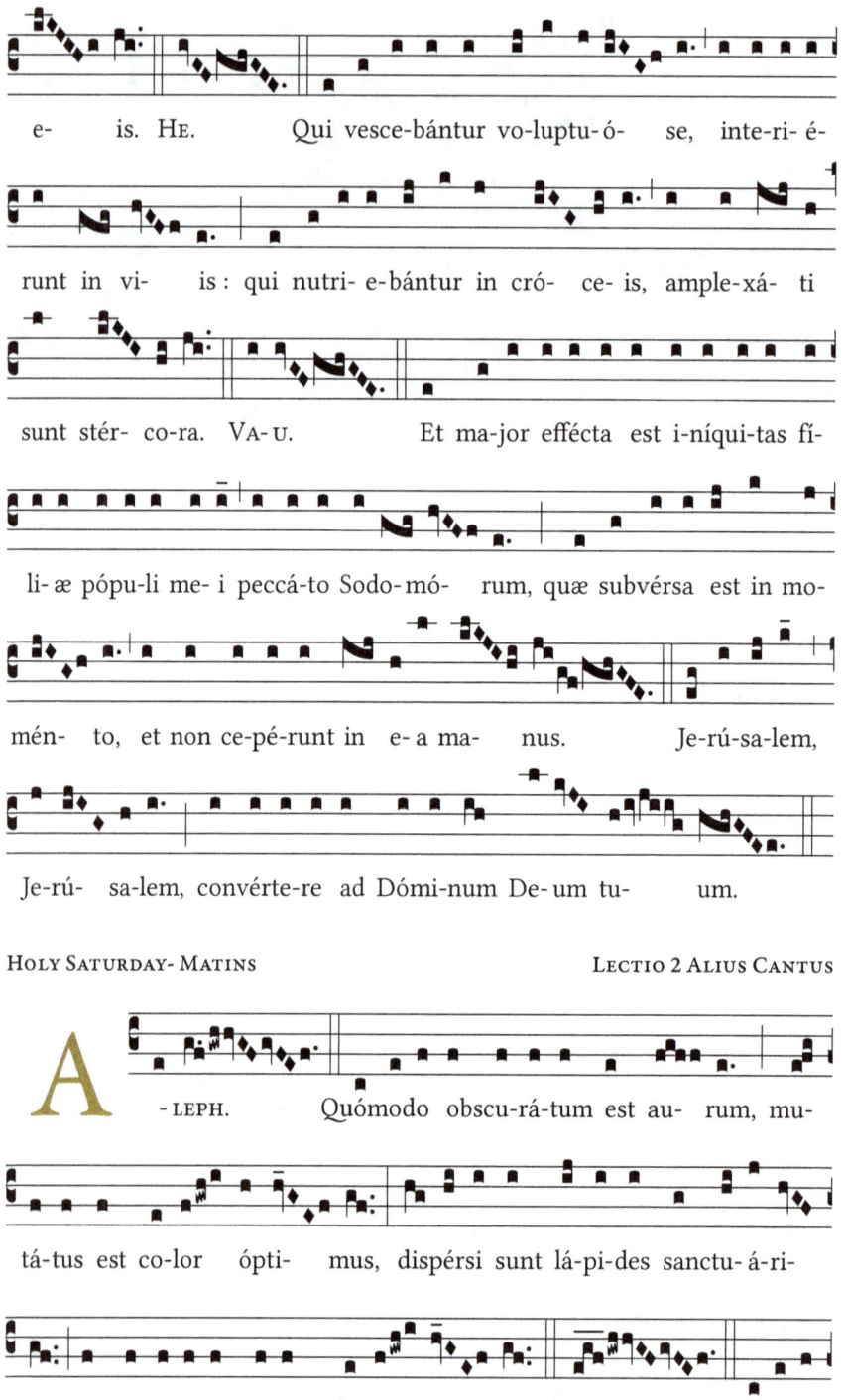

e- is. HE.   Qui vesce-bántur vo-luptu-ó- se, inte-ri-é-

runt in vi- is : qui nutri- e-bántur in cró- ce- is, ample-xá- ti

sunt stér- co-ra. VA-U.   Et ma-jor effécta est i-níqui-tas fí-

li- æ pópu-li me- i peccá-to Sodo-mó- rum, quæ subvérsa est in mo-

mén- to, et non ce-pé-runt in e-a ma- nus.   Je-rú-sa-lem,

Je-rú- sa-lem, convérte-re ad Dómi-num De-um tu- um.

HOLY SATURDAY- MATINS   LECTIO 2 ALIUS CANTUS

A -LEPH.   Quómodo obscu-rá-tum est au- rum, mu-

tá-tus est co-lor ópti- mus, dispérsi sunt lá-pi-des sanctu-á-ri-

i in cá-pi-te ómni- um pla-te- á- rum? BETH.   Fí-li- i

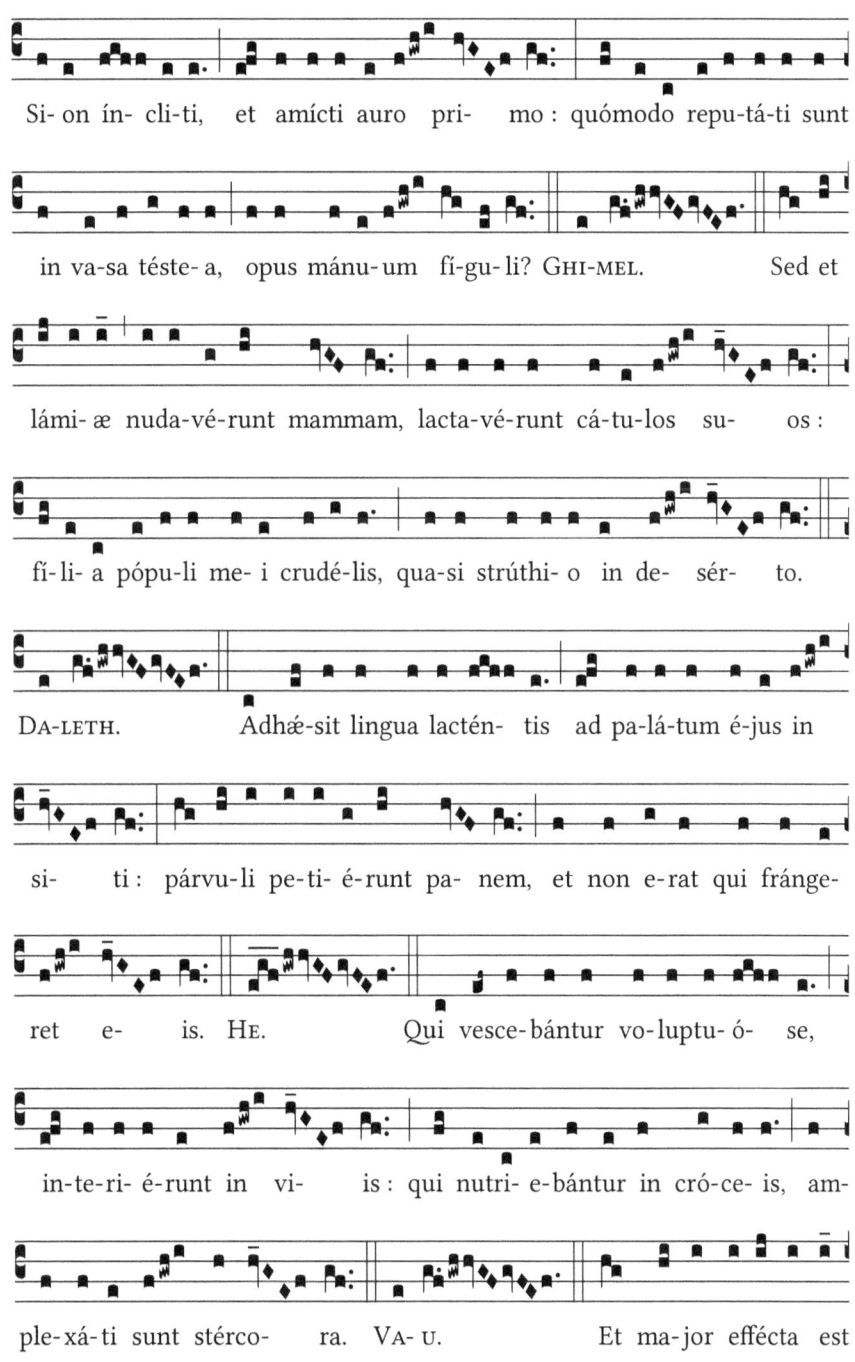

Si- on ín- cli-ti, et amícti auro pri- mo : quómodo repu-tá-ti sunt

in va-sa téste- a, opus mánu-um fí-gu-li? GHI-MEL. Sed et

lámi- æ nuda-vé-runt mammam, lacta-vé-runt cá-tu-los su- os :

fí-li- a pópu-li me- i crudé-lis, qua-si strúthi- o in de- sér- to.

DA-LETH. Adhǽ-sit lingua lactén- tis ad pa-lá-tum é-jus in

si- ti : párvu-li pe-ti- é-runt pa- nem, et non e-rat qui fránge-

ret e- is. HE. Qui vesce-bántur vo-luptu- ó- se,

in-te-ri- é-runt in vi- is : qui nutri- e-bántur in cró-ce- is, am-

ple-xá-ti sunt stérco- ra. VA- U. Et ma-jor effécta est

i-níqui-tas fí-li-æ pópu-li me- i peccá-to Sodo- mó- rum, quæ

subvérsa est in moménto, et non ce-pé-runt in e-a ma- nus. Je-

rú-sa-lem, Je-rú-sa-lem, convérte-re ad Dómi-num De-um tu- um.

IN-CI-PIT O-rá-ti- o Je-re-mí- æ Prophé-tæ. Re-cordá-re, Dómi-

ne, quid accí-de-rit no- bis : intu- é-re, et réspi-ce oppró- bri- um no-

strum. He-ré-di-tas nostra versa est ad a-li- é- nos : domus no- stræ

ad extrá- ne- os. Pu-píl-li facti sumus absque pa- tre, ma-tres no-

stræ qua- si ví- du-æ. Aquam nostram pe-cú-ni- a bí-bi- mus :

ligna no- stra pré-ti- o com-pa-rá- vimus. Cerví-ci-bus nostris mi-

na- bá- mur, las-sis non da-bá- tur ré- qui- es. Ægýpto dé-dimus ma-

num, et Assý- ri- is, ut sa-tu-ra- rémur pane. Patres nostri pec-

ca-vé-runt, et non sunt : et nos i-niqui-tá-tes e- ó-rum portá- vimus.

Servi domi-ná-ti sunt no-stri : non fu- it qui re-díme-ret de ma-

nu e- ó-rum. In a-nimábus nostris affe-re-bámus panem no- bis,

a fá-ci- e glá-di- i in de- sérto. Pel-lis nostra qua-si clí-banus e-

xústa est a fá- ci- e tempe- stá-tum famis. Mu-lí- e-res in Si- on

humi-li- a- vé- runt, et vír-gi-nes in ci-vi-tá- ti-bus Juda. Je-rú-sa-

lem, Je-rú-sa- lem, convér- te-re ad Dómi-num De- um tu- um.

IN-CI-PIT O-rá- ti- o Je-re-mí- æ Prophé- tæ. Re-cordá-

re, Dómi-ne, quid accí- de-rit no- bis : intu- é-re, et ré- spi-

ce oppróbri- um no- strum. He-ré-di-tas nostra versa est ad a-

li- é- nos : domus nostræ ad extrá- ne- os. Pu-píl-li facti su- mus

absque pa- tre, matres nostræ qua- si ví- du-æ. Aquam nostram

pe-cú-ni- a bí- bimus : ligna nostra pré-ti- o compa-rá- vimus.

Cerví-ci-bus nostris mi-na-bá- mur, las- sis non da-bá- tur ré-

qui- es. Ægýpto dé-dimus ma- num, et Assý-ri- is, ut sa-tu-ra-ré- mur

pa- ne. Patres nostri pecca-vé- runt, et non sunt : et nos i-niqui-

tá-tes e- ó-rum por-tá- vi- mus. Servi domi-ná-ti sunt no- stri : non

fu- it qui re-díme-ret de manu e- ó- rum. In a-nimábus no-stris

affe-re-bámus panem no- bis, a fá-ci- e glá-di- i in de-sér- to.

Pel-lis nostra qua-si clí- banus e-xústa est a fá-ci- e tempestá- tum

fa- mis. Mu-lí- e-res in Si- on hu-mi-li- a- vé-runt, et vír- gi-nes

in ci-vi-tá-ti-bus Ju- da. Je-rú-sa-lem, Je-rú-sa- lem, convér-

te-re ad Dómi-num De- um tu- um.

SOLESMES

I N-CI-PIT O-rá- ti- o Je-re-mí- æ Prophé-tæ. Re-cordá-re, Dómi-

ne, quid accí-de-rit no- bis : intu- é-re, et réspi-ce oppró- bri- um no-

strum. He-ré-di-tas nostra versa est ad a-li- é- nos : domus no- stræ

ad extrá- ne- os. Pu-píl-li facti sumus absque pa- tre, ma-tres no-

stræ qua- si ví- du-æ. Aquam nostram pe-cú-ni- a bí-bi- mus : ligna

no- stra pré-ti- o com-pa-rá- vimus. Cerví-ci-bus nostris mi-na-bá-

mur, las-sis non da-bá- tur ré- qui- es. Ægýpto dé-dimus ma- num,

et Assý- ri- is, ut sa-tu-ra- rémur pane. Patres nostri pecca-vé-

runt, et non sunt : et nos in-iqui-tá-tes e- ó-rum portá- vimus. Servi

domi-ná-ti sunt no-stri : non fu- it qui re-díme-ret de ma- nu e-

ó-rum. In a-nimábus nostris affe-re-bámus panem no- bis, a fá-ci- e

glá-di- i in de- sérto. Pel-lis nostra qua-si clí-banus e-xústa est

a fá- ci- e tempe- stá-tum famis. Mu-lí- e-res in Si- on humi-li-

a-vé- runt, et vír-gi-nes in ci-vi-tá- ti-bus Juda. Je-rú-sa-lem,

Je-rú-sa- lem, convér- te-re ad Dómi-num De- um tu- um.

GOOD FRIDAY TRACTS
PSALM TONE

TRACT   DÓMINE AUDÍVI

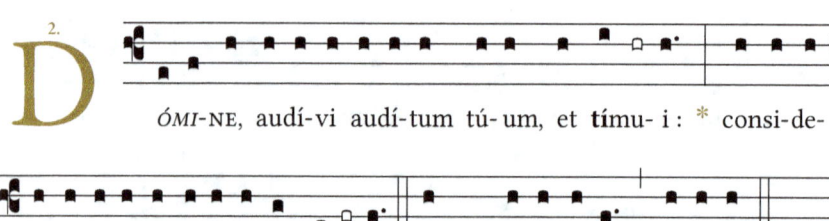

ÓMI-NE, audí-vi audí-tum tú-um, et **tímu-** i : * consi-de-

rá-vi ópe-ra tú-a, et *expá-* vi. *Flex :* inno-tescé-ris : †

O Lord, I have heard Thy hearing and was afraid: * I have considered Thy works and trembled.

℣. *In mé*dio duórum animálium in-notescéris: † dum appropinquáverint anni, cogno**scé**ris: * dum advénerit tempus, o*sténd*eris.

℣. In the midst of two animals Thou shalt be made known: † when the years shall draw nigh Thou shalt be known: * when the time shall come, Thou shalt be manifested.

℣. *In e*o, dum conturbáta fúerit áni-ma **mé**a: * in ira, misericórdiæ me*mor* éris.

℣. When my soul shall be in trou-ble, * Thou wilt remember mercy, even in Thy wrath.

℣. *Deus* a Líbano **vé**niet, * et Sanc-tus de monte umbróso et *condén*so.

℣. God will come from Libanus, * and the Holy One from the shady and thickly covered mountain.

℣. *Opé*ruit cælos majéstas **é**jus: * et laudis ejus plena *est* **ter**ra.

℣. His majesty covered the heavens: * and the earth is full of His praise.

TRACT   ERIPE ME DÓMINE

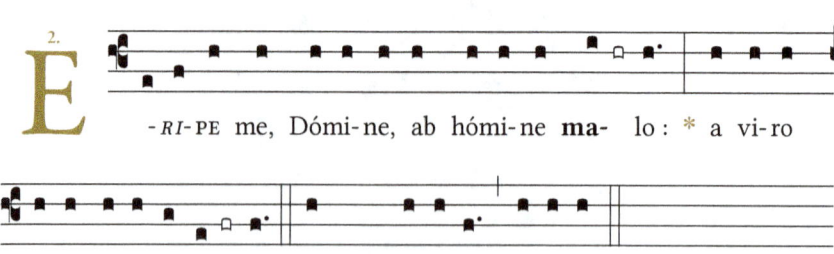

-RI-PE me, Dómi-ne, ab hómi-ne **ma-** lo : * a vi-ro

in-íquo lí-*be*-**ra** me. *Flex :* pecca-tó-ri : †

Deliver me, O Lord, from the evil man: * rescue me from the unjust man.

℣. *Qui co*gitavérunt malítias in **cór**de: * tota die constitué*bant* **prǽ**lia.

℣. Who have devised iniquities in their hearts: * all the day long they designed battles.

℣. *Acu*érunt linguas suas sicut ser-**pén**tis: * venénum áspidum sub lábiis *eó*rum.

℣. They have sharpened their tongues like a serpent; * the venom of asps is under their lips.

℣. *Custó*di me, Dómine, de manu peccató*ris*: * et ab homínibus iníquis lí*be***ra** me.

℣. Keep me, O Lord, from the hand of the wicked: * and from unjust men deliver me.

℣. *Qui co*gitavérunt supplantáre gressus **me**os: * abscondérunt supérbi láque*um* **mi**hi.

℣. Who have proposed to supplant my steps. * The proud have hidden a net for me.

℣. *Et fu*nes extendérunt in láqueum pédibus **me**is: * juxta iter scándalum posué*runt* **mi**hi.

℣. And they have stretched out cords for a snare for my feet; * they have laid for me a stumbling-block by the wayside.

℣. *Dixi* Dómino: Deus meus **es** tu: * exáudi, Dómine, vocem orati*ónis* **me**æ.

℣. I said to the Lord: Thou art my God. * Hear, O Lord, the voice of my supplication.

℣. *Dómi*ne, Dómine, virtus salútis **me**æ: * obúmbra caput meum in di*e* **bel**li.

℣. O Lord, Lord, the strength of my salvation: * overshadow my head in the day of battle.

℣. *Ne tra*das me a desidério meo peccató*ri*: † cogitavérunt ad**vér**sum me: * ne derelínquas me, ne umquam ex*al***tén**tur.

℣. Give me not up from my desire to the wicked: † they have plotted against me. * Do not Thou forsake me, lest at any time they should triumph.

℣. *Caput* circúitus **eó**rum: * labor labiórum ipsórum opéri*et* **e**os.

℣. The head of them compassing me about: * the labor of their lips shall overwhelm them.

℣. *Verúm*tamen justi confitebúntur nómini **tú**o: * et habitábunt recti cum vul*tu* **tú**o.

℣. But the just shall give glory to Thy Name: * and the upright shall dwell with Thy countenance.

ALTERNATE CHANTS FOR CREDO

5.

CREDO in unum De- um, Patrem omni-pot-éntem, factó-rem
cæ-li et terræ, vi-si-bí-li- um ó-mni- um, et invi- si-bí- li- um. Et in
unum Dómi-num Je-sum Christum, Fí- li- um De- i u-ni-gé-ni-tum.
Et ex Patre na- tum ante ómni- a sǽ- cu-la. De- um de De- o, lumen
de lúmi-ne, De- um ve-rum de De- o ve-ro. Gé-ni-tum, non fa- ctum,
consubstanti- á-lem Patri : per quem ómni- a facta sunt. Qui propter nos
All kneel
hómi-nes, et propter nostram sa-lú-tem descéndit de cæ-lis. Et incarná-
tus est de Spí-ri-tu Sancto ex Ma-rí- a Vírgi-ne : Et homo factus est.

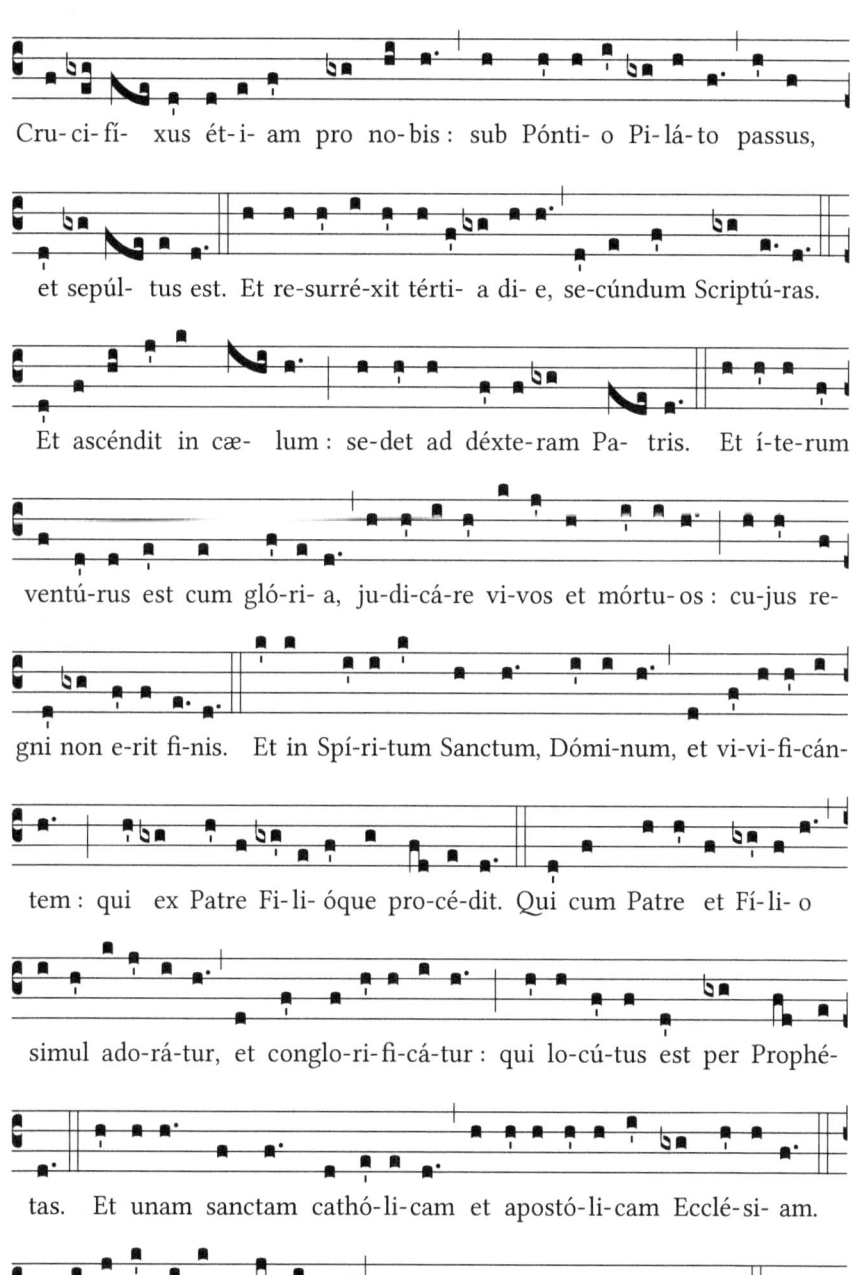

Cru- ci- fí- xus ét-i- am pro no-bis : sub Pónti- o Pi-lá-to passus,

et sepúl- tus est. Et re-surré-xit térti- a di- e, se-cúndum Scriptú-ras.

Et ascéndit in cæ- lum : se-det ad déxte-ram Pa- tris. Et í-te-rum

ventú-rus est cum gló-ri- a, ju-di-cá-re vi-vos et mórtu- os : cu-jus re-

gni non e-rit fi-nis. Et in Spí-ri-tum Sanctum, Dómi-num, et vi-vi-fi-cán-

tem : qui ex Patre Fi-li- óque pro-cé-dit. Qui cum Patre et Fí-li- o

simul ado-rá-tur, et conglo-ri-fi-cá-tur : qui lo-cú-tus est per Prophé-

tas. Et unam sanctam cathó-li-cam et apostó-li-cam Ecclé-si- am.

Confí-te- or unum baptísma in remissi- ónem pecca-tó-rum. Et ex-

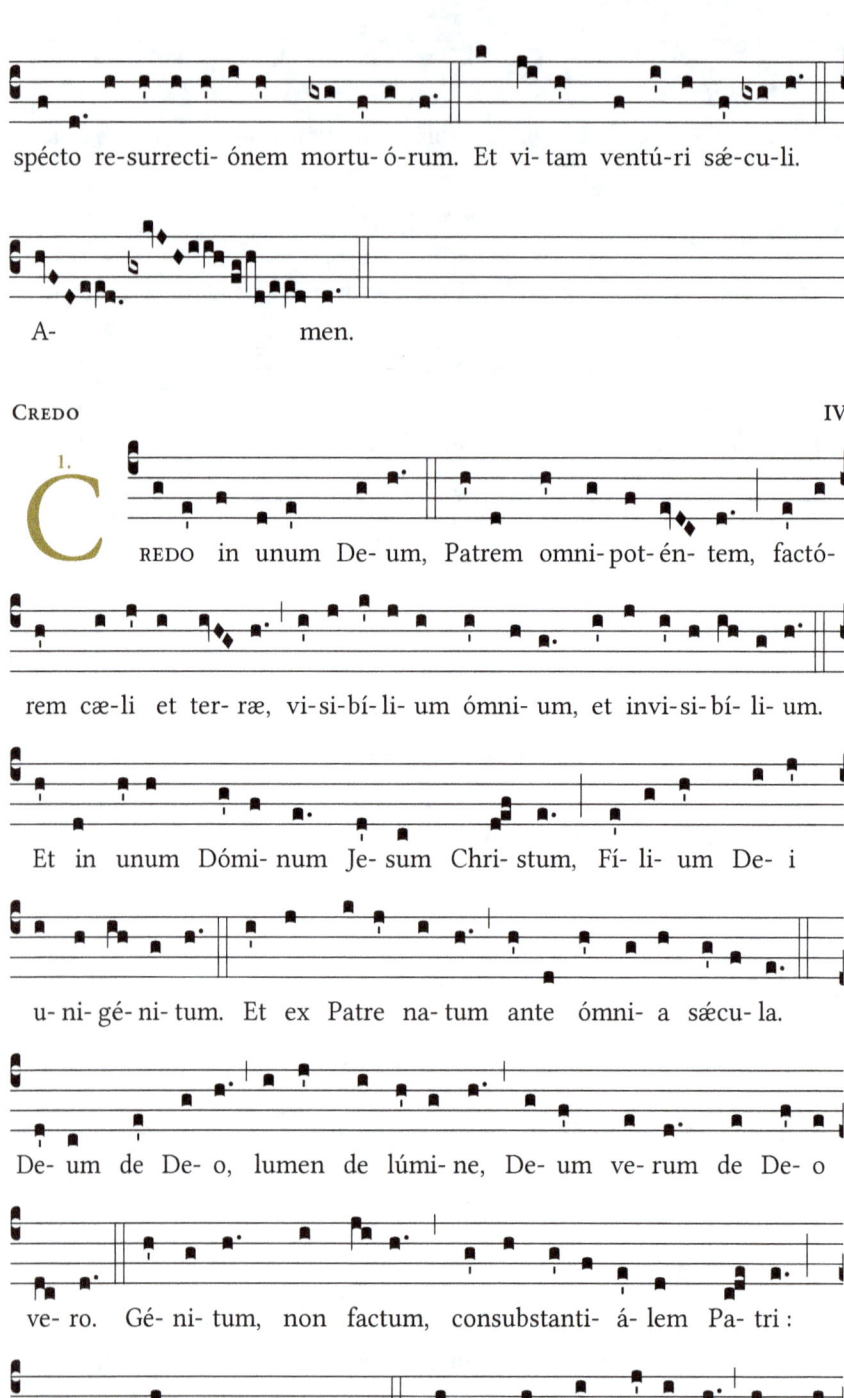

spécto re-surrecti- ónem mortu- ó-rum. Et vi- tam ventú-ri sǽ-cu-li.

A- men.

CREDO IV

CREDO in unum De- um, Patrem omni- pot- én- tem, factó-

rem cæ-li et ter- ræ, vi-si-bí- li- um ómni- um, et invi-si-bí- li- um.

Et in unum Dómi- num Je- sum Chri- stum, Fí- li- um De- i

u- ni- gé- ni- tum. Et ex Patre na- tum ante ómni- a sǽcu- la.

De- um de De- o, lumen de lúmi- ne, De- um ve- rum de De- o

ve- ro. Gé- ni- tum, non factum, consubstanti- á- lem Pa- tri :

per quem ómni- a facta sunt. Qui propter nos hómi- nes, et pro-

All kneel

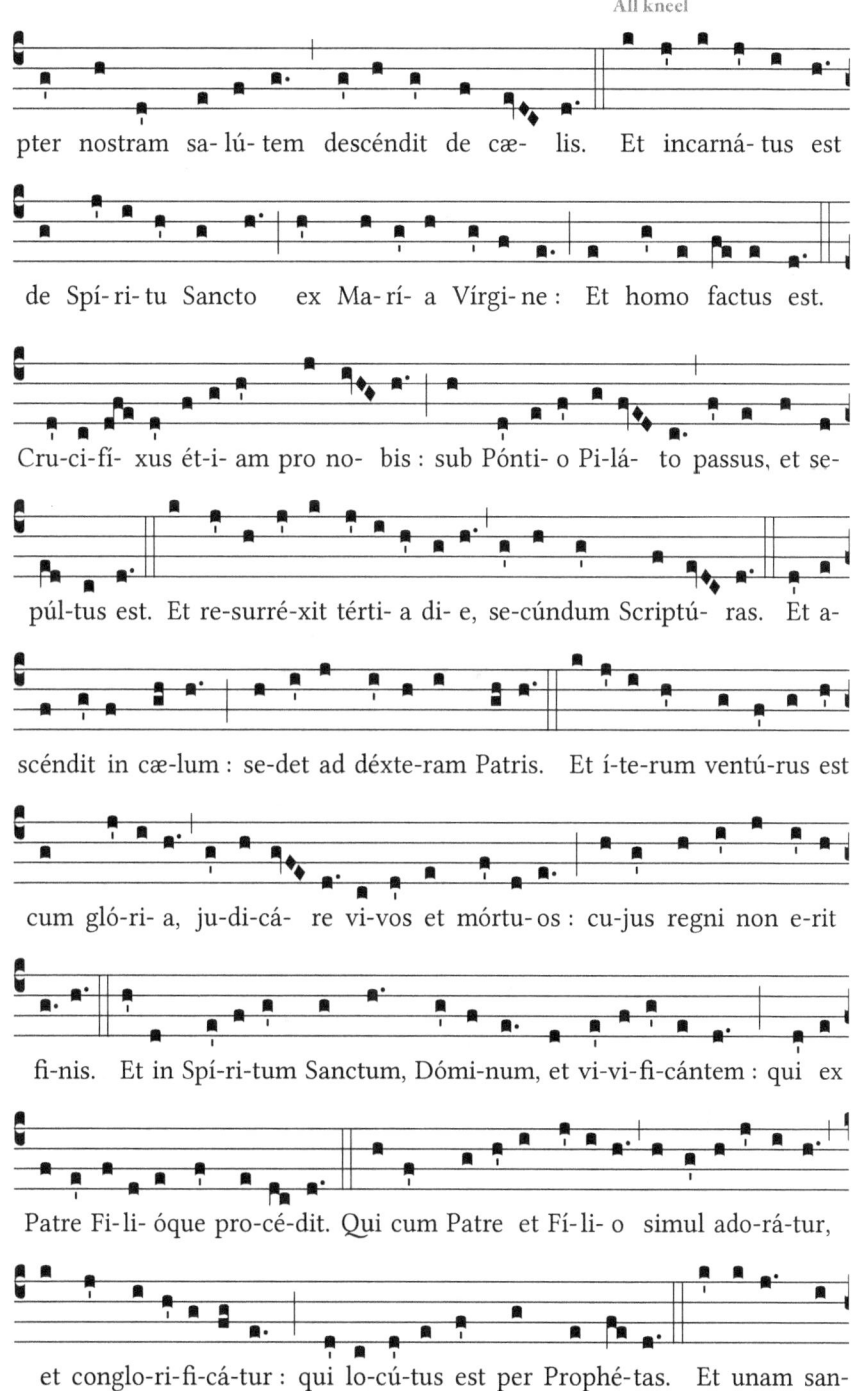

pter nostram sa-lú-tem descéndit de cæ- lis. Et incarná-tus est

de Spí-ri-tu Sancto ex Ma-rí- a Vírgi-ne : Et homo factus est.

Cru-ci-fí- xus ét-i- am pro no- bis : sub Pónti- o Pi-lá- to passus, et se-

púl-tus est. Et re-surré-xit térti- a di- e, se-cúndum Scriptú- ras. Et a-

scéndit in cæ-lum : se-det ad déxte-ram Patris. Et í-te-rum ventú-rus est

cum gló-ri- a, ju-di-cá- re vi-vos et mórtu- os : cu-jus regni non e-rit

fi-nis. Et in Spí-ri-tum Sanctum, Dómi-num, et vi-vi-fi-cántem : qui ex

Patre Fi-li- óque pro-cé-dit. Qui cum Patre et Fí-li- o simul ado-rá-tur,

et conglo-ri-fi-cá-tur : qui lo-cú-tus est per Prophé-tas. Et unam san-

ctam cathó-li-cam et apostó-li-cam Ecclé-si- am. Confí-te- or unum ba-

ptísma in remissi- ónem pecca-tó- rum. Et exspécto re-surrecti- ónem

mortu-ó- rum. Et vi-tam ventú-ri sǽ-cu-li. A- men.

Index

Sources

All Latin texts and English translations:
divinumofficium.com

All chants except Mozarabic Lamentations:
Liber Usualis, 1961

Mozarabic Lamentations:
Cantus Lamentationem, 1934

Scriptural Lessons at Matins:
transcribed by Jason Watson

Psalm Tones:
GABC Psalm Tone Tool

Rubrics:
divinumofficium.com
The Masses of Holy Week (FSSP)
pre1955holyweek.com

Mozarabic Lamentations & Lessons of St. Augustine:
transcribed by Jason Watson

All scores produced using:
GABC Transcription Tool
run.gregoriochant.org

Most chants sourced from:
gregobase.selapa.net